Paulinus of Nola

THE TRANSFORMATION OF THE CLASSICAL HERITAGE

Peter Brown, General Editor

Paulinus of Nola

Life, Letters, and Poems

Dennis E. Trout

UNIVERSITY OF CALIFORNIA PRESS
Berkeley   Los Angeles   London

University of California Press
Berkeley and Los Angeles, California

University of California Press, Ltd.
London, England

© 1999 by the Regents of the University of California

Library of Congress Cataloging-in-Publication Data

Trout, Dennis E., 1953–
    Paulinus of Nola : life, letters, and poems / Dennis E. Trout.
        p.   cm.—(The transformation of the classical heritage ; 27)
    Includes bibliographical references and index.
    ISBN 0-520-21709-8 (alk. paper)
    1. Paulinus, of Nola, Saint, ca. 353–431.   2. Paulinus, of Nola,
Saint, ca. 353–431—Correspondence.   3. Christian poetry, Latin—
History and criticism.   4. Christian saints—Italy—Nola—
Correspondence.   5. Christian saints—Italy—Nola—Biography.
6. Poets, Latin—Italy—Nola—Correspondence.   7. Poets, Latin—
Italy—Nola—Biography.   I. Title.   II. Series.
PA6554.P5Z89   1999
871′.1—dc21   98-31299
[b]   CIP

Manufactured in the United States of America

08   07   06   05   04   03   02   01   00
        10   9   8   7   6   5   4   3   2   1

The paper used in this publication meets the minimum requirements of
ANSI/NISO Z39.48-1992 (R 1997) (Permanence of Paper). ⊗

For my parents
Dorothy I. and Frank E. Trout

CONTENTS

ABBREVIATIONS

Most ancient sources are cited according to the conventions of the *Oxford Classical Dictionary*, 3d ed. (1996); *PLRE*; or *Patrology*, vol. 4, ed. A. di Berardino (1986). Abbreviations for periodical titles generally follow the conventions of *L'Année Philologique*. Note also the following:

ACW	*Ancient Christian Writers*
Atti del Convegno	*Atti del Convegno: XXXI Cinquantenario della morte di S. Paolino di Nola (431–1981).* Rome, 1982.
CCSL	*Corpus Christianorum, Series Latina*
CIL	*Corpus Inscriptionum Latinarum*
CSEL	*Corpus Scriptorum Ecclesiasticorum Latinorum*
CTh	*Codex Theodosianus*
DALC	*Dictionnaire d'archéologie chrétienne et de liturgie*
DHGE	*Dictionnaire d'histoire et de géographie ecclésiastique*
ILCV	*Inscriptiones Latinae Christianae Veteres*
ILS	*Inscriptiones Latinae Selectae*
MGH	*Monumenta Germaniae Historica*
PL	*Patrologia Latina*
PLRE	*Prosopography of the Later Roman Empire.* Vol. 1 (A.D. 260–395). Ed. A. H. M. Jones, J. R. Martindale, and J. Morris. Cambridge, 1971. Vol. 2 (A.D. 395–527). Ed. J. R. Martindale, Cambridge, 1980.
RAC	*Reallexikon für Antike und Christentum*
REAug	*Revue des études augustiniennes*
SC	*Sources chrétiennes*
ZPE	*Zeitschrift für Papyrologie und Epigraphik*

PREFACE

The life and thought of Paulinus of Nola are documented by two modern volumes of his own letters and poems and by various letters and testimonials from his contemporaries. Paulinus emerged as one of my guides to the late Roman world more than ten years ago, when I, perhaps like many, met him as a friend and correspondent of Augustine. I was sufficiently intrigued to write a dissertation on Paulinus's secular renunciation, and I have continued to travel with Paulinus in fits and starts ever since. The erratic pattern of our companionship is owed in part to the exigencies of my own life and in part to the occasional intractability of Paulinus, who a prescient Robert Markus once warned me would not be the kind of candidate for biography that Peter Brown had shown Augustine to be.

It was a good call, and my conception of historical biography has had to evolve in tandem with my appreciation of the nature of Paulinus's works. The "private" Paulinus still eludes me, though some will surely say I am now unwittingly too intimate with my own construction of him. But I have become more at ease with the "public" figure(s) projected in Paulinus's writings. For a long time I thought it my responsibility as the author of a "life" to merge the various images of Paulinus that I detected into a single, all-embracing identity. In the end, I turned away from that summons, for I am not (yet) prepared to perform the reductive collation necessary. Although my negligence may disappoint some, and my study is admittedly less tidy for my decision, I hope my resistance yields a truer reflection of the life Paulinus lived and of the kaleidoscopic character of the age that saw him fulfill so many roles.

Over the years I have accumulated debts well beyond my ability to repay satisfactorily. Many mentors and friends have knowingly and unknowingly made investments here. At Duke, Kent Rigsby and Elizabeth Clark shouldered the yoke of advising my dissertation work. They, as well as another former teacher, Paul Harvey Jr., continue to instruct me by precept and example. An earlier draft of this book was read by Elizabeth Clark and Ray Van Dam; Robert Markus and one anonymous reviewer commented on its penultimate stage. Michael Roberts, Mark

Vessey, and David Hunter responded to select chapters. The advice and sugges-
tions of all these have greatly improved the work; I accept all blame for its short-
comings. Finally, Peter Brown's work has been a constant source of inspiration and
ideas for me, and the completion of this study owes much to his generosity.

My concern with Paulinus has introduced me to a number of friends, some
known (appropriately enough) only through their letters, who have been extremely
generous with their work. For gifts of books, articles, and manuscripts I am deeply
grateful to Yves-Marie Duval, the late Jean Doignon, Giuseppe Guttilla, Carmine
Iannicelli, Sigrid Mratschek-Halfmann, Beat Näf, and Catherine Conybeare. I
warmly acknowledge the generosity of Tomas Lehmann, whose plans of the basil-
ica complex at Nola / Cimitile appear in this book. The proofs of his publication
of a new poem attributed to Paulinus reached me just in time to be introduced
into Appendix A. I hope to address more fully elsewhere the implications of this
exciting evidence. I also especially thank Giovanni Santaniello, who, like Pierre
Fabre, perhaps understands better than most the heart of Paulinus and who in the
spirit of Paulinus's age has sent me so many of the works published by the Centro
di Studi e Documentazione su Paolino di Nola and the Biblioteca Diocesana S.
Paolino. I regret that *Anchora vitae*, the collected papers of the conference held at
Nola in 1995 and edited by Gennaro Luongo, reached me too late for incorpora-
tion.

The broader stream of my debt and gratitude sweeps in Andre Basson, Gillian
Clark, Hagith Sivan, Ralph Mathisen, John Matthews, Michele Salzman, Anne-
wies van den Hoek, and many others who have listened with interest to my talks
on Paulinus. Among institutions that have supported the work appearing in these
pages I thank the Andrew W. Mellon Foundation for both a predoctoral fellowship
and for the postdoctoral grant that permitted me, as a fellow and visiting assistant
professor at Harvard University, to spend a year thinking about biography under
the guidance of William McFeely. At the University of California Press I ac-
knowledge the efforts and experience of Mary Lamprech, Kate Toll, Cindy Ful-
ton, and Erika Büky, who saved me from myself on so many occasions. From the
ranks of my colleagues and former colleagues at Tufts, I thank Steven Hirsch,
Peter Reid, and Ann Van Sant, all of whom maintained their confidence in this
project. The present joy of Cora and Jacob has provided necessary respite from
the past; pride of place I reserve for recognition of the *caritas* and *amicitia* of my
wife, Carlynn.

THE *NATALICIA*:
CHRONOLOGY AND CONCORDANCE

Order in Series	*Year of Performance*	*Number in Corpus*
First	January, 395 (Spain)	*Carmen* 12
Second	January, 396 (Nola)	*Carmen* 13
Third	January, 397	*Carmen* 14
Fourth	January, 398	*Carmen* 15
Fifth	January, 399	*Carmen* 16
Sixth	January, 400	*Carmen* 18
Seventh	January, 401	*Carmen* 23
Eighth	January, 402	*Carmen* 26
Ninth	January, 403	*Carmen* 27
Tenth	January, 404	*Carmen* 28
Eleventh	January, 405	*Carmen* 19
Twelfth	January, 406	*Carmen* 20
Thirteenth	January, 407	*Carmen* 21
Fourteen	After 407	*Carmen* 29

Paulinus's world. Adapted from Brown, *The Body and Society*.

Dnieper

Caspian
Sea

Black Sea

Sinope

PONTUS
Annesi
ARMENIA

Gangrae   Sebaste
Constantinople   Nisibis
                                                              Mosul   Zagros Mountains
Philippi   Ancyra   Nyssa Vanosa
              Tembris Valley   Caesarea   Edessa
Thessalonica   Cotyaion   Nazianzos   Cyrrhus Mabbug
                                                         Telnesin   Tigris
              PHRYGIA   Iconium   Tarsus   Chalcis
       ASIA   CILICIA   Antioch Tel'Ade   Ctesiphon
       Smyrna   Meryemlik   Emesa   Dura-Europos
       Ephesus   Seleucia
              LYCIA   Olympus
Corinth   Termessus   Salamis   Euphrates
            Patara   Beirut
                                   Damascus
CRETE   CYPRUS   Tyre
                          Caesarea   Gerasa
Aegean   Jerusalem
Sea   Bethlehem Wadi Qumran
                     Eleutheropolis Dead Sea
                            Gaza   Engeddi
                        Pelusium
          Alexandria   Memphis
Cyrene   Nitria   Saqqara
            Kellia   SINAI
          Scetis   Moutain of Anthony
            Fayum Arsinoe
CYRENE   Oxyrhynchus

          Bawit
              Tabennisi/   Red
     Aphrodito Phbow   Sea
        Atripe   Thebes
     Nag-Haminadi
              Esna
     THEBAID

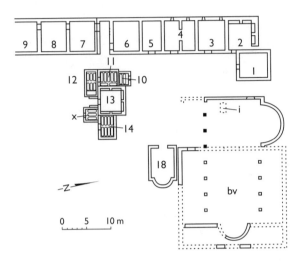

1–9	pagan tombs of the second and third centuries
13	Christian mausoleum of the third century
10–14	Christian mausolea of first half of fourth century
x	tombs of first half of fourth century
18	S. Calionio (before the fifth century)
bv	the Basilica Vetus (fourth century, before 380–81)
i	tomb of Felix

Figure 1. Plans of the basilica complex at Nola / Cimitile. Courtesy of T. Lehman; adapted from *Boreas* 13 (1990).
1a. The basilica complex at the time of Paulinus's Campanian governorship (380–81).

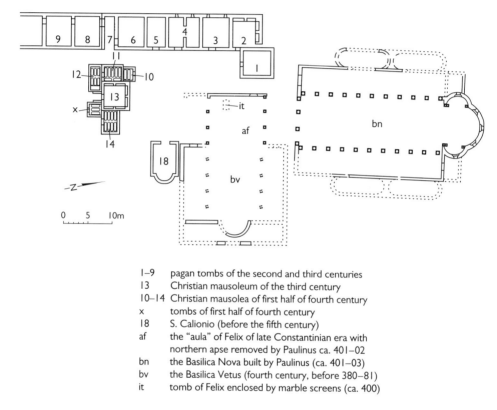

1–9	pagan tombs of the second and third centuries
13	Christian mausoleum of the third century
10–14	Christian mausolea of first half of fourth century
x	tombs of first half of fourth century
18	S. Calionio (before the fifth century)
af	the "aula" of Felix of late Constantinian era with northern apse removed by Paulinus ca. 401–02
bn	the Basilica Nova built by Paulinus (ca. 401–03)
bv	the Basilica Vetus (fourth century, before 380–81)
it	tomb of Felix enclosed by marble screens (ca. 400)

1b. The basilica complex ca. 403 following Paulinus's construction of the Basilica Nova.

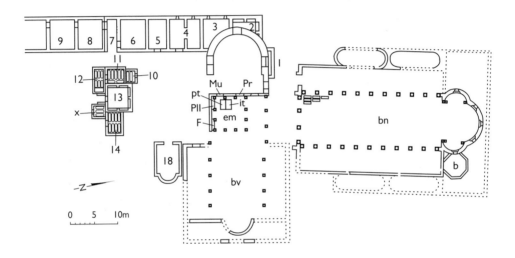

1–9	pagan tombs of the second and third centuries
13	Christian mausoleum of the third century
10–14	Christian mausolea of first half of fourth century
18	S. Calionio (before the fifth century)
21	the great apse (ca. 550?)
b	octagonal structure of fifth or sixth century
bn	the Basilica Nova built by Paulinus (ca. 401–03)
bv	the Basilica Vetus (fourth century, before 380–81)
em	mosaic decorated peristyle (ca. 500)
it	tomb of Felix enclosed by marble screens (ca. 400)
pt	tomb of Paulinus
F	tomb of bishop Felix (d.484)
Mu	tomb of bishop Musonius (d. 535)
PII	tomb of bishop Paulinus II (d. 442)
Pr	tomb of bishop Priscus (d. 523)
S	S. Stefano (sixth century and later)
T	S. Tommaso (sixth century)

1c. The basilica complex in the later fifth and sixth centuries.

CHAPTER 1

—•—

Claiming Paulinus

In the year 394, probably at Barcelona sometime in the late summer or autumn, the Christian senator and noted poet Meropius Pontius Paulinus renounced his secular past and his extensive properties to live for Christ rather than for the world. Paulinus, then in his early forties, had been preparing for the moment for some time. Some five years earlier he had moved away from his estates and friends in Aquitaine and retired with his Spanish-born wife, Therasia, to their properties south of the Pyrenees. Although increasingly attracted to ascetic ideals and already engaged in the formulation of a new Christian poetics, in Spain Paulinus continued at first to live the life of respectable aristocratic retreat, or *otium liberale*, that he had known in his native Aquitaine. In late 394, however, Paulinus yielded to the forces that had been pushing him toward rupture with his social and intellectual past. The spiritual, emotional, and artistic journey of the Spanish years culminated in a *geste spectaculaire*,[1] a sensational rejection of the world in favor of a monastic calling still nascent in the empire's western provinces.

The world, however, was not so easily rejected by a man of Paulinus's rank and wealth. On Christmas Day of 394, a crowd at Barcelona, no doubt eager to lay claim to a rich and influential patron whose wealth had suddenly become disposable, demanded Paulinus's ordination to the priesthood. Their hopes were only partially fulfilled, however, for soon after Easter of the following year, Paulinus, now both monk and priest, left Barcelona for his properties near Nola, a small Campanian town some twenty-three kilometers inland from Naples. Here, at the tomb of the third-century confessor Felix, in the very province where as governor fifteen years before he had wielded "the six-fold *fasces* of authority" (*carm.* 21.395), Paulinus lived until his death on 22 June 431. During the thirty-six years of his

---

1. See J. Fontaine, "Valeurs antiques et valeurs chrétiennes dans la spiritualité des grands propriétaires terriens à la fin du IVe siècle occidental," in *Epektasis: Mélanges patristiques offerts au Cardinal Jean Daniélou*, ed. J. Fontaine and C. Kannengiesser (Paris, 1972), 580.

Nolan residency, Paulinus built lavishly, promoted the cult of Saint Felix, fashioned a local Christianity responsive to the needs of the countryside, and received numerous visitors as Nola became the crossroads of countless letters, texts, and ideas. Prominent bishops, ascetics, and Christian intellectuals embraced the friendship of Paulinus, and he maintained his connections with the Christian aristocracy of Rome by annual trips to the city. By 412 he had become bishop of Nola, and in early 419 he was called on by the imperial court of Honorius to resolve a disputed papal election. Ironically, Paulinus's renunciation of the world and adoption of monasticism propelled him to further prominence within the elite social and ecclesiastical circles of the late Roman west.

But, not unlike the people of Barcelona who had sought to bend Paulinus's new vocation to their own ends, some of those who moved in the competitive and sometimes tense Christian aristocratic circles of the late fourth and early fifth centuries also sought to stake their claims on the remarkable story of his conversion. In their hands, Paulinus quickly emerged as an example for his own age, and the general tone and thrust of contemporary literary representations by the likes of Ambrose, Augustine, and Jerome set in place a framework for generations, even centuries, of thought and writing about Paulinus. Paulinus himself, hardly reluctant to apply his own tale to apologetic ends or to nuance its narrative in the service of issues of the moment, reinforced posterity's natural drift toward selective memory and iconographic representation. For such reasons, and regardless of the other valuable lessons they hold for students of late antiquity, both the testimonials of contemporaries and the letters and poems of Paulinus himself may obscure as well as illuminate the historian's approach to Paulinus. Consequently any new study of Paulinus's life and works or any reappraisal of his world should be prefaced by a consideration of the value and limitations of the ancient literary traditions that have shaped modern images of Paulinus of Nola and by an initial foray into the corpus of Paulinus's own letters and poems, on which, in the end, our assessment of him must largely rest.

VERBAL ICON

Paulinus's "conversion" captured the contemporary imagination, and that conquest lies at the heart of the historian's problem.[2] While some contemporaries immediately decried Paulinus's rejection of normative elite values and his assumed

---

2. The influence on contemporary representation is also observed by B. Näf, *Senatorisches Standesbewusstsein in spätrömischer Zeit* (Freiburg, 1995), 100–101. D. Trout, "History, Biography, and the Exemplary Life of Paulinus of Nola," *Studia Patristica* 32 (1997): 462–67 offers a prolegomenon to this chapter. On *conversio* in the works of Paulinus, see the discussion of J. T. Lienhard, *Paulinus of Nola and Early Western Monasticism* (Köln and Bonn, 1977), 33–51; with Fontaine, "Valeurs," 580, on the process of simplification.

abnegation of domestic and social responsibility,[3] others seized on the didactic power latent in his conversion and his new way of living. Ambrose, Augustine, Jerome, Sulpicius Severus, and others quickly harnessed the edifying force of Paulinus's story by collapsing his "biography" into the act of secular renunciation that seemed to them to epitomize the victory of the Christian present over the errors of the past. Offered as exhortation and defense to a wider public, such a sharply pointed image of conversion to a life lived for Christ, they suspected, could provoke or affirm similar commitments to the values implied by Paulinus's tale. But these influential literary transfigurations performed on the *vita* of Paulinus inevitably veiled or distorted the complexity of his conversion and his subsequent life at Nola. Indeed, they consciously drained Paulinus's life of many of its particularizing details as they fashioned him into a stylized type and assimilated his secular renunciation to a select body of scriptural images and metaphors.

Even our earliest testimonial to Paulinus's conversion reveals the paradigmatic allure of his story. In a letter written soon after the news of Paulinus's renunciation had reached him at Milan, Ambrose, the city's eminent bishop, staged a preemptive strike against those Roman aristocrats who would, he assumed, greet Paulinus's rejection of his rank and patrimony with incredulity and animosity.[4] "What will the nobles (*proceres viri*) say when they have heard these things?" he prodded his correspondent, Sabinus, and immediately offered his own answer: "That a man from that family, with that lineage, of that much talent, endowed with such great eloquence, has abandoned the Senate and broken the continuity of a noble family: this cannot be borne."[5]

To rebut such reproaches and, perhaps most important, to reassure the hesitant, the bishop of Milan suggested to Sabinus that Paulinus's rejection of wealth, home, and family was the equivalent of both David's whirling dance before the Ark (2 Sam 6.14–23) and Isaiah's scandalous nakedness before the people (Is 20). Actions unseemly in the eyes of men, that is, might well appear honorable before God. In fact, Paulinus, like David and Isaiah, had shown himself unashamed to lift up his works "so that they might shine before his Father."[6] Moreover, Ambrose

---

3. For example, the rebuttals at Amb. *ep.* 6.27.3 (*CSEL* 82) = *ep.* 58.3 (*PL* 16); Paul. *ep.* 5.13. Paulinus's *epistulae* and *carmina* are cited from the edition of G. de Hartel, *CSEL* 29 and 30 (1894), unless otherwise noted. See also appendix A.

4. On Paulinus's likely meeting with Ambrose in the early 380s, see chapter 2. On the date and context of the letter, late 394 or early 395, see chapter 5.

5. *Ep.* 6.27.3 (*CSEL* 82): "Haec ubi audierint proceres viri, quae loquentur? Ex illa familia, illa prosapia, illa indole, tanta praeditum eloquentia migrasse a senatu, interceptam familiae nobilis succesionem: ferri hoc non posse." For the potential effect of such social sabotage on a family's social and economic position see B. Shaw, "The Family in Late Antiquity: The Experience of Augustine," *Past and Present* 115 (1987): 3–51.

6. *Ep.* 6.27.8: "ut lucerent coram patre suo."

discouraged any criticism of Paulinus by reminding his readers of the point of Isaiah's behavior. In Isaiah's actions, he duly noted, God had communicated through example (*exemplum*) what he might have expressed openly in words, for Isaiah's shocking nudity prefigured the captivity and nakedness of faithless Jewish youths and maidens.[7] Ambrose left Paulinus's would-be critics to consider for themselves the retribution that might be reserved for them, but the implications of his collation of Paulinus and Isaiah are patent.

They are no less so for the historian. Provoked by an anticipated clamor of hostile reaction, Ambrose had situated Paulinus's subversive rejection of his wealth and career within a framework of a universal and timeless conflict of values. To do so, he screened any peculiarities of Paulinus's conversion behind scriptural typology and presented Paulinus to contemporaries as an edifying example at a time when even many committed Christians were still suspicious of asceticism. Consequently, the defense of Paulinus that appears in this letter perhaps reveals more about Ambrose's rhetorical strategies than about the historical Paulinus.

A year or so later, probably in early 396, Augustine, with an equal show of confidence and even less desire to particularize, also exploited the exemplary force of Paulinus's story. Writing to Licentius, son of his longtime patron, Romanianus, Augustine offered the lesson of Paulinus's conversion to a young man he deemed still too much in love with the world. "Go to Campania (*vade in Campaniam*)," he wrote to Licentius,

> learn (*disce*) about Paulinus, that excellent and holy servant of God, how without hesitation he shook off the great pride of this world from a neck so much more noble for being more humble in order to submit to the yoke of Christ (*Christi iugum*), as he has done. And now at rest (*quietus*) and dispassionate he rejoices with Christ as the governor of his journey (*iter suus*). Go (*vade*), learn (*disce*) with what wealth of mind he offers to Christ the sacrifices of praise, returning to him whatever good he has received, lest he lose all things if he should not restore them to him from whom he has them.[8]

To a young man who had recently expressed in tortured verses the difficulty of following the "secret path" plotted by Varro through the thickets of the liberal arts (*arcanum Varronis iter*), Augustine proposed instead the tranquillity and ease of the *iter Paulini*.[9] Augustine's referral was shrewdly calculated. The example of

---

7. *Ep.* 6.27.11: "Potuit quidem hoc et sermone exprimere, sed exemplo acerbare maluit." Cf. Is 20.2.

8. *Ep.* 26.5 (*CSEL* 34): "Vade in Campaniam, disce Paulinum, egregium et sanctum dei servum, quam grandem fastum saeculi huius tanto generosiore quanto humiliore cervice incunctanter excusserit, ut eam subderet Christi iugo, sicut subdidit; et nunc illo moderatore itineris sui quietus et modestus exultat. vade, disce, quibus opibus ingenii sacrificia laudis ei offerat refundens illi, quicquid boni accepit ex illo, ne amittat omnia, si non in eo reponat, a quo haec habet."

9. Licentius's poem addressed to Augustine is transmitted with Aug. *ep.* 26 (*CSEL* 34). For a recent study, text, and translation see D. Shanzer, "'*Arcanum Varronis iter*': Licentius's Verse Epistle to Augus-

Paulinus, onetime senator but still practicing poet, might be the perfect antidote to the seductions of office, marriage, and *Roma potens* that continued to infect Licentius despite his long association with Augustine.[10] But Augustine, like Ambrose, also offered his correspondent a Paulinus dressed up in poetic metaphors and scriptural images. He prefaced Licentius's summons to Campania, where Paulinus had donned the yoke of Christ, with a quotation of Christ's gospel invitation: "Take my yoke (*iugum*) upon you and learn (*discite*) from me because I am gentle and humble in heart and you will find rest (*requiem*) for your souls. For my yoke is easy and my burden light" (Matt 11.29–30).[11] By traveling to Campania, Augustine implied, Licentius could now learn from Paulinus's example (*disce Paulinum*) what he had so long refused to take from Christ's words.[12] The *iter Paulini* proposed by Augustine to Licentius was, Augustine suggested, far less treacherous than the routes to power and influence that led through the halls of Rome's noble families.

To persuade Licentius, Augustine veiled any potentially troublesome social or psychological dimensions of Paulinus's secular renunciation behind the simple but vivid metaphor of the yoke of Christ. Like Ambrose reporting Paulinus's conversion to Sabinus (but implicitly acknowledging the personal cost), Augustine crafted a stylized Paulinus who could serve Augustine's rhetorical ends. An Augustine who by his own account, soon forthcoming in the *Confessions*, had struggled so hard to find humility and truth held out to Licentius the image of Paulinus "unhesitatingly" shrugging off the pride of the world to shoulder Christ's easy yoke. It is a suggestion of precipitousness and self-confidence hard to sustain on closer inspection of Paulinus's own works, but one that might effectively be contemplated by a young man wracked by the anxieties of public life. For such a man, as apparently for Augustine a decade earlier in Milan,[13] letting go of worldly ambitions might indeed bring the intoxicating calm that validated Christ's gospel claim.[14] Thus it was Augustine's desire to emphasize in

---

tine," *REAug* 37 (1991): 110–43. Shanzer suggests that the *iter Varronis* referenced a work by Varro of Reate containing *compendia* on at least three of the liberal arts.

10. See Paulinus's depreciation of these powerful allurements, which had once entrapped him, in his (partially verse) epistle to Licentius, *ep*. 8.4, with broader discussion by B. Näf, "Paulinus von Nola und Rom," *Studia Patristica* 33 (1997): 448–53, esp. 449.

11. Aug. *ep*. 26.5: "tollite iugum meum super vos et discite a me, quoniam mitis sum et humilis corde, et invenietis requiem animabus vestris, iugum enim meum lene est et sarcina mea levis est."

12. Cp. Aug. *De mendacio* 1.15.30 (*PL* 40.508) on the deeds of the saints as keys to the interpretation of scripture.

13. Aug. *Conf.* 8.12.29.

14. The story has a long sequel: Paulinus, to whom Augustine evidently sent both a copy of Licentius's poem and of his own letter to Licentius (see *ep*. 8.3), did not miss his cue. His own (equally vague and elusive) poetic exhortation to Licentius echoed the plaint of Augustine: "'Quid retrahis fera colla iugo? mea sarcina levis, / Suave iugum' Christi est vox pia, crede deo" (*ep*. 8.3, ll. 27–28). Many years later an aged Augustine would quote a verse of Paulinus's poem to a correspondent named Cornelius; *ep*. 259.5: "Christi est vox pia, crede deo."

his rendering of Paulinus the availability of this relief to anyone who simply took up that yoke.

Paulinus's native Gaul offers a third illustration of the reductive process glimpsed in the two letters of Ambrose and Augustine. About the same time that Augustine composed his letter to Licentius, an embattled Sulpicius Severus, a friend and regular correspondent of Paulinus, was embarking on his own literary defense of ascetic piety. To assist his cause, Severus slipped the story of Paulinus into the pages of his *Life* of Saint Martin, the controversial monk and bishop of Tours.[15] But, like Ambrose and Augustine, Severus fortified his Paulinus by appeal to scripture, in this case to one of the age's most powerful gospel proclamations. "If you wish to be perfect," Jesus had admonished the rich young man of Matthew's gospel, "go, sell what you have, give to the poor, and you will have treasure in heaven; and come, follow me (*sequere me*)" (Matt 19.21). It was this well-known text that provided the language and images with which Severus's Martin would praise Paulinus.

During his own first meeting with Martin, Severus reported that

> [Martin's] talk with us was about not other than the abandonment of the entice-
> ments of the world and the burdens of the age so that we might follow (*sequeremur*) the
> Lord Jesus freely and readily. And he offered to us as the most outstanding example
> (*exemplum*) of our time that illustrious man Paulinus, whom we mentioned earlier. He,
> having thrown away his great wealth and followed Christ (*Christum secutus*), almost
> alone in these times had fulfilled the evangelic teaching. We must follow and imitate
> him, he exclaimed. The present age was fortunate in an example (*documentum*) of such
> great faith and virtue, since, according to the will of God, as a rich man and pos-
> sessing many things, by selling all and giving to the poor, he had made possible by
> example (*exemplum*) what was impossible to accomplish.[16]

"Martin's" discourse here achieved several ends. His endorsement, of course, sanctioned Paulinus's recent secular renunciation by configuring it as the fulfillment of Jesus' gospel proclamation. But Severus simultaneously managed to validate Martin's ascetic practices (and perhaps his own) through association with the conversion of the wealthy and aristocratic Paulinus. Once again, however, a scrip-

---

15. For context see C. Stancliffe, *St. Martin and His Hagiographer: History and Miracle in Sulpicius Severus* (Oxford, 1983), 78–80. See further and on the date (396 or early 397), D. Trout, "*Amicitia, Auctoritas,* and Self-Fashioning Texts," *Studia Patristica* 28 (1993): 124 n. 4.

16. *V. Mar.* 25.4–5 (Fontaine, *SC* 103): "Sermo autem illius non alius apud nos fuit quam mundi in-lecebras et saeculi onera relinquenda, ut Dominum Iesum liberi expeditique sequeremur; praestantis-simumque nobis praesentium temporum inlustris viri Paulini, cuius supra fecimus mentionem, exem-plum ingerebat, qui summis opibus abiectis Christum secutus, solus paene his temporibus evangelica praecepta complesset; illum nobis sequendum, illum clamabat imitandum; beatumque esse praesens saeculum tantae fidei virtutisque documento, cum secundum sententiam Domini, dives et possidens multa, vendendo omnia et dando pauperibus, quod erat factu inpossibile possible fecesit exemplo."

tural image provided the means of encoding complex behavior, as the reader was asked to interpret the story of Paulinus's conversion through the narrative of the gospel story. But with a significant twist, of course: for while the rich man of Matthew's tale balked at Jesus' advice, Paulinus embraced it to become an edifying example of faith and virtue. It was not in Severus's interest in the *Vita Martini*, any more than it had been in Augustine's when he wrote to Licentius, to allow the details or realities of Paulinus's renunciation to intrude on the tale. Subtle censorship might be as effective as invention in shaping a life.[17]

So much may seem too obvious to warrant such attention here, but apology and exhortation like those served up so quickly by Ambrose, Augustine, and Severus frame so many of the surviving *testimonia* on the life of Paulinus that we might be dulled to their force. Paulinus was indeed "something of an exhibit" in his own day and for that reason often subject to staging.[18] The Spanish priest Eutropius, for example, enlisted Paulinus in his *Letter on Condemning Inheritance* addressed to the daughters of a certain Geruntius;[19] Jerome employed his image to exhort his correspondent Julianus to secular renunciation;[20] Eucherius of Lyon recalled the "special and blessed example (*peculiare et beatum exemplum*)" of Paulinus in his *On Contempt for the World (De contemptu mundi)*;[21] while elsewhere Augustine and Severus returned to his name.[22] This fascination with the didactic power of Paulinus's conversion demonstrates the effect of his story on contemporaries; but such passages as those examined above illustrate equally how the very nature of the act that so forcefully brought Paulinus to the notice of his contemporaries also virtually ensured that his biography was simplified, and even distorted, so that he could be set up as an *exemplum* of the (true) Christian life.

Biographical modeling for polemical ends was practically endemic to a late-ancient culture that was itself the product of centuries of "continuity through

17. R. Lane Fox, "The *Life of Daniel*," in *Portraits: Biographical Representation in the Greek and Latin Literature of the Roman Empire*, ed. M. Edwards and S. Swain (Oxford, 1997), 200–210, quote 201.

18. P. Brown, *The Cult of the Saints: Its Rise and Function in Latin Christianity* (Chicago, 1981), 54.

19. *Epistula de contemnenda haereditate* (*PL* 30.45–50, esp. 48C).

20. Jerome *ep.* 118.5 (*Ad Iulianum exhortatoria, CSEL* 55): "Nec est, quod te excuses nobilitate et divitiarum pondere. respice sanctum virum Pammachium et ferventissimae fidei Paulinum presbyterum, qui non solum divitias, sed se ipsos domino obtulerunt, qui contra diaboli tergiversationem nequaquam pellem pro pelle (Hiob. 2.4), sed carnes et ossa et animas suas domino consecrarunt, qui te et exemplo et eloquio, id est et opere et lingua, possint ad maiora producere. nobilis es: et illi, sed in Christo nobiliores. dives et honoratus: et illi, immo ex divitibus et [inclitis pauperes et] inglorii et idcirco ditiores et magis incliti, quia pro Christo pauperes et inhonorati."

21. *Epistola paraenetica ad Valerianum cognatum de contemptu mundi et saecularis philosphiae* (*PL* 50.718D–719A) = *Il rifuto del mondo: De contemptu mundi*, ed. S. Pricoco (Florence, 1990), 385–90: "Paulinus quoque, Nolanus episcopus, peculiare et beatum Galliae nostrae exemplum, ingenti quondam divitiarum censu uberrimo eloquentiae fonte; ita in sententiam nostram propositumque migravit, ut etiam cunctas admodum mundi partes eloquio operibusque resperserit."

22. For example, *De civ. Dei* 1.10; Sev. *Dial.* 3.17.3–4.

replication" of the ethical principles enshrined in stories of exemplary persons.[23] Indeed, we are better equipped to approach and respect the sources that thus enlisted Paulinus if we set them against the background of antiquity's long-standing tradition of moral exhortation and social criticism through biographical portraits. Roman reformers, social critics, and political analysts, drawing on the Hellenic and Hellenistic legacy of rhetorical historiography and panegyric, consistently turned to history and biography as vehicles for political and ethical instruction.[24] Centuries before Paulinus's birth, Sallust's scathing portrait of Catiline and Livy's panorama of Rome's early history canonized the relationship between social or political analysis, the biographic, and the moral exhortation that schoolboys would still meet in the later fourth century.[25] Nearly two centuries after Paulinus's death, this same reliance on both villains and heroes for moral diagnosis and prescription still infused Gregory of Tours's *Liber vitae patrum,* a collection of lives of twenty Gallic saints intended to inspire emulation as well as to build up the church (just as it helped Bede to justify the composition of his *Ecclesiastical History*).[26] Furthermore, this marriage of biography and moral philosophy had been revitalized in Paulinus's own day. Not only were ancient history's leading figures kept alive in texts and classroom exercises, continuing to offer examples of *res sequendas et fugiendas,*[27] but Christian writers also readily took up and reinvigorated this mode of discourse through attention to new subjects. Thus while no less a work than Augustine's *City of God* employed such traditional exemplars as Lucretia, Cato, and

23. P. Brown, "The Saint as Exemplar in Late Antiquity," *Representations* 2 (1983), esp. 1–6.

24. See A. Momigliano, *The Development of Greek Biography* (Cambridge, Mass., 1971), esp. 43–100; J. Geiger, *Cornelius Nepos and Ancient Political Biography* (Stuttgart, 1985); B. Gentili and G. Cerri, *History and Biography in Ancient Thought* (Amsterdam, 1988); S. Swain, "Biography and the Biographic in the Literature of the Roman Empire," in Edwards and Swain, *Portraits,* 1–37, esp. 22–36.

25. See the Gracchan historian Sempronius Asellio on the superiority of *res gestae* over *annales* (Peter frag.1.2 = Gellius *NA* 5.18.9): "Nam neque alacriores, inquit, ad rem publicam defendendam neque segniores ad rem perperam faciundam annales libri commovere quosquam possunt." Cp. Sal. *Jug.* 4.5–6; *Cat.* 3.1–2; Liv. *praef.* 10, with P. G. Walsh, *Livy: His Historical Aims and Methods* (Cambridge, 1961), chapters 3 and 4.

26. *Liber vitae patrum* (*MGH SRM* 1.2), *praef.*: "verum etiam auditorum animos incitate ad profectum." See Bede's preface to the *Ecclesiastical History:* "If history relates good things of men, the attentive reader is excited to imitate that which is good (*ad imitandum bonum*); or if it mentions evil things of wicked persons, nevertheless the religious and pious hearer or reader, shunning that which is hurtful and perverse, is the more easily excited to perform these things which he knows to be good and worthy of God." On the *Liber vitae patrum* see further T. Heffernan, *Sacred Biography: Saints and Their Biographers in the Middle Ages* (Oxford, 1988), 3–6. In the centuries between Livy and Gregory, the same principle had helped to inspire such works as Valerius Maximus's *Memorabilia,* the lives of Plutarch, and the various *De viris illustribus* composed from Nepos through late antiquity. See Nepos, *Att.* 19.1, with comments of T. McCarty, "The Content of Cornelius Nepos's *De Viris Illustribus,*" *CW* 67 (1973–74): 386–91; and the prefaces to Plut. *Aem.* and *Per.*

27. I. Lana, "La storiografia latina pagana del IV sec. d.C.," *Koinonia* 3 (1979): 7–28.

Regulus to debate the ethical, social, and theological conundrums cast up by the Visigothic sack of Rome in August 410,[28] the authors of hagiographical works, notably Athanasius, Jerome, and Sulpicius Severus, consciously presented the lives of their ascetic subjects as models for imitation.

But the literary representation of such figures as the desert hermit Anthony or Martin of Tours, enlisted not from the dim reaches of the Roman past but from the bright light of contemporary debates, introduced new tensions into an old scheme. While these near-contemporary models might be fashioned into "verbal icons"[29] just as readily as those heroes of early Rome whom Livy had wished to set out for all to see like exemplars on a public monument,[30] suspected distortions might quickly draw hostile fire. Thus some criticized Jerome for the fantastic qualities of his *Vita Pauli*, while Sulpicius Severus worried for similar reasons about the reception of his portrait of Martin.[31] Familiarity with a subject could not guarantee an author's truthfulness, accuracy, or independence of mind.[32] More often, in fact, the exemplary status of an individual life was ensured not by an emphasis on the baldly idiosyncratic or peculiar but through close association with expectations now heavily shaped by scriptural images or precepts.[33] That is, like the sculpted portraits of philosophers set out for viewing in late Roman Aphrodisias, whose individualizing features were conflated with standard categorical markers and *topoi* to create an intelligible text,[34] the persuasive power of these new ascetic heroes of the late fourth century was generated as much by their alleged typicality as by their individuality.

It was in a field of discourse charged by such impulses that the "new" Paulinus was quickly seized on and held up for contemplation and imitation. Almost reflexively Ambrose, Augustine, Severus, and others drew on Christianity's rich storehouse of images to suggest to their audiences the ways of comprehending and the means of condoning an act still provocative in the eyes of many. By articulating Paulinus's ascetic conversion through striking scriptural metaphors—the nakedness of Isaiah, the yoke of Christ, the rich young man and the eye of the

28. On Lucretia see D. Trout, "Re-textualizing Lucretia: Cultural Subversion in the *City of God*," *JECS* 2 (1994): 53–70.

29. A. Cameron, *Christianity and the Rhetoric of Empire: The Development of Christian Discourse* (Berkeley, 1991), esp. 57, 141–52.

30. Liv. *praef.* 10: "Hoc illud est praecipue in cognitione rerum salubre ac frugiferum, omnis te exempli documenta in inlustri posita monumento intueri."

31. Jer. *V. Malchi*, praef; Sev. *V. Mar.* 25.

32. See the perceptive remarks of N. McLynn, *Ambrose of Milan: Church and Court in a Christian Capital* (Berkeley, 1994), xvii–xviii, on the shortcomings of Paulinus of Milan as the biographer of Ambrose.

33. See too Swain, "Biography and the Biographic," 33–34.

34. R. R. R. Smith, "Late Roman Philosopher Portraits from Aphrodisias," *JRS* 80 (1990), esp. 144–46, 148–50.

needle—Paulinus's advocates hoped to stamp a potentially renegade act with legitimacy. They focused their readers' attention narrowly upon the moment of Paulinus's conversion and his renunciation of the world, that instant when he danced naked before the people, took up Christ's yoke, and prepared to pass through the needle's eye. Seldom were those who staged his story in this manner concerned with the penumbra of his life on either side of a "conversion" that was best left uncomplicated. The brilliance that flooded that moment might profitably force so much extraneous detail into the shadows.

AN EXEMPLARY LIFE

Paulinus's life remained exemplary long after his death. The virtues that many contemporaries recognized in his tale continued to influence various observers in later antiquity and the early Middle Ages, who were similarly inspired to recall Paulinus's literary talents, his riches, and the conversion to God by which he was made even "more noble."[35] Eucherius of Lyon, writing around the time of Paulinus's death, exhorted his kinsman Valerianus toward contempt for the world by enlisting "the special and blessed example (*exemplum*) of our own Gaul, Paulinus, bishop of Nola."[36] Eucherius not only publicized Paulinus's vast wealth yet again, but, like virtually every other writer who mentioned Paulinus in subsequent centuries, he also stood in awe of Paulinus's eloquence and erudition.[37] Writers of chronicles and collections of the lives of illustrious men compiled lists of his works, including some texts otherwise unknown and some assuredly misassigned.[38] In the

35. Hydatius, *Chronicon* ad annum 424: "Paulinus nobilissimus et eloquentissimus dudum, conversione ad deum nobilior factus, vir apostolicus, Nola Campaniae episcopus habetur insignis." Text at A. Tranoy, *SC* 218 (1974),126; R. Burgess, *The Chronicle of Hydatius and the Consularia Constantinopolitana* (Oxford, 1993), 88–89. There are collections of later *elogia* and *testimonia* at *PL* 61.125–52 and, more usefully, by J. T. Lienhard, "Paulinus of Nola in the Literary Tradition," *Paradosis: Studies in Memory of Edwin A. Quain* (New York, 1976), 35–45.

36. Eucherius, *De contemptu mundi* (*PL* 50.718D): "Paulinus quoque, Nolanus episcopus, peculiare et beatum Galliae nostrae exemplum."

37. Eucherius, *De contemptu mundi:* "uberrimo eloquentiae fonte." Gennadius, *De viris illustribus* 49 (Richardson): "claruit . . . eruditione." Hydatius, *Chron.* ad annum 424 "eloquentissimus." Cassiodorus, *Institutiones* 1.21 (Mynors): "litteris saecularibus eruditus." Gregory of Tours, *De gloria confessorum* 108 (*MGH SRM* 1.2): "rhetoricis litteris eruditus." Gregory the Great, *Dialogues* 3.1.2 (*SC* 260): "vir eloquentissimus atque adprime exterioribus quoque studiis eruditus."

38. Gennadius, *De vir. ill.* 49 (Richardson), supplied the fullest list. Gennadius knew or knew of Paulinus's *carm.* 31 (the *consolatio*), a collection of letters to Severus, and the panegyric to Theodosius. He mentions several otherwise unknown works: Paulinus's letters to his *soror* "de contemptu mundi" (presumably his wife Therasia, but see S. Prete, *Paolino di Nola e l'umanisimo cristiano: Saggio sopra il suo epistolario* [Bologna, 1964], 170); a work on the sacraments and one on / of hymns ("Fecit et sacramentorum [opus] et hymnorum."); a book *de paenitentia* and one *de laude generali omnium martyrum.* Hydatius merely notes the existence of "studia praedicanda." Isidore of Seville, *De viris illustribus* 17 (*PL* 83.1092), mentions only a "concise and brief" book on the Benedictions of the Patriarchs and a *vita* of Ambrose.

manner of Ambrose, Augustine, and Jerome two centuries earlier, Gregory the Great still acknowledged and promoted a version of Paulinus's increasingly diffuse story.[39]

The image of *Saint* Paulinus, however, like that of so many other late-Roman holy men, shifted subtly in the two centuries after his death, as oral tradition supplanted written records and supplemented select collections of his own poems and letters. By the later fifth century Gennadius knew Paulinus not only for his erudition and exemplary life, but also for his power over demons.[40] Indeed, throughout the former provinces of the western empire, anecdote and legend enhanced Paulinus's mystical powers,[41] although in the literary tradition he never fully assumed the mantle of the thaumaturge. It was not so much his Gallo-Roman origin, proudly noted by Eucherius, as his connection to Martin and his presence in Severus's *Vita Martini* that ensured the preservation of Paulinus's memory and the evolution of his image at Tours. Gregory of Tours admitted in his *De gloria confessorum* to having read no life of Paulinus, although he clearly knew Uranius's *De obitu*, an account of Paulinus's final days, as well as some of Paulinus's *natalicia* recounting the life and miracles of Felix.[42] It was rather from "trustworthy sources" that Gregory had heard the colorful anecdotes illustrating Paulinus's simple humility and deep sense of charity that the bishop repeated in his *Glory of the Confessors*.[43] The stories Gregory related, however, at best reflect only very dimly the incidents portrayed in Paulinus's extant works, an illustration perhaps of the "trustworthiness" of the sources that also led to Gregory's mistaken belief that Paulinus of Nola, rather than Paulinus of Périgueux, had versified Severus's *Vita Martini*.[44] Such was the state of "history" in sixth-century Gaul.

In Italy, Gregory the Great's vision of Paulinus was hardly less clouded by legend, misunderstanding, and conflation of sources. Gregory opened the third book of his *Dialogues* with an elaborate tale of voluntary captivity with which he aimed to illustrate Paulinus's humility and charity. The story took Paulinus to the

---

The former is probably the work of Rufinus of Aquileia, introduced by letters from Paulinus (*CCSL* 20.189–90, 203–4 = Paul. *epp.* 46, 47); the latter is misassigned from Paulinus of Milan. Cp. the chronicle of 452, *MGH AA* 9, 630, 650.

39. *Dial.* 3. *praef.*

40. *De vir. ill.* 49: "Claruit . . . potentia adversum daemones."

41. Gregory the Great relied on what his forefathers had told him (*Dial.* 3. *praef.*).

42. *De gloria martyrum* 103 (*MGH, SRM* 1.2), a *vita* of Felix, shows Gregory familiar with at least *carm.* 15, 16, 18, and 23 (the *natalicia* of 398–401), which group might reflect works once sent by Paulinus to Severus. See Paul. *ep.* 28.6 of 402 / 3 and below chapter 9. There is now a translation by R. Van Dam, *Gregory of Tours: Glory of the Martyrs* (Liverpool, 1988). Bede also composed a *vita* of Felix dependent on Paulinus's poems (*PL* 94.789–98). Uranius's *De obitu* is implied at *De gloria confessorum* 108—evidence, perhaps, that the addressee of the *De obitu*, Pacatus, was a Gallo-Roman.

43. *De gloria confessorum* 108: "per relationem fidelium." Translation by R. Van Dam, *Gregory of Tours: Glory of the Confessors* (Liverpool 1988).

44. *De gloria confessorum* 108.

African court of a Vandal king where, to obtain the release of a poor widow's son, he offered himself as a gardener to the king's son-in-law. Subsequently, by foretelling the king's imminent death, Paulinus earned the release of a group of prisoners. In imitation of Christ, Gregory concluded, Paulinus had surrendered to slavery to secure the freedom of others.[45] If the legend bristles with often noted historical impossibilities,[46] like the anecdotes recorded by Gregory of Tours, it nevertheless served to depict a Paulinus whose sanctity was rooted in a deep humility that is, in fact, merely one dimension of the complex historical figure. Like Paulinus's contemporaries, these later writers fashioned Paulinus's "biography" to accord with present issues and immediate tastes. In the waning years of the Roman West Paulinus's life had obviously sacrificed little of its claim on the cultural imagination.

Perhaps, then, it is not surprising that the exemplary elements ascribed to Paulinus's life have drawn the attention of so many of his modern biographers and readers. Paulinus's two premier nineteenth-century biographers, Adolf Buse and François Lagrange, for example, both hoped to edify contemporaries with Paulinus's exceptional piety and devotion. Buse, for whom Paulinus's age was a providential period when a new Christian dawn arose from the night of a dying civilization, believed his goal would be met if his work endowed a single reader with "the unreserved love, the unselfish devotion, the lofty mind of Paulinus."[47] As the nineteenth century closed, Gaston Boissier also defined his Paulinus through moral qualities. For Boissier, however, Paulinus's tolerance and humanity, as well as his delicacy and a simplicity that compensated for a lack of originality, not only characterized the man but also marked him as "one of us," to be reckoned along with Martin and Severus as representative of "l'idéal d'un saint français."[48] Others agreed; Paulinus seemed to have been given to his age to be "le modèle du parfait chrétien." With a heart simple and trusting, unwavering in his doctrine, unruffled by controversy, full of love of God and charity for mankind, he was distinctly a "saint français."[49] More recently Paulinus, by virtue of "sua natura più

45. *Dial.* 3.1.1–8. Cp. Paul the Deacon, *Historia romana*, 14.18 (*MGH AA* 2.207).

46. P. Fabre, *Saint Paulin de Nole et l'amitié chrétienne* (Paris, 1949), 44–46, is judicious. More recently, see G. Santaniello, "La prigionia di Paolino: Tradizione e storia," *Paolino di Nola: Momenti della sua vita e delle sue opere* (Nola, 1983), 221–49; and J. M. Petersen, *The Dialogues of Gregory the Great in Their Late Antique Cultural Background* (Toronto, 1984), 15–18.

47. A. Buse, *Paulin, Bischof von Nola, und seine Zeit (350–450)*,(Regensburg, 1856), quote 1:ix. French translation by L. Dancoisne, *S. Paulin, évêque de Nole et son siècle (350–450)*(Paris, 1858). F. Lagrange, *Histoire de saint Paulin de Nole* (Paris, 1877, 2d ed. 1882). These and earlier studies are usefully glossed by Fabre, *Paulin de Nole*, 9–13.

48. G. Boissier, *La fin du paganisme: Étude sue les dernières luttes religieuses en occident au quatrième siècle*, 3d ed. (Paris, 1898), 2:49, 59.

49. A. Baudrillart, *Saint Paulin: Évêque de Nole (353–431)*(Paris, 1905), i–viii. This image of the pure, simple, and placid Paulinus has not lacked more modern purveyors. See, for example, N. Chadwick, *Poetry and Letters in Early Christian Gaul* (London, 1955), 72 ff.; J. Wright, "Saint Paulinus of Nola," *Clas-*

fine e sensible" as a man, a litterateur, and a poet, has been reclaimed and universalized as a representative of that spirit of humanism "always operating in history."[50] In the wake of such assessments it is no wonder that Paulinus passes through one recent survey of Roman imperial history as "a simple parish priest" or that a new study of friendship in the classical world was able to gloss Paulinus as a humble-spirited man "who, of all his contemporaries, seems to have taken Christian meekness most to heart."[51] It is no small testimony to the legacy of the ancient literary tradition as well as to the power of Paulinus's own words that this facet of his image has endured so long and so well.

But meekness has had its critics. Arnaldo Momigliano's 1959 essay "Christianity and the Decline of the Roman Empire" thus inspired a rather different, but no less sincere and spirited, assessment of the historical importance of Paulinus. When Momigliano, acknowledging his debt to Edward Gibbon, argued that Christianity inadvertently prepared the way for the western empire's collapse, both by diverting men of talent from public service to the church and the monastery and by promoting an ideology of civic ambivalence that encouraged a defeatist attitude before the barbarians,[52] a number of scholars reflexively pointed to the case of Paulinus. C. H. Coster added a cautionary postscript to this effect to a republished article on Paulinus and the German invasions,[53] while P. G. Walsh, who was then engaged with the translation of Paulinus's letters and poems, saw Paulinus as a striking illustration of Momigliano's thesis: Walsh's Paulinus, "a characteristic spokesman" of western monastic Christianity, had not only rejected state service but repudiated "the whole cultural ethos of the Graeco-Roman world."[54] The most influential argument in this direction, however, was set out by W. H. C. Frend in 1969. Although sensitive to the contradictions in Paulinus's thought, Frend ultimately found him "truly representative of the deeper psychological causes that led to the fall of the Roman Empire in the West."[55] Christianity, especially the ascetic element represented by Paulinus, had indeed undermined aristocratic traditions of public service and sanctioned "a failure of nerve."

sica et Iberica: A Festschrift in Honor of the Reverend Joseph M.-F. Marique, S.J., ed. P. T. Brannan (Worcester, 1975), 417–23.

50. Prete, *Paolino di Nola e l'umanisimo cristiano*, x.

51. C. Wells, *The Roman Empire*, 2d ed. (Cambridge, Mass., 1992), 221; D. Konstan, *Friendship in the Classical World* (Cambridge, 1997), 159.

52. "Christianity and the Decline of the Roman Empire," in *The Conflict between Paganism and Christianity in the Fourth Century*, ed. A. Momigliano (Oxford, 1963), 1–16.

53. "Christianity and the Invasions: Paulinus of Nola," in C. H. Coster, *Late Roman Studies* (Cambridge, Mass., 1968), 203.

54. "Paulinus of Nola and the Conflict of Ideologies in the Fourth Century," in *Kyriakon: Festschrift Johannes Quasten* (Münster, 1970), 565–71, quote 566.

55. "Paulinus of Nola and the Last Century of the Western Empire," *JRS* 59 (1969): 1–11, quote 11. The article is the basis of Frend's more discursive "The Two Worlds of Paulinus of Nola," in *Latin Literature of the Fourth Century*, ed. J. W. Binns (London, 1974), 100–33.

Like Walsh, Frend stressed the apparently radical nature of Paulinus's ascetic turn from the world. And while the former even denied to Paulinus the potentially exonerating desire to exercise ecclesiastical leadership despite spurning a public career, Frend chided Paulinus for his failure to rise to the occasion even in the one great public debate that should have stirred him, the Pelagian controversy.[56] For theorists of decline and fall, then, Paulinus's example has been no less enticing, if for some far less uplifting, than it has been for those mesmerized by the moral eddies of his letters and poems.

In an ironically similar vein, others have asserted the mediocrity of Paulinus's thought to champion the typicality of his mind. To such readers Paulinus's exemplary status is ensured precisely because he was a pedestrian figure in an age of so many extraordinary men. Hence one fundamental study of Paulinus's monasticism was justified in part because its author recognized Paulinus as a "typical ascetic" of the age, no towering genius like Augustine, no temperamental scholar like Jerome.[57] Even Pierre Fabre, whose study of Paulinus's spirituality and psychology remains in many ways unsurpassed, would nod towards Paulinus's self-confessed *mediocritas* as justification for his study: to render the soul of Paulinus was to reveal the soul of his age. Too many of Paulinus's better-known contemporaries, like Jerome and Augustine, loomed like summits over their times, and thus above the spirit of the age.[58]

Not all observers, of course, have chosen to smooth out the ruffles of Paulinus's personality or overlook the distinctive qualities of his thought. In his germinal study of Paulinus's passionate articulation of his relationship with Saint Felix, Peter Brown found one reason for awarding Paulinus "a place alongside the mighty Augustine, as a founder of Latin Christian piety."[59] Moreover, Paulinus's poetry, like late Latin poetry more generally, has increasingly been given its due as a fresh and vigorous artistic medium.[60] And recent studies of Paulinus's biblical exegesis and of his conception of friendship, for example, make it difficult to deny the distinctiveness and creativity of his thought.[61] The fruit of such studies as these is largely born from close and sensitive reading of Paulinus's own letters and poems. Consequently, it remains to be seen whether Paulinus's biography, reset

56. Walsh, "Paulinus of Nola," 565; Frend, "Paulinus of Nola," 7–8; Frend, "The Two Worlds," 114–15. On Paulinus and Pelagius, see chapter 8.

57. Lienhard, *Paulinus of Nola*, 5.

58. Fabre, *Paulin de Nole*, 3–6.

59. Brown, *The Cult of the Saints*, 55.

60. Note, for example, the works listed in the bibliography by A. Basson, G. Guttilla, J. Fontaine, and M. Roberts.

61. S. Leanza, "Aspetti esegetici dell'opera di Paolino di Nola," *Atti del Convegno*, 67–91; D. Sorrentino, "L'amore di unitá: Amicizia spirituale ed ecclesiologia in Paolino di Nola," *Impegno e Dialogo* 9 (1991–92): 149–69.

on such foundations, will bear the weight of all the exemplary charges placed on it virtually from the moment of the "spectacular gesture" that signaled Paulinus's conversion and that has largely defined his life ever since.

SELF-PORTRAITS

Unlike Ambrose or Augustine, Paulinus apparently attracted no contemporary biographer with the aims of Paulinus of Milan and Possidius. Indeed, if it were based solely on the terse and pointed witness of his contemporaries, Paulinus's biography might be as intractable as the lives of Pammachius or Marcellinus, those aristocratic correspondents of Jerome and Augustine. Even the Nolan presbyter Uranius, who did offer a final assessment of Paulinus's contemporary importance, restricted his *De obitu Paulini* to an account of the bishop's last days and an encomium of his virtues.[62] While unfortunate for its narrowness, Uranius's limited vision does reveal just how successfully the life of Paulinus of Nola had come to efface the earlier life of Paulinus of Bordeaux. Indeed, Paulinus's own reticence about his pre-Nolan days in the surviving letters and poems may help to explain Uranius's sense of proportion.

Perhaps because of the turmoil brought to Gaul after 406 by the Germanic incursions and settlements, the last two decades of Paulinus's life are also poorly documented. After 408 or so, the flow of Paulinus's preserved letters and poems thins to a trickle, although these and a few other *testimonia* do lend clarity to some events between the Visigothic depredations at Nola in 410 and Paulinus's death in 431. The information provided by occasional letters and stray observations, by a series of exchanges between imperial officials at Rome and the court at Ravenna in 419, and by Augustine's *De cura pro mortuis gerenda,* addressed to Paulinus and composed about 422, form at least an impressionistic picture, while Uranius's *De obitu* provides a proper closure to Paulinus's biography. It is, however, the great middle of Paulinus's life, the years between 393 and 408, that the words of contemporaries as well as his own letters and poems throw into the highest relief.

Only a few of Paulinus's fifty-one *epistulae* and thirty *carmina* can be dated with certainty outside this fifteen-year period.[63] Three examples of Paulinus's early poetry survive,[64] and two letters to Delphinus and Amandus of Bordeaux

---

62. Uranius, *De obitu S. Paulini ad Pacatum.* Text at *PL* 53.859– 866, with an Italian translation by M. Ruggiero, *Cipriano, Paolino di Nola, Uranio: Poesia e teologia della morte* (Rome, 1984), 117–27. My translation is given in appendix D. See also A. Pastorino, "Il *De obitu sancti Paulini* di Uranio," *Augustinianum* 24 (1984): 115–41.

63. For fuller discussion of the corpus see appendix A.

64. *Carm.* 1–3. On the tentative dating of *carm.* 6 (the *Laus Iohannis*) and *carm.* 7–9 (psalm paraphrases) to ca. 393 see chapter 4.

were apparently sent from Spain before 393.[65] On the other hand, only three letters survive from the years after 408, years that must have witnessed significant literary and epistolary activity.[66] The extant works together, however, retain a remarkably vivid imprint of Paulinus and his world. Paulinus's letters sought out their addressees across the reaches of the empire, in Palestine, Gaul, North Africa, and Italy. The correspondence includes letters to Augustine, Sulpicius Severus, Rufinus of Aquileia, and Pammachius as well as to otherwise unknown figures such as the aristocratic Gallo-Romans Aper and Jovius. Paulinus's poems, rich in detail and anecdote, not only celebrate the cult of the Nolan Saint Felix but also commemorate a wedding, bid a friend farewell, and console grieving parents. The immediacy and particularity of these works is never fully sacrificed to the epistolary, poetic, or rhetorical conventions so precious to and so deftly wielded by men of Paulinus's background.

In addition to random and incidental biographical information, Paulinus's works also preserve a number of highly self-conscious passages of autobiographical exposure. Although such moments of reflection on his own past are indispensable for the reconstruction of Paulinus's life, they too demand a cautious approach. Like all of Paulinus's surviving compositions, these passages were written in the full knowledge that they would reach a wide audience.[67] Thus Paulinus's autobiographical projects were equally literary acts, no less conditioned by "the resources of the medium" or the artistic expectations of the audience than, for example, Augustine's *Confessions*.[68] Moreover, like Augustine, Paulinus presented contemporaries with a picture of his past as seen, or reconstructed, through the

---

65. *Epp.* 35 and 36. See P. Fabre, *Essai sur la chronologie de l'oeuvre de Saint Paulin de Nole* (Paris, 1948), 63–65, and chapter 3, this volume.

66. *Epp.* 49–51, to Macarius, Augustine, and Eucherius and Galla.

67. Paulinus evidently expected Severus to make available to others the letters he sent to him in Gaul (*ep.* 24.1); and one correspondent, Sanctus, sent to Paulinus a register (*adnotatio*) of Paulinus's own letters, apparently for the author's verification (*ep.* 41.1). The priest Eutropius, probably writing in Aquitaine, apparently knew Paulinus's *ep.* 13, sent to Pammachius in Rome in 396 (see *PL* 30.48C and Paul. *ep.* 13.4); see Lienhard, "Literary Tradition," 40 n. 34. In 417 Augustine and Alypius could cite back to Paulinus a passage from a letter he had sent to Severus in Gaul some years earlier (see Aug. *ep.* 186.40 with Paul. *ep.* 30.2).

68. See Paul de Man, "Autobiography as Defacement," *MLN* 94 (1979): 920, cited in P. Jay, "What's the Use: Critical Theory and the Study of Autobiography," *Biography* 10 (1987): 44: "We assume that life *produces* the autobiography as an act produces its consequences, but can we not suggest . . . that the autobiographical project may itself produce and determine the life and that whatever the writer *does* is in fact governed by the technical demands of self-portraiture and thus predetermined, in all its aspects, by the resources of his medium?" On the intricate relationship of style, content, and veracity in autobiography see also J. Starobinski, "Le style de l'autobiographie," *Poétique* 3 (1970): 257–59. On the *Confessions*, see P. Courcelle, *Recherches sur les Confessions de Saint Augustine* (Paris, 1950), 188–202; and J. J. O'Meara, "Augustine's *Confessions*: Elements of Fiction," in *Augustine: From Rhetor to Theologian*, ed. J. McWilliam (Waterloo, Ontario, 1992), 77–95.

prism of a radical conversion experience.[69] In such circumstances the impulse to impose retrospective order on unruly reality is especially compelling.[70] Finally, Paulinus's autobiographical notices were no less shaped by the rhetorical context of composition than were the "biographical" observations that others made about him. Much of what Paulinus said about himself, in fact, was similarly said, directly or indirectly, in justification or promotion of his ascetic and monastic endeavors. Paulinus's autobiographical excursions, therefore, are also experiments in self-portraiture (albeit with "la durée et le mouvement" introduced), not exercises in documentary preservation.[71]

The earliest surviving passage of overt autobiographical self-fashioning in Paulinus's works was incorporated into a letter that he sent to Sulpicius Severus within a year of his settlement at Nola. Intent on praising Severus's secular re-nunciation through a corresponding deprecation of his own act, Paulinus con-trasted the gradual progress of his withdrawal from the world with the impetuos-ity that motivated the younger Severus to sunder "the deadly chains of flesh and blood." "You," Paulinus asserted with rhetorical splendor, "were converted to the Lord by a greater miracle; because more youthful in age, more abounding in praise, lighter in the burdens of inheritance, not poorer in your store of riches, both still abiding with fame in that very theater of the world, that is the forum, and also holding the palm for the glory of eloquence, you shattered the servile yoke of sin with sudden impulse and broke the deadly chains of flesh and blood."[72] Ac-cording to Paulinus, neither the additional wealth Severus had acquired with a noble bride nor the license for carnal exploration that her early death afforded him had lured Severus "from the narrow entrance to salvation and the arduous path of virtue."[73] In anticipation of this vivid characterization of Severus's ascetic conversion, Paulinus essayed his own example in far more reserved terms. Firmly rejecting the praise that Severus had offered him in a recent letter, Paulinus re-counted the more protracted stages of his own journey: "My more advanced age and my person honored already from its earliest years were able to bring me to

69. Recognized, but not adequately assessed, by S. Costanza, "Aspetti autobiografici nell'opera poetica di Paolino di Nola," *Giornale italiano di filologia* 27 (1975): 265–77.

70. See, for example, K. Weintraub, "Autobiography and Historical Consciousness," *Critical In-quiry* 1 (1975): 824–27; and Starobinski, "Le style," 261.

71. Further cautionary advice at G. Misch, *A History of Autobiography in Antiquity*, trans. E. Dickes (London, 1950), 1: 5–13. Quote from Starobinski, "Le style," 257.

72. *Ep.* 5.5: "Tu frater dilectissime, ad dominum miraculo maiore conversus es, quia aetate floren-tior, laudibus abundantior, oneribus patrimonii levior, substantia facultatum non egentior et in ipso adhuc mundi theatro id est fori celebritate diversans et facundi nominis palmam tenens, repetino in-petu discussisti servile peccati iugum et letalia carnis et sanguinis vincla rupisti."

73. *Ep.* 5.5: "ab angusto salutis introitu et arduo itinere virtutis." On the importance of this passage for the biography of Severus see, for instance, Stancliffe, *St. Martin and His Hagiographer*, 16–17.

more serious maturity; moreover a body more infirm and a flesh more wasted were able to destroy any devotion to pleasures; furthermore, my very life in the world, frequently vexed in toil and hardship, was able to yield to a hatred for disquieting affairs and, from a need for hope and a fear of doubt, to increase my care for religion."[74] His own circuitous route from the "noise of the forum" to the ascetic way of life (*propositum*), Paulinus added, led rather naturally through "the welcome tranquillity of household retreats" and country leisure (*otium ruris*).[75]

The truthfulness of Paulinus's self-revelation is not necessarily impugned by recognition of the literary and rhetorical forces that shaped its presentation. Artistry and historicity need not stand at odds, and the psychological journey related to Severus is probably reasonably accurate in outline.[76] Nevertheless, Paulinus's literary self-consciousness colors the passage at multiple levels, as structure and language work to heighten the intended contrast between Paulinus and Severus. The cumbersome periodic sentence with which Paulinus describes his own prolonged and hesitant turn away from public life to leisured rural retreat, and eventually to the monastic *propositum,* unfolds over a half-page of text, in marked opposition to the more clipped syntax that inscribes Severus's comparatively headlong conversion. The piled-up clauses of Paulinus's past, grammatically postponing his long-awaited decision—still (*attamen*), moreover (*praeterea*), furthermore (*ad hoc*), afterward (*postea denique*), so that little by little (*ut paulatim*)—lead directly, if painstakingly, into a series of staccato, although gradually lengthening, phrases descriptive of Severus's situation. Diction conspires to increase the effect. If on the one hand Paulinus's verbal constructions emphasize the slow evolution of his own thought (*potuit maturare, augere, iam dimicaverim*), on the other they stress the relative violence of Severus's actions (*conversus es, discussisti, rupisti*). Throughout the passage Paulinus's verbal artistry undergirds the message at the same time that it reaffirms for his readers his undiminished dedication to style.

Other issues may also have played their part in shaping this self-portrait that Paulinus offered up to Severus (and others) so hard on the heels of his settlement at Nola. The passage's harsh self-deprecation, for example, is blunted by guarded self-assertion. Paulinus's humility is carefully countered by his recall of his own *persona* honored from its earliest years, of his vast patrimony, and of the exacting efforts of his public career. While Paulinus readily acknowledged the meritorious zeal of the younger Severus, he nevertheless subtly asserted the respect due to a veteran of the

---

74. *Ep.* 5.4: "attamen mihi aetas provectior et a primis iam annis honorata persona potuit maturare graviorem, praeterea corpus infirmius et decoctior caro obterere studia voluptatum, ad hoc vita ipsa mortalis in laboribus et aerumnis frequenter exercita odium rerum inquietantium parere et de spei necessitate ac dubiorum metu cultum religionis augere."

75. *Ep.* 5.4: "a fori strepitu remotus ruris otium et ecclesiae cultum placita in secretis domesticis tranquillitate celebravi."

76. See further discussion of this passage in chapter 3.

world's storms. At the same time that he belittled his achievements amid such tu-
mult, the former *vir clarissimus* reminded Severus and his other Gallo-Roman read-
ers of his former public successes, which (as Severus required no reminding) had
been garnered not in the cities of Gaul but in the Senate at Rome. And if Paulinus
also expected these words to be seen by critics closer to his new home in Nola, such
as Ambrose's incredulous "noble men" or the ecclesiastical establishment of Rome,
which had received Paulinus with suspicion the year before,[77] then this portrait was
a subtle reminder of the status he had once commanded in more traditional ways.
Of course, neither Paulinus's praise of Severus nor his own avowed humility need
be any less sincere for the self-assertion that also marks this letter; Paulinus's works,
and thus his thought, seem eminently able to entertain ideas and attitudes perhaps
less paradoxical in his world than ours. But in this letter's autobiographical account,
literary and apologetic concerns have patently determined the form, and to some
degree the content, of self-representation.

In this respect, Paulinus's letter to Severus is surely not unique, but its idiosyn-
cratic qualities emerge when it is set against a later self-portrait. A decade after
Paulinus's northward-bound letter had related to friends in southern Gaul the
gradual steps that had led him to his monastic way of life, Paulinus told the story
again, in a different medium and to a rather different audience. In January 407 the
thirteenth *natalicium*, composed to honor Saint Felix, included an extended auto-
biographical excursion, nearly one hundred hexameter lines forming the center-
piece of an 858-line composition. Among the audience for that year's poetic per-
formance were several notable visitors from Rome, including family and friends of
the Elder Melania: her granddaughter, Melania the Younger, and her niece,
Avita, with their husbands, the senators Valerius Pinianus and Turcius Aproni-
anus. At the height of the festival, in the basilica complex that he had erected
around the tomb of Felix, and in the presence of other ascetically inclined mem-
bers of Rome's highest aristocracy, Paulinus now presented a baldly providential
paradigm for the interpretation of his life. The figure of Saint Felix, bypassed
without mention in the passage addressed to Severus, now completely dominates
Paulinus's reconstruction of his conversion story.[78]

The *natalicium* of 407 deeply rooted Paulinus's claim to be the special charge
(*mancipium*) of Felix—and consequently his right to serve as impresario of the
saint's cult—within the intimacies of a relationship whose origins were now ex-
tended back far beyond Paulinus's settlement at Nola in 395. In language strik-
ingly similar to that with which Paulinus had once expressed his profound affec-
tion for an old friend and mentor, he now addressed his devotion to his "revered

77. See chapter 5.
78. Chapter 7 expands on some of the issues only touched on here. The implications of this pas-
sage for the modern reconstruction of Paulinus's earlier life are assessed in appendix B.

father, eternal patron, and guardian, Felix most dear to Christ."[79] To Felix, Pauli-
nus avowed, he owed everything in this life and all hope for the next.[80] From that
moment when as a *puer* he first stood awestruck before the saint's tomb until the
present time, Paulinus told his audience, Felix had ever been his silent guide and
protector. Seeing him safely through the dangers attendant upon two curule
offices, commissioning the construction of a shelter for humble visitors to the
Nolan tomb, recalling him to Gaul, arranging his marriage in Spain, shielding his
life and property in a dangerous lawsuit, Felix had preserved Paulinus and pro-
tected his wealth so that he might finally "renounce the world, native land, and
home" and with his earthly possessions "purchase the hope of the heavenly king-
dom."[81] In this public rehearsal of his story, all was carefully calculated to empha-
size the abiding, if often concealed, care of Felix for Paulinus, a "slave" entrusted
to Felix by none other than Christ himself.[82]

The striking differences in perspective and representation between the more
self-confident and explicit autobiographical vision of the *natalicium* of 407 and the
cautious, impressionistic view offered to Severus a decade earlier evidently owe
their origins to several factors. By January 407 Paulinus had been at Nola for more
than ten years; he had vanquished the suspicion with which some had greeted his
arrival in Italy in 395 and was now secure in his authority at Nola. He could look
around him and see the profits of his forsworn property manifest in the magnifi-
cent new constructions around Felix's tomb. His presence had already drawn
Melania the Elder to Nola upon her return from the Holy Land in 400; now he
could boast the attendance at the festival of her younger kin and protégés. The
presence of Pinianus and Apronianus, both of senatorial families, the former the
son of an urban prefect, further signaled the deep respect due a veteran of the Sen-
ate as well as the ascetic life.[83] These nobles, too, were now self-proclaimed as-
cetics who evidently also hoped to rest their claims to special status simultaneously
on their great wealth and their repudiation of it. For good reasons in 407 Paulinus
might have detected a providential force behind the trials as well as the achieve-
ments of his life. It is unlikely that so much could have been foreseen in 396.

But the same ten years that separate the self-portrait of 396 from that of 407
also witnessed the intrusion of other forces into Paulinus's life. During that time
Paulinus encountered several new literary models that appear to have influenced

---

79. *Carm.* 21.344–45: "nunc ad te, venerande parens, aeterne patrone, / susceptor meus et Christo
carissime Felix." Cf. *carm.* 10.93–96 to Ausonius. On the nuances of Paulinus's relationship with his in-
visible companion, Felix, see Brown, *The Cult of the Saints*, 56–68, and chapter 7, this volume.

80. *Carm.* 21.348–49: "omnia, praesentis vitae rem spemque futurae / quae pariunt, tibi me mem-
ini debere."

81. *Carm.* 21.425–28: "abiurante fide mundum patriamque domumque. . . . res igitur terrae regni
caelestis emit spem."

82. *Carm.* 21.349–50: "cui [Felici] me / mancipium primis donavit Christus ab annis."

83. *PLRE* 1:87 and 1:702.

profoundly the construction and representation of identity as we see it in the thirteenth *natalicium*. In 397 or shortly thereafter both Severus's *Life of Saint Martin* and Augustine's *Confessions* would have become available to Paulinus.[84] The *Vita Martini* was not autobiography in any formal sense, but it reinforced certain currents already evident in Paulinus's own thought. Not coincidentally, for instance, Paulinus would almost immediately after receiving the *Vita Martini* begin the composition of his own biography of a saint, a verse *Vita Felicis*.[85] Moreover the *Life of Martin*, soon supplemented by Severus's *Letters* and *Dialogues*, also suggested how an author might present himself as the confidant and special friend of a holy man even after the latter's death.[86]

Augustine's *Confessions*, however, may appear a more obvious influence on Paulinus's own *confessio* in the thirteenth *natalicium*. Although Augustine raised his voice of praise to God and Paulinus his to Felix, in postulating a guiding, providential hand behind the seemingly unpredictable course of his life, Paulinus's poem adopted a governing motif of the *Confessions*.[87] Indeed, however much these two works may differ in other ways, they share this assertion that a divine will has taken intimate concern in the unfolding mystery of their authors' lives. In this assertion lies a profound difference between the autobiography of the thirteenth *natalicium* and the more introspective musings of the passage written for Severus.

Undoubtedly these two self-portraits, like Paulinus's other less extended reminiscences, were conditioned by multiple factors. Paulinus's situation at the time of composition, his artistic sensibility, and his cognizance of audience expectations all influenced his self-representation. In each case, it seems, Paulinus fashioned an image of himself that refracted the "truth" of his pre-Nolan past through the understanding and purposes of the moment. But despite the differences of these two passages, they are not incompatible as sources for Paulinus's life, and I return to both in the pages below. What I emphasize here is how, in marked contrast to the biographical notices penned by his contemporaries, Paulinus has elected to reveal the determinative background to the turn of events that brought him to Nola. If contemporaries saw the polemical advantages to be gained in the precipitous conversion of a wealthy aristocrat, Paulinus evidently preferred to highlight the social forces that prompted his renunciation of the world and the psychological and spiritual turmoil and growth that anticipated it.

---

84. Paulinus's *ep.* 11.1 (spring 397) records his reception of the *Vita Martini*. Augustine's composition of the *Confessions* dates between 397 and 401, with good reason to prefer the earlier limit; see J. J. O'Donnell, ed., *Augustine: Confessions* (Oxford, 1992), 1:xli–xlii.

85. The *natalicium* of January 398 introduces Paulinus's *vita Felicis*. On this *vita* see chapter 7.

86. D. Trout, "*Amicitia, Auctoritas,* and Self-Fashioning Texts," 123–29.

87. For example, *Conf.* 5.14; 9.23, with the observations of O'Meara, "Augustine's *Confessions,*" 88–93.

Seldom, it seems, did Paulinus write about himself or others without consider-ing the reception of his words. His autobiographical reflections, like his biograph-ical sketches of Melania the Elder and Saint Felix, resonate with polemic, didac-tic, and self-fashioning impulses.[88] The overlapping of the epistolary circles of the late Roman elite only abetted such acute self-consciousness. In this respect, it may indeed be true that Paulinus's works exude the spirit of their age. But Paulinus's life, like most lives, was lived in varying degrees of collision as well as collusion with whatever may be deemed the spirit(s) of this transitional age in the history of the Roman world. Paulinus's world was one of sometimes conflicting political, so-cial, and intellectual forces, and his works reveal some of those fissures. They also reveal tensions of his own mind and thought. Rather than claim Paulinus for one cause or another, I hope the following chapters preserve the unruly, "many-sided self" of Paulinus.[89] The first five chapters bear the heavy imprint of chronological organization. Thereafter the approach is somewhat more thematic.

88. On Melania see Trout, "*Amicitia, Auctoritas,* and Self-Fashioning Texts"; on Felix see chapter 7.
89. C. Heylin, *Bob Dylan: Behind the Shades* (New York, 1991), glossing another artist whose abilty to reinvent himself was "a primary characteristic of his art" (14).

CHAPTER 2

—•—

The Early Years

Aquitaine and Italy

In the spring of 383 the Roman army in Britain elevated its general to the imperial purple, just as three-quarters of a century earlier it had acclaimed another usurper in Constantine. Magnus Maximus, like Constantine before him, quickly crossed into Gaul, and by summer's end the young emperor Gratian was dead at Lyon.[1] These alarming events, it seems, provoked the young senator Meropius Pontius Paulinus, born in the early 350s and thus about thirty years old, to abandon Italy and return to his native Bordeaux. They need not, however, have spelled the end of a promising political career, for behind Paulinus trailed the vestiges of a pattern common among the elite families of the later Roman empire. Well-born, well-educated, and well-served by the familial and patronal webs that embraced late Roman notables, Paulinus had already served the regime of Gratian as suffect consul at Rome and governor of the prestigious Italian province of Campania. Despite the uncertainties raised by the usurpation of Maximus and the murder of the western emperor Gratian, Paulinus may have anticipated only an inconvenient interruption of his public life. In the event, ahead of Paulinus lay a decade of aristocratic retreat to the countryside (*otium ruris*) lived out first on his family's Aquitanian estates—"kingdoms" in the gloss of one contemporary—and then with a recently wed wife in Spain.[2] When he reemerged into public life in the mid-390s, it was the church and the monastery, not the Roman senate and imperial bureaucracy, that provided the institutional framework for his life. The path to both political and religious preferment, however, began in the schoolrooms of

---

1. On these events see J. Matthews, *Western Aristocracies and Imperial Court: A.D. 364–425* (Oxford, 1975), 165, 173.

2. Aus. *ep.* 23.36 Green (EW *ep.* 27): *veteris Paulini regna*. Ausonius's works are cited from the edition of R. P. H. Green, *The Works of Ausonius* (Oxford, 1991). The letters are cross-referenced to the Loeb edition of H. G. Evelyn White (Cambridge, Mass., and London, 1921, rpt. 1985), whose text is that of R. Peiper's Teubner edition (Leipzig, 1886).

one of Gaul's most prominent centers of education and wound through the intricately overlapping social circles of the Roman secular and ecclesiastical aristocracy. Although few of Paulinus's own works from these years survive, his later reminiscences combine with other evidence to offer us intermittent but vivid impressions of these first three decades of Paulinus's life.

BORDEAUX AND THE GUILD OF THE MUSES

In the mid-380s Paulinus returned to an Aquitaine enjoying remarkable prosperity. The security restored to southern Gaul in the late third and early fourth centuries by the military efforts of the Tetrarchs and Constantine on the Rhine frontier had revitalized the region. A countryside "distinguished for its vineyards and rivers" yielded wine and grain in abundance.[3] Bordeaux, ancient Burdigala, the capital of Aquitanica Secunda and perhaps primary residence of the vicar of the diocese of the *Septem provinciarum* as well,[4] thrived on the commerce and shipping that plied the lower Garonne's tidal waters and sheltered in the city's inner harbor.[5] Even the walls and towers of the *castrum*, grim reminders of the darker forces that had disrupted even Aquitaine in the previous century, could evoke a native's sentimental praise.[6] While the amphitheater and some public buildings remained outside these late-third-century walls, the enclosed thirty-two hectares boasted Ausonius's famed fountain of Divona, adorned with Parian marble and pouring out its inexhaustible and limpid waters through a dozen mouths.[7] The city's schools were renowned: more than once they had drawn the attention of emperors in search of tutors and orators.[8] Bordeaux's bishop was already exerting his in-

---

3. Aus. *carm.* 24. 129 (*Ordo urbium nobilium*); Amm. 14.10.2; Sid. *carm.* 22.169–70. Étienne, *Bordeaux antique* (Bordeaux, 1962), 222–23.

4. A. Chastagnol, "Le diocèse civil d'Aquitaine au Bas-Empire," *Bulletin de la société nationale des antiquaires de France* (1970): 272–92, dating the final establishment of the name *Septem provinciarum* to before 381 (279) and the residence of the vicar at Bordeaux since 355 (287–88).

5. See Étienne, *Bordeaux antique*, 202–20; P. Debord and M. Gauthier, *Bordeaux Saint-Christoly: Sauvetage archéologique et histoire urbaine* (Bordeaux, 1982); D. Barraud and M.-A. Gaidon, "Bordeaux," *Villes et agglomérations urbaines antiques du sud-ouest de la Gaule: Histoire et archéologie, Sixième supplément à Aquitania* (Paris and Bordeaux, 1992), 43–48; C. Balmelle, "L'habitat urbain dans le sud-ouest de la Gaule romaine," in Barraud and Gaidon, *Villes et agglomérations*, 355–64; H. Sivan, "Town and Country in Late Antique Gaul: The Example of Bordeaux," in *Fifth Century Gaul: A Crisis of Identity?* ed. J. Drinkwater and H. Elton (Cambridge, 1992), 133–38; and H. Sivan, *Ausonius of Bordeaux: Genesis of a Gallic Aristocracy* (London, 1993), 31–48.

6. Aus. *carm.* 24.141 (*Ordo*).

7. Aus. *carm.* 24.148–62 (*Ordo*). On the amphitheater (the later Palais Gallien) and the old forum (the Piliers de Tutelle), outside the *castrum*, see also M. Maillé, *Recherches sur les origines chrétiennes de Bordeaux* (Paris, 1959), 109–15; *Bordeaux: 2000 ans d'histoire* (Bordeaux, 1973), 36–41.

8. See M. K. Hopkins, "Social Mobility in the Later Roman Empire: The Evidence of Ausonius," *CQ* n.s. 11 (1961): 239–49 and the further discussions of Ausonius's *Professores* cited below.

fluence beyond the confines of Aquitaine. The urban bustle, press, and noise drove the city's notables to seek respite in the lavish rural villas that instantiated their social and economic dominance.[9]

The Pontii of Aquitaine had surely participated in the emergence of a newly emboldened and self-confident Gallo-Roman aristocracy. For the urban elite of Bordeaux and other cities of Gaul, prosperity and peace had ushered in new expectations. Constantine had rejuvenated the senatorial order, increasing several-fold the number of the empire's *viri clarissimi*, in part by elevating to senatorial rank "the flower of the municipal bourgeoisie."[10] And by the later fourth century, with the disturbances of the 350s—the revolts of Magnentius and Silvanus—safely behind, the Gallo-Roman aristocracy had begun to reclaim a place in the imperial administration.[11]

Contemporaries of Paulinus attest to his family's nobility and wealth.[12] The Pontius Proserius Paulinus who followed our Paulinus as governor of the province of Campania almost three decades later is further proof of the family's influence in the late fourth and early fifth centuries.[13] Moreover, the family's fortunes weathered the turmoil of the Visigothic settlement that embroiled Gaul in the early fifth century. Writing in the 460s, three decades after Paulinus's death, the Gallo-Roman aristocrat Sidonius Apollinaris gleefully described an opulent villa at Burgus, near Bordeaux, then inhabited by Sidonius's correspondent Pontius Leontius, a *vir illustris* whose son was named Paulinus.[14] The villa, Sidonius recalled, had been constructed by an earlier Pontius Paulinus, founder of the family (*generis princeps*).[15] Sidonius's Pontii of Bordeaux should be both ancestors (the

9. Aus. *ep.* 4.19–34 (Green).

10. A. Chastagnol, "Les modes de recrutement du Sénat au IVe siècle après J.-C.," *Recherches sur les structures sociales dans l'antiquité classique* (Paris, 1970), 187–89; A. Chastagnol, "L'évolution de l'ordre sénatorial aux IIIe et IVe siècles de notre ère," *Revue historique* 244 (1970): 308–10; and A. Chastagnol, *Le Sénat romain à l'époque impériale* (Paris, 1992), 236–41.

11. J. F. Drinkwater, *The Gallic Empire: Separatism and Continuity in the North-Western Provinces of the Roman Empire* (Stuttgart, 1987), 254. Sivan, *Ausonius of Bordeaux*, 20–22, 97–101, 142–43.

12. See, for example, Aus. *ep.* 24.36 Green (EW *ep.* 27); Amb. *ep.* 6.27.1 (*CSEL* 82) / *ep.* 58.1 (*PL* 16); Eucherius of Lyon, *De contemptu mundi* (*PL* 50.718D).

13. *PLRE* 2.848, "Paulinus 16"; M. Heinzelmann, "Gallische Prosopographie: 260–527," *Francia* 10 (1982): 665, "Pontius Proserius Paulinus 5." He was, perhaps, a nephew of Paulinus and was *consularis Campaniae* probably in 409; see also M. T. W. Arnheim, *The Senatorial Aristocracy in the Later Roman Empire* (Oxford, 1972), 185.

14. On Leontius and his son Paulinus see Sid. *carm.* 22; *epp.* 8.11.3, 8.12.5 with *PLRE* 2.674, "Leontius 30," and 2.847, "Paulinus 10"; Heinzelmann, "Gallische Prosopographie," 636, "Pontius Leontius 2," and 666, "Paulinus 11." Maillé, *Recherches*, 68, conjectured a descent from Paulinus's brother. Sidonius's Burgus is commonly identified with modern Bourg-sur-Gironde at the confluence of the Garonne and the Dordogne; see A. Loyen, "Bourg-sur-Gironde et les villas d'Ausone," *REA* 62 (1960): 115.

15. On Pontius Paulinus see Sid. *carm.* 22.114–19 with *PLRE* 1.681, "Paulinus 19"; Heinzelmann, "Gallische Prosopographie," 665, "Pontius Paulinus 1."

generis princeps) and later representatives of the family of our Paulinus,[16] who, lauded by Ambrose of Milan for the "splendor of a birth second to none in Aquitaine," apparently inherited his senatorial rank, the clarissimate.[17]

Indeed, Paulinus's appointment to a *Roman* suffect consulship about 378 strongly suggests that his father was a member of the Senate at Rome, a costly privilege reserved for a minority of the west's *viri clarissimi*.[18] But the same murkiness that clouds the achievements of and relationships among Paulinus's forebears and ancestors also obscures Paulinus's specific connections of blood and marriage to these attested Pontii of Aquitaine and to other elite families. Even his own declarations of kinship with contemporaries are couched in vague language. He would, for example, merely remind Sulpicius Severus that a blood relationship (*sanguis*) bound him to the revered Melania the Elder, Spanish-born champion of asceticism and veteran of many years in the Holy Land.[19]

But if a faded evidential record and tactful circumlocutions obscure the bloodlines that permeated the *gens* into which Paulinus was born, probably in 352 or 353,[20] there is no doubt that the young Paulinus breathed in the heady atmosphere of the great rural estates of the Aquitanian nobility. In the early 380s the opulent villas that commanded the Aquitanian countryside should not have disappointed a returning ex-governor, even one leaving behind the venerable estates long nestled along the Campanian coast.[21] Paulinus's family properties at Hebromagus,

16. K. Stroheker, *Der senatorische Adel im spätantiken Gallien* (Darmstadt 1948), 188 (no. 215) and 200 (no. 287). But to claim Sidonius's Pontius Paulinus as Paulinus's father or grandfather (so Stroheker, 200, followed by Heinzelmann, "Gallische Prosopographie," 665, "Pontius Paulinus 1") stretches the evidence, even if, on the strength of Ausonius's *veteris Paulini regna* (*ep.* 24.36 Green), either Paulinus's father or grandfather is likely to have carried the diacritical name Paulinus. The family may find its sixth-century representatives in the Bordelais bishops Amelius, Leontius, and Leontius II: see Maillé, *Recherches*, 76, 88; Heinzelmann, "Gallische Prosopographie," 552, "Amelius"; Stroheker, *Der senatorische Adel*, 188, nos. 218–19.

17. Amb. *ep.* 6.27.1 (*CSEL* 82) / 58.1 (*PL* 16): "Paulinum splendore generis in partibus Aquitaniae nulli secundum," with Uranius, *De obitu* 9 (*PL* 53.864C): "Taceamus generis nobilitatem, paternis maternisque natalibus in senatorum purpuras admirabiliter rutilantem."

18. See appendix B.

19. Forwarding to Sulpicius Severus a tunic that he had received as a gift from Melania, Paulinus observed (*ep.* 29.5): "unde te dignior visa est, cuius fides illi [Melania] magis quam noster sanguis propinquat." On the possibility of a marriage connection see F. X. Murphy, "Melania the Elder: A Biographical Note," *Traditio* 5 (1947): 62; and D. Gorce, *Vie de Saint Mélanie, SC* 90 (Paris, 1962), 110–11. The sometimes asserted connection of the Pontii and the powerful Roman Anicii, still considered by Fabre, is commonly rejected now. Nevertheless, the following continue to intrigue: first, Paulinus is a common name among the Anicii as well as the Pontii (*PLRE* 1, "Paulinus 12–17"), although two Pontii Paulini already appear in the early empire: C. Pontius Paulinus (*CIL* 9.3079) and Pontius Paulinus (Ulpian, *Dig.* 24.1.3.1). Second, two of the four known governors of Campania between 378 and 384 (one being Paulinus) were Anicii.

20. See appendix B.

21. See, for example, J. H. D'Arms, *Romans on the Bay of Naples: A Social and Cultural Study of the Villas and Their Owners from 150 B.C. to A.D. 400* (Cambridge, Mass., 1970).

Alingo, and elsewhere would have boasted their own distinctive charm and riches. Throughout southern Gaul, archaeology continues to substantiate the general outlines of Sidonius's surreal picture of the fortified villa of Burgus where Sidonius's contemporary, Pontius Leontius, spent his days amid grand halls, porticos, dining rooms, and baths. All was carefully constructed with attention to the exigencies of seasonal change and the diurnal shifts of sunlight that played on gilded ceilings and walls sheathed in marble or adorned with historical and mythological scenes; there, Sidonius proclaimed, storehouses glutted by harvests rivaled those of Africa or Apulia; and in the villa's *textrina* Sidonius could imagine Leontius's wife dutifully spinning thread of purple and gold.[22]

Archaeology's record is hardly less dazzling. Near Bordeaux the villa of Palat boasts a marble fountain whose octagonal base is resplendent with marine life, mosaics of hunting scenes, and polychrome mosaic floors arranged in geometric patterns and stylized floral designs.[23] Farther south, in the tributary valleys of the Garonne, the villa complexes at Valentine, Montmaurin, and Séviac encompassed grand *thermae* dominating sacred, healing springs.[24] Returning to such familial estates after a long absence was, as one Bordelais poet later imagined,[25] a deeply moving experience, not least perhaps because here the sons of the notable had grown accustomed to opulence and luxury and had first observed, through paternal example, the delicate mechanisms of influence and authority.

Such surroundings bore with them obligations not easily dismissed. The weight of a family's past and its expectations for the future rested heavily on its sons, creating pressures sometimes vented through violence toward the more vulnerable members of the *domus,* its women and slaves.[26] At times paternal authority must have fallen unhappily on the male children of the household as well, but we know too little to say how successfully Paulinus and his father negotiated the charged atmosphere of "punishment and love" that typified the relations of fathers and

22. Sid. *carm.* 22.114–235.

23. C. Balmelle, M. Gauthier, and R. Monturet, "Mosaïques de la villa du Palat à Saint-Émilion (Gironde)," *Gallia* 38 (1980): 59–96, dated here to the early fifth century (95–96). See also H. Sivan, "Town and Country."

24. Valentine: C. Balmelle, *Recueil général des mosaïques de la Gaule; Gallia* supp. 10.4.1 (1980): 58–72; H. Sivan, "Town, Country and Province in Late Roman Gaul: The Example of CIL XIII 128," *ZPE* 79 (1989): 103–13. Montmaurin: G. Fouet, *La villa gallo-romaine de Montmaurin; Gallia* supp. 20 (1969); Fouet, "Le sanctuaire des eaux de 'la Hillère' à Montmaurin (Haute-Garonne)" *Gallia* 30 (1972): 83–124; Balmelle, *Recueil général* 10.4.1 (1980): 74–83. Séviac: R. Monturet and H. Rivière, *Les thermes sud de la villa gallo-romaine de Séviac; Aquitania* supp. 2 (Bordeaux, 1986); Balmelle, *Recueil général* 10.4.2 (1987): 151–94. Also G. Fouet, "Exemples d'exploitation des eaux par de grands propriétaires terriens dans le sud-ouest au IVe siècle," *Caesarodunum* 10 (1975): 128–34.

25. Aus. *ep.* 23.30–52 Green (EW *ep.* 27).

26. Shaw, "The Family in Late Antiquity," 3–51.

sons in the late antique family.[27] These roles, it seems, were constrained by the requirements of paternal domination and control on the one hand and filial respect and obedience on the other. The surviving writings of Paulinus say little of either parent. He would, by constructing and maintaining a *memoria,* dutifully perform the final act of filial *obsequium,*[28] but his later life apparently had little room for the publicly expressed sentiments of family pride and affection that mark such works as Ausonius's *Epicedion in patrem* or his *Parentalia.* It is only in the timely beginning of Paulinus's public life that we can discern the traces of a father's ambition, which—as the case of Patricius and his son Augustine shows—naturally found its first outlet in the choice of a schoolmaster.[29]

At a young age, perhaps seven or eight, Paulinus began his education under Ausonius.[30] In the later 350s Decimus Magnus Ausonius, born about 310 and holder of a chair of grammar at Bordeaux since about 336, would have been a leading figure in a city widely renowned for its educational establishment.[31] Indeed, in the decade after he received Paulinus into his charge, Ausonius was first promoted to a chair of rhetoric at Bordeaux and then summoned to the imperial court at Trier to assume responsibility for the education of Valentinian's eldest son, Gratian.[32] But in the 350s Ausonius was busy inducting the sons of Aquitaine's

27. Shaw, "The Family in Late Antiquity," 25.

28. *Ep.* 12.12. See Shaw, "The Family in Late Antiquity," 27–28 for wider context.

29. Aug. *Conf.* 1.9; 2.3.

30. See appendix B. As recent studies have shown, the evidence does not support the handbook distinctions of a discrete tripartite educational system—*magister litterarum, grammaticus,* and *rhetor*—and the evidence cited below strongly suggests that Ausonius, *praeceptor primus,* instructed Paulinus at both the "primary" and "secondary" stages. See R. A. Kaster, "Notes on 'Primary' and 'Secondary' Schools in Late Antiquity," *TAPA* 113 (1983): 323–46. Note that Arborius taught Ausonius when the latter was "lactantem, puerum, iuvenemque virumque" (*Par.* 3.9–10), that Ausonius's first teacher was a *grammaticus* (*Prof.* 10.12–13), and that Gratian was at most seven or eight when the rhetor Ausonius was summoned to Trier. At *Protr.* 66–75 Ausonius speaks of teaching students in all three stages, although he may have in mind here the successive stages of his own career. See Kaster, "Notes," 331 n. 28, and Kaster, *Guardians of Language: The Grammarian and Society in Late Antiquity* (Berkeley, 1988), 460. Relations between the Pontii and the family of Ausonius may already have been established. Years later, in the 380s, Ausonius reminded Paulinus of the ties between their fathers: see Aus. *ep.* 18.13–14 Green (EW *ep.* 25); Aus. *ep.* 24.8–11 Green (EW *ep.* 27).

31. On the schools of Bordeaux and the academic career of Ausonius much has been written. See Étienne, *Bordeaux antique,* 235–63, 342–44; A. D. Booth, "Notes on Ausonius' *Professores,*" *Phoenix* 32 (1978): 235–49, and Booth, "The Academic Career of Ausonius," *Phoenix* 36 (1982): 329–43; R. P. H. Green, "Still Waters Run Deep: A New Study of the *Professores* of Bordeaux," *CQ* 35 (1985): 491–506; Kaster, *Guardians of Language,* 100–106; Sivan, *Ausonius of Bordeaux,* 74–93. On the number of chairs of grammar (two or three) and rhetoric (one or two) at Bordeaux see Green, "Still Waters," and Kaster, *Guardians of Language,* 455–62, in response to the pioneering work of Booth, "The Academic Career."

32. On ca. 360 as the date of Ausonius's promotion from *grammaticus* to rhetor see Booth, "The Academic Career," 338. For 366–67 as the date of Ausonius's move to Trier see Étienne, *Bordeaux antique,* 342; Booth, "The Academic Career," 332; Matthews, *Western Aristocracies,* 51.

elite into the "guild of the Muses."[33] At least in Paulinus's case, Ausonius's care transcended any merely official role. Years later Ausonius could claim, and Paulinus would ungrudgingly acknowledge, that not only as *magister* and *praeceptor primus*, but also as *pater* and *altor ingenii*—father and nourisher of his character—Ausonius had revealed to Paulinus the "hard-won prizes" of the Muses.[34] Amid the physical intimidations of the ancient school, such rewards were hard-won indeed. Privately, or among the school benches "abuzz with scared confusion," young Paulinus would have learned to "bear the yoke of authority and submit to the jagged bit."[35] For thus, as Ausonius later warned a grandson about to begin his own education, did Bordeaux's "harsh" schoolmasters teach their charges "to pluck sweet fruits from bitter roots."[36] Even the school exercises of the age recalled the minds of the competitive young to the schoolroom's simple alternatives of reward and correction: "If anyone has recited well, he is praised; if he has done so badly, he is curbed."[37]

The discipline of the schoolroom was severe because for the sons of the elite—and for those, like the young Augustine at Thagaste and Carthage, who aspired to join their ranks—the stakes were high. Literature, the grammarians' trade, embodied the past and defined the future; it provided, as Ausonius put it, the links that bound history together.[38] Virgil and Horace, Terence and Sallust bound each generation to the next.[39] At the same time the memorization and recitation of standard texts ensured their continued vitality and transformed them into a common pool of allusions through which, as the later correspondence of Ausonius and Paulinus so well illustrates, the educated could carry on their rich, multivalent, and socially exclusive conversations.[40] Literary acumen signified a man's membership in an intellectual elite, and, enhanced by rhetorical training, it instilled the *mores artesque bonas*—the manners and proper skills—requisite for social authority and administrative responsibility.[41] For this reason, Ausonius could boast of the Bordelais rhetor Tiberius Victor Minervius, one of

33. Aus. *ep*. 22.35 Green (EW *ep*. 28).

34. Aus. *ep*. 19b.23–27 Green, *ep*. 22.33–35 Green (EW *epp*. 25, 28); Paul. *carm*. 10.93–96. Aus. *Protr*. 41–42: "ardua . . . praemia Musarum."

35. Aus. *Protr*. 31: "quod fervent trepido subsellia vestra tumultu," with the felicitous translation of Evelyn White. *Protr*. 75–76: "quamquam imperium cervice negarent / ferre nec insertis praeberent ora lupatis."

36. Aus. *Protr*. 72: "capturi dulcem fructum radicis amarae." See Kaster, "Notes," 332 n. 28, on a possible allusion to a *sententia* of Cato, and M. Irvine, *The Making of Textual Culture: "Grammatica" and Literary Theory, 350–1100* (Cambridge, 1994), 84–87, on wider context.

37. A. C. Dionisotti, "From Ausonius' Schooldays? A Schoolbook and Its Relatives," *JRS* 72 (1982): 83–125; quote 101: "si bene recitavit, laudatur, si quis male, coercetur."

38. Aus. *Protr*. 52–53.

39. The authors specifically recommended by Ausonius at *Protr*. 56–64.

40. On intertextuality as a feature of late Latin poetry see S. G. Nugent, "Ausonius' 'Late-Antique' Poetics and 'Post-modern' Literary Theory," *Ramus* 19 (1990), esp. 37–41.

41. Aus. *Protr*. 74–75: "ad mores artesque bonas fandique vigorem / produxi."

his own teachers, who gave "a thousand young men to the courts and twice a thousand to the Senate's ranks."[42] Thus we must understand the practical and emotional depth of the claims Ausonius later had on Paulinus: "I am your nourisher and first teacher, your first bestower of honors; I first admitted you into the guild of the Muses."[43]

It is possible that Ausonius instructed Paulinus in the rudiments of rhetoric as well as *grammatice*, although this is more difficult to infer from the evidence. If Paulinus was born in 352 or 353, then he would have been only fourteen or fifteen when Ausonius heeded Valentinian's summons to Trier in 366 or 367, perhaps too young for even a precocious student's advance in rhetoric. The issue is moot, however, for the future relationship of Ausonius and Paulinus, as the surviving exchanges of the 380s and early 390s reveal, was rooted in their poetic sympathies. Paulinus had been an ideal student, playing a reckless Icarus, he claimed, to Ausonius's prudent Daedalus.[44] In the 380s, with Paulinus in his thirties and Ausonius approaching eighty, they would still delight in the poetic conceits that led Ausonius to declare Paulinus superior to any Roman *iuvenis* in poetic eloquence.[45] Such steadfast affection between pupil and teacher, further nurtured (as we will see) by Ausonius's political patronage, was probably uncommon. It can be explained in part by the degree to which Ausonius eventually transcended the teacher's social role. In any case, in the 350s Paulinus's family could hardly have envisioned the lifelong influence on Paulinus of Ausonius's teaching and paternal affection; certainly they could not have predicted (though we may wonder if they did not assist) Ausonius's meteoric rise to political power at Trier in the 370s.

The influence of Christianity on Paulinus's early life is less easily detected than the influence of Ausonius. Bordeaux at midcentury was a Christian city; the shadowy late-third-century Christian community, only barely visible behind the name of Orientalis (who as bishop of Bordeaux attended the Council of Arles in 314), would have prospered in the post-Constantinian years.[46] By midcentury the necropolis at Saint-Seurin, to the northwest of the city, may already have been the site of Christian worship and the focus of episcopal attention.[47] When the young

42. Aus. *Prof.* 1.9–10: "mille foro dedit hic iuvenes, bis mille senatus / adiecit numero purpureisque togis." On Minervius see Green, "Still Waters," 498.

43. Aus. *ep.* 22.33–35 Green (EW *ep.* 25): "ego sum tuus altor et ille / praeceptor primus, primus largitor honorum, / primus in Aonidum qui te collegia duxi."

44. Paul. at Aus. *ep.* 17.37–38 Green (EW *ep.* 23) = Paul. *carm.* 3.

45. Aus. *ep.* 17.30–31 Green (EW *ep.* 23): "liquido adiurare possum nullum tibi ad poeticam facundiam Romanae iuventutis aequari."

46. See Maillé, *Recherches,* 17–23; Étienne, *Bordeaux antique,* 265–68; Sivan, *Ausonius of Bordeaux,* 44–48.

47. After 415, the site was associated with the cult of saint Étienne. Maillé, *Recherches,* 118–74, with summary at 173–74; Étienne, *Bordeaux antique,* 271–77.

senator Paulinus returned to Aquitaine from Italy in the early 380s, the Bordelais bishop Delphinus was emerging as one of the foremost clerics in Gaul, consolidating his position as metropolitan of the province and extending his sway into northern Spain.[48] Although earlier prominent cults—Jupiter, Hercules, Mercury, and Cybele—surely maintained their presence and public image in the fourth-century city,[49] Paulinus's milieu appears to have been predominantly Christian: Ausonius's allegiance to Christianity is no longer doubted,[50] and Paulinus's parents must have been Christian by the time of their deaths.

Indeed, the sole piece of Paulinus's early religious history places him as a *puer* standing in awe before the Nolan tomb of Saint Felix. The history of this small Campanian town, tucked against the foothills of the Apennines twenty-three kilometers from Naples and separated from the coast by the bulk of Vesuvius, is distinguished by two significant deaths.[51] Here, on an ancestral estate, the durable *princeps* Augustus died in August of A.D. 14.[52] The consequences of that passing had long been contemplated by many; but relatively few noticed or cared when sometime in the late third century a certain Felix, Nolan priest and confessor, was laid to rest in the cemetery north of town.[53] Yet by the middle of the fourth century Felix's tomb was acknowledged as a special locus of divine power; and Nola, at the junction of the Via Annia—a major artery continuing the Via Appia from Capua to Rhegium—and an important route conveying traffic inland to Avellino,[54] was attracting pilgrims and sightseers. But it was many decades later, in 407, that Paulinus, then in his fifties, told of his boyhood meeting with the figure who was to dominate so much of his later life and thought. In his *natalicium* of that year, presenting the self-portrait discussed above, Paulinus recalled the sense of wonder that accompanied his first encounter

48. Maillé, *Recherches*, 25–39; Étienne, *Bordeaux antique*, 268–71.

49. *Bordeaux: 2000 ans*, 85–96,127–34.

50. For example,, R. P. H. Green, "The Christianity of Ausonius," *Studia Patristica* 28 (1993): 39–48. But see now M. Skeb, *Christo vivere: Studien zum literarischen Christusbild des Paulinus von Nola* (Bonn, 1997), 23–60.

51. For brief sketches of the history of Nola see T. Mommsen, *CIL* 10, 142–43; H. Nissen, *Italische Landeskunde* (Berlin, 1902), 2:756–59; H. Leclercq, *DACL*, s.v. "Nola"; H. Philipp, *RE* XVII.1 (1936): 811–14; and L. Richardson Jr., *Princeton Encyclopedia of Classical Sites* (Princeton, 1976), 627–28. Nola, on the plain, stands at 40 meters above sea level; Avella, six miles away, at 333. Nissen, *Italische Landeskunde*, 2:755–57.

52. Suet. *Aug.* 99.

53. Very little can be said with certainty about the life of Felix or the date of his death. It has been widely held that he achieved his confessor's status under Decius, but there is no explicit evidence. For discussion see P. Testini, "Cimitile: L'antichità cristiana," in *L'art dans l'Italie meridionale: Aggiornamento dell'opera di Émile Bertaux sotto la direzione di Adriano Prandi* (Rome, 1978), 168–69.

54. The route of the Via Annia is well documented, but its name, alternatively the Via Popilla, and the identity of its builder have been debated. See T. P. Wiseman, "Viae Anniae," *PBSR* 32 (1964): 21–37. On the route to Avellino see A. Mercogliano, *Le basiliche paleocristiane di Cimitile* (Rome, 1988) 25.

with Felix: "For as a boy, carried from the western regions of the Gauls, as first I touched your threshold with fearful step, seeing the wonderful proofs of your holy works aglow before your doors, where with your body buried you are enclosed yet spread afar through your lofty merits, with my whole heart I drank in the faith of the divine name and rejoicing in your light I loved Christ."[55]

As testimony to both Paulinus's early connections with Campania, where his family possessed at least one estate,[56] and his early attachment to Felix, this reflection is invaluable, yet in the 360s and 370s the power of literature may have done more to shape Paulinus's life than the power of religion. Certainly the former, not the latter, led Ausonius to Trier in 366–67 to tutor the young Gratian, already Augustus and heir apparent to his father Valentinian I.[57] Valentinian, a Pannonian military officer, had come to the imperial purple some three years before, 26 February 364, elected by the officers of the *comitatus* at Nicaea after the unexpected death of Julian's short-lived successor, Jovian. Recently arrived at Trier, Valentinian, himself not immune to the charms of the Muses despite a reputation for boorishness,[58] selected the sexagenarian professor of Bordeaux to instill in his eldest son the literary skills appropriate to the ruler of the Roman world. Hindsight has inclined some to question the worth of such an education at a time when the problems of the empire seem to have called for outright military solutions, but, as Valentinian was coming to learn, administrative efficiency depended in part on maintaining proper relations with the empire's educated classes.[59] In any case, for Ausonius Valentinian's decision was the first step in a series of events that eventually carried Ausonius and his family to the summits of power and influence; and Paulinus was among those who would benefit in some fashion from the ascendancy of Ausonius.

Even before Valentinian died on 17 November 375, felled by an apparent stroke while venting his wrath at a group of *legati* sent to him by the Quadi,[60] Au-

---

55. *Carm.* 21.367–73:

> nam puer occiduis Gallorum advectus ab oris,
> ut primum tetigi trepido tua limina gressu,
> admiranda videns operum documenta sacrorum
> pro foribus fervere tuis, ubi corpore humato
> clauderis et meritis late diffunderis altis,
> toto corde fidem divini nominis hausi
> inque tuo gaudens adamavi lumine Christum.

56. At Fundi; see *ep.* 32.17. And note that Pontius Proserius Paulinus was *ab origine patronus* at Puteoli (*CIL* 10.1702).

57. For what follows see Matthews, *Western Aristocracies*, 32–87.

58. Matthews, *Western Aristocracies*, 48–52.

59. Still valuable is A. Alföldi, *A Conflict of Ideas in the Late Roman Empire: The Clash Between the Senate and Valentinian I* (Oxford, 1952), with the reservations expressed by Matthews, *Western Aristocracies*, 48.

60. Amm. 30.6.3.

sonius had begun to commute literary skill into political capital. From Valentinian himself came promotion to the rank of *comes* and an appointment as *quaestor sacri palatii*,[61] while Ausonius's presence at the imperial court provided the opportunities to establish useful connections. In 369, for example, Ausonius met Q. Aurelius Symmachus, a junior Roman senator and recent governor (*corrector*) of the Italian province of Lucania and Bruttium, who came to Trier as part of the senatorial embassy charged with delivering the Senate's "gift" of gold (the *aurum oblaticium*) on the occasion of Valentinian's *quinquennalia*,[62] their friendship, nurtured in letters for years to come, would greatly benefit both men. Gratian's accession to the position of senior emperor in the West brought new rewards. Ausonius's quaestorship gave way to the praetorian prefecture, first of Gaul, then of Gaul, Italy, and Africa; and in 379 Gratian magnanimously honored his former tutor with the supreme distinction of the ordinary consulship.[63] It was Ausonius's finest hour.[64] But patronage and *suffragium* (support) were the natural corollaries and expressions of late Roman political capital;[65] and Ausonius used his newfound influence to fill high administrative posts with a coterie of Aquitanian family and friends that included his father, Iulius Ausonius; his son Hesperius; his son-in-law Thalassius; and Magnus Arborius, a cousin or uncle.

A SENATOR'S FRIENDS AND PATRONS

The widening orbit of Ausonius was not without influence on the trajectory of Paulinus's public life, but for Paulinus, unlike Ausonius, Rome, not Trier, stood at the center of political activity. Apart from his boyhood trip to Nola and his literary instruction by Ausonius, we have few details of Paulinus's life before the mid-370s; but between roughly 376 and 383 his political career took on a distinctly Roman character, and he spent much time in Rome and its environs. This consideration, coupled with the character of the offices he held, makes it possible to contemplate the plausible range of Paulinus's social contacts, to observe his likely activities during this first period of Italian residency, and to glimpse the social and religious forces that would eventually draw him back to Italy permanently. In the

---

61. Evidence at *PLRE* 1.140. On what follows and for Ausonius's offices and their context see Matthews, *Western Aristocracies,* 54–87, and Sivan, *Ausonius of Bordeaux,* 106–47. On the office itself, see J. Harries, "The Roman Imperial Quaestor from Constantine to Theodosius II," *JRS* 78 (1988): 148–72.

62. The meeting of Ausonius and Symmachus was preceded by an exchange of letters initiated by Symmachus. See S. Roda, "Una nuova lettera di Simmaco ad Ausonio? (a proposito di Symm., *Ep.* IX, 88)," *REA* 83 (1981): 273–80.

63. Evidence at *PLRE* 1.140–41.

64. Aus. *Protr.* 92–93.

65. For a less flattering discussion of *suffragium* as "purchased recommendation," see R. MacMullen, *Corruption and the Decline of Rome* (New Haven, 1988), 150–51, passim.

late 370s and early 380s, as a *iuvenis* in his mid- and late twenties, Paulinus success-
fully pursued a senatorial career that Ausonius may have aided but which would
have been utterly impossible without the patronage of influential figures at Rome.
Moreover, in these years Paulinus renewed his association with Felix at Nola, lay-
ing the foundations of his later proprietary attitude toward the saint's Nolan shrine.

No later than January 378 Paulinus was in Rome and a member of the Senate,
for by that year he had acquired a suffect consulship. A few years later, probably
in 380–81, he governed the province of Campania.[66] Paulinus's later failure to
speak clearly about his *cursus honorum* has obscured the exact path that led him to
membership in the Roman Senate (as distinct from the hereditary clarissimate).
An entry-level urban quaestorship or praetorship, for example, may well have
preceded Paulinus's suffect consulship, but we cannot document it.[67]

Undoubtedly the influence of Ausonius, emanating from Trier, eased Pauli-
nus's way at Rome. Many years later Paulinus could still recall with undisguised
affection Ausonius's influence exercised on his behalf: "To you, patron, teacher,
and father, I owe my training (*disciplinae*), my dignity (*dignitas*), and my literary skill;
the glory of my eloquence, of my toga, and of my reputation; my preferment, my
nourishment, my education."[68] The language is vague, as are Ausonius's claims to
be Paulinus's "patron" (*fautor*) and "first bestower of honors" (*primus largitor hono-
rum*),[69] but taken together these remarks illustrate the importance of Ausonius's *suf-
fragium* in Paulinus's public life. Yet Paulinus was not just another Gallo-Roman
who came to political office on the coattails of Ausonius. In fact, Paulinus's *cursus*,
however abbreviated, contrasts sharply with the "bureaucratic" careers of the
"Ausoniani"; it suggests how much better placed Paulinus may have been than
many in Aquitaine and hints at other sources of patronage and friendship.

Paulinus's suffect consulship and governorship of Campania placed him in distin-
guished company. If a dearth of evidence renders the social implications of the suffect
consulship difficult to interpret, the Campanian governorship, at least, was clearly the
reserve of the Roman elite under Gratian.[70] Paulinus's near-contemporaries in this

---

66. See appendix B.
67. Appendix B.
68. *Carm.* 10.93–96:

> Tibi disciplinas dignitatem litteras,
>   linguae togae famae decus
> provectus altus institutus debeo,
>   patrone praeceptor pater.

69. Aus. *ep.* 19b.24 Green (EW *ep.* 25); *ep.* 22.34 Green (EW *ep.* 28). The latter claim may equally
refer to Ausonius's role as teacher.

70. This may be true of the suffect consulship as well, but only three other post-Constantinian suf-
fects can be identified. All three belonged to established senatorial families, and one had previously
been both quaestor and praetor at Rome.

post were Anicius Paulinus, Anicius Auchenius Bassus, and Nicomachus Flavianus the Younger, all members of established Roman families. Indeed, the two Anicii, who preceded Paulinus in the posting, carried the enhanced title of *proconsul Campaniae* rather than the normal *consularis Campaniae,* a mark of both their personal prestige and the dignity of the office at the time. Moreover, although this governorship was to be Paulinus's final administrative post, the careers of these others illustrate the place of the office in a fuller *cursus honorum.* The two Anicii moved almost immediately to the urban prefecture, the pinnacle of most Italian careers, while Flavianus in a more regular fashion arrived there ten years later through the proconsulship of Asia.[71]

Paulinus's career track is strikingly unlike the paths of others who owed their promotion primarily to the support of Ausonius. Ausonius himself and members of his family all held palatine posts or appointments as vicars, praetorian prefects, and proconsuls of Africa, conforming to a senatorial career pattern once dubbed "bureaucratic" and considered characteristic of provincials just rising into the senatorial order.[72] Not one of the "Ausoniani" governed an Italian province, and only one appears in an Italian post other than the praetorian prefecture: in 380 Magnus Arborius was *praefectus urbi Romae,* a post frequently given to senatorial "outsiders" by Valentinian, although not by Gratian.[73] Among this group, then, Paulinus is an odd fit.

Turned not toward Trier but toward Rome—the ancient capital of the empire—Paulinus must have cultivated relations with the city's proud and noble families. Even the influence of Ausonius on his behalf would have been channeled through the goodwill of the former's friends at Rome; and among Ausonius's Roman friends one man stands out in our sources. The figure of Symmachus links the Moselle and the Tiber in these years, and he surely served as one of Paulinus's contacts with the Roman nobility.[74] In the decade after they met at Trier in 369, Ausonius and Symmachus assiduously cultivated their friendship and "literary partnership" through numerous letters.[75] Their association offered both men the means to advance various social and political ends.

71. See appendix B; and on the privileged place of the Campanian governorship in senatorial careers see further G. Clemente, "Le carriere dei governatori della diocesi italiciana dal III al V secolo," *Latomus* 28 (1969): 619–44.

72. A. Chastagnol, "La carrière sénatoriale du Bas-Empire (depuis Dioclétien)," *Tituli* 4 (1982): 184–85.

73. See *PLRE* 1.97, "Arborius 3"; Heinzelmann, "Gallische Prosopographie," 585, "Arborius 4."

74. As Glen Bowersock has noted in "Symmachus and Ausonius," *Colloque genevois sur Symmaque à l'occasion du mille-six-centième anniversaire du conflit de l'autel de la Victoire* (Paris, 1986): 1, Ausonius was one of the few individuals to survive Alan Cameron's destruction of the once-renowned "circle of Symmachus." See Cameron, "Paganism and Literature in Late Fourth Century Rome," in *Christianisme et formes littéraires de l'antiquité tardive en Occident* (Geneva, 1977), 1–4. The proof, of course, rests easily and uncontested on the letters of Symmachus and Ausonius.

75. R. P. H. Green, "The Correspondence of Ausonius," *L'antiquité classique* 49 (1980): 198–201.

Symmachus relied on Ausonius, as he did other connections at court, to secure the promotion of his protégés and their interests:[76] of the thirty letters to Ausonius preserved among Symmachus's correspondence, one-third include requests for Ausonius's support of Symmachus's friends and clients or their business at court. Ausonius, in turn, found in Symmachus not only a man eager to distribute and read his poetry at Rome[77] but also a leading senator willing to support him in the capital: the only surviving letter from Ausonius to Symmachus concludes with a cryptic request for such aid.[78] Surely when Ausonius engaged his influence in support of Paulinus's fortunes at Rome, he alerted Symmachus to Paulinus's virtuous qualities.

Although their extant writings provide no explicit proof, the circumstances of Paulinus's years in Italy make it virtually certain that he had contact, perhaps considerable, with Symmachus. These two friends of Ausonius—both boasting literary skills first honed by professors from Bordeaux,[79] both Campanian landowners—were incumbents of a Roman Senate that met at least twice a month.[80] As some years later the eager rhetor Augustine and the aspiring historian Ammianus diligently pursued the *patrocinium* of the *potentiores* of Rome and Milan,[81] so Paulinus, hopeful young senator in a city still able to turn the heads of even the powerful,[82] should have cultivated the goodwill of a leading member of the *ordo amplissimus*, one who was in these years twice designated to read imperial *orationes* in the Senate, an honor normally reserved for the urban prefect.[83] Indeed, to Paulinus the support of Symmachus would have been invaluable; even if the Roman Senate played no formal role in appointments to imperial administrative posts, it did nominate the candidates for its own magistracies—the quaestorship, praetorship, and, notably, the suffect consulship.[84] Moreover, such candidates clearly required

76. For example, Proculus Gregorius, *ep.* 3.19.

77. Aus. *ep.* 12; Sym. *ep.* 1.14.

78. *Ep.* 12.

79. Sym. *ep.* 9.88. Symmachus's Bordelais teacher at Rome may have been the Tiberius Victor Minervius commemorated by Aus. *Prof.* 2. See Roda, "Una nuova lettera," 277–78, with earlier bibliography.

80. It met on the Calends and the Ides according to the Calendar of 354. See Chastagnol, "Le Sénat dans l'oeuvre de Symmaque," *Colloque genevois sur Symmaque*, 82.

81. For Augustine, of course, including Symmachus. See *Conf.* 5.13. On the difficulty of determining Ammianus's specific relations with the Roman aristocracy see Alan Cameron, "The Roman Friends of Ammianus," *JRS* 54 (1964): 15–28; J. Matthews, *The Roman Empire of Ammianus* (Baltimore, 1989), 8–13.

82. *Ep.* 8.3, l.6: "Heu! validos etiam vertere Roma potens." Note, too, Rutilius Namatianus, *De reditu suo* 1.1–18, on the seduction of eternal Rome for another Gallo-Roman.

83. In 376 and 379. See *epp.* 1.95, 3.18, and *Rel.* 10.2, with O. Seeck, *Q. Aurelii Symmachi quae supersunt*, *MGH AA* 6 (1883): LII and J.-P. Callu, *Symmaque: Lettres* (Paris, 1972), 1.141.

84. Sym. *Rel.* 45: "magistratuum nomina, quibus varias functiones designationum tempore amplissimus ordo mandavit, ad aeternitatis vestrae perfero notionem, ut muneribus exhibendis aut subeundis fascibus destinatos cognitio imperialis accipiat." See R. H. Barrow, *Prefect and Emperor: The Relationes of Symmachus, A.D. 384* (Oxford, 1973), 224–25. Elections were held by the Senate in its meeting of

sponsors who would speak in the Senate on their behalf. In early 376 Symmachus delivered a successful oration in support of the son of a certain Trygetius;[85] some twenty years later he spoke in opposition to another candidate.[86] We need not imagine Symmachus delivering an *oratio* in the Senate on Paulinus's behalf in order to envision him exercising his influence in some manner in favor of a well-connected provincial *clarissimus* then enjoying the patronage of a palatine praetorian prefect to whom Symmachus himself was manifestly indebted for the promotion of his own friends and clients.

Paulinus hardly lacked opportunities for association with Symmachus; unlike Augustine or Ammianus, relative strangers in Italy, Paulinus could boast influential connections. The two would have been brought together by numerous well-placed mutual acquaintances who passed through Rome in the years Paulinus was probably there. During the summer of 379, for example, Ausonius's son-in-law Thalassius, en route to Gaul from his proconsular post in Africa and accompanied by his three-year-old son, Paulinus of Pella, met with Symmachus. The latter sent a glowing report of Thalassius's virtues to his father-in-law.[87] Ausonius's son Hesperius, who had preceded Thalassius as proconsul of Africa, should have paid a similar visit during his journeys to and from Carthage. In fact, Symmachus may have met Hesperius earlier at Trier in 369–70, for in early 376 he sent him a copy of his well-received oration *Pro Trygetio,* to which Hesperius responded with the requisite praise.[88] Symmachus's further nineteen extant letters to Hesperius preserve the characteristic combination of polite banter, *commendationes* (*ep.* 81), and requests for intercession on behalf of friends (*ep.* 77). To these mutual *amici* of Symmachus and Ausonius can be added Potitius, who in 379 became *vicarius urbis Romae;* the year before he had carried Symmachus's *commendatio* to Ausonius in Trier.[89]

Other friends of Ausonius as well, although less certainly, could have facilitated Paulinus's movement through the circles that included Symmachus. Proculus Gregorius, for example, was in Rome in 377 as *praefectus annonae,* during which time it appears he became acquainted with Symmachus.[90] In the early 380s, when he

---

9 January; suffect consuls assumed their duties at least by the time of the *Parilia,* the birthday of Rome celebrated on 21 April.

85. Sym. *Or.* 5.4: "[Trygetius], qui vos oratos per me adque exoratos cupit, ut eius filium functioni praetoriae destinatum decimus annus accipiat." *PLRE* 1.376.

86. Sym. *epp.* 4.29, 4.45, 5.9, et al. See Polybius, *PLRE* 1.711. The editors of *PLRE* and Callu, *Symmaque* 2:111 identify Polybius's son as a candidate for the quaestorship, but Symmachus's "ad urbanos fasces resultantem . . . candidatum" suggests the *praetura*. Chastagnol, "Le Sénat dans l'oeuvre de Symmaque," 84.

87. Sym. *ep.* 1.25. *PLRE* 1.887, "Thalassius 1."

88. Sym. *ep.* 1.78. *PLRE* 1.427–28, "Hesperius 2."

89. Sym. *ep.* 1.19. *PLRE* 1.721, "Potitius 1."

90. Sym. *ep.* 3.17 of ca. 379 implies a longstanding relationship. *PLRE* 1.404, "Gregorius 9."

dedicated his *Cupido cruciatus* to this same Gregorius, Ausonius recalled how they had once dined together at Trier in the triclinium of Zoïlus, where the wall was decorated with the mural which inspired Ausonius's ecphrastic rendering of Cupid's torture at the hands of women once beguiled by him. But whether Ausonius's friendship with Gregorius antedates the latter's tenure as imperial quaestor in 379 is unknown.[91] The *praefectus urbi* of 380, Magnus Arborius, recently at Trier as *comes sacrarum largitionum* and surely a relative of Ausonius, could hardly have avoided Symmachus.[92]

Another figure in and out of Rome in these years was the advocate Julianus. Symmachus recommended him to Ausonius as a young man of slender means but notable talent, and by 379–80 he was back in Rome as an agent of Ausonius.[93] Surely, amid the constraining protocols of elite *amicitia*, so relentlessly pursued through the frequent movements of men and letters, the friendship of Ausonius and Symmachus embraced Paulinus as well.

Symmachus, however, is only the most obvious Ausonian link between the young Senator Paulinus and the leading families of Rome. Petronius Probus and Nicomachus Flavianus also warrant consideration. A remarkable succession of administrative appointments, introduced by the urban quaestorship and praetorship and culminating in four praetorian prefectures, eventually distinguished Probus among the Roman aristocrats of his age.[94] Ausonius is likely to have met this emerging "peak of the nobility" at Trier before 371.[95] In any case, to acknowledge Probus's consulship, Ausonius posted to him in that year an ingratiating letter and poem in the company of a copy of Nepos's *Chronica* and the *Fabulae* of Aesop (Aus. *ep.* 9). Moreover, between 375 and 383, the range of Paulinus's first Italian residency, when Probus was out of office and would have found Ausonius an invaluable contact at court,[96] Probus was presumably often in Rome and its environs (Sym. *ep.* 1.58). Probus's attractiveness would have been enhanced for Paulinus by the family's literary pretensions. By 378 Probus had been publicly honored at Rome by his hometown clients as "the light of letters and eloquence";[97] some years later he would feel sufficiently confident in his

---

91. On the date of the *Cupido* see Green, *Ausonius*, 526. Ausonius's *Fasti* were also dedicated to Gregorius.

92. *PLRE* 1.97–98, a cousin; Heinzelmann, "Gallische Prosopographie," 585, "Arborius 4"; and Chastagnol, *Les fastes de la préfecture de Rome au Bas-Empire* (Paris, 1962), 206–7, a nephew.

93. Sym. *ep.* 1.43; Aus. *ep.* 12 (= Sym. *ep.* 1.32).

94. For Probus's *cursus* see *PLRE* 1.736–40; D. Novak, "Anicianae domus culmen, nobilitatis culmen," *Klio* 62 (1980): 474–80; and A. Cameron, "Polyonomy in the Late Roman Aristocracy: The Case of Petronius Probus," *JRS* 75 (1985): 164–82.

95. *ILS* 1265 (August 378): "nobilitatis culmini."

96. So Novak, "Anicianae domus culmen," 488.

97. *ILS* 1265: "litterarum et eloquentiae lumini."

powers as a poet to present his works, along with those of his father and grand-father, to the emperor Theodosius.[98] Moreover, Petronius's family sustained the poet who had already (or soon would) produce the (in)famous *Cento Vergilianus de laudibus Christi*, a Vergilian pastiche destined to attract both the emulation of Paulinus and the sneers of Jerome.[99] Many paths led to Probus. Symmachus and Probus exchanged letters throughout the 370s;[100] and both the secular and ec-clesiastical careers of Ambrose, with whom (as we will see) Paulinus was in con-tact at some time before his return to Aquitaine, owed much to the influence of Probus.

A similar blend of status, connections, and literary interests should have recom-mended even Virius Nicomachus Flavianus to Paulinus. Flavianus, *pontifex maior* and former *consularis* of Sicily (364–65), was not only the intimate friend of Sym-machus but also, in 377, the close associate of Hesperius, the son of Ausonius.[101] As proconsul and *vicarius* of Africa in 376–77, Hesperius and Flavianus together inves-tigated a tangled case of administrative corruption already several years old.[102] Moreover, like Paulinus, Flavianus's son was also *consularis Campaniae* at some point in these years.[103] And, like Probus, Flavianus would eventually offer his literary

---

98. *Ant. Lat.* 1.2.783, ed. Riese. But see the arguments for identification with Aemilius Probus and Theodosius II by L. Traube, "Zu alten Philologie I.3: Zu Cornelius Nepos," *Kleine Schriften: Vorlesungen und Abhandlungen* (Munich, 1920), 3:20–30.

99. For Paulinus's familiarity with the Cento see Y.-M. Duval, "Les premiers rapports de Paulin de Nole avec Jérôme: Moine et philosophe? Poète ou exégète?" *Studi tardoantichi* 7 (1989): 197–205, and chapter 3, this volume. For Jerome's sneer see Jer. *ep.* 53.7, with C. P. E. Springer, "Jerome and the *Cento* of Proba," *Studia Patristica* 28 (1993): 96–105, for the argument that Jerome's aversion may have arisen as much from a distaste for women "teachers" as from theological or literary concerns. The identity of Proba and the date of composition are contested. For the traditional identification of the poet as Faltonia Betitia Proba (*PLRE* I. 732, "Proba 2"), grandmother of the wife of Petronius Probus, and the date of composition as before 370, see E. Clark and D. Hatch, *The Golden Bough, The Oaken Cross: The Virgilian Cento of Faltonia Betitia Proba* (Ann Arbor, 1981), 97; and R. Herzog, *Restauration et renouveau: La littérature latine de 284 à 374 après J.-C.* (Paris, 1993), 385. The attempt of D. Shanzer, "The Anony-mous *Carmen contra paganos* and the Date and Identity of the Centonist Proba," *REAug* 32 (1986): 232–48, to identify the author as Anicia Faltonia Proba, wife of Petronius Probus (*PLRE* I.732, "Proba 3"), and place composition between 385 and 388, drew resistance from J. Matthews, "The Poetess Proba and Fourth-Century Rome: Questions of Interpretation," In *Institutions, société et vie politique dans l'empire romain au IVe siècle ap. J.-C.* (Rome, 1992): 277–304, to which Shanzer in turn responded with "The Date and Identity of the Centonist Proba," *Recherches augustiniennes* 27 (1994): 75–96. H. Sivan, "Anician Women, the Cento of Proba, and Aristocratic Conversion in the Fourth Century," *Vigiliae Christianae* 47 (1993): 140–57, seeks tentatively to save the authorship for Proba 2 and assign an editor's role to Proba 3. Despite the uncertainty of origin, Sivan rightly notes that the Cento was enjoying re-newed life in the mid-390s. Certainty may not be possible.

100. Sym. *epp.* 1.56–61, and, perhaps, 9.112. See Roda, "Una nuova lettera."

101. *PLRE* 1.347–49, "Flavianus 15."

102. Amm. 28.6.28. Matthews, *The Roman Empire of Ammianus*, 385–86.

103. *PLRE* 1.345, "Flavianus 14."

accomplishments to an emperor; the *Annales* of this *historicus disertissimus* were presented to Theodosius while Flavianus held the post of *quaestor sacri palatii* in 388.[104]

If Petronius died as a baptized Christian about the year of Flavianus's imperial quaestorship,[105] Symmachus and Flavianus had by then emerged as beleaguered defenders of the old gods. This later reputation, however, should not eliminate either as likely friends of Paulinus in the late 370s and early 380s. Certainly Paulinus, whose Christian commitment grew stronger in these years, would have sought out like-minded individuals; Rome was also home to Damasus and the Christian Anicii. But the city's elite should not be too hastily separated along religious lines. The fissures that would eventually divide the Senate over religious issues were less obvious in the 370s; Ausonius's relations with Symmachus, for example, were no cooler for what he may then have known of the latter's religious preferences. Only in 382 or 383 would Gratian take the measures—renunciation of the pontifical robe, removal of the statue of victory from the Senate house, and the abolition of state funds for the city's priesthoods—that would force individuals to choose sides.[106] Even so, Symmachus continued to correspond with Ambrose, seeking his *patrocinium* for his clients and his intercession for his friends, long after they had clashed over the Altar of Victory in 384.[107]

In fact, Paulinus's Italian years (ca. 377–83) were a particularly happy period for the Senate and the Roman aristocracy. Gratian's accession and his execution of Maximinus, the dreaded and detested praetorian prefect and former *praefectus annonae* and *vicarius urbis,* had greatly improved relations between the Senate and the imperial court.[108] It was a harmony that few would have wished disturbed, and it should have facilitated Paulinus's relations with those Roman aristocrats who (pagan or not) pursued and entertained the friendship of an Ausonius who had done so well for himself and others at the distant imperial court.

But Paulinus's avowed Christianity, coupled with his economic interests in Spain—where his family apparently had property, among whose aristocracy he

---

104. *CIL* 6.1782: "historico disertissimo." On the *Annales* see *CIL* 6.1783, ll. 19–20. On the date of the quaestorship see T. Honoré, "Some Writings of the Pagan Champion Nicomachus Flavianus," and J. Matthews, "Nicomachus Flavianus's Quaestorship: The Historical Evidence," both at *Xenia* 23 (1989): 9–25.

105. *CIL* 6.1756b. See Matthews, *Western Aristocracies,* 195–97.

106. A. Cameron, "Gratian's Repudiation of the Pontifical Robe," *JRS* 58 (1968): 96–102, for the later date; Matthews, *Western Aristocracies,* 203–4, for the earlier.

107. Sym. *epp.* 3.30–37, with 3.34 dating to 392–95 and 3.37, perhaps, to 395–97. For dates and analysis see M. Patrucco and S. Roda, "Le lettere di Simmaco ad Ambrogio: Vent'anni di rapporti amichevoli," *Ambrosius Episcopus* (Milan, 1976), 2:284–97. For a more cautious assessment see J. Matthews, "Symmachus and His Enemies," *Colloque genevois sur Symmaque,* esp. 173–74; and McLynn, *Ambrose,* 263–75.

108. *PLRE* 1.577. See esp. Sym. *Or.* 4. 10–12; *ep.* 10.2; Amm. 28.1.5–57. He was "homo cum gremitu nominandus" (28.1.36).

would eventually find a wife, and where he would reside in the early 390s—may have provided him with another ready-made network of contacts in Rome during these years when the new emperor Theodosius I, of Spanish background, rose to prominence. Certainly after returning to Italy in 395 Paulinus enjoyed intimate friendship with the family of the Spanish-born Melania the Elder and members of the *gens Turcia*. In 400 Melania came to Nola immediately on her return to Italy after more than two decades in the East; and in January 407 Melania's granddaughter, Melania the Younger, and her niece, Avita, as well as their respective husbands, Valerius Pinianus and the recently converted Turcius Apronianus, attended the feast of Saint Felix at Nola (see below). But Paulinus's relations with this group clearly predated his relocation to Campania and were probably cultivated during his first years in Italy. Melania herself, kin in some fashion to Paulinus, had departed Rome for the East perhaps as early as 372, but her son, Publicola, had been left behind.[109] In the year of his mother's departure, it seems, Publicola was praetor at Rome, and he later became *consularis Campaniae;*[110] Paulinus should not have avoided his company.

Similarly, Paulinus may have already sought out the company of the Turcii. The marriage of Avita, Melania's niece, with Turcius Apronianus must postdate Paulinus's return to Aquitaine in the early 380s,[111] but the Turcii apparently had already contracted a Christian marriage alliance—*perhaps* with a family of Spanish background. The casket of Proiecta, part of the well-known Esquiline treasure, commemorates the marriage of the Christian Proiecta with a certain Secundus. The casket broadly dates to the middle decades of the century,[112] and the bridegroom Secundus was a member of the *gens Turcia*, most likely the son of L. Turcius Apronianus *signo* Asterius, urban prefect in 362–63 and a *quindecemvir sacris faciundis.*[113] If, as is often argued, the casket's Proiecta is the same Proiecta as the young bride commemorated in a epitaph composed by Damasus in 383, then the marriage must have taken place about 380,[114] during the very years that found Paulinus in Italy. Furthermore, if the Damasian Proiecta's father, Florus, is none other

109. On Paulinus's claim of kinship see the remark to Severus at *ep.* 29.5: "unde te dignior visa est, cuius fides illi magis quam noster sanguis propinquat." On the date of Melania's departure for the East see Murphy, "Melania the Elder," 64–65; *PLRE* 1:592, "Melania 1"; N. Moine, "Melaniana," *Recherches augustiniennes* 15 (1980): 24–25.

110. *PLRE* 1.753–54, "Publicola 1."

111. In early 407 Paulinus could refer to Apronianus as still "aetate puerum" (*carm.* 21.211).

112. The "middle decades of the fourth century," with a nod to the early 360s, is argued on stylistic grounds by K. Shelton, "The Esquiline Treasure: The Nature of the Evidence," *AJA* 89 (1985): 150–51.

113. On the filiation see Shelton, "The Esquiline Treasure," 151–52; A. Cameron, "The Date and Owners of the Esquiline Treasure," *AJA* 89 (1985): 144–45.

114. For the argument see Cameron, "The Date and Owners," 136–39, with the objections of Shelton, "The Esquiline Treasure," 148–50.

than the Florus who served Theodosius as praetorian prefect in the early 308s,[115] then a Spanish connection for Proiecta's family, and thus for the Turcii as well, is nearly certain, for Theodosius's prefect was part of that group of new men, many from Spain, who after January 379 found success at the court of Theodosius.[116]

Further Spanish connections can be inferred. The group of Theodosian supporters also included both Maternus Cynegius and Aemilius Florus Paternus. The latter, proconsul of Africa in 393, may have been the son of the prefect Florus,[117] while the former, whose honors culminated in the consulship in 388, was perhaps the father of Antonia Cassia,[118] whose name recalls the paternal side of the lineage of Melania the Elder, granddaughter of Antonius Marcellus, consul in 341.[119] Too much is uncertain in this picture beyond a blurry image of shared bloodlines, Christianity, and Spanish roots, but an important piece of evidence does justify speculation about Paulinus's relations with these individuals prominent in court and aristocratic circles at Rome as well as Constantinople in the early 380s. About the year 421, Paulinus, now bishop of Nola, granted permission to a certain widowed Flora to bury her recently deceased son, named Cynegius, in the basilica complex at Nola. As I discuss later, the episode was significant enough to provoke Augustine's treatise *De cura pro mortuis gerenda;* it is enough to observe here that Flora and her son are likely descendants of those early Theodosian supporters Maternus Cynegius and Aemilius Florus Paternus.[120] Thus the presence of the younger Cynegius at Nola and the request of his mother for *ad sanctum* burial there may well preserve the late traces of an *amicitia* now several generations proven.

The kin of Melania, the Turcii, and the rising Spanish nobility of the early 380s provide tantalizing examples of the kinds of Christian families that Paulinus should have known at Rome. Undeniably, however, Paulinus would also have fallen under the spell of Damasus, bishop of Rome during these years. By the later 370s the storms that had darkened Damasus's contested election in 366 and the early years of his papacy had largely passed.[121] With his rival Ursinus exiled from Rome, Damasus, of Roman clerical family but also with Spanish roots,[122] was

115. *PLRE* 1.367, "Florus 1."

116. See in general Matthews, *Western Aristocracies*, 107–12.

117. *PLRE* 1.671, "Paternus 6"; Matthews, *Western Aristocracies*, 111.

118. *PLRE* 1.235, "Cynegius 3"; Matthews, *Western Aristocracies*, 110–11.

119. Ruf. *Apol.* 2.26; Paul. *ep.* 29.8.

120. Matthews, *Western Aristocracies*, 143–44. On the *De cura* see chapter 8.

121. Amm. 27.3.11–13. J.-R. Palanque, *Histoire de l'église: De la paix constantinienne à la mort de Théodose* (Paris, 1950), 232–34; C. Pietri, *Roma christiana: Recherches sur l'Église de Rome, son organisation, sa politique, son idéologie de Miltiade à Sixte III (311–440)* (Paris, 1976), 1.408–23; Matthews, *The Roman Empire of Ammianus*, 421–22. Damasus's pontificate was never completely free of controversy; see the *testimonia* assembled by A. Ferrua, *Epigrammata damasiana* (Rome, 1942), 59–77.

122. *Liber pontificalis* 39: "Damasus natione Hispanus."

fully embarked on the program of church building, epigraphic commemoration of Christian heroes, and promotion of the cult of the saints that so boldly foreshadows Paulinus's later activities at Nola.[123] In a lesson surely not lost on Paulinus, Damasus was revealing how the material and artistic resources of the church and the Christian elite might be fashioned into powerful instruments of "communication and propaganda" for the faith.[124] Moreover, Damasus's *carmina epigraphica*, established in the *loca sancta* associated with Rome's apostles and martyrs and elegantly inscribed under the guidance of Furius Dionysius Filocalus, a possible client of Melania the Elder as well as Damasus,[125] presented Paulinus with new models for poetic composition at once overtly Christian yet sensitive to centuries of tradition. In Damasus's poems Virgilian allusions resonate alongside scriptural echoes, and the virtues of the entombed find their counterpoint in Damasus's personal appeals for divine intercession.

Indeed, not only at Rome but at Campanian Nola itself Paulinus would have felt the influence of Damasus. In the precinct of Felix's grave an inscribed marble tablet recorded Damasus's visit to the Nolan shrine.[126] Honoring a Felix, "fortunate (*felix*) in body, mind, and soul as well as name," Damasus's seven hexameter lines thanked the saint for preserving the author from death and for vanquishing his enemies "who had spoken falsely." With his verses Damasus, "a humble suppliant, repaid his vows."[127] The specific incident that provoked Damasus's appeal

---

123. On Damasus's churches and the monuments of the catacombs see Pietri, *Roma christiana*, 1.461–68, 529–46.

124. On Damasus's poetry and its context see especially, J. Fontaine, *Naissance de la poésie dans l'occident chrétien* (Paris, 1981), 111–25. Quote 113.

125. On Filocalus see Ferrua, *Epigrammata*, 21–35; A. Cameron, "Filocalus and Melania," *CPh* 87 (1992): 140–44.

126. Ferrua, *Epigrammata*, no. 59, 213–15. For conclusive arguments on the poem's Nolan context see T. Lehmann, "Eine spätantike Inschriftensammlung und der Besuch des Päpstes Damasus an der Pilgerstätte des Hl. Felix in Cimitile / Nola," *ZPE* 91 (1992): 243–81; and Lehmann, "Der Besuch des Papstes Damasus an der Pilgerstätte des Hl. Felix in Cimitile / Nola," *Akten des XII. Internationalen Kongresses für christliche Archäologie* (Rome and Münster, 1995), 969–81, confirming the position of Ferrua and De Rossi.

127.

> Corpore mente animo pariterq(ue) et nomine Felix
> . . . .
> te duce servatus mortis quod vincula rupi,
> hostibus extinctis fuerant qui falsa locuti,
> versib(us) his Damasus supplex tibi vota rependo.

Compare Paulinus's similar puns upon the name of Felix; for example, *carm.* 12.1: "Inclite confessor, meritis et nomine Felix"; and note that his *natalicia* were also composed in fulfillment of a vow to Felix.

to a saint's shrine, which Augustine years later also recognized as an *ara veritatis*, is difficult to determine,[128] but this Damasian inscription preserves tantalizing evidence for the lines of patronage and interest that connected Rome and Nola, the two identifiable poles of Paulinus's life in these years. Localizing the energy of a well-connected Roman bishop at the Nolan tomb of Felix, Damasus's poem suggests the presence of Rome's Christian aristocracy behind the monumentalization, which took place over and around Felix's tomb in the second half of the fourth century (figure 1a):[129] Paulinus is unlikely to have been the first governor of Campania to have attended the saint's January festival or to have expended his resources in the improvement and adornment of the site.[130]

Much in this section has necessarily been speculative, but the incontrovertible facts of Paulinus's life in the late 370s and early 380s encourage sketching out the plausible context within which the aspiring Paulinus of Bordeaux gained appointment to a suffect consulship at Rome and promotion to the prestigious consular governorship of Campania. Such political and social preferment within an almost exclusively Roman theater cannot be credited solely, or even primarily, to the support of Ausonius at Trier. Favor and patronage among the established Roman nobility would have been necessary and, in addition to any inherited relationships that we cannot reconstruct, Paulinus surely secured those prerequisites within the circles of those, like Symmachus, who were bound by the courtesies of *amicitia* to the briefly ascendant family of Ausonius, and those connected to the families of Melania the Elder and the Turcii, his later relationships with whom are well documented. Similarly, Paulinus's Aquitanian provincial background and Spanish interests may have connected him naturally with those identifiable Spanish-based families who came to prominence with Theodosius. Finally, it is tempting to see in

128. Aug. *ep.* 78.3. The charge in question, perhaps *de vi publica* or murder, may have been brought forward by the supporters of Ursinus through the apostate Jew Isaac. See *Liber pontificalis* 39 and the *Epistola Romani Concilii ad Gratianum et Valentinianum* 8–9 (*PL* 13.580–81) with Ferrua, *Epigrammata*, 60–61, 71–74, 215; Pietri, *Roma christiana*, 1:419–22.

129. The architectural history of the site has evaded close delineation. G. Chierci worked at Cimitile in the 1930s and again in the 1950s but never published a comprehensive study of the site. See the bibliography for his intermittent reports. P. Testini, challenging Chierci's methods and many of his pronouncements, called for further archaeological work in "Note per servire allo studio del complesso paleocristiano di S. Felice a Cimitile (Nola)," *Mélanges de l'école française de Rome, Antiquité* 97 (1985): 329–71. Renewed efforts begun in 1988 have yielded a revised understanding of the chronology of the site's development. See T. Lehmann, "Lo sviluppo del complesso archeologico a Cimitile / Nola," *Boreas* 13 (1990): 75–93 and his forthcoming *Paulinus Nolanus und die Basilica Nova in Cimitile / Nola*, as well as E. di Ferrante, "Il restauro delle basiliche di Cimitile," *Akten des XII. Internationalen Kongresses für christliche Archäologie*, 746–55; and M. Exner, "Il Convegno Paoliniano XVI Centenario del Ritiro di Paolino a Nola," *Kunst Chronik* 49 (1996): 145–53. Particular aspects of the site's history are discussed below.

130. See next section.

the later religious and poetic program realized by Paulinus at Nola something of the influence of Damasus, whose foreshadowing enterprise reached beyond Rome's catacombs even to the Nolan tomb of Felix. Without question, in these years of public life and celebrity Paulinus laid down the first mature lines of social relations that would over the next five decades produce that thick and densely cross-referenced palimpsest whose single truly legible surface is preserved in the letters and poems written between 393 and 408.

BETWEEN SENATE AND CHURCH

Moving within closely knit social circles that are as likely to have included Symmachus as Damasus, Paulinus conducted his public life against the contrasting backdrops of metropolitan Rome and small-town Nola. In both places Paulinus's activities affirm hypotheses about how easily the traditional forms of aristocratic life and evolving Christian practices could accommodate each other in the middle decades of the fourth century.[131] To be sure, following Constantine's victory at the Milvian Bridge in 312, the emperor's church-building program began subtly to alter Rome's topography; and for some a great emotional and spiritual gulf had come to separate the ancient *forum Romanum* at the foot of the Capitoline from the new Constantinian foundations—Saint John Lateran, Saint Sebastian, Saint Peter's, and others—which now ringed the city.[132] But Rome's Christian senators had not abandoned the *curia,* where, in a building restored by Diocletian, they still swore fealty to the laws and the emperor at an altar surmounted by a statue of Victory;[133] and the mansions of their pagan counterparts frequently sheltered Christian wives and daughters. Indeed, perhaps no two artifacts of these mid-fourth-century decades better illustrate the relative insignificance of "religious" categories in social relations than the already mentioned casket of Proiecta, with its effortless conflation of Christian and "classical" motifs, and the Codex-Calendar of 354. Magnificently illustrated by Filocalus, presented to the Christian aristocrat Valentinus, it contains a mélange of documents that includes both a calendar of Rome's public "pagan" festivals and a list of saints' days.[134]

---

131. See P. Brown, "Aspects of the Christianization of the Roman Aristocracy," *JRS* 51 (1961): 1–11; reprinted in *Religion and Society in the Age of Saint Augustine* (New York, 1972).

132. R. Krautheimer, *Three Christian Capitals: Topography and Politics* (Berkeley, 1983), 12–28.

133. Sym. *Rel.* 3.5–6. Constantius had removed the Altar, but it was returned to the Curia, presumably under Julian, and remained until it was ordered removed again by Gratian in 382 / 83.

134. For the text of the calendar portion of the codex see A. Degrassi, *Inscriptiones Italiae* (Rome, 1963), 13.2, 237–62; for the *depositiones episcoporum Romanorum* and *martyrum,* a virtual *feriale ecclesiae Romanae,* see T. Mommsen, *Chronica Minora,* vol. 1, *MGH AA* 9 (1892): 70–72. For valuable discussion see M. Salzman, *On Roman Time: The Codex-Calendar of 354 and the Rhythms of Urban Life in Late Antiquity* (Berkeley, 1990), 26, 42–50, 193–231.

In this city, equally accustomed to lavish displays of elite munificence at the annual *ludi* and at the major Christian feasts, we can imagine Paulinus both presiding over games at the Circus Maximus at the foot of the Palatine hill and feeling the press of the crowd before the portals of Saint Peter's across the Tiber. Our sole picture of a suffect consul in these years reveals him ceremoniously conveyed through the city's streets like a *triumphator*, seated in a two-horse chariot (*bigae*), wrapped in the *toga palmata*, and distinguished by the consular insignia. That particular occasion, recalled in fact by Symmachus, was the April 21 celebration of the Parilia, the *natalis urbis*, and the destination of the anonymous suffect may have been the Circus, where the staging of games would mark the day's festivities.[135] The young suffect Paulinus must also have experienced the intoxicating rush of egotism that came with such celebrity, or, as he would warn Licentius, with ostentatious conveyance over the heads of awestruck crowds.[136] In procession like Symmachus's anonymous suffect or with *mappa* in hand at the Circus Maximus, Paulinus's consular *trabea*—resplendent with jewels, segmented, embroidered, and perhaps even emblazoned with portraits of the imperial family—[137] his *sella curulis*, and his fasces conspicuously promoted him, too, among the *plebs Romana*. And although Paulinus's duties as suffect consul may have been costly, largely ceremonial, and restricted to Rome,[138] they were not thereby drained of their social and political significance. The office's regalia and protocols all gave concrete expression to the pretensions and expectations of young men of Paulinus's class and, like the texts they had pored over with their teachers, bound them to senatorial traditions older than the empire itself. Moreover, as suffect, if not by virtue of a previous office, Paulinus should have attended the meetings of the Senate, whose routines emerge from the letters of Symmachus, that *sénateur par excellence*. There, seated among that "best part of the human race," he too would have heard the imperial *orationes* bringing news from the imperial court, weighed the *sententiae* of fellow senators, designated ambassadors to the court, shouted acclamations, and cast votes.[139] All dutifully recorded in the *Acta senatus* and forwarded to Trier or Milan,

135. Sym. *ep.* 6.40. The year was 401, and Symmachus recorded the image only because the unfortunate suffect was tossed from the chariot by a bump and carried off with a broken leg. On the festival's *ludi circenses* see Degrassi, *Inscriptiones Italiae*, 244–45, with Salzman, *On Roman Time*, 186.

136. Reading Paulinus's warning to Licentius as autobiographical. *Ep.* 8.3, ll. 37–38:

> Nec tibi nobilitas videatur libera, quam nunc
> sublimen attonita conspicis urbe vehi,
> quam cernis tanta sibi libertate videri,
> ut dedignetur flectere colla deo.

137. On the components of the *trabea* see, for example, Aus. *Grat. Act.* 11; Claud. *Cons. Hon. IV.* 585–610, *Cons. Stil.* 2.339–61; Sid. *carm.* 15.159–84.

138. Sym. *Or.* 5 on expense. Bagnall et al., *Consuls of the Later Roman Empire* (Atlanta, 1987), 21–22.

139. Chastagnol, "Le Sénat dans l'oeuvre de Symmaque," 81–86.

such actions may ultimately have had little to do with ruling the empire directly, but by engaging in them senators maintained the continuity of senatorial government and justified their claims to social status and public authority in Italy.

But by the early 380s, as Rome was about to be engulfed by a wave of church building that would transform the city's landscape in the decades ahead,[140] the rhythm of urban life at Rome had also begun to reflect the presence of a newer cycle of ceremonies and protocols. By midcentury the church could offer its own annual round of public festivals to the people of Rome. Although not yet on a par with the old civic celebrations of the capital, these new festivals, marking the *depositiones* of Rome's bishops and martyrs, were sufficiently established, as we have seen, to claim their place in the Codex- Calendar of 354.[141] The young senator who during these years dedicated the cuttings of his first beard to Saint Felix at Nola, reenacting the ancient ceremony of the *depositio barbae*,[142] presumably did not forgo the celebrations that punctuated the Christian religious year at Rome. After 395, to be sure, Paulinus regularly journeyed from Nola to Rome each summer for the Feast of the Apostles on 29 June. Much earlier he may also have been part of the crowd that gathered first at the great Vatican basilica and then accompanied the bishop back through the city, out the Porta Ostiensis, and on to the church of Saint Paul on the road to Ostia.[143] Like the Christian senator Pammachius later, equally familiar with the Senate House and Saint Peter's, the young Paulinus in his Roman days must somehow have bridged the distance between potentially dissonant ideas symbolized by these two buildings.

This same dynamic tension appears in Paulinus's relationship with Campania and Nola. As governor Paulinus necessarily managed the harsh judicial apparatus of the state, but he was apparently already sensitive to the expectation that Christian magistrates demonstrate mercy.[144] Moreover, in conformity with a style of

140. Notably, Paulinus's Roman years coincide with the beginning of the second, post-Constantinian, phase of extensive church-building activity at Rome. With the exception of the imperially founded S. Paolo fuori le Mura (begun in 384), this "renascence of church building" was directed by the papacy and, through the replacement of many *domus ecclesiae* with larger basilicas, necessarily occupied more space closer to the city center. See Pietri, *Roma christiana*, 1.461–573; Krautheimer, *Three Christian Capitals*, 94–121, quote 104.

141. On the cult of the martyrs and the development of the Christian festival calendar in the fourth century see Pietri, *Roma christiana*, 1:617–24; R. Markus, *The End of Ancient Christianity* (Cambridge, 1990): 87–106.

142. See appendix B.

143. See Prud. *Peristeph.* 12.57–67. This poem, however, dates from the early 390s, and the basilica described there by Prudentius, S. Paolo fuori le Mura, only begun in 384, postdates Paulinus's first Italian residency. See J. Harries, "Prudentius and Theodosius," *Latomus* 43 (1984): 69–73 on the date; and R. Krautheimer, *Early Christian and Byzantine Architecture*, 4th ed. (London, 1986), 87–89. Cf. the Codex-Calendar of 354 (Mommsen, 71): "III kal. Iul. Petri in Catacumbas et Pauli Ostense, Tusco et Basso cons."

144. The evidence is provided by the much later *carm.* 21.375–76 (407). For the church's emerging

aristocratic behavior well documented in fourth-century Campania,[145] Paulinus easily blended the administrative duties of a *consularis Campaniae* with the philanthropic expectations incumbent on the region's elite families and governors. But unlike the eminent Nolan families of the early empire—the Corelli, Fisii, and Varii Ambibuli—who devoted their patronal energy to the embellishment of the town's civic center,[146] Paulinus's *euergetism* preferred the emerging imperatives of Christian charity. Like the *spolia* that found their way from the town to be reused in the new monumental center rising around the tomb of Felix in the necropolis just north of Nola,[147] so the center of philanthropic gravity was shifting as well. Paulinus, of course, did not initiate that change. The grave of Felix was hardly an *oscura tomba* even in 381:[148] during the Constantinian era an *aula* had replaced the smaller mausoleum that had been erected over the tomb in the opening years of the fourth century, and at least one basilica (the Basilica Vetus) predated Paulinus's governorship (figure 1a).[149] Indeed, Felix's notoriety was already sufficient to attract the patronal and artistic attention of Damasus in addition to the similarly motivated, if less elegant, graffiti of more humble pilgrims.[150] Nevertheless, the improvements made by Paulinus as governor were notable and perhaps long-remembered: almost fifteen years before he settled permanently at Nola, Paulinus built and paved a road from the town to the shrine of Felix, as once the *duoviri* of Capua had paved the road to a suburban temple of Diana,[151] and constructed a shelter to protect the poor who assembled there,[152] expectant no doubt of physical as well as spiritual sustenance. As authority in the late Roman world naturally

position see [Siricius] *ep.* 10, *cap.* 5 (*PL* 13.1190); Ambrose, *ep.* 25 (*PL* 16) / 50 (*CSEL* 82); Innocent, *ep.* 6, *cap.* 3 (*PL* 20.499–500), with discussion in appendix B and chapter 3.

145. B. Ward-Perkins, *From Classical Antiquity to the Middle Ages: Urban and Public Building in Northern and Central Italy, A.D. 300–850* (Oxford, 1984), 23–28. Only one *consularis Campaniae*, Naeratius Scopius (*CIL* 10.1253), is recorded as active at Nola.

146. On these families see H. G. Pflaum, "Q. Planius Sardus L. Valerius Ambibulus, légat de la *legio IIIa Augusta*, à la lumière de découvertes récentes," *Bulletin archéologique du comité des travaux historiques et scientifiques* (1963–64): 141–51, with A. Ferrua, "Cimitile ed altre iscrizioni dell'Italia inferiore, I," *Epigraphica* 33 (1971): 102–4. Varia Pansina, sister of Varius Ambibulus, gave a portico with statues and gardens to the *numen* of Venus Iovia and the colony; see Ferrua, "Cimitile," 102–4.

147. A distinguished example: the inscription recording the second-century generosity of Varia Pansina was used in the construction of the tomb of the Nolan bishop Paulinus II (d. 442). Ferrua, "Cimitile," 102.

148. So A. Ruggiero, "Carme 21: Nola crocevia dello spirito," in *Atti del Convegno*, 186, speaking of Cimitile before Paulinus's relocation.

149. Testini, "Note," 349; Lehmann, "Lo sviluppo," 78–80, esp. figure 18, reproduced here as figure 1a.

150. A. Ferrua, "Graffiti di pellegrini alla tomba di San Felice," *Palladio* n.s. 13 (1963):17–19, dating them to the fourth century before Paulinus's later constructions, for example, "Marcus votum / reddidit / domno Felici s[anc]to."

151. *CIL* 10.3913 = *ILS* 5380.

152. *Carm.* 21.379–86.

welled up from distinct, but often undifferentiated, political, economic, social, and intellectual sources, so authority's public expressions easily remained ambiguous. Already in this, our second glimpse of Paulinus at Nola, Paulinus's actions reveal the seamless mix of public and private, secular and religious, old and new that would characterize his later life at Nola.

In these years one other Italian city and center of innovative Christian activity drew Paulinus's attention. Some time roughly between late 381 and the summer of 383, Paulinus spent time in Milan, by then home to Gratian's court.[153] Again our best evidence is retrospective. In 395, Alypius, a longtime friend of Augustine and by then bishop of Thagaste, recalled while introducing himself to Paulinus how at Milan he had once heard Paulinus's name.[154] Alypius, an aspiring *assessor* seeking professional advancement, came to Milan with the equally ambitious rhetor Augustine in the autumn of 384;[155] Paulinus, who had apparently already departed by the time of Alypius's arrival, must have been in the city not long before. Like Alypius and Augustine, Paulinus would have known Milan not only as an imperial capital but also as the city of Ambrose; and here Paulinus cultivated a relationship with the powerful bishop that later allowed him to gloss Ambrose as *noster pater* and to claim him as his spiritual adviser.[156] Indeed, unlike his socially inferior North African contemporaries,[157] Paulinus, a Christian senator and *vir consularis*, should not have had to wait in the wings for an audience with the former senator and *consularis* of Aemilia and Liguria who had been bishop of the city since 374. Paulinus surely came to this vital link between the imperial court and the Roman aristocracy well recommended. Gratian's court, so recently arrived from Trier, would still have harbored many friends of Ausonius; Symmachus, to whom Ambrose was somehow related, was in frequent, although increasingly strained and formal, correspondence with Ambrose during these years;[158] and Petronius Probus, whom Paulinus could have met at Rome, had years before been the primary patron of Ambrose's administrative career.[159]

If on the one hand it is true, as Paulinus claimed, that Ambrose "nurtured him in the faith," on the other it is also evident that, like Damasus, Ambrose presented

153. T. Mommsen, *Theodosiani Libri XVI* (Berlin, 1905), 1.1. CCLIX. On the summer of 381 as the date of the relocation of the court to Milan, see McLynn, *Ambrose*, 120.

154. Paul. *ep.* 3.4: "quod enim indicasti iam de humilitatis nostrae nomine apud Mediolanium te didicisse, cum illic initiareris." See the judicious assessment of the evidence by S. Costanza, "I rapporti tra Ambrogio e Paolino di Nola," *Ambrosius Episcopus* (Milan, 1976), 220–32.

155. Aug. *Conf.* 6.10. When Augustine arrived in Rome in 383, Alypius was already there (*Conf.* 6.8). O. Perler, *Les voyages de saint Augustine* (Paris, 1969): 134–38.

156. *Ep.* 3.4.

157. Aug. *Conf.* 6.3.

158. Seeck, *Symmachus*, CXXVIII–CXXIX. On the possible relationship see T. D. Barnes, "Augustine, Symmachus, and Ambrose," in *Augustine: From Rhetor to Theologian*, ed. J. McWilliam (Waterloo, Ontario, 1992), 7–13; rejected by McLynn, *Ambrose*, 263–64.

159. Paul. *V. Amb.* 2.5, with *PLRE* 1:52, "Ambrosius 3." McLynn, *Ambrose*, 38, 49–50.

Paulinus with another example of a socially and politically influential churchman intent on extending and reshaping the public role of Christianity. By 382 Ambrose had clearly emerged as a primary influence at Gratian's court, replacing Ausonius in this regard.[160] And if not yet the outspoken "conscience" of emperors he would become in the later 380s, Ambrose was fully prepared to warn Gratian against continuing imperial subsidies for Rome's priestly colleges, maintaining the Altar of Victory in the Senate House, and wearing the pontifical robe.[161] Moreover, by 382, Ambrose's ascetic inclinations had been clearly presented for public consumption by his treatises on virginity,[162] and the bishop was simultaneously a church builder and an advocate of the emerging cult of the saints. Both the Basilica Ambrosiana (S. Ambrogio) and the Basilica Apostolorum (S. Nazaro), for example, must have been under construction at the time of Paulinus's visit to Milan; on 9 May 386 the latter church received the relics of the Apostles Andrew and Thomas and of John the Evangelist.[163] Nor was Ambrose's public stature diminished by Gratian's death in August 383; in the autumn of that year, as ambassador for the new court of Valentinian II and Justina, Ambrose traveled to Trier to negotiate peace with the usurper Maximus. Although Paulinus may never have met with Ambrose again after his departure from Italy, the bishop's influence on the young Christian senator was surely profound, and Paulinus maintained epistolary contact with Ambrose until the latter's death in 397.[164]

Presumably the same series of events that led Ambrose to Trier in the autumn of 383 recalled Paulinus to Aquitaine. In the summer of that year the *comes Britanniarum*, the Spanish-born Magnus Maximus, led his army into Gaul. After the defection of some of Gratian's troops near Paris, the young emperor was caught and murdered at Lyon on 25 August. When this disturbing news reached the Milanese court of Gratian's half-brother, the twelve-year-old Valentinian II, the task of negotiating with Maximus was handed over to Ambrose, who succeeded in buying time from a usurper who apparently hoped to acquire the recognition of Theodosius, emperor in the East, without further battle.[165] But the distress felt in northern Italy in the summer of 383 may have been even more acute in Gaul, where un-

160. Étienne, *Bordeaux antique*, 350. For the cautious view of Ambrose's ascendancy see McLynn, *Ambrose*, 79–157.

161. Amb. *ep.* 17.10 (*PL* 16) / 72 (*CSEL* 82). Cameron, "Gratian's Repudiation of the Pontifical Robe," 96–102.

162. For example, the *De virginibus* of 377 and the *De virginitate* of 378. For context, see McLynn, *Ambrose*, 53–57, 60–68.

163. Krautheimer, *Three Christian Capitals*, 77–81. For Ambrose's possible motivations see McLynn, *Ambrose*, 226–35.

164. See chapter 8.

165. For the course of events see J.-R. Palanque, "Sur l'usurpation de Maxime," *REA* 31 (1929): 33–36; and Palanque, "L'empereur Maxime," in *Les empereurs romains d'Espagne* (Paris, 1965): 255–67, with Matthews, *Western Aristocracies*, 165, 173–77, and F. Paschoud, *Cinq études sur Zosime* (Paris, 1979), 2.2:412–15. On Ambrose's possible motives, again see McLynn, *Ambrose*, 160–63.

certainty over Maximus's intentions would have caused immediate alarm among the landowning aristocracy. Ausonius, although out of office since late 379, was at Trier in the first months of Maximus's regime, while his son Hesperius was en route to Bordeaux and then Italy. Both were apparently seeking to use their influence to ease relations between the new Gallic court and that of Valentinian at Milan.[166] Within this context it is reasonable to place the cryptic remark that follows immediately on Paulinus's reference to his governorship in the autobiographical vignette of 407. "Consequently relieved of the sixfold fasces of authority," he then wrote, "I laid down the axe stained by no slaughter; for with you [Felix] summoning me back to the region of my native soil, I was restored to an anxious mother."[167]

Only the final phrase, "sollicitae matri," perhaps to be understood metaphorically as well as literally, alludes to a troubled situation, but in conjunction with the evidence in favor of dating Paulinus's governorship to 381 (and suggesting his absence from Nola between that date and 395) and the likelihood of a stay in Milan thereafter, it seems justifiable to date the end of this period of Paulinus's life to 383, the year of Maximus's revolt.

As suffect consul and provincial governor Paulinus had surely experienced the sharp anxieties as well as the exhilarating sense of power that came with high office at the ancient capital of the empire. Equally he must have known both the dangers and the rewards of circulation within the social networks of the city's leading pagan and Christian families. These were years when Rome's elite was especially cognizant of the tensions introduced by the absence of the imperial court from Italy and the growing role of Christianity in public and political life. Paulinus apparently negotiated many of these difficulties.

More than a decade was to pass, to the best of our knowledge, before Paulinus set foot on Italian soil again. It remains an open question whether in 383 Paulinus desired or could have anticipated such a long absence from the centers of political and ecclesiastical power in Italy. His years in Gaul and Spain before his return to Nola are still shadowy ones, but they are highlighted by figures and events—Martin of Tours, Victricius of Rouen, baptism, and secular renunciation—that proceed more naturally from certain influences in Paulinus's life in the 370s and early 380s than others. Paulinus's governorship did not lead to higher office; and the ways of accommodation observed in Ausonius, and even Symmachus, yielded

---

166. See Aus. *Pater ad filium* with Bowersock, "Symmachus and Ausonius," 8–12.
167. *Carm.* 21.395–98:

Ergo ubi bis terno dicionis fasce levatus
deposui nulla maculatam caede securim,
te revocante soli quondam genitalis ad oram
sollicitae matri sum redditus.

finally to a less inclusive social outlook. By the early 390s the examples of Dama-
sus and Ambrose, filtered through a decade of personal trials and formative en-
counters, seem to emerge as powerful paradigms in Paulinus's thought. The mid-
390s would find Paulinus himself composing a *Contra paganos*. For many in Gaul
and Italy, the late 380s and early 390s forced critical choices; consensus was
threatened by two usurping regimes, by ever more repressive religious legislation,
and by escalating debate over the proper form of the Christian life.

CHAPTER 3

—•—

From *Otium Ruris* to *Contemptus Mundi*

About the time that Paulinus was leaving Italy for Gaul, others who were to play important roles in his story were arriving. The summer of 382 saw Jerome reach Rome in the company of both Paulinus of Antioch and Epiphanius of Salamis (in Cyprus), the former a frustrated claimant to his city's episcopal office, the latter a zealous upholder of the faith whose passions would help inflame the Origenist controversy in the mid-390s. Over the course of a decade in the East, Jerome had become adept in Greek as well as acquainted with Hebrew, and he had tested ascetic desires for several years in the desert of Chalcis beyond Antioch. Now Jerome's linguistic and exegetical capabilities, as well as his ascetic credentials, earned him the respect and support not only of Damasus but also of two wealthy aristocratic widows, Marcella and Paula. Jerome would serve Damasus until the bishop's death on 11 December 384; Marcella and, especially, Paula, who would accompany him to Bethlehem in 385, would be his friends and intimates into old age.[1] A rather differently employed facility with language brought Augustine to Rome from Carthage in 383 and the next year secured his promotion to Milan as imperial rhetor. In those days Augustine was still intent on making his way in the world.[2] Paulinus met neither Jerome nor Augustine in Italy: although Jerome's family may have been reasonably wealthy by the standards of Dalmatian Stridon,[3] the *vir clarissimus* Paulinus enjoyed considerably superior rank and status. Ironically, when Paulinus eventually did establish his epistolary *amicitia* with these two men in the mid-390s, they were able to claim the authority underwritten by longer and deeper experience with the Christian life.

When he returned to Gaul, Paulinus left behind an Italy now rife with religious and political tensions. Christians who resented the sharp elevation of ascetic ideals

---

1. J. N. D. Kelly, *Jerome: His Life, Writings, and Controversies* (London, 1975), esp. 80–103.

2. P. Brown, *Augustine of Hippo: A Biography* (Berkeley, 1967), 68–72.

3. Kelly, *Jerome*, 6–7.

at Rome under Damasus first found a voice in 383 with the theologian Helvidius[4] and then in late 384 a sympathetic ear with Damasus's successor Siricius. Pagans at Rome were also stirring as the vulnerability of the young Valentinian afforded reactionary opportunities. Also in 384, during the urban prefecture of Symmachus (who as prefect had seen to Augustine's Milanese appointment), a faction of the Roman Senate clashed with Valentinian II and Ambrose over the restoration of the Altar of Victory to the Senate House;[5] and it was most likely the death of the fervent pagan, praetorian prefect, and consul designate Vettius Agorius Praetextatus that provoked the scurrilous *Carmen contra paganos* in the late autumn of that year.[6] Incriminating words were flying not only among Christians but between Christians and pagans as well.

By then, however, Paulinus was far removed form the immediate scene of these conflicts, although he was encountering the concerns of another imperial court. At Trier, Magnus Maximus was settling into his role as emperor in Gaul but continuing both to pursue diplomatic relations with Theodosius at Constantinople and to pressure the Milanese court.[7] In 385 or 386 Ambrose undertook a second embassy to Maximus, hoping (in vain) to negotiate the return of Gratian's body.[8] But if the bishop of Milan returned to Italy humbled and incensed, he had nevertheless learned firsthand that Maximus intended to present himself as the champion of Christian orthodoxy in that region of the empire to which Paulinus had recently returned. The new emperor had already acted against Priscillian and certain of his followers, calling the council that had met at Delphinus's Bordeaux and then staging the trial at Trier that resulted in the execution of the alleged heretic and several followers.[9] Ambrose could attest that the ferment had not yet died down;[10] and soon letters from Maximus to both Valentinian and Pope Siricius pressed this point in Italy.[11]

---

4. See Jerome's rebuttal in his *Contra Helvidium* with further at Kelly, *Jerome*, 104–15 on the effect of these events on Jerome.

5. A much-celebrated incident, on which see Matthews, *Western Aristocracies*, 203–11 and chapter 5, this volume.

6. Text now D. R. Shackleton-Bailey, *Anthologia Latina* 1.1 (Leipzig, 1982). For the identification see L. Cracco Ruggini, "Il paganesimo romano tra religione e politica (384–394 d.C.): Per una reinterpretazione del Carmen contra paganos," *Mem. dell' Accademia Nazionale dei Lincei*, Classe di scienze morali, storiche e filologiche, ser. 8, vol. 23 (Rome, 1979).

7. Zos. 4.37 on overtures to Theodosius. Matthews, *Western Aristocracies*, 176–82; on the dating of these events and review of the evidence, see H. Chadwick, *Priscillian of Avila* (Oxford, 1976), 132–38, favoring 386 as the year of Ambrose's second mission.

8. Amb. *ep.* 24.9 (*PL* 16) / 30 (*CSEL* 82). The exact date is uncertain, depending in part on the date of the trial of the Priscillianists at Trier. On the context of this second embassy see McLynn, *Ambrose*, 217.

9. Sulp. Sev. *Chron.* 2.49–51.

10. Amb. *ep.* 24.12: the exile of Hyginus of Corduba, a former accuser of Priscillian. See H. Chadwick, *Priscillian*, 145.

11. *Coll. Avell.* 39–40 (*CSEL* 35.88–91)

The effect on Paulinus of these contentious events is uncertain. The political tensions and ecclesiastical intrigues of these years surely affected in some measure the course of his actions and the direction of his life in Aquitaine during the mid-380s, but, with one possible exception, to be considered at the end of this section, they left few discernible traces in his extant writings. Indeed, Paulinus's three surviving works from this period, as well as several letters of Ausonius, who abandoned politics with the death of Gratian, rather display Paulinus enjoying the tranquil life of aristocratic leisure on his Aquitanian and Spanish estates; no hint of distress colors these earliest writings.[12] Nevertheless, three poems are meager evidence for the span of six years or so (ca. 383–89) when Paulinus was resident at Bordeaux and Aquitaine. Furthermore, several contrasting images from later recollections belie the tranquillity implicit in these poems. These years saw not only Paulinus's unsurprising marriage at the same age when his coeval, Augustine, had also contracted an (eventually unfulfilled) marital alliance,[13] but also his association with the flamboyant Martin of Tours and his baptism by Delphinus of Bordeaux.[14] Additionally, remarkable events on the immediate horizon—Paulinus's permanent abandonment of Aquitaine for Spain about 389 and then his radical renunciation of his property and secular lifestyle—seem to point to sources of personal turmoil only known to us primarily through the two poignant verse letters that Paulinus sent to the aged Ausonius from Spain (*carm.* 10 and 11), probably in 393 and 394. This period of Paulinus's life, then, between his return to Aquitaine from Italy about 383 and his departure from Spain for Nola in the late spring of 395, is unevenly documented and even spiced with intrigue and bloodshed; yet it is pivotal in his biography, for in this fourth decade of his life Paulinus of Bordeaux experienced the conversion from *vir consularis* to *monachus* that made it possible for some to fashion him as a verbal icon.

AQUITAINE: AUSONIUS AND MARTIN

In returning to Aquitaine, Paulinus reentered a Gallo-Roman world where *potentiores* on their estates were intimately connected by networks of social, literary, and economic exchange; where life still alternated between bustling cityscape and rural villa; and where the *negotia* of urban affairs were recompensed by the sweet freedoms of an *otium ruris* that permitted a man like Ausonius to arrange his own

12. *Carm.* 1–3.
13. *Conf.* 6.13.23.
14. The parallel with Augustine's experience is again notable, for in these years in Milan Augustine too fell under the influence of ascetic teachers and was baptized.

time, to do just what he wanted, or to do nothing at all.[15] A hint of Paulinus's own manner of life in these surroundings is offered by his three contemporary poetic compositions, two preserved in a single manuscript and a fragment of a third enshrined as a quotation in a poem of Ausonius most likely dating from the same period.[16] This poem of Ausonius—and three other pieces probably sent by him to Paulinus in the mid-380s—[17]reinforce the impression of ease created by Paulinus's own *carmina* and depict Paulinus's immersion in the aristocratic protocols of late antique Aquitaine.[18]

In these poems Paulinus appears at ease in a world of privilege. In later years, he would offer gifts of simple Campanian bread or the relics of saints to his correspondents and friends, but in Aquitaine during the 380s more traditional delicacies traveled the paths of *amicitia*. To a certain Gestidius, in return for a gift of exceptional fish, Paulinus sent fig-peckers (*ficedulae*) and shellfish (*testae*) accompanied by poems that cloyingly affirmed the author's literary sensibilities as well as his gastronomic preferences.[19] Similarly, on two different occasions, Ausonius received the proof of Paulinus's "noble soul" (*liberalis animus*) embodied in presents of oil and Barcelona fish sauce (*muria*).[20] Gifts of food represented the proprietary

---

15. Ausonius *ep.* 4 Green (EW *ep.* 6), esp. 31–34:

> dulcia secreti repetantur ut otia ruris,
>   nugis amoena seriis,
> tempora disponas ubi tu tua iusque tuum sit
>   ut nil agas vel quod voles.

On the Horatian echoes see Green, *Ausonius*, 611–12; Fontaine, "Valeurs," 576. On *otium ruris* generally see Fontaine, "Valeurs."

16. *Carm.* 1–2: Voss.Lat.F. 111 (V) of the early ninth century see Hartel V–VIII; Green, *Ausonius*, xli. Paulinus's *carm.* 3 quoted by Ausonius in *ep.* 17 Green (EW *ep.* 23) is preserved in the Z group of Ausonius's mss. Both Green, xlii–xlix, and Herzog and Schmidt, *Nouvelle histoire de la littérature latine*, 310–13, argue anew for a single archetype behind V and Z.

17. Aus. *ep.* 17 Green (EW *ep.* 23) and *epp.* 18, 19, and 20 Green (EW *epp.* 24, 25, and 26) are fairly securely dated by content to before 389, while *ep.* 18 Green (EW *ep.* 24) clearly postdates Paulinus's suffect consulship. On the dating see Fabre, *Essai*, 101 n. 1. For discussion see, for example, Green, "The Correspondence of Ausonius," 197–98, 207–8; and C. Witke, *Numen Litterarum: The Old and the New in Latin Poetry from Constantine to Gregory the Great* (Leiden and Köln, 1971), 7–18, though the latter is not always trustworthy on historical or biographical matters.

18. Topographical references place Paulinus and Ausonius in Aquitaine. Ausonius mentions Hebromagus as the residence of Paulinus at *epp.* 19b.14–15, 20b.35, 23.46 Green (EW *epp.* 25, 26, 27) and at 19b. 24 refers to Paulinus as nearby (*vicinus*), while situating himself at his villa of Lucaniacus. Both must have been relatively near Bordeaux. On the site of Lucaniacus see Étienne, *Bordeaux antique*, 354–57.

19. *Carm.* 1 and 2; on the Ovidian echo in *carm.* 1 see L. Carrese, "I carmi profani di Paolino di Nola," *Annali della facoltà di lettere e folosofia dell'Università di Napoli* 28, n.s. 16 (1985–86): 7–9.

20. Aus. *ep.* 19a.13–14 Green (EW *ep.* 25): "alia huiusmodi documenta liberalis animi." On Spanish oil, the fish sauce of Barcelona, and Ausonius's culinary interests see R. Étienne, "Ausone et l'Es-

rights and social dominance of the landed elite. Paulinus's gift of fig-peckers, he remarked, was the evening prize of his "little slaves" (*pueruli*), while some thrushes that Ausonius would send to his son Hesperius were, the poet noted, "eager to be caught."[21]

But the "storehouse of poetry"[22] offered even more refined materials for cementing social and intellectual bonds among men who "lived and breathed naturally" the literary culture of late-fourth-century Aquitaine.[23] Paulinus's culinary gifts to Gestidius only provided the pretext (*causa*) for poetic banter.[24] To mark the New Year, Paulinus presented Ausonius with a verse epitome of Suetonius's lost *De regibus*,[25] and his offering of Barcelona fish sauce arrived with a learned letter and a poem that a generous Ausonius praised for its "delightfulness" (*iucunditas*).[26] Ausonius, of course, knew how to reciprocate in kind. To Paulinus's versified *De regibus* he responded with his own hexameters;[27] another epistle provided Paulinus with an elegiac New Year's greeting.[28] And Paulinus's former mentor and patron playfully commanded a series of compensatory iambics to demand from Paulinus yet another reply.[29] Reciprocation was fundamental to such a friendship, but poetic exchange was dynamic, not static. Correspondents and the recipients of poems were invited to critique and revise the poems they received and thus to participate in the creation of a living, collaborative text. As Symmachus and his father once coupled an exchange of verses on the legendary history of Campanian Bauli and eulogistic epigrams modeled on the *Hebdomades* of Varro with mutual requests for indulgence and assistance,[30] so Paulinus would implore Ausonius to add the final polish to his poetry.[31] Literary virtuosi were readily appreciative of *concinnitas*, *modulatio*, and *dulcitas* in the work of another, but critique was intended, Ausonius remarked, "to draw out" the literary partner as much as to provide the reader with the self-satisfaction of the critic.[32] In Paulinus's Aquitaine, no less than in

---

pagne," *Mélanges d'archéologie, d'épigraphie et d'histoire offerts à Jérôme Carcopino* (Vendôme 1966), 322–25.

21. *Carm.* 1: "quas pueruli vespere inferunt ficedulas misi." Aus. *ep.* 1.8 Green (EW *ep.* 18): "capi volentes."

22. Aus. *ep.* 19b.46 Green (EW *ep.* 25): "de largitate musici promptarii."

23. Witke, *Numen Litterarum*, 14.

24. *Carm.* 1: "ut et causa mihi esset apud unanimitatem tuam aliquid conloquendi et aliquod sermoni huic obsequium viderer adiungere."

25. *Carm.* 3; Aus. *ep.* 17.9–10 Green (EW *ep.* 23), with Green, *Ausonius*, 637–38.

26. Aus. *ep.* 19a.15 Green (EW *ep.* 25).

27. Aus. *ep.* 17.1–10 Green (EW *ep.* 23).

28. Aus. *ep.* 18 Green (EW *ep.* 24).

29. Aus. *ep.* 19b.18 Green (EW *ep.* 25): "salvere iussum mox reposce mutuum."

30. Sym. *epp.* 1.1–2. For example, 1.2.2: "Sed quae prima conpegi, interim pauca misi, obtestatus te per deos, ut si quid in his displicebit, emendes."

31. Aus. *ep.* 19a.17–20 Green (EW *ep.* 25).

32. Aus. *ep.* 17.27–28 Green (EW *ep.* 23) : "haec tu quam perite et concinne, quam modulate et dulciter . . . enuntiasti," and 44–46: "nam si mihi otium fuerit oblectabile negotium erit ad te prolixius delirare, te ut eliciam, mihi ut satisfaciam."

Symmachus's Italy, the exchanges of epistolary (and poetic) courtesies were the "obligations by which *amicitia* is justly joined."[33]

But successful estate management also demanded vigilance, as the persistent composition of agricultural handbooks from Cato the Elder through Varro and Columella to the fifth-century treatise of Palladius attests.[34] At times, the more immediate problems of estate management might intrude on the tranquillity of villa life, but even these moments offered the true "man of letters" (*homo litteratus*) an opportunity for literary display.[35] Requesting help from Paulinus for the transport of direly needed grain supplies from Paulinus's estate at Hebromagus to his own at Lucaniacus, Ausonius sent Paulinus a letter "adorned and sealed with iambs." Therein Ausonius's parody of the disreputable Philo, once his *vilicus* and now a merchant of questionable ethics, humorously recalled Paulinus to Cicero, Plautus, Horace, and Ovid, and tested his wit, his Greek, and his memory of Republican history. Yet Ausonius's allusive jesting does not mask the seriousness of the situation. Maintaining sufficient food supplies, overseeing the economy of their lands and villas, offsetting local shortages through trade and purchase, and ensuring the trustworthiness and competence of bailiffs and other dependents required skills seldom obvious from the surviving correspondence. Unfortunately the self-conscious surfaces of the letters and poems exchanged by Paulinus and Ausonius in the 380s, although reflecting the ways in which Paulinus and his Aquitanian peers desired to represent themselves, tell us precious little about the direct role they played in the management of their property. Nevertheless, Paulinus's later poetry, revealing a notable sympathy for agricultural work and practices,[36] suggests he had once been attentive to the lives and rhythms of those Aquitanian laborers who worked the land and tended the beasts of his estates.

For Paulinus, however, neither the pleasant, if incessant, demands of *amicitia* and estate management nor the alleged tranquillity of the countryside seem to have inhibited dissatisfaction with the world. For evidence of his spiritual turmoil we must turn to letters and poems written years later. In the letter to Sulpicius Severus already discussed in chapter 1, written at Nola in 396 but apparently referring to his years in Aquitaine and Spain, Paulinus reflected on the relationship between *otium ruris* and monastic conversion.[37] As he then represented it, withdrawal to his country estates had been a necessary step toward renunciation of the world. "At last," he

33. Sym. *ep.* 7.129, cited at J. Matthews, "The Letters of Symmachus," in *Latin Literature of the Fourth Century*, ed. J. W. Binns (London, 1974), 81–82. See also, Matthews, *Western Aristocracies*, 3–9. This aspect is not adequately appreciated by Carrese, "I carme profani," esp. 14.

34. Palladius, *Opus Agriculturae*, ed. R. Rodgers (Leipzig, 1975). On the date, see J. Svennung, "Palladios 7," *RE* 18.3 (1949): 209–11 (early fifth century) and R. Martin, *Traité d'agriculture* (Paris, 1976), xvi (late fifth century).

35. Ausonius's self-designation at *ep.* 20a.10 Green (EW *ep.* 26).

36. Especially, *carm.* 18 and 20, on which see chapter 7.

37. P. Langlois, "Les poèmes chrétiens et le christianisme d'Ausone," *Revue de philologie* 43 (1969): 39–58. Fontaine, "Valeurs," 581: "La vie de retraite aux champs est donc une méthode spirituelle, susceptible de mener à l'ascétisme monastique."

told Severus, "as I seemed to take rest from unjust charges (*calumnia*) and wanderings, and I was not occupied with public affairs and was distant from the noise of the forum (*fori strepitus*), amid the welcome tranquillity of my household retreats, I enjoyed country leisure (*ruris otium*) and care for the church (*ecclesiae cultus*), so that little by little, as my mind was drawn up from the disturbances of this world and adapted to heavenly precepts, it was easier to achieve contempt for the world (*contemptus mundi*) and the comradeship of Christ, as I was already struggling on the path bordering on this way of life (*propositum*)."[38] The conviction of these words, and thus perhaps their essential truthfulness, echoes in the advice he would later give to other wealthy would-be ascetics: the rural estate provided a comfortable and secure setting for pursuit of the monastic life and the companionship of Christ.[39]

Though not mentioned in this letter to Severus, Paulinus's increasing dissatisfaction with his earlier public life and his rising "contempt for the world" may have been hastened by contact with others who were zealously committed to emerging ascetic ideals. At some point after his return from Italy, Paulinus crossed the Pyrenees to marry the Spanish-born Therasia and bring her back to Aquitaine.[40] We may assume that the marriage was calculated to benefit both families. The specific role of Therasia in Paulinus's drift toward asceticism, however, eludes us. One source explicitly announces that Therasia later shared Paulinus's ascetic ideals and, like him, liquidated her personal property; even earlier, as we will see in more detail later, a disgruntled Ausonius ascribed Paulinus's "waywardness" to a Therasia he dubbed Paulinus's "Tanaquil."[41] But the implications of these claims and charges are more ambiguous than once assumed, for in such insinuating ways men regularly invoked womanly influence to justify and condemn each other.[42] In light of recent scholarship, it is now more difficult to assess either Therasia's character or the weight and direction of her influence on Paulinus's intellectual or spiritual development in the 380s,[43] for even the more general

38. *Ep.* 5.4: "postea denique ut a caluminiis et peregrinationibus requiem capere visus sum, nec rebus publicis occupatus et a fori strepitu remotus ruris otium et ecclesiae cultum placita in secretis domesticis tranquillitate celebravi, ut paulatim subducto a saecularibus turbis animo praeceptisque caelestibus accommodato proclivius ad contemptum mundi comitatumque Christi iam quasi de finitima huic proposito via dimacaverim."
39. See, for example, *ep.* 38 to Aper.
40. *Carm.* 21.398–401:

> inde propinquos
> trans iuga Pyrenes adii peregrinus Hiberos.
> illic me thalamis humana lege iugari
> passus es [Felix].

41. Amb. *ep.* 58.2 (*PL* 16) / 6.27.2 (*CSEL* 82); Aus. *ep.* 22.30–31 Green (EW *ep.* 28). See next section.
42. K. Cooper, "Insinuations of Womanly Influence: An Aspect of the Christianization of the Roman Aristocracy," *JRS* 82 (1992): 150–64; Cooper, *The Virgin and the Bride: Idealized Womanhood in Late Antiquity* (Cambridge, Mass., 1996).
43. Others have been more confident: Fabre, *Paulin de Nole*, 28; Lienhard, *Paulinus of Nola*, 27.

theories about the role of women as "conductors of Christianity" within aristocratic households have begun to evaporate.[44] For the influence of Martin of Tours and Victricius of Rouen, although here too the evidence is also later than the 380s, more solid cases can be built.

Paulinus met Victricius at Vienne in the company of Martin. The former had become bishop of Rouen, the metropolitan diocese of Lugdunensis Secunda, by 386, and he held that office when Paulinus met him; Martin had been bishop of Tours since 370 or 371.[45] Both Victricius and Martin had served in the Roman army, and the latter at least perceived his Christian *militia* as a continuation of his military service, openly appropriating idioms of secular and civil authority that might have readily appealed to a former suffect consul and provincial governor like Paulinus.[46] In addition, by the mid-380s both Martin and Victricius commanded reputations for unusual holiness and audacity. Martin's open challenge of Maximus's right to judge Priscillian and his followers had embroiled him in factions at Trier,[47] while Victricius's defiant rejection of his military oath had provoked the beating, torture, and imprisonment that later enabled Paulinus to praise him as a "living martyr."[48] The event that brought Victricius, Martin, and Paulinus together at Vienne may have been the arrival there of relics of Gervasius and Protasius, gifts of Ambrose intended for the churches of Rouen and Tours as well as for the community of Vienne.[49] Such an occasion would have been especially significant for Victricius, whose single surviving work, the *De laude sanctorum*, extols the cult of relics. For Paulinus too it should have been a momentous event: he knew Ambrose well, and at Rome, Nola, and Milan he had learned to appreciate the power inherent in the corpses of the saints, eventually coming to view them as constellations of lights in earthly darkness, echoing the stars of the nighttime sky.[50]

---

44. M. Salzman, "Aristocratic Women: Conductors of Christianity in the Fourth Century," *Helios* 10 (1989): 207–20; Salzman, "How the West Was Won: the Christianization of the Roman Aristocracy in the West in the Years after Constantine," *Collection Latomus 217: Studies in Latin Literature and Roman History VI* (1992): 451–79.

45. Paulinus's *epp.* 18 of 397 / 98 and 37 of 403 / 4 are the fullest sources for Victricius's biography. On Victricius see S. Prete, "Vittricio di Rouen," *Bibliotheca Sanctorum* (1969), 12.1310–15; R. Herval, *Origines chrétiennes: De la IIe Lyonnaise gallo-romaine à la Normandie ducale (IVe–XIe siècles)* (Rouen and Paris, 1966), 25–61; I. Mulders and R. Demeulenaere, *De laude sanctorum*, CCSL 64 (Brepols, 1985), 53–65; D. Hunter, "Vigilantius of Calagurris and Victricius of Rouen: Ascetics, Relics, and Clerics in Late Roman Gaul," forthcoming in *JECS*. On Martin's chronology see L. Pietri, "La succession des premiers évêques tourangeaux: Essai sur la chronologie de Grégoire de Tours," *Mélanges de l'école française de Rome, Moyen Age–temps modernes* 94 (1982): 586–605. See further, on Martin, R. Van Dam, *Leadership and Community in Late Antique Gaul* (Berkeley, 1985), 119–40; Stancliffe, *St. Martin and His Hagiographer*.

46. Van Dam, *Leadership and Community*, 124–28.

47. Sev. *Chron.* 2.49–50; *Dial.* 3.11–13.

48. Paul. *ep.* 18.7.

49. P. Courcelle, "Fragments historiques de Paulin de Nole conservés par Grégoire de Tours," *Mélanges d'histoire du moyen age dédiés à la mémoire de Louis Halphen* (Paris, 1951), 152.

50. *Carm.* 19.1–44.

Nevertheless, the sanctity of Victricius apparently failed to impress Paulinus during their initial meeting. It was only years later, in 397 or 398, inspired by a chance encounter at Rome with Victricius's deacon Paschasius, who apprised Paulinus of Victricius's missionary efforts in northwestern Gaul, that Paulinus renewed contact.[51] His assessment then of his state of mind some ten years earlier offers a valuable check on his nearly contemporary letter to Severus. Recalling Victricius to that earlier meeting, Paulinus wrote:

> I believe you will graciously remember that I once saw your sanctity at Vienne in the presence of our blessed father Martin, to whom the Lord has made you an equal though unequal in age. Although I acquired but little knowledge of you from him, nevertheless I embraced you with great love and I revered your sanctity with all the feeling I could then muster . . . but I lament the heedlessness of my misfortune because, unaware, I lost the opportunity of so great a blessing. At that time not only was I darkened by the sins that even now weigh heavily upon me, but also by the cares of this world (*curae huius saeculi*), from which now by God's kindness I am free; so I saw you only as a bishop, for that was open to all, and I did not know how to see you as what was more distinguished, a living martyr (*martyr vivus*).[52]

Such self-deprecating remarks are not at odds with the self-portrait that Paulinus had presented to Severus. In both reminiscences Paulinus stressed a former worldliness, an abiding concern for the "cares of this world" that may even speak obliquely to hopes he still harbored in the mid-380s for the continuation of the life in public affairs that had begun so auspiciously at Rome in the 370s. Nevertheless, his appearance in the company of Martin and Victricius suggests clearly that he was being pulled in the other direction.

It may also be that at Vienne the personality of Martin simply overshadowed that of Victricius. Martin was the senior prelate, and the only other literary source that brings Victricius into the presence of Martin emphasizes Victricius's deference to Martin.[53] Moreover, the later writings of Sulpicius Severus—his *Vita Martini, Epistolae,* and *Dialogi*—leave little doubt about Martin's charisma. But Paulinus, who was to revere Martin throughout his life and call to him on his deathbed,

---

51. On Victricius's activities see E. A. Thompson, "Christianity and the Northern Barbarians," in *The Conflict between Paganism and Christianity in the Fourth Century,* ed. A. Momigliano (Oxford, 1963), 56–78. On Vitricius see also chapter 8, this volume.

52. *Ep.* 18.9: "Meminisse enim credo dignaris, quia sanctitatem tuam olim Viennae apud beatum patrem nostrum Martinum viderim, cui te dominus in aetate inpari parem fecit. ex illo igitur licet brevi notitia te attigerim, tamen magna dilectione conplexus sum et quanta tunc licuit copia veneratus sum sanctitatem tuam . . . sed lugeo neglegentiam infelicitatis meae, quod occasionem tanti boni ignarus amiserim et contenebrantibus me illo tempore non solum peccatis, quibus etiam nunc premor, sed et curis huius saeculi, quibus nunc propitio deo liber sum, sacerdotem te tantum, quod in medio erat, viderim et, quod inerat insignius, martyrem vivum videre nescierim."

53. Sev. *Dial.* 3.2, a meeting at Chartres.

may have had even more personal reasons for falling under the spell of the icono-
clastic and thaumaturgical bishop of Tours, perhaps to the occasional exclusion of
others around him: during these years Martin may have healed Paulinus of an eye
malady.[54] The story happily found a place in the *Vita* of Martin that Severus had
written only a year or two before Paulinus composed his first letter to Victricius.
"The eye of Paulinus," Severus noted in an account of Martin's miracles, "a man
who would afterwards be a great example, had begun to pain him severely, and a
rather dense cloud (*crassior nubes*) drawn over it had already covered its pupil, when
Martin touched it with a brush (*penicillum*) and restored to it its previous health,
and all the pain was relieved."[55] Perhaps Severus expected his educated readers to
perceive the allegorical possibilities of his rendering of Martin's healing actions
here.[56] Indeed, Paulinus himself would later represent spiritual blindness with im-
ages of vision dimmed by clouds (*nebulae*) of secular attachment drawn across the
inner eye; and, invoking scriptural metaphors, he would portray religious enlight-
enment as the concession of sight to the blind.[57] But allegory does not obviate a lit-
eral reading of this passage of the *Vita Martini*. Martin apparently possessed rudi-
mentary medical knowledge.[58] Paulinus, who frequently alluded to a physical
frailty seemingly belied by his longevity, later isolated miracles of healing as
among the most convincing manifestations of the power of God working through
the figures of his saints; and one of Paulinus's most highly elaborated miracle sto-
ries tells of the restoration of sight to the blinded eye of Theridius, a member of
Paulinus's community at Nola.[59] If Martin indeed saved Paulinus's sight, then the
act of healing could well have created powerful emotional and social bonds be-
tween patient and healer.[60] In any case, in Martin's presence at Vienne or else-
where in these years Paulinus must surely have noted the intimate connection be-
tween Martin's asceticism and his claims to spiritual purity and secular power.[61]

These texts contemporary with or recalling Paulinus's life in Aquitaine during
the 380s leave us with a set of varied, even contrasting, but not irreconcilable im-

---

54. Though there is no compelling reason to place this episode in the context of the Vienne meet-
ing. See Fabre, *Paulin de Nole*, 30 n. 2.

55. *Vita Martini* 19.3 (Fontaine, *SC* 133): "Paulinus magni vir postmodum futurus exempli, cum ocu-
lum graviter dolere coepisset et iam pupillam eius crassior nubes superducta texisset, oculum ei Mart-
inus penicillo contigit pristinamque ei sanitatem, sublato omni dolore, restituit."

56. See Fontaine, *Vie de Saint Martin*, 2:885–88; N. Chadwick, *Poetry and Letters*, 69.

57. *Carm.* 19.39–40: "Nebulae, quibus interiorem / obducent aciem mundi fallentis amores." *Ep.*
30.3–5. Paulinus's extant writings contain no reference to his healing at the hands of Martin.

58. A. Rousselle, "From Sanctuary to Miracle Worker: Healing in Fourth Century Gaul," trans.
E. Forster, in *Ritual, Religion, and the Sacred*, ed. R. Forster and O. Ranum (Baltimore, 1982), 95–127, esp.
110–11; Rousselle, *Croire et guérir: La foi en Gaule dans l'antiquité tardive* (Paris, 1990), 109–22.

59. *Carm.* 23 (*nat.* 7 of 401).

60. Rousselle, "From Sanctuary," 124.

61. For positive assessments of Martin's influence on Paulinus see Fontaine, *Vie de Saint Martin*,
2:885; Lienhard, *Paulinus of Nola*, 94–97. More cautious is Fabre, *Paulin de Nole*.

ages. The life of aristocratic country leisure and literary delights pursued with the respectable "insider" Ausonius is balanced by the image of Paulinus standing in the presence of that sometimes outrageous "outsider," Martin of Tours. If Ausonius practiced a comfortable Christianity, Martin seemed unconventional, even subversive, to many. If we could date texts and episodes with any certainty, we might construct a line of linear development for Paulinus's life and thought in these years, one that leads neatly from one mentor in the old ways of the world, Ausonius, to another, Martin, whose example severed the roots of accommodation with so many of those old ways of thinking. But we cannot, and in any case to do so would surely be reductive. We may, however, detect in the images of these years, as in Italy in the late 370s and early 380s, another pattern of forces pulling Paulinus both toward and away from traditional constructions of aristocratic identity. The estates that had underwritten his political ambitions now offered a sanctuary from the turmoil of political life and, perhaps, the means to realize that particular "contempt for the world" that he would have discerned already in the choices of Ambrose, Martin, and Victricius. At the same time, however, Martin, a man of action, offered Paulinus another, distinctive model of engagement and leadership. If Damasus's poetry expressed Christian and ascetic ideals by adapting traditional meters and language, if Ambrose's churches adopted the architecture of imperial power, then Martin, for all his unorthodoxy, articulated his religious leadership in accessible idioms of military, civic, and social authority.[62] Moreover, although we do not know the extent of Paulinus's familiarity with Marmoutier, Martin's *monasterium* two miles outside the city,[63] its establishment nevertheless demonstrated how religious authority might be localized in a rural or suburban ascetic community yet also be forcefully projected both toward the urban center and into the surrounding countryside.[64] Martin seemed to reconcile those contrary choices of worldly renunciation and ceaseless activity among men, of clerical responsibility and monastic detachment; as Severus would later assert, "full of authority and grace, he discharged the duties of a bishop without, however, deserting the profession (*propositum*) and virtue of a monk."[65] It was a model that Paulinus surely found more appealing than the uncompromising alternative later offered him by Jerome.

Finally, the forces contributing to Paulinus's withdrawal from public life in the later 380s may have been strengthened by a darker turn of events, for his later vague laments about the turmoil and worldly distractions he faced in Aquitaine

---

62. Van Dam, *Leadership and Community*, 132–34.

63. *Vita Martini* 10.3.

64. The latter is underestimated, I believe, by A. Rousselle, "Deux exemples d'evangelisation en Gaule à la fin du IVe siècle: Paulin de Nole et Sulpice Sévère," *Béziers et le biterrois* (Montpellier, 1971), 91–98.

65. *Vita Martini:* 10.2: "plenus auctoritatis et gratiae, inplebat episcopi dignitatem, ut non tamen propositum monachi virtutemque desereret."

and Spain were provoked in part by memories of personal catastrophe. After they relocated to Spain about 389, he and Therasia suffered the death of a newborn baby; and, perhaps while Paulinus was still resident in Aquitaine, he lost a brother to a violent death whose now mysterious circumstances also threw his own property and life into jeopardy. The autobiographical account of the *natalicium* of 407 provides our only explicit evidence for the affair. In that poem, between mention of his marriage to Therasia and recall of his act of renunciation, Paulinus reminded his Nolan audience how Felix had then stood by him in a time of unusual peril:

> When I was troubled by the blood of a slaughtered brother and my brother's case (*causa*) was producing danger for me as his kin, a *sector* [purchaser at a public sale of goods] had already laid hands upon my property, when you, father [Felix], removed my throat from the sword, my patrimony from the treasury (*fiscus*), and preserved me and my possessions for Christ the Lord.[66]

Imaginative modern reconstructions of this episode and diligent searches of Paulinus's works for further references or allusions to it have only deepened its mysteries. Attempts to blame this near-disaster on Paulinus's (unlikely) involvement with Priscillianism[67] or to place it in the context of the usurpation of Arbogast and Eugenius or, more plausibly, during the regime of Maximus remain highly speculative at best.[68]

Most frequently the episode recounted in the poem of 407 has been linked to the contents of two earlier letters, *epp.* 35 and 36, for these letters present Paulinus's replies to condolences on the death of a brother that had come to him from Delphinus and Amandus of Bordeaux.[69] The link appears natural. And since these two letters were clearly written after Paulinus's baptism,[70] probably from Spain, but before his formal renunciation of his property in 394, the fraternal death they record can reasonably be placed between 390 and 394.[71] So if firmly linked to

---

66. *Carm.* 21. 416–20:

> cumque laborarem germani sanguine caesi
> et consanguineum pareret fraterna periculum
> causa mihi censumque meum iam sector adisset,
> tu mea colla, pater, gladio patrimonia fisco
> eximis et Christo domino mea meque reservas.

67. So E.-C. Babut, "Paulin de Nole et Priscillien," *Revue d'histoire et de littérature religieuses* 1 (1910): 97–130, 252–75, esp. 102–4. On Paulinus and Priscillianism see next section.

68. For a political context during the regime of Maximus see U. Moricca, "La morte violenta di un fratello di Paolino di Nola," *Didaskalion* n.s. 4 (1926): 85–90; note the caution of Fabre, *Paulin de Nole*, 33–35; and Walsh, *ACW* 35.220.

69. *Epp.* 35 and 36, the earliest in Hartel's volume of *epistulae*. See, for example, Fabre, *Paulin de Nole*, 33–35; Lienhard, *Paulinus of Nola*, 27–28.

70. *Ep.* 35 (to Delphinus): "ne pietatem tuam, quae nobis filiis gloriabatur."

71. Fabre, *Essai*, 63–65.

these letters the dangerous episode recorded in the thirteenth *natalicium* would also date to Paulinus's years in Spain. But the connection between the *natalicium*'s episode and the consolations of the early 390s is very tenuous. In 1926 Umberto Moricca, who argued that it occurred during the days of Maximus, was justly cautious on this point. Paulinus apparently had more than one brother, and his words to Delphinus and Amandus in *epp.* 35 and 36 hardly fit the traumatic situation described in the *natalicium* of 407.[72] Nothing in Paulinus's two letters suggests that the death that elicited the sympathies of Delphinus and Amandus was unnatural or that its circumstances threatened Paulinus's own life and property, although conceivably Paulinus might have been more circumspect in the immediate aftermath than he was at Nola in 407. Even the fears Paulinus expressed to Amandus and Delphinus about his own spiritual health, and his pleas for their intercession for both his brother and himself, are too general to be conclusive, since such an acute concern with his final judgment colors much of his later correspondence and is prominent in the other poems and letters written in Spain.

At first sight, another text appears a better candidate for helping to unlock the mystery. In 396 Paulinus had reminded Severus of certain "unjust charges" (*calumniae*) that had increased his distaste for the world. These *calumniae* may well represent Paulinus's gloss of the machinations of a *sector* eager to acquire his property.[73] Even so, this passage of *ep.* 5, which could refer to any moment in the 380s or early 390s, resolves neither the chronological or contextual uncertainties of the episode presented in the *natalicium* of 407. In short, the dramatic account of that poem resists historical location, and its true effect on Paulinus's philosophical and spiritual development cannot be weighed. If the crisis unfolded in the latter 380s, it may well have hastened Paulinus's decision to seek baptism or to move to estates in Spain; if it is linked to the two letters sent to the Bordelais clergy and thus dated to the early 390s, it may have encouraged more immediately his formal act of secular renunciation in 394.

We can reasonably suppose that it was amid the tensions produced by the spiritual and philosophical yearning that he later acknowledged—propelled by the examples of figures like Victricius and Martin, whose ascetic commitment undercut the potential satisfactions of a merely traditional life of aristocratic *ruris otium*—and perhaps distressed by a brother's violent death that Paulinus offered himself for baptism to Delphinus at Bordeaux, probably not long before his departure for

---

72. Moricca, "La morte violenta," 88–90. The best evidence for the number of Paulinus's brothers is provided by *ep.* 11.3 of 397, in which Paulinus reinforces his claims on Severus's affection by writing: "ita pro parentibus et fratribus et amicis tu nobis factus a domino es." Aus. *ep.* 23.46 Green (EW *ep.* 27) alerts us to the fact that the estates of one brother of Paulinus bordered his own Hebromagus: "iam praedia fratris vicina ingreditur." Whether this brother was living at the time of composition (394) is unclear; the line is part of a "dream" in which Ausonius imagines Paulinus returning home to Aquitaine. See below.

73. So Moricca, "La morte violenta," 87–88.

Spain in 389.[74] Some contemporary observers would have seen in that act a clear sign of Paulinus's intention to forsake future administrative or secular appointments, for the judicial and religious duties required of office-holders involved them in activities that the Roman church may already have disapproved. Indeed, an epistle *To the Gallic Bishops* had recently declared that those who administered the "law of the world" (*ius saeculi*) could not be "free from sin," and it prohibited those who held secular office after baptism from seeking clerical positions.[75]

Whether Paulinus intended his baptism to signal definitively his withdrawal from imperial and senatorial politics, or whether the event provoked something like the sensation that Augustine reports for the anticipated moment of Marius Victorinus's initiation into the Roman church, is impossible to say, for Paulinus is notably (and curiously) reticent about the event. Although later, at Nola, Paulinus readily acknowledged the vital role of baptism in the life of the Christian and believed that only through this rite could an individual become a member of the mystical body of Christ,[76] his own baptism goes virtually unsung after 395. Most significant, the now familiar autobiographical vignette of the *natalicium* of 407, in which Paulinus might easily have credited to the guardianship of Felix his decision to accept baptism, makes no mention of it. Only in letters written from Spain to Delphinus and Amandus of Bordeaux and in his first letter to Alypius, written soon after his arrival at Nola, is Paulinus explicit. Paulinus honors Delphinus as his "father in the Lord (*in domino pater*)," as the one who "sprinkled me with the salt of his word;" and in reciting his credentials to Alypius he begins with his baptism by Delphinus at Bordeaux.[77] But in Paulinus's later writings, the importance of his decision to seek baptism is overshadowed by his act of secular renunciation. As others would, he came to date his own "conversion" to the moment of his renunciation, and his decision to turn away more radically from a private life apparently unchanged even by baptism became the turning point in his autobiography.[78] An ascetic act by which he had elevated himself above the ranks of merely baptized

74. Although 389 is only a *terminus ante quem;* Fabre, *Paulin de Nole,* 31.

75. [Siricius] *ep.* 10, *cap.* 5 *ad Gallos episcopos* (*PL* 13.1190A). For the argument attributing the decretal to the pontificate of Damasus see Pietri, *Roma christiana,* 764–72; and 769 on the point in question. A more accommodating stance is assumed by Ambrose, *ep.* 25 (*PL* 16) / 50 (*CSEL* 82) and Innocent, *ep.* 6, *cap.* 3 (*PL* 20.499–500). See McLynn, *Ambrose,* 254–55.

76. For instance, *ep.* 5.11, in which a catechumen is explicity excluded from membership in this body.

77. *Ep.* 10.1 (to Delphinus): "tu nobis a domino et in domino pater factus." *Ep.* 9.1 (to Amandus): "quod me verbi sui sale adsperserit." *Ep.* 3.4: "nam ego, etsi a Delphino Burdigalae baptizatus." See further *ep.* 2.4 (to Amandus).

78. On Paulinus's understanding of *conversio* see Lienhard, *Paulinus of Nola,* 33–51; J. M. Petersen, "The Garden of Felix: The Literary Connection between Gregory the Great and Paulinus of Nola," *Studia Monastica* 26 (1984): 215–30; and Skeb, *Christo vivere,*esp. 60–84. On Paulinus's equation of his conversion with his act of renunciation see U. Moricca, "Il *votum* di Sulpicio Severo e di S. Paolino da Nola," *Didaskalion* n.s. 3 (1925): 89–96.

Christians became the defining feature of Paulinus's life and the source of his authority at Nola. Necessarily, perhaps, the importance of his baptism at Bordeaux receded in his own self-understanding.

Our hazy view of Paulinus in the years between his return to Aquitaine and his departure thence for Spain is fortunately relieved by scattered images of his activities and personal contacts. Our knowledge of what lay on the immediate horizon, although surely dangerous to wield in retrospect, can also help us to interpret those years. For Paulinus's association with Martin, his baptism by Delphinus, and, perhaps, the trauma of his brother's violent death are points, however indeterminate, along a trajectory that leads Paulinus from senator to monk and that proceeds to Nola through Spain.

SPAIN: TANAQUIL, BELLEROPHON, AND PRISCILLIAN

It may be merely fortuitous that Paulinus's departure for Spain so nearly coincides with the end of the regime of Maximus in Gaul. The latter was overthrown by Theodosius in the late summer of 388, and it was most likely in 389 that Paulinus and Therasia left Aquitaine for their Spanish estates.[79] Any connection between the political event and the personal decision is now invisible. Moreover, whether or not Paulinus and Therasia initially intended the move to be permanent, they apparently never lived in the Bordeaux region again. During the next six years they conducted their public and private affairs in the orbits of cities such as Caesar Augusta (Saragossa), Tarraco (Tarragona), and Barcinus (Barcelona). The mass of the Pyrenees ensured a degree of separation that provoked some uncharitable speculations, and after Easter of 395, the move to Nola placed even more distance between Paulinus and his family, home, and friends.

Others were in motion during these years as well. Both Jerome and Augustine abandoned Italy in the 380s. Jerome, out of favor with Siricius and forced to defend the ill-tempered diatribe he had aimed at Helvidius, spokesman for the forces of "conventional" Christianity at Rome, set out from Rome for the East late in the summer of 385. Leaving behind friends as well as enemies, the next year he and Paula established the monastic foundations at Bethlehem where they would spend the remainder of their lives.[80] Augustine, the intellectual and social turmoil of his days in Rome and Milan having led to his own embrace of ascetic ideals, returned to North Africa in 388. By the time Paulinus and Therasia were ensconced in their Spanish *villae*, Augustine was already living as a monk with Alypius and other friends in the relative obscurity of Thagaste.[81]

79. Matthews, *Western Aristocracies*, 223–25. On the date of Paulinus's relocation see Fabre, *Essai*, 100–107, based on the information supplied in the letters exchanged by Ausonius and Paulinus.

80. Kelly, *Jerome*, 116–40.

81. Brown, *Augustine*, 132–37.

If Augustine had, in some sense, gone home and was surrounded by friends, in contrast Paulinus's oldest intimate castigated his move to Spain as the desertion of his *patria* and berated him for his withdrawal into an alleged brutish silence. In a series of at least four initially unanswered verse letters, written between 389 and 393, the octogenarian Ausonius complained bitterly about Paulinus's defection from the protocols of an epistolary and poetic exchange that had for so long nourished their *amicitia*. To draw out Paulinus, Ausonius trawled the silent depths between them with the provocative images of the legendary Etruscan queen Tanaquil, the fallen mythic hero Bellerophon, and the ghost of the executed heretic Priscillian. But these ploys and charges of Ausonius, the subjects of this section, may tell us rather more about a rhetor and poet born in the shadow of Constantine or about popular perceptions of ascetic practitioners in the early 390s than they do about the life and thought of Paulinus in these years. For those, I turn in the next chapter to Paulinus's own compositions of this period, for Paulinus finally responded to Ausonius in 393 with a verse letter of his own, and one further poignant exchange between them took place the next year.

This group of epistolary poems composed by Ausonius and Paulinus between 389 and 394 warrants close attention; these pieces have, with justice, entranced modern readers. No other late antique poetry seems so powerfully to evoke the unguarded depths of mutual respect and affection.[82] Moreover, few sources seem so tragically and paradigmatically to chart the social and personal cost of ascetic conversion in the late fourth century or to point so clearly to the course of Gallo-Roman history.[83] But these poems also provide the first significant "conversation" preserved in the modern corpus of Paulinus's works. For the first time we encounter lengthy contemporary texts that permit definitive biographical and historical reconstruction. The change is doubly welcome, for these poems were composed during the critical stage of Paulinus's conversion that immediately preceded his formal adoption of the monastic *propositum*.

After Paulinus and Therasia departed Aquitaine for Spain, communication with Ausonius was broken. As at least four letters went unanswered, Ausonius's impatience grew. Only two letters now survive from this group, but they vividly illustrate Ausonius's suspicions.[84] In the earlier of the two poems, Ausonius laments his previ-

---

82. See, for example, P. de Labriolle, *La correspondance d'Ausone et de Paulin de Nole: Un épisode de la fin du paganisme* (Paris, 1910); N. Chadwick, *Poetry and Letters:* "We feel in the beauty and dignity of these two men, so different in outlook, so incompatible in ideals, the eternal gulf which separates each generation from its predecessor and which no affection or education can bridge" (66).

83. Fabre, *Paulin de Nole*, 166–70; Frend, "The Two Worlds," 109–10; Witke, *Numen Litterarum*, 43–44; Van Dam, *Leadership and Community*, 303–9.

84. Since at least Schenkl's preface to the *MGH* edition of Ausonius the order of these two letters has been recognized as EW *ep.* 28 (*Proxima quae*) followed by EW *ep.* 29 (*Quarta tibi*). See the discussion at Fabre, *Essai*, 100–103. Green has elected to reverse the order; thus he prints Green *ep.* 21 (*Quarta tibi*) followed by Green *ep.* 22 (*Proxima quae*). Unconvinced by Green's reasoning at p. 653, I employ the traditional order here.

ous letter's failure to elicit a response.[85] He wonders if Paulinus is perhaps bound by some sacred "rule of silence" (*lex tacendi*) or if he fears betrayal by some "traitor" (*proditor*) if he should reply. In case the latter should be true, Ausonius rehearses for Paulinus a list of mythological and historical stratagems for conducting secret or confidential correspondence. In the poem's closing lines, however, Ausonius issues a far more serious challenge, recalling Paulinus to the familial and emotional obligations that still bind him and casting Therasia as the source of his social dereliction.[86] "If, Paulinus," he wrote, "you are afraid of betrayal and fear the charge of our friendship (*amicitia*), let your Tanaquil know nothing; scorn others, but do not refuse to address a father with words. I am your sustainer and first tutor, your first bestower of honors, the one who first guided you into the guild of the Muses." Both charges apparently stung deeply, for Paulinus eventually returned to them; in doing so he acknowledged Ausonius's paternal claims but brusquely denounced his comparison of Therasia to the manipulative, imperious Tanaquil, wife of the legendary Roman king Tarquinius Priscus and a woman skilled in pagan religious ritual.[87] "Nec Tanaquil mihi, sed Lucretia coniunx," Paulinus rejoined (no Tanaquil for me, but a wife like Lucretia).[88]

Ausonius's second surviving letter from this early group is longer, its frustration more acute.[89] In the first third of the poem, Ausonius surveys nature itself to prove the perversion of silence. "Nature," he remarks, "has made nothing without voice."[90] Yet, he continues, Paulinus has relentlessly refused to answer his letters, and again Ausonius posits some intrusion on their friendship. He cautions, "Many have given pleasure in a brief reply, none have pleased through silence" (*nemo silens placuit*).[91] But, as before, Ausonius closes his poem with an assault that, though also drawing on classical images, more directly targets his apprehensions. Asserting yet

---

85. *Ep.* 22 Green (EW *ep.* 28), comprising thirty-five hexameter lines. There is discussion at Witke, *Numen Litterarum*, 19–20.

86. *Ep.* 22.30–35 Green (EW *ep.* 28):

> si prodi, Pauline, times nostraeque vereris
> crimen amicitiae. Tanaquil tua nesciat istud;
> tu contemne alios nec dedignare parentem
> affari verbis. ego sum tuus altor et ille
> praeceptor primus, primus largitor honorum,
> primus in Aonidum qui te collegia duxi.

87. On Tanaquil see Livy 1.34, but, as Witke notes (*Numen Litterarum*, 20), it may have been Juv. 6.566 that Ausonius hoped to evoke.

88. *Carm.* 10.192.

89. *Ep.* 21 Green (EW *ep.* 29), consisting of seventy-four hexameter lines. Its opening line indicates that Ausonius has already written three unanswered letters: "Quarta tibi haec notos detexit epistula questus." Therefore Fabre, *Essai*, 106, saw early 393 as the most likely date for its composition, but this assumes an annual exchange that cannot be satisfactorily demonstrated.

90. *Ep.* 21.17 Green (EW *ep.* 29): "nil mutum natura dedit."

91. *Ep.* 21.44 Green (EW *ep.* 29): "nemo silens placuit, multi brevitate loquendi."

again his affection (*pietas*), Ausonius queries, in a phrase Paulinus later echoes, "Have you changed your ways (*mores*), sweetest Paulinus? Are the Vasconian woodlands and the snowy hospitality of the Pyrenees and forgetfulness of our sky the cause?"[92] In contrast with the gentle opulence of Bordeaux, Ausonius imagines Paulinus amid a desolate Spanish landscape. Paulinus, once the glory of his *patria* and a pillar of the Senate, now haunts Birbilis, or Calagurris "clinging to its crags," or "parched Ilerda that looks down upon the roaring Sicoris from its ruins scattered along jagged ridges."[93] Ausonius can envision such unforgiving terrain as the new home of Paulinus's consular *trabea* and his curule chair and as the tomb of his hometown honors.[94] But this inhospitable landscape offers Ausonius more than simply a metaphorical backdrop against which to cast Paulinus's vulgar silence. It also provides a stage on which Ausonius can summon to Tanaquil's side another incriminating figure. To the image of the shrewd and domineering Etruscan queen he now adds that of the errant and deranged Bellerophon:

> But who has encouraged your long silence? Let this impious one (*impius*) turn no sound to advantage; let no joys enliven him, no sweet songs of the poets, no shifting melody of plaint; let no wild beasts, no cattle or birds delight him, nor Echo, who hidden in the woody groves of the shepherds, consoles us, returning our words. Sad, needy, let him dwell in deserted wastes and in silence roam the vault of the Alpine ridge, as it is said once Bellerophon, out of his mind, avoiding the company and traces of men, vagrant, wandered through the trackless places.[95]

92. *Ep.* 21.50–52 Green (EW *ep.* 29):

> vertisti, Pauline, tuos, dulcissime, mores:
> Vasconei saltus et ninguida Pyrenaei
> hospitia et nostri facit hoc oblivio caeli.

93. Aus. *ep.* 21.56–59 Green (EW *ep.* 29). For commentary see further Green, *Ausonius*, 651–52; Witke, *Numen Litterarum*, 23–25. All three cities of Tarraconensis were apparently chosen because of their literary associations rather than any knowledge that Paulinus was actually resident in them.

94. Aus. *ep.* 21.60–61 Green (EW *ep.* 29): "hic trabeam, Pauline, tuam Latiamque curulem / constituis patriosque istic sepelibis honores?"

95. Aus *ep.* 21.62–72 (EW *ep.* 29):

> quis tamen iste tibi tam longa silentia suasit?
> impius ut nullos hic vocem vertat in usus;
> gaudia non illum vegetent, non dulcia vatum
> carmina, non blandae modulatio flexa querellae;
> non fera, non illum pecudes, non mulceat ales,
> non quae pastorum nemoralibus abdita lucis
> solatur nostras echo resecuta loquellas;
> tristis, egens, deserta colat tacitusque pererret
> Alpini convexa iugi, ceu dicitur olim
> mentis inops coetus hominum et vestigia vitans
> avia perlustrasse vagus loca Bellerophontes.

Ausonius's recourse to Tanaquil in his previous letter unambiguously charges Therasia as the agent of Paulinus's dereliction of duty. Here, for us at least, the inimical *impius* apparently stands as an open cipher. In any case, when Paulinus finally responded to these lines, it was primarily the sketch of Bellerophon, and its implications, that drew his eye. "I have not the troubled mind of Bellerophon," his reply announces.[96] In Bellerophon's demented wandering Paulinus detected, as Ausonius perhaps intended, not a curse to be called down on some other but an allusion to his own way of life, to the new, socially subversive *mores* to which Ausonius feared Paulinus had become (unwitting) victim.[97] Paulinus's response leaves little doubt that Ausonius's choice of legendary referents brilliantly expressed his suspicion that an ascetic malignancy was devouring their well-tried friendship and all that it represented about their world. To appreciate Paulinus's reading of Ausonius's lines, however, requires reflection on how images of Tanaquil and Bellerophon could come to gloss perceptions of asceticism and, more specifically, Priscillianism in the early 390s.

Some twenty-five years later the pagan Rutilius Namatianus, perhaps remembering Ausonius, found in Bellerophon an apt personification of the bilious misanthropy that he detected in the *monachi* then gathered on the island of Capraria off the Italian coast. The hearts of such men, Namatianus remarked, were "swollen with black bile."[98] For similar reasons Bellerophon eloquently relayed Ausonius's apprehension that Paulinus had been pulled into the slowly rising stream of radical Christian asceticism. Bellerophon's personal suffering and errant isolation, after a life of heroic action, had been made legendary by Homer and transmitted into Latin literature by Cicero, the apparent source of Ausonius's allusion.[99] Ausonius's Bellerophon, too, was "out of his mind" (*mentis inops*), and now the madness that had provoked Bellerophon's isolation, co-opted by learned critics,

---

96. *Carm.* 10.191–92: "non anxia Bellerophontis / mens est."

97. Witke, *Numen Litterarum*, 23, recognized the *impius* as a "straw Paulinus." More circumspect is Y.-M. Duval, "Recherches sur la langue et la litterature latines: Bellérophon et les ascètes chrétiens: Melancholia' ou '*otium*'?" *Caesarodunum* 3 (1968): 184.

98. *De reditu suo* 1.448–52:

> tristia seu nigro viscera felle tument,
> sic nimiae bilis morbum adsignavit Homerus
>   Bellerophonteis sollicitudinibus:
> nam iuveni offenso saevi post tela doloris
>   dicitur humanum displicuisse genus.

See Duval, "Bellérophon et les ascètes chrétiens," 184–86.

99. Homer, *Il.* 6.201. Cicero, *Tusc.* 3.26.63: "ut ait Homerus de Bellerophonte: Qui miser in campis maerens errabat Aleïs, / Ipse suum cor edens, *hominum vestigia vitans*." Notably, Ausonius's modification of the line "coetus hominum et vestigia vitans" emphasizes the isolation of Bellerophon from human society.

could analogously explain the grievous ascetic renunciation and social sabotage of Christian ascetics.[100]

But why should Ausonius have turned to a symbol of misanthropic dementia— or, for that matter, to one of dangerous feminine independence of mind—to embody his opinions about ascetic practitioners? Surely Ausonius could have based his diagnosis upon casual observance and hearsay in Martin's Gaul. Even at Trier in the 370s an *agens in rebus* might stumble upon the *Life of Anthony* and be induced to consider the friendship of God more valuable than the friendship of the emperor.[101] But a more immediate series of events had shocked Bordeaux in the mid-380s, leaving a deep impression on Ausonius that may explain his choice of Tanaquil to gloss Therasia as well as his recourse to Bellerophon to goad Paulinus out of his silence. In 381, en route to Rome from Spain, Priscillian, a wealthy layman turned religious teacher and bishop of Avila, had arrived at Bordeaux.[102] Delphinus, Bordeaux's bishop, refused him admission to the city.[103] A year earlier Delphinus had attended a council at Saragossa that had condemned a number of practices said to be fomented by Priscillian's teaching, although Priscillian himself was not censured.[104] At that time the church already perceived a "Priscillianist" threat to social order and the institutional hierarchy. Since such separatists, it was held, were wont to assemble in the mountain wilds or in secluded villas, they were forbidden to "inhabit the refuges of cells or of the mountains" during Lent; and they were commanded "to keep the example and precept of the bishops and not gather at the villas of others for the sake of holding meetings."[105] A subsequent canon then extended this prohibition to the season before Epiphany: "Let it be

---

100. Aus. *ep.* 21.71 Green (EW *ep.* 29). In contrast, note the possible Christian adoption of a different Bellerophon, who killed the monstrous Chimera, perhaps as a Christ-Helios corollary; see M. Simon, "Bellérophon chrétien," *Mélanges d'archéologie, d'épigraphie et d'histoire offerts à Jérôme Carcopino* (Paris, 1966), 889–904.

101. Aug. *Conf.* 8.6.

102. Sul. Sev. *Chron.* 2.46–51 (*CSEL* 1 [1986] ed. C. Helm) for Priscillian's story, with Chadwick, *Priscillian*; V. Burrus, *The Making of a Heretic: Gender, Authority, and the Priscillianist Controversy* (Berkeley, 1995), and on Severus's *Chronicle* see H. Inglebert, *Les romains chrétiens face à l'histoire de Rome: Histoire, christianisme et romanités en Occident dans l'antiquité tardive (IIIe–Ve siècles)* (Paris, 1996), 365–85. The primary corpus of Priscillianist writings is found in *CSEL* 18 (1889), ed. G. Schepps, with bibliography at *Patrology* 4.142–43.

103. *Chron.* 2.48: "a Burdigala per Delfinum repulsi."

104. *Chron.* 2.47: "Igitur post multa inter eos nec digna memoratu certamina apud Caesaraugustam synodus congregatur, cui tum etiam Aquitani episcopi interfuere." The record of the council's eight canons (*PL* 84:315–18) is introduced by a list of twelve bishops: "Caesaraugusta in secretario residentibus episcopis Fitadio, Delfino, . . . " On the failure of the council to condemn Priscillian see Chadwick, *Priscillian*, 26–27.

105. Second canon (*PL* 84.315): "et quadragesimarum die ab ecclesiis non desint nec habitent latibula cubiculorum ac montium qui in his suspicionibus perseverant, sed exemplum et praeceptum custodiant sacerdotum et ad alienas villas agendorum conventuum causa non conveniant."

permitted to no one to be absent from the church, nor to hide out in their homes, nor to secede to a villa, nor to seek out the mountains, nor to go about barefoot."[106] The official church clearly had its own concerns about Priscillianist ideas, but these were not far removed from the Ausonian image of wayward Bellerophon wandering beyond the boundaries of civic order and surveillance.

With Bordeaux closed to him by Delphinus in 381, a suspect Priscillian sojourned on the nearby estate of a widow named Euchrotia, who, along with her daughter Procula and a number of other women, eventually accompanied Priscillian on his mission of appeal to Damasus at Rome. Rumor quickly accused Priscillian of the seduction of Procula; an abortion, it was said, destroyed the evidence.[107] Three years later Priscillian was again an issue at Bordeaux. By order of the emperor Maximus, in 384 a synod under the guidance of Delphinus met at Bordeaux itself to reconsider the "blemish" of Priscillianism.[108] The city was soon the scene of violent dissent, and a certain Urbica, a follower of Priscillian, was stoned to death in the streets.[109] Priscillian, however, had refused to appear before the synod and had taken himself to the secular authorities at Trier. His plan proved ill-advised. After a series of court intrigues, and despite the intervention of Martin of Tours, he and several followers, including Euchrotia, were executed on charges not of heresy but of sorcery.[110] Priscillianism (at least as a label) would survive its namesake's death, but Priscillian's career had already profoundly marked the city of Ausonius and Paulinus when both were back in Aquitaine.

These troubling events had touched Ausonius closely. Both Euchrotia, who had received Priscillian in 381 and was executed with him at Trier, and her daughter Procula, allegedly seduced by Priscillian's sexual advances as well as his ascetic teaching, were personally known to Ausonius. Ausonius later commemorated

---

106. Fourth canon (*PL* 84.316): "nulli liceat de ecclesia absentare, nec latere in domibus, nec secedere in villam, nec montes petere, nec nudis pedibus incedere."

107. *Chron.* 2.48: "tamen in agro Euchrotiae aliquantisper morati, infecere nonnullos suis erroribus. inde iter coeptum ingressi, turpi sane pudibundoque comitatu, cum uxoribus atque alienis etiam feminis, in quis erat Euchrotia ac filia eius Procula, de qua fuit in sermone hominum Priscilliani stupro gravidam partum sibi graminibus abegisse."

108. *Chron.* 2.49: "quibus permotus imperator, datis ad praefectum Galliarum atque ad vicarium Hispaniarum litteris, omnes omnino, quos labes illa involuerat, deduci ad Synodum Burdigalensem iubet." The *acta* of this council have not been preserved; see *Concilia Galliae*, ed. C. Munier, *CCSL* 148 (1963): 46.

109. Prosper, *Chron.* ann 385 (*MGH AA* 9, p.462): "Priscillianus in synodo Burdigalensi damnandum se intellegens ad imperatorem [Maximum] provocavit, auditusque Treveris ab Euvodio praefecto praetorio Maximi gladio addictus est cum Euchrotia Delfidi rhetoris coniuge et Latroniano aliisque erroris consortibus. Burdigalae quaedam Priscilliani discipula nomine Urbica ob impietatis pertinaciam per seditionem vulgi lapidibus extincta est."

110. Sev. *Chron.* 2.49–51; Prosper, *Chron.* p.462. On the date, perhaps 386, see Chadwick, *Priscillian,* 132–38.

their husband and father, Attius Tiro Delphidius, in his work on the professors of Bordeaux. "Eloquent, learned, and quick of tongue and wit," Ausonius considered Delphidius fortunate to have died before witnessing the tragedy of his family: "By the gift of God you knew less of evils because you were snatched away in the middle of life, because you were not wounded by the mistake of a deviant daughter or the punishment of a wife."[111] Furthermore, Priscillian's *discipula*, Urbica, stoned to death by a Bordeaux crowd, may also have been known to Ausonius. If she was not the daughter of Ausonius's colleague, the grammarian Urbicus, as some have thought,[112] she may have been the Pomponia Urbica who was the mother of Ausonius's son-in-law Thalassius. The latter identification is particularly tempting, for Ausonius also compared Pomponia Urbica to Tanaquil, apparently to suggest her expertise in the occult, while he hinted that she "courted martyrdom."[113] The high-profile cases of Euchrotia and Urbica would have engendered or reinforced a perception that subversive ascetic teaching, popularly linked with social isolation and pursuit of the occult, found its most fertile ground among the women of the *familia*. Here then was cause to suspect the machinations of a Tanaquilian Therasia behind the silence of a Bellerophonic Paulinus.

The embellishment of Priscillian's story between 384 and the early 390s would have confirmed the aptness of both Tanaquil and Bellerophon as figures for crystallizing certain public perceptions of the ascetic practices and behavior of alleged Priscillianists. Although Priscillian may have less problematically counseled persistent Bible study, along with sexual continence and the renunciation of material goods,[114] his apparent attraction to demonology and occultism made it easy for his opponents to depict him as a crypto-Manichee or a sorcerer.[115] At Trier, as noted earlier, Priscillian had been charged not with heresy but with sorcery (*maleficium*); Priscillian, it was claimed, studied indecent doctrines, conducted nocturnal meet-

---

111. Aus. *Prof.* 5.1, 35–39 Green:

> Facunde, docte, lingua et ingenio celer
> . . . .
> minus malorum munere expertus dei,
>   medio quod aevi raptus es,
> errore quod non deviantis filiae
>   poenaque laesus coniugis.

Note Prosper, *Chron.*, 462: "Euchrotia Delfidi rhetoris coniuge."

112. Urbicus is commemorated at *Prof.* 21. The filiation is confidently asserted by Étienne, *Bordeaux antique*, 269; Green, *Ausonius*, 328, is justly cautious.

113. Aus. *Par.* 30; with Green, *Ausonius*, 328.

114. Chadwick, *Priscillian*, 70–73.

115. Chadwick, *Priscillian*, 57, 96–100. See especially Burrus, *The Making of a Heretic*, for this point and for a lucid discussion of the rhetorical and labeling strategies that permeate this controversy.

ings with disreputable women, and prayed naked.[116] After 384 the *apologiae* of his prosecutors only reinforced these lurid images.[117] Later anti-Priscillianist literature is shot through with charges of sexual deviance and feminine recklessness in a milieu of occultism. Priscillian, it was said, had practiced magical arts since boyhood; and "women desirous of novelty (*novae res*)" and of "prurient curiosity" flocked to him in crowds,[118] a general assertion seemingly too well illustrated by the sordid tales of the widowed Euchrotia and the pregnant Procula. En route to Rome, Severus's *Chronicle* later recorded, Priscillian's entourage included not only these two and the wives of some of Priscillian's followers but even the wives of other men (*cum uxoribus atque alienis etiam feminis*).[119] As the charges brought against Priscillian at Trier had emphasized sex and magic, the *apologia* of Ithacius, one of Priscillian's prosecutors, broadsided his "lusts" (*libidines*).[120]

That such charges were the stock-in-trade of Roman invective need not have diminished their power. In the Roman world the merest hint of clandestine cult or political activity might prompt suspicions of perverted and criminal behavior. In this regard the anti-Priscillianist rhetoric echoes, for example, Livy's account of the infamous Bacchanalian sex and murder scandal of 186 B.C., the alleged excesses of Catiline, and even such pagan slanders of early Christian gatherings as those recorded by Minucius Felix.[121] Yet for all their apparent familiarity, charges of sexual deviance, magic, and secrecy continued to carry emotional force. It was that force that Ausonius hoped to condense into the images of the imperious Tanaquil, learned in the *Etrusca disciplina*,[122] and the errant Bellerophon. Ausonius's letters to Paulinus may not mention the name of Priscillian, but, as Paulinus apparently realized, behind Tanaquil and Bellerophon lurk the vague shadows of the ghost of Priscillian and his followers. Ausonius's poems serve further notice on the resentment many harbored toward the incipient monastic movement.

116. Sev. *Chron.* 2.50: "is [the praetorian prefect, Evodius] Priscillianum gemino iudicio auditum convictumque maleficii nec diffitentem obscenis se studuisse doctrinis, nocturnos etiam turpium feminarum egisse conventus nudumque orare solitum."

117. Chadwick, *Priscillian*, 145, with Isidore of Seville, *De vir. ill.* 15 (*PL* 83.1092) on the *apologia* of Ithacius "in quo detestanda Priscilliani dogmata, et maleficiorum eius artes, libidinumque eius probra demonstrat."

118. Sev. *Chron.* 2:46: "mulieres novarum rerum cupidae." The description of Priscillian and his followers owes a long-recognized debt to Sallust's Catiline, another debauched revolutionary. See J. Fontaine, "L'affaire Priscillien ou l'ère des nouveaux Catilina: Observations sur le 'Sallustianisme' de Sulpice Sévère," *Classica et Iberica: A Festschrift in Honor of Reverend Joseph M. F. Marique, S.J.*, ed. P. T. Brannan (Worcester, Mass., 1975), 355–92, esp. 361–68.

119. Sev. *Chron.* 2.48, quoted above.

120. Isidore of Seville, *De vir. ill.* 15, quoted above. See canons 1 and 8 of the council of 380 (*PL* 84.315, 318).

121. Livy, 19.8–18; Sal. *Cat.* 14–16, 20–22; *Octavius* 9.

122. Liv. 1.34.9: "Tanaquil, perita ut volgo Etrusci caelestium prodigiorum mulier."

It is not clear exactly why Ausonius should have suspected Therasia and Paulinus of association with Priscillianism, however he might have conceived of it. There is, in fact, no convincing reason to connect Paulinus with any Priscillianist "movement" at any time.[123] Paulinus himself seems to deny direct connections with any ascetic groups at all in his eventual reply to Ausonius, and his relations with Delphinus of Bordeaux, a hammer of the Priscillianists, continue unabated through these years. But, at the same time, Paulinus can hardly have been unaware of some version of Priscillianist teachings, and at some point as his own ascetic inclinations matured in these years Paulinus's thought must begin to overlap with the *morale priscillianiste*.[124] Perhaps, as Paulinus later claimed, Ausonius had merely been swept in by gossip and rumor, for if no letters from Paulinus arrived from Spain this kind of (mis)information surely did.[125] Aquitaine and northern Spain were too intimately connected by familial, social, and cultural ties for Ausonius to have been completely ignorant of Paulinus's affairs during these years.[126] Although Ausonius himself appears never to have crossed the Pyrenees, he knew enough about Paulinus to be worried, and he cared enough to persist.[127] Thus he followed his castigation of that "impious one" he deemed guilty of encouraging Paulinus's silence with a plea to the Muses:[128] "These things I pray, divine Boetian Muses, receive my cry and call back your poet with Latin songs (*Latiis camenis*)."

Ausonius's prayer was only partially successful. Paulinus finally received a packet of Ausonius's letters.[129] His response, Paulinus's *carmen* 10, is a remarkable document. Written some twelve years after he had governed Campania as a *con-*

---

123. In 1910 E.-C. Babut, "Paulin de Nole et Priscillien," attempted to prove that Paulinus was deeply influenced by the Priscillianist movement. He claimed that Paulinus had a radical, Pricillianist view of baptism and that his conversion to asceticism was simultaneous with his own reception of baptism (104); that Paulinus's alleged contemporary and subsequent silence about his years in Spain was due to his involvement in the Priscillianist movement (105–8); that it is possible to detect suspicion of Paulinus in such contemporaries as Delphinus and Siricius (109–16); and that Paulinus's works contain verbal reminiscences of the Priscillianist tractates (120 ff.). Babut's specific arguments, highly conjectural and reflecting an outdated view of Priscillian's teaching, are refuted by H. Delehaye, "Saint Martin et Sulpice Sévère," *Analecta Bollandiana* 38 (1920), esp. 66–68, and Fabre, *Paulin de Nole*, 107–16. Nevertheless, as Lienhard remarks, *Paulinus of Nola*, 52, "the refutations have not made the question vanish." That is, both Paulinus's thoughts and Priscillian's are centered on contemporary ideas about the perfect Christian life and ascetic practice. It is worth remembering that Delphinus, an opponent of Priscillian, both baptized Paulinus and remained in contact with him after he moved to Spain.

124. As Fabre admitted, *Paulin de Nole*, 107.

125. *Carm.* 10.265–68.

126. J. Fontaine, "Société et culture chrétiennes sur l'aire circumpyrénéenne au siècle de Théodose," *Bulletin de littérature ecclésiastique* 75 (1974): 241–82.

127. R. Étienne, "Ausone et l'Espagne," 331.

128. Aus. *ep.* 21.73–74 Green (EW *ep.* 29): "Haec precor, hanc vocem, Boeotia numina, Musae, / accipite et Latiis vatem revocate Camenis." Cf. Vir. *Aen.* 4.621, 611.

129. *Carm.* 10.1–8.

sularis, it boldly measures the distance Paulinus had traveled since then, and it surely reflects intervening events: meeting the charismatic Martin of Tours, receiving baptism from Delphinus of Bordeaux, contemplating in apprehension and sadness the deaths of loved ones, and separating, perhaps painfully, from *patria* and old friends. Ironically, however, Paulinus's reply to Ausonius also reveals the degree to which his "contempt for the world" still seemed compatible with many of the ideals shared by men of his background and education. The worst of Ausonius's suspicions about Paulinus were not yet fully warranted, although that fact in no way reduces the latent power invested in the images of Tanaquil and Bellerophon; for the pressure exerted by these hoary figures of revitalized meaning drove Paulinus finally to renew contact.

CHAPTER 4

—•—

Renunciation and Ordination

Having received no written word from Ausonius for at least three years, Paulinus claimed that in 393 a bundle of three overdue letters had at last reached him.[1] Among them, presumably, were the two epistolary poems just discussed. The perplexity and pain, indignation, and self-righteousness that Paulinus felt on reading Ausonius's accusatory pieces still resonate in his elaborate poetic reply, a lengthy poem composed in three different meters.[2] Therein, although Paulinus bluntly rejected Ausonius's charge that he had abandoned the customs of civilized men, he unhesitatingly acknowledged that he was no longer the man he used to be. To Ausonius's suspicious query—"Have you changed your ways (*mores*), sweetest Paulinus?"—he responded frankly, but not without a nod to Horace on poetry and divine "enthusiasm": "Now another power stirs my mind, a greater God, and demands other *mores*."[3] But like Augustine in the troubling months before retiring from his professorial chair at Milan, Paulinus appears still caught in the struggle to understand just what might be required to meet fully the demands of those "other ways." Indeed, both this poem and another written to Ausonius within the year (*carm.* 11) are animated by the same paradoxical tensions that must have been wracking Paulinus's life at the time. These poems, like the few letters that can be dated to these years (ca. 393–94), vividly express the anxieties of a man groping toward the reconceptualization of his life in the face of an uncertain eternity. By 393

---

1. *Carm.* 10.1–8. On the chronology see Y.-M. Duval, "Les premiers rapports," 205–14; Green, *Ausonius,* 648; Trout, "The Dates of the Ordination of Paulinus of Bordeaux and of His Departure for Nola," *REAug* 37 (1991): 237–60.

2. *Carm.* 10 consists of a section of elegiac couplets (1–18), iambics (19–102), and dactylic hexameter (103–331). Green, *Ausonius,* prints the poem as Appendix 3B.

3. Aus. *ep.* 21.50–52 Green (EW *ep.* 29): "vertisti, Pauline, tuos, dulcissime, mores." *Carm.* 10.29–30: "Nunc alia mentem vis agit, maior deus, / aliosque mores postulat." Hor. *carm.* 3.25.1–3 with A. Nazzaro, "Orazio e Paolino," *Impegno e dialogo* 10 (1992–94): 245–48. See further *carm.* 10.131–46.

Paulinus had already begun to implement a new poetic practice, and he was on the verge of radically changing his life. The next year he would do so, and his public announcement of his ascetic vocation would spur a crowd at Barcelona to demand his presbyterial ordination. Moreover, in the months surrounding these events Paulinus would also alert the monastic communities of the East and the clergy of North Africa to his change of ways. The news would draw him into correspondence with both Jerome and Augustine.

TO LIVE FOR CHRIST

The complex testament that Paulinus offered to Ausonius in *carmen* 10 concerned life and poetry equally, for the two were in some sense inseparable for Paulinus. As shared poetic and literary sympathies bound men in intellectual community and provided a language for social relations, so a new poetics was required to articulate a new relation to the world and to God. Since Paulinus was not prepared to forgo poetry, adopting a new way of life necessitated a quest for alternative sources of artistic inspiration as well as revised modes of expression. Spiritual and intellectual transformation, Paulinus avowed, required reconsideration of art's objectives. Thus Paulinus opened the confrontational iambic section of his reply to Ausonius (*carmen* 10) with a direct challenge to the terms of the prayer with which Ausonius had ended his second letter: "Why, father, do you order the Muses I have rejected to return to my care? Hearts dedicated to Christ deny the Camenae and are not open to Apollo."[4]

In practice, however, denial of the Muses was a complicated matter. The iambic and hexameter sections of *carmen* 10, which succeed Paulinus's opening elegiac couplets, are constructed around a series of interlocking and apparently mutually exclusive artistic, moral, and philosophic categories generated from the opposing images of the classical Muses and Christ. Oppositions of old and new, false and true, foolishness and wisdom, visible and invisible, transient and eternal polarize the poem's message, demanding that the reader, Ausonius, locate himself in only one set of categories. To discern God's light and obey His laws, Paulinus asserted, we must renounce the shrewd power of the philosophers, the *ars* of the rhetors, and the fictions of the poets (33–38). These staples of the Ausonian

---

4. *Carm.* 10.19–22:

> Quid abdicatas in meam curam, pater,
>   redire Musas praecipis?
> negant Camenis nec patent Apollini
>   dicata Christo pectora.

Useful discussion by Witke, *Numen Litterarum*, 44–48. The sentiment is expanded at 10.109–18.

schoolroom serve neither truth or salvation (41–42); Christ is the true "teacher of virtues (*magister virtutum*)" (52), who demands our complete submission, our love and our fear (63–66). Faith in a future life with God should inspire us to lend our riches to Christ, to store our treasure in heaven (71–80). The Muses are denounced as mere "names without power (*sine numine nomina*)" (115); God alone can answer Ausonius's prayers (113). In response to Ausonius's interrogation, Paulinus forcefully asserted that he had indeed changed, but for the better; and Ausonius was asked to recognize and accept, even take glory in, the new man Paulinus had become (150–54).

The poem's final section reveals something of the impetus behind Paulinus's binary view of the world and his own future. A frightening vision of judgment and redemption compels Paulinus's decision "to live for Christ as Christ has ordained (*sic vivere Christo ut Christus sanxit*)" (284–85). Paulinus had come to believe that only present losses would purchase eternal rewards (281–82). Fear of "the grave anger of the divine judge" now outweighs any concern for inconsequential human reproach (295–97); and Paulinus's soul trembles to be found ensnared by the cares of the body or the weight of possessions (305–7). His special terror is that the "last day should catch him asleep in the pitch darkness of barren activity" (316–18). Thus resolved to discard his worldly cares, Paulinus closed his address to Ausonius with an ultimatum: "If this pleases you, rejoice in the rich hope of your friend; if you are opposed, leave me to be approved by Christ alone."[5] Ausonius's dismissal of the poem's ethical and spiritual topography would thus require rejection of Paulinus as well.

But the moral and spiritual landscape of *carmen* 10 also has a very real physical and social setting wherein the barriers between the poem's discrete categories begin to collapse; for, despite claims to the contrary, the personal reproaches of Ausonius's letters stung Paulinus acutely. Much of the resentment of *carmen* 10 was reserved for the insinuations Ausonius had cast through the figures of Bellerophon and Tanaquil. Both were vehemently denied. "Therefore, revered father," Paulinus retorted, "don't rebuke me for having turned to these pursuits wrongly or revile me for my wife or the imperfection of my mind; I have neither the troubled mind of Bellerophon nor a Tanaquil, but a wife like Lucretia," he added, turning to a Livian exemplar connoting chastity and marital fidelity.[6] To suggest, as Ausonius had, that Paulinus could be lazy, perverse, or impious, was itself perverse, for *pietas* was the natural mark of a Christian (83–88). But most revealing, perhaps, is the force of

---

5. *Carm.* 10.330–31: "si placet hoc, gratare tui spe divite amici; / si contra est, Christo tantum me linque probari."

6. *Carm.* 10.189–92:

> ne me igitur, venerande parens, his ut male versum
> increpites studiis neque me vel coniuge carpas
> vel mentis vitio; non anxia Bellerophontis
> mens est nec Tanaquil mihi, sed Lucretia coniunx.

Paulinus's refutation of Ausonius's desire to sequester Paulinus in the trackless wastes and backwater towns of Spain, his *patria* deserted, his consular robe dishonored. To Ausonius's Vasconian woodlands and snowy Pyrenees,[7] to his mountainous and rugged Calagurris, Birbilis, and Ilerda,[8] Paulinus opposed his (true) residence "in diverse regions close by proud cities celebrated for the happy refinements of their peoples" (215–17). Spain has its glory, he reminded Ausonius, in Caesaraugusta, in pleasant Barcinus, and in Tarraco looking down upon the sea from its notable heights (232–33). Spain has cities and rivers to rival Bordeaux and the Garonne, and it should not be judged by its rustic regions and folk any more than Aquitaine should be judged by the "pitch-black Boii" or the "skin-clad Bigerri" (239–46). *Otium ruris,* that is, was no less dignified in Spain than on Ausonius's estate of Lucaniacus (256–59); and Paulinus's consular *trabea* was no more disgraced by his Spanish residence than were Ausonius's *curules et trabea* by his own withdrawal to the countryside of Poiteau (249–51). Some topics are fair game for joking, Paulinus admitted, but Ausonius had soured his jests with the vinegar of a biting satire unbefitting a father (260–64). By enlisting Tanaquil and Bellerophon, Ausonius had forced Paulinus's hand. Paulinus was still, and always would be, concerned to project an appropriate public image, even if the elements of that image shifted over time. But it is also clear that in 393, when he wrote this poem, Paulinus had not yet severed the ties that held him to the inherited conglomerate of elite values.

The restraining tug of those values, it appears, also led Paulinus to distance himself from practicing ascetics even if he adamantly defended their way of life. "My mind is not deranged, nor does my way of life (*vita*) shun the society of men, as you write the rider of Pegasus lived in a Lycian cave."[9] Paulinus knew of those who did live in isolation and celibacy (*casti*), but he likened them to those famous philosophers who had withdrawn to pursue learning and inspiration (159–60).[10] Like them, Christian ascetics—turned to the stars, looking on God, and intent to perceive the depths of truth—also loved *otium* and, in accord with the commands of Christ and from love of salvation, abhorred the noise of the forum (*strepitus fori*), the tumult of affairs, and all *negotia* hostile to the divine gifts (163–67). They spurned the visible to win the invisible (172–73). But, Paulinus emphasized, he himself was no such (Platonized) monk: "Why is the same said of me, for whom

---

7. *Carm.* 10.203 with Aus. *ep.* 21.51 Green (EW *ep.* 29).
8. *Carm.* 10.223–25 with Aus. *ep.* 21.56–61 Green (EW *ep.* 29).
9. *Carm.* 10.156–58:

> non etenim mihi mens demens neque participantum
> vita fugax hominum, Lyciae qua scribis in antris
> Pegaseum vixisse equitem.

10. For Paulinus's reliance on Seneca in this picture of philosophical asceticism see Duval, "Bellérophon et les ascètes chrétiens," 187.

there is not the same glory? My faith in the object of my prayer is equal, but even now I inhabit pleasant regions, set among the charming pursuits of a luxuriant coast."[11] Refusing to credit himself with an ascetic life reconfigured as philosophical *otium*, Paulinus rather insisted that he continued to live in honorable aristocratic leisure.[12] Similarly, while he stressed his changing attitude toward material possessions, he nonetheless maintained a philosophically and socially respectable stance. Responsible use, not impulsive rejection, would be repaid by Christ with interest (70–80). Herein Ausonius may have still perceived the dictates of elite civic philanthropy, even if recontextualized.

This confusion of the apparently exclusive categories initially established in *carmen* 10, clearly evident on the surface of the unfolding poem, also reaches deeper. Paulinus elected to state his response to Ausonius in carefully crafted poetry, the medium that had so long bound them together but whose techniques were virtually inseparable from the rhetorical arts that his very words condemned. Although spiritual truths, not poetic fictions, provided the themes, and although Paulinus's sentences teasingly reveal his reading of the Pauline epistles,[13] *carmen* 10 nevertheless delights in the verbal ploys and games that had distinguished Paulinus's earlier "Ausonian" poetry. Paulinus's three meters—elegiac, iambic, and hexameter—consciously echo Ausonius's "threefold page" (8) while also allowing unusual scope for virtuoso performance along conventional lines. Internal rhyme, alliteration, and parallelism distinguish the iambics, elevated diction and complex syntax the hexameters.[14] Wordplay abounds.[15] The same facility with exotic place names that Ausonius had once admired in Paulinus's versification of Suetonius's *De regibus* is given full rein here. Moreover, Paulinus teases out his rebuttals, only openly inscribing the name of Bellerophon (191) after first alluding to Ausonius's *impius* (84) and then employing a periphrasis, "the rider of Pegasus (*Pegaseum equi-*

---

11. *Carm.* 10.181–84:

> at mihi, non eadem cui gloria, cur eadem sit
> fama? fides voti par est, sed amoena colenti
> nunc etiam et blanda posito locupletis in acta
> litoris.

12. Rightly noted by Duval, "Bellérophon et les ascètes chrétiens," 188, but too often ignored.

13. Witke, *Numen Litterarum*, 51–52.

14. Witke, *Numen Litterarum*, 49–51. R. P. H. Green notes, in "Paulinus of Nola and the Diction of Christian Latin Poetry," *Latomus* 32 (1973): 79–85 (more concise than *The Poetry of Paulinus of Nola: A Study of His Latinity. Collection Latomus* 120 [Brussels, 1971], 61–95), that *carm.* 10, like other poems addressed to devoted *litterati*, more readily employs the religious diction of classical poetry than do the *natalicia*, whose immediate audience was largely nonelite. Writing to Ausonius, Licentius (*ep.* 8), or Jovius (*carm.* 22), Paulinus favors periphrases and such pre-Christian words as *numen, genitor, tonans, suboles,* and *spiramen*, eschewing the *sermo humilis* more characteristic of the *natalicia*. Audience influenced diction.

15. For example, *mens demens* (156); *sine numine nomina* (115); the multivalency of *caelum* and *pater* (193–97), with Witke, *Numen Litterarum*, 55.

tem)"(158). And if the fictive themes of the poets have been (mostly) banished, the poets themselves have not: Ausonius would have heard here echoes of Catullus, Virgil, Horace, Ovid, Statius, Persius, and Silius Italicus.[16] A Horatian phrase could describe man's ephemeral nature, Virgilian language be transferred from Jupiter to God.[17]

This seeming dissonance between content and form characterizes virtually all of Paulinus's poetry from this point; it could hardly be otherwise for a man of Paulinus's education and background. More immediately, however, Paulinus's poetics played to the distinct needs of the moment. The polished *ars* of *carmen* 10 encouraged Ausonius's engagement with the poem's ideas at the same time that it palliated the shock of Paulinus's more inflammatory claims. Although both Paulinus's new mores and his ostensible rejection of any art that did not serve God's purposes might seem to target directly Ausonius and his poetic sensibility, nevertheless Paulinus invited Ausonius to read his verses in their customary manner. Moreover, the care Paulinus lavished on this long-overdue letter was tacit recognition of his abiding debt to Ausonius; the choice of medium alone may have facilitated reception of the poem's message and reassured Ausonius that all was not lost.[18]

Thus, despite the poem's closing ultimatum, *carmen* 10 is more an invitation for a rejoinder than a notice of foreclosure; both medium and message offer ample room for understanding and reconciliation. Explicitly and implicitly Paulinus acknowledges his continuing affection for Ausonius: "To you I owe my training, my distinction, my literary skill, the glory of my eloquence, of my political career, and of my reputation; as patron, teacher, and father you have raised me up, nourished me, and taught me."[19] He reassures Ausonius that he is no Bellerophon and even that "to live for Christ" implies not a wayward dementia, such as Ausonius may have suspected behind the followers of Priscillian, but affiliation with a revered concept of philosophical *otium*. Despite Paulinus's anxieties over God's judgment and the eternal fate of his soul, he makes clear that life is still configured as honorable withdrawal to pleasant rural estates. Augustine had offered a similar apology to the Milanese intelligentsia and social elite only a few years earlier. In the months that separated his resignation of his professorial chair in 386 from his

16. See citations at Hartel, *CSEL* 30, 381–82; Witke, *Numen Litterarum*, 56–65.

17. 10.289 with Hor. *carm.* 4.7; discussion at Witke, *Numen Litterarum*, 63–64; 10.121 with *Aen.* 4.210.

18. See further Fontaine, "Valeurs," 579, on "une secrète intelligence, d'ordre culturel et poétique, entre les deux correspondants."

19. *Carm.* 10.93–96:

> tibi disciplinas dignitatem litteras,
>   linguae togae famae decus
> provectus altus institutus debeo,
>   patrone praeceptor pater.

Easter 387 baptism, Augustine composed several dialogues on a country estate near Cassiciacum intended, in part, to assimilate his new Christian way of life with the traditions of *otium ruris*.[20]

Neither the modes nor the messages of this verse letter to Ausonius are unique among Paulinus's compositions of this period. Other texts also relay Paulinus's spiritual discontent and highlight his quest for a new poetry inspired not by the Muses but by Christ. His anxieties over the state of his soul emerge elsewhere, and not without cause, for death had touched Paulinus closely and forced him to confront the troubling issue of his own salvation. Writing to Delphinus and Amandus of Bordeaux (*epp.* 35 and 36) soon after his brother's untimely death, Paulinus expressed deep dissatisfaction with his own spiritual progress. He openly admitted to them his failure to live fully by the gospel precepts; and to Amandus, as to Ausonius, he confessed his trepidation at being caught unprepared by death, as he believed his too worldly brother had been: "Pray for me as well, lest I die in my sins," he wrote. "Let the Master make my end known to me, so that I may know my failings and may hasten to fulfill what remains, so that I am not called back in the middle of my empty days, weaving a spider's web of useless works."[21] He who has lived too much for the "outer man," Paulinus feared, will finally be "condemned to eternal fire."[22] Perhaps even more devastating and determinant for Paulinus and Therasia had been the death of their eight-day-old son, Celsus, so long desired but so soon laid to rest in a saints' shrine at Complutum.[23] Several years later, induced to think of Celsus as he considered in consolatory poetry the meaning of another early death, Paulinus could still evoke the pain of his own loss.[24] He understood the desire of grieving parents to be rejoined with a child seemingly lost

---

20. D. Trout, "Augustine at Cassiciacum: *Otium Honestum* and the Social Dimensions of Conversion," *Vigiliae Christianae* 42 (1988): 132–46.

21. *Ep.* 36.3: "Ora et pro nobis, ne in peccatis nostris moriamur; notum faciat nobis dominus finem nostrum, ut sciamus quid desit nobis et properemus adinplere quod restat, ut non revolvamur in medio dierum inanium [Ps 101.25], texentes operibus vacuis araneae telam [Job 8.14]." Cp. *carm.* 10.316–18: "dies ultimus . . . sterili actu . . . vacuis curis." The dominance of scriptural imagery in *epp.* 35 and 36 reflects the intended audience.

22. *Ep.* 36.3: "quia secundum exteriorem hominem vixerit. . . . quia in ignem damnandus aeternum."

23. *Carm.* 31.602, 607–10:

accitus tempore quo datus est.
. . . .
quem Conplutensi mandavimus urbe propinquis
    coniunctum tumuli foedere martyribus,
ut de vicino sanctorum sanguine ducat,
    quo nostras illo spargat in igne animas.

The shrine in question may have been that of the martyrs Justus and Pastor, remembered by Prudentius at *Pe.* 4.41–44. Complutum was located in the province of Gallaecia.

24. *Carm.* 31 was composed as a *consolatio* on the death of another Celsus, the eight-year-old son of Pneumatius and Fidelis, of whom the former was related to Paulinus in some fashion (624: "nam tua

forever.[25] To the bereft Pneumatius and Fidelis he held out the hope that such a future reunion was indeed possible if they would now learn "to live for Christ (*vivere Christo*)."[26] In the face of death and eternal judgment, once-cherished pursuits become inconsequential.

From such vantage points it was clear that poetry, too, as Paulinus had informed Ausonius, had to change its ways if art were to have legitimacy, value, and meaning. Thus at this time Paulinus was composing poems that would boldly fulfill the poetic program that he delineated for Ausonius in *carmen* 10.[27] The four extant poems of this period—a panegyric on John the Baptist (*carm.* 6), and three Psalm paraphrases (*carm.* 7–9)—self-consciously shunned both the Muses and the poetic *ficta* of the past in favor of Heaven-sent inspiration and scriptural themes. In the former, the so-called *Laus Sancti Iohannis,* a lengthy invocation of the God of the prophets and evangelists aligned Paulinus's poetic work with that of David.[28] The Gospel of Luke loosely underlies the 330 hexameters of that poem, while the text of the Psalms provides the material for paraphrase and adaptation to classical meter in *carmina* 7–9.[29] And although these pieces seem devoid of the urgency and anxiety that characterize parts of *carmen* 10 and letters 35 and 36 to Delphinus and

---

de patrio sanguine vena sumus"). The poem is dominated by a theological and Christological discourse that has led some critics to doubt its consolatory effect and artistic integrity: C. Favez, "Note sur la composition du *carmen* 31 de Paulin de Nole," *REL* 13 (1935): 266–68; and Fabre, *Paulin de Nole*, 212–17. The case for unity of structure and purpose is made by S. Costanza, "Dottrina e poesia nel carme XXXI di Paolino da Nola," *Giornale italiano di filologia* 24 (1972): 346–53; A. Quacquarelli, "Una *consolatio* cristiana (Paul. Nol., *Carm.* 31)," *Atti del Convegno*, 121–42; G. Guttilla, "Una nuova lettura del *carme* 31 di S. Paolino di Nola," *Koinonia* 11 (1987): 69–97. See also Green, *The Poetry of Paulinus*, 37–38. Guttilla, 91–94, attempts to narrow Fabre's range of composition for this piece, 393–408 (*Essai*, 124), to 393–96, by arguing that Paulinus's reluctance here to admit almsgiving by survivors as beneficial for the soul of the deceased must predate the promotion of this same claim in Paulinus's *ep.* 13 of 396 / 97 to Pammachius. In any case, the death of Paulinus and Therasia's Celsus is reasonably dated to 392 or 393, while the couple were in Spain but before their ascetic renunciation.

25. *Carm.* 31.545–46: "si desiderium est Celsi sine fine fruendi, / sic agite, ut vobis aula eadem pateat."

26. *Carm.* 31.499–500: "his monitis sanctam discamus vivere Christo / iustitiam et partem ponere pauperibus." The emphasis on almsgiving is characteristic of Paulinus's later thought on redemption, but in this developed form is anachronistic for the early 390s.

27. For one argument in favor of the contemporaneity of *carm.* 10 and 6 see Green, "Paulinus of Nola and the Diction of Christian Latin Poetry." Like *carm.* 10, *carm.* 6 freely combines classical terminology and Christian *sermo humilis* to describe Christian religious phenomena. For another, as also noted by Duval, "Les premiers rapports," the treatment of John the Baptist's ascetic withdrawal parallels the images and, to some extent, the diction of Paulinus's description of Spanish ascetics in *carm.* 10: cp. *carm.* 6.226–28 and 10.157–68.

28. *Carm.* 6.1–26. On David (22–23): "inspirante deo quicquid dixere priores / aptavit citharis nomen venerabile David." On the theme of the cithara in Paulinus see further J. Fontaine, "Les symbolismes de la cithare dans la poésie de Paulin de Nole," *Romanitas et christianitas: Studia J. H. Waszink* (Amsterdam, 1973), 123–43.

29. *Carm.* 6 relies primarily on Luke for the narrative, but Paulinus is quite free with his own additions in describing the Annunciation, for example, or filling out the years of John's childhood. John is

Amandus, in both choice of subject and topics for rhetorical expansion (*exaedifica-tio*) they too signal Paulinus's attention to asceticism and his apprehensions over divine judgment.[30]

These poems, then, would seem to confront the canons of an "Ausonian" poetics more radically than the roughly contemporary *carmen* 10 does, but they too are saturated with classicizing motifs and echoes of the classical poets. Paulinus's depiction of the desert solitude sought out by John the Baptist in *carmen* 6 draws heavily on the Golden Age imagery of Virgil and the Augustan poets.[31] And Paulinus applied to John the language of heroic epic; like the Argonauts in Statius's *Thebaid,* John became a *semideus vir,* a demigod.[32] It was Horace, however, who facilitated Paulinus's paraphrase and transformation of the first Psalm. The opening of *carmen* 7—"Beatus ille qui procul vitam suam / ab impiorum segravit coetibus"—conflates the Psalm's "Beatus vir qui non abiit in consilio impiorum" with the first line of Horace's second epode, "Beatus ille qui procul negotiis." Thus allusion to a well-known (if somewhat ambiguous) Horatian endorsement of rustic simplicity establishes a common ground for the reconfiguration of "happiness." In Paulinus's paraphrase *impii* replace *negotia* as impediments, while the study of God's *praecepta* replaces physical labor as the sanctioned activity.[33] Ultimately, then, even these poems on explicitly Christian themes derive much of their allure from their confusion of boundaries and from Paulinus's desire to appropriate the poetics of the past for new ends.

The emotional, spiritual, and artistic contradictions characteristic of Paulinus's writings in this period, though never fully resolved, achieve a brilliant equilibrium in Paulinus's final known letter to Ausonius, *carmen* 11. After so many years of silence broken only by rumor, Paulinus's *carmen* 10 had finally apprised Ausonius directly of the new forces active in his life. With the deep dismay brought by surer knowledge, Ausonius had then penned the poetic reply that *carmen* 10 had invited. Reflecting on the rift now separating him from Paulinus, Ausonius enlisted a dis-

---

Romanized, and Paulinus includes several passages of castigation, exhortation, or praise (163–78, 236–54, 276–302). On *carm.* 6 as both hagiography and encomium see S. Prete, "Paolino di Nola: La parafrasi biblica della *Laus Iohannis* (carm. 6)," *Augustinianum* 14 (1974): 625–35; for an argument on behalf of Iuvencus's influence on the poem see P. Flury, "Das sechste Gedicht des Paulinus von Nola," *Vigiliae Christianae* 27 (1973): 129–45. Brief notice at Witke, *Numen Litterarum,* 75–79; Green, *The Poetry of Paulinus,* 21–24. *Carm.* 7–9 paraphrase Ps. 1, 2, and 136.

30. A Platonizing conception of ascetic withdrawal is prominent at 6.226–28 and 7.5–7. On judgment, compare 7.30–43 with 10.294–323 and *epp.* 35 and 36; and note the elaboration of this theme over the original in *carm.* 8.

31. Compare *carm.* 6.240–46 with Vir. *Aen.* 8.319–36, Ovid *Met.* 1.89 ff. See also Prete, "La parafrasi biblica," 628 n.10.

32. *Carm.* 6.249–54 and *Theb.* 5.373, 3.518.

33. See also P. G. Walsh, "Paulinus of Nola," 568; A. Nazzaro, "Orazio e Paolino," 244–45, and especially A. Nazzaro, "La parafrasi salmica di Paolino di Nola," *Atti del Convegno,* 99–104, on the theological as well as literary implications of the poem. In Paulinus's latter poetry the paraphrase as a free-standing set piece gives way to paraphrase within poems; see Guttilla, "Una nuova lettura," 86–88.

tinctly vivid metaphor, one Paulinus would find eminently appealing: "We are shaking off a yoke (*iugum*), Paulinus, which its familiar balance once made easy, a yoke lightly placed and worthy of the respect of those who joined it, which mild Concord used to guide with even reins."[34] For this violent disruption, however, Ausonius accepted no blame; the fault was Paulinus's alone.[35] Nor would Ausonius fully acknowledge the complaints and countercharges of Paulinus's verse letter to him (*carmen* 10). Although Ausonius now banished Bellerophon and Tanaquil from his page, he did not otherwise eschew the fictions of the poets: Theseus and Peirithous, Nisus and Euryalus, the bow of Ulysses and the spear of Achilles were surely enlisted not only to substantiate through venerable examples Ausonius's unwavering loyalty to Paulinus but also to proclaim his abiding commitment to the poetics of the past.[36] Similarly, Ausonius might this time address not the Muses but rather "the Father and the Son of God (*genitor natusque dei*)" with his prayer for Paulinus's return to Aquitaine,[37] but only his desire not to "weep for a home scattered and plundered nor for the realms of old Paulinus broken up amid a hundred masters" obliquely acknowledged the ascetic impulses Paulinus had so openly inscribed in *carmen* 10.[38] Like Paulinus, Ausonius still entertained hopes of reconciliation: the last line of his poem was a calculated bid to elicit yet another poetic response. Concluding his letter with a dreamlike reverie of Paulinus's return to Bordeaux, Ausonius asked himself, "Can I believe this, or do lovers fashion dreams for themselves?"[39] Paulinus recognized the line as the penultimate verse of Virgil's eighth *Eclogue*, a poem whose theme was a lament on rejected love.

Perhaps Paulinus's response was spurred as much by the poetic challenge of that last line as by depth of affection. His response, *carmen* 11, probably of late 393 or early 394, began by repeating many of the charges against him contained in Ausonius's earlier letters, only to rebuke Ausonius for falling prey to gossip. Deploying

---

34. Aus. *ep.* 23.1–3 Green (an abbreviated EW *ep.* 27):

> Discutimus, Pauline, iugum, quod nota fovebat
> temperies, leve quod positu et venerabile iunctis
> tractabat paribus Concordia mitis habenis.

Translation by EW. Contrary to most editions, Green prints two versions of this poetic epistle, viewing the second longer version, *ep.* 24 (in which *nota* replaces *certa* and *venerabiles* replaces *tolerbiles*), as Ausonius's own adaptation based on his subsequent reading of Paulinus's *carm.* 11.

35. *Ep.* 23.6–7 Green.

36. *Ep.* 23.19–29 Green.

37. *Ep.* 23.33–34 Green. Perhaps only in the revised version of the letter, Sarragosa, Tarragona, and Barcelona replace the desolate wastes and trackless regions as the residences of Paulinus. See *ep.* 24.79–81 Green.

38. *Ep.* 23.35–36 Green.

39. *Ep.* 23.44–52 Green with Vir. *Ecl.* 8.108. See M. Roberts, "Paulinus Poem 11, Virgil's First *Eclogue*, and the Limits of *Amicitia*," *TAPA* 115 (1985): 271–82.

the traditional language of friendship, Paulinus pledged anew his obligations to "sweet friendship (*dulcis amicitia*)" (42). No perverse gossip could loose the yoke (*iugum*) of friendship from his neck.[40] More subtly, however, Paulinus engaged Ausonius in the allusive literary discourse that had expressed their deepest bonds for so many years. Ausonius's poetic epistle had asked Paulinus to see the eighth *Eclogue* as descriptive of their situation and to imagine Ausonius as a rejected lover. Paulinus in turn suggested that, against the background of Virgilian pastoral, an allegorical reading of the first *Eclogue* was more appropriate to his perspective on their troubled relationship: as Tityrus's god-given *otium* had disrupted his association with Meliboeus, so Paulinus's divinely inspired decision to live in Christian *otium* might also necessitate unwelcome separation from old friends.[41] To engage Ausonius in this manner was to honor him highly: *carmen* 11 declares that not even Cicero or Virgil is fit to share the yoke (*iugum*) of literary pursuits with Ausonius.[42] However far apart Paulinus and Ausonius might have drifted in recent years, poetry and Virgilian imagery still provided a vital bridge between their worlds. At the same time, of course, Paulinus's subtly crafted poetic allusions once again both elevate the very rhetorical arts that *carmen* 10 had decried and seek to elicit anew the schoolmaster's praise that Ausonius had once lavished on him.[43]

But perhaps Ausonius would have detected an even more poignant poetic allusion at the conclusion of *carmen* 11, one whereby Paulinus sought both to affirm and reconfigure in confident Christian terms his unlimited affection for Ausonius. Not many years before, Ausonius had commemorated in verse a number of Bordeaux's famous teachers.[44] His elegy for Tiberius Victor Minervius, first in the series, whose passing Ausonius had mourned as the loss of a father (*pater*),[45] ended with a reflection upon the uncertain fate of the soul after death: "And now, if anything remains after death, you live still, recalling the life which has passed away. But if nothing survives and our long repose knows no feeling (*sensus*), you have lived for yourself; your fame pleases us."[46] As Paulinus ended his last known poem to a teacher whom he, too, readily designated *pater*, he turned at this moment with greater certainty to that same question. In death—wherever their common Father should place him—

---

40. *Carm.* 11.44–45: "hoc nostra cervice iugum non scaeva resolvit / fabula."
41. For the possible range of application see Roberts, "Paulinus Poem 11," 278–82.
42. *Carm.* 11.38–39: "vix Tullius et Maro tecum / sustineant aequale iugum."
43. For example, Aus. *ep.* 17.30–31 Green (EW *ep.* 23).
44. Green, *Ausonius*, 328–29, dating the *Professores* to the later 380s. An argument for original composition in the late 360s with publication in the 380s is offered by Sivan, *Ausonius*, 160.
45. *Prof.* 1.38: "fletus es a nobis ut pater et iuvenis."
46. *Prof.* 1.39–42:

> et nunc, sive aliquid post fata extrema superfit,
>   vivis adhuc aevi, quod periit, meminens;
> sive nihil superest nec habent longa otia sensus,
>   tu tibi vixisti; nos tua fama iuvat.

as in life, Paulinus avowed, he would ever hold Ausonius in his mind, for "though the limbs slip away, the mind (*mens*), which survives because of its heavenly birth, must retain its feelings (*sensus*) and affections as it retains its life. And admitting forgetfulness no more than death, it lives and remembers for ever."[47]

It must have been soon after these lines were written that Ausonius died.[48] His life had spanned a remarkable period. Born in the opening years of Constantine's reign, Ausonius had risen from municipal professor to imperial tutor under Valentinian I, finally serving Gratian as praetorian prefect and ordinary consul. His patronage had assisted the careers of family and friends alike, including the precocious Paulinus. In his retirement, Ausonius had witnessed apparently with alarm the rising tide of ascetic fervor and Christian belief in imperial court and society under Theodosius. Such changes, particularly when they seemed to disrupt proven friendships, were surely hard to assess dispassionately. Thus Ausonius's final poems to Paulinus may appear nostalgic, even reactionary.

Addressed as it is to the fading figure of Ausonius, Paulinus's *carmen* 11 seemingly stands poised between an easily recognized, Ausonian past and an uncertain future. Understandably, therefore, many readers have discovered fragments of the age's turbulent social and religious history condensed into the intensely personal sentiments of this poem and the series of letters that it concludes. *Carmen* 11 is a moving final poetic testament to Paulinus's long relationship with this man who shaped his intellect and his life in ways we cannot fully know, while its allusive richness deftly memorializes the high literary culture of the late empire's aristocracy. At the same time, Paulinus's thinking here and in *carmen* 10 suggests the degree to which some, under the force of new spiritual impulses "to live for Christ," had begun to perceive traditionally construed *amicitia* and purely secular literature as insufficient. In these years Paulinus was finding both inadequate. His solution, notwithstanding the bold language of *carmen* 10, was not radical rejection but calculated reconceptualization. Such, perhaps, is the hallmark of Paulinus's thought hereafter: old ways could be reshaped and revitalized by new ideas and personalities. In late 394 and early 395 the forces of new ideas and the intrusion of new personalities propelled several rapid and remarkable turns of events.

---

47. *Carm.* 11.63–68:

> mens quippe, lapsis quae superstes artubus
>   de stirpe durat caeliti,
> sensus necesse est simul et affectus suos
>   retineat ut vitam suam;
> et ut mori sic oblivisci non capit,
>   perenne vivax et memor.

See also Walsh, "Paulinus of Nola," 570, for the observation that in these lines "Paulinus is telling Ausonius that Christian friendship at once deepens and transcends" the traditional notion of *amicitia*.

48. Étienne, *Bordeaux antique*, 344.

FOR MY YOKE IS SWEET

As he was composing these final exchanges with Ausonius and thereby deliberately making public his own anxieties about his past endeavors and his vast wealth, Paulinus was also engaged in a program of scriptural study. Scriptural reading looms behind such poetic projects as the *Laus Sancti Iohannis* (*carm.* 6) or the psalm paraphrases of *carmina* 7–9. Guidance was provided, perhaps through precept as well as example, by Amandus of Bordeaux, apparently a regular correspondent through these years. Paulinus's efforts are especially manifest in one of his letters (*ep.* 9) to this priest who had earlier prepared him for baptism.[49] Heavily imbued with images from the Psalms and the Gospels, assuring Amandus of Paulinus's continuing effort to "scale the heights of the virtues through the teaching (*doctrinae*) of the prophets and the apostles," Paulinus's letter already displays the allegorizing tendencies of his exegesis. His approach apparently found favor with Amandus, for the latter's praise of Paulinus led Delphinus—Bordeaux's notable bishop and the "common father" (*ep.* 9.1) of Amandus and Paulinus—to request from the latter "some discourse (*sermo*) on the Scriptures" that might reveal the treasure (*thesaurus*) of his heart.[50] With (feigned) reluctance Paulinus complied. His artful manipulation, through Biblical citation and allusion, of the *thesaurus* image suggested by Delphinus's own letter appropriately undercuts his own self-deprecating claim of inadequacy: "But I am a barren land; what can I do?"[51] A similarly subverted *recusatio,* also energized the roughly contemporary *carmen* 11, but now a Biblical rather than Virgilian chamber offers its literary riches.

It was, perhaps, Paulinus's desire to progress as a reader of scripture, as much as his ascetic inclinations, that led him to write to Jerome in the spring or early summer of 394, initiating an epistolary relationship that persisted, despite problems, until at least 400.[52] By 394 Jerome had been established in his monastery at Bethlehem for eight years. He had amassed a significant reputation not only as a Biblical scholar, translator, exegete, and historian but also as an ardent defender of asceticism. In virtually no area of his endeavors, however, had Jerome avoided controversy. After serving Damasus until the latter's death, he had left Italy in 385 under a cloud of suspicion and the indictment of the Roman church; his fanciful *Vita* of the hermit Paul of Thebes had drawn criticism; and more recently his furious attack upon the anti-ascetic Jovinian had scandalized many in Rome.[53]

---

49. *Ep.* 9. On the date see Fabre, *Essai,* 62–63.

50. *Ep.* 10. 1: "iubes nos in epistolis, quas ad te facimus, aliquem praeter officii de scripturis adicere sermonem, qui tibi thesaurum nostri cordis revelet."

51. *Ep.* 10.2: "sed quid faciam ager sterilis?"

52. For reconstructions and the chronology of the exchanges between Jerome and Paulinus (Paulinus's letters to Jerome do not survive) see P. Courcelle, "Paulin de Nole et Saint Jérôme," *REL* 25 (1947): 250–80; P. Nautin, "Études de chronologie hiéronymienne (393–397): III. Les premières relations entre Jérôme et Paulin de Nole," *REAug* 19 (1973): 213–39; Trout, "The Dates."

53. Kelly, *Jerome,* 180–89. On Jovinian see also D. G. Hunter, "Helvidius, Jovinian, and the Virginity of Mary in Late Fourth-Century Rome," *JECS* 1 (1993): 47–71.

How much Paulinus knew about Jerome before he wrote to him in 394 is not clear. He appears to have read Jerome's *Adversus Jovinianum*, for traces of it have been detected in both Paulinus's *carmen* 10 to Ausonius and in the *Laus Sancti Io-hannis*.[54] He may have known firsthand Jerome's *Vita Pauli* and the widely circulated *ep.* 22 to Eustochium,[55] as well as Jerome's commentaries on select Pauline letters and the minor prophets.[56] We may reasonably assume that something of Jerome's reputation had found its way to Paulinus in Spain through the letters of friends in Gaul or Italy, or perhaps through Nummius Aemilianus Dexter. The latter was the son of Pacianus, recent bishop of Barcelona, where Paulinus was soon to be ordained to the priesthood, and he had been proconsul of Asia between 379 and 387; he was about to become praetorian prefect of Italy (395).[57] He was also a committed Christian and the historian to whom Jerome's *De viris illustribus* (392–93) was dedicated.[58] Geography and interests make Dexter a likely acquaintance of Paulinus and a possible intermediary between Paulinus and Jerome. At the other end of the Mediterranean, one Eusebius of Cremona, a member of Jerome's Bethlehem monastery, was in a position to relate to Jerome something of Paulinus's character, his love of Christ, and his *contemptus saeculi*.[59] Paulinus and Eusebius may have met earlier at Milan.[60] In any case, Paulinus knew enough to turn to Jerome in 394 for advice on *divinarum scripturarum studia*.[61]

Paulinus's letter is lost, but Jerome's reply (*ep.* 53) suggests clearly that it dealt with scriptural matters. Jerome cites scriptural study and the fear of God as the common bonds that unite them (53.1); and the bulk of his letter is given over to a rapid exposition of the hermeneutical mysteries of the biblical books, intended to verify Jerome's assertion that a well-trained guide was requisite for anyone seeking real understanding of the truths embedded in the apparent "simplicity (*simplicitas*)" and "verbal crudity (*vilitas verborum*)" of Scripture (53.10). Throughout the letter Jerome parades his knowledge of Greek and Hebrew, as well as his classical learning, in order to offer himself as a mentor. Accordingly he invited Paulinus to join him in Bethlehem, where they would be not master and pupil, but scholastic

---

54. Duval, "Les premiers rapports," 179–93, 211–12; contra Nautin, "Études de chronologie III" 225–26.

55. See G. Guttilla, "Paolino di Nola e Girolamo," *Orpheus* 13 (1992): 278–94, for possible reflections of these works in Paulinian compositions of the later 390s.

56. Nautin, "Études de chronologie III," 226.

57. *PLRE* 1.251, "Dexter 3."

58. *De vir. ill. praef.* and 132 (Dexter). See further Kelly, *Jerome*, 174; and S. Rebenich, *Hieronymus und sein Kreis* (Stuttgart, 1992), 223.

59. So Jerome in his response to Paulinus's first letter. Jer. *ep.* 53.11: "[Eusebius] qui litterarum tuarum mihi gratiam duplicavit referens honestatem morum tuorum, contemptum saeculi, fidem amicitiae, amorem Christi."

60. Courcelle, "Paulin de Nole et Saint Jérôme," 265.

61. Jer. *ep* 53.1.

"comrades *(comites)*" (53.10). Jerome's enthusiastic response to Paulinus's letter—like his invitation several years later to another wealthy Spaniard aspiring to asceticism—may have been prompted by a vision of his correspondent as a potential patron for his Bethlehem foundation,[62] for Paulinus's letter had apparently also carried the news of his desire to divest himself of material goods. To this revelation Jerome responded with a passionate exhortation to precipitous secular renunciation: "If you hold your property in your own power, sell it; if not, throw it away. . . . To be sure, always procrastinating and dragging it out day after day, you say that unless you sell your little estates carefully and gradually, Christ will have nothing with which to nourish His poor. Nay, he has given everything to God who has offered himself. . . . He easily disdains everything, who always considers that he is going to die."[63]

The uncompromising demand of Jerome's letter, though it was not strictly heeded, must have reinforced Paulinus's doubts and anxieties and helped push him to declare his secular renunciation. Thus some time in late 394, between the time when he first wrote to Jerome and Christmas Day, when he was ordained to the priesthood,[64] Paulinus made public his plan "to purchase heaven and Christ for the price of his brittle riches."[65] Sexual relations with Therasia were now surely set aside,[66] and Paulinus must have begun the disposition of property through which he would, as he told both Ausonius and Severus, lend his riches to Christ through the medium of the poor and needy.[67] In such a salvation economy the prudent investor had limited options for the proper disposition of wealth. Paulinus

---

62. Rebenich, *Hieronymus und sein Kreis,* 229–30. Cp. Jer. *ep.* 71 with Kelly, *Jerome,* 213–14.

63. Jer. *ep.* 53.11: " si habes in potestate rem tuam, vende; si non habes, proice. . . . scilicet, nisi tu semper recrastinans et diem de die trahens caute et pedetemptim tuas possessiunculas vendideris, non habet Christus, unde alat pauperes suos. totum deo dedit, qui se obtulit. . . . facile contemnit omnia, qui se semper cogitat esse moriturum."

64. Trout, "The Dates."

65. So in *ep.* 1.1, written a few months after Paulinus's renunciation, Paulinus described the recent renunciation of Severus: "fragilis substantiae pretio caelum Christumque mercatus."

66. *Ep.* 1.1: "praesentium onerum decoctione." Jerome, *ep.* 58.6, is explicit on Therasia. F. E. Consolino, "Modelli di santità femminile nelle più antiche Passioni romane," *Augustinianum* 24 (1984): 95–96.

67. *Carm.* 10.71–76:

> non ut profanas abicit aut viles opes,
> > sed ut magis caras monet
> caelo reponi creditas Christo deo,
> > qui plura promisit datis,
> contempta praesens vel mage deposita sibi
> > multo ut rependat fenore.

Cp. Matt 19.21. *Ep.* 1.1: "vere intellegens super egenum et pauperem, quem in Christo esse et in quo Christum, ut ipse docuit, tegi pasci fenerari credidisti." Cp. Matt 25.37–40.

may also have formally renounced his senatorial rank.[68] Grand gestures were not inappropriate: Augustine had announced his conversion through the resignation of his professorial chair, and Marius Victorinus had made a greater stir by entering a church and publicly professing his faith.[69] Paulinus, a former provincial governor and suffect consul, well aware of the importance of public ritual, should have chosen his moment well for the *geste spectaculaire* that registered his renunciation.[70] That he did so is suggested both by the nearly immediate hostility that greeted his ascetic conversion in some circles and also by his forced presbyterial ordination at Barcelona on 25 December 394.

The storm foreshadowed in Paulinus's exchanges with Ausonius in 393 and 394 now broke. The wicked and foolish voices of worldly men began to clamor around him.[71] In Gaul Sulpicius Severus, who soon after learning of Paulinus's renunciation had followed suit,[72] was called on to defend both Paulinus and himself from the recriminations of certain *infideles*.[73] Although taking consolation in scriptural precedent and predictions of persecution (Matt 5.11), Paulinus nonetheless cautioned Severus against overzealous defense; "Let us displease these men, and be thankful that we displease those who find God displeasing."[74] Let them enjoy their pleasures, their offices (*dignitates*), and their wealth; let them be rich men in worldly goods, for they are without God's.[75] Moreover, too close association with such men, Paulinus feared, might infect Severus with their depravity or undermine his resolve.[76] So as Jerome had invited him to Bethlehem, Paulinus now invited Severus to join him in Barcelona, where they could offer each other support.[77] The rancor that in some quarters of southern Gaul had greeted the news of Paulinus's

68. See Amb. *ep.* 58.3 (*PL* 16) / 6.27.3 (*CSEL* 82): "migrasse a senatu." However, baptism may have already signaled his intention to avoid holding further offices.

69. Aug. *Conf.* 8.2.

70. Fontaine, "Valeurs," 580.

71. *Ep.* 1.2: "si nos interdum profana vel stulta quorundam saecularium verba circumlatrent." Paulinus's letter was written between Christmas 394 and Easter 395, but here it concerns events in late 394. Severus was clearly in southern Gaul, most likely in the region of Narbo, when Paulinus wrote, for Paulinus records that Severus's courier had required eight days to make the journey from Elusio to Barcelona, the Pyrenees presenting no obstacle (1.11). Elusio may be identified with a stop on the *Itinerarium Burdegalense* between Toulouse and Carcassone. See Fontaine, *Vie de Saint Martin*, 32–38, for the location of Severus's estate of Primuliacum between Toulouse and Narbo, "probablement aux confins mêmes de la Narbonnaise," and for Severus's residence here in the period 394–96. Chastagnol, in "Le diocèse civil d'Aquitaine," 284, accepted Fontaine's identification of Primuliacum with the area of modern Nauroze, but argued that this area was not near the border of the provinces of Narbonensis and Aquitaine.

72. Stancliffe, *St. Martin and His Hagiographer*, 18.

73. *Ep.* 1.2.

74. *Ep.* 1.6: "displiceamus ergo his et gratulemur isdem nos displicere, quibus et deus displicet."

75. *Ep.* 1.7.

76. See, for example., *ep.* 1.9.

77. *Ep.* 1.10.

renunciation was also expected in Italy. Writing to Sabinus of Piacenza after he learned of Paulinus and Therasia's decision to sell their property and confer the proceeds upon the poor, Ambrose, as we have seen, anticipated the outcry of the *proceres viri:* "That a man from that family, with that lineage, of that much talent, endowed with such great eloquence has abandoned the Senate and broken the continuity of a noble family: this cannot be borne."[78] Undoubtedly facilitated by his own public acts, and perhaps by his communications with friends in Italy as well,[79] the inflammatory news of Paulinus's conversion had traveled quickly through western aristocratic circles, in which ascetic claims were then eminently capable of provoking both deep respect and sharp disdain.[80]

No doubt public knowledge of Paulinus and Therasia's renunciation of their wealth also prompted the highly unusual presbyterial ordination of this *vir clarissimus* at Barcelona on 25 December 394.[81] The same letter that contained Paulinus's fervent admonitions to Severus also included a report of his recent unexpected ordination: "On the day of the Lord, when He deemed it fit to be born in the flesh, as He Himself is witness, by the sudden compulsion of the crowd yet, I believe, seized by His command, I was consecrated to the priesthood."[82] If the bishop Lampius and the church at Barcelona had hoped to profit financially from Paulinus's ascetic conversion, they were disappointed. Paulinus accepted ordination only on the condition that he was not attached to the church of Barcelona. By late 394 Paulinus was already planning his relocation to Nola and, perhaps, hoping for an ecclesiastical career in Campania.

If Paulinus openly testified that his mind was already set on another place,[83] he was considerably more circumspect regarding his clerical aspirations. It was his intention to settle at Nola, he informed Severus, that had prompted his resistance to ordination, not any distaste for the (mere) presbyterial rank (*locus*). Indeed, Severus was assured that Paulinus had hoped to begin his "holy slavery" at the bottom of the ladder, as a sacristan (*aedituus*).[84] Paulinus's humility was not necessarily disingenuous, but his thwarted desires conveniently buttressed one recently expressed attempt of the Roman church to formulate an ecclesiastical *cursus*. In 385 Siricius of

---

78. Amb. *ep.* 58.3 (PL 16) / 6.27.3 (CSEL 82).

79. See chapter 5.

80. Hence the animosities provoked by Jovinian and the counterattack upon him.

81. On the paucity of even bishops of senatorial background in the fourth century see F. Gilliard, "Senatorial Bishops in the Fourth Century," *HTR* 77 (1984): 153–75.

82. *Ep.* 1.10: "die domini, quo nasci carne dignatus est, repentina, ut ipse testis est, vi multitudinis, sed credo ipsius ordinatione correptus et presbyteratu initiatus sum." See also the contemporary *ep.* 2.2 (to Amandus): "vi subita invitus, quod fateor, adstrictus et multitudine strangulante conpulsus"; and *ep.* 3.4 (to Alypius), written later in the same year: "nam ego . . . a Lampio apud Barcilonem in Hispania per vim inflammatae subito plebis sacratus sim."

83. *Ep.* 1.10: "sed ut alio destinatus, alibi, ut scis, mente conpositus et fixus."

84. *Ep.* 1.10: "nam testor ipsum, quia et ab aeditui nomine et officio optavi sacram incipere servitutem."

Rome had offered one such plan to Himerius, bishop of Tarragona, a city that Paulinus considered one of his Spanish homes in the early 390s. For older converts to the *sacra militia*, Siricius advised a *cursus* that progressed with proper temporal interval from lector and exorcist to acolyte and subdeacon, and only later to deacon, presbyter, and bishop.[85] Indeed, Paulinus might have known that the irregularity of Ambrose's episcopal ordination had been mitigated only by his rapid promotion through the ranks in the week before his consecration.[86] In other ways as well Paulinus's actions colluded with papal attempts to regulate admission to clerical orders. His baptismal renunciation had not been sullied by further exercise of secular authority; and his sexual renunciation conformed to demands iterated by Siricius in his letter to Himerius.[87] If during the fall of 394 Paulinus was indeed envisioning a clerical career at Nola, then the unforeseen turn of events at Barcelona on Christmas Day was a spanner in the works because it had the potential to bind him to that city.

This development evidently caused Paulinus grave consternation on other grounds as well. In his letter to Severus and another to Amandus, Paulinus reflected on this intrusion of the divine will into his life. He publicly doubted his worthiness for such responsibility, although his neck (so recently chafed by the yoke of literary partnership with Ausonius) had necessarily if unwillingly accepted the "yoke of Christ (*iugum Christi*)."[88] In his new calling he requested the support of Severus and the continued guidance of Amandus, particularly with respect to his presbyterial duties.[89] Yet Paulinus also assured Severus that his ordination would not derail the plan (*ratio*) that he and Therasia had previously conceived.[90] Paulinus was acutely sensitive to the potential conflict between his recently undertaken monastic *propositum* and the demands of the priesthood. He wrote again to Jerome, someone from whom he might reasonably expect advice on reconciling clerical responsibilities with an ascetic or monastic calling and someone who had responded so warmly to his first letter in the previous year. But when Paulinus wrote that first letter to Jerome in 394 he had been neither monk nor priest; in early 395 (before Easter), he would claim to be both.

---

85. Siricius, *ep.* 1, *cap.* 10 (*PL* 13.1143). Cf. [Siricius] *ep.* 10 (*ad Gallos episcopos*), *cap.* 5 stating that only clerics should become bishops. On the *cursus* see Pietri, *Roma christiana*, 1:690–96; A. Rousselle, "Aspects sociaux du recrutement ecclésiastique au IVe siècle," *Mélanges de l'école française de Rome: Antiquité* 89 (1977): 358.

86. Paul. *V. Amb.* 3.9.

87. Siricius, *ep.* 1, *cap.* 6 (*PL* 13.1137–41), concerning deacons, priests, and bishops. The demand had already been lodged by canon 33 of Elvira and [Siricius] *ep.* 10 (*ad Gallos episcopos*), *cap.* 2 and would be restated by Innocent, *epp.* 2, *cap.* 9 and 6, *cap.* 1. See Pietri, *Roma christiana*, 689; Rousselle, "Aspects sociaux du recrutement ecclésiastique," 343–44, 362.

88. *Ep.* 1.10: "data igitur cervice in iugum Christi video maiora me meritis et sensibus opera tractare."

89. *Ep.* 2.3–4.

90. *Ep.* 1.10: "scito tamen voti communis eodem domino praestante salvam esse rationem."

The reply, probably reaching him later that summer (395) in Nola,[91] was markedly different in tone from Jerome's first letter. It was a seemingly suspicious and irritated Jerome who now addressed Paulinus's questions. The previous invitation to join Jerome in the Holy Land was now tactfully, if surprisingly, withdrawn. Jerome uncharacteristically pleaded his own inadequacy as a teacher and assured Paulinus that God's power was not limited to a narrow strip of earth in the Holy Land; true Christians have no need to worship at Jerusalem, for "the kingdom of God is within you" (Luke 17.21).[92] And while Jerome understood the dilemma provoked by Paulinus's ordination, this monk who had refused to fulfill his own presbyterial functions would offer Paulinus no compromising solution. Considering Paulinus's *propositum* and the ardor with which he had renounced the world, Jerome wrote, Paulinus's only choice was to abandon cities (including Jerusalem) and seek Christ in the deserted places of the countryside.[93] The same man could not be both cleric and monk: "Because then you ask me as a brother by which path you should proceed, I will speak with you frankly. If you wish to perform the duty of a priest, if perhaps the labor or the honor of the episcopate delights you, live in the cities and strongholds (*castella*) and make the salvation of others the profit of your soul. But if you desire to be what you are called, a monk (*monachus*), that is alone (*solus*), what are you doing in cities, which are surely not the dwelling places of solitaries but of crowds?"[94] A brief list of ascetic precepts followed. Jerome encouraged both Paulinus and his "holy sister" (Therasia) to limit their social associations and to complement simple habits of eating and dress with biblical study, prayer, and vigil. On dietary matters, Jerome noted, more could be gleaned from his *Adversus Jovinianum*. Significantly, Jerome further advised Paulinus to distribute alms to the poor and to the monastic communities only with his own hands, for "faith (*fides*)" was rare among men.[95] Do not, he commanded, by immoderate judgment give the property of the poor to those who are not poor.[96] Always acutely self-conscious, and now writing to a renowned poet, Jerome care-

91. Again, Paulinus's letter is lost. On the chronology see Trout, "The Dates."

92. Jer. *ep.* 58.1–4.

93. *Ep.* 58.4: "considerans et propositum tuum et ardorem, quo saeculo renuntiasti, differentias in locis arbitror, si urbibus et frequentia urbium derelicta in agello habites et Christum quaeras in solitudine."

94. *Ep.* 58.5: "Quia igitur fraterne interrogas, per quam viam incedere debeas, revelata tecum facie loquar. si officium vis exercere presbyteri, si episcopatus te vel opus vel honos forte delectat, vive in urbibus et castellis et aliorum salutem fac lucrum animae tuae. sin autem cupis esse, quod diceris, monachus, id est solus, quid facis in urbibus, quae utique non sunt solorum habitacula, sed multorum?" Amb. *ep.* 63.66 (395), describing Eusebius of Vercella as a monk-bishop, offers a pointed contrast to Jerome's words here; see Lienhard, *Paulinus of Nola*, 89–90.

95. Jer. *ep.* 58.6: "pauperibus et fratribus refrigeria sumptuum manu propria distribue; rara est in hominibus fides."

96. Jer. *ep.* 58.7: "ne inmoderato iudicio rem pauperum tribuas non pauperibus."

fully rounded off this admonitory passage of his letter with allusions to both Lucan and Persius. In Jerome's next words, however, Paulinus may have detected not only an echo of Sallust but also, perhaps, unknown to Jerome, of the very advice he himself had recently offered to Severus: "To be a Christian is the great thing," Jerome wrote, "not to seem one. And somehow those things which are more pleasing to the world, displease Christ."[97]

The curiosities and ambivalence of Jerome's response find explanation both in the troubled state of his affairs in Palestine and in his emerging suspicions about Paulinus. Both factors would impede the promise of friendship raised by their first epistolary exchange in the previous year and prompt Paulinus's turn instead to Augustine and to Jerome's former comrade turned rival, Rufinus of Aquileia. When Paulinus's second letter, carried by his Gallo-Roman compatriot and Jerome's future adversary, the priest Vigilantius,[98] reached Jerome in Bethlehem, the latter was apparently already under a ban of excommunication issued by John of Jerusalem. The opening volleys in the complicated Origenist controversy, destined to drag on for years, had been fired the previous year when Epiphanius of Salamis began a campaign to expose Origenist sympathizers; by the summer of 395 the Christians of Palestine were "in a state of declared war."[99] Unwittingly Paulinus's letter (and his letter carrier) entered the fray. Vigilantius apparently spent the first part of his Palestinian visit at Jerusalem in the company of the "other side," that is, at the monastic foundation of Paulinus's relative Melania the Elder and Rufinus.[100] The latter had been Jerome's friend since youth but now stood accused by Epiphanius of Origenist leanings and was perceived by Jerome as the ally of his enemy John of Jerusalem. Indeed, Jerome's caustic remarks on the appropriate methods of alms distribution had perhaps been provoked by Vigilantius's perceived favoritism to the (apparently better endowed) monasteries of Melania and Rufinus.[101] And when Vigilantius abruptly cut short his stay at Bethlehem despite Jerome's calculated displays of anti-Origenist orthodoxy,[102] Jerome's

97. *Ep.* 58.7: "esse Christianum grande est, non videri. et nescio quomodo plus placent mundo, quae Christo displicent." Cp. Jer. *ep.* 125.7. Sallust, *Cat.* 54: "esse quam videri bonus [Cato] malebat."

98. Vigilantius was born, according to Jerome's *C. Vig.* 1, at Calagurris. Apparently a *viculus* of the *civitas* of Convenae, Calagurris was in the Gallic province of Novempopulana. The site has been identified with modern St.-Martory; see M. Massie, "Vigilance de Calagurris face à la polémique hiéronymienne," *Bulletin de littérature ecclésiastique* 81 (1980): 89, with bibliography; and the map at M. Labrousse, *Toulouse antique* (Paris, 1968), 324. On Vigilantius see chapter 8.

99. P. Nautin, "Études de chronologie hiéronymienne (393–397): I," *REAug* 18 (1972): 209–17; "II," *REAug* 19 (1973): 69–86; "III,"*REAug* 19 (1973): 213–39; "IV," *REAug* 20 (1974): 251–84. Kelly, *Jerome*, 195–209, quote 201. E. Clark, *The Origenist Controversy: The Cultural Construction of an Early Christian Debate* (Princeton, 1992). See also chapter 8, this volume.

100. Nautin, "Études de chronologie III," 231.

101. Nautin, "Études de chronologie III," 237–38; Kelly, *Jerome*, 193.

102. Jer. *ep.* 61.3. See further Nautin, "Études de chronologie III," 232.

suspicions about Paulinus's letter carrier, whom he would subsequently dub Paulinus's "insignificant client courier," duly increased.[103] Seemingly snubbed by Vigilantius and embroiled in theological controversy, Jerome surely deemed it an inopportune time to renew his earlier invitation to Paulinus. Jerome's letter, however, was largely silent on these problems, and it would have been left to Vigilantius to provide the background that, in the event, only fanned the flames of discord.[104]

If the activities of Vigilantius troubled Jerome, so too, it seems, did the news contained in Paulinus's letter and the works that Paulinus sent with it, which included a recent prose panegyric to the emperor Theodosius and, most likely, his poetic encomium and mini-epic (*epyllion*) on John the Baptist (*carm.* 6). While Jerome's blunt claims for the exclusivity of the monastic *propositum* and his referral of Paulinus to his *Adversus Jovinianum* apparently adumbrated suspicions about the depth of Paulinus's ascetic commitment, the panegyric and poems that Paulinus had forwarded to Jerome prompted him to reactivate the "literary criticism" with which he ended *ep.* 53. In his first letter, as he had steered Paulinus away from false teachers of scripture, Jerome had also knowingly cautioned (the poet) Paulinus against guides previously trained in secular literature or those, such as the unnamed but surely intended Proba, who composed puerile Virgilian centos.[105]

Jerome now employed the opportunity provided by his receipt of Paulinus's panegyric and other works to advance the critical front he had established in *ep.* 53. Jerome did praise Paulinus's panegyric effusively, proclaiming Theodosius fortunate to be defended by "such an orator of Christ."[106] But his comments dwell most heavily on matters of style, diction, and organization,[107] and he rounded off his observations on the work with rather backhanded praise. If such are your first efforts (*rudimenta*), Jerome announced to Paulinus, what a "soldier" you will be when disciplined (*exercitatus*)![108] This prediction Jerome quickly clarified. He ended his letter by exhorting Paulinus to add scriptural knowledge to his already proven talent, discretion, and eloquence. Then, surely, Paulinus would "hold our citadel and ascending with Joab the summit of Zion sing upon the housetops what he had learned in his chambers."[109] Or as Jerome had phrased it some lines earlier, if Paulinus could but learn to understand the inner meaning of scripture and add this final foundation to his work, then "we would possess nothing more beautiful,

103. Jer. *ep.* 58.11. Cp. Jer. *ep.* 61.3: "portitorem clientulum." The letter was written a year or two after Vigilantius's stay in Bethlehem; see F. Cavallera, *Saint Jérôme, sa vie et son oeuvre* (Louvain, 1922), 2:45.
104. On Vigilantius's later activities see chapter 8.
105. Jer. *ep.* 53.7. For the identification of Jerome's target, the *garrula anus*, as Proba, see Duval, "Les premiers rapports," 193–205.
106. Jer. *ep.* 58.8. On the panegyric see chapter 5.
107. Cp. Jerome's searing indictment of Jovinian on similar grounds (*Ad. Jov.* 1.1–3).
108. Jer. *ep.* 58.8: "qui talia habes rudimenta, qualis exercitatus miles eris!"
109. Jer. *ep.* 58.11.

nothing more learned, and nothing more Latinate than your books."[110] Then might Paulinus surpass Tertullian, Cyprian, Victorinus, Lactantius, Arnobius, and Hilary.[111] Paulinus's "books," that is, were being sent back for revision.

If Jerome considered his remarks flattering,[112] they may have sounded much more ambiguous to Paulinus. But surely Paulinus's poetry did puzzle (and even infuriate) Jerome, for Paulinus's attempt to repackage biblical passages into classicizing verse for elite consumption produced some curious transformations of both scripture and theology. Jerome, it seems, had read and apparently disapproved of Paulinus's encomium on John the Baptist. Perhaps Jerome already knew it when he wrote his first letter to Paulinus.[113] More certainly he did when he wrote his second, for he quickly signaled his discomfort with *carmen* 6 by uncustomarily excluding John from the series of Biblical "first men (*principes*)" of the monastic *propositum* that he offered to Paulinus as incentives and exemplars. If we turn to the authority of scripture, Jerome informed Paulinus, we have as our *principes* Elijah and Elisha.[114] In similar contexts elsewhere, however, Jerome regularly enlisted John as the *princeps monachorum:* preaching on the Gospel of John, commenting on Mark, exhorting another would-be monk, and in his widely circulated letter to Eustochium, a text probably known to Paulinus, Jerome consistently invoked the image of the Baptist.[115] Having recently composed an *epyllion* presenting John as the prototypical ascetic *exemplum,* Paulinus could not have missed the slight, an omission whose own anomalous status in Jerome's practice suggests that it was provoked by the latter's reading of Paulinus's idiosyncratic work. For as biblical epic Paulinus's *Laus Sancti Iohannis* may adroitly link the New Testament paraphrases of Iuvencus and Sedulius,[116] but as exegesis it contrasts sharply with the thought of Jerome as well as other contemporaries. Against the current, Paulinus invented an infancy and youth for John,[117] and he reconfigured Christian history

110. Jer. *ep.* 58.9: "si haberes hoc fundamentum, immo quasi extrema manus in tuo opere duceretur, nihil pulchrius, nihil doctius nihilque Latinius tuis haberemus voluminibus."

111. Jer. *ep.* 58.10.

112. Jer. *ep.* 58.11: "quin potius vel errare me aestimato vel amore labi quam amicum adulatione decipere."

113. Duval, "Les premiers rapports," 203–5, arguing that Jerome's denunciation of Proba in *ep.* 53 was triggered by an echo of her cento in Paulinus's *carm.* 6. Cp., for example, *Cento* 29–30 and *carm.* 6.1–2.

114. Jer. *ep.* 58.5: "ad scripturarum auctoritatem redeam, noster princeps Helias, noster Helisaeus."

115. Jer. *Homilia in Iohannem Evangelistam (CCSL* 78, 517–18); *Tractatus in Marci Evangelium (CCSL* 78, 453–54); *ep.* 125.7; *ep.* 22.36.

116. Paulinus knew Iuvencus's text; see Flury, "Das sechste Gedicht." And Sedulius apparently knew *carm.* 6; cp., for example, *Carm. Pasch.* 2.35 and *carm.* 6.14. See C. Springer, *The Gospel as Epic in Late Antiquity* (Leiden, 1988).

117. *Carm.* 6.205–18. Absent from Luke and Matthew of course, but also from Iuvencus and Proba. Ambrose explictly denied John a regular childhood (*Expositio Evangelii secundam Lucam* 2.30 [*SC* 45, 85–86]).

and theology to credit John's baptism of repentance with the salvific power that
Jerome and others were so carefully preserving for the baptism of forgiveness
through Christ's grace.[118] Moreover, to Jerome's John, "first of the monks (*princeps
monachorum*)," Paulinus opposed a John glossed as a "demigod (*semideus vir*)," which
was not only Statius's term for the legendary Argonauts but also, according to Au-
gustine, the term with which Porphyry's contemporary Cornelius Labeo had en-
rolled Plato among the "divine powers (*numina*)."[119] Understandably then,
Jerome's praise of Paulinus as a Christian writer had to be highly qualified.

It is probable that Paulinus received Jerome's "literary criticism," especially in the
light of Vigilantius's report of other events in Palestine, with some chagrin. If, like
some modern scholars, Paulinus also detected a slight to Ambrose in Jerome's as-
sessment of Latin Christian letters, he may have had further reasons to reconsider his
overtures to the monk and scholar of Bethlehem.[120] Nonetheless, Paulinus's relations
with Jerome continued for another five or six years after this epistolary exchange of
395.[121] The only surviving letter from their further correspondence, Jerome's *ep.* 85
to Paulinus from 399, reveals Paulinus persisting in referring exegetical questions to
Jerome: requesting a commentary on Daniel and explanations of God's hardening
of Pharaoh's heart (Exod 7.13; Rom 9.16) and of Paul's designation of the children of
baptized parents as *sancti* (1 Cor 7.14).[122] Jerome's responses, despite his protestations
of friendship, were terse; and the commentary on Daniel, when it was finally com-
pleted in 407, was dedicated to Pammachius and Marcella, not Paulinus.

It is perhaps surprising that relations between Paulinus and Jerome were main-
tained at all in the later 390s. The years after Vigilantius's return from the east saw
Jerome engaged in full-scale assault against this priest and former familiar of
Paulinus who now accused Jerome of Origenism (and eventually even attacked his
asceticism).[123] Moreover, in the summer of 397 Rufinus returned to Italy, and
shortly thereafter Paulinus struck up a friendship with this learned monk who had
been Melania's companion in Jerusalem for many years, but whose divisive quar-
rel with Jerome now spilled over into aristocratic Christian circles in Italy.[124] In

118. *Carm* 6.255–75, esp. 258–67. See Amb. *Expos. Luc.* 2.79; Chrys. *Hom.* 10.2; Jer. *Tract. in Marci
Evangelium* 1 (*CCSL* 78, 453): "Illud datum est in paenitentia, hoc in gratia. Ibi paenitentia tribuitur, ibi
venia: hic victoria." Prudentius, on the other hand, appears more comfortable with this notion: cp.
Cath. 71–77 with S. Costanza, "Rapporti letterari tra Paolino e Prudenzio," *Atti del Convegno*, 36.

119. Aug. *De civ. Dei.* 2.14

120. See Inglebert, *Les romains chrétiens*, 281.

121. Courcelle, "Paulin de Nole et Saint Jérôme," 274–79 for the difficulty of reconstructing any
later exchanges. See further chapter 8.

122. See Courcelle, "Paulin de Nole et Saint Jérôme," 266–71; Kelly, *Jerome*, 240–42.

123. Jer. *ep.* 61 of 396 or 397 and the *C. Vig.* of 406. See Kelly, *Jerome*, 206–7; Clark, *The Origenist
Controversy*, 34–36. For Paulinus's close relations with Vigilantius in 396 see Paul. *ep.* 5.

124. On the presence of Rufinus at Rome or the monastery of Ursacius at Pinetum near Terracina
between 397 and his departure for Aquileia in 399 see, F. X. Murphy, *Rufinus of Aquileia (345- 411): His
Life and Works* (Washington 1945), 82, 89–92; and C. P. Hammond, "The Last Ten Years of Rufinus'

400 Melania herself returned to Italy after twenty-seven years in the Holy Land and was magnificently received at Nola.[125] Finally, in late 395, Paulinus discovered in Augustine a mind more compatible with his than Jerome's.[126] If Jerome seemed hostile to Christian poetry, Augustine, in the letter of 396 that spurred Paulinus's correspondence with Licentius, virtually invited its composition.[127] And if Jerome endorsed a "professional" discipline of biblical interpretation that privileged the skills of the trained guide, Augustine came to champion the more egalitarian "biblical conference" as the path to advanced understanding of scripture.[128] Perhaps taking his cue from Paulinus himself, Augustine's unfinished *De doctrina christiana* of 396 / 97 and then the *Confessions*, appearing between 397 and 401,[129] offered an *Apologia contra Hieronymum* whose emphasis on human love (*caritas*) as the wellspring of revelation would have both flattered and appealed to Paulinus, whose poems and letters consistently celebrated the ideals of friendship.[130] As he wrote his second letter to Jerome from Barcelona in early 395, however, Paulinus could have foreseen none of these developments. Nevertheless, such were the fruits of Paulinus's decision, in the wake of his renunciation and ordination, to send letters of announcement via Vigilantius to the monastic communities of the East and to the bishops of North Africa through the courier Julianus (*ep.* 3.1). It was not at Barcelona but at Nola that Paulinus received the replies to those letters.

Paulinus left Barcelona for Italy some time after Easter of 395 (25 March).[131] The first stage of his journey probably took him overland through Narbonensis, but he seems to have arrived in Italy by sea, stopping in Rome before continuing to Campania and Nola.[132] A few months before abandoning Spain forever,

---

Life and the Date of His Move South from Aquileia," *JTS* 28 (1977): 379–80. Murphy, "Rufinus of Aquileia and Paulinus of Nola," *REAug* 2 (1956): 79–81, seems not to consider the possibility of a meeting at this time; the earliest proof of their friendship is a letter from Paulinus to Severus in 404 (*ep.* 28.5). On these matters see chapter 8.

125. Paul. *ep.* 29.12. This letter, dated by Fabre, *Essai,* 32–33, to 400 is the cornerstone of the chronology of Melania's movements. Ancillary evidence in support of (or at least not in contradiction) is examined by N. Moine, "Melaniana," 24–45.

126. See chapter 8.

127. Aug. *ep.* 31.7 with Paulinus's *ep.* 8 to Licentius. See also Aug. *ep.* 26.5 (to Licentius). Pace H. Westra, "Augustine and Poetic Exegesis," in *Grace, Politics and Desire: Essays on Augustine,* ed. H. A. Meynell (Calgary, 1990), 95.

128. M. Vessey, "Conference and Confession: Literary Pragmatics in Augustine's *Apologia contra Hieronymum.*" *JECS* 1 (1993): 175–213.

129. O'Donnell, *Confessions,* xli–ii.

130. Vessey, "Conference and Confession," 185–213. For another perspective on the *De doctrina christiana* as a response to Jerome's *ep.* 58 see J. Doignon, "'Nos bons hommes de foi': Cyprien, Lactance, Victorin, Optat, Hilaire (Augustin, *De doctrina christiana,* IV, 40, 61)," *Latomus* 22 (1963): 795–805. On Paulinus and *amicitia* see chapter 8.

131. *Ep.* 1.11.

132. Paulinus's route is uncertain. *Carm.* 12.25–27, the *nat.* of 395, shows Paulinus undecided, suggesting he might travel by land or sea. *Carm.* 13.32–34, the *nat.* of January 396, indicates an arrival (the previous summer) at Italy or Nola by sea, although the language is obviously heavily metaphorical as

shortly after his Christmas ordination, Paulinus composed the first of his (extant) *natalicia*, the series of poems that annually commemorated Saint Felix on his "birthday," 14 January. The appearance of this poem suddenly reminds us of an element of Paulinus's piety little in evidence in his other writings of the Spanish years: his profound reverence for the cult of the martyrs. Yet in this respect, too, the period of Paulinus's Spanish residence may have been a vital link between his earlier years—when as a boy he had first stood in awe before the tomb of Felix or as governor of Campania had attended the feast day celebrations and financed the construction of a road and a shelter for the poor at the site—and the years from 395 until his death in 431, when he lived almost all his days near the *aula* of Felix. For Spain, too, possessed its martyrs; and Paulinus surely paid them respect. At Complutum, as we have seen, Paulinus and Therasia laid their newborn Celsus to rest *ad sanctum*. Complutum, however, was not alone in claiming a *martyrium* and martyr's cult in the late fourth century. In the *Peristephanon* of Paulinus's contemporary, Prudentius, Complutum shares this distinction with, most notably, Caesaraugusta, Tarraco, and Barcino, three cities that Paulinus had proudly opposed to Ausonius's less flattering list of Spanish towns. Indeed, the eighteen martyrs of Caesaraugusta and Fructuosus of Tarraco provided the primary subjects for two of Prudentius's hymns, poems perhaps composed while Paulinus and Therasia were living in Spain.[133] In fewer lines, Prudentius recalled the cult of Cucufas at Barcino, city of Lampius and site of Paulinus's ordination.[134] Visitors to these shrines shed their tears and implored the heavenly intercession of the tombs' occupants.[135] Like Paulinus, they must have hoped that the recently deceased would add their voices to those of the saints.

If Paulinus did attend the tombs of these Spanish saints, by late 394 anticipation of the joy he expected to feel on reunion with Felix must have tempered his enthusiasm.[136] To Severus in early 395 and in the first *natalicium* Paulinus expressed his longing to return to Nola and the threshold of Felix.[137] Throughout the

---

well. *Ep.* 1.11 suggests the possibility of meeting Severus en route, presumably in Narbonensis, while a letter of 396 to Severus (*ep.* 5.22) speaks of Paulinus's property interests at Narbo. On Paulinus's cold reception at Rome by Pope Siricius see *ep.* 5.14 (summer 396).

133. Caesaraugusta: Prud. *Peristeph.* 4; Tarraco: *Peristeph.* 6, *Peristeph.* 4.21–24. Many believe Prudentius to have been a reader of Paulinus; see, for example, J.-L. Charlet, "Prudence, lecteur de Paulin de Nole: A propos du 23e quatrain du *Dittochaeon*," *REAug* 21 (1975): 55–62; S. Costanza, "Rapporti letterari," 25–65. But although the geography of the lives and careers of Paulinus and Prudentius overlaps considerably (northeastern Spain and Italy) and poetic borrowing seems demonstrable in some cases, the uncertain chronology of Prudentius's biography and poetry makes the lines of dependence difficult to verify. See A. M. Palmer, *Prudentius on the Martyrs* (Oxford, 1989), 20–31; and for literary and social aspects of the *Peristephanon* see M. Roberts, *Poetry and the Cult of the Martyrs* (Michigan, 1993).

134. *Peristeph.* 4.33–34.

135. For example, Prud. *Peristeph.* 1.7–15.

136. *Carm.* 12.13–14: "liceat . . . pia reddere coram / vota et gaudentes inter gaudere tumultus."

137. *Ep.* 1.10; *carm.* 12.10–14.

years he had spent away from Nola, he could then say, he had never been absent in mind.[138] In the *natalicium* he wrote at Nola for the festival of 396, he claimed that even during the previous three *lustra* of his life lived elsewhere he had always called on Felix in times of distress.[139] In January 395, as he contemplated his imminent move to Nola and addressed his thoughts in poetry to Felix, Paulinus returned again to the metaphor that had served him well in his final exchange the previous year with Ausonius: "There, under your dominion, Felix, we well bear the sweet yoke (*iugum*), the light burden, and pleasant servitude."[140] Indeed, under that yoke, Paulinus, now monk and priest, eventually bishop, would fulfill the exhortation with which Jerome had closed his second letter to Paulinus: "Let the church esteem you noble, as before the Senate did."[141]

138. *Carm.* 12.17: "quamvis non mente remoti."

139. *Carm.* 13.10–17: "nam te mihi semper ubique propinquum / inter dura viae vitaeque incerta vocavi" (12–13).

140. *Carm.* 12.32–33: "illic dulce iugum, leve onus blandumque feremus / servitium sub te domino." Cp. Matt 11.30: "Iugum enim meum suave est, et onus meum leve."

141. Jer. *ep.* 58.11: "nobilem te ecclesia habeat, ut prius senatus habuit."

CHAPTER 5

—•—

Paulinus at Nola

395–431

Paulinus arrived in Rome sometime in the summer of 395, spending time there before proceeding to Nola. Although rebuffed at the empire's ancient capital by Pope Siricius, Paulinus was soon grandly received by the clergy of Campania. Nola now became his home and remained so until his death in 431. These long Nolan years unfortunately are not evenly documented, for the majority of Paulinus's surviving letters and poems are concentrated in the years 395–408. Thereafter the record is woefully erratic. Nevertheless the rich and varied works composed at Nola, coupled with the observations of outsiders, permit sometimes vivid reconstructions of parts of Paulinus's world. Subsequent chapters explore particular aspects of Paulinus's life and thought as these bear on the problem of ascetic renunciation, the development of the cult of Felix, and the paramount theological controversies of the age. This chapter first considers the evidence for Paulinus's engagement with and reaction to some of the decisive political and military events unfolding in the empire around him and then examines his role in the emerging monastic movement in the pre-Benedictine West. Together these two perspectives help to situate Paulinus's life within the complicated nexus of political, military, cultural, and spiritual forces shaping the late antique world. Although Paulinus's role in shaping the emerging forms of the monastic life has continually attracted attention, few have recognized that neither in Spain nor at Nola was Paulinus insulated from the political uncertainties and military troubles of the regimes of Theodosius and Honorius.

EMPERORS, POPES, AND BARBARIANS

The poems and letters that survive from Paulinus's years in Spain yield virtually no hint that the remarkable events transpiring elsewhere in the empire interested or concerned him. Writings now lost, however, as well as comments made later by Paulinus himself, suggest that he was well informed, perhaps in part by old friends in Rome and Milan, about developments in Italy in the early and mid-390s.[1] Indeed, it is unlikely that a man of Paulinus's previous political background and current ascetic inclinations would have relocated his household to central Italy without some reconnaissance. Thus it may be more than coincidence that Paulinus abandoned Spain for Italy at the first possible moment after the usurping regime of Arbogast and Eugenius met its end at the battle of the Frigidus River in September 394. In fact, it is tempting to link the timing of Paulinus's renunciation to the new horizons opened up by Theodosius's victory. Both the tense political climate in Italy under the usurpers and the public resurgence of reactionary religious sentiments among some of the Roman aristocracy, a movement facilitated by Eugenius's need to secure a power base, should have cautioned against an earlier move. Thus a review of these events and their aftermath is in order because they demonstrate both the continuing vitality of paganism in Paulinus's Italy and the sharp political and religious divisions that could still fracture the Italian aristocracy.

In the late summer of 394 the eastern emperor Theodosius I had once again marched from Constantinople with a Roman and Gothic army against a western usurper.[2] Like his defeat of Maximus's forces in the late summer of 388, the battle of the Frigidus River was a demonstration of the diplomatic and military resourcefulness with which Theodosius thwarted political fragmentation and ensured dynastic continuity. In May 392, as Ausonius was seeking to prod Paulinus from his silence, the young Valentinian II, reinstalled in the West after Maximus's fall, had died at Vienne under circumstances still mysterious, either by suicide or as the victim of his Frankish *magister militum* Arbogast.[3] In any case, three months after Valentinian's death the pagan Arbogast raised to the purple Eugenius, a former teacher of rhetoric, a minor palatine official, and a Christian.[4] When the new regime's attempts to win recognition and legitimacy from Theodosius foundered,[5] Arbogast and Eugenius turned their attention to the aristocracy of Italy and Rome. Here they found a more receptive audience, some of whom, including perhaps Virius Nicomachus Flavianus, may have been troubled by the prospect of yet another child emperor signaled by Theodosius's elevation of Honorius to the rank

1. Contact with Milan, and perhaps Ambrose himself, is indicated by Ambrose's nearly immediate knowledge of Paulinus's renunciation and (intended) move to Nola. Amb. *ep.* 58.1 (*PL* 16) / 6.27.1 (*CSEL* 82). For Paulinus's contact with Rome through Endelechius, see below.

2. On the events of these years see O. Seeck, *Geschichte des Untergangs der antiken Welt* (Stuttgart, 1920), 5:217–59; E. Stein, *Histoire du Bas-Empire*, trans. J.-R. Palanque (Paris, 1959), 1:191–218, 2:520–35; A. H. M. Jones, *The Later Roman Empire, 284–602: A Social, Economic and Administrative Survey* (Norman, 1964), 159–69; Matthews, *Western Aristocracies*, 223–52; A. Lippold, *Theodosius der Grosse und seine Zeit*, 2d ed. (Munich, 1980), 45–51, 134–35. McLynn, *Ambrose*, 335–60.

3. Ruf. *HE* 11.31; Zos. 4.53–54; *et al.* See B. Croke, "Arbogast and the Death of Valentinian II," *Historia* 25 (1976): 235–44, and F. Paschoud, *Zosime: Histoire nouvelle* (Paris, 1979), 2.2:455–57, arguing respectively for and against suicide.

4. On Eugenius see J. Straub, "Eugenius," *RAC* 6 (1966): 860–77.

5. Straub, "Eugenius," 862–64; Matthews, *Western Aristocracies*, 239.

of Augustus on 23 January 393;[6] and some, to judge by the later tone of Eugenius's regime, may have been disquieted by Theodosius's increasingly severe anti-pagan legislation.[7] By April 393 the new court had moved to northern Italy, and Eugenius had been recognized at Rome.[8] As early as the summer of 393 the new emperor may have co-opted the influential pagan Nicomachus Flavianus as praetorian prefect and appointed his son, the younger Flavianus, *praefectus urbi*.[9] The Elder Flavianus's Eugenian prefecture, although effectively limited to Italy, was crowned by the highly esteemed ordinary consulship for 394 (unrecognized by Theodosius).[10]

Although probably not the original intentions of Arbogast or Eugenius, who initially hoped to avoid religious confrontation and sought reconciliation with the devoutly Christian eastern court,[11] the overtures to Rome's aristocracy produced the grounds for a revitalized public paganism. Despite the earlier efforts of Gratian and Theodosius to bankrupt the state cult and to hinder its ritual life, pagan sym-

6. The case is made by T. Honoré, "Some Writings of the Pagan Champion," 16–17. Flavianus's inclusion among the disaffected hinges upon the attractive thesis that he should be identified as the historical figure behind the senator Maecius Faltonius Nicomachus of the *Historia Augusta*'s *V. Tac.* See also T. Grünewald, "Der letzte Kampf des Heidentums in Rom? Zur postumen Rehabilitation des Virius Nicomachus Flavianus," *Historia* 41 (1992): 472–73, although the latter underestimates the possible extent of dissatisfaction with Theodosius's religious policies.

7. *CTh* 16.10.10 (24 February 391); 16.10.11 (16 June 391); 16.10.12 (8 November 392). On 16.10.10 and 11 as two constitutions deriving from a single imperial decision see J. Gaudemet, "La condemnation des practiques païennes en 391," *Epektasis: Mélanges patristiques offerts au Cardinal Jean Daniélou*, ed. J. Fontaine and C. Kannengiesser (Paris, 1972), 597–602. See further P.-P. Joannou, *La législation imperiale et la christianisation de l'empire romain, 311–476* (Rome, 1972), 47–48; Lippold, *Theodosius der Grosse*, 45–47; Matthews, *Western Aristocracies*, 237–38. Both Arbogast and Eugenius had connections to the senatorial aristocracy of Italy. See, for example, Sym. *ep.* 3.60–61 (389, 385) to Ricomer, uncle of Arbogast, in which Eugenius is styled *frater meus*.

8. *ICUR* n.s. I.1449 (= *ILCV* 2971A) of 14 April 393.

9. On Flavianus see below; on the urban prefecture of Flavianus Iunior see Chastagnol, *Les fastes*, 241–42, and Chastagnol, *La préfecture urbaine à Rome sous le Bas-Empire* (Paris, 1960), 163–64, and *PLRE* 1:346, "Flavianus 14."

10. For Flavianus's career between his vicariate in Africa (noted in chapter 2) and 393 see *PLRE* 1:347–49, "Flavianus 15"; with J.-P. Callu, "Les préfectures de Nicomaque Flavien," *Mélanges d'histoire ancienne offerts à William Seston* (Paris, 1974), 78–79; J. J. O'Donnell, "The Career of Virius Nicomachus Flavianus," *Phoenix* 32 (1978): 134–35; D. Vera, "La carriera di Virius Nicomachus Flavianus e la prefettura dell'Illirico orientale nel IV secolo d.C.," *Athenaeum* 61 (1983): 41–42; T. Honoré, "Some Writings of the Pagan Champion"; J. Matthews, "Nicomachus Flavianus's Quaestorship"; R. Malcolm Errington, "The Praetorian Prefectures of Virius Nicomachus Flavianus," *Historia* 61 (1992): 446–48. It is not certain when Flavianus became prefect under Eugenius, but it is unlikely that he moved directly from his Theodosian prefecture to his Eugenian one with no temporal or constitutional hiatus, as Callu, "Les préfectures," 77, and Errington, "The praetorian Prefectures," 445–46, argue. For the case that Flavianus's Theodosian prefecture ended well before his Eugenian one began (perhaps as early as late 391) see Vera, "La carriera," 58, esp. n. 127. For the consulship of 394 see *CIL* 6.1782 and R. Bagnall et al., *Consuls*, 322.

11. Straub, "Eugenius," 864–65; Matthews, *Western Aristocracies*, 240–41.

pathies had persisted among the Roman aristocracy. Undeterred by the failures of 383 and 384, wherein Ambrose had marshaled the court's effective resistance, pagan senators continued their requests for the restoration of the Altar of Victory to the Curia and the renewal of state subsidies for the priestly colleges.[12] Eugenius's elevation renewed their hopes. After two refusals, the new emperor, increasingly dependent on the support of the senatorial aristocracy and perhaps pressured by Flavianus, conceded. The appropriate funds were discreetly provided to prominent individuals, and the Altar of Victory was restored to the Curia.[13]

Eugenius himself may have hoped matters would go no further,[14] but the pattern of subsequent events reveals that others favored a more general reconstitution of traditional state and civic paganism.[15] Thus in the summer of 394 Rome was again the scene of public sacrifices, divination, and haruspication—venerable preliminaries to a military campaign—credited by one hostile source to the machinations of Nicomachus Flavianus.[16] In the same period the oracular temple of Hercules at Ostia—dating to the late Republic and located in a section of the

12. Amb. *ep.* 17.10 (*PL* 16) records the embassy to Gratian. After the famous mission of 384 to Valentinian II, memorialized by Symmachus's *Rel.* 3 and Amb. *epp.* 17 and 18 (*PL* 16), the Senate sent further embassies to Theodosius and to Valentinian (Amb. *ep.* 57.2–4). The course of events has often been discussed. See, for example, J. J. Sheridan, "The Altar of Victory: Paganism's Last Battle," *L'antiquité classique* 35 (1966): 186–206; A. Cameron, "Gratian's Repudiation of the Pontifical Robe," 96–102; Matthews, *Western Aristocracies*, 203–11, 240.

13. Amb. *ep.* 57.6 (*PL* 16, to Eugenius) describes the compromise: "compertum est postea donata illa esse praecellentibus in republica, sed gentilis observantiae viris." Paulinus, *V. Amb.* 26, adds the restoration of the Altar of Victory and makes Flavianus ("tunc praefecto") and Arbogast the primary instigators. McLynn, *Ambrose*, 344–47, argues (unconvincingly) for misrepresentation by Ambrose.

14. Straub, "Eugenius," 868.

15. The essentially conservative character of this pagan restoration is clarified by the elimination of the so-called *Carmen contra paganos* from the context of 394. T. Mommsen, "Carmen codicis Parisini 8084," *Hermes* 4 (1870): 350–64, identified Flavianus as the poem's subject, and, despite challenges, was followed in this respect by H. Bloch, "A New Document of the Last Pagan Revival in the West, 393–394 A.D.," *Harvard Theological Review* 38 (1945): 230; J. Matthews, "The Historical Setting of the 'Carmen contra Paganos' (Cod. Par. Lat. 8084)," *Historia* 20 (1970): 464–79, with a review of the question to date; Matthews, *Western Aristocracies*, 242–43. Secure attribution of the poem, however, is unlikely; O'Donnell's "dogmatic agnosticism" ("The Career," 140) and Vera's rejection ("La carriera," 54) of the poem as evidence for Flavianus's activities are warranted. Cracco Ruggini's argument, at "Il paganesimo romano," 74–116, for Agorius Praetextatus finds support in F. Dolbeau, "Damase, le carmen contra paganos, et Hériger de Lobbes," *REAug* 27 (1981): 38–43. For the conversion of T. D. Barnes to this point of view see Barnes, "Religion and Society in the Age of Theodosius,"in *Grace, Politics, and Desire: Essays on Augustine,* ed. H. Meynell (Calgary, 1990), 166–68. Grünewald, "Der letzte Kampf," dating the poem to the 430s and arguing that the poem's subject is a composite of several figures and periods, represents a resourceful, if desperate, attempt to make sense of a perplexing document.

16. Ruf. *HE* 11.33 of 402–3. Rufinus's lurid description of pagan cult activity is substantiated by the contemporary observations of Ambrose (*ep.* 57.6, *ep.* 61.2, where Eugenius is "qui se sacrilegio miscuisset") and of Prudentius in book 1 of the *Contra Symmachum,* perhaps the remarks of an eyewitness. See *Con. Sym.* 1.1–41, esp. 415–505 (the picture of Rome presented in the speech of Theodosius) and

city recently gentrified by the construction of lavish urban villas—was restored by the *praefectus annonae* Numerius Proiectus, a subordinate of the *praefectus urbi*, the younger Flavianus.[17] These reactionary views found their ultimate expression at the Frigidus: in the final confrontation Eugenius, Arbogast, and Flavianus met the cross-bearing standards of Theodosius under the protection of this same Hercules and of Jupiter, gods whose home had been Italy since time immemorial but whose names equally evoked memories of the halcyon days of Diocletian and Maximian.[18]

Some Christians clearly sensed the acuteness of pagan animosity in these days: shortly after the Frigidus, Ambrose, who had deserted Milan before Eugenius's arrival, hinted at the possibility of outright persecution of Christians in the wake of a Eugenian victory.[19] The alleged threat of Arbogast and Flavianus to convert the *basilica* of Milan into a stable and the possible calculated circulation of an oracle prophesying the end of Christianity's allotted 365-year span should only have heightened the tension in the weeks before the battle.[20] At the Frigidus,

529–37. On a date of late 394 or early 395, not 402, for book 1 of the *Contra Symmachum* see J. Harries, "Prudentius and Theodosius," 68–84, and the more elaborate argument of D. Shanzer, "The Date and Composition of Prudentius's *Contra Orationem Symmachi Libri*," *Rivista di filologia e d'istruzione classica* 117 (1989): 442–62, esp. 458–59, maintaining Harries's date for at least the Theodosian material of book 1. This dating is not vitiated by the attempt of T. D. Barnes and R. W. Westfall, "The Conversion of the Roman Aristocracy in Prudentius's *Contra Symmachum*," *Phoenix* 45 (1991): 50–61, to date the composition of lines 552–56 to ca. 384.

17. Bloch, "A New Document," 199–202, 232–35; R. Meiggs, *Ostia*, 2d ed. (Oxford, 1973), 347–50, 401–3; M. Cébeillac, "Quelques inscriptions inédites d'Ostie," *Mélanges de l'école française de Rome* 83 (1971): 39–88. Regions I and III of the city, to the north and west of the temple, saw substantial villa construction in the fourth century (e.g., the House of Amor and Psyche and the House of the Dioscuri). See Meiggs, *Ostia*, 258–61; C. Pavolini, *Ostia* (Roma-Bari, 1983), 118–19, 159–61. Symmachus had a *domus* at Ostia: *epp.* 2.52.2, 3.82.2, 6.72, with Meiggs, *Ostia*, 264.

18. Aug., *De civ. Dei.* 5.26 records statues of Jupiter; Theodoret, *HE* 5.24, images of Hercules. Amb. *De obitu Theo.* 4 may be a veiled reference to the *simulacra* of Eugenius. See Prud. *Con. Sym.* 1.464–64 on Theodosius's standards. Characteristically, Claudian, *Con. Hon. III.* 138–42, records only eagles, dragons, and serpents on Theodosius's standards. See also W. Seston, "Jovius et Herculius, ou l'épiphanie' des Tétrarques," *Historia* 1 (1950): 257–66.

19. *Ep.* 57.1 (*PL* 16): Ambrose returned to Milan only about 1 August 394, after Eugenius's departure (*ep.* 61.2). Amb. *En. in Ps. 36* 25 (*PL* 14.979, 20 March 395): "Saepe enim iacula in ipsos qui ea iecerint, refunduntur. Quod etiam proximo accidit bello, cum infideles et sacrilegi lacesserent aliquem in Domino confidentem, et regnum eius ereptum ire contenderent, ecclesiis Domini persecutionum saeva minitantes."

20. On the threat see Paul. *V. Amb.* 31, with Straub, "Eugenius," 867. The oracle, assigning to Christianity a limit of 365 years, is reported more than thirty years later by Augustine at *De civ. Dei.* 18.53–54. The attempt of L. Herrmann, "Claudius Antonius et la crise réligieuse de 394 ap. J.-C.," *Mélanges Henri Grégoire* (Brussels, 1950), 2:329–42, to credit the circulation of the oracle to Flavianus in 394, although accepted by J. Doignon, "Oracles, prophéties, 'on-dit' sur la chute de Rome (395–410): Les réactions de Jérôme et d'Augustin," *REAug* 36 (1990): 125–26, remains hypothetical. Augustine himself believed the oracle referred to the year 398, not 394; see J. Hubaux, "La crise de la trois-cent-

however, the old gods offered no succor.[21] The armies of Eugenius and Theodosius met in the valley of the Frigidus River, thirty-six miles from Aquileia, near the border of Venetia and Illyricum, and the battle took place on 5 and 6 September. Theodosius's desperate situation after the first day was relieved by the nighttime defection of Eugenius's general Arbitio. The next day Arbogast's troops were routed during a panic provoked by the bora, an unusually strong wind endemic to the region but unknown to the antagonists. Flavianus committed suicide,[22] and Eugenius was taken prisoner and beheaded. Arbogast took his own life several days later. Theodosius quickly sent news of his victory to Milan, calling upon Ambrose to offer suitable thanksgiving to God.[23] The bishop in turn prevailed on the emperor to show clemency to the defeated, some of whom had appeared as suppliants at the Milanese churches, and immediately set out to meet Theodosius at Aquileia.[24] Theodosius, having once again united East and West, survived his victory by less than six months, dying at Milan on 17 January 395. Not much more than another six months had passed when Paulinus and his household arrived in Rome, although there is good reason to believe that he had given ample (literary) notice beforehand.

In Italy Christian observers had immediately capitalized on the Frigidus's apologetic potential. Theodosius himself had quickly promoted his victory as divinely sanctioned, and Ambrose, in a letter sent to Theodosius just days after the battle, claimed that the outcome of the Frigidus, like the victories of Moses, Joshua, Samuel, and David, resulted from the action of heavenly grace rather than human calculation.[25] The bishop publicly reprised the idea in the funeral oration he delivered for Theodosius on 25 February 395, explicitly describing the war as an anti-pagan crusade wherein faith and piety were the instruments of victory.[26] Prudentius, too, in the battle's immediate aftermath, visualized Theodosius's campaign as a skilled surgeon's strike against a "renewed plague" of *error* and *superstitio*.[27] Indeed, both Ambrose and Claudian had already advanced the

soixante-cinquième année," *L'antiquité classique* 17 (1948): 343–54. The oracle may have originated with Porphyry; see H. Chadwick, "Oracles of the End in the Conflict of Paganism and Christianity in the Fourth Century," *Mémorial A.-J. Festugière* (Geneva, 1984), 125–29.

21. On the battle, see O. Seeck and G. Veith, "Die Schlacht am Frigidus," *Klio* 13 (1913): 451–67, and F. Paschoud, *Zosime: Histoire nouvelle* 2.2:474–500, with a collection of sources.

22. Ruf. *HE* 11.33 improbably places Flavianus's suicide before the actual battle.

23. Amb. *ep.* 61.4–5 (*PL* 16).

24. Amb. *epp.* 61.7, 62.3 (*PL* 16); Paul. *V. Amb.* 31.

25. Amb. *epp.* 61.4–5, 62.4 (*PL* 16).

26. *De obitu Theo.* 4 (*PL* 16): "qui [Theodosius] imitatus Jacob supplantavit perfidiam tyrannorum, qui abscondit simulacra gentium; omnes enim cultus idolorum fides eius abscondit, omnes eorum ceremonias oblitteravit." Cf. 7, 23. Discussion of Ambrose's "general theory of divine victory" is offered by Inglebert, *Les romains chrétiens*, 299–304.

27. *Con. Sym.* 1.1–41 and the "speech" of Theodosius at 408–505. Prudentius provides few details; neither Theodosius nor his opponents are specifically named.

"miraculous" wind of the battle's second day as proof of the divine favor accorded Theodosius.[28]

It was in the midst of the scramble to canonize a version of these events that Paulinus, still in Spain, penned the (lost) panegyric on Theodosius that he sent to Jerome in early 395 (eliciting an ambivalent response)[29] and probably also posted to Italy in anticipation of his arrival there. With that work, Jerome noted, Paulinus not only ennobled the emperor's purple but also consecrated the "usefulness of his laws for future generations."[30] But Paulinus may have harbored other, more personal motives for composing and circulating such a panegyric. Despite the fact that a letter written to Severus some years later (402–4) excuses the panegyric as a "trifle" (*nugae*) and blames its composition on the request of Paulinus's friend Endelechius,[31] Paulinus, preparing for his return to Italy after more than a decade of absence, may well have intended the work to serve as both an announcement of his new commitments and advance notice of his arrival. Indeed, the Endelechius in question, who also engineered the initial circulation of the panegyric, can reasonably be identified with a known rhetor and poet active in Rome in the 390s. Moreover, this Endelechius's apologetic poem, *De mortibus bovum,* has reasonably been claimed as another voice in the religious debates of the late Theodosian

28. Amb. *En. in Ps. 36* 25 (20 March 395): "ut subito ventus oriretur, qui infidelibus excuteret scuta de manibus, ac tela omnium, atque missilia in peccatoris exercitum retorqueret." Perhaps alluded to earlier at *ep.* 62.4. Claudian described the war in three different works written for the court between late 394, when Theodosius was still alive, and late 397 (the panegyrics on the consulship of Olybrius and Probinus [395] and on the third [396] and fourth [398] consulships of Honorius), although he refused to present the conflict in other than political and civil terms, and his treatment of the windy miracle, with its references to Aquilo and Aeolus, is ambiguous at best. At *Con. Oly. et Prob.* 136–41 the victory of Theodosius is described as the victory of *libertas* over *servitium,* while at *Con. Hon. III.* 63–64 Arbogast has provoked *civilia bella* and *discordia.* At ll. 93–98 of the same work, although Honorius is called "*O nimium dilecto deo,*" the wind in question is Aquilo, and it is sent forth by Aeolus. While such language need not have a religious connotation, and may represent more aesthetic than religious resistance, it does show Claudian's reluctance to engage in the style of presentation favored by his Christian contemporaries.

29. See Jer. *ep.* 58.8 (early 395). Courcelle, "Paulin de Nole et Saint Jérôme," 261, preferred a date of composition soon after the death of Theodosius; but G. Guttilla, "Il *Panegyricus Theodosii* di S. Paolino di Nola," *Koinonia* 14 (1990): 139–54, argues with some force for a date of composition between the Frigidus and Theodosius's death. Gennadius, *De vir. ill.* 48, records that Paulinus "composuit . . . ad Theodosium imperatorem, ante episcopatum, prosa panegyricum super victoria tyrannorum; eo maxime quod fide et oratione plus quam armis vicerit." The thesis of H. Sivan, "The Last Gallic Prose Panegyric: Paulinus of Nola on Theodosius I," *Collection Latomus* 227; *Studies in Latin Literature and Roman History* 7 (1994): 577–94, dating the composition to ca. 389, will not sustain criticism.

30. Jer. *ep.* 58.8: "felix Theodosius, qui a tali Christi oratore defenditur. illustrasti purpuras eius et utilitatem legum futuris saeculis consecrasti." Presumably he refers to the provocative anti-pagan laws of 391 and 392. Paulinus may have considered Theodosius's victory over Maximus as well as that over Arbogast and Eugenius. Note Gennadius's plural: "prosa panegyricum super victoria tyrannorum." Sivan, "The Last Gallic Prose Panegyric," 592, notes the inappropriateness of this term for Arbogast.

31. *Ep.* 28.6.

age.[32] Although Paulinus's later claims on behalf of Endelechius's role in the genesis and publication of the work need not be disingenuous, Paulinus must also have weighed the likely benefits and disadvantages of such a text's circulation in Italy in the months after the Frigidus, especially as this work apparently deployed the same themes of "divine victory" preferred by many in Italy.

Thus Paulinus's timely composition of a panegyric honoring Theodosius not only may demonstrate his cognizance of the events unfolding in Italy during these years (and suggest that Endelechius was one source of his information) but may also hint at his sympathy with, if not collusion in, the interpretive scheme that Ambrose and others were imposing on the Frigidus.[33] For faith and piety were also the dominant Theodosian instruments of war in Paulinus's panegyric. A few years later Paulinus would declare that he undertook the work's composition, the Christianization of a venerable genre, so that he might "proclaim in Theodosius not so much an emperor as a servant of Christ, a man mighty not through his pride over ruling but through his humility of serving, *princeps* not in his kingship but his faith."[34] Moreover, if, as has been suggested, Paulinus's panegyric lies somewhere behind Rufinus's slightly later account of Theodosius's victory at the Frigidus, then an even sharper image of Paulinus's approach emerges.[35] For Rufinus, by then in contact with Paulinus, would narrate his version of the tale by rigidly contrasting the emperor's Christian *religio* with Flavianus's pagan *superstitio;* in the *Ecclesiastical History* faith and prayer prevail over demons, while victory is achieved "more by prayers than by power (*orationibus magis quam virtute*)."[36] Much later Gennadius would summarize in similar terms: Paulinus's Theodosius, Gennadius remarked, had defeated the *tyranni* "by faith and prayer more than arms (*fide et oratione plus quam armis*)."[37] If, in fact, Rufinus's representation of the conflict, with its

32. On the identification and placement in Rome see W. Schmid, "Tityrus Christianus: Probleme religiöser Hirtendichtung an der Wende von vierten zum fünften Jahrhundert," *Rheinisches Museum für Philologie* 96 (1953): 120–22; and F. Corsaro, "L'autore del *De mortibus boum*, Paolino da Nola e la politica religiosa di Teodosio," *Orpheus* 22 (1975): 3–26. Severus's ignorance of the panegyric in Gaul might also suggest that it was published in Italy.

33. On the Ambrosian background see further Ingelbert, *Les romains chrétiens,* 304 n. 47.

34. *Ep.* 28.6 (to Severus): "ut in Theodosio non tam imperatorem quam Christi servum, non dominandi superbia sed humilitate famulandi potentem, nec regno sed fide principem praedicarem." Gennadius's "quod fide et oratione plus quam armis vicerit" offers support. On the *novitas* of Paulinus's approach see Guttilla, "Il *Panegyricus Theodosii,*" 148–51.

35. P. Courcelle, "Jugements de Rufin et de Saint Augustin sur les empereurs du IVe siècle et la défaite suprême du paganisme," *REA* 71 (1969): 100–130, esp. 110–11. For Augustine's dependence on Rufinus see also Y.-M. Duval, "L'éloge de Théodose dans la *Cité de Dieu* (V, 26, 1): Sa place, sons sens et ses sources," *Recherches augustiniennes* 4 (1966): 135–79, with 169 n. 123 suggesting Rufinus's use of Paulinus.

36. Ruf. *HE* 11.33. See further F. Thélamon, "L'empereur idéal d'après l'*Histoire ecclésiastique* de Rufin d'Aquilée," *SP* 10 (1970): 310–14; G. W. Trompf, "Rufinus and the Logic of Retribution in Post-Eusebian Church Histories," *Journal of Ecclesiastical History* 43 (1992): esp. 361, 366–67. So, too, for Augustine (*De civ. Dei* 5.26) Theodosius fought "magis orando quam feriendo."

37. It may be, however, that Gennadius knew only Paulinus's *ep.* 28.6, as noted by Courcelle, "Paulin de Nole et Saint Jérôme," 261 n. 3, and Duval, "L'éloge," 169 n. 23.

graphic denunciation of the demonic enthrallment of the losing side, was foreshadowed in Paulinus's panegyric, then we are afforded a further plausible indication of Paulinus's sensitivity to the "official" position being staked out by Theodosius, Ambrose, and others in the months after the Frigidus.

Paulinus's panegyric would have circulated in an atmosphere thick with tension and suspicion. The battle of the Frigidus was only a first step towards the restoration of order in Italy. Although from the very moment of Theodosius's victory the battle had served ideological and partisan ends, the clemency advocated by Ambrose as well as the calculations of Claudian reveal that the debate over the regime of Eugenius was initially conducted with delicacy. Theodosius himself openly expressed to the Senate his regret over the death of Flavianus (and perhaps others as well),[38] and most offenders were quickly pardoned for their involvement with the usurping regime. In the critical period of transition and regency in Italy that followed Theodosius's death, the victorious side, desiring reconciliation with Rome's senatorial aristocracy, preferred leniency.[39] By imperial edict the immediate past was consigned to oblivion: "The period itself shall be judged as if it never was."[40] Those who had served or been honored by Eugenius returned to the rank they had enjoyed before the "tyranny," and, although property was not confiscated, salaries received under the usurper were to be repaid.[41] Some, perhaps the younger Flavianus among them, prudently converted to Christianity.[42] In this atmosphere direct accusation and incrimination were best eschewed. If culprits

38. Rehabilitating Flavianus in 431, Theodosius II and Valentinian III reminded the Senate that Theodosius I had desired Flavianus "vivere nobis, servariq(ue) vobis—quae verba eius aput vos fuisse pleriq(ue) meministis" (*CIL* 6.1783). Theodosius's regrets were most likely delivered to Rome by imperial emissary or letter (*oratio*). Against the thesis derived from Zosimus (4.59) that Theodosius visited Rome in the months between the Frigidus and his death (e.g., A. Cameron, "Theodosius the Great and the Regency of Stilico," *HSCP* 73 [1969]: 247–67) see F. Paschoud, *Cinq études sur Zosime*, 100–124; Harries, "Prudentius and Theodosius," 80–81.

39. Matthews, *Western Aristocracies*, 264–70, with the apprehensive tone of Ambrose's *De obitu Theo.* and the conciliatory policy advocated at *Con. Hon. IV.* 111–21 (398).

40. *CTh* 15.14.9: "tempus vero ipsum, ac si non fuerit, aestimetur."

41. By *CTh* 15.14.11 (18 May 395) Arcadius and Honorius confirmed the conditions of pardon already established by Theodosius (cp. *CTh* 15.14.12). *CTh* 15.14.9 (21 April 395) validated legal and financial arrangements made during the period. On the repayment of salaries see Sym. *epp.* 4.19, 4.51, 5.47, 6.12: with the help of Symmachus, the younger Flavianus was apparently relieved of the obligation to repay his father's salary. See also Aug. *De civ. Dei.* 5.26.

42. See the exaggerated picture of mass conversion offered by Prudentius at *Con. Sym.* 1.545–78. Although it may be logical to assume Flavianus's conversion, the only evidence that can be cited in support is Aug. *De civ. Dei.* 5.26 (e.g., Seeck, "Flavianus 15," *RE* 6.2512; Chastagnol, *Les fastes,* 242; A. Marcone, *Commento storico al libro VI dell'epistolario di Q. Aurelio Simmaco* [Pisa, 1983], 44). This passage, however, is not explicit, referring only to Theodosius's mild treatment of the sons of his enemies (specifically those killed in the battle) who took refuge in a church and whom Theodosius "Christianos hac occasione fieri voluit." Against the sincerity of Flavianus's conversion see Grünewald, "Der letzte Kampf," 481.

needed to be singled out, they could be found in Arbogast and, as Ambrose real-
ized, in his straw man Eugenius; both were relative outsiders.[43]

Thus, heralded in some quarters by his panegyric, Paulinus arrived in a Rome
still tense in the summer of 395. Ambrose, who may have known something of the
repercussions of the panegyric as well as of Paulinus's secular renunciation in
Spain, predicted a rough reception at the hands of Rome's pagan senators for this
self-proclaimed monk freshly minted from a former suffect consul and *consularis
Campaniae:* "Although they shave their heads and brows whenever they undertake
the rites of Isis, they call it a shameful outrage if perhaps a Christian man, more
intent on holy piety, has changed his clothing." But Ambrose's prognostication
may have been intended as much to shame Paulinus's Christian detractors
through implicit association with caricatured pagans as to denounce his pagan
critics, for although the cult of Isis had retained a high profile in Rome through-
out the fourth century,[44] no sensible pagan was likely to be flaunting his sympa-
thies in the summer of 395. The previous summer's boldness was surely out of the
question. Unfortunately, we cannot say whether Ambrose's prophecy of pagan
polemic was fulfilled. Of those previously posited as friends of the ambitious
young senator, Paulinus of Bordeaux, in the late 370s and early 380s, the Elder
Flavianus was now dead, and his son, who had been *consularis Campaniae* about the
time of Paulinus's tenure, was striving (successfully, in the event) to salvage his fu-
ture and his property.[45] Symmachus, who had miscalculated in 388 by delivering
a panegyric to Maximus and then remained aloof from the usurping regime of
392–94, was equally cautious. Perhaps Paulinus now renewed contact with this
onetime correspondent and friend of the recently deceased Ausonius, but Pauli-
nus's imminent composition of a now lost work "against the pagans (*adversus
paganos*)" may rather signal his desire to distance himself from such old friends and
acquaintances.[46]

In fact, Ambrose's prediction may have missed the mark. The only known stir
caused by Paulinus's arrival was in Rome's clerical establishment. Months later he

43. Straub, "Eugenius," 875.

44. For example., the issues of brass coins with images of Isis from Diocletian through Theodosius;
see A. Alföldi, *A Festival of Isis in Rome under the Christian Emperors of the Fourth Century* (Budapest, 1937). The
temple of Isis at Portus was restored under imperial command as late as the reign of Gratian; see
A. Chastagnol, "La restauration du temple d'Isis au *Portus Romae* sous le règne de Gratien," *Hommage à
Marcel Renard, Collection Latomus* 102 (1969) 2:135–44. The calendar of 354 records five different festivals
associated with Isis; see Salzman, *On Roman Time,* 169–76. For epigraphical evidence of initiates see *ILS*
4413, 4153, 1259, 1260, 4154.

45. He held the urban prefecture in 399–400 and again in 408 and served as praetorian prefect of
Italy, Illyricum, and Africa in 431–32. See *PLRE* 1:346, "Flavianus 14."

46. Aug. *ep.* 31.8 to Paulinus: "Adversus paganos te scribere didici ex fratribus," but the nature and
form of the work are not clear.

was still venting his frustration at the clerical ill will that had greeted him at Rome. Jealousy and envy, he informed Severus, singling out for special complaint the "haughty separation" of Pope Siricius,[47] had provoked some of the Roman clergy to hate him and refuse fellowship with him.[48] Paulinus's excessive assurances to the contrary reveal the lack of equanimity with which he viewed this affront to the privileges of his rank, while his consternation suggests he had drastically miscalculated the mood of the Roman church. The ecclesiastical politics of Rome, a city notorious for its social exclusivity, could be every bit as contentious and rancorous as those of the Senate or the imperial court, although the ultimate reasons for Siricius's hostility are now impossible to discern clearly. Perhaps Siricius was truly scandalized by the apparent irregularities of Paulinus's presbyterial ordination. Not only had Paulinus, in contravention of the *cursus* instructions Siricius had issued to Himerius of Tarragona, leapfrogged the lower clerical orders, but he also exemplified the pattern of popular elections and migratory habits that the church labored to restrict.[49]

But other concerns may have weighed more heavily with Rome's bishop. In the mid-390s the prickly issue of asceticism still divided even the Christian elite of the city,[50] and, as Jerome had learned a decade earlier, Siricius did not share Damasus's congenial attitude toward the ascetic movement. And despite his condemnation of Jovinian's anti-ascetic teachings in the early 390s, Siricius apparently still entertained suspicions about the Manichaean sympathies of some ascetic leaders.[51] Moreover, Siricius also knew from Himerius himself all about Spanish monks who employed the cover of their *propositum* as a shield for illicit sexual relations.[52] In this context, doubt about Paulinus's motives for moving to estate-studded Campania, rather than concern for the irregularities of his ordination, may explain Siricius's rebuff of Paulinus. If, as is likely, Paulinus, who had written his second letter to Jerome that spring, also paid his respects at Rome to Pammachius (to whom he later wrote a still-extant letter), Marcella, Domnio, and others of Jerome's Roman circle, Siricius may have felt further justified in his

---

47. *Ep.* 5.14: "urbici papae superba discretio."

48. *Ep.* 5.12.

49. Siricius, *ep.* 1, *cap.* 9–10 (*PL* 13.1142–43); *ep.* 6, *cap.* 2 (*PL* 13.1165–66, against the ordination of wandering monks); [Siricius] *ep.* 10, *cap.* 5.13 (*PL* 13.1190, on popular election) and 5.16 (*PL* 13.1192, forbidding the movement of bishops from church to church).

50. On the anti-ascetic teaching of Sarmatio and Barbatianus at Verona in 395 / 97 see Amb. *ep.* 63.7–9 (*PL* 16).

51. Siricius's condemnation of Jovinian centered on the latter's denial of the claims of superiority being made on behalf of the virginal or celibate life. See Sir. *ep.* 7 (*PL* 13.1168–72). Jovinian's arguments would have undermined Siricius's support for clerical celibacy. On charges and countercharges of Manichaeism see D. Hunter, "Resistance to the Virginal Ideal in Late-Fourth-Century Rome: The Case of Jovinian," *Theological Studies* 48 (1987): 45–67.

52. Siricius, *ep.* 1, *cap.* 6 (*PL* 13.1137–41).

stance.[53] Pammachius was already fully identified as Jerome's advocate in Rome,[54] and the beginnings of the Origenist controversy may have been stirring along an axis that ran from Bethlehem to the houses of Jerome's friends in the city of Siricius.[55] These are complications that Paulinus may not have foreseen from Barcelona.

However much the Roman sojourn of 395 discomfited Paulinus, the mesmerizing city that had been the scene of his earlier political and social ambitions would continue to attract him in the decades ahead. Annual trips to Rome for the celebration of the June 29 festival of Peter and Paul provided regular opportunities to cultivate friendships with the city's Christian aristocracy that eventually encouraged reciprocal attendance at the January festival of Felix at Nola.[56] Moreover, after the death of Siricius on 26 November 399, Paulinus's relations with the church at Rome improved dramatically. Siricius's successor, Anastasius, immediately sent letters of recommendation on Paulinus's behalf to the Campanian bishops, thereby publicly embracing this victim of Siricius's "haughty separation" and officially reversing what must have been for Paulinus a painful and awkward ostracism from the Lateran community.[57] Indeed, when Paulinus appeared in Rome for the Feast of the Apostles in June 400, Anastasius received him "with as much flattery as honor"; he subsequently invited Paulinus to attend the anniversary of his ordination, an honor, Paulinus emphasized to his correspondent, normally reserved for bishops.[58] From Anastasius, who also proved more vulnerable to the anti-Origenist rhetoric of Jerome's Roman friends,[59] Paulinus received the welcome he must have hoped for in 395.

If a proper welcome had come belatedly at Rome, it had been more readily forthcoming in Campania. The fawning attention showered by the Campanian clerics upon the landowning former governor compensated to some degree for his humiliation before Siricius.[60] This regional recognition was complemented by the assurance offered from farther afield in the course of the summer and fall of 395.

53. Paulinus was in contact with Domnio no later than the autumn of 395 (*ep.* 3.3); the next year finds Paulinus in correspondence with Pammachius, the recipient of *ep.* 13.

54. Nautin, "Ètudes de chronologie IV," 253–55; Kelly, *Jerome*, 187–89.

55. Jerome's unfaithful translation of Epiphanius of Salamis's letter to John of Jerusalem is dated to 395 by Nautin, "Ètudes de chronologie II," 78–79. See Kelly, *Jerome*, 202–3, and chapter 8, this volume.

56. On Paulinus's regular attendance at the Feast of the Apostles see *epp.* 17.2 (with an account of his busy schedule) and 20.2. By 406 Paulinus had changed his visit to soon after Easter; see *ep.* 45.1.

57. *Ep.* 20.2 to Delphinus (401).

58. *Ep.* 20.2: "tam blande quam honorifice excepit." Paulinus sent his regrets on the latter occasion.

59. Kelly, *Jerome*, 246–49.

60. *Ep.* 5.14, on the Campanian clergy and bishops who paid court to Paulinus during his illness of early to mid-396.

By that summer Ambrose had magnanimously embraced Paulinus by letter as one of Milan's "long-distance" clergy.[61] Perhaps in Rome, Paulinus's courier, Julianus, probably dispatched to North Africa from Barcelona, had reached him with letters from a group of African bishops that evidently included Aurelius of Carthage.[62] Also in Julianus's packet was an unanticipated and flattering letter from Alypius of Thagaste.[63] Accompanied by five books of Augustine, Alypius's letter shrewdly provoked the initiation of Paulinus's lifelong correspondence with the future bishop of Hippo.[64] About the same time, a letter must have arrived from Severus in Gaul, holding out the tantalizing (but unfulfilled) promise of a personal visit.[65] Only the arrival of Jerome's second letter might have cast any shadow over these happy contacts.

In any case, ensconced at Nola by the autumn of 395, Paulinus set about creating the life for which posterity knows him best. He adopted the monastic lifestyle that would bolster his later reputation; at the same time, he worked to extend his network of epistolary *amicitia*. While he began to forge new friendships, as with the North Africans Alypius and Augustine, he also assiduously cultivated old ones, as with Severus and Victricius of Rouen. The stature of Paulinus as well as the name of Saint Felix eventually brought to Nola not only such renowned visitors as Melania the Elder and Nicetas of Remesiana but also Augustine's future adversary, Julian of Eclanum. Paulinus's annual trips to Rome kept him in personal contact with such members of the city's Christian elite as the Turcii, Melania's granddaughter (the Younger Melania), and her husband Valerius Pinianus. These influential circles would bring Paulinus to the attention of such scholars and theologians as Rufinus and Pelagius.[66]

---

61. Paul. *ep.* 3.4 (autumn 395), informing Alypius that Ambrose "wished to claim me for his own cleric, so that, although I live elsewhere, I consider myself his priest (*ipsius presbyter censear*)." There is no evidence that Paulinus visited Milan in 395; perhaps Ambrose's communication reached Paulinus in Rome.

62. See *ep.* 3.1 (Julianus had left from Carthage). Perhaps Julianus reached Paulinus when the latter was still in Rome, for Paulinus sought out Domnio for a copy of Eusebius's *Chronicle*.

63. For Alypius as the instigator of his correspondence with Paulinus see Trout, "The Dates," 240 n. 13.

64. The five "libri" were from among Augustine's anti-Manichaean works (cp. *ep.* 4.2).

65. So much is implied by *ep.* 5.1 of summer 396. Paulinus had just received a letter of excuse for an earlier promise to visit. It is reasonable to assume that Severus had made the promise by a letter of the previous summer or autumn.

66. See chapter 8. I have not been convinced by the argument of T. Piscitelli Carpino, *Paolino di Nola: Epistole ad Agostino* (Naples, 1989), 47–70, which credits Paulinus with a voyage to Carthage in the winter of 408–9. In addition to the still-valid considerations of Fabre, *Essai*, 72–73, this thesis requires Paulinus to have undertaken the trip very late in the sailing season (at a time when he had already adjusted even his trips to Rome to avoid summer heat) and therefore to be absent from Nola for the feast of Felix. Striking is the absence of any mention of such a visit in the letters that Augustine and Paulinus exchanged only a few months before the alleged journey (Paul. *ep.* 45 and Aug. *ep.* 95).

While he was constructing these relationships with the living, Paulinus was also acutely concerned with the dead. His fashioning of the cult of Felix stretches from the mundane to the sublime. His own "friendship" with Felix took its cue from the intricate patterns of late Roman social relations, while his physical aggrandizement of the cult complex transposed and adapted long-proven forms of aristocratic philanthropy and community action. Under Paulinus's direction the annual festival of Felix emerged as the supreme opportunity both for validating his own claims to social and religious authority and for promoting an especially populist interpretation of the Christian faith. Undeniably Paulinus's presence and activities at Nola affected the community and the region in ways now only barely visible: in the virtual anonymity of Paul, the bishop of Nola,[67] or in the bitter struggle to control the city's water supply. But these facets of Paulinus's life[68] were necessarily subject to the empire's political and military vicissitudes, the latter spreading inexorably from the Danube to Italy itself in the opening years of the fifth century. Occasionally Paulinus's writings reflect the impact of events unfolding in this wider arena. At least once these events collided resoundingly with his life.

The Gothic federate settlement arranged by Theodosius in the aftermath of Valens's defeat at Adrianople in 378, the increasing prominence of Gothic soldiers in the imperial army reconstituted by that same emperor, and the mutual suspicions after Theodosius's death that sabotaged cooperation between the eastern court of Arcadius and the Milanese court of Honorius all conspired to create unforeseen opportunities for ambitious barbarian leaders.[69] From this unhealthy mix the Visigothic tribal leader and Theodosian commander Alaric extracted the means of rampaging virtually uncontested through the Balkans between 395 and 397. Briefly appeased by an agreement with the eastern court that gave him a high military command but subsequently alienated by power struggles within that court, Alaric eventually led his Gothic supporters into Italy.[70] He entered Italy in November 401, prompting the restoration of the Aurelian wall at Rome.[71] He besieged (though apparently did not capture) Aquileia and Milan before being stopped by Honorius's *magister militum* Stilicho at Pollentia on 6 April 402 and again at Verona, most likely in the summer of that same year (although possibly not until 403).[72]

67. *Ep.* 32.15.
68. See chapter 7.
69. The complex story can be followed in P. Heather, *Goths and Romans, 332–489* (Oxford, 1991), 157–218.
70. On Alaric's background and these events see Heather, *Goths and Romans*, 196–208.
71. *CIL* 6.1188–90.
72. On the chronology see Seeck, *Geschichte des Untergangs*, 5:329–31, 572–74, now generally accepted, with P. Heather, *Goths and Romans*, 209 contra the date of 403 for Verona argued anew by T. D. Barnes, "The Historical Setting of Prudentius's *Contra Symmachum*," *AJP* 97 (1976): 376. On the siege of Aquileia see Jer. *Con. Ruf.* 3. 21 and Claud. *De bel. Goth.* 562, with Seeck, *Geschichte des Untergangs* 5:572.

Such an unfortunate turn of events under Christian emperors required expla-
nation. After Pollentia Prudentius, in the second book of the *Contra Symmachum,* at-
tempted to bolster Christian morale and to rebut pagan grumblings that linked
the Gothic invasion to the demise of traditional cults.[73] Likewise Rufinus, encour-
aged by Chromatius, bishop of ravaged Aquileia, now produced his *Ecclesiastical
History* as suitable medicine for sick times; his avowed purposes were to distract
worried minds from present suffering and to reassure them by demonstrating the
beneficent hand of divine providence behind the events of history.[74] Before victory
had been achieved, however, Paulinus offered his own literary response to the fear
that Alaric's invasion had spread as far south as Nola. In the *natalicium* of January
402 Paulinus tried to dispel the gloom that seemed to have settled over Felix's feast
day. His words, too, wavered between opposing but well-proven poles of consola-
tion. Although no physical imprisonment can enchain the heart, he announced,
and although the barbarians may in any case be instruments to convey God's dis-
pleasure at the sins of Christians, nevertheless, Christ, through Felix, will surely
crush the enemy and place them prostrate at the saint's feet.[75]

Despite Paulinus's desire to banish sadness from the celebration and embrace
the immediate joy of Felix's day, that year's poem was clearly conceived and com-
posed in the shadows cast from northern Italy. That darkness called forth exhor-
tations to a confidence that Paulinus claimed was fully warranted by countless bib-
lical examples of God's eventual defense of his people. Steadfast faith, prayers,
and tears were the weapons now available to the Nolan crowd, and Paulinus en-
couraged his listeners to wield them: "Arms have always needed faith; faith has
never needed arms."[76] Characteristically, however, Paulinus also advocated re-
course to Felix as "go-between with the Lord (*interventor ad dominum*)," and he urged
the crowd to direct their prayers to one no less capable than Daniel of calming
fierce beasts.[77] "Distinguished for his power" even among the martyrs, piously ap-
proached by his suppliants, their patron Felix would ensure that only rumors of
war reached Nola; and no bloodshed would pollute the saint's shrine.[78]

73. Barnes, "The Historical Setting," 381–84, is even more specific, suggesting that Prudentius
was responding to yet another request of the Senate, through the agency of Symmachus, for the
restoration of the Altar of Victory and of pagan cult, but see the reservations of Harries, "Prudentius
and Theodosius," 82–84.

74. Ruf. *HE* praef., with F. Thélamon, *Païens et chrétiens au IVe siècle: L'apport de l'"Histoire ecclésias-
tique" de Rufin d'Aquilée* (Paris, 1981), esp. 21–25. On both Prudentius and Rufinus see Inglebert, *Les ro-
mains chrétiens,* 309–55.

75. *Carm.* 26.22–28; 70–79; 246–58. Note the similar tension between passivity and activism that
marks the so-called *Epigramma Paulini* composed in Gaul between 406/07 and 418. See M. Roberts,
"Barbarians in Gaul: The Response of the Poets," *Fifth-Century Gaul: A Crisis of Identity?* ed. J. Drinkwa-
ter and H. Elton (Cambridge, 1992), 97–106.

76. *Carm.* 26.156–57: "arma fide semper, numquam cognovimus armis / indiguisse fidem."

77. *Carm.* 26.195–96. On the comparison with Daniel see 294–306.

78. *Carm.* 26.208: "martyres, e quibus est insigni robore Felix"; 211 (*patronum*); 413–29. Further
commentary on this poem by G. Guttilla, "S. Paolino e i barbari nei *Natalicia*," *Koinonia* 13 (1989): 5–29.

The defeat of Alaric in the months ahead would prove the accuracy of Paulinus's vision. Five years later events confirmed it once more. The *natalicium* of 407 was again composed against a background of military crisis, but this time amid the satisfaction that followed the defeat of another Germanic force in Italy. Radagaisus had led a Gothic group across the Danube in late 405 and maintained his momentum into Etruria.[79] His advance, like Alaric's, had spread a "cloud of grim war" over Latium and Campania, but Felix, with Paul, Peter, and the other martyrs, successfully prevailed on the "King of kings" to preserve Rome's dominion: Radagaisus was defeated by Stilicho at Faesulae, near Florence, in August 406.[80] In January 407, the opening of Paulinus's *natalicium* celebrated this victory achieved by the saints through the agency of the "boy emperor" Honorius.[81] It was perhaps in deference to Paulinus's distinguished guests from Rome that Felix was asked to share his intercessory role with Peter, Paul, and the countless martyrs of Rome and the empire of Romulus.[82]

In 401 and 402 and again in 406 only the threat of war had disrupted life at Nola, and Paulinus's poetry duly records its effect while also revealing much about Paulinus's assumptions concerning the role of the cult of Felix in securing temporal peace and security in an increasingly fragile world.[83] In 410, however, the breakdown of order finally engulfed Nola itself. Unfortunately, Paulinus's extant writings preserve no notice of this catastrophe, whose immediate origins lay in the overthrow and death of Stilicho in August 408 and whose reverberations echoed throughout the Roman world.[84] Honorius's court was now dominated by figures unwilling to pursue the conciliatory policies that had served Stilicho in his relations with Alaric after the confrontation at Verona. Once again, therefore, Alaric advanced into Italy, and a series of sieges and negotiations culminated in Alaric's sack of Rome over three days in late August 410.[85] The menace of Alaric, however, drove some of Rome's aristocrats out of the city as early as the autumn of 408; at that time Paulinus received at Nola Melania the Younger, Pinianus, and Albina, the Elder Melania's daughter-in-law.[86] By August of 410 this group was to

---

79. On the dating see Seeck, *Geschichte des Untergangs*, 5: 375–77, 587. See also Stein, *Geschichte*, 1:380–81, and Matthews, *Western Aristocracies*, 274–75.

80. *Carm.* 21.1–38.

81. *Carm.* 21.21: "Augusti pueri."

82. *Carm.* 21.29–38.

83. The practical as well as the theological implications of Paulinus's thought are evaluated by F. Heim, *La théologie de la victoire de Constantin à Théodose* (Paris, 1992), 293–322.

84. For the circumstances see Matthews, *Western Aristocracies*, 278–83.

85. See Matthews, *Western Aristocracies*, 284–306; Heather, *Goths and Romans*, 213–16.

86. A passage of the Greek text of the *Vita Melaniae* 19 (Gorce 166–69) states that they visited Nola on their journey south. Murphy, *Rufinus*, 205, dates their departure from Rome to October 408. P. Courcelle, "Les lacunes de la correspondance entre Saint Augustin et Paulin de Nole," *REA* 53 (1951): 268–69, keeps the group at Nola after their visit of 406–7, but see E. Clark, *The Life of Melania the Younger* (New York, 1984), 101–9.

be found on their estates in Sicily, with Rufinus in their company.[87] Thus they were not at Nola when Alaric's force arrived from Rome. The extent of the destruction at Nola is not known,[88] although it is worth recalling that Alaric did not pillage Rome's churches. Like Marcella at Rome,[89] however, Paulinus was apparently interrogated as to the whereabouts of his riches. This moment later became another instructive scene in Paulinus's iconographic portrait. As he was being held by the barbarians, Paulinus later informed Augustine, he had prayed, "Lord, let me not be tortured for gold and silver, for you know where all my possessions are."[90] Paulinus's treasury (like Marcella's) was beyond the barbarians' reach; it was another lesson, Augustine realized, well illustrated by the teacher to whom the bishop of Hippo had referred the worldly Licentius some fifteen years earlier. It is only a somewhat later reference, also preserved by Augustine, that reveals Felix's role in the defense of Nola in 410: the *De cura pro mortuis gerenda* recalls the saint's miraculous appearance during the siege of the city.[91] Augustine had heard the story from "trustworthy witnesses," but almost surely Paulinus's poetry had also recounted it.

Against this backdrop of terrible uncertainty and national catastrophe, the changes in Paulinus's life can also be gauged in more personal measures. Therasia, who never truly emerges from the penumbra of our texts, finally fades entirely from view; her death can be placed between 408 and 415.[92] Similarly obscure is the passing of Nola's bishop Paul. Only Augustine's reference to Paulinus as "bishop" in the first book of the *City of God* signals his attainment of the Nolan episcopate sometime between 407 and 413.[93] Uncertainty over both of these significant transformations aptly illustrates the paucity of our sources on Paulinus's life after 408.

Both the shrine of Felix and Paulinus himself recovered from any misfortunes they suffered in 410. The basilica complex continued to attract the attention of patrons who desired a prestigious final resting place for themselves or their kin; so about 420 Paulinus granted to the widow Flora the *ad sanctum* interment of her son Cynegius.[94] Paulinus's own reputation as a moral exemplar only grew in the years after the Visigothic depredations. Indeed, his report to Augustine of the prayer he

---

87. Murphy, *Rufinus*, 213–16; Clark, *Melania*, 110. See chapter 8, this volume.

88. Augustine, our only source, who had the information from Paulinus ("ut ab eo postea cognovimus"), speaks of destruction; *De civ. Dei* 1.10 (413): "quando et ipsam Nolam barbari vastaverunt."

89. Jer. *ep.* 127.13.

90. *De cura pro mortuis gerenda* 19. New light may be shed upon this entire episode by T. Lehmann, "Zu Alarichs Beutezug in Campanien: Ein neu entdecktes Gedicht des Paulinus Nolanus," *Römische Quartalschrift* 93 (1998): 181–99.

91. *De cura pro mortuis gerenda* 19.

92. Fabre, *Paulin de Nole*, 47.

93. *Carm.* 21.619 (January 407) implies that Paul was still bishop. See Fabre, *Paulin de Nola*, 46–47.

94. Chapter 2. See further chapter 8.

offered while in the hands of the barbarians reveals Paulinus's willingness to turn tragedy to public and moral advantage.[95] After 410 North African aspirants to the Christian life could still expect to find guidance and tutelage at Nola,[96] while the leaders of the incipient monastic community at Lérins—destined to play central roles in the intellectual and ecclesiastical life of fifth-century Gaul—reached out for contact with this fellow Gallo-Roman whose life was now so closely identified with Italy.[97] Paulinus's stock in ecclesiastical politics rose as well. From North Africa Augustine saw clearly the value of Paulinus's friendship; in 417 he would seek to secure and fortify Paulinus as an ally in his campaign against Pelagius.[98] In 419, when the imperial court's attempts to broker a contested papal election proved futile, it may have been Honorius's own half-sister, Galla Placidia, who made the epistolary appeal for mediation of the crisis by Paulinus.[99] Brief glimpses though they are over a long span of time, such episodes confirm the status that Paulinus had achieved through the community he had created at Nola in the years after 395. In the final analysis, that status rested on Paulinus's claim to have renounced the world, as many of his peers understood the act, and to have taken up the monastic life.

DECENTLY UNCULTIVATED AND HONORABLY CONTEMPTIBLE

Paulinus defined himself more readily as a monk than a cleric. When he wrote his second letter to Jerome in early 395, he at last laid claim to the title of *monachus* that he had disowned in his recent exchange with Ausonius. At Nola he set about establishing and organizing the community that he would immediately designate a *monasterium*.[100] By his choice of terms Paulinus consciously placed himself in the broad context of a vital but still fluid western religious movement, one apparently defined no more clearly for Paulinus's contemporaries than for modern observers. The cross-fertilization of western and eastern ascetic thought and practice in the later fourth century yielded a heterogeneous crop of ascetic lifestyles and practices that resists the imposition of any simple taxonomy.[101] Thus Paulinus drew on a

95. The *Martyrologium Hieronymianum* lists Paulinus as a confessor (*PL* 30.463).
96. Aug. *ep.* 149.34.
97. The evidence is supplied by Paulinus's *ep.* 51 to Eucherius and Galla. See further chapter 9.
98. Aug. *ep.* 186. Chapter 8.
99. *Coll. Avell.* 25. Chapter 9.
100. On Paulinus's use of these terms see Lienhard, *Paulinus of Nola*, 60–69.
101. The point is stressed by many. See, for example, G. Gordini, "Origini e sviluppo del monachesimo a Roma," *Gregorianum* 37 (1956): 220–60, esp. 250; G. Penco, "La vita monastica in Italia all'epoca di S. Martino di Tours," *Studia Anselmiana* 46 (1961): 67–83, esp. 68; R. Lorenz, "Die Anfängen des abendländischen Mönchtums im 4. Jahrhundert," *Zeitschrift für Kirchengeschichte* 77 (1966): 1–61, esp. 31; and S. Pricoco, "Aspetti culturali del primo monachesimo d'Occidente," *Società romana e impero tardantico*, vol. 4: *Tradizione dei classici: trasformazioni della cultura* (Bari, 1986), 189–204.

spectrum of personal experience and literary models to fashion the community of ascetics at Nola. Their daily lives apparently came to be governed by a regimen of physical deprivation through fasting and sexual continence and by prayer, vigil, and attendance at the basilica complex that continued to rise around the tomb of Felix. Both the example of monastic life as lived at Nola and the exhortations of Paulinus's letters contributed to the refinement of western monastic practice in the century before Benedict of Nursia.

Paulinus may well have confronted advocates of the *vita ascetica* quite early in his life. At Bordeaux itself Ausonius could boast of *virgines devotae* on both sides of his family: a maternal aunt, Aemilia Hilaria, died a virgin at sixty-three, and his father's sister, Julia Cataphronia, unwed and vowed to virginity, similarly lived to an advanced age.[102] Both could have provided Paulinus with examples of the house asceticism he surely met later in Rome. The early development of ascetic practice in Gaul, however, has left few distinct traces. Hilary may have established a community at Poitiers in midcentury, and Martin's monastery at Marmoutier, founded about 371, may have been preceded by an anchoretic experiment at Ligugé near Poitiers in the 360s, but the contemporary influence of such excursions into the ascetic life was arguably negligible.[103] Even the extremely accidental nature of the conversion of two *agentes in rebus* at Trier in the early 370s, as recorded and made famous by Augustine's *Confessions*, suggests the relative ease with which ascetic practitioners could be overlooked. Conceivably Paulinus in the 360s and early 370s was no more alert to ascetics in his midst than the ambitious Augustine initially was at Milan in the mid-380s.[104]

During Paulinus's Roman days of the late 370s and early 380s, however, encounters with asceticism's champions (and detractors) were virtually unavoidable. The city that had welcomed Athanasius of Alexandria in the early 340s had by the 370s seen notable figures attracted to an asceticism whose cause the embattled eastern bishop had evidently promoted in the West.[105] In the mid-350s Marcellina, the daughter of a praetorian prefect and sister of a future *consularis* of Aemilia and Liguria, Ambrose, took the virgin's veil from Pope Liberius himself.[106] Some time thereafter the noble young widow Marcella, a descendant of consuls, dedicated herself to "perpetual chastity" (against the wishes of her mother).[107] Mar-

---

102. Aus. *carm.* 10 (*Parentalia*) 6 and 26.

103. On Hilary see *V. Mar.* 7.1: "monasterium conlocavit." See also Stancliffe, *St. Martin and His Hagiographer,* 22–24.

104. Aug. *Conf.* 8.6.15.

105. Against exaggerated claims for the influence of Athanasius see Giordini, "Origine e sviluppo," 223–29.

106. Amb. *De virginibus* 3.1; Paul. *V. Amb.* 4. On the date see McLynn, *Ambrose,* 34.

107. Jer. *ep.* 127.2: "si vellem nubere et non aeternae me cuperem pudicitiae dedicare, utique maritum quaererem, non hereditatem." See *PLRE* 1:542–43, "Marcella 2." On the difficulty of the exact date see Giordini, "Origine e sviluppo," 226–27; Kelly, *Jerome,* 92. Jerome, *ep.* 127.5, insists she was the first of the *nobiles feminae* to adopt the *propositum monachorum.*

cella would be followed in her monastic *propositum* by a remarkable line of as-
sertive, aristocratic Roman women whose renown now rests heavily on the testi-
mony of Jerome.[108] Marcella and the like-minded women who gathered around
her conducted their fasts, study, and prayer largely in their urban and suburban
Roman homes;[109] in 372 the Elder Melania raised the stakes and the public profile
of women ascetics when she embarked for the Holy Land and founded a
monastery on the Mount of Olives.[110] Thus by the time of Paulinus's suffect con-
sulship, about 378, the ascetic vocation heeded by such women had significantly,
even scandalously,[111] affected the Roman elite.

Monasticism and worldly renunciation also had their male champions and role
models. More influential in the long run than Athanasius's sojourn in Rome dur-
ing the early 340s were the translations into Latin of his *Life* of the desert monk An-
thony, the first appearing about 360 and another by Evagrius of Antioch about
370.[112] If, as Jerome claimed, firsthand stories about Anthony told by Alexandrian
visitors had fired the ardor of the young Marcella,[113] the Latin *Vita Antonii* now
opened up the ascetic, and exotic, world of the Egyptian desert to a much wider
audience. This text, and other accounts of eastern ascetics that followed, fulfilled
the need both for information about the ascetic life and for models to adapt and
imitate.[114] Augustine is perhaps only one—and the most famous—of several
figures whose conversion stories are refracted through the tale of Anthony.[115] It is
reasonable to think that Anthony's "life" was well known in the monastic *diversoria*
that the same Augustine discovered while at Rome in the mid-380s.[116] We cannot
say whether Paulinus came to know the *Vita Antonii* at Rome in the 370s or early
380s, or, like Augustine a few years later, heard of those Roman *diversoria* where,
"in eastern fashion (*Orientis more*)," men fasted, prayed, and worked to sustain

108. See further A. Yarbrough, "Christianization in the Fourth Century: The Example of Roman
Women," *Church History* 45 (1976): 149–65; E. Clark, "Ascetic Renunciation and Feminine Advance-
ment: A Paradox of Late Ancient Christianity," *Anglican Theological Review* 63 (1981): 240–57; and, more
broadly, F. E. Consolino, "Il monachesimo femminile nella tarda antichità," *Codex Aquilarensis* 2 (1988):
33–45. For the argument that ascetic withdrawal at Rome was an expression of resistance to the reli-
gious policies of Constantius II, see R. Lizzi, "Asceticismo e monachesimo nell'Italia tardoantica," *Codex
Aquilarensis* 5 (1991): 56–61.

109. Jer. *ep.* 127.4, 8. Gordini, "Origine e sviluppo," 238–47; Pietri, *Roma christiana*, 639–40.

110. Murphy, "Melania the Elder," 64–65.

111. Jer. *ep.* 127.3.

112. See J. Fontaine in Herzog, *Restauration et renouveau*, 592–95. On the Athanasian authorship of
the Greek text see Averil Cameron, "Eusebius' *Vita Constantini* and the Construction of Constantine,"
in Edwards and Swain, *Portraits*, 170–72.

113. Jer. *ep.* 127.5.

114. For example, P. Rousseau, *Ascetics, Authority, and the Church in the Age of Jerome and Cassian* (Ox-
ford, 1978), 93–94.

115. *Conf.* 8.6.15.

116. Aug. *De mor. ecc. cath.* 33.70 (*PL* 32.1339–40). See further Gordini, "Origine e sviluppo,"
248–49; Pietri, *Roma christiana*, 640–43.

themselves. Like the "virile" assertiveness of certain aristocratic Roman women, however, the ascetic sympathies of the city's bishop, Damasus, were impossible to miss. Both Damasus's prose works and his public poetry espoused ascetic virtues, while his friendship embraced the more adventuresome of Rome's noble Christian families.[117] His own sister died as a young virgin who "had vowed herself to Christ";[118] and not long after Paulinus's departure from the city, Jerome, now a veteran of the Syrian desert, found Damasus a ready patron.[119] For an observant Paulinus, Damasus's advocacy of virginity would have sanctioned ascetic practices by bringing them within the purview of the institutional church at Rome.

This link between ascetic piety and ecclesiastical patronage was no less visible at Milan in the early 380s. When the future Martin of Tours, abandoning Poitiers, briefly set himself up there as a monk about 356, he was soon driven off by the "Arian" bishop Auxentius.[120] By the late 370s, however, ascetic interests and monasticism at Milan were solidly identified with Auxentius's "Nicene" successor Ambrose. The literary dossier of Ambrose is tellingly framed by extravagant praise of the virginal life at one end and by vociferous defense of Mary's perpetual virginity at the other.[121] Moreover, Ambrose "catapulted the virginal ideal to prominence" by actions as well as words.[122] Seeking to solidify his tenuous position in the late 370s, Ambrose organized a corps of virgins—"highly visible symbols for Christian Milan"—under the direction of his church.[123] This alliance with ascetic interests was further publicized by Ambrose's support of a *monasterium* in the Milanese suburbs, which, when Augustine knew it in the mid-380s, was under the immediate control of a presbyter.[124] Ambrose's austere persona, enhanced by his reputation for continence, fasting, and vigils,[125] was firmly grounded by the time Paulinus established friendly relations with him no later than the early 380s.

During the years of Paulinus's first Italian residency, then, both Damasus at Rome and Ambrose at Milan offered him models of highly cultivated and influential churchmen who endorsed monastic practices and whose churches spon-

---

117. See Jer. *ep.* 22.22 on Damasus's writings in prose and poetry.

118. See the *epitaphium* (*carm.* 11) at Ferrua, *Epigrammata*, 108–9: "voverat haec sese Christo, cum vita maneret, / virginis ut meritum sanctus pudor ipse probaret. . . . Bis denas hiemes necdum compleverat aetas."

119. Jer. *ep.* 22.7; Kelly, *Jerome*, 82–90.

120. Sev. *V. Mar.* 6.4. See Lizzi, "Ascetismo et monachismo," 63–64.

121. P. Brown, *The Body and Society: Men, Women, and Sexual Renunciation in Early Christianity* (New York, 1988), 345–65; D. Hunter, "Helvidius, Jovinian, and the Virginity of Mary in Late Fourth-Century Rome," *JECS* 1 (1993): 47–71.

122. On this description see K. Cooper, *The Virgin and the Bride*, 78.

123. Amb. *De virginibus* 1. 57–60. See Lizzi, "Ascetismo e monachismo," 69–70; Lizzi, "Una società esortata all'ascetismo: misure legislative e motivazioni economiche nel IV-V secolo d.C." *Studi storici* 30 (1989): 136–38; McLynn, *Ambrose*, 66–68 (quote 68).

124. Aug. *Conf.* 8.6.15; *De mor. ecc. cath.* 33.70. See Lizzi, "Ascetismo e monachismo," 71.

125. Paul. *V. Amb.* 38.

sored and cultivated practitioners of ascetic piety. The voices raised in opposition, adumbrated for us particularly by Helvidius's denunciation of the perpetual virginity of Mary in 383, may only have further ensured public notice of these issues.[126] Paulinus necessarily returned to Gaul in the early 380s acutely sensitive to, perhaps even inspired by, the ways in which not only the cult of the martyrs but also the imperatives of secular renunciation were reconfiguring Christian faith and practice in Italy. Gaul in the 380s was also subject to the tremors that everywhere accompanied this reshaping of the Christian landscape. Not only had the Italian-bred Martin of Tours, having weathered the initial opposition to the election of one so unepiscopally shabby and ill-kempt,[127] now emerged as a prominent (but still controversial) exponent of the monastic life, but another outsider, the Spanish ascetic Priscillian, had also set the tongues of Bordelais society wagging. His rumored seduction of the young heiress Procula while he was passing through Bordeaux in 381 reifies the ill will many must have harbored toward the ascetic movement.[128]

The likely influence, direct and indirect, that both Martin and Priscillian apparently had on Paulinus's life in the later 380s and early 390s has already been broached. In addition to problematizing any complacency Paulinus may have felt about his life of Christian aristocratic *otium*, Martin also provided Paulinus with a model of an aggressive cleric whose personal asceticism was rather more severe than that of the great bishops of Rome and Milan. If he had not seen it, Paulinus at least would have heard about the small wooden cell that served as Martin's home in the "desert solitude" outside Tours.[129] There the community of *fratres* held all property in common, and the only work they performed was the copying of texts assigned to younger members. Prayer and fasting, communal meals, and abstention from wine characterized their lives.[130] When Paulinus met Martin, probably at Vienne, the latter should have been strikingly garbed in the camel's-hair clothing virtually mandated by the Marmoutier community.[131] The clash between Martin's ragged appearance and the extravagance of the Gallo-Roman nobility to whose ranks Paulinus had returned mirrors the tension that charges Paulinus's own representation of his life.

Later, when Paulinus declared to Ausonius his knowledge of *casti* who lived apart from other men, the monks of Marmoutier may not have been far from his

---

126. See Jerome's *Contra Helvidium*, with Kelly, *Jerome*, 104–97.

127. Sev. *V. Mar.* 2.1: "intra Italiam Ticini altus est"; see chapter 9.

128. Sev. *Chron.* 2.48.

129. Sev. *V. Mar.* 10.4: "Qui locus tam secretus et remotus erat, ut eremi solitudinem non desideraret. . . . Ipse ex lignis contextam cellulam habebat."

130. Sev. *V. Mar.* 10.5–7. See also Lienhard, *Paulinus of Nola*, 95–97; Stancliffe, *St. Martin and His Hagiographer*, 25–26.

131. Sev. *V. Mar.* 10.8: "Plerique camelorum saetis vestiebantur: mollior ibi habitus pro crimine erat."

mind, but in the 390s a Spain still roiling from the aftershocks of Priscillian's exe-
cution sustained a native ascetic movement. In Gallaecia, where Paulinus and
Therasia buried their newborn son Celsus, Priscillian was honored as a martyr,
and some bishops there, despite the opposition of the Spanish episcopate else-
where, still espoused his cause.[132] Less controversial would have been the ascetic
practices of the majority of those "monks," women as well as men, who inhabited
the *monasteria* of northeastern Spain. The alleged sexual indiscretion of some of
their number led Himerius of Tarragona to seek the advice of Damasus in 384,
but the *monasteria* of Tarraconensis, a region where Paulinus lived in cultivated
retirement during the early 390s, were themselves implicitly sanctioned by
Himerius.[133] In Gaul and Spain any predilection for the monastic life that Pauli-
nus might have acquired in Rome and Milan could have been nurtured and
affirmed, but not without a full realization of its social cost.

When Paulinus founded his *monasterium* at Nola in the late summer or early au-
tumn of 395, therefore, he could have drawn on a surprisingly rich range of expe-
riences, some surely acquired firsthand in Italy, Gaul, and Spain, others obtained
through hearsay and report. Despite variations in organizational detail and in de-
grees of severity or enthusiasm, the fundamental components of ascetic piety evi-
dently differed little from community to community. Against the restraining ele-
ments of sexual continence and dietary abstinence were set the constructive
routines of prayer, vigil, contemplation, and scriptural study.

In the late-fourth-century Latin West, ascetic ideals found their clearest pre-
sentations outside scripture in tracts of exhortation or defense and in the *vitae* of
ascetic heroes. Jerome's epistles 53 and 58, addressed to Paulinus himself, fall
comfortably within the former category. Therein Jerome encouraged a radical
rejection of property, concentrated scriptural study, and life divorced from the city
and from clerical duties. Although Jerome's second letter offered only terse guide-
lines for celibate and abstinent living—social isolation, frugal diet, study, prayer,
and vigil—its author carefully referred Paulinus to his recent *Against Jovinian* for
further reading.[134] Book 1 of this searing treatise was a relentless, erudite rebuttal
of Jovinian's assertion of the moral and spiritual equivalence of the married and
virginal states; book 2 contained a lengthy, albeit largely borrowed,[135] philosophi-
cal and scriptural justification of fasting and dietary restraint.[136] Paulinus evidently
read this work, and dietary frugality emerges as one of the hallmarks of his ascetic
program.

132. Chadwick, *Priscillian*, 148–56.
133. The reply actually came to Himerius from Siricius. See Sir. *ep.* 1, *cap.* 6 (*PL* 13.1137B-C). Cp.
the complaints of Jer. *ep.* 22.13–14.
134. *Ep.* 58.6.
135. From Porphyry; see P. Courcelle, *Late Latin Writers and their Greek Sources*, trans. H. E. Wedeck
(Cambridge, Mass., 1969), 73 ff.
136. *Ad. Jov.* 2.5–17.

Some of the more practical advice that Jerome offered in his second letter took its cue from the problem posed by Paulinus's *soror* Therasia. Jerome was all too familiar with the difficulties presented by aristocratic women who fancied the ascetic life for the wrong reasons,[137] and Paulinus may already have encountered Jerome's strictures on feminine dress and deportment through a copy of his widely circulated letter to the young Eustochium. Similarly, Paulinus is likely to have known Ambrose's two treatises on virginity and his defense of widowhood, all published at about the time of Paulinus's suffect consulship at Rome.[138] Although Paulinus's writings are remarkable for their discretion on matters of sexuality, these works on virginity may have left their mark on him. While his own corpus preserves no prose tract of exhortation or defense like Ambrose's *De virginibus* or Jerome's *Adversus Jovinianum*, it is replete with letters of exhortation to a renunciation of the world that necessarily embraced sexual continence.[139] Although ostensibly addressed to individual recipients, these letters, like Jerome's to Eustochium or to Paulinus himself, were surely intended to convey their carefully crafted messages to a much wider audience.[140]

Such hortatory and apologetic works of Ambrose and Jerome as Paulinus might have known left no doubt about the priorities of the ascetic piety they promoted, but the same strictures emerged in more subtle ways from another genre that also attracted Paulinus's pen in later years. In the "lives" of the desert monks, the narrative and romantic element added an enchanting luster to the excruciating realities of the monastic life. The Latin translations of Athanasius's *Vita Antonii* were followed by the three "lives" of Paul, Hilarion, and Malchus by Jerome. All depicted the rigorous discipline, self-denial, and spiritual combat of holy men in the deserts of the East; but these could offer well-born western ascetics only inspiration and a generalized ethos. Two years after Paulinus arrived at Nola, however, he received a copy of Sulpicius Severus's *Vita Martini*. Severus's Martin lived in a cell near the city and waged one front of his spiritual war against the demons of a familiar countryside populated by superstitious rustics, not in unknown deserts inhabited by nefarious spiritual forces. The year after he received the *Vita Martini* Paulinus issued the first installment of his own verse *Vita Felicis*, wherein Felix is carefully cloaked in the attitudes of a proto-monk.[141]

Although the engaging beat of these hagiographic works sounds steadily for some two decades, no more than the treatises on virginity were these *vitae* meant

---

137. For example, *ep.* 22.16.

138. The treatises in question are the *De virginibus*, the *De viduis*, and the *De virginitate*, dated to 377–78.

139. But note Gennadius's reference to (lost) letters *de contemptu mundi* given to his *soror* (presumably Therasia) and "de diversis causis diversa disputatione tractus." *Carm.* 25, an epithalamium for Julian (later of Eclanum) and Titia is more direct on sexual issues.

140. For example, *ep.* 16 to Jovius and *ep.* 25 to Crispianus.

141. Paulinus received the *Vita Martini* in the spring of 397 (*ep.* 11.1); the *natalicium* of January 398 (*carm.* 15) initiated his "vita Felicis." See chapter 7.

to offer guidelines for the organization and regulation of monastic communities. Jerome's description of the three types of Egyptian monks at the end of his letter to Eustochium or the picture of Marmoutier that might emerge from the *Vita Martini* may have suggested possibilities, but western readers were offered no plan for monastic life until Rufinus translated the rule of Basil of Caesarea for Ursacius of Pinetum in 397.[142] Thus Paulinus founded his *monasterium* near the tomb of Felix at a moment when certain principles were widely accepted as defining the ascetic life but their implementation varied greatly.

Paulinus's decision to establish his *monasterium* beside the tomb of Felix was significant. Like Rufinus and Melania on the Mount of Olives or Jerome and Paula at Bethlehem, Paulinus founded his religious community in close proximity to an acknowledged *locus sanctus*.[143] At Nola, in contrast to the environments of both the urban and suburban house-monasteries of the Roman aristocracy and, at least initially, to that of Severus's new villa-monastery at rural Primuliacum,[144] Paulinus's asceticsm was not only an announcement of his heightened sense of piety but also a concrete expression of his devotion to a particular holy person and his tomb. While this meant that Paulinus's fasts, vigils, and prayers focused narrowly on the life and miracles of Felix, it also meant that he played his ascetic role under the nearly constant scrutiny of the pilgrims and visitors to the shrine of Felix. Hs claim to Felix's legacy rested largely on how convincingly he, and those around him, played the part of monk.

Although the physical details of Paulinus's *monasterium* remain elusive despite both his own random observations and the continuing work of archaeologists, it is certain that Paulinus and those he gathered around him lived virtually in view of the saint's tomb. Within a year of his arrival Paulinus invited Severus to join him and thus become not only a "tenant (*inquilinus*) of the neighboring martyr" but also a "*colonus* of his garden."[145] Although Severus never would become Felix's *inquilinus*, the Elder Melania did. During her visit in 400, Melania and her entourage stayed with Paulinus in his residence, a simple *turgurium*—Varro's term for a peasant's hut—that nevertheless proved capacious enough to house not only the *sancti* who came with Melania from the East but also the band of wealthy relatives and friends who descended on Nola from Rome. This "cloister," occupying a second story and separated from the guest rooms proper (*cellulae hospitales*) by a portico, ev-

142. *PL* 103.487–554; preface at *CCSL* 20.241. Rufinus translated an abbreviated edition of 203 questions of the *Asceticon*, to be followed by Jerome's translation of the rule of Pachomius in 404 (Kelly, *Jerome*, 280). Note also Rufinus's translation of the *Historia monachorum* in the same year.

143. On the fundamental link between the cult of the martyrs and the genesis and spread of the idea of the Christian *locus sanctus* in the fourth century see, R. Markus, "How on Earth Could Places Become Holy? Origins of the Christian Idea of Holy Places," *JECS* 2 (1994): 257–71.

144. On Primuliacum see Stancliffe, *St. Martin and His Hagiographer*, 30–38.

145. *Ep.* 5.15: "tum ego te non in monasterio tantum vicini martyris inquilinum, sed etiam in horto eiusdem colonum locabo."

idently replaced the shelter for the poor that Paulinus had erected earlier as governor.[146] Its rooms were so close to the tomb that the singing of choirs in the *turgurium* resounded from the "neighboring roofs" of Felix's basilica.[147] By 403, following the massive construction projects of the preceding years (figure 1b), these *cellae* had apparently been transformed into a second story standing over the atrium that now divided the new basilica (of the Apostles) from the older basilica of Felix; the windows of these rooms, Paulinus observed, looked down on the altars.[148] If, as is likely, they are the same rooms described by Paulinus a few years later in the *natalicium* of 407, they served not only as guest quarters but also as the dwelling of Paulinus and the more permanent members of the community.[149] In the porticoes below these rooms the poor and sick congregated. In perfect symbiosis, the poor were kept warm in return for their prayers.[150] Thus, however much this residential structure was transformed in the years after Paulinus's arrival at Nola in 395, it remained intimately connected to the basilica of Felix, and it still sheltered, though at respectable distance from Paulinus and his friends, the destitute and sick.

Paulinus's daily exposure to the public gaze in a world that generally viewed dress and deportment as fundamental social markers partially explains the preoccupation with appearances in his comments on monastic practices. The monk was revealed to others primarily through his dress and the physical signs of his ascetic regimen.[151] An absence of such outward signs cast doubt on inner commitment; their presence validated a monk before his monastic brothers and announced him to the outside world. But Paulinus's apparent privileging of monastic externals was also a facet of communication among elite participants in a still poorly defined religious movement. Social equals, for example, might be validated or castigated through their subordinates, because a man's own piety was displayed in the dress and behavior of those who carried his letters or represented his community abroad.[152] For these reasons, the ensemble of the monastic practices advocated by

146. According to *carm.* 21.384–94 the *tegimen* of Paulinus's governorship was extended with a second story to serve as quarters for Paulinus. This structure can reasonably be identified with the second-story rooms remarked in *ep.* 29.13 and *carm.* 27.395–454.

147. *Ep.* 29.13 (to Severus): "Turgurium vero nostrum, quod a terra suspensum cenaculo una porticu cellulis hospitalibus interposita longius tenditur, quasi dilatatum gratia domini non solum sanctis <cum> illa plurimis, sed etiam divitum illorum catervis non incapaces angustias praebuit, in quo personis puerorum ac virginum choris vicina dominaedii nostri Felicis culmina resultabant." Varro, *De re rustica* 3.1.3.

148. *Carm.* 27. 395–454: "nam quasi contignata sacris cenacula tectis / spectant de superis altaria tuta fenestris" (400–401).

149. *Carm.* 21.389. See also *carm.* 23.106–28.

150. *Carm.* 21.392–94.

151. So too Lienhard, *Paulinus of Nola,* 81.

152. See also M.-Y. Perrin, "*Ad implendum caritatis ministerium:* La place des courriers dans la correspondance de Paulin de Nole," *Mélanges d'archéologie et d'histoire de l'école française de Rome, Antiquité* 104

Paulinus is revealed not in passages of systematic exposition but in a series of vivid, rhetorically charged individual portraits. Not "rules" but *exempla,* fortified by praise or condemnation, alerted Paulinus's like-minded contemporaries to the limits of appropriate and inappropriate behavior.

Thus it is, in a sense, accidental knowledge that Paulinus advocated that the monk take only one vegetarian meal late in the day and limit his consumption of wine; that he avoid bathing and dress simply in a rough hair-shirt and a cloak bound with a rope; that he crop his hair closely and shave part of his head; and that he participate in common prayer, vigils, and hymn singing.[153] Indeed, the richest source of such information, Paulinus's *ep.* 22, was written primarily to chasten Severus at the nadir of his relationship with Paulinus.[154] The letter, a pungent diatribe against the carrier of Severus's two most recent letters, a certain "inspiritalis monachus" named Marracinus, obliquely and cautiously indicts Severus, who has begged off too many of Paulinus's invitations.[155] Although Paulinus had not even seen Marracinus on the second occasion, for at Rome the latter had entrusted Severus's Nola-bound letter to another *tabellarius,* Sorianus, Paulinus had encountered Marracinus at Rome the previous year. The surprise he had expressed then[156] was now turned into an indignation that settled swiftly on Marracinus's demeanor: his military cloak and boots, his ruddy cheeks, his belching, and his gluttony all betrayed him. In striking contrast, Paulinus depicted the *tabellarius* Sorianus as "vere spiritalis." Such men, true monks, are pale, garbed in the *cilicium* (hair shirt) and the roped *pallium* (cloak). Their half-shorn heads and nauseous odor declare their profession; they stagger not from drunkenness but from the strain of vigils and meager diets. Unadorned physically, such men were adorned with chastity; they were "decently uncultivated and honorably contemptible."[157] These were the men, ascetic paradox embodied, whom Paulinus hoped to receive as Severus's letter carriers henceforth.

Presentation of the same ascetic, anticonventional elements in the service of praise or denigration is at the heart of other literary portraits in Paulinus's writings. Paulinus praises the recently converted letter carrier Cardamas, for example, to affirm the sanctity of Delphinus and Amandus of Bordeaux. Cardamas, represented as a former actor and drunkard, had been ordained an exorcist at Bordeaux and subsequently acquitted himself well during visits to Nola. Along with

---

(1992): 1034–35; C. Conybeare, "The Expression of Christianity: Themes from the Letters of Paulinus of Nola." Ph.D. diss., University of Toronto, 1998, 47–55.

153. See Lienhard, *Paulinus of Nola,* 73–81; and Lienhard, "Paulinus of Nola and Monasticism," *SP* 16 (1985): 29–31.

154. Probably in 399. See Fabre, *Essai,* 27–38, and chapter 8, this volume.

155. For a dossier of Paulinus's couriers see Perrin, "La place des courriers,"1053–68.

156. *Ep.* 17.1. Marracinus is not named, but the identification is clear. He was attached to a friend of Paulinus and relative of Severus named Sabinus.

157. *Ep.* 22. 2: "et ornatu pudicitiae inornati et decenter inculti sint et honorabiliter despicabiles."

the community there, he fasted and was satisfied with the single vegetarian meal and meager cups. His emaciated body and pallid face were proof not only of his "devoted service" but also of the "blessing (*benedictio*)" of Delphinus's hand.[158] Paulinus's most elaborate piece of this type is the compelling account of Melania the Elder's visit to Nola in a letter sent to Severus in 400. As Sorianus had provided contrast to Paulinus's scathing depiction of the too-worldly Marracinus, so Paulinus raised Melania's ascetic simplicity into high relief by casting it against the ornate but empty display of the senatorial aristocrats who hastened to join Melania on her arrival in Campania. As the Appian Way groaned and gleamed with the gilded coaches and carriages of the senators, Melania approached Nola from Naples on a small, thin horse, "cheaper than any ass."[159] Dressed in silk, these nobles rejoiced to touch her thick tunic, with its bristle-like threads, and her cheap cloak (*palliolum*).[160] They hoped to cleanse themselves of the pollution of their riches by gathering the dirt from her vile clothing and her footsteps.[161] Crimson silk and golden ornaments bowed to old black rags, "a confusion of this world worthy of God."[162] That night, as the less dedicated slept, Paulinus and the faithful kept vigil and sang the Psalms.[163] Validating Paulinus himself as it praises Melania, Paulinus's letter lingers over the sharply contrasting visual details that measured the distance between Christian humility and the "utter emptiness of this world."[164]

If such passages impart vivid impressions of Paulinus's ascetic principles, illustrate his debt to his monastic precursors, and suggest some of the practices that governed the routines of the *monasterium* he founded at Nola, they nevertheless shed scant light on the organization and administration of this community. Neither the relationship of the *monasterium* to the church at Nola nor the official position of the presbyter Paulinus is clear. That Paulinus was the community's guiding authority seems certain. His clerical office may have mattered less in this respect than his social rank and wealth.[165] Moreover, a number of those who formed or served the community evidently were Paulinus's dependents and perhaps former

---

158. On Cardamas see *epp.* 14.1 (to Delphinus); 15.4 (to Amandus); and 19.4 (to Delphinus). *Ep.* 19.4: "quod etiam pristinae conditionis ingenium religioso mutavit officio."

159. *Ep.* 29.12: "macro illam et viliore asellis burico sedentem."

160. *Ep.* 29.12: "illi sericati . . . crassam illam velut spartei staminis tunicam et vile palliolum gaudebant manu tangere."

161. *Ep.* 29.12: "expiari se a divitiarum suarum contagio iudicantes, si quam de vilissimo eius habitu aut vestigio sordem conligere mererentur."

162. *Ep.* 29.12: "vidimus dignam deo huius mundi confusionem, purpuream sericam auratamque supellectilem pannis veteribus et nigris servientem."

163. *Ep.* 29.13. Cp. *carm.* 23.110–13.

164. *Ep.* 29.12: "de huius saeculi vanitate ipsa." See further Trout, *"Amicitia, Auctoritas,* and Self-Fashioning Texts," 126.

165. So, too, on Olympias, Melania, and Paula, E. Clark, "Authority and Humility: A Conflict of Values in Fourth-Century Female Monasticism," *Byzantinische Forschungen* 9 (1985): 17–33.

slaves; the steep social hierarchy that structured the late antique world did not level out at the monastery door. Much of the work of maintaining the basilica complex and staging the annual festival must have been overseen by those, like Theridius, whom Paulinus styles *fratres,* but they are seldom visible in such roles. Rather, *pueri* can be found tending the lamps (but also keeping vigil with the *fratres*),[166] and the basilica's attendants may be styled *aeditui.*[167] The physical labor required to run the complex must have been entrusted to these anonymous figures, whose sustenance may well have been provided by Paulinus himself.

Besides the details fortuitously preserved in his extant letters and poems, Paulinus's contemporaries would have had other information about his efforts. News traveled through travelers and letter carriers, and these surely relayed the practical information that might have interested Paulinus's ascetic or aspiring correspondents. If Paulinus and Severus troubled themselves to coordinate their building projects at Nola and Primuliacum through the exchange of texts and painted renderings,[168] they must also have shared organizational ideas. The flow of travelers between the monasteries of North Africa and Nola and the aristocratic foundation at Lérins must also have facilitated an approximation of community standards and styles. Paulinus is likely to have borrowed as much as he gave, but the *monasterium* of Nola has a recognizable place in the evolution of western monasticism in the late fourth and early fifth centuries.

Although seemingly far removed from each other, the monastic community at Nola and the papal and imperial courts of Rome and Milan were linked by Paulinus's personal asceticism. Paulinus's audiences with the bishops of Rome and his eventual summons by a pious Christian emperor and his sister were underwritten by the quotidian routines of monastic life at Nola. By founding his *monasterium* at Nola in 395 and living henceforth as a *monachus,* Paulinus strengthened the claim to social and religious authority that his secular renunciation had so boldly laid before the late-fourth-century imagination in the previous year. But as the next chapter shows, both secular renunciation and monastic life at Nola were more complex phenomena than they might at first appear.

166. *Carm.* 23.148–53.
167. *Carm.* 19.445–47.
168. *Ep.* 32.10. See also chapter 8.

CHAPTER 6

—•—

Salvation Economics

The Theory and Practice of Property Renunciation

When Paulinus arrived at Nola in the late summer or early autumn of 395, he had but recently announced his decision to forsake the tumult of the world. He wished others to think of him as a spiritual novice, still an "infant" with respect to the "birthdays of his soul."[1] Presumably he and Therasia had begun to sell or transfer the ownership of their estates in earnest only within the year. Although Paulinus's first verse letter to Ausonius, written before his formal act of renunciation, had already voiced the sound investment principle that encouraged the commutation of worldly into heavenly treasure,[2] now at Nola he quickly elaborated that earlier bald assertion into a rich and nuanced theory of salvation economics. Constructed from the pith of sometimes contrary philosophic and gospel precepts, Paulinus's theory denigrated the value of traditionally conceived worldly goods at the same time that it advised calculated monetary investment to benefit the poor and humble. As Paulinus perceived it, wealth could be either immensely deleterious or exceedingly salutary to one's spiritual well-being; but his various discourses on goods, property, and redemption are also firmly ensconced in economic and social realities of the temporal world. Despite his occasionally bold rhetoric of renunciation, Paulinus recognized and honored the complex practical and emotional obstacles facing men and women of elite background. By emphasizing, instead of complete renunciation, intellectual detachment from wealth and mastery over, or proper use of, riches, Paulinus's writings frequently obscured the more radical implications of the ascetic project. At the same time, Paulinus's publicly articulated attitudes toward his own property and estates in Gaul and Italy and toward the buildings and basilicas of Felix's Nolan shrine underscore the

---

1. *Ep.* 4.3 (to Augustine): "in natalibus autem animae illius adhuc mihi tempus infantiae est, quae intentatis Christo vulneribus inmolata digno sanguine agni victimam praecurrit et dominicam auspicata est passionem." Cp. Matt 2.16.

2. *Carm.* 10.71–76; with above chapter 4.

complex issues surrounding his own secular renunciation. Indeed, in many ways Paulinus's implementation of his secular renunciation necessarily embraced long-familiar patterns of elite behavior. The society in which he moved was accustomed to granting status and authority to those who employed their wealth for civic and communal purposes. In this sense Paulinus's own perception and public articulation of his renunciation, although intricately bound to his relationship with the shrine and cult of a Christian saint, overlap the philanthropic ideals and actions of the earlier empire's civic and senatorial elites.

THE EYE OF THE NEEDLE AND THE BOSOM OF ABRAHAM

In 394 Paulinus had given dramatic expression to his *contemptus mundi* by renouncing the *saeculum*. In just such terms, at any rate, Paulinus described his actions when, five years or more after his arrival at Nola, he wrote a letter of exhortation to a soldier and potential ascetic convert named Crispianus. Crispianus, Paulinus hoped, would take the course that Paulinus had earlier judged best for himself: renunciation of the world with all its pomp and empty allurements, and safe refuge against the anger to come with Jesus Christ, the sole salvation of the human race.[3] In 396, writing to the young Licentius at the request of Augustine, Paulinus had expatiated in greater detail on the particular pomp and allurements likely to matter most to the son of a wealthy *curialis*. With frequent echoes of Virgil, whom Licentius had studied under Augustine's tutelage, Paulinus paraded a litany of well-worn Platonic and Christian admonitions on the ontological inferiority of temporal goods: the "wise mind," Paulinus reminded Licentius, sees through appearances, recognizing the slippery hazards inherent in state service (*milita*) and the evil slavery lurking behind the enticing titles of public office (*honos*).[4] Accordingly Paulinus encouraged Licentius to submit to the yoke of Christ while he was still free from the chains of the marriage bed and high office;[5] the true freedom found in servitude to Christ far surpassed such *bona falsa*. Even without an explicit reminder that marriage and *honores*, the sole objects of Paulinus's derision here, had once been the goals of an ambitious Augustine (as well as the achievements of a younger Paulinus), Licentius should still have detected in Paulinus's verses the echoes of Augustine's conversations with him at Cassiciacum a decade earlier.[6]

---

3. *Ep.* 25*.1: "ut renuntiantes huic saeculo et omnibus pompis et inlecebris vanitatis eius fugiamus ab ira ventura et confugiamus ad unicam generis humani salutem, Iesum Christum." On the date, about 401–2, see Fabre, *Essai*, 48–49.

4. *Ep.* 8.3 vv. 1–14. On this letter see also chapter 1. On the widespread diffusion of generalized Platonic material in this period see S. Gersch, *Middle Platonism and Neoplatonism: The Latin Tradition*, 2 vols. (Notre Dame, 1986).

5. *Ep.* 8.3. vv. 31–32: "Nunc potes hoc, dum liber agis, dum nulla retenant / vincula, nulla tori cura nec altus honor."

6. For example, the prefaces of the *De ordine*, written while Augustine and Licentius were at Cassiciacum.

But Paulinus's exhortation to Licentius, written so soon after his own secular renunciation, is perhaps most telling for its silence on one crucial matter. Paulinus avoided confronting his wavering correspondent with the blunt possibility that renunciation of the world might require massive property divestment. Indeed, henceforth Paulinus's letters show a marked ambivalence toward the problem of reconciling property ownership with ascetic practice. He is seldom strident and often evasive when speaking to those, like Licentius, still resistant or perhaps tottering on the edge of commitment. Paulinus's apparent sensitivity in the matter that so largely shaped public representations of his own claims to Christian perfection is closely linked both to the particular circumstances of his correspondents and to deeply seated upper-class assumptions about property and inheritance. If Paulinus rarely offered to potential candidates for the ascetic life the kind of radical advice on material renunciation that Jerome had offered to him in *ep.* 58, it was perhaps precisely because he was better placed to understand the issue's inflammatory nature. The assimilation of Christian *contemptus mundi* to aristocratic *otium ruris,* or the blurring of boundaries between new ascetic and older philosophic precepts, could be accomplished rather more smoothly than any justification of dismemberment of a patrimony built up over several generations.

Accordingly, Paulinus far preferred the gospel story of Lazarus to that of the rich young man seeking the path to eternal life. It was easier, Jesus apprised his disciples, for a camel to pass through the eye of a needle than for a rich man to enter the kingdom of Heaven.[7] If that utterance apparently barred heaven's door to those who still possessed substantial property, in contrast Lazarus's tale, wherein the rich man who had refused alms to the sore-ridden Lazarus suffered endless torment in Hell, suggested that wealth might be employed to secure a place in Abraham's bosom.[8] Perhaps in consequence, Paulinus studiously avoided exhortation to secular renunciation on the basis of the exacting story of the rich young man in Matthew. That passage might have been credited with the ascetic conversion of Anthony,[9] but Paulinus offered it as incentive neither to Licentius nor, more surprisingly, to Crispianus. Indeed, on several occasions when Paulinus did openly discuss Jesus' admonition to the young man, it was ostensibly to refute correspondents, like his fellow ascetic Severus, who had too simplistically employed its language as the terms of praise for Paulinus's own actions. Paulinus might admit to fulfilling the first part of Christ's command by divesting himself of worldly goods; but truly following Christ, he avowed, was far more crucial and difficult.[10] If the former was a singular act of departure, the latter was a protracted journey. Ridding oneself of property merely cleared the site; construction of the

7. Matt 19.16–24. Cp. Mk 10.17–27.
8. Luke 16.19–31.
9. *V. Ant.* 2.
10. Especially, *ep.* 24.4–5, 21; *ep.* 11.12; *ep.* 40.11.

new spiritual edifice was the work of a lifetime.[11] In fact, the crucial possessions to be sold to comply with Christ's counsel were not money and estates but "the inner wealth of our minds." To sell this "property" was the greater victory.[12] This shift in exegetical emphasis from externalized to psychological action characterizes the evolution of Paulinus's thought on the question of property; once a man has torn down the walls and ripped up the pavements of his earthly mansions, he is forced to face the "inner part" of his house, the "entire darkness" of his unhappy state.[13] In these haunting circumstances Paulinus regularly turned the light of examination from action to attitude, a subtle deflection but one that somewhat paradoxically allowed the approbation of a significant range of behavior and pragmatic relationships between committed Christians and their worldly goods.

Others before Paulinus had grappled with the troubling aspects of Christ's counsel to the rich young man. Christian communities in urgent need of resources and patrons had been obliged to mitigate the force of such gospel injunctions and offer the hope of salvation to the rich as well as the poor.[14] Thus in the late second or early third century Clement of Alexandria closely anticipated, albeit with greater reliance on allegory, Paulinus's revisionist reading of the rich young man's story.[15] Two centuries later, but paradoxically in an age of ascetic fervor, a carefully selected complex of scriptural images and texts enabled Paulinus to reopen the celestial door to property holders and ultimately to find justification for the possession of wealth, first in its proper use, and second in the more slippery rationalizations of mental detachment and mastery. And it was the tale of Lazarus, in particular, that Paulinus seized on as the answer to the conundrum of Matthew 19.21–24. If Paulinus was circumspect in his use of the latter, he enlisted the story of Lazarus in a wide range of contexts; better than any other image, the heavenly refreshment of the beggar Lazarus and the corresponding torment of the greedy rich man came to embody the principles of Paulinus's spiritual economics.

Paulinus's sole surviving letter to Pammachius, a lucid monument to his thinking about the redemptive deployment of property in the life of the wealthy Christian, presents the earliest of his extended reflections on Luke's story of the *mendicus* Lazarus and the anonymous *dives* (Luke 16.19–31). Writing to Pammachius, Roman senator and friend of Jerome, in the winter of 396–97 to offer his consolations on the death of Pammachius's wife, Paulinus praises the meal for the poor and

---

11. *Ep.* 24.20–22.

12. *Ep.* 40.11.

13. *Ep.* 24.20.

14. L. W. Countryman, *The Rich Christian in the Church of the Early Empire: Contradictions and Accommodations* (New York, 1980); H. C. Kee, "Rich and Poor in the New Testament and in Early Christianity," in *Through the Eye of a Needle,* ed. E. A. Hanawalt and C. Lindberg (Kirksville, 1994): 29–42.

15. *Quis dives salvitur.* On broader context see B. Ramsey, "Almsgiving in the Latin Church: The Late Fourth and Early Fifth Centuries," *Theological Studies* 43 (1982): 226–59.

distribution of alms with which Pammachius observed Paulina's funerary rites.[16] While so many Roman nobles purchased only death through lavish outlay on beast hunts and gladiatorial games, Paulinus declares, Pammachius has purchased life through a *spectaculum* that truly nourished the poor, the "patrons of our souls."[17] Pammachius's surety, Paulinus continues, is provided by Lazarus's tale, for therein lies the counterpoint to "that saying . . . that would have shut the kingdom of heaven to almost every rich man [Matt 19.23], if God the only Good, had not exacted from his omnipotence this gift: that He might enrich the wealthy through the will (*voluntas*) of the poor."[18] Thus the compassionate rich man might also pass through the needle's eye.[19] Wealth used to succor the indigent, Paulinus asserts, is treasure stored in heaven, for Christ himself was fed, clothed, and visited in the person of every man succored in need.[20] "In short," Paulinus remarks, "not riches but men through their use of them are blameworthy or acceptable to God."[21] Such thinking could claim good company, for in 386 the recently converted Augustine, inspired by Cicero, had staked out a similar position at Cassiciacum.[22]

Again and again in the years ahead Paulinus returned to this argument, goading the wealthy into developing a self-interested sense of charity toward the less fortunate who crowded around their doors, waiting to catch sight of them.[23] His single extant sermon (bearing the title "On the alms table"), a letter to Severus, and even his exhortation to the soldier Crispianus, all redeploy at length the calculated reasoning of the letter to Pammachius.[24] To Paulinus even the starkly unequal distribution of material resources that made the late-ancient city such a volatile place was, in fact, divinely sanctioned. In this harsh inequality Paulinus detected the outlines of the scheme through which God sought to stitch together the lives of men from vastly different walks of life. Despite the gulfs of lifestyle, law, and social protocol so sharply dividing them, rich and poor were bound in an intimate interdependence that could be fully perceived only from a perspective that

16. *Ep.* 13.11ff. Cp. Jerome, *ep.* 22.32.

17. *Ep.* 13.15–16.

18. *Ep.* 13.16–19: "erat enim, inquit, habens multas possessiones [Matt 19.22], et idcirco secuta est illa sententia, quae regnum caelorum omni diviti pene clauserat, nisi deus ut solus bonus omnipotentiae suae excepisset hoc donum, ut divites pauperum voluntate ditaret" (13.19).

19. *Ep.* 13.18.

20. *Ep.* 13.22, referencing Matt 25.40 ("quamdiu fecistis uni ex his fratribus mei minimis mihi fecistis"), another important text for Paulinus and one he frequently employed in the letters to Severus.

21. *Ep.* 13.20: "Denique, ut scias non divitias sed homines pro earum usibus esse culpabiles vel acceptos deo."

22. *De ord.* 2.9.27; *Sol.* 1.10.17.

23. For example, *ep.* 34.7.

24. *Epp.* 34, 32.21, and 25*.3. On this issue see further S. Prete, *Paolino di Nola e l'umanesimo cristiano*, 69–71; and Prete, "I temi della proprietà e della famiglia negli scritti di Paolino di Nola," *Augustinianum* 17 (1977): 266–71, reprinted in *Motivi ascetici e letterari in Paolino di Nola* (Naples and Rome, 1987), 67–72.

encompassed the view of eternity providentially afforded men by Lazarus' tale. The poor depended on the generosity of the rich to survive; the rich required the poor to drain off the lethal superfluity of their wealth. The refreshment the rich offered on earth would be duly repaid in heaven. "If you give only a little from your abundance," Paulinus advised, "the prayers of all the poor and the vows of the sick are conferred on you. Be sure that they are not forced to exchange such devoted affection, transforming their prayers into complaints. . . . If you love yourself, beware of loving yourself alone."[25] Neither before such already committed ascetics as Pammachius and Severus nor before the presumably more moderate audience and readers of his sermon does Paulinus ever advocate the reckless abandonment of wealth. Used in accord with God's plan, property is too valuable to both social order and individual salvation to be disregarded. Our temporal goods, he informed Severus, are allotted to us by God like "a fleece to be shorn." They are given to us, he continued, "as the means for our virtue to win merit," for by using them to do the work of God, we transform our possessions into "a blessed kind of merchandise," one that we even send on before us into the "bosom of the Lord."[26] Although God could have made all men equally rich, Paulinus observed elsewhere, He mercifully made some men poor in order to test the minds (*mentes*) of others.[27]

Hence Paulinus's attention was inevitably drawn to the state of mind that visible acts of charity and munificence illuminated. Charitable use of wealth signaled the deeper frequencies of a mind attuned to God. Thus the benefactor of the poor announced himself as the master of his passions as well as of his riches. "You are free from greed, because you are a slave to justice. . . . You are the master, not the slave of your money, because you are possessed by Christ," Paulinus informed Pammachius.[28] When Severus expressed anxiety over his failure to divest himself completely of his properties, Paulinus echoed Paul's admonition that those who are buying property should act as if they possessed none to reassure Severus that, even in his role as owner, he was still "perfect," for his mind (*mens*) was free from the "chains of possession."[29] Such emphasis on the more recondite mental matrix from which social action emerged also facilitated an allegorical reading of the critical passage at Matthew 19.21–24, a reading that might override any impulse to take Jesus' words to the rich young man too literally. A passage of a letter written sometime after 400 and addressed jointly to Amandus and a certain Sanctus—

25. *Ep.* 34.7–8.

26. *Ep.*11.9: "quasi tonsile vellus . . . ut materiam nobis virtutis ad merita parienda. . . . ea per omnipotentis dei opus beato mercimonii genere vertentes non modo nobiscum efferimus, sed ante nos etiam in sinum domini seminata praemittimus" (Cp. Gal 6.8).

27. *Ep.* 34.6: "ut tuam in illis mentem probet." Cp. *ep.* 32.21.

28. *Ep.* 13.22.

29. 1 Cor 7.30: "et qui emunt, tamquam non possidentes [sint]"; *Ep.* 24.3: "Itaque et in quo possessor videris, soluta a possessionum vinculis mente perfectus es."

perhaps to be identified with the poet and rhetor Endelechius— illustrates well a stage of this exegetical progression. Troubled by the praise that his correspondents had bestowed on him and referring to God all credit for what he might seem to have accomplished, Paulinus cautions them further,

> From the very paths of virtue we can slip down into sin, and as I said, unless we arrange and balance in sure position the forces of our mind (*animus*), we may take haughtiness from our humility, and the splendor of our piety will pass away if through praise of our poverty vanity creeps in. What good will it do us to be free from riches if we remain rich in sins? Whence I ask you not to flatter me because I have fulfilled that saying of the Lord: "Sell what you possess," for that which follows is greater: "And come follow me." . . . For these words, "Go and sell all you have," like almost all divine scripture, have a double meaning. For we possess not only money and estates, external goods, but even the inner wealth of our mind (*animus*), which is truly our substance. To sell this, that is, to alienate this inner wealth, is the greater victory, as it is more difficult to set apart what is innate than what is placed before us, and to tear away what is inwardly attached than to reject what is outwardly affixed.[30]

So Paulinus simultaneously underscores his own more literal fulfillment of the first part of the gospel precept and drastically undercuts the ultimate value of any simple *contemptus patrimonii* unaccompanied by self-contempt (*nostri contemptus*).[31] Addressing Sanctus and Amandus in this letter, Paulinus shifted his exegesis of the problematic gospel injunction away from the emphasis on the proper use of riches that characterizes his letter to Pammachius and toward a notion of radical mental (self-)dispossession expressed in metaphors of violent intellectual and psychological reconfiguration. "He who renounces his character (*qui renuntiat moribus suis*) and

---

30. *Ep.* 40.11:

> quia per ipsas virtutum vias in vitia delabi possumus, et nisi certo, ut dixi, statu dirigentes animi momenta libremus, de ipsa humilitate capiemus superbiam, et evanescet species pietatis, si per laudem paupertatis obrepat inflatio. Et quid proderit caruisse divitiis, si remanemus divites vitiis? Unde quaesumus, ne ex illo nobis verbo domini blandiamini, quia fecerimus: "vendite quae possidetis," quia plus est quod superest illud: "et veni, sequere me." . . . nam et iste sermo, sicut omnis fere scriptura divina, in bivium patet: "vade et vende omnia tua." Non enim pecuniam tantum et fundos, extraneas facultates, sed etiam animi nostri internas, opes quae vere nostra substantia est, possidemus. Hanc vendere hoc est alienare a nobis tanto maior victoria, quanto altior difficultas est ingenita quam adposita separare et intus infixa divellere quam adfixa extrinsecus reicere.

On the letter's date, between 400 and 408, see Fabre, *Essai*, 83–86, and on the identification of Sanctus see chapter 8.

31. *Ep* 40.11: "Quamobrem orate solliciti ut . . . qui accepimus contemptum patrimonii accipiamus etiam nostri contemptum."

disowns himself for himself," Paulinus continues his admonition to Sanctus and Amandus, "changes and overcomes himself so that he fulfills that most potent saying of God: He who will lose his life on account of me will find it."[32] Paulinus's concern here penetrates to the most intimate reaches of personal identity, the "inner part" of our earthly mansion, and he reaffirms in uncompromising terms the link between renunciation of the *saeculum* and renunciation of *mores* that he had announced to Ausonius some years earlier,[33] though now in a manner that perhaps transcends even his own previous understanding. Secular renunciation may have less to do with the rejection of wealth than with the construction of a radically new identity.

A letter that Paulinus wrote to a certain Jovius carries this line of reasoning to its intriguing conclusion—or, from another perspective, brings it full circle back to Paulinus's final verse correspondence with Ausonius. If Pammachius, Sanctus, and Amandus were committed Christians with ascetic tendencies already evident, Jovius's religious affiliation is ambiguous.[34] Although he harbored Christian sympathies, approving even of Paulinus's way of life (*propositum*), Jovius was strongly attracted to pagan philosophy.[35] Wealthy, apparently residing in Gaul while owning property in Campania,[36] and well-read in classical literature, Jovius engaged Paulinus in a debate, one deeply seated in the western consciousness, over the respective roles of fortune and providence in human affairs. The single extant letter from Paulinus's correspondence with Jovius[37] and the poem (*carmen* 22) that Paulinus addressed to him are isolated fragments of this debate, but we know that in its course Paulinus urged Jovius to lift up his mind (*mens*) to the height of wisdom (*sapientia*), that is, to "Christ, the very tinder of the true light, who enlightens faithful souls."[38] Pressed by Jovius, who had previously countered Paulinus's summons to conversion with the reasonable claim that his involvement with "earthly affairs and concerns" prevented his full engagement with heavenly matters, Paulinus confronts bluntly the issue of wealth's impediment to the true philosophical or religious life. To meet Jovius's objections, moreover, Paulinus carried forward and

---

32. *Ep.* 40.11: "Se enim ipsum mutat et superat qui renuntiat moribus suis et se abdicat sibi, ut illud fortissimum dei verbum inpleat: qui perdet animam suam propter me inveniet eam" (Matt 10.39).

33. See chapter 4.

34. For sketches of Jovius see Fabre, *Paulin de Nole*, 171–75; Stroheker, *Der senatorische Adel*, 186, no. 206, who offers possible identification with a legate sent by Constantine to Honorius in 409 (Zos. 6.1.); W. Erdt, *Christentum und heidnisch-antike Bildung bei Paulin von Nola* (Meisenheim, 1976), esp. 10–14; *PLRE* 2, "Jovius 1." For the argument that Jovius was the author of *carm.*32 of Hartel's edition of Paulinus see F. G. Sirna, "Sul cosidetto 'poema ultimum' ps-Paoliniano," *Aevum* 35 (1961): 87–107.

35. See Erdt, *Christentum*, 11–12.

36. Inferred from reference at 16.1 to the couriers Posthumianus and Theridius, who carry Paulinus's letter to Jovius on their return to their *patria*. See *ep.* 27.2. On the family properties in Gaul see, for example, 16.9. At 16.1 Paulinus refers to a *patrimonium* that the context suggests should be located on the Campanian coast. See also Erdt, *Christentum*, 11.

37. On the letter's date, between 400 and 402, see Fabre, *Essai*, 47.

38. *Ep.* 16.6: "Erige in summam sapientiae mentem tuam et ipsum veri luminis fomitem Christum pete, qui fideles animas inluminat et pectora casta perlabitur."

recontextualized the argument he had made or soon would sketch out for Sanctus and Amandus. After rehearsing for Jovius the theme of secular *bona falsa* played some years earlier to Licentius, Paulinus turned squarely to the issue of Jovius's vast family wealth. It might be true that some pagan philosophers had dumped their money into the sea, Paulinus wrote,

> but you must make a division with God and render thanks to the highest Father as if for a favor (*beneficium*) on loan. Of all those things He has given you, however, inwardly or added from outside, He demands from you only yourself. It is permitted to you and your family to keep all that you possess, so long as you admit that God is the bestower (*largitor*) of these things also. For we have nothing which we have not received, who, as I said, came into this world naked.[39]

The severity of inner reorientation demanded of Jovius, notified that God "demands from you only yourself," may approach the level of commitment that Paulinus asks of Sanctus, to "disown himself for himself"; but for Jovius the proof of this self-abnegation and reidentification was not to be signaled in a renunciation of property and patrimony, the *contemptus patrimonii* that was the public mark of Paulinus's own conversion and his allegorically muted suggestion to Sanctus and Amandus. Rather, Jovius was implicitly being offered an opportunity to face the daunting eye of the needle by selling off the worthless literature and philosophy of the past and redirecting his future literary endeavors: "Dedicate to God the powers of your natural ability (*ingenium*) and the resources of your mind (*mens*) and tongue, offering to Him, as it was written, the sacrifice of praise, with eloquent tongue and devoted heart."[40] As *carmen* 22 makes equally clear, Paulinus envisioned the same conversion of poetics for the *litteratus* Jovius that he had himself experienced in the early 390s and urged on Ausonius, but he was fully willing to help Jovius "wield his lyre" on greater themes and "conceive thoughts of God" without demanding that he shunt off the impediments of material wealth and property.[41] Paulinus thus offers Jovius an unprecedented opportunity for "writing [his] way into a right relationship with the divine."[42] Although Paulinus may have seen a significant distinction between the Christian life he envisioned for Jovius and his own monastic calling, he does not suggest to Jovius, any more than he did to Licentius, that what he advocates to them is inferior in any way to his own *propositum*.

---

39. *Ep.* 16.9: "Sed tu divisionem cum deo facito et quasi mutuo beneficio redde summo patri gratiam, qui tamen de his, quaecumque tibi donavit ingenita aut adiecit extrinsecus, te tantum a te reposcit. Habeas licit tibi et tuis cuncta quae possides, tantum id curans, ut horum quoque largitorem deum esse fatearis. Nihil enim habemus quod non accepimus, qui in hunc, ut dixi, mundum nudi venimus" (1 Cor 4.7; Job 1.21).

40. *Ep.* 16.9: "Ingenii autem tui facultates et omnes mentis ac linguae opes deo dedica 'immolans ei,' sicut scriptum est, 'sacrificium laudis' ore facundo et corde devoto" (Ps 49.14).

41. *Carm.* 22.1–20.

42. Witke, *Numen Litterarum*, 99.

The subtly nuanced visions of Christian renunciation articulated across these letters to Crispianus, Licentius, Pammachius, Sanctus, and Jovius may have arisen from Paulinus's own experience of conversion, his sensitivity to the attitudes of individual correspondents, or even from the rich humanity of his spirit,[43] but Paulinus's apparent circumspection also speaks to broader and deeper social issues. If the later fourth century was an age "exhorted to asceticism" even by some financially shrewd churchmen,[44] property management and inheritance still mattered deeply to most wealthy families. Apparently even the ascetic impulses of such renowned figures as Melania the Elder, Paula, and Albina did not prohibit them from making provisions for heirs and attending to the responsibilities incumbent on the representatives of senatorial families.[45] Some of the resistance that met the news of Paulinus's own secular renunciation, like that later encountered by Melania the Younger and Pinianus, was rooted in the potential conflict between the ideal of ascetic repudiation of worldly attachments and aristocratic devotion to patrimonial continuity and the preservation of a powerful family's landed *regna*.

Paulinus appears to have understood that these social forces exercised power even on an individual already convinced of the necessity of renouncing the *saeculum*. Three letters survive from the correspondence of Paulinus with the otherwise unknown Aper. In telling ways Aper's life seems to echo that of Paulinus. Presumably a wealthy Gallo-Roman, Aper was well educated and eloquent, and he had earlier acted as an *advocatus* and served the imperial administration as a provincial governor (*iudex*).[46] Aper was ordained to the priesthood but withdrew from the urban and ecclesiastical world to live quietly on his estates while (as Paulinus eventually learned) his wife, Amanda, managed the family properties.[47] The couple lived in continence as Aper pursued scriptural study.[48] Paulinus had apparently known Aper before the latter's ascetic conversion and rural retreat, but these events, communicated to Paulinus in a letter now lost, apparently initiated the series of Paulinus's extant letters.[49]

The news from Aper was not all good: the image of placid, ascetic *otium* was apparently marred by inimical pressures. Aper's *secessio* had drawn hostile fire from

---

43. For example, Prete, *Paolino di Nola*, 78–82.

44. Lizzi, "Una società esortata all'ascetismo," esp. 140–44.

45. J. Harries, "'Treasure in Heaven': Property and Inheritance among Senators of Late Rome," in *Marriage and Property*, ed. E. Craik (Aberdeen, 1984), 54–70.

46. *Epp.* 38, 39, 44. Fabre, *Essai*, 75–83, dates them only to between 396 and 406, but tentatively with a relative chronology of 38, 44, 39 and a narrower time frame of 399–402. More recently it has been suggested by Leanza, "Aspetti esegetici," 78–80, that *ep.* 39 shows Paulinus's reading of Jerome's *Comm. in Ioel*, indicating a *terminus post quem* of 406 for that letter. Nothing in the letters indicates the whereabouts of Aper, but Gaul (and perhaps Aquitaine) are likely. On Aper's learning and public career see *epp.* 38.7–8, 44.1. See further Heinzelmann, "Gallische Prospographie," 555, "Aper 1."

47. *Epp.* 38.10, 44.4.

48. *Epp.* 39.1, 44.3, 38.10.

49. See Walsh, *ACW* 36:238.

some quarters, but Paulinus was by now adept at fielding such criticism. He reassures Aper—now a stranger and enemy to the world, a true imitator of Christ—[50] that his critics hate not him but Christ who exists in him; they despise most his Christian *humilitas* and *castitas*.[51] They are men who "intent only on the things before their eyes, excel in lust and avarice rather than belief in God."[52] Paulinus advocates persistence in his way of life, continued humility, and patience. Paulinus similarly attempts to soothe Aper's doubts over his retention of property; Aper feared that his *propositum* was hindered by the intrusive realities of estate management and the needs of his children.[53] In his first extant letter, in phrases echoing his praise of Pammachius, Paulinus tells Aper, "You have emptied yourself of the rich man so that you may be enriched as a poor man; and, hungering for justice, you have been freed from the satiety of useless fullness so that you may be filled by the true goods of a pious poverty."[54] Perhaps only later did Paulinus learn of the arrangement by which Aper had turned management of the family properties over to Amanda. Still, Paulinus approves: "She takes care of secular concerns, lest you care for them; she takes care of them so that you may take care of heavenly matters. She seems to have possessions, so that you may not be possessed by the world, but by Christ."[55]

Paulinus does not suggest to Aper, as he did not to the more worldly Jovius, that he abandon his estates or abrogate his responsibilities to his sons. Again the logic of mental detachment from and mastery over riches facilitates the approbation of Aper's discreet retention of his property. Moreover, Paulinus recognizes a deeper justification. He sees in Aper's situation, as he had in an anxious Severus's, outlines of the grand divine economy that links rich and poor and provides the opportunity for virtue to win merit:

> I judge these things to have been determined by divine plan, which has provided you rather with manifold opportunity for practicing your faith and for perfecting your virtue. For since the entire possession of the world seems established for man and subjected to men, who doubts that everywhere in the world and in every part of nature advantages have been prepared for the human race and that we may not only take from these carnal benefits, but we may even more greatly reap spiritual ones?[56]

---

50. *Ep.* 38.2.

51. *Ep.* 38.3.

52. *Ep.* 38.6: "qui praesentibus tantum rebus intenti praestant avaritiae et libidini, ne credant deo."

53. *Ep.* 39.2.

54. *Ep.* 38.8: "inanitus es a divite, ut diteris in paupere, et ab illa supervacuae distentionis saturitate vacuatus es, ut veris piae pauperitatis bonis implearis esuriens iustitiam."

55. *Ep.* 44.4: "Curat illa saeculi curas, ne tu cures; curat ut <caeli> cures. Possidere videtur, ne tu possidearis a mundo et ut possidearis a Christo."

56. *Ep.* 39.2: "in multimodam potius vobis exercendae fidei perficiendaeque virtutis materiam divino haec esse proposita consilio iudicamus. Cum enim haec universa mundi possessio propter

The nature of those spiritual benefits, Paulinus suggests, may be gleaned from allegorical or analogic exploration of images of agriculture or animal husbandry, just as, for instance, Wisdom directs us for edification to the ants and the bees, "both country creatures."[57] Or Aper's estates could offer him, like Pammachius, the opportunity to translate wealth into spiritual capital through the alchemy of alms. Here, too, Paulinus envisions Amanda as Aper's dutiful agent: "Throwing open her hands to the pauper and extending the fruit of her work to the helpless, she weighs out the spiritual tax (*vectigal*) and assigns the revenue of her possessions to your soldier's salary (*stipendium*), more eager of a salutary loss (*damnum*) than a deadly profit (*lucrum*)."[58] Thus Aper's carefully managed secular renunciation frees him from secular attachment and drains his wealth of its pernicious potential without seriously disrupting his estates or threatening the welfare and rank of the next generation. It remains unclear whether Aper's renunciation and the consequent reorientation of his secular economy to bring it into conformity with a more pressing divine economy actually involved the loss of any family holdings.

To be sure, these passages from Paulinus's letters should not be deployed along a single axis of hermeneutical evolution; they are rather, at least to our eyes, only fortuitously preserved markers in an exegetical field whose exact contours and boundaries are now difficult to discern. Moreover, the addressees of these letters are of such varied, and in many cases uncertain, background and commitments that facile generalization would be imprudent. In these letters theological and intellectual justifications jostle with sometimes conflicting practical and apologetic issues. Nevertheless, a persistent tendency does emerge forcefully from these texts. Like other contemporary exegetes constructing new texts and new meaning out of Biblical intertexts, Paulinus often undercuts the primary or literal meaning of a "recalcitrant" passage by "constraining" or "expanding" it with the help of another passage or with the aid of allegory.[59] In such manner, for example, Luke's tale of Lazarus and the *dives* provides a philanthropic wedge with which Paulinus can pry open the needle's eye of Matthew 19.24. In similar fashion Paul's warning to property owners "to be as if not possessing" (1 Cor 7.30) helps Paulinus to shift the lethal weight of vast temporal goods onto the props of mental detachment and mastery. Thus, writing from Nola, Paulinus endorses a partial détente between an

---

hominem constituta hominique subiecta videatur, quis ambigat in omni loco mundi, in omni parte naturae utilitates humano <generi> paratas, e quibus non solum carnalia emolumenta capiamus, sed multo magis spiritalia perlegamus."

57. *Ep.* 39.2 with Prov 6.6–8, 30.25 and Sir. 11.3.

58. *Ep.* 44.4: "'manus suas adaperiens pauperi' [Prov 31.20] et fructum operae suae porrigens inopi spiritale vectigal pensitat et reditum possessionis in tuae militiae stipendium suggerit, salutaris damni avarior quam letalis lucri."

59. As do, for example, both Chrysostom and Jerome, though to different ends. See E. Clark, "Reading Asceticism: Exegetical Strategies in the Early Christian Rhetoric of Renunciation," *Biblical Interpretation* 5 (1997): 82–105.

ascetic impulse perceived as subversive of traditional elite values and aristocratic families still deeply imbued with those values. To privilege mental detachment, the reconfiguration of *mores,* and a spiritual economy centered on charitable use was to open the door not only to Aper, who in his own understanding had renounced the world for Christ, but even to Jovius, still searching for the common ground between his philosophical preoccupations and the monastic *propositum* exemplified for him by Paulinus's life.[60] Recognition of the range and subtlety of Paulinus's thinking about property and redemption is critical to our appreciation of his relationship to and use of his own patrimony after 394.

CHARITY, CHURCH BUILDING, AND A PROPRIETARY SENSIBILITY

Even for those intent on doing so, offloading the property accumulated by a wealthy family over several generations could not have been easy. Other family members might strenuously object, as apparently did Severus's father, abandoned as he was in the entangling nets of his possessions when his son tied his lot to a heavenly *pater.*[61] But family resistance was only part of the problem: the market might become saturated, questions of tax liability might impede the process, and the anticipated plight of agricultural laborers and tenants might intervene. Thus Melania the Younger and Pinianus required the assistance of Serena, wife of Stilicho, to realize the sale of some estates,[62] and Severus complained to Paulinus about his inability to sell one of his properties.[63] Indeed, we may reasonably suspect that the latitude with which Paulinus approached the renunciation of his friends and correspondents was in part a pragmatic response to the various logistical problems faced by those who sincerely wanted to divest but found their way blocked by circumstances beyond their easy control. But more often than not in such matters our sources fail us, for, although their ascetic leanings may be richly documented, the exact arrangements made by even the better-known members of the ascetic elite for the sale or distribution of their property are seldom preserved.

Characteristically, Paulinus's letters and poems offer only incidental insight, often vague and allusive, into the nature of his own property divestment. Conjecture is possible, of course. Paulinus, like other ascetic converts, may have honored the conventions of elite society by passing on some property to agnate heirs or to collateral branches of the family, and he may have sold some property outside the

60. *Ep.* 16.1: "cum certe studiosus Christiani nominis conprobatorque propositi etiam nostri amore docearis."

61. *Ep.* 5.6.

62. *Vita Melaniae* 12, with E. Clark, *Melania,* 101–2.

63. *Ep.* 24.1, though the issues are vague.

family;[64] but no such instances can be documented. It is also likely, and quite reasonable to suspect, that Paulinus transferred some estates from his legal control to the ownership of the church, as Severus, whom Paulinus calls both a seller (*venditor*) and a donor (*largitor*), seems to have done.[65] Such donated estates would have been free from at least the extraordinary compulsory state services that would still have encumbered them if Paulinus had retained ownership after his ordination.[66] In any case, the legal alienation of a senator's wealth and landed property is unlikely to have happened quickly, and this aspect of secular renunciation should be envisioned as a protracted process rather than a sudden reversal. Paulinus apparently retained control, if not ownership, of some property for many years after his conversion in Spain in the fall of 394 and certainly never relinquished the proprietary attitudes that had so long governed his relations with his lands and his dependents.

In the summer of 396, for example, the year after his arrival at Nola, Paulinus is found sending north a substantial group of *pueri*—slaves and freedmen—to attend to business and property interests in Aquitaine. This group was specifically charged with acquiring oil and wine and shipping them back to Nola; the wine, a *vinum vetus* that presumably came from Paulinus's Aquitanian estates, was then in storage at Narbo.[67] Paulinus's transitional years at Nola, during which he transformed himself from a conventional landowner into a more ambiguous *dominus*, may have seen a number of similar parties set out for properties or former properties in Spain and Gaul. The ambivalent nature of Paulinus's relationship with his patrimony after 395, however, is better highlighted by his participation in and oversight of the construction of two churches on or near former estates, one in Aquitaine and the other in Latium. Paulinus's explicit comments on his motivations for undertaking the latter project provide a valuable context for assessing the more opaque Aquitanian affair.

We learn of Paulinus's activities at Fundi, a town of southern Latium midway between Nola and Rome, from a letter that he sent to Severus in 403 or 404. Much of that letter is given over to descriptions of Paulinus's building and renovation work around the tomb of Felix. But Paulinus also includes in his letter copies of various *tituli* inscribed or painted on the walls of the Nolan complex, and he appends a report on his construction project at Fundi. Here, where Paulinus once

---

64. So Harries, "Treasure in Heaven," 63–64; Lizzi, "Una sociatà esortata all'ascetismo," 148–52.

65. *Ep.* 24.1: "venditor largitorque fundorum et ideo sine animi captivitate possessor, quia quae reservasti ecclesia te serviente possideat."

66. See *CTh* 16.2.15 (359 / 60), but note the apparent violation of this exemption suggested by 16.2.40 (411 / 12). For wider context see M. Salzman, "The Evidence for the Conversion of the Roman Empire to Christianity in Book 16 of the *Theodosian Code*," *Historia* 42 (1993): 362–78, esp. 367 on this issue. More broadly Jones, *The Later Roman Empire*, 894–99.

67. *Ep.* 5.21–22, essentially an attachment to the letter. The nature of the requested *nigellatum* is unclear. Perhaps it refers to a dark oil or wine (Walsh, *ACW* 35:223) or a medicinal oil (Santaniello, *Le lettere*, 257).

owned property and had visited often,[68] he is now building a basilica, and he sends to Severus a copy of the verse inscription he had composed for its apse.[69] Although the Fundanan property in question had by the date of this letter apparently passed out of Paulinus's ownership, perhaps sold outright or donated to the church there, the previous visits to which Paulinus refers in this letter of 403 or 404 may have included some made in the course of his regular journeys to Rome after 395, for Fundi was conveniently located on the Via Appia. A letter of 408, for example, finds Paulinus spending a day of rest at Formiae, near Fundi, en route to Rome.[70] On one point, however, Paulinus's letter is explicit. Severus is meant to see clearly the wellsprings of Paulinus's philanthropy: "I longed to found a basilica in that very town," he informs Severus, "either as a pledge of my civic affection (*pignus quasi civicae caritatis*) or as a memorial of my former paternal estate (*memoriam praeteriti patrimonii*), since the town was in need of one, its own being ruinous and small."[71]

Similar combinations of civic affection, familial pride, and patronal sensibility had goaded elite euergetism for centuries. The Younger Pliny, motivated by such a constellation of private and public forces, had given liberally to his home town of Comum. His gifts included a library and an endowment for its maintenance, public baths, and an alimentary fund that supported some 175 children. Subsequently Pliny's will supplemented these gifts with a large sum for the decoration and upkeep of the baths and a fund for the maintenance of one hundred of his freedmen, the proceeds of which were eventually to be used for providing an annual banquet for the *plebs urbana* of Comum.[72] Such patterns of largesse and patronage, which had underwritten the splendor of early imperial cities at the same time that they memorialized powerful families, now provided much of the revenue for church building and adornment, equally satisfying secular and religious needs.[73] For if the objects of aristocratic munificence had begun to change under the influence of Christian *caritas*,[74] Paulinus's words serve notice that the complexity of the social forces driving such projects had not diminished. In Paulinus's view building a church at Fundi was an apt way to serve the congregation there,

---

68. *Ep.* 32.17: "Egrediamur iam Nolana hac basilica et in Fundanam transeamus. Fundis nomen oppido est, quod aeque familiare mihi fuit, dum maneret possessio, quam illic usitatiorem habui."

69. See *ep.* 32.17 for the *titulus* describing the apse painting and an epigram recounting the relics to be placed in a casket under the altar. For reconstructions of the apse painting see J. Gadeyne, "Alcuni considerazione sulla descrizione Paolina del mosaico absidiale di Fondi," *Boreas* 13 (1990): 71–74.

70. *Ep.* 45.1.

71. *Ep.* 32.17.

72. Sources and discussion at R. Duncan-Jones, *The Economy of the Roman Empire: Quantitative Studies* (Cambridge, 1974): 27–32; J. Nicols, "Pliny and the Patronage of Communities," *Hermes* 108 (1980): 365–85, esp. 379–81.

73. On this point see Ward-Perkins, *From Classical Antiquity to the Middle Ages*, concisely at 70–71.

74. See, for example, F. Consolino, "Sante o patrone? Le aristocratiche tardoantiche e il potere della carità," *Studi storici* 30 (1989): 969–91, esp. 976.

to declare his love (*caritas*) for the town, and to provide a permanent reminder of his family's former status. Not unlike Pliny's library at Comum, the new basilica at Fundi, its walls bearing Paulinus's verses, eloquently translated landed property (or its proceeds) into a public monument that spoke more loudly about Paulinus's patronal stance before the civic and ecclesiastical community than any rural or suburban estate could have done. By the late fourth century church building had come to unite in an incomparable way the age's secular and religious activity.[75]

Although we do not know the details of the financial transactions that underwrote Paulinus's construction project at Fundi, they may have differed little from those that facilitated similar commemoration and philanthropy in the region of Bordeaux. The tantalizing clues to this affair appear in two letters addressed to Amandus and Delphinus, priest and bishop at Bordeaux, that Paulinus wrote between 397 and 400. In the earlier letter Paulinus commended to the care of Amandus a certain Sanemarius.[76] Paulinus had recently manumitted Sanemarius, who was carrying Paulinus's letter to Bordeaux, and he now asked that his new *libertus* be assigned to the alternative "holy slavery" of tending the *memoria* of Paulinus's parents. At the same time, Paulinus requested that a certain priest named Exsuperius be instructed to award Sanemarius a small plot (*terrula*) on the estate of the church (*in casa ecclesiae*). And finally Paulinus suggested that Amandus might employ "one of the Alingonenses" to carry on into Gaul certain letters of Paulinus related to other business. This bundle of requests strongly suggests, first, either that the *memoria* to Paulinus's parents and the *ecclesia* of the priest Exsuperius were near to each other or that the land of the church of Exsuperius contained the *memoria*, and, second, that both church and *memoria* were located on or near a (former) family estate in the territory of Alingo, perhaps the modern Langon, 47 kilometers up the Garonne from Bordeaux.[77]

Further details emerge in a letter of 400 or 401 addressed to Bordeaux's bishop Delphinus, which records the construction and dedication of a new church (*ecclesia*) at Alingo. Paulinus's words to Delphinus in this letter demonstrate his considerable involvement in the ecclesiastical building project. He fully expects the work will redound to his spiritual credit. "I rejoice and glory in the Lord," he told Delphinus, "because both visibly and invisibly, as truly a good father and the patron of my salvation, you work for the salvation of my house . . . visibly you work for me in the building of churches, so that you give us a share with that one [the Centurion] whose house deserved to be visited by Christ."[78] Here, of course, resonate the echoes of that investment principle justified elsewhere by the story of Lazarus

---

75. Ward-Perkins, *From Classical Antiquity to the Middle Ages*, 84.

76. *Ep.* 12.12, following up on a request he had already made to Delphinus.

77. Maillé, *Recherches*, 30 ff.

78. *Ep.* 20.3: "Nos vero gaudemus et gloriamur in domino, quia et visibiliter et invisibiliter operaris salutem <in>domum nostram vere pater bonus et salutaris patronus . . . visibiliter autem nobis operaris in fabricis ecclesiarum, ut partem nobis facias cum illo, cuius domus a Christo meruit visitari." Cp. Luke 7.2–10.

and the *dives*, but church building is now construed, like almsgiving, as a form of wealth devoted to Christ. But at least one of Paulinus's other motives at Alingo, as seen in these two letters, was to provide a system of maintenance for the *memoria* that, like the newly built church at Alingo, both memorialized Paulinus's parents and reified the family's local influence. Indeed the *ecclesia* of Alingo, apparently home to Paulinus's parental *memoria* and now seemingly a *parochia* of Delphinus's episcopal see, was probably created out of a parcel of Paulinus's Aquitanian lands. At Alingo as at Fundi we sense a melding of familial and civic or ecclesiastical interests and a conflation of religious and secular motives; and, in consequence, we may even sense the inadequacy of such categories for capturing the essence of the cultural moment.

Perhaps even more than Paulinus's remarks on the church at Fundi, the events at Alingo blur the distinctions between formal ownership and a more vaguely defined patronal sensibility. If Paulinus had ceded ownership at Alingo, he had nevertheless not fully yielded his proprietary interest. He requested a grant of church land for Sanemarius, a freedman and legal *cliens;* he advised Amandus to chose a letter carrier from among the Alingonenses, that is, from among those who were likely to have been his former tenants or *coloni;* and in the construction of the church at Alingo he presented himself as, by implication, the son and client of Delphinus, who appears here and elsewhere as Paulinus's agent in Aquitanian affairs.[79] But if the presence of his parents' tomb at Alingo helps to explain his claims there, that fact may not account for another moment of intervention in the property concerns of the Bordelais church. In 399 Paulinus again asked Amandus to supply a small plot of land (*manci-piolum*) to the wife of his courier, an exorcist named Cardamas.[80] Thus Cardamas's wife, like Sanemarius, may have found herself settled on land that had once been Paulinus's property but which was now held by the church at Bordeaux; and, like the new church at Alingo, Cardamas, his wife, Sanemarius, and surely other dependents of Paulinus as well, represented constant, if more humble, reminders of Paulinus's persistent role in the social and ecclesiastical life of the *patria* he had abandoned.

If in the years after his permanent relocation to Italy Paulinus still maintained proprietary claims on lands and friends in Aquitaine, his presence must have loomed even larger over those Campanian lands that he still possessed or had transferred to the church. Although we lack specific evidence for the juridical fate of these properties, the implications of Paulinus's program of philanthropy and church building at Nola largely offset that loss. Paulinus's various projects at Nola must have been partly, if not largely, funded by the proceeds from the sale of properties or from the annual revenues of the estates he retained or donated to the church, and both Paulinus's own writings and the witness of archaeology suggest that Paulinus displayed his munificence at Nola on a grand scale.

---

79. See chapter 7 on the Daducii affair.
80. *Epp.* 15.4 with 19.4.

As we have seen, Paulinus's letter to Pammachius made care of the poor the piv-
otal act in the salvation drama that equalized the divinely ordained imbalance of
material wealth. By securing the temporal welfare of Sanemarius and of Cardamas
and his wife, Paulinus managed to pursue such philanthropic ends even in the area
around distant Bordeaux. But after 395 the primary scenes of Paulinus's offerings
to the less fortunate were played out around the shrine of Felix. Here, as governor
in the early 380s, Paulinus had raised a structure to shelter the poor who gathered
at the saint's tomb. When, in the opening years of the fifth century, he erected new
buildings for this purpose, he candidly asked those who sought out the new porti-
coes to pay for their food and shelter with prayer: "So that we may perform friendly
services for each other in turn," Paulinus remarked publicly in January 407, "they
strengthen our foundations by praying and we warm the bodies of our destitute
brothers under our roof."[81] The annual January festival was a particularly high-
profile setting for such reciprocity, as wealthier visitors were encouraged to give
alms to the substantial crowds of country folk (*rustici*) or to provide them with meals
through the slaughter of previously pledged cattle or pigs.[82] But, as elsewhere in the
cities and towns of the late empire,[83] there must have been at Nola a more regular
system of daily provision for those *pauperes* whose distress was not regulated by the
festival calendar. In the image of Paulinus's deathbed payment of forty gold coins
to local merchants who had been supplying clothing for the poor, we may glimpse
the more quotidian operation of almsgiving and social relief at Nola.[84]

The most visible sign of wealth turned redemptive at Nola, however, recalls us
more readily to Paulinus's building projects at Fundi and Alingo. The explicit mo-
tives that encouraged Paulinus to erect the basilica at Fundi here coalesced with his
devotion to Felix to spur the construction of a new monumental complex around
the saint's tomb. The architectural details, exact plans, and spatial relationships of
the structures erected or renovated by Paulinus at Cimitile in the first years of the
fifth century remain elusive despite several periods of modern excavation and
study,[85] but enough can be said to illustrate the grandeur of Paulinus's designs

---

81. *Carm.* 21.392–94:

> commoda praestemus nobis ut amica vicissim,
> fundamenta illi confirment nostra precantes,
> nos fraterna inopum fovemus corpora tecto.

82. See chapter 7.
83. E. Patlagean, *Pauvreté économique et pauvreté sociale à Byzance, 4e–7e siècles* (Paris and The Hague,
1977), 191–95.
84. Uranius, *De obitu,* 3; see appendix D.
85. On the excavations see above chapter 2. Two of the *natalicia, carm.* 27 and 28 (of 403 and 404),
and one letter, *ep.* 32 (of 403 or 404) provide most of the textual information on Paulinus's buildings at
Nola (Cimitile). More recent than Hartel's edition of the relevant sections of these texts is that by R. C.
Goldschmidt, *Paulinus' Churches at Nola: Texts, Translations, and Commentary* (Amsterdam, 1940), 34–89,

(figure 1b). The centerpiece was a new church, the Basilica Nova, constructed just to the north of the older funerary basilica of the saint.[86] Paulinus described it to Severus in the same letter that contains his reference to the church at Fundi:[87] oriented on a north-south axis, the new basilica's northern end terminated in an innovative triple-lobed apse (*absis trichora*).[88] The apse vault was adorned with a mosaic depicting the Trinity, the Apostles, and the Evangelists, and its floor and walls were faced with marble.[89] The altar, located in the apse, housed the relics of numerous saints and martyrs as well as a fragment of the true cross, a gift from Melania the Elder.[90] The nave, some thirty meters long, was divided by a twin colonnade and had on each side two chapels for prayer and for the burial of "the clergy and their friends."[91] Throughout the basilica were verse *tituli* such as one that explained to viewers the symbolism of the vault mosaic.[92]

The construction of this new basilica between 400 and 403 also involved a modification of the plan of the older one, the so-called Basilica Vetus, which contained the actual tomb of Felix.[93] Part of the north wall of this funerary basilica was removed to permit a line of sight from the apse of Paulinus's new basilica through a triple archway to the tomb of Felix in the western end of the funerary

---

with invaluable commentary, 92–195. The difficulties of reconstructing architectural realities from Paulinus's poetic descriptions are well illustrated by Testini's article, "Paolino e le costruzioni di Cimitile (Nola): Basiliche o tombe privilegiate?" *L'inhumation priviligiée du IVe au VIIIe siècle en Occident: Actes du colloque tenu à Creteil les 16–18 mars 1984,* ed. Y. Duval and C. Picard (Paris, 1986), 213–19.

86. See the plan by A. Mercogliano in Testini, "Note," 331, reprinted in Mercogliano, *Le basiliche paleocristiane,* 276–77. See further Testini, "Note," 358–60, Mercogliano, 175–92, and Lehmann, "Lo sviluppo," 80–81.

87. *Ep.* 32.10–16.

88. On the place of this apse in the early evolution of the Christian basilica with triconch apse see T. Lehmann, "Zur Genese der Trikonchosbasiliken," *Innovation in der Spätantike: Kolloquium Basel 6. und 7. Mai 1994* (Wiesbaden, 1996), 317–57, denying the Basilica Nova its commonly assigned status as a prototype by stressing the disproportionate size of the central apse and the nature of sightlines that precluded views of the side apses from the central nave.

89. On the in situ remnants of the mosaic and the *opus sectile* see Lehmann, "Lo sviluppo," 81. For the possible arrangement of the accompanying *tituli* see Lehmann, "Eine spätantike Inschriftensammlung," 255–58, 281. See also Mercogliano, *Le basiliche paleocristiane,* 175–79, which reprints several attempts by art historians to reconstruct the apse mosaic on the basis of Paulinus's description and compares with it the mosaic of St. Apollinare in Classe (Ravenna), whose iconography was anticipated by the Nolan work.

90. The altar's relics are enumerated at *carm.* 27.406–39. *Ep.* 31.1: Melania was given a fragment of the cross by John of Jerusalem; she in turn presented Paulinus with a fragment. When Severus was searching for relics for his new church at Primuliacum, Therasia sent some of the cross to Bassula, his mother-in-law, who resided with him. Paulinus subsequently composed a poem for the altar relics at Primuliacum (*ep.* 32.7–8).

91. *Ep.* 32.12: "religiosi ac familiares." Cf. the gloss by Goldschmidt, *Paulinus' Churches,* 107. See also A. Grabar, *Martyrium: Recherches sur le culte des reliques et l'art chrétien antique* (Paris, 1946; rept. London, 1972), 1:489–90. Mercogliano, *Le basiliche paleocristiane,* 175, indicates eleven columns per side.

92. *Ep.* 32.10.

93. At *carm.* 28.268–69 (of 14 January 404) Paulinus noted the completion of the building in the third year after its commencement. If the construction was finished in 403, it must have been begun in 400.

church.[94] The old basilica was also extensively renovated. Craftsmen were hired to install marble facings and wooden ceiling panels designed to simulate ivory, and the building's old pillars were replaced with marble columns. Painters were commissioned to embellish the interior with "the likenesses of divine countenances," and a New Testament fresco cycle was added to the area around the tomb.[95] This and other internal spaces were also demarcated by the addition of new marble *cancelli*, or barriers, inscribed with biblical maxims.[96]

Paulinus's massive efforts on behalf of these two basilicas were complemented by expenditure on various auxiliary structures not yet revealed by archaeology: Paulinus identifies a baptistry, a series of handsome courtyards, and lodgings for guests as well as the permanent members of the community. The baptistry was attached in some fashion to the new basilica, and its domed roof was decorated with stars.[97] The primary courtyard (*vestibulum* or *atrium*), perhaps occupying the space between Pauli-

94. *Ep.* 32.13.

95. On these renovations see *carm.* 27.382–94. On the work of the painter see 386: "pictor imaginibus divina ferentibus ora." On the new columns see also *carm.* 28.200. On the New Testament cycle see D. Korol, "Zu den gemalten Architekturdarstellungen des NT-Zyklus' und zur Mosaikausstattung der 'Aula' über den Gräbern von Felix und Paulinus in Cimitile / Nola," *JbAChr.* 30 (1987): 156–71.

96. See A. Ferrua, "Cancelli di Cimitile con scritte bibliche," *Römische Quartelschrift* 68 (1973): 50–68, which publishes thirty-four whole or fragmentary inscriptions and concludes that the screens were carved and inscribed during the period of Paulinus's building activity. Ferrua bases this conclusion on the correspondence between the maxims selected for presentation and both the thought of Paulinus and verses quoted by him in his letters and poems; the style of the *cancelli* and of the lettering; and the divergences between the form assumed by the verses cited and their later form in the Vulgate tradition. For photographs of some of these *cancelli* see Mercogliano, *Le basiliche paleocristiane*, 122–23. The mosaic-decorated peristyle still in place around the tomb is now dated to the later fifth century and not attributed to Paulinus (Lehmann, "Lo sviluppo," 83). Around the inside of this peristyle, in mosaic, runs a series of eight lines of verse recording an enhancement of the basilica. Hartel included these in the corpus of Paulinus's poems as *carm.* 30.2 (see, however, the corrected edition of the inscription by Ferrua, "Le iscrizioni paleocristiane di Cimitile," *Revista di archeologia cristiana* 53 [1977]: 105–7), although they are attested by none of the manuscripts of Paulinus. Their attribution to Paulinus is now explicitly denied by Lehmann, "Eine spätantike Inschriftensammlung," 248–50.

97. It is not clear whether this baptistry was attached, but external, to the new basilica or a separate room in the basilica itself; but it is clearly considered part of the basilica. *Carm.* 28.180–84 (Goldschmidt):

> est etiam interiore sinu maioris in aulae
> insita cella procul quasi filia culminis eius,
> stellato speciosa tholo trinoque recessu
> dispositis sinuata locis.

Testini, "Paolino e le costruzioni di Cimitile," 216, using Hartel's reading of line 180, "interiore situ," and remarking that Paulinus did not employ the word *baptisterium* in his description, concluded that the room in question was within the basilica. This is too confident. Other elements of the description, the *tholus* and the undulating walls with their recesses, point to a structure distinct but attached, as so many baptistries were. The recently discovered octagonal structure to the east of the apse of the Basilica Nova, perhaps a baptistry, is post-Paulinian (Lehmann, "Lo sviluppo," 81–82).

nus's new basilica and the older funerary church, was dominated by a large fountain, and the porticoes that ran along its sides were decorated with paintings depicting Old Testament scenes.[98] Above the porticoes, which provided shelter for poorer pilgrims, was a second story with lodgings (*habiticula*) for more distinguished visitors and the permanent community.[99] Around an outer courtyard were more lodgings.[100] Paulinus himself eventually lived in one of these structures.[101]

The new church, the courtyards and fountains, the marbles and frescoes of this martyrial complex represent a bold new instantiation of financial resources that Paulinus commanded either from the profits of sale or the revenues of leftover private property and lands assigned to the Nolan church.[102] The scale and magnificence of these buildings entailed the commitment of significant funds. And, although Paulinus is likely to have solicited other contributions,[103] justly might he have turned back on himself his praise of Severus as "rich in wealth lavished on Christ."[104] In that sense as well, these building projects vividly illustrate the redirection of Paulinus's social action into the channels of thought adumbrated in his correspondence. On the one hand, riches bestowed on Christ through the medium

98. See *carm.* 27.365–66. On the fountains, 27.463–64, 28.29 ff; on the paintings, 27.511–41.

99. *Carm.* 27.395–405.

100. *Carm.* 28.53–59.

101. It is almost impossible to distinguish among the various courtyards and lodges mentioned by Paulinus, in part because his remarks are often vague, in part because they date from different periods of the complex's architectural history. As governor in the early 380s Paulinus had erected the covering (*tegimen*) for the poor near the tomb, and, after the addition of a second story, Paulinus was living there in 407 (*carm.* 21.384–94). When this work was done is not certain. In 400, before the building of the new basilica, Paulinus informed Severus that he lived in a cottage (*tugurium*) raised off the ground and separated from the guest apartments (*cellulae hospitales*) by a portico. It was here that he housed Melania the Elder and her relatives in 400 (*ep.* 29.13). It seems likely that these remarks refer to the same structure. Whether this is also to be identified with the *habiticula* surrounding the inner courtyard (*carm.* 27.395–405) is not clear. There must have been several different structures built to accommodate the more prestigious visitors to the shrine. Others, we know, found lodging in town during the festival or spent the night in the open porticoes (cf. *carm.* 20.337; 21.90). For a fuller discussion see Lienhard, *Paulinus of Nola*, 70–72, with bibliography.

102. Prete, "I temi," 260–63.

103. Possibly to be seen in the "argentum illud sancti comercii" that Jovius had been forwarding to Paulinus (*ep.* 16.1), but this is uncertain. Walsh, *ACW* 35:244.

104. *Ep.* 32.3: "Dives opum Christo." The translation is Walsh's. Paulinus employed the phrase in a *titulus* composed to commemorate the baptistry erected by Severus at Primuliacum. At the same time that Paulinus was building at Nola, Severus was building on his Aquitainian estate. See esp. *ep.* 32.1–10. The two men exchanged ideas and information: Severus sent the regular courier Victor to Nola with sketches (*picturae*) of his new basilicas and copies of its *tituli*, and Paulinus returned Victor to Severus with pictures of the Nolan churches and their inscriptions (32.9–10). Paulinus also composed a number of verses for the decoration of Severus's churches (32.6–7). Earlier Severus had asked Paulinus to send a portrait of himself to Primuliacum for inclusion in the baptistry there (*ep.* 30.2), and when Paulinus declined Severus had one painted from memory. This portrait of Paulinus was placed along with one of Saint Martin in the baptistry that connected the two churches built by Severus. The deed

of his saints, like those used by Pammachius to succor the poor,[105] were cleansed of their debilitating taint. Church building thus emerged as another mode of the appropriate use of wealth motivated by a complex sense of *caritas,* but it was one that, like Paulinus's conception of almsgiving, kept the benefactor very much at the center of attention. But at the same time, Paulinus articulates his own relationship to the newly embellished *locus sanctus* of Felix in a dense and multivalent language that recalls both the reluctance of his correspondence with Aper to draw a firm line between ownership and control and also the elision of property ownership and property stewardship that characterizes the compromise offered to Jovius.

In January 403, as at least the initial stage of the project was nearing completion, Paulinus used a portion of that year's *natalicium* to lead the visiting Nicetas of Remesiana and the rest of his audience on a verbal tour of the structures so far finished.[106] These new buildings of Felix's shrine, Paulinus announces, are his own achievements (*mea gesta*), and with this proclamation Paulinus, perhaps merely by reflex, locates his *gesta* within a civic context easily understood by an aristocratic elite accustomed to receiving commemoration and honor in return for munificence expressed in the funding of public buildings. For if such acts of munificence had long confirmed and enhanced the status of donors, they also obligated the community to acknowledge benefactors in both concrete and intangible ways. And beyond public statues and honorary inscriptions, financial contributions were still more readily rewarded socially and politically than economically.[107] Pliny, because of his senatorial rank, may have garnered only prestige from his gifts to Comum and other towns,[108] but prestige was a valuable commodity. Indeed, *laus* and *honor* were singled out by Paulinus as the twin fruits of his work in brick and concrete, marble and fresco. Felix, Paulinus observed in another *natalicium,* had permitted his "halls" to grow through the effort of Paulinus, furnishing to him thereby the "esteem of praise" in the present and the "title of honor" for the future.[109]

---

having been done, Paulinus composed two epigrams to accompany the paintings (32.2), and other poems for the baptistry (32.5). Paulinus's name as well as his face could be seen on the walls of Severus's church complex: the poem Paulinus composed for the tomb of Martin's disciple Clarus specifically mentioned both Paulinus and Therasia (32.6). See chapter 8.

105. *Ep.* 13.20.

106. *Carm.* 27.345–53: "nunc, age, sancte parens, aurem mihi dede manumque. . . . nam cui iure magis mea gesta retexam / Felicisque manu nobis operata revolam, / quam cui cura sumus?"

107. Patlagean, *Pauvreté économique,* 182–83.

108. Nicols, "Pliny and the Patronage of Communties," esp. 379–83.

109. *Carm.* 21.572–76:

> illa etiam, quibus et nunc gratia laudis
> quaeritur et post <nos> retinetur nomen honoris,
> addidit, ut tantis numquam retro conditus aevis
> nostro opere extructas adcrescere vel renovari
> porticibus domibusque suas permitteret aulas.

In this same work, the *natalicium* of 407, Paulinus also elaborates at some length on his current status as the impoverished client of Felix and the happy resident and steward of these magnificent earthly "halls"—which, however, truly belong to the saint. But Paulinus's elaboration only further blurs the categories of ownership and proprietary rights. The crucial passage follows Paulinus's account of the events that have led him to abandon his home and his patrimony in exchange for the family of Felix at Nola and the hope of salvation. "What things similar to these," he declares, "did I have when I was called senator such as I now have here, when I am called poor . . . on all sides and everywhere alike, whatever is cultivated, celebrated, and kept in the name of the blessed Felix, in every area is my house (*domus*). Nor is there any place," he continues, "joined to these sanctuaries or within them which is not accessible to me as if it were my own."[110] Then, giving rein to the metaphorical possibilities latent in the image of the "house of Felix," and perhaps intending to forestall potential critics of his poverty, Paulinus observes, "But why do I boast in this gift, if I, a house-born slave and guest, possess (*possideam*) this property of my beloved Felix, with its visible covering of stones? How much more it means to me that Felix himself is, by the gift of God, a house for me, in whom my life possesses a living house which will never fall down."[111] And this turn to Felix as a spiritualized "house" leads to reflections in which literal and metaphorical understandings of "possession" strain vigorously and without resolution against each other: "As to the fact that the house of Felix is also my house, he himself granting to me free rein

---

110. On the narrative that precedes these remarks see the discussion in chapter 4. *Carm.* 21. 458–68:

> Quid simile his habui, cum dicerer esse senator,
> qualia nunc istic habeo, cum dicor egenus?
> Ecce mihi per tot benedicti martyris aulas
> et spatiis amplas et culminibus sublimes
> et recavis alte laquearibus ambitiosas
> inriguas et aquis et porticibus redimitas,
> undique ubique simul, quodcumque per ista beati
> nomine Felicis colitur celebratur habetur,
> omnibus in spatiis domus est mea. Nec locus ullus
> aedibus illius coniunctus et insitus extat,
> qui mihi non quasi res pateat mea.

111. *Carm* 21. 468–73:

>   Sed quid in isto
> munere me iactem, si rem Felicis amati
> visibili lapidum tecto vernaculus hospes
> possideam? Quanto plus est mihi, quod mihi Felix
> ipse dei dono domus est, in quo mea vivam
> vita domum nullis lapsuram possidet annis?

with his possessions, even my boldness (*audacia*) attests through these favors (*officia*): for as a host I have received my comrades under these roofs and now we all hold the rights of Felix with equal right."[112] "Now deprived of my wealth," Paulinus sums up, "not of wealth but more truly free from hateful burdens, free of possessing (*liber habendi*), I enjoy serene poverty."[113]

By 407 Paulinus was fully prepared to express his relationship to the cult complex he had constructed with a tour de force of elusive metaphor, rhetorical antithesis, and ascetic paradoxes. A proprietary sensibility is asserted even as ownership is denied, and the distinctions may have been no clearer to many in Paulinus's audience then than they are for us today. Indeed, if elsewhere in the Roman world ecclesiastical architects and their patrons were co-opting the elements of imperial style and reloading the already intimidating force of monumental architecture with blatantly Christian significance,[114] at Nola Paulinus was advancing this synthesis in an intensely personal way. As resident and caretaker of a holy shrine, he had constructed a complex that replicated the courtyards, reception halls, porticoes, and fountains that were the architectural hallmarks of power and social status in the suburban and rural villas of late antiquity's elites. The same power aesthetic that conditioned late Roman aristocrats' reception of their guests also informed Paulinus's manner of welcoming Felix's faithful into their common domicile. Like Paulinus's words, so too did his manipulation of space and form assert his patronal bearing.

In the *natalicium* of 407, then, renunciation theory and practice merge in a passage that subtly restates ideas we have already met in, for example, Paulinus's praise for Pammachius and others who knew how to possess wealth but remain free of possessing, or in his approbation of Aper, who also relied on the surrogate ownership of another to secure his own serene poverty. "She seems to have possessions so that you may not be possessed by the world, but by Christ," Paulinus said of Aper's wife.[115] By 407 Paulinus could represent his relationship to the halls of Felix

---

112. *Carm* 21. 474–78:

> Nam quod Felicis domus et mea sit domus, ipso
> permittente sui licitas mihi iuris habenas,
> his etiam probat officiis audacia nostra,
> hospita quod socios in tecta recepimus et nunc
> omnes iure pari Felicis iura tenemus.

113. *Carm* 21. 500–502:

> At modo cassus opum, nec opum sed verius expers
> damnatorum onerum, secura liber habendi
> paupertate fruor.

114. For example, Krautheimer, *Early Christian and Byzantine Architecture*, 39–42 passim.
115. *Ep.* 44.4.

in similar terms. Although he had transformed landed wealth into a monumental cult center, these magnificent buildings and their accoutrements belonged not to him, but to his companion Felix. It was a technical transfer of ownership that hardly diminished Paulinus's proprietary spirit, however, and much of the thinking of the former master of Hebromagus and governor of Campania still informs these verses expressing his *audacia,* reciprocating *officia,* and receiving his aristocratic friends under the roofs of his magnificent *domus.* This same way of thinking typifies other aspects of Paulinus's interaction with the region around Nola.

The audacity of Paulinus in these matters of asceticism and property may be evident only if set in a wider context, for if his various discourses on property and salvation and his actions and words at Nola are understandable within a social and cultural context illuminated by the lives of other western aristocrats lured by ascetic precepts,[116] they nevertheless set him at variance with a number of contemporary monastic thinkers. While Paulinus, for example, offered Jovius the distinctive image of pagan philosophers casting their wealth into the sea only to counter it with a less stringent Christian alternative, Jerome had earlier presented the new monk Paulinus with the same image for the opposite purpose of proving the necessity of true poverty for the committed Christian. Indeed, Jerome brought this image into explicit and natural conjunction with the text of Matthew 19.21.[117] Moreover, when Jerome first wrote to Paulinus in 394 to encourage his renunciation of the world, he advised him immediately to reject all his possessions, explicitly warning him against the type of progressive distribution of his wealth that seems to have been Paulinus's method after 394.[118]

Other monastic writers in the decades ahead would be as adamant on this matter as Jerome. Between 420 and 429 John Cassian, addressing the issue of covetousness (*filargyria*), demanded absolute poverty of the monk. He condemned the practices of those of "lukewarm and wretched condition" whose renunciation was incomplete.[119] He criticized both those who kept back a portion of their money or property as well as those who, like Aper, relied on the services of a woman to provide surrogate ownership.[120] As for those who hoped to blunt the literal edge of Matthew 19.21 by recourse to a theory of charitable giving "and under this color judge that they do not have to throw away their riches; indeed pronouncing themselves more blessed if, supported by their old fortune, they also give to others from their superabundance," Cassian proclaimed, "they know they are deceiving themselves and know that clinging to their former riches they have renounced this

---

116. For further discussion see Ramsey, "Almsgiving in the Latin Church."

117. *Ep.* 16.8 with Jer. *ep.* 58.2.

118. *Ep.* 53.11.

119. *Institutiones* 7.18: "tepido ac miserabile statu." *CSEL* 17 (1888), ed. M. Petschenig; and more recently J.-C. Guy, *Institutions cénobitiques* SC 109 (Paris, 1965).

120. 7.14; 7.11.

world not at all (*nequaquam renuntiasse huic mundo*). If they truly and indeed desire to put to the test the *professio* of the monk," he continued, "having given up and forsaken all things and reserving nothing from those things that they have renounced, let them glory with the apostle 'in hunger and thirst, in cold and nakedness' (2 Cor 2.27)."[121] Moreover, the underlying assumption of Cassian's *Institutes* was that only within a monastic community was true renunciation (and the quest for perfection) possible. Aper's *secessus in villam*, approved by Paulinus, should have fallen extremely short in Cassian's sterner view.[122]

And perhaps under that of Eucherius of Lyon as well. Eucherius's *De contemptu mundi et saecularis philosophiae*,[123] written like Cassian's *Institutes* in the 420s, parallels Paulinus's letter to Jovius in important ways. As we saw in chapter 1 it too was a protreptic tract addressed to a wealthy and educated monastic outsider, Valerianus. Eucherius's *paraenesis* develops many of the same philosophical themes as Paulinus's letter.[124] But Eucherius's Gaul of *fames, vastitas,* and *bella* appears much grimmer than Paulinus's Gaul of some thirty years earlier, and a more urgent eschatological vision informs his exhortation.[125] Eucherius, like Paulinus, emphasizes that Valerianus's possessions were not truly his: "Because whatever you now love, is His; His, I say, it is His."[126] In this context he does not, however, promote the compromise by which Paulinus was willing to facilitate Jovius's retention and enjoyment of his property in exchange for a literary and intellectual turnaround.

If it is even generally true that monastic spirituality rejected the concept of the neutrality of riches argued earlier by Clement of Alexandria[127] and that both Cassian and Eucherius exercised an almost unsurpassed influence on the spirituality of Gaul in the fifth century,[128] then Paulinus's contrary claims would seem to marginalize him. Paulinus's thinking on property renunciation and on the role of wealth in the lives of those who would be perfect locates him closer to Clement

---

121. 7.16.

122. On the role of the monastery see, for example, *Institutiones* 7.29. Rousseau, *Ascetics, Authority, and the Church,* 199–205, softened the hard line drawn by Cassian in this text between the monastery and the world.

123. *Epistola paraenetica ad Valerianum cognatum de contemptu mundi et saecularis philosphiae* (*PL* 50.711–26) = *Il rifiuto del mondo: De contemptu mundi,* ed. S. Pricoco (Florence, 1990).

124. For instance, the well-worn contrast between the transitory and the eternal (714); between the true and the real, and the spurious and the apparent (722B–C); between the errors of the many and the truth perceived by the few (718A). *Opum voluptas* and *honorum dignitas* enmesh men in the *negotia saeculi,* and these in turn "blanda desideriis vitia inspirant" (716A).

125. 722C–723B. If Paulinus had been prepared to admit to Jovius that some pagan thinkers had indeed "reached the outlines of the highest truth" (ep. 16.8), Eucherius offers Valerianus no such concession.

126. 721A: "Quia et quidquid nunc amas, suum est; suum, inquam, suum est."

127. So Pricoco, *L'isola dei santi: Il cenobio di Lerino e le origini del monachesimo gallico* (Rome, 1978), 148.

128. F. Consolino, *Ascesi e mondanità nella Gallia tardoantica* (Naples, 1979), 10.

than to the Cassian of the *Institutes*.[129] His spiritual economy credits properly used wealth with a fundamental role in God's salvific plan. He could sanction mental renunciation of ownership as the virtual equivalent of physical repudiation. But rather than marginalize him, the distinctiveness of Paulinus's voice on these fundamental problems of Christian society and monastic self-definition should stand as a further demonstration of the intensely fluid and formative character of this period, for even Eucherius honored Paulinus's claim to membership in the monastic and ascetic community of the age.[130]

129. But see also, J.-C. Guy, "La place du 'mépris du monde' dans le monachisme ancien," *Le mépris du monde: La notion de mépris du monde dans la tradition spirituelle occidentale* (Paris, 1965), 5–17, suggesting that Cassian, inspired by the Stoic theory of *adiaphora*, was prepared to argue that wealth was neither intrinsically good or bad but neutral (*media*). See *Conf.* 3.7.11. Guy concluded that Cassian was aware of the difficulties of renunciation and in the *Conferences* tried to accommodate them by shifting the emphasis to use and inner conversion. Guy's survey of contemporary writers does not include Paulinus.

130. *PL* 50.718D–719A. See chapter 1.

CHAPTER 7

The Cult of Saint Felix

It was probably in the year 406 that a "sudden prodigy" disquieted the keepers of the tomb of Saint Felix.[1] The perfumed oil that was customarily poured into and extracted from the sepulchre unexpectedly emerged contaminated by dust, fragments of bone, and shards. Those withdrawing the oil were visibly shaken, fearing that some small animal, as was the way of such "forsaken beasts (*monstra*)" of the countryside, had violated the inner coffin (*arca*).[2] Not only was the sanctified oil's medicinal power made suspect by this turn of events, but the very integrity of the entombed corpse was challenged. Such ominous ripples in the cosmological order had always demanded pontifical response. Entrusted with the responsibility by Nola's bishop, Paulinus and several other priests, following the delay forced by yet another eruption of earth from the tomb, supervised a group of anxious workmen as they disassembled the sepulchre. The railings were removed from their sockets and the silver-covered, fenestrated, upper marble slab of the tomb lifted off. To the relief and wonder of all, the coffin beneath appeared intact, and, as Paulinus later reported, "faith confirmed drove the danger of error from wavering hearts."[3] Expiation was unnecessary after all; no crime (*piaculum*), as reflexively feared, had provoked the "strange event."[4] Sight and touch had confirmed the integrity of Felix's *arca*.[5] The saint's bones retained their honor, Felix still lay in tranquil repose, not putrefying death, and the tomb was secure as the abode not only of the martyr's body but also of the Holy Spirit and living grace.[6]

---

1. The events are narrated in the *nat.* of 407: *carm.* 21.558–642. 600–602: "Nova res movet omnes / et studium accendit subiti disquirere causam / prodigii."

2. *Carm.* 21.610–14. On this oil's use see also *carm.* 18.38–39.

3. *Carm.* 21.626–27: "tunc secura fides dubio de corde periclum / erroris pepulit."

4. *Carm.* 21.629–30. 21.600: "nova res."

5. *Carm.* 21.627: "cum tactu oculoque probaret."

6. *Carm.* 21.632–33. Following G. Chierici's excavation in 1955 of the supposed sepulchre of Felix, examination of "Felix's" bones was conducted by Prof. V. Palmieri of the University of Naples at the

When Paulinus presented his account of these events in the *natalicium* that he recited during the festival of Felix in January 407, he reformulated the initially misread "prodigy" as yet another sign of Felix's "great love" for him. His autopsy of Felix's physical remains now emerged as yet another manifestation of the saint's *pietas* for the man who had lavished untold wealth and care on his halls.[7] Felix's desire to have Paulinus gaze on his tomb's "holy secrets" and "terrible mystery,"[8] was the gift of a "generous patron."[9] As a kind father, Felix wished to demonstrate his "special love (*amor*)" by allowing his tomb, "so silent and undisturbed for so many previous generations," to be opened during Paulinus's lifetime.[10] In the aftermath of events, Paulinus, self-styled object of the saint's love, his client and son, used his poetic performance to transform a traumatic disruption of the shrine's routines into a further affirmation of his unique relationship with Felix. Following Paulinus's supervision of the tomb's inspection, which allowed him to stage-manage events as closely as possible, his verses sought a similar control over the meaning of those events. Staging and explaining were the twin prerogatives of a saint's impresario.[11]

By 407, indeed, Paulinus was exceptionally well positioned to orchestrate affairs at the tomb of Felix and to offer exegesis of the miraculous events that transpired there. He had arrived at Nola more than a decade earlier and immediately begun to fashion in verse and deeds his distinctly personal claims on the affection and patronage of a saint whose entombed body, lying in silent repose, and vital soul, enjoying celestial life, were, as he supposed, two brilliant points on an arc bridging heaven and earth.[12] Moreover, Paulinus's authority, soon heavily underscored by his well-publicized relationship with Felix, also empowered him to effect the further Christianization of the region and to exercise an influence on secular affairs that defies any simple definition of religious leadership.

THE *NATALICIA:* PAULINUS AS *AUCTOR* AND *ACTOR*

Arriving at Nola in 395, Paulinus immediately assumed a role that others had surely already developed, perhaps to a high degree. Undoubtedly the tomb and

---

request of the Bishop of Nola, Mons. Adolfo Binni. Palmiere reported that the bones belonged to a man of forty or more and were many centuries old. See A. Ruggiero, "Carme 21," 206; D. Korol, "Alcune novità riguardo alla storia delle tombe venerate e del complesso centrale nel luogo di pellegrinaggio di Cimitile / Nola," *Akten des XII. Internationalen Kongresses* (Rome, 1995), 933–34.

7. *Carm.* 21.579–80: "ut magnae pietatis luceat instar, / qua nos indignos tanto dignatus amore est."

8. *Carm.* 21.577–78: "secreta sancta"; 581: "acranum verendum."

9. *Carm.* 21.644–45: "profusi patroni."

10. *Carm.* 21.561–65.

11. The felicitous term is Brown's, from *The Cult of the Saints*, 90, a study to which this section owes debts all too obvious.

12. See, for example, *carm.* 18.82–97.

festival of Felix had long required caretakers and managers. The patronage of Damasus implied by his poetic celebration of Felix, the rise of at least a rudimentary complex of buildings around the shrine, even Paulinus's own acts of patronage and attendance at the festival in the later 370s and early 380s, all speak to the cult's importance and sophistication decades before Paulinus's settlement beside the tomb. Only Paulinus's first *natalicium* composed at Nola, however, provides contemporary literary evidence for the size and character of the cult and festival. In that short, thirty-six–verse poem written for the festival of 396, Paulinus described the crowds of people with the hyberbolic images that became common in his later poems. Even in midwinter, he announced, a multicolored folk converging on Nola painted the roads with its mottled throng, as one city welcomed into its midst the citizens of countless others. Already Nola, boasting Felix as its protector (*praesul*) and heavenly patron (*patronus*), yielded first place only to a Rome honored by the Apostles' tombs.[13] The *natalicium* of 397 enhanced these images of surfeit, in part through allusion to Virgil's well-known description of the "gathering of the clans" and in part by cataloging the notable cities of Latium and Campania whose peoples hastened to Felix's feast. Even the Appian Way, Paulinus claimed, disappeared beneath the throngs.[14]

Accommodating such a host of pilgrims and fairgoers, even discounting their number in accord with the poet's license for exaggeration, must have honed the organizational skills of Nola's clerics and townsmen and called forth a managerial coterie well before Paulinus's arrival in 395. If not the Nolan bishop Paul,[15] then surely others of notable local or regional stature had been managing the cult and festival of Felix for some time. Indeed, we should not allow Paulinus's natural ease in the role of impresario to deflect attention from the presumptuous character of his takeover. Tensions may well have marred his intrusion into affairs at Nola, and initial resentment of his self-assertion may have anticipated the conflicts that eventually disrupted relations between Paulinus's new suburban community and the town.

Paulinus's initial claim on the impresario's role at the shrine of Felix presumably rested most heavily on the deference due a senatorial aristocrat, a great landowner, and a former governor and local patron. It was surely not Paulinus's tenure of clerical office but rather this deep reserve of influence, with its promise of liberality (whose sources were paradoxically enriched by his recent assumption of the ascetic aura), that so quickly drew Campania's bishops to his door and en-

13. *Carm.* 13.26–30. On Paulinus's use of *patronus* and other terms in this context see C. Iannicelli, "Note al lessico Paoliniano: Indagine su alcuni apellativi riferiti a S. Felice," *Impegno e Dialogo* 8 (1990–91): 183–204.

14. *Carm.* 14.44–88, 14.70: "confertis longe latet Appia turbis."

15. On Paul: *ep.* 32.15 gives the name; *carm.* 19.520 places the *antistes* performing service in the basilica (nova?); *carm.* 28.180 credits baptism in the baptistry to the bishop. In *carm.* 21.619 it is the bishop who entrusts inspection of the tomb to the priests.

abled him to establish himself as the special friend of a saint and the architect of his sacral time and space. Moreover, although Paulinus may well have observed both Damasus and Ambrose perfecting their administrative and exegetical skills as the clients of saintly patrons, from the outset Paulinus's situation at Nola was strikingly unlike that of these two men. Damasus and Ambrose were bishops; Paulinus, during the years illustrated by the *natalicia*, was a priest, albeit one whose poems and letters seldom remind his audience that official ecclesiastical authority at Nola resided with Paul.[16] And although Paulinus reveals no tension between himself and Paul, who must have been drastically overshadowed by the rank and wealth of Paulinus, elsewhere in these years bishops exercised, or sought to exercise, control of the cults of local martyrs and confessors. Thus Sulpicius Severus eventually lost his bid for the cult of Martin to the bishops of Tours,[17] and Ambrose's *inventio* and translation of the relics of Gervasius and Protasius into the Basilica Ambrosiana, another drama known to Paulinus, provides a case study of episcopal manipulation.[18]

These two examples highlight a further contrast with the Nolan situation. Both the cult of Martin at Tours and that of Gervasius and Protasius at Milan, like many others in the West outside Rome in this age, were new cults emerging under episcopal sponsorship. From the perspective of an episcopally centered church, Paulinus's anomalous position placed the sanctuary of Felix, now also the residence of Paulinus, rather nearer to the private periphery. Established in the suburbs of Nola, aloof from the urban cathedra, free from many of the constraints that hemmed in a bishop in a city crowded with Christian *potentiores* and imperial agents, and enjoying the prerogatives of ambiguous status, Paulinus cut a figure substantially different from Damasus, Ambrose, or the bishops of Tours.

Perhaps in part for such reasons, when Paulinus appeared as a new monk and freshly ordained presbyter to assume control within a ritual setting whose structures must already have been reasonably well established, he almost immediately began to articulate, enact, and inscribe his claims on the cult and person of Felix in terms that echo, but in a strikingly different key, those of his arrival on the scene. From our vantage point, it appears that much of the responsibility for conveying to others Paulinus's claims, his new self-understanding, and his conception of the central place that Felix and the saints should enjoy in private, rural, and civic life fell to the *natalicia* declaimed every January at Felix's festival.[19] For that

16. The *tituli* composed by Paulinus for the basilica complex did recognize Paul's episcopacy. See *ep.* 32.15.

17. L. Pietri, *La ville de Tours du IVe au VIe siècle: Naissance d'une cité chrétienne* (Rome, 1983), 103–12.

18. McLynn, *Ambrose*, 209–15, with Paulinus's remarks at *carm.* 19.317 ff.

19. Internal references to the audience at, for example, *carm.* 18.8, 18.62–64, 18.210, 26.318, 19.385–86. See further Fabre, *Paulin de Nole*, 341–43; J. Fontaine, "Les symbolismes de la cithare," 135 n. 9.

reason, and also because Paulinus used these performances to present striking images from the panorama of spectacles that unfolded at the shrine, the fourteen extant *natalicia* now preserve a rich, idiosyncratic ledger of life and events in the vicinity of a holy tomb.

Moreover, as Paulinus's enthusiasm for performance apparently increased with time, so did the length of the *natalicia*. From short pieces in 395 and 396, they grow unsteadily to the 858-verse poem of 407, and consequently these hexameter works make up well over half of Paulinus's surviving poetic corpus.[20] We meet in this poetry a happy cross-fertilization of the confessional qualities evident in Paulinus's poetic epistles to Ausonius and the descriptive, exegetical, and apologetic techniques he had explored, for example, in his earlier *epyllion* on John the Baptist. Richly allusive to both classical precursors and scriptural themes, boldly episodic and yet driven forward by their persistent focus on Felix, these poems fulfill the promise made earlier of a divinely inspired Christian poetics of praise.[21] At the same time, by virtue of their status as performance art, they harness the exegetical potential of "liturgical" poetry to the service of a saint and his self-proclaimed client. But Paulinus's *natalicia* did much more than proclaim to contemporaries a record of events and miracles or display before them Paulinus's fruitful marriage of classical poetics and Christian themes. Paulinus also employed this poetry as a powerful medium for the assertion of his claims to authority at Nola and for the explicit (re)construction of his public identity, for these poems presented Paulinus as both *auctor* and *actor*. He appeared before the *natalicia*'s audiences (or readers) simultaneously as a narrator of sacred tales and as a character in the dramas he recounted; these roles were easily elided, for they reinforced Paulinus's claim to be both the impresario and the spokesman of Felix.

As we have already glimpsed in the affair of the prodigy at Felix's tomb, the *natalicia* provided Paulinus a public platform from which he could attempt to determine the meaning of events, to draw out their morals, or to strip away the veil that concealed the divine will directing them. But as this poetry slipped toward homily it also provided opportune moments for conspicuous self-representation. Hence the *natalicia* preserve in vivid strokes the nuances of a bold relationship entwining a saint and his special earthly ward. Like the narrator of the *Confessions*, the narrator of the *natalicia* sometimes makes forays into his past to delineate the moral shape of his present self.[22] Paulinus, however, is less inclined than Augustine to

---

20. The *natalicia* constitute fourteen of the thirty poems ascribed to Paulinus and approximately 63 percent of the extant lines in the corpus. Note that the fourteenth *natalicium* (*carm.* 29) is really a short collection of fragments.

21. Cf. *carm.* 15.26–49 on the rejection of the Muses for the poetic inspiration of Christ, with H. Junod-Ammerbauer, "Le poète chrétien selon Paulin de Nole: L'adaptation des thèmes classiques dans les *Natalicia*," *REAug* 21 (1975), esp. 22–28; G. Guttilla, "Preghiere e invocazioni nei *carmi* di S. Paolino di Nola," *Annali del liceo classico 'G. Garbaldi' di Palermo* 28–30 (1991–93): 93–188. On praise see S. Costanza, "I generi letterari nell'opera poetica di Paolino di Nola," *Augustinianum* 14 (1974): 637–50.

22. J. Winkler, *Auctor & Actor: A Narratological Reading of Apuleius's* The Golden Ass (Berkeley, 1985), esp. 135–42, quote 141. Most notably the autobiographical excursus of *carm.* 21.

configure his earlier years as enemy territory; he prefers to sketch out his identity through constant reminders of the special relationship that has bound him then and now to Felix and after 395 overrides his previous, more traditional claims on the people of the region. It is to the subtle modulations of this relationship with Felix that I turn attention before considering Paulinus's choreography of space and time at the shrine and festival of Felix.

A PRIVATE STAR

Paulinus began promoting his distinctive relationship with Felix even before his arrival in Campania. The first *natalicium*, composed in Spain, anticipates Paulinus's imminent journey to Nola and stresses the depth and longevity of his commitment to Felix;[23] it introduces much of the lexicon that Paulinus subsequently employs to represent his relations with Felix. Already designated here as *pater* and *dominus*, Felix dominates Paulinus and his household, cast as *servi* and *famuli*. But however sweet and pleasant the yoke of holy servitude, Felix's further role as Paulinus's *comes* hints at more intimate and less threatening bonds, merging the saint with those *daemones* and astral "companions" long believed to aid and care for their terrestrial counterparts.[24] The themes of dependency, intimacy, and continuity expressed in the images and metaphors of holy slavery, of friendship, and of Felix's resolute guardianship of a Paulinus so long away from Nola reemerge boldly in the *natalicium* of the next year, the first composed at the shrine. Now, however, Felix's companionship also explicitly attains a critical new dimension. Paulinus now champions this confessor, set by Christ in his Father's hall, as a potent intercessor, an intermediary capable of channeling on to Christ prayers addressed to him and of exercising such influence in the court of heaven that Felix's love can be sensed even behind the protective hand of Christ himself.[25] To be sure, this was a vision of divine hierarchy deeply indebted to the workings of an imperial court where results were often most readily produced by favor and influence. But by virtue of this fact, Paulinus's self-representation as Felix's *comes* authorized his own superior status in the chain of intercessors that reached heavenward. For as Felix represented Paulinus before the heavenly court, so Paulinus represented Felix before men. In a discretely layered universe,[26] Paulinus, too, was an intermediary.

23. For example, *carm.* 12.17: "sede tua procul heu! quamvis non mente remoti."

24. *Comes* at 12. 25; *dulce iugum* at 12.32–33. Felix's astral abode is specific at *carm.* 13.23 of the next year. See further Brown, *The Cult of the Saints*, esp. 55–56.

25. *Carm* 13.2–3, 15–16, 18–19: "redit alma dies, qua te sibi summus / adscivit patriam confessum Christus in aulam. . . . nam tua sensi / praesidia in domino superans maris aspera Christo. . . . hunc [Christum], precor, aeterna pietate et pace serenum / posce tuis . . . Felix." Following Ruggiero, *Paolino di Nola: I carmi. Testo latino con introduzione, traduzione italiana, note e indici* (Naples, 1996), 1:214–15.

26. P. Brown, *Authority and the Sacred: Aspects of the Christianisation of the Roman World* (Cambridge, 1995), 8–11.

These paradoxical constructions of intimacy and hierarchy, so forcefully as-
serted in the first two *natalicia,* would be reiterated and refined yearly. At the festi-
val of 403, with Nicetas of Remesiana present, Paulinus was frank as he recast and
melded venerable images of political and spiritual guardianship: "For although
the crowds of people from various regions may today pour out their pious joy with
similar vows, nevertheless it is fitting that I rejoice more richly and remarkably,
because no one is bound more closely to Felix as a debtor than me, for whom this
day brought forth so great a patron without end (*sine fine patronum*)—more pecu-
liarly my own than a private star (*privatus aster*)."[27] Incident after incident demon-
strates Felix's special love for Paulinus; and favors repay favors in customary man-
ner as each exchange further reinforces the links of patronage and friendship that
connect the earthly tomb preserving Felix's body and the heavenly *aula* adorned
by his soul.[28] Moreover, Felix's intercessory role soon expands to encompass spon-
sorship of the faithfuls' souls before the supreme Judge (*iudex*): verbally foreshad-
owing the scene later painted in the apse of the Fundanan basilica, Paulinus envi-
sions himself among Felix's followers, set not with the goats on the Lord's left, but
among the sheep on his right.[29] The enduring quality of the bond uniting the saint
and his ward is spelled out in remarkable detail in the autobiographical section of
the *natalicium* of 407. As *auctor* in that year Paulinus offers himself as the *actor* in a
lifelong drama whose script is never far removed from Felix's hand.

These images of affection and care binding a saint and his ward float easily on
the surfaces of Paulinus's *natalicia,* but before 407 Paulinus had already enlisted
Felix's aid in a more subtle construction of his public identity. In January of 398
and 399, Paulinus recited before the festival crowds the earliest known "passio po-
etica," a two-part life of Felix.[30] Embellishing freely on oral tradition,[31] Paulinus

27. *Carm.* 27.142–47:

nam licet e varia populi regione frequentes
conparibus votis hodie pia gaudia fundant,
me tamen uberius decet atque insignius isto
exultare die, quia nemo obstrictior est me
debitor huic, cui privato specialius astro
ista dies tantum peperit sine fine patronum.

28. *Carm.* 18.105–6: "[Christus] addidit ornatum caelis nec pignore terras / orbavit."
29. *Carm.* 14.124–35, with Matt 25.31–34. Cp. *ep.* 32.17.
30. S. Prete, "Paolino agiografo: Gli atti di S. Felice di Nola (*carm.* 15–16)," *Atti del Convegno* 149–59
= *Motivi ascetici e letterari* 103–16, quote 104. On the unified structure and integrity of the two poems see
W. Evenpoel, "The Vita Felicis of Paulinus Nolanus," *Aevum inter Utrumque: Mélanges offerts à Gabriel
Sanders* (Steenbrugis, 1991), 143–52.
31. On this and other issues see also A. Ruggiero, "La 'Vita Felicis' di Paolino di Nola come fonte
per la conoscenza della religiosità popolare in Campania nei secoli IV e V," *Paolino di Nola: Momenti
della sua vita e delle sue opere* (Nola, 1983),163–97; G. Luongo, *Lo specchio dell' agiografo: S. Felice nei carmi XV
e XVI di Paolino di Nola* (Naples, 1992), 18–26.

reached back across the decades that separated the present time from the heroic age of persecution to draw Felix close. The *natalicium* of 398, nearly three times longer than the previous year's poem, carries the *vita Felicis* from Felix's boyhood devotion to Christ, through his fulfillment of the lower clerical orders and his presbyterial ordination,[32] to his confessor's witness and his invincible loyalty to the aged Nolan bishop Maximus during a period of persecution. Unwavering in his faith, Felix withstands torture to win the crown of martyrdom, be wondrously released from prison by an angel, and restore a dying Maximus with the help of miraculously produced fruit.

In the installment of Felix's tale presented as the *natalicium* of the next year, renewed persecution provides the context for further displays of Felix's fortitude and for the divine favor it prompted. A spider's web, God's handiwork, deceives pursuers, while food prepared by a pious but unaware old woman sustains Felix in hiding. During six months of seclusion in a dry cistern, Felix's only companion is Christ, who converses with Felix, feeds him with his own hand, and quenches his thirst with the sweet dew of a cloud. With the end of persecution and the death of Maximus, Felix declines the episcopal office offered him, preferring to serve a more deserving successor, the aged Quintus. Likewise Felix refuses to reclaim the estates and houses of his patrimony and, despite the protestations of others, lives as a tenant on a small property whose garden he cultivates with his own hands and whose produce he bestows on the Lord by sharing it with the poor. Often attired in rags, "unkempt in body while adorning his mind," in the fullness of time Felix "changed rather than closed the days of his holy life."[33]

Paulinus's *vita Felicis* is a rich tapestry of miracle story, biblical and classical echoes, hagiographic themes, and ascetic precepts interwoven with exhortation and moral instruction.[34] Like the other *natalicia*, the *vita* was meant to educate and delight. The *passio* lifted up Felix before his Nolan *patria*,[35] reassuring the audience of the wisdom of their allegiance to the saint by recounting the astonishing events that warranted his claim to the nurturing and intimate friendship of Christ.[36] But Paulinus's verses, of course, also accomplished other ends. The poet's words and images ineluctably drew the audience's attention from biographical subject to biographical *auctor*. The ascetic virtues espoused by Felix were instantly recognizable as those advocated by Paulinus and epitomized by his own life of secular renunciation. Urged to take back his possessions, "Felix" echoes the sentiments we have already met in Paulinus's letters: "It is better to have salvation without

---

32. On contemporary context and Paulinus's possible apologetic aims here see Luongo, *Lo specchio dell' agiografo*, 80–87.

33. *Carm.* 16.296: "exornans inculto corpore mentem." 16.299: "mutavitque piae, non clausit saecula vitae."

34. See further Prete, "Paolino agiografo"; Luongo, *Lo specchio dell' agiografo*, for example, 49–60.

35. *Carm.* 15.54.

36. Cp. *carm.* 18.103–4: "cum Christus amicam / adsumens animam casto deus hausit ab ore."

wealth," Felix replies, "than riches without life. As a rich man I will be without God, but as a poor man I will have Christ. The grace of Christ will enrich the man poor in wealth."[37] Though smaller in scale, the wealth of Felix's garden, like that of Pammachius, Aper, or Paulinus himself, was returned to Christ through the medium of the poor.[38] And when Paulinus describes the ascetic regimen adopted by Felix after the restoration of peace, he explicitly links the trials of the confessor with the self-imposed hardships of the ascetic: "Nor did Felix overcome lesser battles in peace," Paulinus remarks, "than as a confessor he had waged with strong arms. In grim times he had spurned bodily health; likewise, during untroubled peace he disdained both riches and honors."[39] As the confessor Felix posthumously validated Paulinus's ascetic precepts, so the *monk* Paulinus, ostentatiously rejecting riches and *honores*, now embodies the confessor's witness. Asceticism, the *vita Felicis* proclaims, is the equivalent of martyrdom in an age that no longer knows imperial persecution.

Through such constructions, biography slides almost imperceptibly into autobiography.[40] But this subtle elision of subject and narrator is underscored by striking parallels, some quite obvious, between the *vita Felicis* and the emerging *vita Paulini*. Like Paulinus, the *vita*'s Felix was noble and wealthy; and though Felix was born at Nola, his "Syrian" family's origins too were distant.[41] Like Paulinus, the *vita*'s Felix rejected vast *patrimonia* in favor of being the co-heir of Christ.[42] With allusion to Paulinus's ecclesiastical rank, Felix preferred to remain a priest, though one of noticeably episcopal profile,[43] even when offered the bishopric. And, perhaps prompted by the model of Jacob and Esau, Paulinus developed at some length a reference to Felix's worldly brother who, like his own lamented brother, had preferred the transient to the eternal.[44] If this fraternal connection was obscure for some listeners (though perhaps less so for Gallic readers), the *vita*'s vivid closing image of Felix the *colonus* tending a small garden (*hortus*) should have helped his audience to bridge the gap between narrator and subject, for by then Paulinus himself had also assumed the role of ascetic gardener. In 396, pressing his request

37. *Carm.* 16.281–83: "praestat, opes salvo desint quam vita opulento; dives egebo deo, nam Christum pauper habebo. divitiis inopem ditabit gratia Christi."

38. *Carm.* 16.287–89.

39. *Carm.* 16.246–50.

40. Also recognized by Prete, "Paolino agiografo," 111–12; Luongo, *Lo specchio dell' agiografo*, 86–90. On the autobiographical use of biography see further Trout, "*Amicitia, Auctoritas*, and Self-Fashioning Texts."

41. *Carm.* 15.50–53.

42. *Carm.* 15.82–84: "iste [Felix] solum caelo vertit, patrimonia regnis; / ille heres [Hermias] tantum proprii patris, iste [Felix] coheres / Christi." Cf. the expansion of this idea at *carm.* 16.254–83. Notably, however, Felix even seems to reject the argument that he might use his wealth to support the poor (16.272–73).

43. Luongo, *Lo specchio dell' agiografo*, 71–74.

44. *Carm.* 15.76–101, with Gen 25.22 ff.

that Severus join him at Nola, where he would welcome him into the "bosom of Felix," who was to be henceforth their "common patron," Paulinus had added: "Then shall I set you in the monastery not only as a tenant (*inquilinus*) of the martyr close by, but as a *colonus* in his *hortus*."[45] When Severus made light of this invitation to become Paulinus's fellow laborer in the garden of Felix, Paulinus bristled in his next letter: "I have not abandoned Hebromagus for the sake of a little garden (*hortulus*), as you write, but have preferred that garden of paradise to my patrimony and my country."[46] The metaphorical possibilities of Paulinus's horticultural imagery do not preclude a more literal reading.[47] Presumably Paulinus could have been seen on occasion "working" in the garden of Felix, and such images might have enhanced for his audience the biographical overlap of the saint and his client. As it blurred the boundaries of identity, then, the *vita Felicis* did its part to help erode the distinctions between Paulinus and the saint, who, more peculiarly his than a "private star," was near to becoming an upward extension of himself.

Felix's astral immortality and celestial companionship with Christ, and thus his viability as Paulinus's heavenly patron, were also confirmed for contemporaries through familiar images of heavenly ascension. Like the language of *amicitia* and *clientela*, metaphors of the released soul's heavenward flight had tenacious roots in the pagan milieu Paulinus had once known well. In the *natalicium* that he presented in January 400, having completed his *vita Felicis* the previous year, Paulinus prefaced a long miracle story about a rustic and his oxen with an account of Felix's death, burial, and ascension.[48] After Felix's body has been laid to rest in a field outside the city, a "joyful crowd of saints" meets him as he mounts the heights in smooth flight (*placidus volatus*). They escort him through the ethereal clouds until a band of angels takes over to accompany him triumphantly into the presence of the King and Highest Father.[49] With less vivid embellishment would Sulpicius Severus depict Martin's journey upward in a cloud to join the Apostles and prophets,[50] but in strikingly similar fashion does the British Museum's roughly contemporary Consecratio diptych depict the flight of a soul to heaven in the company of two wind gods, where it is welcomed by the outstretched hands of a group of *dei* or, perhaps, *maiores* already inhabiting the celestial halls.[51] Paulinus's verses only subtly translate this image into the terms required for the consecration of a Christian saint.

---

45. *Ep.* 5.15: "Tum ego te non in monasterio tantum vicini martyris inquilinum, sed etiam in horto eiusdem colonum locabo."

46. *Ep.* 11.14: "Ebromagum enim non hortuli causa, ut scribis, reliquimus, sed paradisi illum hortum praetulimus et patrimonio et patriae."

47. On the later importance of this image see Petersen, "The Garden of Felix," 215–30.

48. *Carm.* 18.70–189.

49. *Carm.* 18.138–44.

50. Sev. *ep.* 2.

51. W. Volbach, *Elfenbeinarbeiten der Spätantike und des frühen Mittelalters* (Mainz, 1976), 52, Nr. 56. See also A. Cameron, "Pagan Ivories," *Colloque genevois sur Symmaque*, 45–49, and S. MacCormack, *Art and Ceremony in Late Antiquity* (Berkeley, 1981), 141–44.

From the moment of his resettlement at the tomb of Felix, then, through both direct assertion and subtle allusion Paulinus began to fashion a persona rooted in a relationship of deep and abiding intimacy with the omnipresent and potent saint whose body rested close by but whose soul shared Christ's heavenly halls. Regardless of the extent to which Paulinus's self-understanding may have charted new psychological, spiritual, or emotional terrain, the logic of culture and language nevertheless demanded expression in conventional terms and images.[52] Thus the tightly managed protocols of *amicitia* and *clientela* among men, and their upward sweep through metaphors of celestial ascent or notions of the private *genius* and astral *daemon*, provided familiar and comprehensible images for describing personal dependency and divine companionship.[53] But through them Paulinus also explained and validated his control of Felix's *terrestrial* halls, for at the tomb of Felix Paulinus ultimately justified his claim on the saint's cult in profoundly personal terms. These terms had rather little to do with formal legal or ecclesiastical authority but drew their vitality both from Paulinus's personal history and from the pre-Christian legacies that the *natalicia* constantly invoked and simultaneously transformed.

As the narrator of the *natalicia* Paulinus had absolute control over his own appearances as a character in their tales, but Paulinus was an *actor* at the shrine of Felix in an even more fundamental sense. In the verses of the *natalicia*, as they roll on from year to year, we glimpse Paulinus's determination to impose his own sense of order on sacral space and time and to manage the spectacles that drew crowds to the holy shrine now under his care. For if from one point of view the complex of new buildings and courtyards so painstakingly described in the *natalicia* of 403 and 404 represented the hard proof of Paulinus's salutary transformation of private wealth, from the perspective of the impresario and poet these buildings provided an elaborate theater for the January festivities and a vivid backdrop for the saint's displays of miraculous power. Before taking up in the next section the miracles of Felix, the forms of piety expressed by those who visited the site, and Paulinus's efforts to evangelize and educate those who came there, I want first to consider Paulinus's thinking about and his own role in the sacral space and time of the cult center.

Paulinus's reorganization of the Felix's precinct entailed both its expansion and the sharper definition of its spatial and temporal boundaries.[54] This enlargement and remapping required at least one rather heavy-handed act of expropriation,

---

52. D. Kaspin, "Chewa Visions and Revisions of Power: Transformations of the Nyau Dance in Central Malawi," in *Modernity and Its Malcontents*, ed. J. Comaroff and J. Comaroff (Chicago, 1993), 53: "Virtually no aspect of Christian conduct, real or imagined, can be interpreted independent of the cultural logic of the Nyau."

53. Again, see Brown, *The Cult of the Saints*, 50–68.

54. On the Christian sacralization of place and time see more generally Brown, *The Cult of the Saints;* Markus, *The End of Ancient Christianity*, esp. 85–155; Markus, "How on Earth Could Places Become Holy?"

whose retelling by Paulinus both epitomizes many of the principles guiding his re-design of the site and illustrates the extent of his proprietary and patronal disposi-tion. The incident began when Paulinus decided that two wooden huts adjacent to the refurbished complex were obstructing light and detracting from the beauty of the basilica. He ordered their demolition.[55] The inhabitants, however, refused to vacate them. Paulinus later asserted his reluctance to bring about a dispute or to force eviction, but he also conceded that he would have done so had not a mir-acle intervened. Recourse to violence was forestalled by an opportune fire that de-stroyed one hut and so seriously damaged the other that the *colonus* who possessed it finally tore it down. Paulinus recounted this affair to the festival crowd in the *na-talicium* of 404 for several reasons. First, the outbreak of the mysterious but fortu-itous fire is offered as another *signum* of Felix's guiding presence. The revelation that Paulinus himself employed a fragment of the Cross, a gift of Melania the Elder housed in the altar of the Basilica Nova, to ward off the rampaging flames when they began to threaten even the "palaces of the saints," also endorses the thaumaturgical power of the church's relics.[56] If the careful listener notes with some curiosity that a relic of the Cross has been enlisted to restrain a conflagration just credited to Felix, Paulinus's concluding sentiment, the most sharply pointed moral of the tale, is far less compromised: had that fire not destroyed these hovels, Paulinus asserts, his own hands certainly would have.[57] Paulinus harbors no sym-pathy for the wretched, dispossessed *colonus*. The latter's ill-considered obstinacy has cost him not only his buildings, Paulinus stresses, but even the favor (*gratia*) that he might have earned through deference (*obsequium*).[58]

The obstinacy of social inferiors seldom earned the goodwill of their betters, but Paulinus's harsh response was provoked by more than the affront to his aes-thetic sensibility embodied in the hovels. Paulinus also desired a transitional zone around the shrine's major buildings, free of the "unsuitable" and the "disgrace-ful,"[59] because he was acutely concerned to influence people's perception of and response to architecturally defined space. To this end, for those able to read or willing to listen, numerous *tituli* signaled the passage from quotidian to sacred

55. *Carm.* 28.60–166.
56. *Carm.* 28.60: "signum"; *carm.* 28.115–19: the cross; *carm.* 28.97: "sanctorum palatia."
57. *Carm.* 28.145–48:

> et nihil exustum nisi quod debebat aduri
> cernimus ex illisque unum flagrasse duobus
> hospitiis, quae nostra manus, nisi flamma tulisset,
> abstulerat.

58. *Carm.* 28.165–66: "se tantum miser accusat, quem gratia nulla / manserit obsequii." The same fire seems to be described much more briefly and in different terms in the *natalicium* of two years ear-lier (*carm.* 26.395–412). There no background is given and the role of the Cross goes unmentioned.
59. *Carm.* 28.64: "inportuna situ simul et deformia visu."

space and explained the symbolic significance of architectural elements and ground plans. Above the doors of the basilicas, visitors could read in verse as they entered, "Let there be peace for you, whoever pure with a peaceful heart enters the sanctuary of Christ God";[60] or, above a more private entrance, the words of Paulinus: "Christ's worshippers, enter on the heavenly path through this pleasant green. An approach from cheerful gardens is fitting for this place from which entrance into holy paradise is given to those who merit it."[61] Walls, Paulinus wanted others to realize, may or may not make Christians, but they do make a church.[62] Thus the basilicas' doors were portals to another world, their resplendent inner atmosphere a vast airlock in which the soul might prepare for the journey.

This special significance of the components of sacred architecture was reinforced in other ways throughout the site. As they passed through a triple archway between the new and the old basilica, visitors read: "That single faith which worships One under a threefold name receives those of single mind with a threefold entrance."[63] In verses that he composed for the twin basilicas erected by Severus at Primuliacum, Paulinus drew attention to the unity of the two Testaments symbolized in Severus's two churches.[64] Sacred architecture, like miracles, required exegesis to reveal its deeper meaning.

With similar intentions Paulinus attempted to draw firm distinctions between ritual and quotidian time. God has provided the feast days of the saints, Paulinus proclaimed in the *natalicium* of 403, especially to assist the worldly in their climb to the "citadel of virtue."[65] More to the point, Paulinus had announced two years earlier that the crescendo of healings and exorcisms that peaked on 14 January provided unassailable proof that Felix reserved his powers especially for his feast day.[66] Like the space inside the walls of Felix's churches, that is, his festival day was promoted

---

60. *Ep.* 32.12: "Pax tibi sit, quicumque dei penetralia Christi / pectore pacifico candidus ingrederis."

61. *Ep.* 32.12:

Caelestes intrate vias per aemona virecta [cp. *Aen.* 6.638],
Christicolae; et laetis decet huc ingressus ab hortis,
unde sacrum meritis datur exitus in paradisum.

62. See Victorinus to Simplicianus at *Conf.* 8.2: "Ergo parieties faciunt Christianos?"

63. *Ep.* 32.15: "Una fides trino sub nomine quae colit unum / unanimes trino suscipit introitu."

64. *Ep.* 32.5. See further S. Leanza, "Aspetti esegetici," 71–73.

65. *Carm.* 27.119–21:

inde bonus dominus cunctos pietatis ut alis
contegat, invalidis niti virtutis ad arcem
congrua sanctorum dedit intervalla dierum.

66. *Carm.* 23.45–60.

as a palpable intrusion of the extraordinary into the rhythms of the mundane. And as the *natalicia* lengthen and increasingly focus on the miracles and wondrous events taking place at the tomb, they reveal incidentally and purposefully how Paulinus was himself prepared to occupy the stage during Felix's midwinter festival.

Years spent before a public conditioned to read the nuances of power in the details of dress, insignia of office, and posture and demeanor prepared Paulinus for such self-assertion.[67] In 407, as he delivered his *natalicium*, Paulinus appeared before the audience flanked by the Roman *nobiles* Pinianus and Apronianus.[68] In 403 he was seated beside Nicetas of Remesiana, the bishop who had come to Nola from distant Dacia. In these formal settings, "unkempt in body" as he had once described Felix, Paulinus's ascetic dress reinforced the distance that separated him from the audience as well as from the more worldly elite. It was a highly self-conscious posturing. Clothing carried a heavy symbolic charge in antiquity, and, as noted earlier, the stark simplicity of monastic garb now proclaimed rejection of the world's values.[69] But the garment of a true monk also held a talismanic charge.[70] Melania's silk-clad children took joy in touching her tunic and cheap cloak, her "old black rags." Through sympathetic contact, Paulinus told Severus, they hoped to cleanse the pollution of their own riches. Years later, Paulinus demanded of another correspondent of what value might be purple cloth, swelling togas, or embroidered tunics in comparison with the rags of a man who had experienced the kindness of God.[71]

Paulinus's letters and poems, and particularly the *natalicia*, depict with unusual clarity the dominant features of the intensely personal yet brilliantly public relationship that he forged with an invisible patron, companion, and intercessor. At the same time, these works depict the manner in which Paulinus set about orchestrating the cult of Felix at Nola by recalibrating sacral space and time and by assuming an overt part in the festival activities. But it was no simple drive for power or control that led Paulinus to seek such intimacy with Felix or to advance in this fashion his claim on the saint's tomb. Paulinus sensed clearly that both his personal salvation and the realization of his vision of a Christian society were inextricably bound up with a power and influence whose immediate source was a holy corpse.

CHRISTIANIZATION

On a snowy 14 January in 400, Paulinus partially honored his annual vow to Felix by recounting an emotionally overwrought tale, rich in pathos, relieved by moments

---

67. R. MacMullen, "Some Pictures in Ammianus Marcellinus," in *Changes in the Roman Empire: Essays in the Ordinary* (Princeton, 1990), 78–106.

68. *Carm.* 21.269 ff.

69. For example, Macmullen, *Corruption and the Decline of Rome*, 61–62, 238 n. 8.

70. Thus beggars might parade as monks. See Paulinus's denunciation at *carm.* 24.319 ff.

71. *Ep.* 49.12.

of gentle humor.[72] A local rustic, Paulinus reported, had awoken one morning to find that his two oxen had been stolen from their stalls. These beloved beasts, the "cherished consolation" of his life, were the source of the poor man's livelihood.[73] A futile search for the animals was followed by immediate recourse to the tomb of Felix. Weeping and suppliant, the rustic rebuked Felix for his dereliction of duty as the oxen's guardian. The saint, who had always received the man's prayers and watched over his two beasts, now seemed responsible for having let him sleep too heavily to hear the thieves. Indeed, the wretched fellow proclaimed that he would consider Felix to be the burglars' accomplice if the oxen were not restored. Acquit the guilty, but return my oxen, was his final demand.

In heaven, Paulinus noted, Felix joked and laughed with the Lord at these ill-mannered rebukes, but, stirred by the man's faith, the saint hurried to bring aid. Late that same night the rustic was startled out of his lamentation, tears, and prayer by an ominous banging at his cottage door. Fearing the thieves had returned, he cautiously peered out through a crack. There, illumined by a beam of heavenly light, stood his oxen. They had traversed the rugged countryside, driven by Felix and guided with invisible reins. Overcome by anxiety and joy, the poor man rightly saw the oxen's return as the work of his heavenly patron, Felix; and at morning light he led the two animals to the saint's shrine. The people already gathered there parted to receive the rustic and his oxen and immediately "hymned the glory of Christ revealed in these dumb beasts."[74] In turn, the man now happily fulfilled his vows to Felix with a witness of praise, which, he audaciously concluded by asking that the saint now also restore his fading eyesight. Although those present at the shrine smiled at such impudence, Felix nevertheless also heeded this request of his tactless suppliant. Soon the rustic felt Felix's holy right hand touch his eyes, and his vision became clear once more. And thus vouchsafed assurance of Felix's abiding care and protection, the man returned home rejoicing in the "happy triumph of his double vow."[75]

Paulinus's telling of this tale consumes more than half of the *natalicium* of 400, and the episode stands out as a narrative tour de force wherein Paulinus's seriousness, his dramatic flair, and his playfulness work together to remarkable effect. The affair merits such elaboration, Paulinus claims at the outset, because it epitomizes the power (*virtus*) of Felix revealed in countless other events left un-

72. *Carm* 18 (*nat.* 6 of 400); the tale of the oxen occupies over half of the poem, vv. 219–468. Snow: 16 ff. On this poem see also R. Argenio, "Il miracolo dei buoi nel xx [*sic*] natalizio di S. Paolino di Nola," *Rivista di studi classici* 17 (1969): 330–38; Witke, *Numen Litterarum*, 83–89; and W. Evenpoel, "Saint Paulin de Nole, *carm.* 18, 211–468: Hagiographie et humour," *La narrativa cristiana antica: Codici narrativi, strutture formali, schemi retorici* (Rome, 1995), 507–20.

73. *Carm.* 18.234: "cara solamina."

74. *Carm* 18.438–40: "dat euntibus ingens / turba locum et muto celebratur gloria Christi / in pecore."

75. *Carm.* 18.467–68: "et illum / laeta sequebatur gemini victoria voti."

recorded.[76] To illustrate so precisely this single display of Felix's power was sufficient to direct his audience's attention away from the earthly life of Felix, whose story Paulinus had completed in the *natalicium* of the previous year, and toward the miracles now regularly unfolding at his tomb. The *miracula* transpiring at Felix's shrine demonstrated without question that "greater power (*virtus*) survives in the death of pious men than force (*vis*) in the lives of wicked ones."[77] Though laid to rest with care in a fertile field outside Nola's walls, as the first part of the poem reminds his audience, the saint continued to watch over his faithful followers.[78] The grace (*gratia*) divinely implanted in his holy limbs could not die nor be interred with his flesh.[79] Although now a "jewel" set among the surrounding buildings, Paulinus continues, from its humble beginning Felix's tomb had shone forth with a healing light that "proved the life of the dead martyr."[80]

As a sequel to the *vita Felicis* of the previous two *natalicia*, the performance of January 400 quite naturally turned to those strange events that proved Felix's vitality in a new register. Paulinus was here determined, as he was again several years later when he reported the anxious opening and inspection of Felix's tomb, to provide the evidence that death had gained no hold on Felix. Felix, like the divinized heroes of the classical past, continued to confound certain assumptions about the mutual exclusiveness of life and death. Reassurance on this point was crucial. Upon it now rested not only Paulinus's (public) self-identity, but also the strategies for Christianization that emerge so forcefully from this and other *natalicia*. By so casting and staging the miraculous tale of the impetuous rustic and his pilfered oxen, Paulinus was endorsing the story's implicit religious attitudes and its explicit forms of piety. Moreover, the beliefs and practices that Paulinus thus encouraged, and subtly reshaped in their new context, were deeply rooted in the traditions of the Mediterranean world. Thus the *natalicia* bear witness to both the assumptions that worshippers brought to the tomb of Felix and the manner in which Paulinus tried to bring those assumptions into parallel with his own vision of a Christian society. Far more than Paulinus's letters or other poems, the verses of the *natalicia* signal the distinctive missionary impulse that was a further motivation behind the claims Paulinus laid on the cult of Felix.[81]

76. *Carm.* 18.206–10.

77. *Carm.* 18.90–91: "ut ostendat maiorem in morte piorum / virtutem quam vim in vita superesse malorum."

78. *Carm.* 18.131 ff.

79. *Carm.* 18.155–56: "at in sanctis divinitus insita membris / gratia non potuit cum carne morique tegique."

80. *Carm.* 18.162: "[lux] martyris haec functi vitam probat"; 177: "et manet in mediis quasi gemma intersita tectis."

81. Ideas in this section are also discussed in my two articles "Christianizing the Nolan Countryside: Animal Sacrifice at the Tomb of Saint Felix," *JECS* 3 (1995): 281–98; and "Town, Countryside, and Christianization at Paulinus's Nola," in *Shifting Frontiers in Late Antiquity*, ed. R. Mathisen and H. Sivan (Aldershot, 1996),175–86.

People had worshipped at the shrine of Felix long before Paulinus attempted to impose his vision on the site. His earliest extended description of the saint's festival, the *natalicium* of 397, begins to catalog forms of piety presumably manifest at the tomb long before. Prayer (and laughter) punctuated the long night, whose darkness was dispelled by flaming torches.[82] In the daylight hours, while some presented Felix with gifts of food, snow-white curtains, or lamps and candles to be burned on the altars and hung from the ceiling,[83] others attached their vows (*vota*) to the doorposts of the shrine, sometimes inscribed on polished silver foil.[84] Fragrant oil was poured into the tomb and extracted as an unguent endowed with healing power.[85] The less fortunate sought release from pain and anguish or the exorcism of demons.[86]

Many surely came to Felix like the rustic who had lost his oxen, seeking solace, protection, and compensation in the face of life's hardships. In the region around Paulinus's Nola, no less than in Augustine's Hippo,[87] matters of health, so vulnerable to the malignant power of demons, drove people to the shrines of the saints. But the concerns of the *rustici* who populate the *natalicia* extended beyond their own well-being to include the health of their livestock and the fertility of their land. Thus sick beasts were led to the shrine and select newborn animals vowed to Felix.[88] For many, Felix was a first line of defense against the vagaries of life in the towns or on the rural estates of late Roman Italy.

Many others who traveled to the festival of Felix were motivated by desires more mundane but no less pragmatic. Nola had long been known as a market town, and the festival of Felix, like other pagan and Christian celebrations, must have been accompanied by a market or fair.[89] Thus those rustics attested as driving their pigs and cattle to the Nolan festival likely had profit on their minds as

82. *Carm.* 14.51–52: "votis avidis mora noctis / rumpitur et noctem flammis funalia vincunt," with *Aen.* 1.727 ("et noctem flammis funalia vincunt"). The evidence of *carm.* 14 can be rounded out with references from later *natalicia*.

83. *Carm.* 14.98–100 with, for example, *carm.* 18.30–37. 18.45: food.

84. *Carm.* 14.44–45: "omnes / vota dicant sacris rata postibus." With *carm.* 18.33–34 on silver *tituli*.

85. *Carm.* 18.38–39.

86. *Carm.* 14.21–43.

87. For example, *sermo* 286.7, with the acknowledgment that recourse to magicians was not uncommon.

88. On sick cattle led to the shrine see *carm.* 18.198–205. On the dedication of newborn animals see below.

89. On Nola see Cato, *De agr.* 135 and the imperial *nundinae* at Degrassi, *Inscriptiones Italiae*, 13.2 (1963): 50, 51, 53. On fairs and religious festivals in Roman Italy see E. Gabba, "Mercati e fiore nell' Italia romana," *Studi classici e orientali* 24 (1975): 155–56; J. M. Frayn, *Markets and Fairs in Roman Italy* (New York, 1993), 133–44; and on the peasant character of fairs see L. de Ligt, *Fairs and Markets in the Roman Empire: Economic and Social Aspects of Periodic Trade in a Pre-industrial Society* (Amsterdam, 1993), 78–82.

well as worship.[90] The shrines of the martyrs, Basil of Caesarea complained, were too readily turned into common markets,[91] a warning deemed necessary perhaps because fairs offered a host of those less sober enticements also present at pagan religious festivals. The latter had often served up theater and spectacle along with food and drink,[92] and many Christian holidays were clearly little different. Many who attended the feast of Felix, Paulinus himself conceded, expected such diversions. Too many, he acknowledged, had but recently abandoned those pagan cults in which "their belly was their god." So here, as at the *memoria* of the North African saints,[93] they drank and reveled late into the night, and, perhaps mindful of pagan funeral banquets (*refrigeria*), even doused Felix's tomb with their wine.[94] With daybreak came further diversions amid the spectacles of exorcism and healing and the theatrics of poetic recitation. No doubt Felix's midwinter festival succored body as well as soul in a rich variety of ways.

Neither Paulinus's recognition of the varied motives that brought people to the vicinity of Felix's shrine nor his sensitivity to the different degrees of their commitment to Christianity diminished his concern for them. Rather Paulinus encouraged indigenous religious assumptions and forms of piety at the same time that he sought to Christianize them. In part, promoting confidence in Felix's power meant affirming his guardianship of all his followers, beyond the special and intimate relationship that Paulinus was claiming for himself. From the outset the *natalicia* stressed the bond between Felix and the Nolan community. "O Nola, happy with Felix as your protector (*praesul*), renowned with him as your sacred citizen, and strengthened with him as your heavenly patron (*patronus*)," Paulinus addressed the city in his first *natalicium* composed at the shrine.[95] The refrain echoed through successive Januaries; recounting Felix's burial in 400, Paulinus recalled that when Felix died Nola, the city "vowed to him," had gained "a patron in heaven."[96] Repeatedly Paulinus credited the safety and prosperity enjoyed by Nola to Felix or to Felix's friendship with Christ and the saints, as Romans had

90. For instance, *carm.* 18 and 20.

91. Basil, *Reg. Fusius* 40 (*PG* 31.1020B–1021A).

92. For example, R. MacMullen, *Paganism in the Roman Empire* (New Haven, 1981), 18–34.

93. Aug. *C. Faustum* 20.4, 21.

94. *Carm.* 27.547–67. On the *refrigerium* so troublesome to some churchmen see Amb. *De Elia et jejunio* 17.62; Zeno, *Tract.* 1.15.6; and Aug. *ep.* 22.2–6.

95. *Carm.* 13.26–27: "O felix Felice tuo tibi praesule Nola, / inclita cive sacro, caelesti firma patrono."

96. *Carm.* 18.110–12:

    namque sacerdotem sacris annisque parentem
    perdiderat sed eum caelis habitura patronum
    urbs devota pium.

long attributed the security and vitality of cities and peoples to tutelary deities. Protection against a threatening army, the defeat of a rampaging barbarian horde, the preservation of the city's water supply were all attributed to Felix.[97]

But Felix's corporate care filtered down to his most humble followers. All these might one day be set among the sheep in paradise, but they could also expect more immediate benefits. Paulinus's miracle stories relentlessly drove home this point. As Felix's love secured the return of the rustic's stolen oxen, his "favoring hand" healed another's severely gouged eye and dispelled another's acute madness.[98] Sensitive to the ailments that drove so many to seek magical or religious cures, Paulinus dwelt on Felix's power over the forces that brought agony to men and women and to their children. In January 401 he riveted his audience's attention on Felix's "miracles brilliant with salvation-bringing signs."[99] Felix might be seen besetting demons daily, lashing and torturing them until they cried out, but the warfare was hottest on Felix's feast day, either because the saint wished those who justly served as the vessels of malignant demons to expiate fully their sins or because he desired to be most generous with his gifts on his birthday.[100] So on 14 January, Paulinus continued, the shrine was packed with those hoping to be restored to health. Then the demons burned more fiercely, howled more tearfully, and moaned out their final torments.[101] Then the miserable demoniac might be raised aloft and left to hover above the ground until the demon was captured and the man set free.[102] One man long possessed was suddenly seized from among the crowd of the sick, thrust before the holy *cancelli* that marked the tomb, and suspended there upside down. As the demon possessing him was tortured into submission, the man's loose clothing defied nature and preserved modesty by continuing to cover him as if sewn to his feet. "Events like this," Paulinus concluded, "are strange but significant, all will agree."[103] Their strangeness, of course, was the proof of their significance, and by emphasizing such episodes, Paulinus simultaneously affirmed Felix's authority and his compassion.

While Paulinus's *natalicia* worked hard to depict a saint "powerful in his holiness,"[104] they also reinforced at every possible turn the reciprocal obligations of men. A votive concept underlay the composition of the *natalicia* and the construc-

---

97. *Carm.* 26.22–28; *carm.* 21.1–36, 643–858.

98. The healing of the eye of Theridius is recounted in detail at *carm.* 23.106–265, "manus prospera" at 255; one graphic description of madness appears at *carm.* 26.307–23.

99. *Carm.* 23.44: "clara salutiferis edens miracula signis."

100. *Carm.* 23.45–59.

101. *Carm.* 23.59–63.

102. *Carm.* 23.64–73.

103. *Carm.* 23.96: "mira haec sunt et magna (quis abnegat?)." See further graphic description of exorcism at *carm.* 14.21–43.

104. *Carm.* 26.346: "sic Felix pietate potens."

tion work at the shrine; both poems and buildings thus offered indisputable evidence of vows discharged.[105] But in the world of Paulinus's poetry *vota* are also made and fulfilled frequently by others. Visitors to the shrine attached their written *tituli* to the doorposts.[106] They discharged *vota* through gifts (*donaria*).[107] "Every day," Paulinus alerted his audience in 402, "we witness dense crowds on all sides either of those restored to health discharging their vows of gratitude or of sick people seeking and experiencing various remedies."[108] Moreover, dereliction might bring punishment. A broken vow, Paulinus made clear, might bring sudden paralysis;[109] an act of sacrilegious theft might induce Felix's "hidden hand" to fetter a man with confusion and bewilderment.[110]

Perhaps no more forceful statement about the intricate relationship of these themes of power and obligation, and, incidentally, no more intriguing picture of the conflation of pre-Christian and Christian practice, issued from Paulinus's pen than the *natalicium* of January 406. In the poem of that year, adapting the themes and imagery of bucolic poetry to the service of Christianity, Paulinus related three wondrous tales of votive practice and ritual slaughter at the tomb of Felix. The poem's three "sacrificial" animals, two hogs and a heifer, have been vowed to Felix at birth. When the time is right their owners set out to butcher them at the saint's shrine. The first tale focuses on the actions and punishment of a master who hopes to avoid full compliance with his vow; the second and third tales relay the miraculous means by which the animals themselves reach the shrine despite their owners' hesitations. In the end, all three beasts are slaughtered, and their flesh is served to the poor.[111]

In telling the seemingly simple and folkloric tales of these rustics and their livestock, Paulinus draws heavily on the language and conventions of animal sacrifice in the classical Mediterranean world.[112] And although such sacrificial language

105. On the buildings as vows fulfilled see *carm.* 28.1–2.

106. For records of vows scrawled on the basilica's walls, see A. Ferrua, "Graffiti di pellegrini," 17–19.

107. *Carm.* 18.29: "donaria."

108. *Carm.* 26.384–86.

109. *Carm.* 20.86 ff.

110. *Carm.* 19.378–730 is a lengthy account of the theft of a cross from the basilica. 598–99: "operta manu."

111. *Carm.* 20. Fuller discussion of the issues broached here is given in Trout, "Christianizing the Nolan Countryside." On the literary qualities of this poem see, for example, J. Doignon, "Un récit de miracle dans les 'Carmina' de Paulin de Nole: Poétique virgilienne et leçon apologétique," *Revue d'histoire de la spiritualité* 48 (1972): 129–44; S. Prete, "Il Carme 20 di Paolino di Nola: Alcuni aspetti letterari e culturali," *Augustinianum* 21 (1981): 169–177 = *Motivi ascetici e letterari*, 87–99; and W. Evenpoel, "La phrase et le vers dans les Carmina de Paulin de Nole," *Eulogia: Mélanges offerts à Antoon A. R. Bastiaensen* (Steenbrugis, 1991): 95–108.

112. Bibliography at Trout, "Christianizing the Nolan Countryside," 281–82.

may have been largely metaphorical when Paulinus applied it to the "offering" of his own poetry,[113] in this narrative context its literal associations are clear. Paulinus designates the animals as *victimae*, each is set aside as *sacer* at birth, and each is slaughtered in fulfillment of a vow.[114] Furthermore, Paulinus insists on the cooperation of each animal,[115] a crucial component of animal sacrifice in non-Christian cult; and, in harmony with previous literary and sculptural depictions of sacrifice, Paulinus's narratives avoid description of the animals' deaths in favor of the preparations that precede and the meals that follow the ritual killing.[116] Finally, the meat is distributed to the crowd according to gender and age, replicating the social hierarchy and repeating a pattern recognizable in earlier cultic practice.[117] In short, Paulinus's verses, simultaneously reflecting and seeking to mold contemporary practice at Felix's tomb, promote an understanding of the ritual slaughter of farm animals that can readily be accommodated within the boundaries of traditional pre-Christian sacrifice.

Just as significant, however, Paulinus develops the miraculous elements of these animal tales in a manner that underscores both the authority of Felix and the binding force of *vota*. In the first tale, the narrative centers on Felix's punishment of the owner of one of the pigs, who seeks to reserve some of the meat for himself.[118] The man's horse, however, "as if endowed with human reason,"[119] throws its master to the ground as he attempts to leave the shrine. While the culprit sprawls there paralyzed, the animal returns the purloined meat to Felix. Only the eventual intercession of the assembled poor, who have enjoyed the fresh pork, and the man's own doleful supplication of the saint elicit Felix's compassion. In the other two tales Paulinus offers a similar and equally blunt lesson in the binding force of vows by recounting the miraculous means by which the votive animals themselves, a pig and a heifer, journey from their distant farms to Felix's shrine.[120] The pig, dedicated at birth to Felix but grown too plump under his protection to make the long march from Apulia to Nola, is left behind by its masters, only to appear inexplicably before their lodgings at the shrine. "Divine power," Paulinus suggests, has staged this "remarkable portent," perhaps by wafting the pig through

---

113. Junod-Ammerbauer, "Le poète chrétien," esp. 18–22.

114. *Carm.* 20.431: "victima." *Carm.* 20.67: "solvere votum." *Carm.* 20.317: "in vota." *Carm.* 20.392: "votivo munere."

115. For instance, *Carm.* 20.351–52, 434.

116. For example, Tibullus 2.1; the *suovetaurilia* reliefs of the Altar of Domitius, of a panel of Marcus Aurelius reused on the arch of Constantine, or the *vicennalia* monument of Diocletian. Citations at Trout, "Christianizing the Nolan Countryside," 291.

117. *Carm.* 20.114–16 with S. Stowers, "Greeks Who Sacrifice and Those Who Do Not: Toward an Anthropology of Greek Religion," in *The Social World of the First Christians: Essays in Honor of Wayne A. Meeks,* ed. L. M. White and O. L. Yarbrough (Minneapolis, 1995), 325–29.

118. The longest of the three tales: *carm.* 20.62–300.

119. *Carm.* 20.129: "velut humana ratione repletus."

120. *Carm.* 20.301–444.

the air concealed in a cloud.[121] The heifer, the star of her tale, refuses to be harnessed to her owners' wagon, preferring to guide them herself through a dark forest to Nola. There, Paulinus concludes his account, "offering her neck to the ax . . . she joyously poured out her blood in fulfillment of her masters' vow."[122] Blending learned poetic allusions with engaging narrative, Paulinus employs these remarkable tales not only to highlight the thaumaturgical power of Felix but also to illustrate the contractual obligations that exist between men and the saints. These mute beasts virtually sacrifice themselves to honor their masters' vows.

Constant repetition, dramatic presentation, and straightforward admonition denote clearly Paulinus's approval of such attitudes and practices as well as his aim to establish Felix's cult as a distinctive locus for their enactment. But whom did Paulinus hope to influence through the verses of the *natalicia*, and what other initiatives complemented the poems? One audience for the sophisticated poetry of the *natalicia*, and thus one target of its missionary front, must have been those individuals sufficiently educated to recognize Virgilian allusions and to interpret tales allegorically.[123] But Paulinus apparently hoped his messages would also reach ears less well trained in the literary arts. Presumably his audience was socially diverse. Certainly in an earlier age the festival performances of skilled declaimers and of poets specializing in hymns and panegyrics to the gods might hold spellbound even *hoi polloi*,[124] while in Paulinus's day some accomplished big-city preachers captured the attention of crowds that, particularly on holidays and feast days, were swollen with ordinary folk.[125] Even the manner in which Augustine's sermons were simplified by one sixth-century preacher inversely suggests the superior "aural" understanding of early fifth-century audiences.[126] Moreover, the *natalicia* are Paulinus's least classicizing poems, readily employing the diction of the Christian *sermo humilis*.[127] Like Paulinus's privileging of dramatic narrative and his frequent recourse to explicitly drawn morals, his lexical choices seem designed to appeal to a broad audience. And if the crowds' more cultivated members might be asked to share the poet's occasional smile at the naïveté of the simple souls who populate the poems, they are not invited to mock or deride them.[128] In short, Paulinus's language, his themes, and his messages reveal that he intended these

121. *Carm.* 20.353–87.

122. *Carm.* 20.434–35.

123. See *ep.* 49.14, however, for Paulinus's explicit claim that the allegorical possibilities of a miracle tale do not obviate its simple and literal meaning.

124. MacMullen, *Paganism*, 14–18, with Dio Chrysostom, *Or.* 27.5; Lucian, *Rhetoron didaskalos* 20.

125. For example, R. Macmullen, "The Preacher's Audience (A.D. 350–400)," *Journal of Theological Studies* 40 (1989): 503–11.

126. J. Cavadini, "Simplifying Augustine," paper presented to North American Patristic Society, Loyola University of Chicago, 31 May 1996.

127. Green, "Paulinus of Nola and the Diction of Christian Latin Poetry," 79–85; see also Fabre, *Paulin de Nole*, 368–85.

128. Evenpoel, "Hagiographie et humour."

poems to win the allegiance of his more humble listeners, particularly those from the countryside, as well as his more cultivated ones.[129]

The Christianizing mission manifest in the *natalicia* was expressed in other media too. Like Paulinus's choice of doorway inscriptions, his decorative schemes were informed by a desire to fashion a space of such otherworldly aura that all minds, but especially the less refined, might become receptive to new messages. Paulinus imagined the cult complex's buildings as "a marvel for the eyes."[130] The murmur of fountains, the fragrance of perfumed oil, the play of sunlight through latticework or across marble and mosaic surfaces, the rippling mirage of sculpted ceiling panels above swaying lamps could calm and soften coarser spirits.[131] But mollifying such worldly souls was only the means to a far greater end. "On eyes bemused (*attoniti*) a new light dawns," proclaimed one inscription,[132] glossing Paulinus's conviction that the basilicas' flood of sensual stimuli would induce an awe conducive to revelation.

Wonderment and edification in equal measure were the goals of the elaborate program of figural paintings commissioned by Paulinus. Narrative scenes drawn from both the Old and New Testaments adorned the walls of the two main basilicas.[133] The porticoes of the courtyard displayed the portraits and names of martyrs of both sexes flanked by representations of the *sacra gesta* of such biblical witnesses as Job, Tobias, Judith, and Esther.[134] This rich visual panorama not only violated at least one earlier conciliar canon that, despite the striking development of Christian art in the third century, had condemned the painting of *picturae* on the walls of churches; but it also, as Paulinus admitted, contradicted normal practice in the opening years of the fifth century.[135] Yet, anticipating by nearly two hun-

129. Pace Walsh, "Paulinus of Nola," 568, who sees *rustici* as "hardly the audience for a *recitatio*." The influence of landlords and patrons on their tenants and *coloni* offered a less direct path from performance to the lower social levels.

130. *Carm.* 28.43: "mirum óculis."

131. On these various components and Paulinus's sensitivity to their psychological effect see, for example, *ep.* 32.10–15, *carm.* 18.181, *carm.* 27.360–94, *carm.* 28. 1–49. For the literary and philosophical background shaping Paulinus's understanding of *decorum, venustas, gratia,* and *varietas,* see H. Junod-Ammerbauer, "Les constructions de Nole et l'esthétique de Saint Paulin," *REAug* 24 (1978): 22–57, esp. 47–52.

132. *Ep.* 32.15: "Adtonitis nova lux oculis aperitur, et uno / limine consistens geminas simul adspicit aulas." The felicitous translation is from Walsh, *Paulinus,* 36.148.

133. *Carm.* 27.511–41; 28.170–79. New Testament scenes were reserved for the older basilica, while Old Testament scenes served the new one (*carm.* 28.173–74). The list of subjects offered to Nicetas at *carm.* 27.607–35 (Adam, Lot, Jacob, Isaac, et al.) probably reflects the Old Testament cycle. For possible remains of the New Testament cycle see Korol, "Zu den gemalten Architekturdarstellungen des NT-Zyklus.'"

134. *Carm.* 28.16–27.

135. Council of Elvira, *can.* 36 (Hefele-Leclerq, *Histoire,* 1.240): "Placuit picturas in ecclesia esse non debere, ne quod colitur et adoratur in parietibus depingatur," with M. Meigne, "Concile ou collection d'Elvire?" *RHE* 70 (1975): 361–87, for a date after 325. *Carm.* 27.544: "raro more." On third-century painting see, for example, A. Grabar, *Early Christian Art,* trans. S. Gilbert and J. Emmons (New York, 1968), 67–121.

dred years Gregory the Great's "theory of missionary art,"[136] Paulinus unhesitat-
ingly justified his methods by stressing the didactic potential of such figural im-
ages. The passage merits quotation:

> Everyone is aware of the crowds that Saint Felix's fame brings here. Now the greater
> number among these crowds are country folk (*rusticitas*), not without belief but unskilled
> in reading. For years they have been accustomed to following the profane cults in which
> their god was their belly. . . . This was why we thought it useful to enliven all the houses
> of Felix with paintings on sacred themes, in the hope that these sketches painted in vari-
> ous colors might seize the beguiled minds (*adtonitas mentes*) of the rustics (*agrestes*) through
> their wondrous appearance (*spectacula*). Over these paintings are explanatory inscriptions,
> the written word revealing the theme outlined by the painter's hand. So when they point
> out and read over to each other the subjects painted, they turn more slowly to thoughts
> of food. . . . In this way, as the painting deceives (*fallit*) their hunger, their astonishment
> may allow better behavior to develop in them. Thus a sense of propriety inspired by
> saintly examples steals up (*subrepit*) as they read those holy accounts of spotless actions.[137]

The sense of wonder inspired by sheer physical splendor, painted images, and in-
scribed texts lowered defenses, and those thus mentally disarmed were vulnerable
to the transformative power so long credited to figural representations and por-
traits. *Imagines*, Paulinus reminded one correspondent, persuasively embodied
both what to imitate and what to avoid.[138]

Paulinus's commentary on the paintings of the basilica complex, like his tales of
rustics and their livestock, illustrates his desire to advance Felix's authority into the
world of the Campanian *agrestes*.[139] The countryside was seen by bishops and town
dwellers as the final preserve of paganism, and Paulinus's desire to Christianize it
aligns him with other contemporary churchmen. But if the missionary activities of
Martin of Tours or Vigilius of Trent often assumed a confrontational or combat-
ive posture,[140] Paulinus's efforts at the suburban shrine of Felix, where town began
to fade into countryside, appear more nuanced. The third *natalicium*, for example,

136. H. Kessler, "Pictorial Narrative and Church Mission in Sixth-Century Gaul," in *Pictorial Nar-
rative in Antiquity and the Middle Ages*, ed H. Kessler and M. Simpson (Hanover, 1985), 75–91, with refer-
ence to the Martin cycle in the cathedral reconstructed by Gregory of Tours. Notably Paulinus does
not refer to scenes that illustrated the life of Felix.

137. *Carm.* 27.546–50, 580–91.

138. *Ep.* 32.3, on Severus's planned installation of a portrait of Paulinus near one of Martin in the
baptistry at Primuliacum: "et vitandum et sequendum pariter conspicarentur." On the alleged inspi-
rational power of the *imagines maiorum* among the Roman nobility see, for example, Polybius 6.53 and
Pliny *NH* 35.6–8. See also Junod-Ammerbauer, "Les constructions de Nole," 41–47.

139. At Aquitanian Alingo Paulinus's construction of a basilica may signal his intention of pro-
moting Christianity among the inhabitants of his former estates. Pace A. Rousselle, "Deux exemples
d'évangélisation en Gaule," 91–98.

140. For example, *Vita Martini* 12–15; Vig. *epp.* 1–2 (*PL* 13.549–58) with Trout, "Town, Country-
side, and Christianization," 176–79.

reveals his sensitivity to the agricultural world and his willingness to clothe Christ in solar vestments. Paulinus linked the mid-January festival of Felix with the end of winter and the rebirth of flowery spring, and he counted the telltale few days separating Felix's birthday anniversary from Christ's "solstice" advent, "when Christ was born in the flesh and transformed the cold winter season with a new sun (*novus sol*)." Now with his salvation-bringing rising (*ortum*), Christ orders the nights to shorten and the days to grow longer.[141] Most notably, however, Paulinus's *natalicia* endorse a technology of piety deeply embedded in the rhythms of rural life.[142]

When Paulinus encouraged *rustici* to entrust their animals to the protection of Felix, to vow newborn beasts to the saint, and to conduct ritual butcherings at his tomb, or when he encouraged gifts to the saint as recompense for health restored or insurance for prosperity preserved, he asked them to replicate traditional acts of piety. In rural pre-Roman and Roman Italy, religious practice had included animal sacrifice as well as vows undertaken for the health of animals. In the mid-second century B.C., Cato the Elder advised that a vow for the health of the cattle (*votum pro bubus*) be made annually: the offering to Mars Silvanus consisted of meal, bacon, meat, and wine.[143] A similar offering of roasted meat and wine (*daps pro bubus*) was to be made to Jupiter Dapalis just before the spring plowing, and the sacrifice of a pig to Ceres should precede the harvest or the thinning of a grove.[144] But perhaps the best-known rite described in Cato's agricultural handbook—one recalled by Varro in the closing decades of the Republic and prominent in monumental art as late as the early fourth century—is the *suovetaurilia*.[145] This expiatory or lustral sacrifice of a pig, a lamb, and a calf for the purification of the fields was accompanied by a very specific prayer whose opening lines epitomize the intention of the rite: "Father Mars, I pray and entreat you that you be favorable and well disposed to me, my house, and my household, to which end therefore I have

141. *Carm.* 14.15–19:

[dies] quae post solstitium, quo Christus corpore natus
sole novo gelidae mutavit tempora brumae
atque salutiferum praestans mortalibus ortum
procedente die secum decrescere noctes
iussit.

142. On the correlation of ritual and agricultural calendars see, for example, E. Wolf, *Peasants* (Englewood Cliffs, N.J., 1966), 100; W. Mitchell, *Peasants on the Edge: Crop, Cult, and Crisis in the Andes* (Austin, 1991), 135–37; M. H. Jameson, "Sacrifice and Animal Husbandry in Classical Greece," in *Pastoral Economies in Classical Antiquity*, ed. C. R. Whittaker (Cambridge, 1988), 106–7.

143. Cato, *De agr.*, 83, ed. R. Goujard, *Caton: de l'agriculture* (Paris, 1975).

144. *De agr.* 131–40.

145. *De agr.* 141. Cp. Varro, *Rust.* 2.1.9–10, with text at *Varron: Économie Rurale: Livre II*, ed. C. Guiraud (Paris, 1985), 16–17. On the *suovetaurilia* as a *piaculum* see the sources at M. Krause, *RE supp.* 5 (1931): "Hostia," 240–41.

ordered this *suovetaurilia* to be led around my land, my ground, and my farm; so that you may keep away, avert, and remove sicknesses seen and unseen, sterility and ruin, destruction and intemperate weather."[146] The vows made and discharged by the crowds who gathered several centuries later at a rural temple rebuilt by the Younger Pliny must have had many of the same goals.[147]

In short, while the *natalicia* did validate the more elevated sentiments of Christian *caritas* and urged the philosophical detachment from material possessions so often advocated by Paulinus's letters, they also endorsed traditional techniques for assuring secular security and prosperity. Nor is it necessary to believe that this endorsement represents compromise or condescension on Paulinus's part; his own understanding of secular renunciation, as we have seen, was heavily contractual, while his conception of his relationship with Felix reproduces contemporary social and political structures. Paulinus's spirituality and his Christianizing vision were quite naturally "synthesized into the established order."[148] If Paulinus seems to blur the distinction between old and new, as Gregory the Great was perhaps more self-consciously prepared to do in seeking the conversion of the English,[149] his methods appear rooted in a sympathy rather than a disdain for the conventions and rhythms of traditional piety.[150] In any case, the result of his efforts must have been a Christianity more relevant to the concerns of those who lived so close to unruly nature in this *terra di lavoro* and who felt themselves exposed to the machinations of demonic powers.

In the end, it was this very real power of the demonic that warranted maintenance of the cult of Felix and required someone to assume the impresario's duties. In the *natalicium* of 405 Paulinus tendered his explanation of a problem that has animated many later historians: the origin of the cult of the saints.[151] The awesome and holy power now made manifest through miracles at the tombs of martyrs and confessors, Paulinus then observed, merely signaled the current stage of God's plan to establish fully His light in the world and drive out the forces of demonic darkness. Earlier, during their own lifetimes, the confessors and martyrs had been

---

146. *De agr.* 141: "Mars pater, te precor quaesoque uti sies volens propitius mihi, domo familiaeque nostrae: quoius rei ergo agrum, terram fundumque meum suovitaurilia circumagi iussi, uti tu morbos visos invisosque, vidueratem vastitudinemque, calamitates intemperiasque prohibessis, defendas averruncesque."

147. *Ep.* 9.39.

148. Comaroff and Comaroff, *Modernity and Its Malcontents*, xxii.

149. Bede, *HE* 1.30, text and translation at *Bede's Ecclesiastical History of the English People*, ed. B. Colgrave and R. Mynors (Oxford, 1969), 106–9. Discussion of the Gregorian context by R. Markus, "Gregory the Great and a Papal Missionary Strategy," reprinted in *From Augustine to Gregory the Great: History and Christianity in Late Antiquity* (London, 1983), chapter 11. For parallels see Gregory of Tours, *Liber in Gloria Confessorum* 2, as noted by J. Wallace-Hadrill, *Bede's Ecclesiastical History of the English People: A Historical Commentary* (Oxford, 1988), 45; and Aug. *ep.* 29.9.

150. Recognized as well by Ruggiero, "La 'vita Felicis' di Paolino di Nola," concisely at 196–97.

151. *Carm.* 19.1–282.

the agents of this illuminating plan; now they carried on that work from the "sacred tombs" apportioned by the Creator throughout the world as the stars were scattered through the night sky.[152] As a Nola dying in the pernicious darkness of pagan worship was first awarded the presence of the living Felix the physician (*medicus*),[153] so now at his tomb Felix continued to torment the few remaining demons, compelling them to shout out and to acknowledge their deceptions.[154] Thus from among the number of that heavenly firmament of martyrs established on earth, Nola boasted in Felix its own star, "for every martyr, wherever the region to which his body is committed, is both a star (*stella*) for that district and a source of healing (*medicina*) for its residents."[155] It was in the cosmological context of this agelong battle against the darkness that the cult of Felix assumed its ultimate meaning. But Felix's protective power was experienced by his faithful in far more immediate and mundane ways, wherein Paulinus, who had linked his own destiny to Felix as his special "star," was not without his role. But that role also eventually extended well beyond the precinct of Felix's shrine and involved Paulinus in affairs only remotely religious.

BROKERING THE POWER OF FELIX

Sometime in the weeks before 29 November 384 the urban prefect of Rome, Q. Aurelius Symmachus, representative of the emperor's justice, faced a complicated case of intimidation, violence, and obstruction of due process—a case that starkly reveals the gap between theory and practice in the administration of the later Roman Empire.[156] A certain Scirtius, a *vir perfectissimus* and thus relatively small fry in these waters,[157] came before Symmachus to report that he had been driven from an estate that he possessed at nearby Praeneste. Symmachus apparently conducted an inquiry (*praeiudicium*) and ordered Scirtius's reinstatement as *possessor* of the property in question. But when Scirtius returned to the estate to resume possession, he was blocked by a certain Artemisius, an agent (*actor*) of the influential senator, *vir illustris*, and recent ordinary consul, Q. Clodius Hermogenianus Olybrius,[158] whose men had forced Scirtius from the property in the first place. With Scirtius locked out despite his ruling, Symmachus sent a subordinate of his own,

---

152. *Carm.* 19.18–19: "sic [creator] sacra disposuit terris monumenta piorum, / sparsit ut astrorum nocturno lumina caelo."

153. *Carm.* 19.164–248; 195–97: "Felix . . . medicus."

154. *Carm.* 19.249–82.

155. *Carm.* 19.14–15: "omnis enim quacumque iacet mandatus in ora / martyr stella loci simul et medicina colentum est."

156. *Sym. Rel.* 28, with translation and helpful commentary at Barrow, *Prefect and Emperor*, 153–61.

157. Otherwise unknown. *PLRE* 1:810.

158. *PLRE* 1:640, "Olybrius 3."

named Rufinus, to haul the estate's inhabitants (*habitores*) back to Rome for questioning. En route, however, Olybrius's men seized these folk and whisked them off to one of Olybrius's suburban villas, a deed Symmachus denounced as "barbaric (*incivilis*)." To get to the bottom of things, a stymied Symmachus summoned to his tribunal the town councilors of Praeneste, who confirmed that Scirtius had been paying the land tax on the property, a sure sign of possession. But unfortunately Symmachus also unearthed a complication: Scirtius had actually shared possession of the estate with one Theseus, recently deceased. Symmachus also now began edging the investigation closer to the powerful Olybrius, whom he considered the real villain in the affair. He summoned Olybrius's procurator, a man of senatorial rank named Tarpeius,[159] who alleged that Olybrius had actually obtained Theseus's half of the estate on the latter's death. This much even Scirtius was willing to concede, but the legal representative (*defensor*) of Theseus's children was also present, and he now claimed the other half of the estate (the portion left for Scirtius) on their behalf. An exasperated Symmachus sensed the collusion between Olybrius's procurator Tarpeius and the *defensor* of Theseus's children, and he insisted on assigning half of the contested property to the dispossessed Scirtius, a decision against which officially there could be no appeal.[160] Nevertheless, the next day Tarpeius and the *defensor* were back to do just that. Indeed we only learn this whole tale because a clearly disgruntled Symmachus did send the case's thick dossier and his *relatio* north to Milan, so that, he began his summary, "such a disgraceful a case of trespass (*invasio*)" might be brought to the attention of the imperial court.

Readers of Ammianus, of any church historian of the period, or even of Augustine's account of the ethical dilemma that a senator's bribe posed for the young Alypius, *assessor* at Rome in this very period,[161] will not be surprised by any report that unmasks the divergence between theory and practice in the late Roman administration of justice or that highlights the role of coercion and force in contemporary social and economic relations. It may not matter at all in this particular clash of Roman aristocrats that Symmachus and Olybrius stood on different sides of the age's growing religious divide. It is evident, however, that Symmachus, although urban prefect and thus the direct representative of the Christian imperial court, found himself unable to restrain the agents of Olybrius, a well-connected member of Rome's Christian aristocracy who had risen to the praetorian prefecture of the East in 378 and shared the ordinary consulship with Ausonius in 379. As for Olybrius, although he remains in the margins of Symmachus's *relatio*, he is ultimately responsible, at least in Symmachus's eyes, for the acts of intimidation and chicanery that characterize this land grab.

159. Otherwise unknown. *PLRE* 1:875.
160. Sym. *Rel.* 28.1.
161. *Conf.* 6.10.16.

By the time Symmachus had to grapple with this unsavory affair in late 384, the young Paulinus had already abandoned Italy for Aquitaine. But when Paulinus returned to Nola and the tomb of Felix in 395, he too presumably pressed his spiritual and proprietary claims through such ambiguous prerogatives of rank and status as those that enabled Olybrius to frustrate Symmachus at Praeneste. But Paulinus's ambitions in this regard did not end at the confines of the basilica complex. In the several episodes to be examined here, Paulinus reveals his willingness to extend his reach well into the mundane affairs of men and to redirect the channels of his influence therein through the tombs and relics of the saints. In these efforts, too, Paulinus elided his own *auctoritas* as a former senator with the *potentia* of his new astral companion. As a broker of the holy and the agent of Felix, Paulinus intervened in a complicated lawsuit at Rome, tried to resolve a rancorous quarrel with the citizens of Nola, and, presumably, settled a property dispute whose chain of litigants reached from nearby Capua to distant Aquitaine. Like Symmachus's twenty-eighth *relatio*, Paulinus's accounts of his engagement in these affairs draw our attention back to the blurred edges of public and private authority in late Roman Italy, but they also reveal how the *potentia* of Christ and his saints was emerging as a nearly palpable force in the disputatious relations of men.

Paulinus's forty-ninth letter, like Symmachus's twenty-eighth *relatio*, recounts a curious tale of intrigue and disputed property, but one that showcases a talismanic ear as well as quarreling senators and Roman officials. Addressed sometime after 408 to a high-ranking Roman whose name may have been Macarius,[162] Paulinus's letter, one of the few documents surviving from his episcopacy,[163] records his attempt to influence the outcome of a dispute between a shipowner named Secun-

---

162. Macarius is identified only by a superscription in a second hand. If the identification is correct several possibilities exist: (1) After he returned to Italy in 397, Rufinus was in contact with a Macarius, "vir fide, eruditione, nobilitate iuxta clarus," who sought his counsel on matters concerning the *mathematici* and who requested his translation of Origen's *Peri Archon*. See Ruf. *Apol.* 1.11 and the preface of *Peri Archon*. To *PLRE* 2:696, "Macarius 1" add Gennadius 28. (2) Palladius, *Hist. Laus.* 62, speaking of Pammachius, mentions Macarius, a former *vicarius*, who also gave away his wealth. Although identified as "Macarius 2" at *PLRE* 2:696, Palladius's Macarius could be Rufinus's. (3) According to Cornelius *apud* Augustine, *ep.* 259.1, Paulinus wrote a (lost) *epistula consolatoria* to a Macarius on the death of his wife. If true, this fact may bring some support to the manuscript superscription by corroborating a friendship between Paulinus and a Macarius. Note that *PLRE* 2:696, "Macarius 2," incorrectly identifies Paulinus's *ep.* 49 as a consolatory letter.

163. At 49.14 Paulinus styles himself "pastor exigui gregis." See Fabre, *Essai*, 86–87, dating only to after August 408. For other treatments of this letter see J. Rougé, "*Periculum maris* et transports d'état: La lettre 49 de Paulin de Nole," *Studi Tardoantichi* 2 (1986): 119–36; F. Foerster and R. Pascual, *El naufragio de Valgius: Estracto comentado de la Epistola n. 49 de San Paulino de Nola* (Barcelona, 1985); and G. Guttilla, "Tre naufragi di contenuto cristiano del IV secolo d.C. (Ambrogio, *De exc. fratr.* 1,43–48; Paolino, *carm.* 24,1–308 ed *epist.* 49)" (forthcoming). Rougé, "*Periculum maris*," 134–36, reviving an argument of Reinelt relating the episode to the invasion of Alaric, argues for a date of 411, but I retain Fabre's skepticism.

dinianus[164] and a senator named Postumianus.[165] Although it was winter, a ship owned by Secundinianus had set sail under imperial orders from Sardinia with grain destined for Rome. Buffeted by a storm, the crew, with the exception of an old sailor named Valgius, abandoned ship. Fierce winds then drove the ship and its single crew member across the sea until it was found and brought to harbor in southern Italy by fishermen. The ship landed on an estate belonging to the senator Postumianus, whose *procurator* quickly seized the vessel and stripped it. When he learned of these events, Secundinianus, the ship's owner, petitioned the governor (*iudex*) of Lucania for the restoration of his property. But the governor proved uncooperative. In the meantime Postumianus's *procurator* slipped off to Rome, whither Secundinianus soon followed to press his claims.[166] At some point Paulinus became embroiled in this affair on the side of Secundinianus, whom he styles his *amicus* and *frater*,[167] and whose sailor, the old Valgius, he sheltered at Nola for some time after the end of his high-seas ordeal. This Valgius and his wondrous adventure tale then became the currency with which Paulinus set out to contract Macarius's support for Secundinianus's suit against Postumianus.

Indeed Paulinus wrote letter 49 to the Roman Macarius precisely because the latter was in a position to intervene with Postumianus and secure the restoration of Secundinianus's property. Paulinus still had powerful *amici* at Rome, and, as we have noted, after his relocation to Campania in 395 he made annual journeys to the capital, initially for the Feast of the Apostles in late June and in later years for Easter.[168] While there, fulfilling the obligations of friendship and piety, he visited and resided with families who possessed estates scattered throughout Latium and Campania.[169] His relations with the ecclesiastical establishment of the city, as we have seen, improved after the death of Siricius; in 400 Pope Anastasius received him warmly and invited him to return to the capital to attend the anniversary of his election. But if it is therefore not surprising to find Paulinus enlisting the help of Macarius at Rome, nevertheless his attempt to triangulate this dispute among men by introducing into these decidedly human affairs a pure and potent spiritual vector remains a spectacular turn of events.

164. *Ep.* 49.1: *navicularius*.

165. Possibly to be identified with either *PLRE* 1:718, "Postumianus 2" or his son. See Rougé, "*Periculum maris*," 126.

166. So much can be reconstructed from Paulinus's letter. For the imperial legislation and legal issues underlying this affair see Rougé, "*Periculum maris*."

167. *Ep.* 49.1.

168. *Ep.* 45.1.

169. At *ep.* 17.2 Paulinus describes his activitites during the ten days he spent in Rome in June 398 (or 399). He remained quite busy. The mornings were spent at the *memoriae* of the apostles and martyrs. Then, returning to his *hospitium*, he was occupied with innumerable meetings (*frequentationes*), some required by *amicitia*, others by *religio*.

To win Macarius's support for Secundinianus, Paulinus offered to him the old sailor Valgius. And to make abundantly clear the value of this "spiritual gift (*xenium spiritale*),"[170] Paulinus recounted at some length for Macarius the harrowing and miraculous shipwreck tale, which is the centerpiece of his accompanying letter. For six days Valgius had been alone on the storm-tossed vessel, without food, praying for death amid the sea's desolation, when at last the Lord gave him the strength to chop down, with two light blows of an ax, the ship's imperiling mast. Hailed now with the name Victor by the Lord, the weary old man began to triumph over the storm, performing by himself the tasks of a full crew. With a gentle hand, Paulinus continued, the Lord stroked Victor and, whenever the old man was in danger of sleeping too long, tweaked his ear to rouse him. At last a band of angels descended to assist with the sails, the rigging, and the bailing of water, while armed men, soldiers of the heavenly army, stood watch over the ship. The Lord himself, Paulinus proclaimed, sat at the ship's stern, sometimes with the appearance described in the Apocalypse, sometimes "in the revered appearance of His *amicus* and *confessor,* my lord and our common patron, Felix."[171] Valgius, throwing himself at the feet of the Lord or His martyr, laid his head on their laps. Christ himself, Paulinus assured Macarius, was present in the holy Felix. Finally the Lord commanded the storm to stop, pitying the humble Valgius as He pitied all men who toss on the seas of this world.[172] And as the ship, through God's mercy, at last approached the shore of Lucania after twenty-three days at sea, it was met by fishermen, who towed the vessel into harbor after they had first enjoyed a rich feast on board.

Paulinus's Virgilian allusions and the other classical references that punctuate his retelling of Valgius's tale were meant to engage the sympathies of an educated reader,[173] while its allegory and typology offered Macarius the means for extrapolating higher ethical and philosophical truths from its miraculous events.[174] But it was at its most literal level that the tale of Valgius's close encounter with the divine was intended to persuade Macarius to intervene in the dispute. "Is there any worldly distinction," Paulinus asked Macarius, "that you would prefer . . . more than the kindness of God experienced by this old man? A great proportion of mankind accounts it a privilege to see an earthly king at close quarters. . . . How

---

170. *Ep.* 49.14.

171. *Ep.* 49.4.

172. *Ep.* 49.5.

173. For example, Vir. *Aen.* 3.193 at *ep.* 49.2; the denunciation of the Argo at 14.8–9 in comparison with the ship of Valgius.

174. *Ep.* 49.10: an extended comparison between Valgius's ship and both Noah's ark and Jonas's ship and the whale that swallowed him. The latter is in turn explained as a type of the Passion and Resurrection. *Ep.* 49.11 compares Valgius's journey to Paul's trip to Rome, "in quibus similiter mystica argumenta formantur."

much more blessed . . . is Valgius whom the King of Kings honored! . . . for like Israel he saw Christ, like Moses he spoke face to face with the King of Heaven."[175]

With his case made in such fashion, Paulinus became refreshingly straightforward. "I who am the shepherd of a small flock," Paulinus continued as he drew near his point, "make this gift of one I greatly cherish. I pass him over to your affection as a spiritual gift." But, he confessed, "I have so incessantly fingered his ear, that I have almost worn it away; I should even have liked to cut off a part of that . . . ear, except that such a token (*pignus*) would have meant wounding him!"[176] Valgius was a treasure, Paulinus asserted, whose influence (*gratia*) even outstripped that of a pinch of dust from the holy places where Christ walked, suffered, and rose again. "My brother," Paulinus concluded, "you now have my gift (*xenium*). Take it in the spirit of charity. . . . I'm sure you will seek and desire some means of demonstrating the love you bear for Christ toward Valgius. An opportunity is at hand; you must direct the zeal of your pious devotion and assist with all the love of your faith his patron, Secundinianus. . . . I do not doubt that our brother Postumianus will be stirred both by your intervention and by his own faith and righteousness."[177]

Only several decades separate the affair of Scirtius, Olybrius, and Symmachus from that of Secundinianus, Postumianus, and Paulinus, and the latter is not distinguished from the former either by Paulinus's attempt to deploy private influence to resolve a property dispute or even by any manifest vulnerability of due process to private interests. Rather it is the attempt of a bishop to short-circuit a legal case by certifying and bartering a "living relic" that marks the psychological distance. Paulinus, who had once cemented the bonds of elite friendship and favor with gifts of birds and oysters, now sought to energize the *amicitia* of Macarius with a gift appropriate to a bishop whose see included the tomb of a powerful saint. Men were, of course, still recommended to others on the traditional bases of education, wealth, or family, but Paulinus's "recommendation" of Valgius had little to do with the latter's personal accomplishments, beyond his native simplicity,[178] and everything to do with an astonishing intervention of the Lord and Felix into his life. Certified now by the letter of Felix's client and impresario, Valgius could, like other relics, travel the pathways of friendship and turn the wheels of patronage. Valgius's ear, tweaked by the Lord, worn raw by Paulinus, and a talisman with which Macarius, too, might access a purer heavenly force, could be brokered for favors of a far more mundane kind. In such small but telling ways did the "sacred," in the hands of men like Paulinus, invade the realms of the "secular" in these decades.[179]

175. *Ep.* 49.12.
176. *Ep.* 49.14.
177. *Ep.* 49.15.
178. *Ep.* 49.13.
179. Markus, *The End of Ancient Christianity*, 16–17.

In this affair Paulinus has obviously extended the impresario's role far beyond the orchestration of events at the saint's shrine. As an agent of holy power, distributing "relics" at Rome and chronicling the mysterious actions of Christ and Felix in a manner reminiscent of his earlier *vita Felicis*,[180] Paulinus was defining a base of social and political power quite different from, but perhaps no less potent than, that which undergirded the authority of more traditional late Roman aristocrats. But by the time Paulinus had positioned himself as the intermediary between Valgius's ear and a high-ranking Roman, he was already well practiced in representing the "holy" in the disputes of men. I have already noted various ways in which Paulinus presented himself as the representative of Felix's celestial will at the saint's tomb, but the final section of the long *natalicium* of 407 testifies with unusual clarity to the manner in which Paulinus was prepared to exploit his relationship with Felix to intervene directly in the secular affairs and civic life of Nola. In Paulinus's rendition of a dispute over the "waters of Felix," the tenets of civic patronage have been amplified to accommodate the power of a patron saint whose influential earthly representative resided just beyond the city walls.

In the final verses of the *natalicium* of 407, Paulinus responded to a rancorous dispute over water resources that had recently divided Nola and the inhabitants of Paulinus's suburban basilica complex.[181] The new buildings and lavish fountains that Paulinus had constructed at Felix's shrine, coupled with the growth in permanent residents and temporary visitors, had apparently overtaxed the water sources of the old site and of Nola itself. Initially the shrine's new requirements were met by rain-collecting cisterns[182] and with water from the town's supply, which was received both through the grand *Aqua Augusta* restored by Constantine[183] and from a small aqueduct descending from the hills of nearby Abella.[184] But when Nola began to experience shortages and a disturbance (*tumultus*) broke out in the town, generosity withered and the water stopped flowing to Paulinus's basilicas.[185] The crisis was apparently resolved to the satisfaction of townsmen and

---

180. For the parallels see G. Guttilla, "Tre naufragi."

181. *Carm* 21.650–858.

182. Even during the construction phase Paulinus knew that supplying water to the fountains might be difficult. In *carm.* 27 of 403 he rhetorically asked Nicetas, "unde replenda sit haec tot fontibus area dives" (464), and answered by informing Nicetas that, trusting in God to meet their needs, they had built cisterns to collect the *de nubibus amnes* (471).

183. Nola received water from the famous *Aqua Augusta*, which ran from Avellinum some ninety-six kilometers to Misenum. An inscription published in 1938 by I. Sgobbo, "L'acquedotto romano della Campania: 'Fontis Augustei Aquaeductus,'" *Notzie degli scavi* 16 (1938): 75–97, records the restoration of the aqueduct by Constantine in 323 or 324. It was apparently still supplying Naples when Belisarius laid siege to the city in 536 (Procop. *Goth.* 5.9). At *carm.* 21.712–17, Paulinus describes the hydraulic system that collected water from the surrounding mountains in a reservoir (*arca*) at Abella and led it through pipes (*calices*) to Nola and the nearby country estates (*multa rigans et in agris praedia passim*).

184. *Carm.* 27.465–66: "cum procul urbs et ductus aquae prope nullus ab urbe / exiguam huc tenui dimittat limite guttam."

185. See especially *carm.* 21.758–67.

Paulinus alike by refurbishing and extending the aqueduct system that brought water down to the Nolan plain from upland Abella.

Paulinus's poetic account of this episode in the life of an extramural basilica complex is rich in incidental detail, but its primary intention was to control the representation and meaning of the events that had just taken place. Regardless of the realities of the conflict and negotiations between Felix's caretaker and the communities of Nola and neighboring Abella, Paulinus intended to establish the will of Felix as the basis of this and all such future transactions. To this end Paulinus put his poem to work confirming Felix's social vision and authority, while he once more situated himself as the medium through which these were communicated. Accordingly, he praised the goodwill and obedience (*obsequium*) of the Abellans, who, he asserted, had alleviated the tensions by spontaneously repairing at their own expense the old aqueduct system that carried water down to Nola.[186] He emphasized that the Abellans had acted "for the honor of Felix,"[187] while he chastised the Nolans both for their reluctance to share their resources and for their lack of faith in God as a provider.[188] But with the dispute resolved by the time he spoke, Paulinus could forgive the former arrogance of the Nolans[189] and urge them to join him in praising Christ. For it was Christ, acting through his *amicus* Felix, who had restored Nola's water by inspiring the Abellans' act of service. Thus, Paulinus observed, Nola, which had once begrudged Felix, was now indebted to him.[190] Favors inevitably left obligations in their wake.

No less than the Nolans, the Abellans found themselves enmeshed in the web of reciprocity that governed relations between Felix and those who enjoyed his protection. Their spontaneous *obsequium*, Paulinus now informed them, had earned them the reward of being included in his praise of Felix and of being remembered "as the wards of so great a patron."[191] But *alumni* have their responsibilities, too. "Now there is this task," Paulinus continued, "to which the spirit of Felix urges you. Your whole citizenry, people and council, must harmoniously

---

186. *Carm.* 21.708–9: "laborem / sponte sibi sumpsit," and 21.718: "pro munere." Paulinus also mentions bands of men who worked without pay at 21.728: "manus . . . inemptas." It is not at all clear from Paulinus's descriptions exactly what the Abellans accomplished. It appears that the work, which required only a few days to complete (21.742), was limited to repairing smaller channels that led into the collecting reservoir. This effort would, of course, have had the desired effect of increasing the water available to Abella itself, and then to Nola and Cimitile (cf. 21.718–53).

187. *Carm.* 21.708: "pro Felicis honore."

188. See esp. *carm.* 21.767–87.

189. *Carm.* 21.820: "qua fueras felicibus ante superba."

190. *Carm.* 21.822–35.

191. *Carm.* 21.791–93:

> hoc pensabo tibi pretium mercedis honore,
> Felicis sancti scribaris ut addita semper
> laudibus et tanti memoreris alumna patroni

attack this work that will be accomplished only with great effort."[192] And remind-
ing the Abellans of an aqueduct long forgotten, unused, and overgrown, he
charged them with its restoration. In this way, Paulinus proclaimed, the "waters of
Felix'" would further increase.[193]

It is possible to view this passage as further evidence of the manner in which Pauli-
nus promoted the Christianization of the region by asserting the protective power of
Felix over the fundamental concerns of daily life and by extending the saint's au-
thority into the surrounding small towns like Abella. If Felix had inspired the Abel-
lans' service (*obsequium*), then the waters that now flowed to Nola were rightly Felix's
waters. But in consequence all who benefited from these waters—Abellans, Nolans,
and Paulinus's own community—were bound to Felix as they would be to any great
patron. Those so obligated must praise Felix, and Christ who worked through the
saint, and contribute to the glorification of his house. By thus asserting guardianship
over such a precious resource as water, as well as over personal health and economic
welfare, might a cult establish regional prominence and control.

But Paulinus's representation of these negotiations and transactions concern-
ing the "waters of Felix," no less than his reports of miracles at the saint's tomb,
also highlights his own highly self-conscious place in the chain of favors and pa-
tronage now linking heaven and the region of Nola. As panegyrist and intimate
friend of Felix, Paulinus situated himself as a vital intermediary in the power rela-
tions between patron saint and indebted communities. He meant to control the
channels of communication as well as the flow of information. He represented
men before Felix and the *spiritus* of Felix before men. At the same time, as in other
moments in the *natalicia*, the boundary separating his public identity from that of
Felix begins to dissolve in the nuances of his poetic language. By 407 the familiar
outlines of the returning provincial governor had surely faded after years of Pauli-
nus's insistence that he was the special friend of a special friend of Christ. And if
the private influence that Roman aristocrats wielded even in their *otium* still re-
mained visibly rooted in the familiar forms of their public *negotia* and their secular
honores, the wellsprings of Paulinus's *auctoritas* must have by now looked rather

192. *Carm.* 21.795–97:

> nunc tuus iste labor, quo te Felicis adegit
> spiritus, ut tota tibi plebe vel ordine concors
> adgredereris opus magno sudore parandum.

193. *Carm.* 21.812–15:

> [Nola] quae fruitur Felicis aquis, quia copia non est
> haec ipsi sua nunc urbi, quam nuper adepta est
> Felicis studio, modicae pro munere guttae
> ex ope divina largis ditata fluentis.

more private and mysterious. Yet it was explicitly by virtue of this new kind of private authority, buttressed by ascetic paradoxes, that Paulinus sought to intervene in the urban affairs of Nola. But even so, Paulinus at Nola shares at least one thing with, let us say, Symmachus at Capua or Beneventum.[194] For although as the client of Felix and the broker of his *virtus* Paulinus may have been tapping a source of influence quite different from that which grounded the weight of other Roman aristocrats visiting their Campanian estates, he was still performing in that liminal zone where public and private merged.

The same mélange of authority and influence must lie behind the resolution of another dispute whose negotiations and posturings entwined Nola, Capua, and Bordeaux, for the shadowy affair of Basilius and the Daducii shares a number of qualities with the dramas that unfolded later around Valgius and the waters of Felix. In the year 397 or 398, Paulinus wrote from Nola to a certain Daducius in Gaul to complain about the latter's ill-treatment of an aged Capuan priest named Basilius.[195] At the same time that he wrote to Daducius, Paulinus encouraged Delphinus and Amandus to intervene with "our son" Daducius on behalf of Capua's "most holy presbyter."[196] Basilius, in an episode that recalls the eviction of Scirtius at Praeneste, had been ousted from his Capuan house in a dispute over ownership with the Daducii, a family that had sufficient property interests in Campania to warrant frequent journeys there by their "men."[197] A year or two later the dispute had been resolved and, to the joy of the Capuans, their priest had been restored. Paulinus credited much of this success to the intervention of Delphinus and Amandus with the Gallo-Roman Daducii. He thanked Delphinus effusively for settling the matter in accord with Paulinus's desires;[198] and he gratefully acknowledged the importance of Amandus's intercession, requesting as well that Amandus extend his gratitude to the Daducii. They should know, Paulinus told Amandus, that they had offered a sacrifice acceptable to God through the obedience (*oboedientia*) of their faith (cf. 1 Sam 15.22); and that their response to his request (*petitio*) and their devotion (*devotio*) had given Paulinus great joy and enhanced their prospects for salvation. The Daducii were especially worthy of gratitude (*gratia*), Paulinus informed Amandus, because "they were able to transgress and did not" (Eccles 31.10), and they preferred to do what was advantageous rather than what

194. For example., Sym. *Epp.* 1.3.4 (Beneventum) and 1.10 (Capua) with D. Vera, "Simmaco e le sue proprietà: Struttura e funzionamento di un patrimonio aristocratico del quarto secolo d.C," *Colloque genevois sur Symmaque* (Paris, 1986), 231–76.

195. We are informed about this episode by Paulinus's remarks in two letters to Amandus, *epp.* 12.12 of 397 or 398 and 15.2–3 of 399, and one to Delphinus, *ep.* 14.3–4 of 399.

196. *Ep.* 12.12: "filium nostrum"; "sanctissimus presbyter."

197. *Ep.* 12.12 records only that Basilius has suffered violence: "vim sustinet." *Ep.* 14.3–4 makes it clear that the dispute was over a "domus" that was eventually restored to Basilius. *Ep.* 15.3: "homines."

198. *Ep.* 14.3: "illud videlicet curae nostrae negotium de sancti presbyteri Basili domo per operam tuam, ita ut desideravimus, explicatum."

was permissible. "Because with a heart so committed and pure," Paulinus concluded, "they deigned to obey me, no one may dispute their *beneficium*."[199]

The language of secular and of religious authority overlaps easily in this passage as the deference and compliance of the Daducii are reconfigured in the terminology of spiritual sacrifice and the obedience of faith. But if Paulinus's attitudes here point toward concepts worked out more fully later, it was not, explicitly at least, as the client and voice of Felix that Paulinus directed his *petitio* to either the clergy of Bordeaux or, presumably, to the Daducii. Perhaps in the later 390s Felix's influence could not yet carry its charge to distant Gaul. Indeed the change of heart and mind displayed by the Daducii and the "favor" they bestowed on Basilius and his advocates may have been provoked above all by Paulinus's residual prestige as a member of a wealthy Aquitanian family and by the moral and political weight of the episcopal establishment of Bordeaux. But if Paulinus was willing to concede to Delphinus credit in Gallic circles for the successful resolution of this dispute,[200] closer to home matters may have been different.

"Almost all of Capua and the crowded church of that city, sharing the joy of its priest, praised God who aided a poor man in his need and humbled the proud hearts of the rich," Paulinus informed Delphinus afterwards.[201] This Capuan congregation may have been alerted to Delphinus's long-distance role in the affair; we may justly imagine they were made aware of Paulinus's intercession and presumably of a role played by Felix as well. Capua, like Nola, was an inland Campanian town on a heavily traveled highway. Long an important urban center, during the fourth century it was also the province's administrative capital.[202] It is thus virtually certain that Paulinus, governor in the early 380s, had old connections there. Moreover, Capua's Christian establishment could boast of early imperial patronage, for Constantine himself was said to have founded a basilica there.[203] Three decades later, as Paulinus lay on his deathbed, he was attended by Capua's bishop.[204] In any case, regardless of whether Paulinus employed the Basilius affair

---

199. *Ep.* 15.3: "ut sciant et intellegant quam acceptum deo sacrificium dederint hac oboedientia fidei suae, quacum petitionem nostram in vestro interventu exorabiles receperunt, nobis quidem gaudium praesens de sua devotione praestantes, sed saluti suae aeternum commodum providentes. . . . tamen gratia largiter habenda digni sunt pro ipso bonae voluntatis affectu, quo potuerunt transgredi et non sunt transgressi et maluerunt id facere, quod expediebat quam quod licebat, et quod tam absoluto et puro corde nobis parere dignati sunt, ut de beneficio eorum disputari non posset."

200. *Ep.* 14.4: "Veniat tota illa benedictio super caput tuum et in coronae tuae cumulum supertexta florescat."

201. *Ep.* 14.4: "sed tota propemodum Capua et celeberrima urbis ipsius ecclesia gaudio presbyteri coexultans dedit laudem deo, qui adiuvisset pauperem de mendicitate et humiliasset alta divitum corda."

202. A. Chastagnol, "L'administration du diocèse Italien au Bas-Empire," *Historia* 12 (1963): 362–66; G. D'Isanto, *Capua romana: Ricerche di prosopografia e storia sociale* (Rome, 1993), 15–44.

203. *Lib. Pont.* 34 (Silvester).

204. Uranius, *De obitu* 2.

as an opportunity to promote the cult of Felix, his actions once more signaled his willingness to deploy his influence in regional affairs far beyond the immediate vicinity of Felix's tomb.

No simple retirement from the world, Paulinus's secular renunciation appears to us a terribly complex affair, and at the heart of its complexity lie the figure and cult of Felix. Paulinus's intimate relationship to both of these entities precludes us from ever seeing him merely as a monk, a priest, or even a simple bishop. At Nola in 395 Paulinus stepped forcefully back onto the public stage that he had apparently largely eschewed during the previous decade or more. But where he had once stood in resplendent senatorial attire, he now moved in the shabby garb of a monk. He developed a genre of Christian public poetry, the *natalicia*, through which he could define and publicize his friendship with Felix, control the interpretation of events at his tomb, and promote the Christianization of the region. He arrogated to himself the right of representing Felix before men to such a degree that on occasion his voice became the voice of Felix, tuned to the frequencies of the saint's heavenly will. He was prepared to employ his role as Felix's *cliens* to advance causes recommended by his own or others' interests. Despite his protestations of humility, his disposition often appears patronal, and he continued to organize his social relations as well as his spiritual preoccupations in accord with traditional notions of reciprocity and obligation. If Paulinus had renounced one world in 394, many of its principles continued to condition his responses in the new one he was fashioning beside the tomb of Felix. Moreover, his actions here as impresario and friend of a saint continually challenge the exclusivity of such categories as public and private, secular and sacred, or even political and ecclesiastical. In this sense especially, Paulinus's biography embodies some of the most powerful currents of his age.

CHAPTER 8

—•—

Paulinus and Latin Christian Culture

In the late spring of the year 400, Melania the Elder, returning to Italy after nearly three decades of ascetic life in the Holy Land, stopped first at Nola. She was accompanied by a coterie of Rome's Christian aristocracy.[1] Earlier that same year Nicetas, bishop of Remesiana in Dacia Mediterranea, had been with Paulinus for the celebration of the feast of Saint Felix.[2] Both Nicetas and Melania had listened to their host declaim the *Life* of Saint Martin of Tours, which Paulinus had recently received from its author, his longtime Gallo-Roman intimate Sulpicius Severus.[3] Not long after Melania's departure for Rome, Paulinus sent to Severus a carefully crafted account of her Nolan *adventus;*[4] to celebrate Nicetas's earlier departure for Dacia he had composed a *propemptikon,* subverting the conventions of that classical genre in much the same manner that his account of Melania's ascetic heroism had transformed the terms of praise.[5] Friendship and literary pursuits, defining elements of Paulinus's life in Aquitaine and Spain, were no less cultivated at Nola, but bishops and fellow ascetics now dominated the ranks of Paulinus's epistolary friends, and the poetic program announced to Ausonius found new opportunities for expression in the occasions that brought like-minded Christians to Paulinus and the tomb of Felix.

But in the late Roman world even like-minded friends might divide along the lines of rising controversies. The year of Melania's visit saw Paulinus in corre-

---

1. Paul. *ep.* 29.6–14.

2. On Nicetas see A. E. Burn, *Niceta of Remesiana: His Life and Works* (Cambridge, 1905). He appears in *ep.* 29.14, "venerabili episcopo atque doctissimo Nicetae" and *carm.* 27 (*natalicium* 9) of 403; and he was the recipient of *carm.* 17, a *propemptikon.* On the dating and the visit see Fabre, *Essai,* 36–38, 115–16. As Nicetas was at Nola for the January feast of Felix in 400 (cf. *carm.* 27.187–93), his visit apparently preceded that of Melania.

3. *Ep.* 29.14.

4. *Ep.* 29.6–14.

5. On the date of *carm.* 17 see Fabre, *Essai,* 115–16. For brief discussion see Green, *The Poetry of Paulinus,* 34–35, and the next section.

spondence with other Gallo-Roman friends in addition to Severus;[6] Venerius, bishop of Milan;[7] Rome's bishop, Anastasius;[8] probably with Jerome in Palestine and Augustine in Hippo.[9] Several of these correspondents were already entangled in the acrimonious disputes swirling around the writings and ideas of the third-century theologian Origen. Although by 400 Paulinus's relations with the anti-Origenist Jerome had withered, his friendship with Rufinus, the central figure in the Italian theater of the Origenist controversy, was probably well established. Indeed, it was in 400 that Paulinus visited with Anastasius in Rome, only a few months before that bishop formally condemned Origenism and then received Rufinus's letter of personal defense.[10] But while the Origenist affair was a convoluted controversy in its own right, it also "stands as the prehistory of the Pelagian debate," another debacle that eventually brought attention to Paulinus and Nola.[11]

Paulinus may have made Nola a "crossroads of the spirit," but the hum of incessant activity must often have disrupted the silence of the monastery.[12] By couriers and letters, through visitors and annual trips to Rome, Paulinus nourished a far-flung network of friends and correspondents. As the fifth century began this web of relationships apparently grew in density and extent, stretching from northern Gaul through North Africa to Palestine and, after Paulinus's introduction to Nicetas, to at least one point in Upper Moesia. At a time when classical ideals were being transformed and many of the fundamental doctrines and precepts of western Christianity were being determined, Paulinus was exceptionally well connected to influential thinkers and churchmen, and Campanian Nola was strategically located on the empire's routes of travel. Not only was Paulinus reformulating

---

6. In 400 Severus received Paulinus's *epp.* 23, 24, and 29. See Fabre, *Essai,* 29–34. Some or all of the following may also date to 400: *Carm.* 24 addressed to Cytherius, *ep.* 16 and *carm.* 22 to Jovius, some of the letters to Aper (*epp.* 38, 39, 44), *ep.* 14 to Delphinus, and *ep.* 15 to Amandus.

7. Reported to Delphinus in *ep.* 20.3 of 401. Venerius succeeded Simplicianus, who died 15 June 400, and wrote to Paulinus after his consecration. Paulinus was forwarding a letter to Venerius by Delphinus's courier, Cardamas, who stopped at Milan en route to Bordeaux.

8. *Ep.* 20.2.

9. Courcelle, "Paulin de Nole et Saint Jérôme," 271–73; and Courcelle, "Les lacunes," 264–65, 295.

10. Paul. *ep.* 20.2 (401): soon after his election following the death of Siricius on 26 November 399, Anastasius wrote to the bishops of Campania commending Paulinus. During his trip to Rome for the feast of Peter and Paul on 29 June 400, Paulinus was received by Anastasius "tam blande quam honorifice." Paulinus was invited to the celebration of the anniversary of Anastasius's election in late 400. On the dating see Fabre, *Essai,* 57–59. For Anastasius's condemnation of Origenism see Anas. *ep.* 2 (*PL* 20.73–76 = Jer. *ep.* 95); for Rufinus's letter see *CCSL* 20.25–28. On these affairs see also the next section of this chapter.

11. Clark, *The Origenist Controversy,* 6.

12. Ruggiero, "Carme 21," *Atti del Convegno,* 186: "Da quando Paolino è a Nola, dove si è ritirato nella povertà e nel silenzio, questo centro della Campania è diventato come crocevia dello spirito."

Christian practice at Nola after 395, but his presence also placed Nola at the center of crisscrossing lines of communication and controversy.

A NETWORK OF FRIENDS

We seldom meet late Roman aristocrats outside the social and intellectual relationships that help us to define them. Paulinus is no exception: he is always seen in relationship with others. His letters naturally imply a correspondent and his poetry an audience, one that may in theory eventually include all educated readers of Latin but that often originates with one or a few direct addressees, like Nicetas of Remesiana or Titia and Julian, recipients of a wedding hymn. Friendship was an important component of Paulinus's emotional and social world, and his network of friends, broadly understood, was also the medium through which he accomplished a wide range of practical, artistic, and spiritual ends.

On the eve of his conversion Paulinus may have initiated contact with Jerome and others in the Holy Land, but henceforth we most frequently see his letter carriers either traveling north to Gaul or crossing the sea to Carthage. Obviously Paulinus's relocations to Spain and then Campania had not foreclosed either his economic interests or his friendships north of the Alps. He remained in regular epistolary contact with some old friends in Gaul, and he extended his reach to embrace new contacts. We have already examined his dialogues on the topic of secular renunciation with Jovius, with Aper and Amanda, and with Sanctus, all of whom he apparently had known before abandoning his homeland.[13] This group of older Gallic friends and acquaintances also included Paulinus's correspondents Sulpicius Severus and Victricius of Rouen, to whom I return below, and Delphinus and Amandus of Bordeaux, whose profiles can be rounded out here.

Delphinus of Bordeaux had baptized Paulinus and apparently had been his regular correspondent since Paulinus had left Aquitaine for Spain.[14] He had assisted Paulinus's church-building scheme at Alingo and intervened on his behalf with the Daducii in the affair of the Capuan priest Basilius. From Nola, Paulinus in turn kept Delphinus abreast of developments in Italian ecclesiastical circles.[15] In 405, not long after Delphinus's death, Paulinus repaid his attention and affection by ranking his tomb with the shrines of Ambrose at Milan and Martin at Tours.[16] The Bordelais priest Amandus, with whom Paulinus appears to have been more intimate than with the city's bishop, eventually succeeded Delphinus at Bordeaux,

---

13. See chapter 6 and chapter 5, if the Sanctus to whom Paulinus addressed *epp.* 40 and 41 is to be identified with the rhetor Endelechius.

14. *Epp.* 35, 10, 14, 19, and 20 (ca. 390 to 401) are addressed to Delphinus.

15. Paul. *ep.* 20.2–3; cp. Amb. *ep.* 87 (*PL* 16) to Delphinus.

16. *Carm* 19.153–54.

but Paulinus's six letters to him all predate his episcopal accession.[17] He too was a valuable agent for Paulinus's interests in Aquitaine.

Paulinus's known relations with several other Gallo-Roman families were perhaps initiated only after his arrival at Nola in 395. By the opening years of the fifth century, Paulinus was corresponding with Florentius and Alethius, successive bishops of Cahors in southern Aquitania Prima. Florentius apparently wrote to Paulinus soon after his episcopal election; Paulinus's reply acknowledged the news of Florentius's appointment and repaid his compliments.[18] Alethius, who later succeeded his brother Florentius at Cahors, received Paulinus's now fragmentary *ep.* 33 and a copy of Paulinus's sermon entitled *On the Alms Table*, a small taste of the "talent and eloquence" he had requested.[19] In addition to these two documented correspondents, a decade or more later Paulinus commenced an epistolary relationship with Honoratus and Eucherius of Lérins, future bishops of Arles and Lyon.[20]

Paulinus's likely communication with several other Gallic episcopal and ecclesiastical leaders is signaled by a letter fragment preserved only by Gregory of Tours in his *Historia Francorum*.[21] Gregory's eye was drawn to Paulinus's letter by the group of eight bishops from southern Gaul whom Paulinus had therein identified as "worthy of the Lord." Paulinus's list is tantalizing: Exsuperius of Toulouse, Simplicius of Vienne, Amandus of Bordeaux, Diogenianus of Albi, Dynamius of Angoulême, Venerandus of Auvergne, Alethius of Cahors, and Pegasius of Périgeux. Amandus and Alethius are documented correspondents of Paulinus, and the other six plausibly were as well. Paulinus's displaced notice, however, provides virtually all that is known about Diogenianus, Venerandus, Pegasius, and Dynamius,[22] and Simplicianus, whom Paulinus could have met at Vienne in the 380s, is otherwise attested only as a signatory of the Council of Turin in 400.[23] Exsuperius of Toulouse, on the other hand, cuts a rather full and interesting figure in our sources.

17. *Epp.* 36, 9, 2, 12, 15, and 21. Maillé, *Recherches,* 41–43; L. Duchesne, *Fastes épiscopaux de l'ancienne Gaule* (Paris, 1910, 2d ed.), 2:60.

18. *Ep.* 42, which cannot be dated. See Duchesne, *Fastes* 2:44; Heinzelmann, "Gallische Prosopographie," 610, "Florentius"; Fabre, *Essai,* 50–51.

19. Duchesne, *Fastes,* 2:44; Heinzelmann, "Gallische Prosopographie," 550, "Alethius." Fabre, *Essai,* 50, dates *ep.* 33 to after 400, and probably after 402. The *tituli* of three manuscripts identify Alethius as Florentius's brother (*CSEL* 29.301), and *tituli* designate Alethius as the recipient of Paulinus's *ep.* 34, *De gazophylacio* (*CSEL* 29.303). On Alethius's request for Paulinus's eloquence, see *ep.* 33.2: "ingenii quoque et oris opes subpetere nobis arbitrareris."

20. *Ep.* 51, and chapter 9.

21. *Hist. franc.* 2.13 = Paul. *ep.* 48. On the identification see Courcelle, "Fragments historiques," 146–48. Paulinus's letter, the source of this fragment, must date after 401, since Amandus succeeded Delphinus at Bordeaux between 401 and 404.

22. See respectively Duchesne, *Fastes,* 2:42, 34, 87, 68; Heinzelmann, "Gallische Prosopographie," *ad nomina* except Diogenianus. Gregory adds that Venerandus was "ex senatoribus" (*Hist. franc.* 2.13) and records the construction of a basilica on the site of his tomb (*In gloria confessorum* 34–38).

23. Duchesne, *Fastes,* 1:146; the suggestion is Courcelle's at "Fragments historiques," 147 n. 3.

Exsuperius apparently shared many of Paulinus's ideals as well as acquaintances. He, too, promoted monastic life and the cult of the saints, completing Toulouse's church of Saint Saturninus and translating the saint's relics to it.[24] He also cultivated connections in Italy and in the East, appealing to Pope Innocent on topics ranging from clerical marriage to the scriptural canon and the transfer of alms to monks in the Holy Land and Egypt.[25] Contact with Sulpicius Severus, whose Primuliacum lay not far from Toulouse, is plausible enough, but Exsuperius's correspondence with Jerome is documented.[26] Indeed, it was Exsuperius's messenger, Sisinnius, who carried Jerome's *Contra Vigilantium* back to southern Gaul.[27] Thus even Vigilantius stands as a troublesome link between Paulinus, Severus, Jerome, and Exsuperius, though by this time Paulinus's relations with both Jerome and Vigilantius were exhausted.[28]

As he did in Gaul, Paulinus presumably also had longstanding contacts with Rome's North African provinces. Office-holding patterns and patronal obligations tied many members of the Roman aristocracy to North African communities. Many of the same senatorial families who possessed pleasure and working estates in Campania also owned substantial properties in North Africa, where they monopolized the governorship of the proconsular province.[29] It is not surprising then to find Paulinus, a former governor of Campania and an Italian landowner, quickly sending letters to North African churchmen in the aftermath of his secular renunciation. Paulinus's earliest extant letter to a North African was written at Nola in late 395 and addressed to Alypius, bishop of Thagaste, who had just introduced himself by letter to Paulinus. But the presence of Paulinus's courier, Julianus, in Africa in the summer of 395 indicates that he had already made overtures to prominent African bishops, as he did to Jerome, before he left Spain for Italy.[30]

One of Paulinus's early North African correspondents was Aurelius, the influential bishop of Carthage, with whom he appears to have been familiar even be-

---

24. Labrousse, *Toulouse antique*, 558–66; H. Crouzel, "Saint Jérôme et ses amis toulousains," *Bulletin de littérature ecclésiastique* 73 (1972): 129–38.

25. Innocent, *ep.* 6 (*PL* 20.495–502); Jer. *Commentariorum in Zachariam*, book 2, *praef.; Contra Vigilantium* 17.

26. See the prefaces to Jerome's Zechariah commentary, and the mention of Exsuperius in Jer. *epp.* 123.16 and 125.20.

27. *Contra Vig.* 17.

28. On Vigilantius see chapters 4 and 8. The identification of Exsuperius of Toulouse with Paulinus's Exsuperius of Alingo (Santaniello, *Le lettere*, 1:138) is unlikely, and any identification with the Exsuperius of Jer. *ep.* 54 is tenuous; see Crouzel, "Saint Jérôme et ses amis toulousians," 131, against Labrousse, *Toulouse antique*, 560, 565.

29. For example, Arnheim, *The Senatorial Aristocracy*, 157–59; Matthews, *Western Aristocracies*, 24–30.

30. *Ep.* 3.1. On this letter and on Paulinus's correspondence with North Africans generally see Courcelle, "Les lacunes," 253–300; Piscitelli Carpino, *Paolino di Nola: Epistole ad Agostino;* Trout, "The Dates," esp. 239–48. See also chapter 4, this volume.

fore 395.[31] At the center of Paulinus's African correspondence, however, is the figure of Augustine. Four letters from Paulinus and eight from Augustine survive, although internal references hint at as many as twenty-six more exchanged by the two men.[32] Paulinus, prodded by Alypius, opened the series in late 395 with a letter of self-introduction (*ep.* 4). Thereafter the two men probably wrote annually.[33] Augustine's *De cura pro mortuis gerenda,* addressed to Paulinus about 422, is the latest sure evidence of contact, but the correspondence surely continued.[34] In his initial quest for direction in the thickets of Christian scripture and teaching, Paulinus may have sensed as early as 395 or 396 that Augustine promised to be a more congenial and sympathetic guide than the skeptical and apparently uncompromising Jerome.[35] In fact, Augustine frequently played the role of exegetical conferee; the exchanges of courtesies and books that characterized the early letters were soon supplemented by discussions of scripture and Christian moral philosophy.[36] As time passed, queries on the means of recognizing the will of God or about the nature of the activities of the blessed after the resurrection led to consideration of the best manner of living in this world.[37] Although Paulinus and Augustine apparently never met,[38] more than a quarter of a century of communication through letters and intermediaries fostered a candid and resilient relationship founded on mutual

31. *Ep.* 3.3. At *ep.* 6.2 Paulinus may be referring to an earlier letter from Aurelius, presumably carried by Julianus, who brought Alypius's first letter to Paulinus. Aurelius was bishop of Carthage from ca. 392–ca. 430. See A. Audollent, "Aurelius 19," *DHGE* (Paris, 1931), 5:726–38; and G. Zannoni, "Aurelio," *Bibliotheca Sanctorum* (Rome, 1962), 2:609–11.

32. H. Lietzmann, "Zur Entstehungsgeschichte der Briefsammlung Augustins," *Sitzungsberichte der preussischen Akademie der Wissenschaften, philo.-histor. Klasse* (1930): 365–70, identified nine lost letters of the correspondence. Courcelle, "Les lacunes," (254), supplementing the arguments of Lietzmann, added another seventeen. For a synopsis, see the table at "Les lacunes," 294–96.

33. Fabre, *Paulin de Nole,* 71 n. 6. Courcelle, "Les lacunes," 297.

34. On the date of the *De cura pro mortuis gerenda,* see A. Mutzenbecher, *Sancti Aurelii Augustini retractionum libri II; CCSL* 57 (Turnholt, 1984), xxi. See further the fourth section of this chapter.

35. Chapter 4, with Vessey, "Conference and Confession," and Doignon, "'Nos bons hommes de foi.'"

36. Alypius supplied Paulinus with five books of Augustine against the Manichees (*ep.* 3.2), identified by Lietzmann, "Zur Entstehungsgeschichte," 365 n. 1, and Courcelle, *Recherches sur les Confessions de Saint Augustine,* 2d ed. (Paris, 1968), 29 n. 3, as *De vera religione: De Genesi contra Manichaeos libri II, De moribus ecclesiae catholicae,* and *De moribus manichaeorum.* Through Romanianus in 396 Augustine made available to Paulinus all his treatises written to that time (Aug. *ep.* 27.5). Augustine sent his three books *De libero arbitrio* to Paulinus through Romanus and Agilis (Aug. *ep.* 31.7). Alypius requested from Paulinus Eusebius's *Chronicle* (*ep.* 3.3), and Augustine requested Paulinus's own rumored treatise against the pagans and a copy of Ambrose's *De philosophia* (Aug. *ep.* 31.8). On the broader implications see H. Gamble, *Books and Readers in the Early Church: A History of Early Christian Texts* (New Haven, 1995), 132–40. Augustine's *ep.* 149, an answer to Paulinus's *ep.* 50, is almost entirely given over to the exegesis of difficult scriptural passages.

37. Aug. *epp.* 80 and 95; Paul. *ep.* 45.

38. *Contra* Piscitelli Carpino, *Paolino di Nola: Epistole ad Agostino,* 47–70, discussed in chapter 5.

respect.[39] Even the disruptive Origenist and Pelagian controversies failed to sunder these ties.

In the closing decade of the fourth century, the name of Paulinus outweighed that of Augustine, at least beyond the clerical circles of North Africa. Paulinus's reputation was known to Alypius, and therefore presumably to Augustine, at the time of their residence in Milan in the mid-380s, when the wealth and political accomplishments of Paulinus would still have commanded the attention of Augustine. Yet in 395 Alypius remained unfamiliar to Paulinus; and if he knew of Augustine as a Christian writer, Paulinus had not yet read his major works against the Manichees. This imbalance of public exposure partially explains the request for personal information that Paulinus incorporated into his first letter to Alypius (*ep.* 3.4). It may also have provided some of the motivation behind an ambitious Augustine's composition of the *Confessions*. But even if Augustine was provoked by Paulinus to write a version of the biography of Alypius that eventually found a place in the *Confessions*, the final form of Augustine's "autobiography" owes considerably more to Augustine's genius than to any inquiry from Nola.[40] Still, in 396, Paulinus's social rank and connections, his reputation as a poet, and his letters "flowing with milk and honey" must have been as decisive as the recently revealed proof of his moral strength (*exemplo roboris tui*) in recommending him as an Italian correspondent and as the antidote to the alluring but hollow worldly honors still distracting Augustine's former student Licentius.[41]

Presumably this same combination of qualities also recommended Paulinus's monastery as a valuable warehouse and way station for Augustine's books, friends, and ideas in Italy. Nola quickly became a repository of Augustine's writings. Alypius sent Paulinus Augustine's anti-Manichaean works in 395, and the next year Augustine made available to Paulinus all his treatises. Subsequently he could refer the Roman Manichee Secundinus to Paulinus for a copy of his *De libero arbitrio*.[42] African friends and associates of Augustine sojourned at Nola, including the deacon Quintus, who met Paulinus at Rome with a letter from Augustine,[43] and Pos-

39. G. Casati, "S. Agostino e S. Paolino di Nola," *Augustinianum* 8 (1968): 46.

40. Augustine, *ep.* 27.5, promised to write the biography of Alypius for Paulinus, but all that survives is *Conf.* 6.7.11. Courcelle's elaborate arguments at *Recherches sur les confessions*, 29–32; "Les lacunes," 264–66, and *Les confessions de Saint Augustin dans la tradition littéraire* (Paris, 1963), 559–607, are deflated by O'Donnell, *Confessions*, 2:360–62. Paulinus's influence on Augustine's style may be another matter.

41. Aug. *ep.* 27.2, 6.

42. Aug. *ep.* 27.5; *Contra Secundinum*, 11. Courcelle, "Les lacunes," 269, may go too far in calling Nola "le dépositaire officiel de ce traité [*De libero arbitrio*], et probablement de ses autres oeuvres, pour l'Italie." See also P. Brown, "The Patrons of Pelagius: The Roman Aristocracy between East and West," *JTS* n.s. 21 (1970), reprinted in *Religion and Society in the Age of Augustine* (New York, 1972), 212.

43. *Ep.* 45.1.

sidius of Calama, on a mission to the imperial court in 408.[44] In addition to the travelers and couriers who passed through on their journeys, some came from Africa with Nola as their destination. In 396 Augustine recommended the *puer* Vetustinus to Paulinus (*ep.* 31.7). Vetustinus, having left his home amid unspecified difficulties, desired to devote himself to the service of God. A decade and a half later a certain Paulinus, *filius* of Augustine, appeared at Nola under somewhat similar conditions; Augustine was confident he would find Paulinus's way of life instructive.[45] With different intentions, in 404 Augustine sent to Nola Spes and Boniface, a monk and priest of Hippo, hoping that divine judgment at the tomb of Felix would resolve a dispute between them that had disrupted the church at Hippo for some time.[46]

Nola also served other African clerics and travelers as an Italian outpost and hospice. Paulinus remained in correspondence with Alypius probably until the latter's death sometime after 419.[47] Romanianus, Alypius's kinsman, a former magistrate in the latter's see of Thagaste, and a patron of Augustine, visited Nola carrying Augustine's *ep.* 27 in 396, and while still in Italy he received Paulinus's *ep.* 7, accompanied by *ep.* 8, addressed to his son Licentius.[48] When Melania the Younger and Pinianus, dear friends of Paulinus, relocated to their estates near Thagaste soon after 410, Paulinus's letter carriers had further reason to visit that city. But Paulinus's couriers circulated widely in North Africa. In 395, for example, Paulinus had written to Aurelius of Carthage with instructions on copying a manuscript of Eusebius's *Chronicle.*[49] The next year, when the couriers Romanus and Agilis returned to Nola with a letter from Aurelius, they also carried letters from Profuturus, bishop of Cirta, and Severus, bishop of Milevis, as well as from Alypius and Augustine.[50] If Severus of Milevis is identified with the like-named bearer of Augustine's *ep.* 42 of 398, then he too was a visitor to Nola.[51] Evodius of Uzalis and his fellow bishop, Theasius, were, like Possidius of Calama, conducting official church business in 404, when they stopped at Nola on their return from Ravenna, where they had gone as representatives of the ninth Council of

---

44. Aug. *ep.* 95.1. On Possidius, bishop of Calama and Augustine's biographer, see H. Leclercq, "Guelma," *DACL* 6.2 (Paris, 1925), 1861–73. Possidius came to Italy in 408 to complain of the violence exhibited by the pagans of Calama against the Christian community there. See Aug. *ep.* 91.8–9.

45. Aug. *ep.* 149.34.

46. Aug. *ep.* 78, with section 4, this chapter.

47. See *ep.* 7.1; Aug. *epp.* 45 and 186 of 399 and 417 are consigned by Alypius.

48. On Romanianus, Alypius, Licentius, and Thagaste see C. Lepelley, *Les cités de l'Afrique romaine au Bas-Empire:* vol. 2, *Notices d'histoire municipale* (Paris, 1981), 178–82.

49. Cf. *ep.* 3.3.

50. *Ep.* 7.1. On Cirta and Milevis see Lepelley, *Les cités,* 2: 383–99; 438–39. On Profuturus see H. Leclercq, "Constantine," *DACL* 3.2 (Paris, 1914), 2722. On Severus see Leclercq, "Milève," *DACL* 6 (Paris, 1933), 1102–3.

51. Aug. *ep.* 42.1.

Carthage.[52] Certainly many other North African clerics, the necessity of whose Italian journeys Augustine regretted (*ep.* 95.1), paid calls at Nola.

Such evidence amply documents the lines of personal friendship and ecclesiastical business that kept Nola and Paulinus linked to various towns of Gaul, Africa Proconsularis, and Numidia. Moreover, the presence of so many North African couriers and clerics in Campania underscores the fluidity of Paulinus's community and allows us to animate his monastery with scenes of arrival, conversation, and farewell that must have been often repeated over the years. Spring and fall in particular would have been regularly enlivened by the arrival and return of couriers.[53] And unlike communications between Nola and Gaul, which were disrupted by the military and political misfortunes of the first decade of the fifth century, the movement of travelers between Nola and Africa probably increased as aristocratic refugees fled to their North African estates and then gradually filtered back to Latium and Campania. In a different way, as I will show, the age's theological controversies also added to the flow of traffic through Nola.

Meetings and conversations at Nola, Rome, and points in between would more often have complemented Paulinus's contact with friends in Italy, but Paulinus's letters and poems still preserve the outlines of his relations with some of the secular and ecclesiastical elite of Italy. Unfortunately no letters exchanged by Paulinus and Ambrose survive, though we can take their correspondence for granted. Nor did communication with the episcopal see of Milan end with Ambrose's death in 397, for in 401 Paulinus was corresponding with Milan's new bishop, Venerius, who had recently replaced Ambrose's successor Simplicianus.[54] Paulinus may also have exchanged letters with the Roman church before Anastasius restored cordial relations with him in late 399, but his relations with the Roman aristocracy are more evident. In 396 Paulinus addressed to Pammachius, a former proconsul and member of the powerful *gens Furia*, a long letter of consolation on the death of his wife Paulina, the daughter of Jerome's companion, Paula.[55] The composition of this letter probably reveals Paulinus's desire to reach out to Jerome as well as to nurture friendly relations with a branch of the Christian aristocracy whose ascetic aspirations were highly visible; though Pammachius, like Paulinus, was related to Melania the Elder, he was better known as a companion and friend of Jerome.[56] Indeed, Paulinus's lengthy development of the tenets of secular renun-

---

52. Aug. *ep.* 80.1. On Evodius see A. M. LaBonnardière, "Evodius 4," *DHGE* 16 (Paris, 1967), 133–35. On Uzalis, a city of Africa Proconsularis, see Lepelley, *Les cités*, 2:246–47.

53. For example,, *ep.* 7.1.

54. *Ep.* 20.3 to Delphinus. Paulinus's phrase, "filius vester hucusque, nunc frater," suggests a previous relationship between Bordeaux's bishop and Venerius.

55. On Pammachius see the evidence collected at *PLRE* 1:663, "Pammachius"; for Paulina see *PLRE* 1:675, "Paulina 3." On the *gens Furia* see Arnheim, *The Senatorial Aristocracy*, 129–30.

56. On relations with Melania see Paul. *ep.* 29.5; Palladius, *Historia Lausica* 62 (*The Lausiac History of Palladius, Texts and Studies* 6, ed. C. Butler, [Cambridge, 1904]). Jerome knew Pammachius during his student days in Rome in the 360s; see, for example, Jer. *ep.* 66.9.

ciation in this consolatory letter may be his indirect response to the suspicions that Jerome had voiced in his second letter to Paulinus (*ep.* 58), received at Nola only a few months earlier.[57]

Paulinus moved with ease among the Roman circles with which Jerome was increasingly at odds. As Jerome's relations with Melania and Rufinus in Palestine were rapidly deteriorating,[58] Paulinus was cultivating friendships with Melania's kin and laying the foundations for a strong friendship with Rufinus, who returned to Italy in 397. These connections crystallized spectacularly when Paulinus received Melania at Nola in 400 on her epic return to Italy from the Holy Land.[59] Those of Melania's family who are likely to have assembled with her at Nola in the spring of that year include her son, the former *consularis Campaniae* Publicola, his wife Albina, their daughter, Melania the Younger, and perhaps the latter's husband Pinianus.[60] Paulinus appears at ease and intimate with this branch of the Christian aristocracy whose vast wealth fomented the introspection and anxiety that Paulinus understood so well.[61]

57. On the date of the letter, *ep.* 13, and the death of Paulina early in the winter of 395–96, see the discussion by Fabre, *Essai,* 65–67. Paulinus received the news of Paulina's death during the winter and could not travel (13.2).

58. Jerome had honored Melania with a place in his *Chronicle* but later was accused of erasing her name. Jer. *Chron.* ann. 374 (*Die Chronik des Hieronymus, Eusebius Werke,* vol. 7, ed. R. Helm, [Berlin, 1956], 247): "Melanium, nobilissima mulierum Romanorum"; Ruf. *Apol.* 2.26. Cf. Murphy, "Melania," 59.

59. The chronology of events in the life of Melania is still debated. The most complete sources are Paulinus's *ep.* 29.6–14 and Pall. *Hist. Laus.* 46, 54, and 55. See also Paulinus *epp.* 28.5, 31.1, 45.2–3. For recent discussions see Moine, "Melaniana," 3–79, and Hammond, "The Last Ten Years of Rufinus' Life," 372–429. See also Gorce, *Vie de Sainte Mélanie,* 20–26, passim; and Murphy, "Melania the Elder," 59–77. Fabre's date of 400 for *ep.* 29, in *Essai,* 32–33, is the cornerstone of the chronology of Melania's return. Ancillary evidence is examined by Moine, "Melaniana," 24–45. It is likely that Melania arrived at Nola in the spring, but Palladius's reckoning of twenty days for the voyage from Caesarea to Rome is suspect. Perhaps he meant the distance to Naples, as Murphy, "Melania," 73, suggests, but even in this case the time may be too short. See Moine, "Melaniana," 43–45. On Paulinus's account of Melania's arrival (*ep.* 29.12) see also chapter 5; on Rufinus see section 3, this chapter.

60. Paulinus, *ep.* 29.12, is not specific: Melania was met "filiorum nepotumque occursu." See Moine, "Melaniana," 40, on the identity of the group. Valerius Publicola was Melania's only living child, two others having died in the same year as her husband, when she was twenty-two (Pall. *Hist. Laus.* 46). See *PLRE* 1:753–54, "Publicola 1 and 2." He was urban praetor ca. 377. See Jer. *Chron.* ann. 374 (Helm, 247): "unico praetore tunc urbano filio derelicto [Melania] Hierosolymam navigavit." See *CIL* 9.1591 on his governorship. His father is usually assumed to have been Valerius Maximus, urban prefect in 361–62. See *PLRE* 1:582, "Maximus 17," and Chastagnol, *Les fastes,* 154–56. Moine, "Melaniana," 39–43, would date Publicola's birth no later than 367–68. His wife was Albina (*PLRE* 1:33, "Albina 2"), daughter of the urban prefect of 389–391, Ceionius Rufius Albinus (*PLRE* 1:37, "Albinus 15"), and sister of the future urban prefect of 417–18, Volusianus (*PLRE* 2:1184, "Volusianus 6," and Chastagnol, *Les fastes,* 276–79). On Melania the Younger and Pinianus see below.

61. Melania controlled a great deal of wealth, and her son, Publicola, controlled his share as well. See Murphy, "Melania," 65, 72; and Moine, "Melaniana," 39. Melania's granddaughter, Melania the Younger, possessed estates in the Spains, Gaul, Campania, Sicily, and Africa, according to Palladius

In late 406 or early January 407, some members of this group of "slaves of Christ, once nobles of the earth," reassembled at Nola for the feast of Saint Felix, perhaps having abandoned Rome some months earlier before the advance of Radagaisus.[62] On that occasion, Paulinus represented them all as the strings of a mystical lyre.[63] The matriarch was absent, and Publicola was probably now dead,[64] but the younger generation displayed the same dynamic combination of firmly held ascetic aspirations and high social status underwritten by political prominence and wealth. Turcius Apronianus, converted several years before through the combined influence of Rufinus and Melania the Elder,[65] once a senator of the *curia*, was now a "senator for Christ." Paulinus's poetry attested to the antiquity of his nobility; the *fasti* confirm his family's recent urban prefectures and provincial governorships.[66] Also present at Nola that January was Pinianus, the husband of Melania the Younger. Sprung from Valerius, the first consul of the city, he was now a consul of Christ.[67] One breath, Paulinus boasted, spoke the thoughts

---

(61), and in Mauretania, Britain, and Numidia as well, according to the *Vita* 11 and 20. On anxiety see *carm.* 21.506–25, delivered before members of Melania's family.

62. On the date and circumstances of *carm.* 21, following the defeat of Radagaisus in August 406, see chapter 5. It is not clear when the group arrived at Nola, or even whether they arrived together. Paulinus's words at ll. 836 ff., designating Albina, Pinianus, and Melania the Younger as *famuli* of Christ and "tuis [Nola] modo finibus ortos," may indicate a sojourn extending beyond the January festival, but it is unlikely they intended permanent residence as Courcelle, "Les lacunes," 268–69, suggests. See also Ruggiero, "Carme 21," 188–89.

63. *Carm.* 21.205 (*natalicium* 13): "mancipia Christi, nobiles terrae prius"; 328–29: "Omnes ex nobis cytharam faciamus in unum / carmen diversis conpositam fidibus."

64. The date of Publicola's death has been debated. Moine, "Melaniana," 52–64, argues persuasively that it occurred in 405 or, more likely, 406. Courcelle, "Les lacunes," 275–76, placed Publicola's death in 407 at Nola (276 n. 2), sometime after the gathering recorded in *carm.* 21. He is followed on the date by Hammond, "The Last Ten Years of Rufinus' Life," 416. If Publicola died in 406, as Moine argues, then Melania the Elder would have been in Africa when the January 407 gathering took place, for it was apparently there that she received the news of her son's death. Cf. Paulinus, *ep.* 45.2, and Courcelle, "Les lacunes," 270.

65. On the respective roles of Rufinus and Melania in his conversion see Murphy, *Rufinus of Aquileia*, 112; Hammond, "The Last Ten Years of Rufinus' Life," 379; Moine, "Melaniana," 33–34.

66. *Carm.* 21.210–15:

Apronianum Turciae gentis decus,
aetate puerum, sensibus carnis senem,
veteri togarum nobilem prosapia
sed clariorem Christiano nomine,
qui mixta veteris et novi ortus gloria
vetus est senator curiae, Christo novus.

On his filiation and the family's offices see Shelton, "The Esquiline Treasure," 151–52 and Cameron, "The Date and Owners," 144–45, against *PLRE* 1:1147.

67. *Carm.* 21.219–23: "in principe urbe consulis primi genus. . . . Valeri modo huius Christiani consulis." See *PLRE* 1:702, "Pinianus 2." His father, Valerius Severus, had been urban prefect in 382.

of all; although three in number, Apronianus, Pinianus, and Paulinus were singular in mind.[68] Therasia, Avita, the wife of Apronianus, and Albina, wife of the late Publicola, knew a similar mystical harmony. They were three leaders of the hymning chorus,[69] while their daughters, Eunomia and Melania the Younger, conducted an entourage of noble ladies and virgins.[70] Elite solidarity was announced in the metaphors of spiritual union and Christian affection, and it was affirmed by a common sympathy for the paradoxes of renunciation. The novelty of ascetic Christian senators was fresh enough to inspire poetic irony.

Even such a cursory survey of some of the influential personalities whose names decorate the correspondence and poems of Paulinus reveals both the geographical breadth and the steep social pitch of the world traversed by his letter carriers. A network of friends so far-flung could, of course, serve many social, economic, and political ends, but Paulinus's letters and the ideals of friendship that they embodied also worked to hold together the members of a Christian elite that was always vulnerable to unpredictable flare-ups of personal animosity or theological controversy. Perhaps this was one reason that Paulinus, like others of his contemporaries, was struggling to define the concepts and the language that would allow Christian friendship to transcend the apparent limits of the more traditional relationships of the late Roman world.

FRIENDSHIP, LETTERS, AND POETRY

True friendship may be our primary solace in a human society fraught with misunderstandings and calamities, but even its currency, Augustine once lamented, was difficult to recognize and debased by its own intrinsic pangs of anxiety.[71] Augustine's hesitation before the allure of intimacy was not new. Among the elites of the ancient world, friendship had long been a problematic philosophical concept as well as a revered social institution, assuaging existential isolation while also serving pragmatic ends. Thus, along with most other aspects of intellectual and social life, the meaning and implications of friendship were being reconsidered by

68. *Carm.* 21.271, 278: "uno loquente spiritu affectu trium"; "tres etenim numero sumus, idem mentibus unum."

69. *Carm.* 21.281–83:

> prima chori Albina est cum pare Therasia;
> iungitur hoc germana iugo, ut sit tertia princeps
> agminis hymnisonis mater Avita choris.

70. *Carm.* 21.77–78: "has procerum numerosa cohors et concolor uno / vellere virgineae sequitur sacra turba catervae." On Eunomia see *PLRE* 2:421, "Eunomia." Her brother, Asterius (*PLRE* 2:171, "Asterius 3") was also present on this occasion. Cf. *carm.* 21.313–25.

71. *De civ. Dei* 19.8.

Christian men and women in the late Roman world.[72] Ambrose may have remained firmly rooted in the ethical concepts virtually canonized for the Latin west by Cicero in his *De amicitia* and other works, by Seneca, and by other writers of an earlier age; but Paulinus, like Augustine from at least the time of the *Confessions*, was more consciously bending Ciceronian notions to accommodate a conviction that the grace and love of God, not individual human sympathy or mutual recognition of traditionally construed virtues, must be the source and medium of true Christian friendship.[73] But at the same time, and in a further display of their common sensibility, both Paulinus and Augustine adamantly preserved a role for individual friendships and intimate relations within the broader, all-inclusive Christian sodality.[74] In his poetry as well as in his letters, Paulinus vigorously pursued this spiritualization of desire by simultaneously abstracting friendship and solidly recentering old relationships and anchoring new ones in the love of God.

This reconfiguration of the emotional terrain of social relations, especially of the deeper reaches of masculine intimacy, introduced dilemmas of which Paulinus was acutely conscious. His writing displays persistent engagement with the language of friendship and love at the same time that it challenges the assumptions and assertions of earlier generations. By asserting the unanimity that swept all the baptized into spiritual communion Paulinus would, for example, counter Cicero's restriction of psychological *unanimitas* to only the closest friends, a conceit retained by Symmachus.[75] Similarly Paulinus subverted the Ciceronian claim that friendships required time to arise and develop by announcing to Pammachius that their friendship (*amicitia*), sprung from God and joined by a hidden similarity of spirits, was born already strong and great.[76] More radically still, Paulinus informed Alypius in the first letter that he wrote to him that their love (*caritas*) was predestined by God.[77] Anchored in the love of Christ (*caritas Christi*), such mystical love between men, Paulinus suggested here and elsewhere, existed from the origin of the world

---

72. The topic is vast. On Paulinus's place and for further bibliography see, for example, Fabre, *Paulin de Nole*, 137–54; J. Lienhard, "Friendship in Paulinus of Nola and Augustine," *Collectanea Augustiniana* (Leuven, 1990), 279–96; C. White, *Christian Friendship in the Fourth Century* (Cambridge, 1992), 146–63; D. Sorrentino, "L'amore di unità," 149–69; L. Pizzolato, *L'idea di amicizia nel mondo antico e cristiano* (Turin, 1993), 287–96; D. Konstan, "Problems in the History of Christian Friendship," *JECS* 4 (1996): 87–113; Konstan, *Friendship in the Classical World*, 157–60; and Conybeare, "The Expresssion of Christianity," esp. 72–110.

73. Konstan, *Friendship in the Classical World*, 122–48, offers a recent survey of the earlier Roman background. On Ambrose and Augustine see Lienhard, "Friendship in Paulinus of Nola and Augustine," 289–96; White, *Christian Friendship*, 111–28, 185–217; Pizzolato, *L'idea di amicizia*, 269–76, 296–319; Konstan, *Friendship in the Classical World*, 149–53; and Conybeare, "The Expression of Christianity," 72–77.

74. Cp. Paul. *ep.* 11.6 and Aug. *Conf.* 4.4, with Rom 5.5.

75. Perrin, *La place des courriers*, 1038–41.

76. Cic. *Amic.* 19.67–68; Paul. *ep.* 13.2, cp. *epp.* 42.1, 51.3.

77. *Ep.* 3.1.

and, in contrast to mere human friendship, would last forever.[78] Moreover, since Paulinus affirmed that such Christian friendship anticipated physical acquaintance, he told Augustine that it could bind even those who had never met face to face.[79]

Such revisions of inherited notions made it possible to begin to rank relationships on a scale that privileged Christian over worldly friendship. Writing to his new correspondents Eucherius and Galla, for instance, Paulinus contrasted any mundane relationship defined by human friendship (*humana amicitia*) with the transcendental affection that now bound them through divine grace (*divina gratia*) and the love of Christ (*caritas Christi*).[80] Even an old acquaintance could be informed that their former friendship had been deficient precisely because it had been established only in the rootless "friendship (*amicitia*) of *human* intimacy," not in the "love (*dilectio*) which is of Christ" and is founded on a rock.[81] Indeed, from the loftiest perspective that Paulinus could imagine, all individual relations among Christians might simply dissolve into their common membership in that three-dimensional, mystical Pauline body of which Christ was the head. With this view in mind, Paulinus informed Augustine in 396 that becoming familiar with him was more like resuming a long-standing love (*caritas*) than beginning a new friendship (*amicitia*).[82]

Clearly Paulinus's perception of the sources and context of true friendship sometimes led him to deny traditionally conceived *amicitia* access to the upper reaches approached through friendship rooted in the heart and "built up in Christ."[83] But Paulinus apparently realized that such spiritualized and universalized formulations of friendship ran the risks of rarefying human emotions beyond recognition and of precluding the cultivation of intense individual relationships, something he was ill-prepared to do both by temperament and by sensibility. His letters to Sulpicius Severus show how Paulinus resolved this dilemma by retaining some theoretical value for the more mundane aspects of intimate relations while he simultaneously adapted the conventional sense and language of *amicitia* to embrace Christian friendship's upward sweep. In 397, Paulinus represented his pre-conversion friendship with Severus both as the special gift that continued to distinguish Severus from Paulinus's other spiritual friends (*spiritales*) and as the first

78. *Epp.* 3.1, 11.2, 51.3.

79. *Ep.* 4.1, cp. *epp.* 6.3, 20.1. On these points see also G. Santaniello, "Momenti del percorso teologico di Paolino nel dialogo epistolare con Agostino," *Impegno e Diologo* 11 (1997): esp. 265–69.

80. *Ep.* 51.3: "Non enim humana amicitia sed divina gratia invicem nobis innotuimus et conexi sumus per viscera caritatis Christi" (Phil 1.8).

81. *Ep.* 40.2: "Sancte frater, diligere coepi te; et dilexi iugiter, quamquam non ista dilectione quae Christi est, sed illa familiaritatis humanae amicitia, quae blandimenta in labiis habet et radicem in cordibus non habet, quia non est fundata super petram quae non aedificatur in Christo."

82. *Ep.* 6.2 with, for example, Rom 12.4, 1 Cor 10.17, 12.12. See also Piscitelli Carpino, *Paolino di Nola: Epistole ad Agostino,* 195–96; and Sorrentino, "L'amore di unità," 155–60.

83. *Ep.* 40.2, just quoted.

stage of a journey, however inadequate in retrospect, that had early on marked them out for each other "in the love of Christ." "But yet," Paulinus continued, "we have grown into this bond, by which now we are joined by the intervention of God, through the habit of that former intimacy (*familiaritas*), so that by loving each other faithfully even on that path of unbelief we still learned to love spiritually. For we always loved each other so scrupulously that no affection (*affectio*) could be added to the love (*dilectio*) between us except the love (*caritas*) of Christ, which alone transcends every feeling and affection."[84]

At a time when Paulinus was hoping to lure Severus to Nola, his emphasis lay on eliding, not segregating, the friendship of the preconversion past and the Nolan present. The infusion of Christ's *caritas* through God's intervention recalibrated rather than effaced the bonds of earlier friendship.[85] Indeed, just as Paulinus had recently presented Severus with *otium ruris* as a preparatory school for the monastic *propositum* (*ep.* 5.4), he now positioned their early mutual affection as the prolegomenon to their current elevated spiritual friendship. Continuity, not discontinuity, prevailed in this context, and for both Paulinus and Severus their former intimacy (*familiaritas*) and their earlier *otium* became corresponding points on the continuum that extended from their Gallic estates to their monastic foundations. In practice, reflecting on a relationship complicated by preconversion bonds of intimacy, Paulinus would deny neither the emotional weight nor the theological significance of that former love. By such means it was possible to preserve the legitimacy of human love and friendship as features that distinguished some Christian friends from others. In such cases, physical desire was washed over but not washed away by the "love of Christ," which allowed this desire to transcend its mundane limits.

We are fortunate that the sentiments Paulinus expressed to Severus in this letter of 397 can be viewed as part of an extensive dialogue between the two men, for, like Paulinus's correspondence with Ausonius, this long conversation also reminds us that the public reconceptualization of social and emotional life under Christian imperatives was shaped by the vagaries of longing and emotional turmoil. Within the theoretician of friendship, that is, beat "the heart of a man."[86] Read in series, Paulinus's thirteen letters to Severus, more than one-fifth of the collection,[87] seem to lay bare the emotional and psychological lives of two men perhaps not well matched in all ways. Their story illuminates the struggle within each of humility

84. *Ep.* 11.5: "Sed tamen in hanc, qua modo interventu dei nectimur, copulam per consuetudinem illius familiaritatis inolevimus, ut diligendo nos et in infideli via fideliter diligere etiam spiritaliter disceremus, quia tam religiose nos semper uterque dileximus, ut ad nostram inter nos dilectionem nulla adici posset affectio nisi caritas Christi, quae sola omnem sensum affectumque supereminet."

85. So too F. Ghizzoni, *Sulpicio Severo* (Rome, 1983), 66–67; Pizzolato, *L'idea di amicizia*, 291; Sorrentino, "L'amore di unità," 160–65.

86. Fabre, *Paulin de Nole*, 293, animating his view of the theoretician of friendship.

87. *Epp.* 1, 5, 11, 17, 22–24, 27–32; but for the chronology see Fabre, *Essai*, 19–46.

and vanity, of honesty and irony, and of impulse and consideration, all amid the most intimate expressions of affection. And eventually, out of the debris of frustration, jealousy, and recriminations, they apparently salvage an equilibrium founded on transcendental ideals and cooperative enterprise.[88]

Paulinus's letters to Severus tell the story of an emotionally tangled friendship that began no later than the 380s in Aquitaine and followed both men across the precipitous divide of their ascetic conversion. The support that they gave each other in the mid-390s, as their monastic plans attracted criticism, eventually yielded to bristling irritation when Paulinus's repeated invitations failed to bring Severus south to the "garden of Felix."[89] Shared assumptions and common goals, however, eventually provided the anodyne for this proclaimed betrayal; and it was especially in the service of the cult of the saints, a topic I take up below, that Paulinus and Severus pooled their literary and economic resources. Simultaneously, Paulinus employed his letters as a medium of spiritual communion for the "abstraction" of their friendship,[90] while, more pragmatically, representing Severus before Italian ascetic circles.[91] Paulinus's letters to Severus do not offer us a treatise on friendship; they are the contrary fragments of its practice.[92]

Other such fragments glitter among Paulinus's verses. In Spain poetry had offered Paulinus and Ausonius the medium for articulating the limits of friendship; at Nola Paulinus employed it to elevate friendship's horizons. The amicable relationships that provided the occasions for Paulinus's redirection of such traditional poetic genres as the *propemtikon* and the epithalamium, as well as the *consolatio* and the *protreptikon*,[93] also created the opportunities for further revision of friendship's boundaries. Even Paulinus's annual celebration of Felix could become a vehicle for exploration and announcement. The *natalicium* of 407 (*carm.* 21), the poem that put on display the mystical communion of Paulinus and the kin of Melania, is the longest of Paulinus's poems written for Felix's feast. From one perspective it presents an apparently disjointed patchwork of episodes, many of which I have already examined, whose discontinuity seems only highlighted by Paulinus's shifting

<hr/>

88. For example, Fabre, *Paulin de Nole*, 277–338; and more succinctly Santaniello, *Le lettere* 1:79–85; Sorrentino, "L'amore di unità," 150–55.

89. *Epp.* 17 and 22.

90. For instance, *ep.* 32.1 of ca. 404; see also Conybeare, "The Expression of Christianity," 81–107, on letters as a crucial, constitutive part of the fashioning of friendship.

91. For example, by redirecting the latter's historical questions to Rufinus *Ep.* 28.5. Note, too, Severus's reworking of Paulinus's *ep.* 31.3–6 at *Chron.* 2.33–34. See Inglebert, *Les romains chrétiens*, 381–83.

92. Thus they vitiate modern attempts to tidy up Paulinus by, for example, relegating his use of the term *amicitia* (and its assumed limited connotations) solely to the field of "inferior" human friendship; so Fabre, *Paulin de Nole*, 148–52; 292–93. For the debate see White, *Christian Friendship*, 158–59; Pizzolato, *L'idea di amicizia*, 290–91; Konstan, "Problems," 97–101; and most sensibly Conybeare, "The Expression of Christianity," 77–80.

93. *Carm.* 31 and 22.

meters. The piece opens with expressions of relief for the victory over Radagaisus at Faesulae; moves on to recognition and praise of Paulinus's Roman guests, "new flowers" in the field of Felix; continues with the now-familiar autobiographical vignette; and concludes with the scenes re-creating for the crowd the recent examination of Felix's tomb and the water dispute with Nola. But each panel may also be approached as a discrete study of the multiplex gifts, joys, and rewards of Christian love and friendship. In verses harmonious and profound,[94] Paulinus dwells on forms of intimacy whose nearly unfathomable human depths are simply the obverse of their long reach upward to embrace the saints and Christ. As a companion (*sodalis*) of Christ, Felix receives the gifts that he in turn gives to Paulinus (194–95); united as they are in "body, mind, and faith" (339) Paulinus's Roman friends form the lyrical assembly of parents and affectionate children that Christ plucks with the quill of Felix (326–43); the opportunity to examine Felix's tomb is fashioned as a gift of the saint's "special love (*amor*)" (561), while Felix merits his share of Nola's water as a companion (*consors*) of God (770). It is Christ, through His beloved friend (*amicus*) Felix, who has bestowed the resources of heaven and earth on Nola (822–35). As in the other *natalicia*, Paulinus's compulsion to give poetic expression to his overwhelming sense of Felix's patronal and caring presence pervades these verses. But in this poem especially, the circles of human and divine love and friendship overlap in dizzying array as they also work to hold together the fabric of a performance on the verge of narrative disintegration.

The *natalicium* of 407 is only one example of the fertile concourse of friendship and poetry in the corpus of Paulinus. Paulinus's Christian reanimation of the classical *propemptikon*, or farewell poem, celebrated the departure from Nola of Nicetas, bishop of Remesiana in Dacia, setting out in early 400 to catch ship to Epirus and make his way home. Under Paulinus's eye the conceits of Horace, Tibullus, Propertius, and Ovid were banished or transformed.[95] The calm waters, full sails, and placid sea beasts desired by traveler and poet alike are no longer simply the stuff of the poet's prayers or the gifts of the old gods. Nature would now reflexively relax at the approach of a holy bishop who embodied Christ himself (15–16). As Nicetas set out, Paulinus presented him with an idealized image of the pristine harmony between man and nature that apparently drew its inspiration from ascetic visions of conditions before the Fall.[96] In the Christian poet's imagination the early imperial desire to dominate nature was accomplished effortlessly in a world

---

94. Ruggiero, "Carme 21," 187.

95. F. Jäger, *Das antike Propemptikon und das 17 Gedicht des Paulinus von Nola* (Rosenheim, 1913); Green, *The Poetry of Paulinus*, 34–35; A. Basson, "A Transformation of Genres in Late Latin Literature: Classical Literary Tradition and Ascetic Ideals in Paulinus of Nola," in Mathisen and Sivan, *Shifting Frontiers in Late Antiquity*, 267–72. See also H. Sivan, "Nicetas' (of Remesiana) Mission and Stilicho's Illyrican Ambition: Notes on Paulinus of Nola *Carmen* XVII (*Propemticon*)," *REAug* 41 (1995): 79–90, arguing that Nicetas was returning to Illyricum as an agent of western imperial and papal ambitions.

96. Basson, "A Transformation of Genres," 271–72.

deemed thoroughly attuned to the Word through which it was created (125–26), and the spiritualized natural world responded in full measure to Nicetas's sanctity.

Years earlier, in Spain, Paulinus had sketched John the Baptist's desert in somewhat similar terms; there peace had reigned in a biblical-Saturnian paradise.[97] Now, however, Nicetas's missionary efforts to convert the barbarians of his district offered Paulinus scope to rearticulate the Augustan ideal of Rome's civilizing mission at a time when that ideal must have seemed desperate and embattled. Paulinus emphasized the universal pacifying and civilizing power of Nicetas's Christianizing endeavors among the Bessians, the Scythians, the Getae, and the Dacians: necks unsubdued by war bend in submission to the yoke of the Lord (209–12); mountain brigands turn their plundering urges on the kingdom of heaven (217–28); wolves are turned into calves and the lion yoked with the ox (253–55). In Paulinus's vision, the discipline of Christ displaces the more martial assignment Virgil's Aeneas had received from Anchises, although the Christianized barbarians whom Paulinus fashioned in his verses are no less Roman than those the Augustan poet envisioned as subject to the might of Roman arms and laws.[98] "Through you," Paulinus praised Nicetas, "the barbarians learn to resound the name of Christ with Roman heart and to live chastely in tranquil peace" (261–64). *Pax romana* and *pax christiana* blended seamlessly.[99]

Paulinus framed his distinctive reworking of such literary and ideological themes with passages that also rejected the *propemptikon*'s traditional "poignancy of separation."[100] Through the departure of a friend he again asserted Christian friendship's transcendence of the boundaries of time and space, for, as friends in Christ need never meet, so they could never be truly separated. There was no need for the expression of loss. Unity of heart and mind, Paulinus assured Nicetas, prevailed over physical separation; love was surpassing.[101]

This same surpassing Christian love and friendship provided Paulinus with the subject as well as the occasion for another assault on generic conventions.[102] In the opening years of the fifth century Paulinus celebrated the wedding of Julian, future bishop of Eclanum, and Titia with the composition of a poem that still sits rather uncomfortably within the corpus of late Latin epithalamia.[103] Paulinus's

---

97. *Carm* 6.233–35 and chapter 4.

98. *Aen.* 6.851–53.

99. S. Costanza, "*Pax romana–pax christiana* in Paolino di Nola," *Studi tardoantichi* 1 (1986): 57–61.

100. Green, *The Poetry of Paulinus*, 35.

101. *Carm* 17. 1–12; 77: "superante amore"; 317–32.

102. *Carm* 25; Green, *The Poetry of Paulinus*, 35–37.

103. On the date of the poem and the marriage see Fabre, *Essai*, 122–23. The *terminus ante quem* is 408: Julian was a deacon by that year (Aug. *ep.* 101 addressed to Memor), although apparently the office was recently acquired; and deacons were forbidden to marry. Nor could the wedding have taken place in 405–6, when Aemilius, depicted as present by Paulinus (*carm.* 25.225 ff.), was absent from Italy on an embassy to Constantinople (Palladius, *de vita S. Iohann. Chrys.* 4). Fabre, therefore, preferred 400–404 for the date of the poem; although, as Walsh noted, *ACW* 40:400, the year 407 is theoretically possible.

friendship with Julian's father, the bishop Memor, and with the wedding cere-
mony's presiding bishop, Aemilius of Beneventum (the tenth string of *carmen* 21's
mystical lyre),[104] presumably secured Paulinus's invitation to the festivities. His
own proven commitment to secular renunciation and conjugal celibacy deter-
mined the poem's exegesis of marriage and marital love. True once more to the
proclamation made a decade earlier to Ausonius, Paulinus banished the classical
gods and mythical referents from a genre still heavily saturated with them; only a
few years earlier, in the poetry of Claudian, a secularized Venus and Cupid had
easily joined in the nuptials of Honorius and Maria celebrated at the Christian
court of Milan.[105] Paulinus, however, refused the marriage of Julian and Titia
such lewd accomplices, perhaps in conscious reply to Claudian.[106] The newly-
weds, particularly Titia, were warned against the snares of vain, physical display
and self-adornment (39–139); their wedding, torn from the anticipated context of
erotic fabric, was set against a biblical backdrop.

To encourage the couple to "chaste partnership (*par inviolabile*)" (191), Paulinus
recalled his audience to iconic, Ambrosian images of Mary's perpetual virginity
and of the Church's status as sister as well as bride of Christ.[107] He held out before
the young couple the consummate "angelic form (*speciem angelicam*)" toward which
the baptized had already begun their journey and in whose final enjoyment sexual
distinctions would dissolve and marriage would be irrelevant, as it had been be-
fore the Fall (179–90). By these reversals, Paulinus subsumed the particular and at
least potentially intimate relationship of Julian and Titia into the overarching love
(*amor*) that entwined Christ and the Church (197–98), and he situated their conju-
gal relations in a pre-Augustinian eschatological framework.[108] Viewed from the
same lofty perspective that brought friendship's true dimensions into clear focus,
the moment's joyful celebration of two "harmonious souls" being joined in
"chaste love"[109] also became an incipient point, diminished in retrospect, on a

A. Brückner, *Julian von Eclanum: Sein Leben und seine Lehre; Texte und Untersuchungen* 15.3a (Leipzig, 1897):
18 n. 1, suggesting that a subdeaconate of several years must have preceded the deaconate, dated the
marriage to ca. 403. On the problem of genre see R. Herzog, "Probleme der heidnisch–christlichen
Gattungskontinuität am Beispiel des Paulinus von Nola," *Christianisme et formes littéraires de l'antiquité tar-
dive: Entretiens sur l'antiquité classique 23* (Geneva, 1977), esp. 381–89; R. Gelsomino, "L'epitalamio di
Paolino di Nola per Giuliano e Titia (Carme 25)," *Atti del Convegno*, 213–14; M. Roberts, "The Use of
Myth in Latin Epithalamia from Statius to Venantius Fortunatus," *TAPA* 119 (1989): 337–38; Basson,
"A Transformation of Genres," 273.

104. *Carm.* 21.326–30.
105. Roberts, "The Use of Myth," 328–34.
106. *Carm.* 25.9–10. Gelsomino, "L'epitalamio di Paolino," 220.
107. *Carm.* 25.153–82. See H. Crouzel, "L'epitalamio di San Paolino: Il suo contenuto dottrinale,"
Atti del Convegno, 145–47; T. Piscitelli Carpino, "La figura di Maria nell'opera di Paolino di Nola," *Im-
pegno e Dialogo* 9 (1991–92): 199–204.
108. Basson, "A Transformation of Genres," 273–75.
109. *Carm.* 25.1: "Concordes animae casto socientur amore."

continuum that reached into the unbounded mystical future. With so much at stake, Paulinus refused to construct a literary backdrop that endorsed the sexuality of marriage, an overriding implication of the classically inspired images drawn from the lore and iconography of Venus. Rather, Paulinus petitioned Christ at his poem's end, let the newlyweds remain virginal, or at least let them be the parents of consecrated virgins (231–34). If Paulinus preferred the former, even Jerome had endorsed the latter, praising the decision of Laeta, Paula's daughter-in-law, to consecrate to Christ her as yet unborn daughter.[110]

Protreptic dominates this wedding poem, which finds no known imitators in later antiquity[111] but whose exhortations run easily enough in the broader stream of Paulinus's thought about love and friendship among Christians. Like friendship, marital relations clarified only when seen from a distant vantage point. So Paulinus encouraged Julian and Titia to view themselves through the lens of the pre-Fall Adam and Eve, whose paradisaical relations in turn forecast the eternal life to be lived in "immortal bodies" (190). Similarly, Paulinus had alerted correspondents like Alypius and Severus that friendship's earthly span revealed its true nature only when seen against the wider expanse projected by God's foreknowledge (*praescientia*) and the intimacy to be shared by friends even in the life to come.[112] Addressing Julian and Titia, Paulinus found those Pauline images of the corporeal unity of the community of believers appropriate for the expression of his vision of transcendental human relations, marital as well as amicable. "All who acknowledge Christ as Head of our body are one body (*unum corpus*)," Paulinus reminded the couple;[113] to Severus several years before, he had observed, "Now indeed through the favor of Him 'who made both one,' we two are one, because in both of us there is a single spirit, and we are not separate since we belong to one body."[114] In this mystical corporeal unity, as in the sweep of eternity, Paulinus allowed individual ties of love and affection to be both submerged and distinguished, flooded with God's overwhelming love and the *caritas* of Christ and elevated beyond the bounds of terrestrial time and space.

Paulinus's letters and poems persistently recalled the thought of correspondents and friends scattered around the Mediterranean world to the matrix of divine love and grace in which he sensed their own idiosyncratic feelings of desire and affection were suspended and given meaning. Surely, in some measure, Paulinus's richly metaphorical articulation of this mystery arose from spiritual experiences that convinced him of the deeply seated unity of all who entered into the

---

110. Jer. *ep.* 107.3.

111. Roberts, "The Use of Myth," 338; Basson, "A Transformation of Genres," 273–74.

112. *Epp.* 3.1; 32.1.

113. *Carm.* 25.179–82 with Gal 3.28 and 1 Cor 12.27.

114. *Ep.* 11.5: "Nunc vero propitio ipso, qui fecit utrumque unum (Eph 2.14), et duo unum sumus, quia unus spiritus in duobus et nulla discretio, quorum corpus unum." See also A. Salvatore, "Immagini bibliche e strutture discorsive: La lettera 11 di Paolino," *Atti del Convegno*, 266–70.

community of believers.[115] Surely as well his effort to lift these fundamental human relationships out of the mire of sometimes recalcitrant and erratic human emotions reflects his own frustrations with friendship that find expression in the correspondence with Ausonius and Severus. Perhaps, too, Paulinus's search for the fundamental forces that brought all Christians together in the Pauline body of Christ was a response to the fragility of social relations in an age of acute doctrinal and ecclesiastical controversies.

THEOLOGICAL CONTROVERSY:
THE ORIGENIST AND PELAGIAN DEBATES

Many of Paulinus's friendships seem stacked up squarely on one side of the two theological debates that passionately divided western clerics and interested laymen in the first decades of the fifth century.[116] Yet modern observers have long maintained that Paulinus showed little interest in, or aptitude for, the biblical exegesis and speculative theology that distinguished the Origenist and Pelagian controversies.[117] Some have found this apparent lack of commitment to systematic theology to be commendable, others lamentable.[118] Many have considered Paulinus's detachment from the period's rancorous name-calling and sometimes duplicitous maneuvers a mark of his better nature.

But while the sharp proclivity of Paulinus's social relationships away from the circles of Jerome and towards the "friends of the friends of Rufinus" has resisted erosion,[119] the image of a Paulinus unschooled in exegesis or disengaged from theological issues has not.[120] Paulinus was much better read than his reputation suggests. His reliance on Ambrose's *Expositio Evangelii secundam Lucam* has been long noted and recently reaffirmed,[121] and he was obviously familiar with various polemical works of Augustine and Jerome. But we now have good reason to be-

---

115. Sorrentino, "L'amore di unità," 155 and passim.

116. For example,, Brown, "The Patrons of Pelagius," 211–13; Clark, *The Origenist Controversy*, 33–35, however, recognizes Paulinus's links to Jerome; Santaniello, *Le lettere,* 74.

117. For example, Fabre, *Paulin de Nole,* 3–4; G. Casati, "S. Agostino e S. Paolino di Nola," 53; Lienhard, *Paulinus of Nola,* 128–33 ("he remained a man of letters"), 141–44; R. Eno, *Saint Augustine and the Saints* (Villanova, 1989), 29, 33.

118. For example, respectively, Coster, "Christianity and the Invasions," 194, finding Paulinus's lack of interest in speculative philosophy " a very agreeable quality"; Frend, "The Two Worlds," 114–15: "Had he risen to the occasion, western Christendom might have been spared the final fateful injection of theological rigorism from North Africa."

119. Brown, "The Patrons of Pelagius," 211.

120. For a sense of the new direction see S. Leanza, "Aspetti esegetici," 67–91; Piscitelli Carpino, "La figura di Maria," 208–15.

121. *CSEL* 30.378; Piscitelli Carpino, "La figura di Maria," 208–15.

lieve that Paulinus's library also housed, for example, Gregory of Elvira's homily on Samson,[122] Jerome's commentary on Joel,[123] Rufinus's translations of Origen, works of Clement of Rome,[124] Ambrosiaster's commentary on the Pauline Epistles,[125] and works in Greek by Origen, Gregory of Nyssa, and others.[126] Moreover, although Paulinus's apparently eclectic reading and conflation of sources did at times yield idiosyncratic exegeses,[127] and his delight in figurative language, paradox, and *catenae* of associated images may challenge the patience of modern readers,[128] he shows himself quite capable of adapting older texts to present needs,[129] of weaving mesmerizing passages of scriptural reflection, and of wielding the tools of typological interpretation and intertextual exegesis. At the least, we can no longer accuse Paulinus of theological naïveté.

Nevertheless, in an age of acute controversies, Paulinus was seldom overtly polemical. It is rather the recognizable pitch of his social relations toward the circles of Rufinus and Melania after 400 that signals his intellectual inclinations. But Paulinus also remained in formal contact with Jerome long after developing his friendship with Rufinus, and he apparently harbored Pelagians at Nola while preserving his friendship with Augustine, testimony perhaps as much to Paulinus's stature and his desirability as an ally as to any wish on his part to mediate among friends or avoid conflict. Moreover, even in this age's contentious debates, Paulinus displays the independence of mind that we might well expect from a senatorial monk and a sometimes brash impresario of the cult of a saint. It is for such reasons that Paulinus has been hard to label. In any case, more can be revealed about both Paulinus and the age by preferring an account of his relations with the figures of controversy.

Paulinus's relations with Jerome had begun well enough but soon became prickly. In 394 Paulinus's initial request for scriptural mentoring had elicited Jerome's invitation for Paulinus to join him in Bethlehem; but Jerome's letter to Paulinus the next year had withdrawn the invitation, offered backhanded praise of Paulinus's literary accomplishments, and obliquely questioned Paulinus's ascetic

122. A. Salvatore, "Due *omelie su Sansone* di Cesario di Arles e l'*epistola* 23 di Paolino da Nola," *Vet. Christ.* 7 (1970): 83–113, esp. 93–94.

123. Leanza, "Aspetti esegetici," 78–80.

124. *Ep.* 46.2 to Rufinus, on which see below; and Leanza, "Aspetti esegetici," 83. Jer. *ep.* 85 offers reason to give greater credit to Paulinus's Greek.

125. A. Nazzaro, "La parafrasi salmica," 101–4.

126. Leanza, "Aspetti esegetici," 79–82.

127. Leanza, "Aspetti esegetici," 89–91.

128. For a notable exception see Conybeare, "The Expression of Christianity," 128–41.

129. E. Cattaneo, "Il *Christus patiens* nel giusto perseguitato: reminiscenze melitoniane in S. Paolino di Nola," *Koinonia* 9 (1985): 141–52. See also S. Leanza, "Una pagina di Melitone di Sardi in Paolino di Nola," *Orpheus* 5 (1984): 444–51, and S. Leanza, "Una precisazione a proposito di due recenti articoli su Melitone di Sardi e Paolino di Nola," *Koinonia* 10 (1986): 89–90.

commitment.[130] Although correspondence between Paulinus and Jerome contin-
ued until at least 399 or 400, relations appear tense and unfruitful.[131] Unfortu-
nately, Paulinus had made his overtures to Jerome just as the Origenist contro-
versy was erupting in Palestine. Like so many others Paulinus became entangled
in a web of incrimination, misunderstanding, and misapprehension that centered
on such problematic doctrines of Origen as the premundane existence of the soul,
the universality of salvation (which might even encompass the devil), and the na-
ture of the resurrection body. Initially the figure of Vigilantius disrupted the in-
cipient friendship of Paulinus and Jerome, but not long after 397 Rufinus, with far
more damaging effect, also intruded directly on the channels of communication
that Paulinus had sought to establish between Nola and Bethlehem. By 400 Pauli-
nus appears largely aloof from Jerome and his Roman friends. It is, however, a
blighted relationship worth closer inspection, for it well illustrates the interplay of
friendship, suspicion, and ideas around Paulinus.

Jerome's invectives ensured both Vigilantius's contemporary notoriety and his
future as a caricature. Vigilantius had been born at Calagurris in the *civitas* of
Convenae, whose capital was Lugdunum (modern St.-Bertrand-de-Comminges),
in the southwest Aquitanian province of Novempopulana. There he became a
priest perhaps as early as 395.[132] In that year he carried Paulinus's second letter to
Jerome, along with alms to be distributed to monks in the Holy Land and Egypt.
Vigilantius spent some troubled weeks with Jerome before leaving Bethlehem
abruptly, although in Palestine he probably lodged as well on the Mount of Olives
with Melania and Rufinus, the latter now in open rupture with Jerome and even-
tually portrayed by Jerome as the real source of Vigilantius's Origenist tests and
accusations.[133] Late in the season Vigilantius returned west, spending some
months with Paulinus while he recovered from illness. When in 396 Vigilantius set
out for Gaul, he took with him a letter from Paulinus to Severus (*ep.* 5), but en
route, it seems, he also began to spread the word of Jerome's alleged Origenism.

130. See chapter 4.

131. See further Courcelle, "Paulin de Nole et Saint Jérôme," esp. 271–80.

132. The most important sources for Vigilantius are Jer. *ep.* 58.11, *epp.* 61 and 109, and the *Contra
Vig.*; Paul. *ep.* 5; Sev. *Dial.* 1.9; and Gennadius, *De vir. ill.* 36. For attempts to reconstruct the activities
of Vigilantius see H. Crouzel, "Saint Jérôme et ses amis toulousains," 141–42, 265–66; M. Massie,
"Vigilance de Calagurris," 81–108; H. Crouzel, "Un 'piccolo cliente' di San Paolino di Nola: Vigi-
lanzio di Calagurris," *Paolino di Nola: Momenti della sua vita e delle sue opere* (Nola, 1983), 199–219;
Rebenich, *Hieronymus und sein Kreis*, 240–51; Perrin, "La place des courriers," 1065–68; G. Jenal, *Italia
ascetica atque monastica: Das Asketen- und Monchtum in Italien von dem Anfangen bis zur Zeit der Langobarden*
(Stuttgart, 1995), 1:466–71; and Hunter, "Vigilantius of Calagurris and Victricius of Rouen." Jerome
puts Vigilantius's birth at Calagurris and Convenae (*Contra Vig.* 1,4). For the identification with St.-
Bertrand-de-Comminges, see Massie, "Vigilance de Calagurris," 89. Jer. *ep.* 58.11 of 395 attests to Vig-
ilantius's priesthood, and *ep.* 109.2 of 404 places this office at Calagurris. Gennadius places Vigilantius's
priesthood in Barcelona, but it is unclear whether this is an early or late stage, or a mistake.

133. Nautin, "Études de chronologie III," 231 with Jer. *C. Rufin.* 3.19 of 402.

Furthermore, at some point after returning to Italy, Vigilantius had sent to Jerome a letter of self-defense that provoked Jerome's abusive response, *ep.* 61 of 396. Having returned to Calagurris, leaving as traces of his activity in the Holy Land only the ambiguous remarks that closed Jerome's second letter to Paulinus, *ep.* 58, and the fiery sparks of Jerome's letter 61 to him, Vigilantius disappears from view until 404.

When he reemerges, it is once more as a target in Jerome's sights. News from southern Gaul had alerted Jerome to Vigilantius's campaign denouncing ascetic practices, clerical celibacy, the cult of the martyrs, and the transmission of alms to the Holy Land. To the incriminating letters and materials forwarded to him in Bethlehem, Jerome responded with his own letters and then, in 406, with his vitriolic pamphlet *Contra Vigilantium,* which is less an answer to the real questions raised by Vigilantius than satirical invective. Jerome knew well, it seems, that Vigilantius's brand of old-fashioned Christian practice was now too conservative and required no reasoned response.[134] Submerged now in the wake of the *Contra Vigilantium,* Jerome's adversary vanishes for good.

Paulinus's relationship with Vigilantius goes undocumented much earlier. Paulinus's *ep.* 5 of 396 contains his final mention of Vigilantius, leaving too little evidence to support the claim that Vigilantius was a dependent of Paulinus. Certainly the arc of Paulinus's life crossed that of Vigilantius then and in the previous year, and this conjunction contributed to the corrosion of Paulinus's relations with Jerome, but Vigilantius cannot on these grounds be cast primarily as a client of Paulinus. Indeed, Paulinus had recommended Vigilantius to Jerome in 395, and in 396 Jerome dismissed Vigilantius as Paulinus's "little letter-carrying client."[135] But the protocols of correspondence and the manipulations of invective respectively explain these claims.

Nor can Vigilantius otherwise be made a menial member of Severus's household at Primuliacum. Paulinus's language in the letter that Vigilantius carried north to Severus in 396 (*ep.* 5) carefully distinguishes the presbyter, "our" Vigilantius, from the *pueri,* slaves, and freedmen, some recently dispatched to Nola by Severus and others being sent north by Paulinus.[136] Vigilantius apparently deserves to be given more intellectual and social independence from Paulinus and

134. For this portrayal of Vigilantius see Massie, "Vigilance de Calagurris," but note Crouzel's defence of Jerome, "Un 'piccolo cliente,'" 217–18.

135. Jer. *ep.* 58.11; *ep.* 61.3: "portitor clientulus."

136. Compare, for example, *ep.* 5.1, *tuis pueris;* 5.3, *tuorum;* 5.14, *conservi nostri, pueri tui;* and 5.11, *pueros nostros* with 5.11, *Vigilantius quoque noster.* The latter had been recovering at Nola for some time; Severus's *pueri* have only been at Nola a few days (5.14: *paucis ipsis diebus*). Also noted by Perrin, "La place des courriers," 1066 n. 183a. This reading thus revises Stancliffe, *St. Martin and His Hagiographer,* 304–5, and the modifications of Perrin, 1066 n. 183b, and thereby eliminates the chronological and nomenclature misunderstandings that led Rebenich, *Hieronymus und sein Kreis,* 250–51, and Jenal, *Italia ascetica,* 466 n. 105, to reject the identification of Jerome's Vigilantius with the Vigilantius of Paul. *ep.* 5.

Severus, even in the mid-390s, than is usually allowed. Moreover, we should not follow Jerome's caricature too far. Not only is his denunciation of Vigilantius's *rusticitas, simplicitas,* and uncouth speech countered by Gennadius (otherwise no defender of Vigilantius), who marked Vigilantius as "a man of polished language,"[137] but Jerome's dismissal of Convenae as the backwoods abode of brigands and misfits is belied by the archaeological record of a late Roman town well stocked with the amenities of urban life.[138]

Unfortunately only Jerome's increasingly florid reports are witness to what took place during Vigilantius's brief stay with Jerome in 395.[139] In that year Jerome pleaded reluctance to speak to Paulinus candidly about Vigilantius, lest he give offense (*ep.* 58.11), but Jerome's letter to Vigilantius in 396 portrays Origenist issues as the center of the tensions and disputes that marred Vigilantius's stay at Bethlehem. Jerome, it appears from this letter, had done his best to highlight for Vigilantius (and for Rufinus, whom he probably perceived as the real audience) the propriety of his critical reading of the "heretic" Origen, even preaching an anti-Origenist display on the corporeality of the risen body (61.3). If Jerome thought the performance convincing, Vigilantius apparently felt otherwise.

We do not know how Paulinus would have received the accusations of Origenism that Vigilantius leveled against Jerome in Italy. Perhaps, having just opened his correspondence with Bethlehem, he advised reconciliation.[140] Certainly Sulpicius Severus, who had received Vigilantius at Primuliacum in 396, later employed a section of his first *Dialogue* to defend Jerome's orthodoxy.[141] But Paulinus could not have missed the palpable ambiguity that undercuts Jerome's ostensible exculpation of Paulinus for his recommendation of his "little client" Vigilantius.[142] Jerome's suspicions about Paulinus filtered through Vigilantius, his implied doubts about the sincerity of Paulinus's ascetic calling, and his likely awareness of Paulinus's relationship with Melania the Elder all obstructed growth of their friendship.

Surely, however, Paulinus had no sympathy for Vigilantius's later turn against ascetic practices and the cult of the martyrs; and if it is difficult to envision him penning the acerbic *Contra Vigilantium,* he can be imagined agreeing with its general premises. But by 406, when Jerome sent this piece west, he and Paulinus had already edged away from each other. Taken generously, Paulinus's repeated re-

---

137. Jer. *ep.* 61.3: "rusticitatem et simplicitatem"; *C. Vig.* 3: "sermone inconditus"; Gen. *De vir. ill.* 36.

138. J. Guyon, "St.-Bertrand-de-Comminges," *Villes et agglomérations urbaines antiques du sud-ouest de la Gaule: Hüstoire et archéologie. Sixième supplément à Aquitania* (Paris, 1992), 140–45.

139. For example, *C. Vig.* 11, Vigilantius's emergence from his cell naked during an earthquake.

140. So Courcelle, "Paulin de Nole et Saint Jérôme," 263, suggesting that Paulinus urged Vigilantius to write to Jerome the letter provoking Jer. *ep.* 61.

141. *Dial* 1.9.

142. *Ep.* 61.3; cf. 58.11.

quests to Jerome for a commentary on Daniel represent a sincere attempt to resolve exegetical issues that emerged during Vigilantius's stay with Jerome in 395.[143] But Jerome's third extant letter to Paulinus, *ep.* 85 of 399, is formal and curt, ironically substantiating the very complaint against Jerome's brevity that Paulinus himself had already lodged with Jerome over a previous, now lost, letter (85.1). In *ep.* 85 Jerome put off once again Paulinus's request for a commentary on Daniel; and he replied to Paulinus's inquiries on Romans 9.16 and Exodus 4.21, concerning the hardening of Pharaoh's heart, and 1 Corinthians 7.14, on the "holiness" of children of mixed pagan and Christian couples, by referring him to Origen's *On First Principles* and Tertullian's *De monogomia.* But by mentioning Origen Jerome did create an opportunity to reissue his complaint against those injudicious friends of Origen who mistakenly claimed that Jerome condemned everything that Origen had written (85.4). Jerome's real intent here may have been to acknowledge his awareness of the place Rufinus was beginning to occupy in Paulinus's network of friends.

Rufinus, born near Aquileia, had in the late 360s and early 370s lived in that city along with Jerome and others as members of an ascetic community.[144] Like Jerome, Rufinus left for the East about 372, but for Egypt, not the Syrian desert. Unlike Jerome, however, Rufinus remained in the East, joining Melania the Elder in a double monastery on the Mount of Olives sometime around 380, where they eventually developed close relations with John, bishop of Jerusalem, and received Evagrius Ponticus, the "prime theoretician of late fourth-century Origenism."[145] If Paulinus was unfamiliar with Rufinus before 395, then certainly the news and letters that Vigilantius brought back from the Holy Land would have introduced to him this "companion of the holy Melania" (*ep.* 28.5). In any case, in 397 Rufinus returned to Italy, and by 404 Paulinus could inform Severus that an "intimate affection" now joined him to Rufinus, a "truly holy and piously learned man."[146] Presumably Paulinus met Rufinus between the latter's arrival in Italy in the spring of 397 and his departure for Aquileia in 399, for during those years Rufinus lived

143. Jer. *ep.* 61.4; 85.3, with Courcelle, "Paulin de Nole et Saint Jérôme," 268–71.

144. On the life and literary activities of Rufinus see Murphy, *Rufinus;* Murphy, "Rufinus of Aquileia and Paulinus of Nola," *REAug* 2 (1956): 79–91; C. Hammond, "The Last Ten Years of Rufinus' Life"; G. Fedalto, "Rufino di Concordia: Elementi di una biografia," *Storia ed esegesi in Rufino di Concordia* (Udine, 1992), 19–44; Clark, *The Origenist Controversy,* esp. 159–93.

145. Clark, *The Origenist Controversy,* 22.

146. *Ep.* 28.5, replying to Severus's request for historical information for the *Chronicle* he was then composing. On the date see Fabre, *Essai,* 39–40. On the whereabouts of Rufinus at this time, see the discussion of Hammond, "The Last Ten Years of Rufinus' Life," esp. 378, 420, arguing (against the assumption that Rufinus remained at Aquileia until 407 [e.g., Murphy, *Rufinus,* 201–2]) that he had returned to Rome and its environs perhaps as early as 403 or 404. See also Murphy, "Rufinus of Aquileia and Paulinus of Nola," 83–84.

both at Rome and in the monastery of Ursacius at Pinetum near Terracina, where he prepared a translation of the *Rule* of Basil of Caesarea and of Pamphilus's *Apology for Origen*.[147] Certainly the confidence of Paulinus's description of 404 indicates some years of amicable contact.[148]

The esteem for Rufinus that Paulinus then expressed to Severus would have blossomed during the very years when Jerome's relations with Rufinus had reached their nadir. In 398, at the request of a certain Macarius (perhaps Paulinus's later Roman correspondent of the same name), Rufinus had translated Origen's *On First Principles* and thereby instigated the tumultuous final phase of the Origenist controversy in Italy. Alerted to Rufinus's translation by Pammachius and Oceanus, a monk of Jerome's Bethlehem monastery recently arrived in Italy, Jerome responded with a critique of Rufinus's translation, charges of Rufinus's Origenist sympathies, and his own translation of *On First Principles*.[149] It was in this same year, 399, that Jerome's reserved *ep.* 85 tactfully alerted Paulinus to the accusations being aimed at him by Origen's "injudicious friends." Matters in Italy deteriorated rapidly, however, as the machinations of Jerome's zealous Roman friends soon elicited a condemnation of Origen's teachings from Pope Anastasius, who in November 398 had succeeded a much less cooperative Siricius.[150] Subsequent attempts to impugn the orthodoxy of Rufinus himself, however, led Rufinus to write an *Apology* in his own defense to Anastasius.[151] Herein he affirmed his Nicene faith and asserted once more his belief in the resurrection of the body and the final damnation of the devil, although he admitted his uncertainty on the nature and origin of the soul. Moreover, claiming yet again to have translated Origen accurately and to have excised clearly heretical, interpolated passages, Rufinus exonerated himself as a translator of Origen.[152] Rufinus's *Apology* at least convinced a still-skeptical Anastasius to leave its author's fate in the hands of God.[153] But both reputation and scandal prefer a public context, and in 401 and

147. The first dedicated to Ursacius (*CCSL* 20.241); the second, to which was appended Rufinus's own *De adulteratione librorum origenis* (*CCSL* 20.7–17), dedicated to Macarius (*CCSL* 20.233–34). See further Murphy, *Rufinus of Aquileia*, 82, 89–92; Hammond, "The Last Ten Years of Rufinus' Life," 379–80; G. Santaniello, "Un'amicizia sofferta in silenzio: Rufino di Concordia e Paolino di Nola," *Teologia e vita* 5 (1997): 76–77.

148. Santaniello, "Un'amicizia sofferta in silenzio," 104–9.

149. Jer. *epp.* 83 and 84.

150. Anas. *ep.* 2 to Simplicianus of Milan (*PL* 20.73–76 = Jer. *ep.* 95.3). On affairs in these years see further Kelly, *Jerome*, 246–58; Clark, *The Origenist Controversy*, 171–83.

151. *CCSL* 20.25–28.

152. And, more unwittingly, underscored his status as a pioneer in that contentious territory where "patristic" texts were being authenticated and disciplined with the "critic's rod" to satisfy the needs of the post-Theodosian age's "new order of books." See M. Vessey, "The Forging of Orthodoxy in Latin Christian Literature: A Case Study," *JECS* 4 (1996): 495–513.

153. Anas. *ep.* 1.6 to John of Jerusalem (*PL* 20.73).

402 Rufinus and Jerome openly aired their grievances in five books of apology and invective, Rufinus's two books of *Apology against Jerome* and Jerome's three books *Against Rufinus*.[154]

Paulinus, who must have watched these matters closely, was not deterred by Jerome's campaign. His relations with the wider circle of Melania and Rufinus appear only stronger in the first decade of the fifth century; and any potential that Paulinus had to mediate between the circles of Jerome and Rufinus,[155] severely weakened by the intrusion of Vigilantius, was surely dissolved by his drift toward Rufinus after 397 and by his explicit praise of Melania and her family in his letters and poetry. Melania's well-publicized stopover at Nola in 400 was buttressed by the close contact with the next generation that anticipated the Nolan visit of Melania the Younger and other kin in 407. The Roman noble Turcius Apronianus, married to a niece of Melania, and present with Paulinus in January of 407, had been closely involved on the side of Rufinus in the dispute with Jerome: he had provided Rufinus with a copy of Jerome's accusatory letter to Pammachius and Oceanus and had received the dedication of Rufinus's *Apology against Jerome* as well as several later works of translation.[156] Aemilius of Beneventum, whose cordial relations with Paulinus are announced by the latter's epithalamium for Julian and Titia and by the *natalicium* of 407, and who was bishop of the town where the Elder Melania's son, Publicola, may have been hereditary *patronus*, can also be associated with Melania and her circle through Melania's sometime companion and eventual "biographer," Palladius.[157] For Palladius, who stayed with the Younger Melania and Pinianus in Rome in 405, was subsequently in contact with Aemilius in Constantinople, where both had gone on behalf of the cause of John Chrysostom.[158] Palladius himself attests to another link, the friendship of Melania and the noble ascetic, Silvia, sister-in-law of the former praetorian prefect Flavius Rufinus.[159] On Silvia's return to Italy she inspired Rufinus's eventual translation of the Pseudo-Clementine *Recognitions*, a text that Paulinus himself apparently translated with the help of Rufinus;[160] and, as Paulinus notified Severus in 402 or

154. Ruf. *Apol. contra Hieronymum* at *CCSL* 20.37–123; Jer. *Apol. contra Rufinum* at *PL* 23.398–492.

155. Clark, *The Origenist Controversy*, 35–36.

156. *Apol. contra Hieronymum* 1.1. Rufinus dedicated to Apronianus translations of Basil's homilies, of Origen's *Explanatio super Psalmos XXXVI–XXXVIII*, and of nine sermons of Gregory Nazianzen. See *CCSL* 20.237, 251, and 255.

157. *Carm.* 25.211–26; *carm.* 21.326–30; *CIL* 9.1591 with *PLRE* 1.754, "Publicola 2"; Pall. *Hist. Laus.* 46, 55, with Clark, *The Origenist Controversy*, 22–23, 188–89.

158. Pall. *Hist. Laus.* 61; *Dialogus* 4.15 (Coleman-Norton, 22).

159. Pall. *Hist. Laus.* 55. See *PLRE* 1.842; Heinzelmann, "Gallische Prosopographie," 695, "Silvia 1".

160. Rufinus dedicated the translation to Gaudentius of Brescia after the death of Silvia (*CCSL* 20.281); Paul. *ep.* 46.2 reveals Paulinus translating "sanctus Clemens," presumably the *Recognitiones*.

403, she had promised to send to Primuliacum a collection of martyrs' relics.[161] Finally, and most significant, through these years Paulinus was apparently in regular and direct contact with Rufinus himself. The four extant letters, two sent by Paulinus to Rufinus between 406 and 408 (*epp.* 46 and 47) and two from Rufinus to Paulinus, allude to other correspondence.[162] Indeed, Paulinus's friendship with Rufinus provoked one of Rufinus's few original works, an explanation of the benedictions of Jacob in Genesis 49 known as the *De benedictionibus patriarcharum.* Book 1 of that work responded to Paulinus's request for an explanation of the prophecy of Jacob delivered to Judah (Gen 49.8–12); book 2 met Paulinus's further request for exegesis of Jacob's eleven remaining blessings.[163]

When Paulinus wrote his *ep.* 46 to Rufinus in 406 or 407, the latter was in Rome; when Rufinus answered *ep.* 47 with book 2 of the *De benedictionibus patriarcharum,* probably during Lent in 408, he was back at the monastery of Pinetum, near Terracina between Rome and Nola.[164] During these years, as Rufinus moved about Latium and Campania, he and Paulinus surely met. Both of Paulinus's extant letters issue invitations for Rufinus to visit Nola, and his first implies time spent together.[165] In the early fall of 408, when the advance of Alaric drove Pinianus, Melania the Younger, and Albina out of Rome, Rufinus was most likely in their company when they visited Paulinus for what may have been the last time.[166] In the late summer of 410, Alaric's army descended on Nola itself, but by that time Rufinus was in Sicily with Melania the Younger and Pinianus. Only the narrow straits between Rhegium and the island, Rufinus informed Ursacius, protected them from barbarian attack.[167] Some months later, still in Sicily, Rufinus died. Not long before, Melania the Elder, his companion of so many years, had

---

161. *Ep.* 31.1.

162. On the dates and authenticity of these two letters of Paulinus, preserved only in the manuscripts of Rufinus, see Fabre, *Essai,* 88–97; Murphy, "Rufinus of Aquileia and Paulinus of Nola," 85–86; and Santaniello, "Un'amicizia sofferta in silenzio," 116–17. In *ep.* 46.1 (406 / 7) Paulinus mentioned the (lost) *brevis epistula* he had just received from Rufinus. Rufinus complained, *De benedictionibus patriarcharum* 1.1, that the more he excused himself, the more persistent became Paulinus's requests; and *De benedictionibus* 2.1 referred to the writings "semel atque iterum dedi." See also Hammond, "The Last Ten Years of Rufinus' Life," 413, 418–20. It remains open whether the *sanctus doctissimus vir* of Paul. *ep.* 40.6 is Rufinus or Jerome; see Courcelle, "Paulin de Nole et Saint Jérôme," 271–73, arguing for Jerome, and Hammond, "The Last Ten Years of Rufinus' Life," 381–82 for doubts.

163. For text and commentary see Rufin d'Aquilée, *Les bénédictions des patriarches, SC* 140, ed. M. Simonetti (Paris, 1968), reprinting the text of *CCSL* 20 (1951). On the threefold style of exegesis—historical, typological, and moral—the influence of Origen, and the originality of the work see 27–31.

164. *Ep.* 46.1; *De benedictionibus* 2.2.

165. *Epp.* 46.1, 47.1. At *ep.* 46.2 Paulinus complained that his Greek studies would never progress unless the Lord allowed him to enjoy Rufinus's fellowship for a longer period: "ut diutius consortio tuo perfruar."

166. *Vita Melaniae,* 19, recording a visit to Nola and the unrealized intention for another. Murphy, *Rufinus,* 205; Hammond, "The Last Ten Years of Rufinus' Life," 372, 412–14.

167. Ruf. *Praef. ad lib. Orig. in Num.* (*CCSL* 20.285); *Vita Melaniae,* 19.

passed away in Jerusalem, whither she had recently returned and Rufinus himself had hoped to follow.[168] The Younger Melania and Pinianus were bound for North Africa and, eventually, the East, where they would live until their deaths in the 430s.[169] By late 410 this community of friends that Paulinus had nurtured in Italy over the course of a decade or more had dissolved in death and the disruptions of Alaric's invasion.

In 396, when Paulinus wrote his consolatory letter to Pammachius, it may have seemed possible to maintain good relations with both Jerome and his friends and the family and friends of Melania the Elder. Regardless of kinship and social affiliations, all were apparently united by their ascetic endeavors. Even as late as 406, Jerome would still offer a young ascetic aspirant the inspirational examples of Pammachius and Paulinus, a "priest of most fervent faith."[170] But by then Paulinus's relations with Jerome seem quite hollow. The misunderstanding and controversy caused by the campaigns of Vigilantius as well as the animosities generated by the Origenist dispute surely took their toll, even if Paulinus himself seems to have kept his distance from Origen's more inflammatory ideas.[171] Another strain would have been the growing friendship between Paulinus and Rufinus, whose exegetical skills and intellectual capabilities,[172] as well perhaps as his more even temperament, should have recommended him, like Augustine, as the partner in scriptural study that Jerome declined to be. But Paulinus's associations with Melania and Rufinus also brought within his circle of friends and protégés Pelagius, whose life and writings soon disturbed Paulinus's relations with Augustine as well as with Jerome.

Unfortunately the controversy generated by Pelagius's perceived assault on divine grace and original sin through his emphasis on the absolute freedom of the human will flares most intensely just as our corpus of Paulinus's poems and letters grows thin. Indeed, only two letters of Paulinus can be securely dated after 411, the year that saw the first formal denunciation of Pelagian ideas and initiated escalation of the war of treatises and councils that demanded so much of the aging Augustine's time and energy, even after the imperial and ecclesiastical condemnation of Pelagianism in 418.[173]

---

168. Murphy, *Rufinus of Aquileia*, 213–16; Murphy, "Melania the Elder," 76–77. Paulinus, *ep.* 47.1, knew of Rufinus's intention to return east.

169. *Vita Melaniae*, 49, 62–68.

170. Jer. *ep* 118.5.

171. See, for example, Paulinus's assertion of the eternal damnation of the devil (*ep.* 23.44) and his adamant insistence on the corporeality of the resurrection body in *ep.* 45.6–7 addressed to Augustine in 408. Christ, Paulinus avows, was resurrected in the same flesh (*caro*) in which he died, while for men, "their bodies after the resurrection will be spiritual (*spiritalia*), but the glorified flesh (*glorificata caro*) will retain all its limbs in all their shape and number."

172. Clark, *The Origenist Controversy*, 7–8, 180–83.

173. Paul. *epp.* 50 and 51 to Augustine, and Eucherius and Galla. The following summary draws especially on Brown, *Augustine*, 340–75; Kelly, *Jerome*, 309–23; Pietri, *Roma christiana*, 2.1177–244; B. R. Rees, *Pelagius: A Reluctant Heretic* (Bury St. Edmunds, 1988); Clark, *The Origenist Controversy*, 194–244.

Before 409, however, the primary theater of Pelagius's activities was Rome; and Paulinus was undoubtedly in contact with Pelagius and surely in some sympathy with a moral reform movement that attracted the support of a number of the capital's Christian aristocracy. In 411, however, when a council at Carthage censured Pelagius's associate Caelestius for his more bluntly articulated rejection of original sin and the necessity of its remission through infant baptism, Pelagianism became the matter of a divisive public debate. From Carthage the contest expanded to Palestine, where Pelagius had gone not long after 409, joining the aristocratic exodus from Rome to North Africa provoked by Alaric. In Palestine, however, Pelagius confronted a hostile Jerome, whose personal animosity toward Pelagius may date to as early as the mid-390s and who now saw the Origenist controversy reborn in Pelagius.[174] Local reaction was seconded by the accusations of the Spanish priest Orosius, sent east by the African clergy, and Augustine, whose own opposition to Pelagius had now firmly crystallized around his perception of the threat posed by Pelagius's ideas to positions won in hard debate with Manichees and Donatists. Nevertheless, accused of heresy before synods at Jerusalem and Diospolis in 415, Pelagius successfully dissociated himself from Caelestius and defended his orthodoxy by staunchly asserting belief in the necessity of grace.

The next year Augustine, unsatisfied by Pelagius's defense at Diospolis, secured condemnation of Pelagianism in councils at Carthage and Milevis and provoked a "studiously vague," even if politically prudent, denunciation of Pelagius and Caelestius from Innocent of Rome in 417.[175] In that same year, however, Zosimus, who succeeded Innocent, reversed his predecessor's position. Motivated more perhaps by papal politics than by theological meditation,[176] Zosimus ostentatiously exonerated both Caelestius and Pelagius after they presented their cases before him at Rome. But Zosimus, too, eventually acquiesced with the view promulgated by the North African church, this time through Ravenna: on 30 April 418 an imperial edict, urged by the African bishops and encouraged by partisan rioting at Rome, banished Pelagius and his supporters from Rome. On 1 May the Council of Carthage condemned Pelagianism; and in the same year Zosimus sanctioned the decrees of the Carthaginian Council. By imperial edict, conciliar pronouncement, and papal *tractoria*, Pelagius's doctrines were vanquished in the West by a "Christian theology whose central concerns were human sinfulness, not human poten-

174. On the implications of the inconclusive debate over the identification of the monastic opponent of Jerome's *C. Jov.* recorded by Jerome in *ep.* 50, see R. Evans, *Pelagius: Inquiries and Reappraisals* (New York, 1968), 26–42; Y.-M. Duval, "Pélage est-il le censeur inconnu de l'*Adversus Iovinianum* à Rome en 393? Ou: du 'portrait-robot' de l'hérétique chez S. Jérôme," *Revue d'histoire ecclésiastique* 75 (1980): 525–57; Rees, *Pelagius*, 4–6.

175. J. Merdinger, *Rome and the African Church in the Time of Augustine* (New Haven, 1997), 127–30; Pietri, *Roma christiana*, 2.1197, 1207–12; quote from Brown, *Augustine*, 358.

176. Pietri, *Roma christiana*, 2.1223.

tiality; divine determination, not human freedom and responsibility; God's mystery, not God's justice."[177] But the condemnation of Pelagianism was perhaps also a sign of the newfound willingness of the majority of the Roman elite to set aside an endemic spirit of divisive competition and to close ranks in the aftermath of the terrible blow dealt to their world by Alaric's forces in 410.[178] Surely, too, the victory of Augustine's more inclusive and less austere "idea of the Church," checking Pelagius's demand that Christians set their "moral sights" higher, made it far easier for that church "to swallow Roman society whole."[179]

Paulinus's response to these events and his relations with Pelagius in the decade leading up to them are revealed only in intermittent flashes. Perhaps the most brilliant example appears in a letter written by Augustine and cosigned by Alypius, in 417.[180] Even in that late year, well into the controversy but at a critical moment of uncertainty before the condemnation issued by the imperial government and a chastened Zosimus, there were still professed Pelagians at Nola, or at least so Augustine thought. For this reason Augustine and Alypius, already acutely sensitive to the favor Pelagius still enjoyed at Rome,[181] could address a long letter to Paulinus deliberating the errors of Pelagius without overtly making Paulinus partner in them. Augustine reviewed for Paulinus his own initially generous but ultimately unyielding reaction to Pelagius's doctrines, and he reported the response of the recent councils of Carthage and Milevis. He noted his correspondence with Innocent and Innocent's "right and fitting" denunciation of Pelagius's "new and deadly error."[182] At considerable length Augustine expounded for Paulinus the scriptural passages that supported the decisions reached by Pelagius's critics, including Paul's troublesome comments on the Genesis account of the hardening of Pharoah's heart, about which Paulinus had once queried Jerome.[183] Thorough exposition was necessary, Augustine asserted, because he had heard that individuals could be found at Nola who still shared Pelagius's views on the reception of grace as a reward for merit or on the sinless state of newborn infants. Indeed, Augustine understood that these people—as much his audience as Paulinus, and whose names Augustine had entrusted to his courier—would sooner condemn Pelagius himself, if he should repudiate his views, than renounce what seemed the truth of his opinions.[184]

177. Clark, *The Origenist Controversy*, 250.

178. Brown, "Pelagius and His Supporters: Aims and Environment," *Religion and Society*, 185–92.

179. Brown, "Pelagius and His Supporters," 204–7; Markus, *The End of Ancient Christianity*, 42–43.

180. Aug. *ep.* 186. See also Courcelle, "Les lacunes," 284–88; Piscitelli Carpino, *Paolino di Nola: Epistole ad Agostino*, 70–79.

181. For example, Aug. *ep.* 177.2 with Pietri, *Roma christiana*, 2.1185–86.

182. Aug. *ep.* 186.2–3: "quo fas erat atque oportebat apostolicae sedis antistitem"; "novellum et perniciosum errorem."

183. Aug. *ep.* 186.16–17 on Rom 9.14–21. See further below.

184. Aug. *ep.* 186.29, 41.

All this, including further assessment of what Augustine saw as the contradictions between Pelagius's recent statements about original sin, grace, and human free will and his earlier self-defense,[185] Augustine insisted he offered not to support Paulinus's unquestionable faith, but to assist his confession of it against those who favored Pelagius.[186] Augustine had opened with a similar tactful apology: like Paulinus, Augustine admitted, he too had once loved Pelagius as a man of true faith, but that was before Pelagius's writings had unveiled opinions hostile to the grace of God.[187] Paulinus's earlier affection for Pelagius, it was implied, might be similarly explained (and excused). In any case, Augustine confidently concluded, Paulinus's own letters demonstrated his painful awareness of the "ancestral poison (*virus*)" bequeathed by Adam and revealed the bishop of Nola now anxiously, but appropriately, awaiting that grace of Christ, through which we are all delivered from "the body of this death."[188]

When they wrote this letter to Paulinus in 417, Augustine and Alypius were intently seeking an ally against Pelagius in an Italy that, under the Roman lead of Zosimus, might have seemed to be slipping away from the cause.[189] Nola had long offered Augustine an Italian outpost. Although a lapse in their correspondence the previous year may have undercut Augustine's confidence in Paulinus,[190] he was now asking Paulinus to commit his resources to a campaign whose gravity even drew the North African church into direct negotiations with the imperial court at Ravenna.[191] The immediate effect of this letter on Paulinus and his relations with Augustine is not known. Certainly Paulinus's correspondence with Augustine continued, and their later relations were cordial, even allowing them to slide over a difference of opinion that emerged a few years later in the *De cura pro mortuis gerenda*.[192]

There is no good reason, however, to doubt either the general outline of Paulinus's previous relations with Pelagius drawn by Augustine in his letter or the sincerity of Augustine's careful culling of Paulinus from the flock of Pelagius's current allies at Nola. Ample evidence suggests that Augustine's understanding was well informed. Paulinus surely had once "loved" Pelagius,[193] but his letters and poems even from those more optimistic days show little sympathy for what would emerge as the characteristic Pelagian positions. In the closing years of the fourth century

185. Aug. *ep.* 186.32–38.

186. Aug. *ep.* 186.39.

187. Aug. *ep.* 186.1.

188. Aug. *ep.* 186.40–41 with Rom 7.24. Augustine here quotes back to Paulinus a passage from Paulinus's *ep.* 30.2 to Severus.

189. See, too, Piscitelli Carpino, *Paolino di Nola: Epistole ad Agostino*, 77.

190. Courcelle, "Les lacunes," 287.

191. Pietri, *Roma christiana*, 2.1230–34.

192. Courcelle, "Les lacunes," 288–94. See next section.

193. Aug. *ep.* 186.1: "Pelagium . . . quod ut servum Dei dilexeris, novimus; nunc autem quem ad modum diligas, ignoramus."

and the opening decade of the fifth, however, Pelagian questions were being discussed at Nola, and Paulinus was in direct contact with Pelagius. When Paulinus wrote to Jerome in 399, in addition to once more urging Jerome's completion of a commentary on Daniel, he had also asked for explication of the hardening of Pharaoh's heart (Exodus 4.21) and of Paul's related claim that "it is not a matter of the one who wants or who runs, but only of God having mercy" (Rom 9.16). Both passages seemed to Paulinus to take away free will (*liberum arbitrium*). Paulinus's further question to Jerome pointed to the debate over the nature of inherited sin, for he asked in what sense Paul (1 Cor 7.14) called "holy (*sancti*)" those who were born of baptized parents, since without the gift of grace afterward received and guarded they could not be saved.[194] The texts and issues circumscribed by Paulinus's questions to Jerome in 399 were central both to the emerging consciousness of the inherent tension between the claims of divine sovereignty and freedom of the human will in the drama of salvation and to the related issues of original sin and infant baptism.[195] Indeed, an anonymous Pelagian tract of this period, *De induratione cordis pharonis,* devoted itself specifically to study of one of the texts being probed by Paulinus.[196] Not surprisingly then, when Pelagius wrote a long letter to Paulinus around 405, its topic was, as Pelagius himself later glossed it, a confession of "God's grace and aid and our own inability to do anything at all without God." Augustine, who preserves this notice of Pelagius's correspondence with Paulinus in his *De gratia Christi,* a treatise composed in 418 and addressed to Albina, Pinianus, and Melania, disputed Pelagius's description of his letter, but he did not question its authenticity.[197]

Paulinus's contact with Pelagius in the opening decade of the fifth century is quite natural, as is his apparent unease over the competition between divine grace and free will, for this discomfort had percolated in close concert with the ascetic movement itself. Even without Augustine's direct testimony, relations between Paulinus and Pelagius would have been surmised. And although images of Pelagius introduced to Augustine's *Confessions* in the company of Paulinus or studying

194. Jer. *ep.* 85.2.

195. Courcelle, "Paulin de Nole et Saint Jérôme," 268–69; T. de Bruyn, *Pelagius's Commentary on St. Paul's Epistles to the Romans* (Oxford, 1993), 22.

196. *PLS* 1 (1958–59) 1506–39. The treatise was requested by "Christi minister" and by one "qui saeculum ridet et sub chlamyde monachum gerit" (1506). G. Martinetto, "Les premières réactions antiaugustiniennes de Pélage," *REAug* 17 (1971): 106 (following G. de Plinval, *Essai sur le style et la langue de Pélage* [Fribourg, 1947], 133–34), identified the source of the request as Paulinus, despite Courcelle, "Paulin de Nole et Saint Jérôme," 270–71. See also Courcelle, "Les lacunes," 287. Against identifying the author as Pelagius see F. Nuvolone-Nobile, "Problèmes d'une nouvelle édition du *De induratione cordis Pharaonis* attribué à Pélage," *REAug* 26 (1980): 116–17.

197. *De gratia Christi* 38 (*CSEL* 42, p. 154) of 418; Augustine quotes Pelagius as having written to Innocent: "legant . . . illam epistulam, quam ad sanctum virum Paulinum episcopum ante duodecim fere annos scripsimus, quae trecentis forte versibus nihil aliud quam Dei gratiam et auxilium confitetur nosque nihil omnino facere posse sine Deo." Pelagius's letter to Paulinus should then date to ca. 405.

Augustine's anti-Manichaean treatises in the library at Nola are alluring,[198] be-
yond doubt, as we have seen, are Paulinus's associations with "Rufinus and the
friends of the friends of Rufinus" who eventually constituted the Pelagian "circles"
in Rome.[199] Indeed, after the return of Rufinus and Melania the Elder from the
East, Pelagius was apparently often in their company. For his own commentary
on the Pauline epistles, Pelagius utilized Rufinus's translation of Origen's com-
mentary on Romans, even before its "publication."[200] And it was in the "distort-
ing medium" of Rufinus's translation of the *Sentences of Sextus,* requested by Avita,
niece of Melania the Elder and wife of Turcius Apronianus, that Pelagius found
further support for his convictions.[201] Even after his condemnation in 418, Pelag-
ius could still be found, as Augustine's *De gratia Christi* shows, in the company of
such intimate friends of Paulinus as Melania the Younger and Pinianus.[202]

But also to be found in reasonably close association with Paulinus in these
years was Julian of Eclanum, the young, noble, and well-educated cleric who,
after 418, became the persistent and unusually capable opponent of Augustine in
the later stages of the debate over original sin and free will.[203] For Julian's wed-
ding with Titia, conducted by Aemilius of Beneventum in the first years of the
fifth century, Paulinus had composed the epithalamium examined above.
Shortly thereafter Paulinus may have provided the link that facilitated an intro-
duction to Augustine for Julian's father, Memor, perhaps bishop of Capua.[204] In
the years ahead Julian would prove himself a particularly creative reader of
Rufinus as well as, in Gennadius's estimation, "a man of clever genius, learned in
divine scripture."[205] But by the time Julian's relentless barrage of the 420s, aimed

198. So Brown, "The Patrons of Pelagius," 211–12, following the suggestions of Courcelle, "Les la-
cunes," 273–74, on the former. See *De dono persev.* 20.53.

199. Brown, "The Patrons of Pelagius," 208–26, quote 211, is the fundamental study of these rela-
tionships.

200. C. Hammond Bammel, "Rufinus' Translation of Origen's Commentary on Romans and the
Pelagian Controversy," *Storia ed esegesi in Rufino di Concordia* (Udine, 1992), 131–42; de Bruyn, *Pelagius's
Commentary,* 5.

201. Evans, *Pelagius,* 43–65, quote 65.

202. *De gratia Christi* 1.1–2.

203. On Julian see the fundamental study of Brückner, *Julian von Eclanum.* The attempt of F. Re-
foulé, "Julien d'Éclane, théologien et philosophe," *Recherches de sciences religieuses* 52 (1964): 42–84,
233–47, to rehabilitate the thought of Julian, long denigrated by theologians and historians (e.g., Plin-
val, *Pélage,* 357: "Il [Julian] est loin d'avoir les qualités supérieures d'intelligence que des auteurs mod-
ernes [Harnack] lui ont complaisamment prêtées") drew the criticism of F.-J. Thonnard, "L'aris-
totélisme de Julien d'Éclane et Saint Augustin," *REAug* 11 (1965): 296–304, but shows its legacy in
Brown, *Augustine,* 381–97, and Brown, *The Body and Society,* 408–27.

204. Aug. *ep.* 101 with Brown, *Augustine,* 381. For the problematic evidence of the location of
Memor's southern Italian bishopric see Brückner, *Julian von Eclanum,* 15.

205. Gennadius, *De vir. ill.* 46: "vir acer ingenio, in divinis scripturis doctus"; Y.-M. Duval, "Julien
d'Éclane et Rufin d'Aquilée: Du concile de Rimini à la répression pélagienne. L'intervention impériale
en matière religieuse," *REAug* 24 (1978): 243–71.

especially at Augustine's cataclysmic relocation of the sexual urge to the domain of Adam's punishment, was uncharacteristically provoking from Augustine an "unintelligent slogging match,"[206] Paulinus's relations with Julian had long gone undocumented.

In sum, Paulinus surely associated both with Pelagius and with Julian, at least before the events unfolding between 411 and 418 forever changed all relationships with these two figures. In the opening years of the fifth century, moreover, Paulinus had sought out answers to Pelagian questions. Nevertheless, Paulinus's frequent assertions of a fundamentally prerequisite divine grace and his public laments over the taint of original sin seem unconditionally to distance him from Pelagius.[207] "We have been taken," Paulinus informed Severus about 397, "not through our own merit, but through the grace of God (*gratia dei*), 'whose gifts and calling are without repentance' (Rom 11.29)."[208] About the same time Paulinus advised Amandus that Jesus had spurned the wise things and taken up the foolish "so that there might be equality (2 Cor 8.14), and no one could claim anything as his own since it was necessary for everyone to boast in the Lord, as each attains salvation and wisdom only by God's gift (*munus*)."[209] Similarly, when replying to Ausonius a few years earlier, Paulinus had credited his startling conversion solely to God's agency—a force that Paulinus was to rechannel through Felix some years later.[210] On the vexed matter of original sin, even Augustine and Alypius could astutely quote from a letter of Paulinus the passage that has become the proof text of Paulinus's adamant affirmation of the enduring consequences of Adam's fall.[211] Such beliefs, buttressed by the notable latitude Paulinus was willing to allow a wealthy, potential convert like Jovius, might seem sufficient to separate Paulinus from the optimistic rigor associated with the thought of Pelagius.

Yet Paulinus's works also relay the contrary notions that were, perhaps, necessary for sustaining a difficult life of renunciation undertaken for the reward of eternal salvation. Elsewhere, for example, Paulinus wavered on the severity of Adam's transgression, stressing the divine justice that eternally condemned the agent of deception, the devil, but punished the victim only with temporary exclusion from

206. Brown, *The Body and Society*, 412–13; Brown, *Augustine*, 387.

207. So Fabre, *Paulin de Nole*, 88–92, echoed by Brown, "The Patrons of Pelagius," 212; Santaniello, *Le lettere*, 1.70–78; Ruggiero, *I carmi*, 1.62, with fuller citation of passages. For G. de Plinval, *Pélage: Ses écrits, sa vie et sa réforme* (Lausanne, 1943), 403, Paulinus found some middle ground: "Si l'on jete un regard sur les contemporains, on ne voit guère que saint Paulin de Nole qui eût pu trouver, sinon un terrain d'entente, du moins la possibilité d'un apaisement."

208. *Ep.* 11.6: "Adsumpti autem non nostro merito sed gratia dei, cuius dona et vocationes sine paenitentia sunt," but the sentence continues, "neque ex operum praerogativa sed ex fide bonae voluntatis (and not because our works give us preference, but because of our faith of right disposition)."

209. *Ep.* 12.5.

210. *Carm.* 10.128–30, 142–43; 21.421–27.

211. Aug. *ep.* 186.40–41 with Paul. *ep.* 30.2. Cf. *carm.* 21.180–81: "peccator utero peccatricis excidi / conceptus atris ex iniquitatibus."

paradise.[212] Moreover, Paulinus, who returned several times to 1 Timothy 2.4, "He wants everyone to be saved," should have been uncomfortable with any theology that seemed to threaten the freedom of the human will with the cancer of predestination.[213] Finally, Pelagius's "Christianity of discontinuity" may have held certain attractions for a man whose own conversion had driven such a precipitous chasm between his present and his earlier life,[214] leading him to balance his elevation of grace with reflections on faith and merit. Thus, although Paulinus voiced to Severus unequivocal rejection of works as the catalyst of grace, his next words seem paradoxically to preserve that prerogative for "faith of right disposition (*fides bonae voluntas*)." And, perhaps not without similar contradiction, Paulinus nuanced his understanding of the nature of the "gift" of the Lord's crucifixion and resurrection by explaining to Amandus that these events had fashioned the present life "wherein we obtain the merit (*meritum*) through which possession of the eternal life of the blessed is made ready."[215] A "spiritual economy" that privileged the tale of Lazarus over that of the rich young man and the eye of the needle, and according to whose tenets God had purposely made some men poor to test the minds of those whose wealth "provided them with the opportunity for virtue to beget merit," was unlikely to push individual effort and responsibility into the margins of the scheme of salvation.[216] On the forge of such strongly held yet sometimes contrary convictions Paulinus fashioned his own distinctive answers to the questions of the day.

Paulinus's extant writings do not depict him as a theological controversialist in the style of Jerome or Augustine, but they do attest to his biblical study, his exegetical enterprise, and his serious engagement with issues of moral philosophy. All these endeavors, it is also clear, were conducted in full view of the theological questions caroming around the Mediterranean basin in these years. Paulinus, who in the mid-390s had defined himself through an act of radical renunciation just as the ascetic movement was giving new life to old ruminations about grace and merit, struggled continually to justify and explain his conversion by reference to the interplay of divine and human forces that had then generated and now sustained his new life and that established that new life as a proving ground for the life of eternal blessedness. Any push for a tightly reasoned reconciliation of the competing claims of still dimly understood divine grace and human free will raised

---

212. *Ep.* 23.44, with Clark, *The Origenist Controversy,* 201.

213. Fabre, *Paulin de Nole,* 90–91; Piscitelli Carpino, *Paolino di Nola: Epistole ad Agostino,* 78–79.

214. Lienhard, *Paulinus of Nola,* 115, echoed by Piscitelli Carpino, *Paolino di Nola: Epistole ad Agostino,* 78–79; the quote is from Brown, "Pelagius and His Supporters," 200. Cf. the intuitions of R. Marandino, "I dolci colloqui di Paolino nell'epistolario," *Impegno e dialogo 9* (1991–92) 146.

215. *Ep.* 12.6: "qua meritum adquirimus, quo vitae illius in aeternum beatae possessio praeparatur."

216. Above chapter 6 with *epp.* 34.6, 11.9: "ut materiam nobis virtutis ad merita parienda proponat."

problems whose very intractability and ultimate threat to the unity of the mystic body of the church were tragically demonstrated to Paulinus in the quarrels and condemnations of 411–18 and the renewed assault of Julian thereafter.

Thus Paulinus, like many others outside Africa and especially in the monastic centers of southern Gaul over the next half-century, may have been unable to take with Augustine the final steps toward rigid predestinarian doctrine.[217] It is likely, therefore, that Paulinus listened carefully to Pelagian arguments before the dispersion of 410; it is likely that he respected those Pelagian sympathizers whom Augustine detected at Nola in 417; and it is also likely that Nola continued discreetly to harbor Pelagians for years thereafter, if indeed they numbered among the outsiders readmitted to communion by Paulinus upon his deathbed.[218] It is especially telling that when Augustine once sought Paulinus's opinion on the activity of the blessed after the resurrection of the flesh, Paulinus instead invited Augustine to discuss with him the present state of his life. It was by withdrawing from the life of this world, Paulinus avowed, that we anticipate the loosening of the flesh.[219] Such withdrawal, regardless of the ultimate force that enabled its accomplishment, required constant realization in the daily life of each person who chose "to live for Christ."

By the time Paulinus wrote this letter to Augustine, about 408, his life of renunciation was also inextricably bound up with the tomb of Felix, where Paulinus encouraged the devout to bargain for the succor and favor of Christ and the saint. Here, where by his efforts Paulinus had accomplished so much, people continued to seek out the privilege of burial near the tomb of Felix. Perhaps not surprisingly, discussion of the place of the cult of the saints in this life and the next provided a topic of conversation that would lead the correspondence of Paulinus and Augustine along an arc that we can trace much further than that formed by the Pelagian controversy.

THE LIVING AND THE DEAD

In 402, or shortly thereafter, scandal rocked the church at Hippo. A priest named Boniface and a monk named Spes each accused the other of making a "vile and immoral" proposal.[220] When the accusations became public, the congregation divided its support. Some members refused to attend services unless Boniface was

217. See, for example, R. Markus, "The Legacy of Pelagius: Orthodoxy, Heresy, and Conciliation," *The Making of Orthodoxy: Essays in Honour of Henry Chadwick,* ed. R. Williams (Cambridge, 1989), 214–34; T. Smith, *De Gratia: Faustus of Riez's Treatise on Grace and Its Place in the History of Theology* (Notre Dame, 1990), 39–55, and especially 44–46 on Cassian. The way has been pointed by Piscitelli Carpino, *Paolino di Nola: Epistole ad Agostino,* 79.

218. Uranius, *De obitu* 2, as suggested by Brown, *Augustine,* 384.

219. *Ep.* 45.4: "praesenti vitae meae statu."

220. *Ep.* 78.2: "motum inpudicum et inmundum." The episode is recounted in Aug. *epp.* 77 and 78 (*CSEL* 34). It appears that Boniface was the first to make the charge (*ep.* 78.2). On the date 402, not

removed from the roll of presbyters.[221] This disruption of internal harmony pro-
vided both Donatists and non-Christians an opportunity to gloat: one fallen
monk, they announced, was merely manifest evidence of the masked intemper-
ance of all.[222] Although Augustine believed in the innocence of Boniface, he was
unable to demonstrate it satisfactorily. So in a letter to the clergy and church of
Hippo, he announced his decision to submit the difficult matter to divine judg-
ment.[223] Spes and Boniface, Augustine informed his people, had agreed to travel
to Nola and stand trial before the tomb of Felix.[224] In a case that clearly con-
founded the minds of men, the "divine power" would now pass judgment through
the miraculous action of a saint at a "holy place" where the "dreadful works of
God" were often made manifest.[225]

Augustine's decision to appeal the case to Felix must be credited largely to the
promotional efforts of Paulinus, who by then had been resident just outside Nola
for seven years. Although the tomb of Felix had become known as an "altar of
truth (*ara veritatis*)" as early as the 360s—for even Damasus had visited Felix to
clear himself of allegedly false charges—since 395, when he arrived at Nola, Pauli-
nus had significantly advanced Felix's claim to be an efficacious heavenly *comes*
and a vigilant guardian of justice and truth.[226] In fact, Augustine explained his
own recourse to this particular locus of *virtus* in terms familiar to readers of Pauli-
nus. God might be everywhere, Augustine acknowledged, but he had appointed
some places to be the special scenes of "miraculous action." And in this respect,
Augustine continued, "the holiness of the place where the body of the blessed Felix
of Nola is buried is very well known to many."[227] Although Africa might be full of
the bodies of martyrs and Milan possessed tombs where thieves as well as demons
confessed their crimes, Augustine acknowledged the particular appropriateness of
Felix's tomb for the type of miraculous display now required.[228] But, acutely con-
scious of the potential for fraud in such matters of the saints, Augustine also further
assured his congregation that the verdict of the case, though revealed in miracle,

---

secure, see Courcelle, "Les lacunes," 266–67; Perler, *Les voyages*, 244–45; and more broadly (401–8),
Piscitelli Carpino, *Paolino di Nola: Epistole ad Agostino*, 42.

221. *Ep.* 78.4.

222. *Ep.* 78.6.

223. *Ep.* 78.3–4: "ne divinae potestati, sub cuius examine causa adhuc pendet, facere viderer ini-
uriam" (78.4).

224. *Ep.* 78.3. *Ep.* 77, addressed to Felix and Hilarinus, "domini dilectissimi meritoquo honorandi
fratres," also explains and justifies this action.

225. *Ep.* 78.4: "divinae potestati." 78.3: "se ambo constringerent ad locum sanctum se pergituros,
ubi terribiliora opera dei non sanam cuiusque conscientiam multo facilius aperirent."

226. For example, *carm.* 19.515 ff. (but of 405).

227. *Ep.* 78.3: "quare in aliis locis haec miracula fiant, in aliis non fiant? multis enim notissima est
sanctitas loci, ubi beati Felicis Nolensis corpus conditum est."

228. *Ep.* 78.3.

would eventually return to Hippo in the form of a trustworthy written report.[229] It may well have been the presence of Paulinus at Nola, as much as the reputation of Felix, that led Augustine to single out this particular *locus sanctus* in 402.

By the time Spes and Boniface made their mutual accusations, Augustine's epistolary friendship with Paulinus was nearly seven years tried. By then their letters were occupied with matters of scriptural interpretation and discussions of Christian life and belief. Around 404 they were engaged in a "pleasant conversation," as Augustine put it, about the means by which men might rightly discern the will of God—a will, Augustine then tellingly remarked, much more often revealed in the "accidents of circumstance" than in any voice from heaven, dream, or ecstatic seizure.[230] And after 408, in addition to tackling together a series of thorny biblical passages, Augustine and Paulinus initiated an extended epistolary conference whose topics, the resurrection body and the life of the saints in heaven, occupied them for some time and reappeared in what we might consider the final installment of their correspondence, the last book of *the City of God*.[231]

Among the lost letters of the correspondence of Augustine and Paulinus must be counted the letter from Augustine that Spes and Boniface should have carried with them to Paulinus. Its loss is especially unfortunate, for its survival presumably would have given us another valuable view of Augustine's wavering opinion on the place of the tombs and miracles of the martyrs in Christian dogma. For Augustine's was a vacillating response to the cult of the saints, his attitude shifting as his experiences unfolded.[232] In the *De vera religione,* for example, written at Thagaste more than a decade before the eruption of the controversy that drove Boniface and Spes to Nola (and a text that Alypius apparently sent to Paulinus in 395),[233] Augustine had declared the impossibility of legitimate miracles in the postapostolic age: the visible signs that had been necessary for the growth of faith during the infancy of the church, he then wrote, would now be stumbling blocks to the appreciation of Christianity's metaphysical truths, the visible would distract attention from the invisible. Let us not, he added, worship with religious rites dead men who lived piously, but rather let us honor and imitate them.[234] Despite the

---

229. *Ep.* 78.3: "quia inde nobis facilius fideliusque scribi potest, quicquid in eorum aliquo divinitus fuerit propalatum."

230. Aug. *ep.* 80.

231. Paul. *epp.* 45 and 50; Aug. *epp.* 95 and 149. On the chronology see Courcelle, "Les lacunes," and Piscitelli Carpino, *Paolino di Nola: Epistole ad Agostino,* 45–70.

232. Well documented by D. De Vooght, "Les miracles dans la vie de Saint Augustin," *Recherches de théologie ancienne et médiévale* 11 (1939): 5–16. See also T. J. Van Bavel, "The Cult of the Martyrs in St. Augustine: Theology versus Popular Religion," *Martyrium in Multidisciplinary Perspective: Memorial Louis Reekmans,* ed. M. Lamberigts and P. Van Deun (Leuven, 1995), 351–61.

233. On the date, ca. 390, see Perler, *Les voyages,* 149–51.

234. *De vera religione* 25.47, 55.108. Brown, *Augustine,* 415; Eno, *Augustine and the Saints,* 75.

apparently contrary decision about 402 to subject Boniface and Spes to the scrutiny of Saint Felix, the strain of resistance to contemporary practice that surfaces in the *De vera religione* reemerged in another text, the *De cura pro mortuis gerenda*, which also eventually traveled from North Africa to Nola.

Augustine's recourse to the tomb of Felix to resolve the dilemma presented by Boniface and Spes signals the powerful pull that Paulinus might exercise even on a hesitant mind that had already thought through the theological and doctrinal implications of the cult of the martyrs. For Paulinus was an active agent of the saints, disseminating, along with holy relics, the precepts manifest in the *natalicia*, precepts that elevated the Christian saint to the status of heavenly *comes* and established the saint's tomb as a locus of special power. Paulinus's staunch advocacy, however, was displayed with more immediate success before such Gallo-Roman friends as Victricius and Sulpicius Severus. Events at Rouen and Primuliacum, therefore, allow us to see more clearly how friendship and the promotion of the cult of the saints were intertwined at the end of the fourth century and the opening of the fifth.

Having met Victricius at Vienne in the late 380s, Paulinus did not renew his acquaintance with him until 397 or 398.[235] Victricius had recently composed his only extant treatise, *De laude sanctorum,* delivered to celebrate the installation at Rouen of a new "crowd of saints," whose arrival augmented a force that already included relics of Milan's Gervasius and Protasius.[236] Although Victricius appears in this text as rather different in temperament and attitude from Paulinus, the two clearly shared interests and views announced by their common passion for the collection and transfer of sacred relics. If Victricius's reasoned and tempered public justification of the value of relics in the *De laude sanctorum* contrasts with the more dramatic and confessional mode of Paulinus,[237] he nonetheless also stresses the role of the saints as physicians and intercessors.[238] And if Victricius's *sancti* are not here the personal *comites* of the *natalicia*, they nevertheless are domiciled in heaven, and the faithful are their *hospites*.[239] Moreover, both men apparently hoped that the distribution of relics, enabling "the blessed martyrs now to provide kindly presents from their tombs" to those in distant regions,[240] might help bind far-flung Christian communities in a network of piety and patronage; and they expected that unrefined converts could be both at-

---

235. *Ep.* 18 and chapter 3.

236. Text and translation at Herval, *Origines chrétiennes,* 108–53. An English translation is forthcoming by G. Clark in *JECS. De laude* 12: "dum recens est turba sanctorum incumbamus." See *De laude* 6 for a list of relics already installed.

237. See esp. *De laude* 10–11. Victricius is quite restrained in his use of miracles and his mention of demons.

238. *De laude* 11–12.

239. *De laude* 5: "Horum quidem domicilia superna sunt sed nos ut hospites praecemur."

240. Paul. *Carm.* 19.309–10: "Ut iam de tumulis agerent pia dona beati / martyres."

tracted by the power of these bits of dead bodies and led to see through them to the "postmortem effectiveness" that constituted the "real life" of the martyr's body.[241]

Victricius's courier, Paschasius, may have been impressed by what he found at Nola; he certainly reported the endeavors by which Victricius had turned Rouen into the image of Jerusalem, including even the presence of the Apostles.[242] In turn Paulinus's letter endorsed both Victricius's ascetic program and his incorporation of the power of relics into his strategies of Christianization in the town and region. For this reason, it seems, Paulinus took the rare step of introducing Felix into his letter and crediting the saint with the healing of Paschasius's traveling companion, Ursus. "Through the prayers of the saint," Paulinus assured Victricius, "the Lord restored him to Paschasius."[243] We might assume that Paulinus should have sought to assist Victricius's efforts more assiduously, but the only other letter of their correspondence dates to 403 or 404 and is devoted to rather different matters.[244]

Better documented than Paulinus's support of Victricius are his efforts with Sulpicius Severus on behalf of the saints and their relics. Indeed, Paulinus's letters to Severus reveal in unusual detail how Christian friendship served the promotion of the personal ends and spiritual ideals that met in the cult of the saints. At Primuliacum Severus established his own monastic and cultic complex centered on the legacy of one saint, Martin; the bones of another, Martin's disciple Clarus; and the accumulated *virtus* of an assortment of relics that eventually included a fragment of the cross sent north by Paulinus. Few sources reveal as clearly as these letters how literary enterprise, the traffic in relics, and the lines of friendship could conspire to redirect Christian worship. These letters and the texts they included or supplemented form a network of cross-referenced and self-referential documents that extend local interests to the interprovincial level. Not only the cults of Martin and Felix, and more broadly the principles that shaped the role of *sancti* in worship, but also Paulinus and Severus were the beneficiaries of these efforts.

The *vita Martini*, inspired by Severus's visits with Martin and written before Martin's death, arrived at Nola probably in the spring or early summer of 397.[245] Though the friendship of Paulinus and Severus was then approaching its low point,

241. *Ep* 18.4 with P. Cox Miller, "'Differential Networks': Relics and Other Fragments in Late Antiquity," *JECS* 6 (1998): 113–38, quote 125.

242. *Ep.* 18.3.

243. *Ep.*18.3: "Praestabit idem dominus, qui illum orationibus sancti fratri nostro Paschasio . . . redonavit."

244. *Ep.* 37. Victricius had recently journeyed south to defend himself before Innocent, apparently against a charge of Apollinarianism. When he also failed to visit Nola, he both drew a rebuke from Paulinus and elicited one of Paulinus's rare affirmations of his own orthodoxy (37.5–6). See Innocent, *ep.* 2 (*PL* 20.469–81) with Fabre, *Paulin de Nole*, 56–66.

245. *Ep.* 11.11, 13.

Paulinus eventually became the eager agent of this text that, as even he immediately saw, was destined to bring Martin "fame among men."[246] Paulinus read the story to visitors, and he saw to its circulation in Rome and beyond.[247] In a world where the *vita Antonii* had already done so much to fire enthusiasm for, or at least curiosity about, the ascetic life, the influence of this text, which illustrated so dramatically the thaumaturgical power of the "confessor" (11.11), should not be underestimated. Indeed, as Paulinus elsewhere makes clear, Severus's text even scripted the protocols of monastic humility at Nola, where in *imitatio Martini* Paulinus washed the hands of ascetic visitors.[248]

But as Severus found an Italian agent for the cult of Martin in Paulinus, so Paulinus took the unusual step of employing his letters to Severus to spread the name of Felix.[249] At first it was merely the saint's humble "garden," with its implicit embodiment of the ideals of secular renunciation and poverty, that took its place in Paulinus's letters.[250] But in the difficult days of their friendship between 397 and 399, when Severus's frequent promises to visit Nola remained frustratingly unfulfilled, an embittered Paulinus found opportunity to remind Severus of the awesome power of the saints. Writing probably in 397, Paulinus rebuked Severus for honoring Martin while mocking their "common patron" Felix by failing to visit him, and he curtly warned Severus not to offend a saint "who is most dear to God."[251] "Although I want Christ's grace to overflow for you in every saint," Paulinus wrote, "I should not like you to encounter a stumbling block, especially not in the saint in whom God's love is notable and outstanding."[252] The love of Christ and the saints might offer an appropriate matrix for elevating human friendship, but Paulinus's hovering threat intimated that it might also create powerful disincentives to breaching friendship's protocols. For at the same time that Paulinus and Severus set about abstracting their friendship, they also expanded it to accommodate the utterly palpable presence of Martin and Felix, a presence whose immediacy would be heightened when Severus's *amicus* Martin joined Paulinus's *comes* Felix in heaven.[253] Indeed, as the fifth century dawned and Paulinus and Severus were reconciled, it was especially this reconfiguration of the terms

246. *Ep.* 11.11.

247. *Ep.* 29.14. Sev. *Dial.* 1.23; 3.17.

248. *Ep.* 23.4.

249. Felix is notably absent from Paulinus's extant correspondence. Outside the letters to Severus he appears only in *ep.* 18.3 to Victricius and the late *ep.* 49 to "Macarius."

250. *Epp.* 5.15; 11.14.

251. *Ep.* 17.3: "communis patroni"; 17.4: "carissimum dei."

252. *Ep* 17.4. "et dum in omni sancto abundare tibi gratiam Christi cupio, nolim te in eo potissimum, in quo dei caritas est insignis et eminens, lapidem offensionis incurrere."

253. Martin's death in November 397 is commemorated in Sev. *ep.* 2 and 3. *Ep.* 17.4 seems to assume Martin is still living, and therefore the letter should have been written before or shortly after that date.

of their friendship that motivated an energetic effort to triangulate Nola and Primuliacum with points among the stars and provide and promote suitable earthly contexts for the *virtus* of the saints.

Paulinus read the *Vita Martini* to guests like Melania and Nicetas to teach them as much of Severus as of Martin;[254] and his letters to Gaul found other ways to bolster the image of Severus while also praising Martin and his disciple Clarus, now buried at Primuliacum.[255] Thus, about 401 Paulinus boldly announced his understanding that in Severus "Martin wholly breathes, Clarus blooms, and the Gospel is brought to ripeness."[256] A year or so earlier he had highlighted the lines of blood and spiritual sympathy that bound Severus to that towering figure of ascetic victory, Melania the Elder.[257] Severus meanwhile persisted in offering Paulinus, and even Felix, further roles in his Martinian *Dialogues*. Indeed, Severus's *Dialogues* end with a request to the interlocutor Postumianus, about to return to the East, that en route he share with others their recent conversations about Martin. Postumianus's first duty, Severus's readers learned, was to visit Paulinus, "a man renowned and praised throughout the world."[258] The interlocutor Severus assured Postumianus that because Paulinus harbored no jealousy toward Martin and was a most pious appraiser of his saintly powers in Christ, he would further spread the word, not even refusing "to compare our protector (*praesul*) with his own Felix."[259] Severus also reciprocated Paulinus's promotion of his literary works in Italy by collecting at least some of Paulinus's writing at Primuliacum. About 403, for example, Paulinus honored a request and sent to Severus a *libellus* containing at least one of the *carmina natalicia*, those "annual invocations," as he remarked, "to the patron of our house . . . offered on the feast of his admission into heaven," as well as a copy of his panegyric on Theodosius.[260]

Such texts and letters could be expected to reach a wide audience. Cooperative work of another kind was being done to define and enhance the local authority of

254. *Ep.* 29.14.

255. Clarus first appears in Paulinus's letters in *ep.* 23.3 (400), where Paulinus claims to recognize the pattern of Martin and Clarus in the courier Victor.

256. *Ep.* 27.3: "totum in te spirare Martinum, florere Clarum, maturari evangelium praedicabant."

257. Paulinus's *vita Melaniae* appears in *ep.* 29 to Severus and the association with Severus is explicit at 29.5; see also Trout, "*Amicitia, Auctoritas*, and Self-Fashioning Texts."

258. *Dial.* 3.17: "quin illic [Campania] adeas inlustrem virum ac toto laudatum orbe."

259. *Dial.* 3.17: "ille Martini non invidus gloriarum sanctarumque in Christo virtutum piissimus aestimator non abnuet praesulem nostrum cum suo Felice conponere."

260. *Ep.* 28.6: "Habes ergo libellos a me duos, unum versibus natalicium de mea solemni ad dominaedium meum catilena." The courier Victor had previously carried *volumina* to Primuliacum (*ep.* 28.4). The *libellus* of 28.6 is likely to have contained a single *natalicium*, perhaps *carm.* 26 or 27. See S. Mratschek, "Einblicke in einen Postsack: Zur Struktur und Edition der 'Natalicia' des Paulinus von Nola," *ZPE* 114 (1996) : 165–72.

the cult site. Gifts and relics laden with spiritual significance, holy power, and prestige moved between Nola and Primuliacum. It was probably in 400 that Severus sent Paulinus several camel's-hair cloaks, received by a self-deprecating Paulinus like "a bag of dung" offered "to a barren fig tree."[261] Paulinus, who a few years earlier had sent north an equally humble but no less eloquent gift of simple Campanian bread and a wooden platter, now reciprocated with the present of a special tunic. The tunic, he informed Severus, had been a gift to him from Melania the Elder, and he had worn it himself before sending it on. Paulinus had donned the tunic, he continued, so that his presence might travel with it and also so that he could steal a prior blessing from a shirt that would soon belong to Severus.[262] Presumably, this tunic assumed, as Paulinus's letters apparently did at times, the power of a contact relic.[263]

But full-fledged relics, too, traveled from Nola to Primuliacum. About 402 or 403 Severus wrote to Paulinus requesting sacred relics to install in the basilica of his new "family church" at Primuliacum. Unable to supply "sacred ashes," Paulinus instead forwarded to Severus a tiny sliver of the holy Cross, part of a gift from Melania, who had received it from John of Jerusalem.[264] Eventually this nearly invisible fragment of the Cross joined relics of the martyrs in Severus's new church.[265] As purveyor of such a powerful relic, Paulinus was already playing the role that he ascribed a few years later, in the *natalicium* of 405, to Constantine and Ambrose.[266] He too was now an agent in that plan by which God would distribute more broadly the remains of the saints and multiply their *memoria*. Thus, with the help of friends, Primuliacum too was plotted on the expanding grid of Christendom as a point where the special dead could offer their gifts and the entombed protect the living.[267]

It was ultimately within the walls of Severus's new basilica complex itself, however, that texts and artifacts merged to offer the most eloquent manifestation of Paulinus's reach into southern Gaul and to reveal a remarkable picture of the managerial side of the cult of saints and the traffic in relics. Paulinus's complex at Nola and that of Severus at Primuliacum arose in tandem, joined by a "chain of letters."[268] Victor and other couriers kept Paulinus and Severus apprised of the details of plans and construction at each site, sometimes verbally, sometimes by transporting drawings and copies of paintings and *tituli*.[269] Thus Paulinus rejoiced

261. *Ep.* 29.1–3. Cf. *ep.* 23.3.
262. *Ep.* 29.5.
263. Uranius, *De obitu* 9.
264. *Ep.* 31.1–2.
265. *Ep.* 32.7.
266. *Carm.* 19.307–77.
267. *Carm.* 19.309–10: "ut iam de tumulis agerent pia dona beati / martyres et vivos possent curare sepulti."
268. *Ep.* 32.10: "epistolae serie."
269. *Ep.* 32.5, 9–10.

that, by bestowing basilicas simultaneously on the Lord's fold, he and Severus "exhibited a single likeness of heart and body."[270] Indeed, Paulinus appears as more than simply a "consultant" in these letters. For Severus's baptistry he composed verses that explicated the mystery of baptism and offered the same symbolic exegesis of space and architectural relationships that adorned the walls at Nola.[271] He wrote further verses to advertise and celebrate the relics of the Cross and the martyrs now housed in "our second basilica" at Primuliacum.[272] Similarly, he wrote verses to celebrate Clarus, the "permanent guest" of Severus's church, whose ascent to heaven Severus had already given literary fame.[273] Now Clarus's bones rested beneath the altar, Paulinus's hexameters proclaimed, but his mind rejoiced among the stars.[274]

But Paulinus was more than a long-distance impresario, for at Primuliacum Severus found it worthwhile to tap the potential allure of Paulinus's name and reputation, and to supplement the physical presence of the relics of Clarus with the power of the names and images of the "outsider" Martin and the supreme Gallo-Roman insider Paulinus. It was an impulse that Paulinus tempered but did not deny. Thus he composed self-deprecating verses to accompany his portrait, which Severus had paired with one of Martin in his new baptistry. Whether Severus added Paulinus's verses to those, surely more assertive, that Severus himself had written remains unknown.[275] Still Paulinus insisted that the verses he had composed for Primuliacum be specifically denoted as his, lest someone inadvertently blame Severus for them.[276] Thus an elaborate inscription commemorating Clarus also linked Severus, Paulinus, and Therasia in a network of friendship and favors that ascended from Nola through the mediation of Severus to the astral home of Clarus and Martin.[277] If in Martin Severus had sent a "heavenly patron" on ahead of him, at the tomb of Clarus he worked in cooperation with Paulinus to establish firmly the terrestrial anchor of a line that stretched upward to Clarus's home in Paradise.[278]

270. *Ep.* 32.1: "Perquam enim gratulor, quod unam cordis et corporis nostri, operum quoque et votorum similitudinem ostenderimus, eodem tempore basilicas dominicis adicientes ovilibus."
271. *Ep.* 32.5.
272. *Ep.* 32.7: "aliam apud Primuliacum nostram et priore maiorem basilicam."
273. *Ep.* 32.6: "perpetuum tibi hospitem"; Sev. *Ep.* 2.5.
274. *Ep.* 32.6: "sed membra caduca sepulchro, / libera corporeo mens carcere gaudet in astris."
275. *Ep.* 32.2–4.
276. *Ep.* 32.9.
277. *Ep.* 32.6.
278. Sev. *ep.* 2.8: "Praemisi quidem patronum"; *Ep.* 32.6:

Sive patrum sinibus recubas dominive sub ara
   conderis aut sacro pasceris in nemore,
qualibet in regione poli situs aut paradisi,
   Clare, sub aeterna pace beatus agis.

Perhaps especially because the tombs of holy men stood as shining portals to those "holy halls of tranquil peace," burial in the vicinity of the martyr's bones became highly desirable.[279] Paulinus would eventually be buried near Felix, but others were already claiming the privilege of resting in the "refreshing house of Felix" until, called back to their bodies by the "dreaded trumpet," they might enjoy Felix's comradeship "before the tribunal."[280] In fact, it was just such a claim that brought Paulinus and Augustine back into conversation about the role of the holy dead in Christian life. Not long before 422 a certain Flora, a widow and a spiritual daughter of Augustine living in Africa, requested of Paulinus that her son, recently deceased near Nola, be permitted burial close by the tomb of Felix.[281] Paulinus complied, interring Cynegius in the basilica of Felix and apparently composing the verse epitaph just quoted. He also wrote a (now lost) letter of consolation to Flora and took the opportunity to send with Flora's returning couriers a letter to Augustine requesting the latter's thoughts on the true benefits of such burial *ad sanctum*. Paulinus queried Augustine specifically about the power of the martyrs to intercede for the dead and even about the efficacy of the prayers of the living in this regard, for Paulinus was unable to reconcile 2 Cor 5.10—"For we must all appear before the judgment seat of Christ, so that each one may receive good or evil,

279. *CIL* 10.1370 (= Diehl *ILCV*, 3482), the Nolan epitaph of Cynegius: "[et paci]s sancta placidae requiescit in aula." I follow here Walsh's suggestion of [et paci]s for the restoration of the second line (40:421).

280. *CIL* 10.1370 (= Diehl *ILCV*, 3482). Mommsen notes, "Cimitile in S. Felicis, postea Nolae, in seminario ubi nunc non extat." He knew it only from copies:

[Exegit v]itam florente Cinegius aevo
[et laetu]s sancta placidae requiescit in aula;
[illum nu]nc Felicis habet domus alma beati
[atque ita per lo]n[g]os susceptum possidet annos;
[patronus pl]acito laetatur in hospite Felix;
[sic protec]tus erit iuvenis sub iudice Christo;
[cum tuba terri]bilis sonitu concusserit orbem
[humanaeque ani]mae rursum in sua vasa redibunt,
[Felici merito] hic sociabitur ante tri[bunal];
[interea] in gremio Abraham [cum pace quiescit].

Courcelle, "Les lacunes," 289 n. 3, wondered why Hartel omitted the piece from the edition of Paulinus's *carmina*. Walsh, *ACW* 40:345 and Ruggiero, *I carmi*, following 413, admit it.

281. *De cura pro mortuis gerenda* 1 (*CSEL* 41). The date of the treatise is ca. 422, and Augustine noted therein that he had received Paulinus's letter *diu*. Flora appears to live in Africa, perhaps at Hippo, for Augustine refers to her as *filia nostra religiosa;* and the same men who brought to her Paulinus's letter of consolation also brought his letter to Augustine. See Y. Duval, "Flora était-elle africaine? (Augustin, *De Cura gerenda pro mortuis*, 1, 1)," *REAug* 34 (1988): 70–77, and Y. Duval, *Auprès des saints: Corps et âme. L'inhumation "ad sanctos" dans la chrétienté d'Orient et d'Occident du IIIe au VIIe siècle* (Paris, 1988), 87–88; Courcelle, "Les lacunes," 289–90; and chapter 2, this volume.

according to what he has done in the body"—with the idea of *any* intercession on behalf of the dead.

Augustine responded with the treatise *The Care to Be Taken for the Dead* (*De cura pro mortuis gerenda*). This work must have disturbed Paulinus deeply, for therein Augustine directly, if gracefully, counters some of the fundamental tenets of Paulinus's thought.[282] For several decades Paulinus had been working to establish the distinctive otherworldly sanctity of the martyrs' tombs and the paradoxical vitality of their corpses and relics. For years he had argued for the intimate involvement of the celestial saints in the lives of their earthly clients, and he had predicated much of his own public identity on the affection and care that he experienced as the special friend of Felix. In a few brief pages, the bishop of Hippo, reluctantly it seems, expresses a serious challenge to those claims. In addressing Paulinus's questions Augustine shifts the focus of investigation from the dead to the living, he privileges the hidden and the notional over the visible and the tangible, and he erects a solid barrier between the affairs of the living and the concerns of the dead.[283] In the end, the doubts that Augustine offered Paulinus in the *De cura* were a corrosive affront to the ideology and the pastoral initiatives expressed so often in the annual poems with which Paulinus had honored Felix.

The *De cura* is in some ways an ambiguous work, perhaps because Augustine was genuinely uncertain, perhaps because he did not want to risk giving grave offense. Augustine does not fully discount the value of *depositio ad sanctum*, but he locates its worth quite differently from, for example, Paulinus's epitaph for Cynegius, which so confidently assigns to Felix care of the deceased young man who rests simultaneously in the saint's "holy halls of tranquil peace" and the "bosom of Abraham." Burial itself, Augustine reminds Paulinus, with a footnote to book 1 of the *City of God*, is a rite that benefits the living, not the dead. The dead are no longer bodies, but souls. The body is nothing to those deceased who are "now at rest in the hidden abodes of the pious."[284] Neither good nor bad actions, disfigurement nor burial, performed on the dead body impinge on the detached soul; thus funerary rites comfort only the living, and burial, even inhumation *ad sanctum*, is essentially an act of "human affection" toward the remains of friends (6). Still, Augustine concedes, interment at a *memoria sanctorum* may be beneficial for the soul of the deceased to the extent that the prominence of the *memoria* ensures that the deceased is more likely to remain in the memory of the living and thus be more frequently recalled in prayer. These prayers and supplications on behalf of the deceased, sometimes directed to the martyr, could profit those dead who lived pious lives. The power of assistance, however, comes not from the "place" where

282. See also V. Saxer, *Morts martyrs reliques en Afrique chrétienne aux premiers siècles* (Paris, 1980), 165–68; Y. Duval, *Auprès des saints*, esp. 3–21, 171–201; Eno, *Augustine and the Saints*, 66–70.

283. *De cura* 23: Augustine had to be coerced by Paulinus's courier to complete the piece.

284. *De cura* 5: "in occultis piorum sedibus iam quietos."

the body is buried, Augustine emphasizes, but from the "living affection" that a place might inspire.[285]

If such thinking could be seen as justification for the continued maintenance of the martyrs' tombs, it hardly endorsed the grander conceptions that undergirded Paulinus's project at Nola. Nor were Augustine's radical separation of the post-mortem body and soul or his rejection of the utility of burial for the deceased consistent with the widely held assumptions that mistreatment of the dead body or exposure without burial brought suffering to the deceased or that the final resurrection of the flesh would be facilitated by the preservation of the entombed body.[286]

Augustine's troubling reservations about *loca sancta* were linked to a profound mistrust of assumptions about too easy relations between the living and the dead. He devoted the second half of the *De cura* to commentary on the cognitive barrier that divided these respective realms. The dead may care about the living just as the living care about the dead, Augustine again concedes, but they care in mutual ignorance. The souls of the dead know no more about the plight of the living than the living know about the conditions of the dead.[287] Even dreams and visions, Augustine warns, should not be accepted as legitimate communication across the divide: it is not the true soul of the dead that appears to the living, but a "likeness."[288] Still, Augustine, who had after all sent Boniface and Spes to Nola for judgment at the tomb of Felix, would admit exceptions to this natural order. Angels, who journeyed between the realms of the living and the dead, might, with God's permission, enlighten the dead about the living (18). And sometimes God even empowered the martyrs to breach the divide and bestow their *beneficia* on those who prayed to them. Thus, Augustine recalled, he had been informed that Felix had actually appeared at Nola when the city was being threatened by barbarians (19). If this concession was welcome to Paulinus, it was perhaps small consolation for a man who had repeatedly stressed Felix's intimate sympathy for and knowledge of every detail of his life, and who had many years before sought consolation by burying his own newborn son *ad sanctum* in Spain.[289] The *De cura*, anxiously awaited at Nola, left little room for the Christian *sanctus* as heavenly *comes*. As so often, Augustine took a position that confounded contemporary expectations and subverted, however cautiously, a deeply rooted confidence in the power of the holy dead both to protect the deceased from demonic forces and to intercede with God on their behalf.[290]

<hr/>

285. *De cura* 7: "adjuvat defuncti spiritum, non mortui corporis locus, sed ex loci memoria vivus matris affectus."

286. Y. Duval, *Auprès des saints*, 23–47.

287. *De cura* 16–17.

288. *De cura* 13: "non eius animam, neque corpus, sed hominis similitudinem sibi apparuisse non dubitet."

289. *Carm.* 31.605–10.

290. Y. Duval, *Auprès des saints*, 171–201.

Augustine ends his treatise by inviting Paulinus's epistolary response, just as he did a few years earlier when, together with Alypius, he fired an anti-Pelagian warning shot across Paulinus's bow.[291] But when Augustine closes the *De cura* by suggesting that Paulinus might be more grateful for the return of the courier Candidianus than for the reception of the text, his humility may be more than protocol. Ironically, however, Augustine would soon move much closer to the line of Paulinus's thought, for not long after Augustine wrote the *De cura* the relics of the proto-martyr Stephen arrived in Hippo. Stephen's cult had been moving like a "tidal wave" across the Mediterranean since his relics had been discovered in Palestine in late 415.[292] Since then Stephen had busily settled in Roman towns as the "spiritual equivalent" of a powerful earthly patron.[293] By 418 or 419 Stephen had made his way into Africa Proconsularis, where Augustine's disciple and friend Evodius, bishop of Uzalis, who had visited Paulinus at Nola in 404, soon welcomed Stephen to his city amid a frenzy of miracles.[294] Soon another friend of Augustine and former guest of Paulinus, Possidius, similarly received Stephen's relics at Numidian Calama.[295] Stephen's North African advent was timely. Free of partisan contamination, the "dust" of Stephen facilitated the integration of Catholics and Donatists, many of whom shared that confidence in the *virtus* of martyrs that Augustine had so long resisted.[296] And now, fortified by the examples of Evodius and Possidius, recalling his days in Ambrose's Milan,[297] and surely pondering the long-tried commitment of Paulinus, a friend of nearly three decades, Augustine began to reconsider the place of the miraculous in the contemporary struggle to strengthen belief or to encourage conversion.

Any shift that Augustine made toward the acceptance of *contemporary* miracles would have been facilitated by the "theology of miracle" that he had already hammered out in defense of the seemingly wondrous events recorded in the Old and New Testaments. These historical miracles, Augustine had argued in *De Trinitate*, assumed their wondrous quality merely from the relative rarity that distinguished them from the equally marvelous but overlooked complexity of the everyday, natural world. The miracles of the biblical age, therefore, were no less natural than the otherwise inexplicable but underappreciated wonders of the created order. Nor had they occurred outside God's purview. Indeed, even those wonders once wrought by nefarious magical arts in Egypt had their hidden source in the dispensation made by God at the Creation. Just as farmers were not the "creators"

291. Aug. *ep.* 186.41.

292. Saxer, *Morts martyrs reliques*, 245–79, quote 245. A concise summary of events appears in S. Bradbury, *Severus of Minorca: Letter on the Conversion of the Jews* (Oxford, 1996), 16–25.

293. Brown, *Augustine*, 413.

294. *De civ. Dei* 22.8 (*CSEL* 40. p. 608.12). Saxer, *Morts martyrs reliques*, 245–54; Aug. *ep.* 95.1.

295. *De civ. Dei* 22.8 (*CSEL* 40. p. 608.9); Aug *ep.* 80.1.

296. Brown, *Augustine*, 414.

297. *Serm.* 318.1 (*PL* 38.1437); *De civ. Dei* 22.8 (*CSEL* 40. p. 596.28).

of corn, Augustine had argued, neither had men, nor even good or bad angels, been the true source of the biblically recorded miracles. The distinguishing power of angels and demons, rather, was a suprahuman sensitivity to the invisible "seeds of things," which, as God permitted, they had turned to the production of unusual events. All, even these apparent contradictions of the natural order, was encompassed within the work of Creation.[298]

Now, in the face of Stephen's onslaught, as Augustine set aside his reluctance to accept reports of contemporary miracles, he could return to this "theology of miracle" to justify a new effervescence of the unusual at the tombs and shrines of the saints. Early miracles, he had concluded in *De vera religione* (25.47), had been granted by God to bolster the faith of a nascent and struggling church; now miracles could be understood as affirmations of faith in the final resurrection of the flesh.[299] The *virtus* now manifest in the relics of martyrs signaled the truth of that problematic carnal reassembly. Bolstered by this confluence of recent events and earlier thinking, the bishop of Hippo became, as the bishop of Nola had so long been, an impresario of sorts.

In 424 Stephen finally entered Hippo. Augustine himself may have personally escorted the "little bit of dust" of this potent "friend" of God on its journey from Evodius's Uzalis to Hippo.[300] In any case, he received Stephen's relics into the city with a sermon welcoming but cautionary. Augustine warned a large crowd that it was the example of Stephen's fulfillment of divine precepts *before* his death that should motivate their imitation.[301] Probably in the summer of 425, Augustine supervised the intramural transfer of Stephen's relics to a newly built *memoria* financed by his deacon Eraclius.[302] For this new shrine's walls Augustine himself apparently composed the verses that his sermon admonished the congregation to learn by heart. "Let that little room be your book," he told them.[303] For the illiterate (as at Nola, where mural texts and painted images buttressed each other), Stephen's story was also told in a wall painting.[304] Moreover, Augustine now employed his sermons to announce God's miracles worked through Stephen's relics,

---

298. *De Trinitate* 3.5–10. See further D. De Vooght, "La théologie du miracle selon Saint Augustine," *Recherches de théologie ancienne et médiévale* 11 (1939): 197–222.

299. *De civ. Dei.* 22.8 (*CSEL* 40, p. 609).

300. *Serm.* 317.1 (*PL* 38.1435): "exiguus pulvis"; *serm.* 316.1 (*PL* 38.1431): "Stephanus de servo amicus." Saxer, *Morts martyrs reliques*, 259; with Perler, *Les voyages*, 380, 472.

301. *Serm.* 317 (*PL* 38.1435–37). On the order and dates of Augustine's sermons on Stephen see C. Lambot, "Les sermons de Saint Augustine pour les fêtes de martyrs," *AB* 67 (1949): 263.

302. *Serm.* 318 (*PL* 38.1437–40); *serm.* 356.7 (*PL* 39.1577). On the date see also Perler, *Les voyages*, 377. On the absence of archaeological remains see Y. Duval, *Loca sanctorum Africae* (Rome, 1982), 627.

303. *Serm.* 319.7 (*PL* 38.1142): "camera illa codex vester sit." There were four verses (*serm.* 319.7): "Legite quattuor versos quos in cella scripsimus." Augustine also composed verses for the tomb of a deacon named Nabor, a victim of Donatist violence; see Y. Duval, *Loca sanctorum Africae*, 182–83.

304. Placing the *pictura* of *serm.* 316.5 (*PL* 38.1434) at Hippo.

not only at Hippo but also at Ancona in Italy and at Uzalis.[305] He now asked his congregation to invoke the prayers of Stephen on their own behalf;[306] and he encouraged them to seek cures at Stephen's shrine rather than through illegal, clandestine sacrifices.[307] And Augustine now began reading out the *libelli beneficiorum* composed by those who had experienced miraculous cures at the *memoria*.[308] Soon he also set about collecting and publishing the miracles of Stephen, creating a dossier of Stephen's victories over demons and illness whose intent parallels Paulinus's *natalicia*. To this end Augustine urged all who had personally experienced the saint's power to share their stories, and he encouraged other bishops to document events and prepare them for public recital.[309]

The rationale behind these initiatives eventually found systematic expression, and a considerably larger audience, in the final book of the *City of God*, written less than two years after Stephen's arrival in Hippo. Therein Augustine gave a condensed catalog of miracle stories, primarily healings and exorcisms, effected through the power of prayer, the sacraments, and the relics of the saints. He recalled a number of these incidents from his own experiences at Milan and Carthage before his ordination but turned quickly to events connected with the relics and shrines of Stephen in and around Hippo. He dramatically retold the story of the Easter healing of a brother and sister who had wandered the Mediterranean in search of a cure for a malady provoked by a mother's curse—a tale whose daily unfolding can also be followed across a series of four sermons contemporary with the events.[310] The miraculous signs of the church's infancy had now reappeared, Augustine admitted, and it was necessary to record and document such stories. Trustworthy accounts of recent miracles would strengthen belief in the even greater miracles of the Gospels and the promised resurrection of the flesh.[311] At Hippo, Augustine realized, the "eloquence of God" had found a new and effective outlet in the miracles at Stephen's shrines.[312] And with the arrival of Stephen's relics, Augustine must also have recognized that Hippo became, like Paulinus's Nola, another star in the constellation of martyrs' shrines where God poured out his protective grace.

This recognizable slippage in the bishop of Hippo's personal "center of gravity,"[313] of course, also signals the momentous shift in practices long sanctioned by,

---

305. *Serm.* 323 (*PL* 38.1445–46).

306. *Serm.* 316.5 (*PL* 38.1434).

307. *Serm.* 318.3 (*PL* 38.1439–40).

308. *Serm.* 319.7 (*PL* 38.1442); *serm.* 322 (*PL* 38.1443–45) for an example. For fuller discussion see H. Delehaye, "Les premiers 'libelli miraculorum'," *AB* 29 (1910): 427–34; Delehaye, "Les recueils antiques de miracles des saints," *AB* 43 (1925): esp. 73–84.

309. *De civ. Dei* 22.8 (*CSEL* 40, p. 607–9).

310. *Serm.* 320–24.

311. *De civ. Dei* 22.8 (*CSEL* 40, p. 609).

312. *De civ. Dei* 22.8 (*CSEL* 40, p. 611.11).

313. Brown, *Augustine*, 415.

among others, Paulinus at Nola. If there were those, like Augustine, who had re-
sisted the proliferation of *loca sancta* or who, like Vigilantius, had scoffed at the ado-
ration of "a bit of powder wrapped up in a cloth" and denied the intercessory role of
deceased martyrs,[314] nevertheless many more were eager to accept the aid offered
by the saints. In their defense Jerome had rebuked Vigilantius for doubting that the
demons cried out in the presence of the relics of the saints, and he assured his read-
ers that sleep, not death, had overcome the martyrs.[315] The "bishops of the whole
world," Jerome proclaimed, now performed divine service in basilicas that housed
holy relics.[316] With somewhat less fanfare, anonymous attendants at the Imolan
shrine of the martyr Cassian assured visitors that the martyr listened to all prayers
and answered those that seemed acceptable.[317] At Rouen, Primuliacum, and Imola,
as at Nola, and now at Hippo, suppliants to the saints shed their tears and uttered
their petitions over the remains of holy men, while poets and bishops transformed
those moments into literary accounts.[318] At Hippo the communications blackout
imposed on the living and the dead by Augustine's *De cura* had been officially lifted.

Even before departing from Spain in the spring of 395 Paulinus had begun to
reach out to like-minded converts to the ascetic life. Thereafter his letters and
couriers connected him with ever-widening circles of "friends" throughout the
empire. These relationships were constantly refined, both abstracted within the
unifying and elevating medium of divine love and sharply pointed under the pres-
sures of personal joy and disappointment or of theological and doctrinal debate.
Connected to so many of the participants in the key controversies of his day and
instrumental in the reformulation of piety before the tombs and relics of the holy
dead, Paulinus's activities and writings helped to shape the religious transforma-
tions of his age. We are fortunate in our ability to eavesdrop on the discussions in
which men like the aging Paulinus and Augustine struggled to make sense of and
gain control over a world that had changed considerably since the days of their
youth in mid-fourth-century Bordeaux and Thagaste.

Thus when the final book of the *City of God* arrived at Nola, as we can presume
it did, Paulinus must surely have read it as a further, and especially satisfying, stage
of his decades-long conversation with Augustine. Not only did that book offer the
retractatio of the troublesome second half of the *De cura* that the *Retractationes* them-
selves had not,[319] but it also took up anew their earlier discussion of the nature of

314. *Contra Vig.* 4, 6.

315. *Contra Vig.* 5–6.

316. *Contra Vig.* 8.

317. Prud. *Peristeph.* 9.97–98: "audit, crede, preces martyr prosperrimus omnes, / ratasque reddit
quas videt probabiles."

318. Prud. *Peristeph.* 9.99–104; for example, *De civ. Dei.* 22.8 (*CSEL* 40, p. 607).

319. The *De civ. Dei* was complete when Augustine wrote the *Retract.* (2.69), but Augustine's entry
there on the *De cura* (*Retract.* 2.90) did no more than present the circumstances of composition and sum-
marize the work in a few words.

life in heaven. About 408, provoked by Augustine to consider the "activity of the blessed after the resurrection of the flesh,"[320] Paulinus, taking his cue from Psalm 83.5—"Blessed are they that dwell in Thy house; they shall praise Thee forever and ever"—had devoted several paragraphs of speculation to the kind of tongue and voice that would be appropriate to the postresurrection "spiritual body."[321] But, confessing his own uncertainty, Paulinus had also called on Augustine to express his views about "the immortal voices of heavenly creatures."[322] In his reply, Augustine had agreed that in the "city of the holy" men and angels would surely praise God with voices emanating from organs of speech, but he had begged off full discussion until a later time.[323]

Whether later correspondence did take up the question of the "activity of the saints," we do not know, but the final book of the *City of God* surely did so. Although Augustine maintains his earlier reservations about any full understanding of the nature of the spiritual body, he nevertheless directly reengages the problem of just "what the saints are going to do in their immortal and spiritual bodies."[324] It was postresurrection vision, not the question of the postresurrection voice raised by Paulinus two decades before, that now occupied Augustine, but Paulinus should still have been able to detect in the closing pages of the monumental *City of God* the echoes of a "pleasant conversation" that he and the bishop of Hippo had begun many so years earlier. Such a recall to the pleasures of friendship and intellectual communion may have been especially welcome in the late 420s, because by the time the final installment of the *City of God* reached Nola, Paulinus, like Augustine, was enjoying the virtually unrivaled regional status that brought endless business and petitions to an eminent bishop's door.

320. Paul. *ep.* 45.4: "quare vero post resurrectionem carnis in illo saeculo beatorum futura sit actio, tu me interrogare dignatus es."

321. Paul. *ep.* 45.4–7. 6: "spiritalia corpora."

322. Paul. *ep.* 45.7.

323. Aug. *ep.* 95.7–8.

324. *De civ. Dei* 22.29: "nunc iam quid acturi sint in corporibus immortalibus adque spiritalibus sancti."

CHAPTER 9

—•—

The Final Years

The opening decades of the fifth century were excruciatingly difficult ones for Aquitaine and for southern Gaul more generally. On 31 December 406 a combined force of Vandals, Suebi, and Alani crossed a frozen and undefended Rhine. Wreaking havoc on the countryside, they slowly proceeded across Gaul and in the late summer of 409 broke through the Pyrenees into Spain. In 412 Athaulf, Alaric's brother-in-law and successor, led the Visigoths out of Italy and into war-ravaged southern Gaul, where they temporarily joined the usurper Jovinus. By the late summer of 413 Athaulf, desiring friendly relations with the court of Honorius at Ravenna, had established himself at Narbo. There, in January 414, he married in a Roman-style ceremony the imperial hostage Galla Placidia, Honorius's half-sister, who soon bore him a son, named Theodosius. This bid for amicable relations with Ravenna was rejected, however, and by the end of the year Honorius's general Constantius, future husband of Galla Placidia and coemperor with Honorius, had forced Athaulf and his new emperor Priscus Attalus to withdraw from Narbo to Barcelona. Constantius, however, continued to pressure the Goths in Spain; and in 418 Vallia, the Gothic leader since 415, and the Goths were transferred to Aquitaine. From Toulouse to Bordeaux, they were settled in the Garonne valley of Paulinus's Hebromagus, but perhaps on terms still favorable to the empire and the Gallo-Roman elite.[1] These disruptions facilitated the temporary success of a series of Gallic usurpers, such as Constantine III in 407 and Jovinus in 411, who offered inhabitants at least the hope of protection and order that the imperial court in Italy seemed unable to provide.[2]

These traumatic events threw the aristocracy and the church of southern Gaul into disarray and tested their loyalty to the Italian court and to Rome in a fashion

---

1. On the status of the Goths thus settled see Heather, *Goths and Romans*, 221–22.

2. I summarize here, for example, Matthews, *Western Aristocracies*, 307–28; Heather, *Goths and Romans*, 213–24; J. Harries, *Sidonius Apollinaris and the Fall of Rome* (Oxford, 1994), 57–67.

that became typical of the decades ahead. Some, like Sidonius Apollinaris's grandfather, who became Constantine's III's praetorian prefect,[3] and Proculus, bishop of Marseilles,[4] allied themselves with the usurping regimes; others leaned toward accommodation of sorts with the Germans, like that Ingenius whose house provided the setting for the marriage of Athaulf and Placidia. Still others sought refuge in retreat; it is not purely coincidental that the monastery founded by Honoratus on the small island of Lerino sometime between 400 and 410 became a haven for aristocratic ascetics in these troubled years.[5] At Nola Paulinus may have been safely removed from the scene of these events, but his friends at Bordeaux and elsewhere were not. Indeed, another Paulinus, the grandson of Ausonius, briefly but with little enthusiasm served the regime of Athaulf and Prisus as *comes rei privatae*, only to see his Bordelais property sacked by the Visigoths and his life turned topsy-turvy.[6]

In hindsight it is possible to think that between 406 and 418, Roman Gaul ceased to exist;[7] more optimistically, the history of Gaul after 418 became regional history.[8] Communication and travel between Gaul and Italy were certainly severely hampered.[9] Moreover, as the Gallo-Roman elite turned inward, the imperial court at Ravenna also increasingly narrowed its field of vision. Paulinus's corpus reflects these changes in small but telling ways. With Italy threatened by Alaric and Radagaisus, Paulinus had used the *natalicia* of 402 and 407 to bolster courage and proclaim victory, but Gaul went unmentioned.[10] Indeed, Paulinus's extant correspondence with friends in Gaul, so rich for the late 390s and the opening years of the fifth century, dries to a trickle by 405.[11] But despite the hardships abroad and the Gothic attack on Nola in 410, Paulinus remained active in ecclesiastical affairs. Moreover, Paulinus's name remained as potent within the ranks of Gaul's asceticizing aristocrats as it did among the clergy of North Africa. But in 419 Paulinus's hard-won connections with the political and ecclesiastical elite of Italy merged with his prestige in the provinces to recommend him to an imperial

3. Harries, *Sidonius Apollinaris*, 27–32. And *perhaps* Paulinus's correspondent Jovius; see *PLRE* 2:622, "Jovius 1." R. Mathisen, *Ecclesiastical Factionalism and Religious Controversy in Fifth–Century Gaul* (Washington, D.C., 1989), 27–28, may be overconfident on the identification.

4. Mathisen, *Ecclesiastical Factionalism*, 28–31.

5. Mathisen, *Ecclesiastical Factionalism*, 82–83.

6. Paul. *Euch.* 286–90, with Matthews, *Western Aristocracies*, 324–25. On Paulinus's career and the context of the poem's composition see N. McLynn, "Paulinus the Impenitent: A Study of the *Eucharisticos*," *JECS* 3 (1995): 461–86.

7. J. F. Drinkwater, "The Bacaudae of Fifth-Century Gaul," in *Fifth-Century Gaul: A Crisis of Identity?* ed. J. F. Drinkwater and H. Elton (Cambridge, 1992), 216.

8. Matthews, *Western Aristocracies*, 321.

9. R. Mathisen, *Roman Aristocrats in Barbarian Gaul* (Austin, 1993), 22–24.

10. See chapter 5.

11. Only *ep.* 43 to the Aquitanian Desiderius (probably of 406) and *ep.* 51 to Eucherius (on the date, see next section) postdate 405.

court desperately seeking a way to resolve a violent papal schism. So far had Paulinus traveled since renouncing the world a quarter-century earlier.

ROME, RAVENNA, AND PAPAL SCHISM

On 26 December 418, only two days after he had assumed office as *praefectus urbi*, Aurelius Anicius Symmachus faced an administrative crisis of daunting proportion. The death that day of Zosimus, the long-ailing bishop of Rome who had given a sympathetic hearing to Caelestius and Pelagius, prompted a scramble for power among the capital's ecclesiastical factions that on several occasions in the months ahead would erupt in rioting and bloodshed. Symmachus's immediate attempts to forestall trouble went unheeded. Despite a cautionary *allocutio* delivered to the people, calculated threats to the *maiores* of the urban regions, and a frank conference with the city's presbyters, three days after Zosimus's death, on 29 December, two rival bishops were ordained in different parts of the city. In a *relatio* written that same day, Symmachus, favoring the claim of the archdeacon Eulalius over that of the priest Boniface, referred the matter of the disputed papal election to Honorius in Ravenna. So the emperor, who had just extricated himself from the latest phase of the Pelagian controversy, became entangled in yet another unsavory ecclesiastical affair. Shortly thereafter the dispute also impinged on the life of Nola's septuagenarian bishop.[12]

Paulinus's involvement began only after Honorius failed in his first efforts to resolve the matter. Symmachus's *relatio* of 29 December, as well perhaps as the advice of the Patrician Constantius and his wife, the emperor's half-sister, Galla Placidia,[13] induced Honorius initially to champion Eulalius and to exile Boniface from Rome, but the prefect's report was immediately undercut by an appeal to Honorius from Boniface's advocates. Contradicting Symmachus's assertion that Eulalius was supported by the majority of the clergy, they presented their own version of the events of late December. Eulalius, Boniface's supporters claimed, was a usurper who had crept into another's place by force and *ambitus*, while Boniface, approved by acclamation and by the *consensus meliorum civitatis*—a phrase surely de-

---

12. The affair in question is well documented by the letters and rescripts of *Collectio Avellana* 14–37 (*CSEL* 35, pp. 59–84), with *Lib. Pont.* 44. See E. Caspar, *Geschichte des Papsttums von den Anfängen bis zur Höhe der Weltherrschaft* (Tübingen, 1930), 1:360–64; G. Bardy, *Histoire de l'église; De la mort de Théodose à l'élection de Grégoire le Grand*, ed. P. de Labriolle, G. Bardy, G. de Plinval, and L. Brehier (Paris, 1937), 251–53; Chastagnol, *Les fastes*, 279–81, and *La préfecture urbaine*, 172–76; S. I. Oost, *Galla Placidia Augusta* (Chicago, 1968), 156–61, 167–68; Pietri, *Roma christiana*, 452–60, 948–50; S. Cristo, "Some Notes on the Bonifacian-Eulalian Schism," *Aevum* 51 (1977): 163–67. Symmachus's *relatio* of 29 December is *Coll. Avell.* 14.

13. So Oost, *Galla Placidia*, 158 and 167, and Cristo, "Some Notes," 164–65; but see the reservations of Pietri, *Roma christiana*, 459. For the wider factional background see also Mathisen, *Ecclesiastical Factionalism*, 61.

signed to capture the emperor's eye—had been consecrated in the presence of some seventy priests and nine bishops. So, on 15 January 419, a confused Honorius rescinded his previous announcement in favor of Eulalius and summoned the contenders to a hearing at court. By mid-February, as disturbances continued at Rome, Honorius had passed the matter on to a synod of Italian bishops gathered at Ravenna, who in turn failed to resolve the dispute. As the potentially volatile Easter holy days approached, emperor and synod determined to banish both Eulalius and Boniface from Rome until a larger synod could consider the case. To this end a rescript of 15 March informed the prefect Symmachus that Achilleus, bishop of Spoleto, would perform the Easter services in Rome. In the meantime the bishops of Italy, Gaul, and Africa, including Augustine and Alypius, were invited to convene at Spoleto on 13 June 419.[14]

Paulinus had declined attendance at the midwinter synod at Ravenna. The difficult journey would have severely taxed his health.[15] As the schism widened, however, the imperial court renewed its efforts to enlist his influence and leadership for the Spoleto meeting. An adulatory imperial letter of 20 March, perhaps bearing the hand of the willful Galla Placidia—whom Paulinus could have met in 410 when the Visigoths, holding Placidia captive, ravaged Nola—explicitly, if somewhat disingenuously, credited the failure of the Ravenna synod to Paulinus's absence.[16] Consequently, judgment had been deferred, the letter announced in the grandiloquent language of the imperial chancery, so that Paulinus's mouth might disclose the divine precepts, for no one was more suitable for this responsibility than Paulinus, worthy disciple of the Apostle. "And so," the letter concluded, "holy lord, father venerable in merit, just servant of God, disdaining the labor, concede this divine work and grant us the service (*munus*), if it must be so called, of your attendance, so that, with all else set aside, and as the tranquillity of the temperate weather favors, you may deign to preside over the synod without interruption and to fulfill both our wishes and the blessing we desire."[17]

14. *Coll. Avell.* 15–26. On the order given to both Eulalius and Boniface to leave Rome see also *Coll. Avell.* 31.1 and *Lib. Pont.* 44.

15. *Coll. Avell.* 25.1: "cum beatitudo tua de corporis inaequalitate causata itineris non potuerit inuriam sustinere."

16. Almost certainly *Coll. Avell.* 27 to Aurelius of Carthage and *Coll. Avell.* 28 to Augustine, Alypius, and five other African bishops were sent under the name of Placidia. The strong similarity in wording of *Coll. Avell.* 25 to Paulinus ties this letter closely to the other two. On the question of authorship see Oost, *Galla Placidia,* 158–59, 167–68, with earlier bibliography. Cristo, "Some Notes," 165, also posits a meeting of Galla Placidia and Paulinus in 410.

17. *Coll. Avell.* 25.2–3: "dilatum itaque iudicium nuntiamus, ut divina praecepta ex venerationis tuae ore promantur. . . . nec potest alius eorum praeceptorum lator existere, quam qui dignus apostoli discipulus approbaris specialiter. itaque domine sancte, merito venerabilis pater, iustus dei famulus, divinum opus contempto labore tributurus hoc nobis visitationis tuae, si ita dicendum est, munus indulge, ut postpositis omnibus, quoniam temperati aeris tranquillitas suffragatur, synodo praefuturus sine intermissione etiam desideriis nostris et benedictioni, quam cupimus, te praestare digneris."

As matters turned out, Paulinus was deprived of the opportunity of honoring this imperial *desiderium*. The rash actions of Eulalius, set in motion even before the letter to Paulinus had left the imperial secretariat, made the Spoleto synod unnecessary. On 18 March 419, contravening the Ravenna synod's decision and the accompanying imperial command, Eulalius entered Rome and soon seized the Lateran basilica. Three days later, when Achilleus arrived in the city, such intense rioting broke out in the Forum between the supporters of Eulalius and those of Boniface that Symmachus and the *vicarius,* who had ventured to the Forum of Vespasian in an attempt to restore peace, preserved their lives only by effecting a hasty retreat. On Sunday, 23 March, Symmachus reported the situation to the *comes* Constantius, Honorius's virtual coregent by 419, requesting a ruling before Easter, only one week away. On Good Friday the *cancellarius* Vitulus delivered the strident imperial response: Eulalius was once again commanded to comply with the imperial *praeceptum* and the synodical *ordinatio* and leave the city. Further obstinacy would elicit severe punishment. Warned immediately by Symmachus, Eulalius nonetheless refused to abandon the Lateran. The next day, Saturday, he was expelled by force and removed form the city. On Easter Sunday Achilleus celebrated services.[18]

Eulalius's final *usurpatio* had tested the limits of imperial *clementia;* a rescript dated 3 April recognized Boniface as bishop of Rome. On 10 April, according to Symmachus's report, Boniface entered the city amid widespread rejoicing. After four months of disruption, order had been restored.[19] Symmachus had weathered the storm and would retain his urban prefecture at least until January 420, when he dedicated a statue to Constantius—"restorer of the *res publica* and kinsman of the unvanquished *principes*"—in honor of the Patrician's third consulship.[20] Constantius himself, elevated to the rank of Augustus in early 421, died later that year, followed by Boniface in 422[21] and Honorius in 423. Paulinus, summoned back to the center of imperial and ecclesiastical politics in Italy, outlived them all by nearly a decade.

The events of late 418 and early 419 are not without their historical lessons and their ironies. The Christian riots and besieged basilicas of those months reprised on a larger scale the bloody rivalry of Damasus and Ursinus a half-century earlier.[22] But, as one modern observer has pointed out, the greater disruption wrought by this contested papal election, which engaged the passions of the whole city, including the senatorial elite both as individuals and as a corporate body, is striking evidence for the changed character of political life at Rome by 418.[23] Dur-

---

18. *Coll. Avell.* 29–32.
19. *Coll. Avell.* 33–34.
20. *CIL* 6.1791 = *ILS* 801.
21. F. Caraffa, "Bonifacio I," *Bibliotheca Sanctorum* (Rome, 1963), 3:328–30.
22. Amm. Mar. 27.3.11–14.
23. Pietri, *Roma christiana,* 458–60. *Coll. Avell* 23 is an imperial *oratio ad senatum*.

ing Paulinus's life, the politics of the city of Rome had become virtually indistinguishable from the politics of the Roman church. Thus it is not merely a curious twist of fate, but a signal of the deeper currents of historical flow, that the newly appointed urban prefect of December 418, who found himself trying to adjudicate a messy papal election and restore order to a city torn by the riots of opposing Christian factions, was the nephew of the author of the now-famous third *relatio*.[24] If the better-known Q. Aurelius Symmachus, urban prefect some thirty-five years earlier, had been openly pagan and an advocate of toleration for the traditional religion, his nephew was not only most likely a Christian[25] but apparently also an active ally and agent of one of the episcopal contenders, the aristocratically backed Eulalius, against the more populist Boniface, whose support arose from the ranks of the city's presbyters.[26]

But the social and political dimensions of this Roman affair are also revealing of the problems faced by the imperial administration in the West. At a time when external threats demanded inner cohesion and order, the confusion, reversals, and indecision at the court of Honorius, perhaps exacerbated by favoritism and power struggles,[27] testify to the seriousness of the internal distractions and disunity that ecclesiastical competition was capable of generating. Indeed, it is telling that Constantius, who had been such a vital imperial agent of "determination and vigor" against the usurper Constantine in 411,[28] had successfully dabbled in ecclesiastical politics in southern Gaul by installing Patroclus as bishop of the vital see of Arles,[29] and had overseen the Visigothic settlement in Aquitaine in 418, was so abruptly and ineffectively pulled into the vortex of ecclesiastical politics in Italy the very next year. Moreover, the ultimate failure of Constantius's candidate, Eulalius, may further have undermined Patroclus of Arles's already contested claim to the extraordinary metropolitan rights he had received from Pope Zosimus, surely with the cooperation of Constantius.[30] Indeed, it may be precisely the "interprovincial" implications of the papal schism of 418–19 that led the imperial court eventually to enlist the prestige of Paulinus in an effort to bring the affair to an end.

The reports and orders that flew between Rome and Ravenna sketch a context notably reminiscent of Paulinus's earlier political life and one quite distinct from the private world of his letters. The choice of Paulinus to preside over the Spoleto synod suggests, of course, that some figures at the imperial court perceived him to

24. On the relationship see Chastagnol, *Les fastes*, 279–80; *PLRE* 2:1043, "Symmachus 6."

25. Chastagnol, *La préfecture urbaine*, 175.

26. Pietri, *Roma christiana*, 456–58.

27. For the argument that Galla Placidia favored Eulalius over Boniface see Oost, *Galla Placidia*, 167–68, contra Bardy, *Histoire de l'église*, 252–53, and Chastagnol, *La préfecture urbaine*, 175.

28. Matthews, *Western Aristocracies*, 312–19.

29. Mathisen, *Ecclesiastical Factionalism*, 35–36.

30. Mathisen, *Ecclesiastical Factionalism*, 48–61.

be the leading bishop in Italy after the pope.[31] It is less likely that Honorius's or Placidia's choice of Paulinus was dictated by a sincere belief that his "disdain of worldly goods" placed him above factional ambitions.[32] Rather, Paulinus should have been offered this honor because of the extensive reach and longevity of his friendships and because of the respect his name commanded in Italy and the western provinces. Few if any Italian bishops in 418 could match Paulinus's connections in Gaul and Africa, two provinces whose bishops had been invited to Spoleto and two provinces recently given good reason by Zosimus to be apprehensive of papal ambitions and therefore interested in the choice of Zosimus's successor.[33] Nor, as we have seen, had Paulinus's prestige and claims among the Roman aristocracy withered despite his absence. Indeed, Paulinus might well have been acquainted with Symmachus, the current urban prefect, a member of a family with whom Paulinus had probably once and perhaps still had connections. Moreover, Paulinus had earned a reputation for conciliation and neutrality in controversy and had shown his willingness to exploit the obligations of *amicitia* to resolve other disputes, as, for example, when he intervened in the legal dispute between the *navicularius* Secundinianus and the senator Postumianus.

But if Paulinus's status and reputation recommended him for the role of mediator at Spoleto, his claim to rank among the leading bishops of Italy and to preside over a synod to settle a disputed papal election was paradoxically conditioned and fortified by his decision some twenty-five years earlier to forsake the "cares of this world."[34] The path back to political, that is ecclesiastical, authority for Paulinus led through secular renunciation—a path he may not have anticipated in the mid-390s, but one whose track was to become increasingly well worn by others as the fifth century advanced, particularly in southern Gaul, where Paulinus's name and example retained their magnetism.

LÉRINS

Sometime about 420,[35] a group of young men traveled from southern Gaul to call on Paulinus at Nola. They had been sent to Italy by Eucherius, the future bishop

31. Fabre, *Paulin de Nole*, 48.

32. So Buse, *Paulin*, 553.

33. On Zosimus's interventions see Mathisen, *Ecclesiastical Factionalism*, 44–60, noting in passing Paulinus's relationships with Gallic clergy known for appealing outside the province (47); Merdinger, *Rome and the African Church*, for example, 113–120 on the case of Apiarius.

34. *Ep.* 18.9.

35. The key piece of chronological information is Paulinus's *ep.* 51. Fabre, *Essai*, 87–88, dates this letter between 423 and 426. Pricoco, *L'isola dei santi:*, 36–37, argued that these dates were too narrow to be supported by the evidence. Fabre held that Eucherius did not establish himself at Lero until ca. 422, but this date is unproven. Pricoco placed Eucherius's arrival at Lerino, where he spent some time prior to relocating to Lero, between 412 and 420. Fabre's *terminus ante quem* of 426 was based on the fact that Paulinus referred to Honoratus as *conpresbyter* (51.1), which would place the letter before Honora-

of Lyon, who was then residing on the island of Lero, off the coast of Provence.[36] From these couriers, and presumably from the letter they carried, Paulinus learned how Eucherius, fleeing from "the din of the world," had taken up the monastic *propositum*.[37] Paulinus also heard from these men about the monastic community founded by Honoratus, the future bishop of Arles, on the neighboring island of Lerino.[38] Eucherius's Lerinian couriers had established a Nolan connection destined to continue, for the next year Paulinus received another delegation of three *filii et conservi*, Gelasius, Augendus, and Tigridius, this time sent by Honoratus himself. On their leave to return to Lerino, Paulinus also entrusted them with a letter to Eucherius and his wife Galla, both still residing on Lero near Honoratus. Of this known correspondence between Nola and the monks of Lérins, and the epistolary exchanges that probably followed, only this second letter from Paulinus to Eucherius and Galla survives.[39] Its fortuitous preservation testifies to the continuity of Paulinus's links with Gallic ascetic circles in a way that complements his association with Severus's more distant monastic center at Primuliacum and extends it beyond the years documented by his letters to Severus.

Paulinus's extant letter to Eucherius fulfilled with grace and sensitivity the protocols of *amicitia* become Christian. Now a bishop, Paulinus painstakingly established his humility before Eucherius while warmly praising the beneficence of a God who fulfills the *vota* of men. Paulinus expressed his concern for the good health of Eucherius and offered his brief letter as a token of affection (*caritas*) and a testimony of his heart (*animus*) and love (*amor*),[40] while he reassured his aristocratic correspondents that they were bound to him not by mere *humana amicitia*, but by a *divina gratia* that left him no less desirous of a letter in return.[41] Paulinus's

tus's elevation to the bishopric of Arles. Fabre understood the latter event to have occurred in 426. See also Duchesne, *Fastes,* 1:110, 249. More recent arguments, accepted by Pricoco, *L'isola dei santi,* 36, date Honoratus's move to Arles to late 427 or early 428. The approximate date of 415 for the *terminus post quem* is based on two facts: Eucherius spent some time at Lerino before moving to Lero, and he had been at Lero for at least a year when Paulinus wrote *ep.* 51 (51.2). Thus *ep.* 51 could date between 415 and 428.

36. *Ep.* 51.2.

37. *ep.* 51.2: "ab istius mundi strepitu profugam."

38. Lero (Ste.-Marguerite) and Lerino (St.-Honorat) together form Lérins. Honoratus established the monastic community on the smaller island, Lerino, between 400 and 410, and it quickly became a center of learning and a training ground for bishops. See, for example, the succinct article by H. Leclerq, "Lérins," *DACL* 8.2, 2596–2627. The more recent and thorough study of the early history of the community by Pricoco, *L'isola dei santi,* esp. 25–59, supplies some necessary corrections of detail, particularly on chronological matters. See also, Mathisen, *Ecclesiastical Factionalism,* 76–85.

39. A number of Eucherius's literary works survive, and much has been written about him. See the bibliography in Stroheker, *Der senatorische Adel,* 168, no. 120; Pricoco, *L'isola dei santi,* 44; and *Patrology* 4:504–7. See also *PLRE* 2, "Eucherius 3."

40. *Ep.* 51.2.

41. *Ep.* 51.3.

richly nuanced discourse reveals both his knowledge of Eucherius's life and his sympathy for the ascetic and literary culture already forming at Lérins, which in many ways were reminiscent of Paulinus's own background.

Eucherius was younger than Paulinus, perhaps by a generation, but in outline at least his life strikingly reprises that of his older contemporary. Of aristocratic family, Eucherius had been moved to renounce the world in favor of the "desert" of Lerino.[42] Arriving at the small island with his wife Galla and two young sons sometime between 412 and 420, he joined the monastic community presided over by Honoratus.[43] A plan to travel to Egypt never materialized, and after some time with Honoratus, Eucherius relocated to the neighboring island of Lero. While there Eucherius wrote, corresponded, began or continued his reading of Augustine, Jerome, Rufinus, Ambrose, and Lactantius,[44] and saw to the education of his sons. During these years he initiated contact with the expatriated Paulinus and eventually composed, among other works, the two extant treatises, *De laude eremi* and *De contemptu mundi*, eloquent testimonies to the ideals of those who withdrew to Lerino and Lero in those years.[45] Eucherius himself became a figure of increasing eminence in southern Gaul. At about the same time that Paulinus wrote *ep.* 51 to him, Cassian dedicated the second part of his *Conferences* to Eucherius.[46] And after 430, but before 441, Eucherius's prestige issued in a summons to the episcopal chair of Lyon, which he occupied until his death about the year 450.[47]

---

42. The following sketch is based largely on that of Pricoco, *L'isola dei santi*, 44–48. Full documentation is included there. Eucherius himself equates Lerino with the desert at *De laude eremi* 42, ed. S. Pricoco (Catania, 1965): "Equidem cunctis heremi locis quae piorum illuminantur secussu, reverentiam debeo, praecipuo tamen Lirinum meam honore complector." He continues, however, by noting: "aquis scatens, herbis virens, floribus renitens, visibus odoribusque iucunda paradisum possidentibus se exhibet" (42).

43. For a review of the social and political context in which Lérins should be placed—"era una crisi di potere e di ruolo sociale, alle quale si accompagnava una crisi di valori" (62)—a crisis that surely influenced Eucherius's decision to come there, see Pricoco, *L'isola dei santi*, 61–69.

44. P. Courcelle, "Nouveaux aspects de la culture lérinienne," *Revue des études latines* 46 (1968): 379–409.

45. The former is the earlier and dates to late 427 or early 428. On the date and for an analysis of the piece see Pricoco, *L'isola dei santi*, 154–64. The *De contemptu mundi* (*PL* 50, 711–26 and now Pricoco, *Il rifiuto del mondo*), can be dated between 430 and 432. See Pricoco, *L'isola dei santi*, 144–45.

46. See the preface to *Conference* 11. The second series of *Conferences* (11–17) was dedicated to Honoratus and Eucherius when Honoratus was still at Lerino. When the third series was dedicated shortly thereafter, however, Honoratus was bishop of Arles. See E. Pichery's introduction to *SC* 42 (Paris, 1955). As Pichery dated Honoratus's move to Arles to 426, he placed the composition of the second and third series of conferences in that year. See *SC* 42, 28–29. Following the dating preferred by Pricoco and followed here, they would have been dedicated in 427.

47. Eucherius was still at Lero when he wrote the *De contemptu mundi* between 430 and 432 but was bishop of Lyon when he participated in the council of Orange in 441. Eucherius was only one of many in this period who left Lérins to assume an episcopal see. See Pricoco, *L'isola dei santi*, 66, and the prosopographical sketches, 40–59.

In the 420s, however, the elder and established Paulinus offered the emerging Eucherius a vital point of contact beyond the still parochial literary and ascetic circles of Lérins[48] and perhaps also served as an influential patron in Honoratus's own confrontations with the local ecclesiastical establishment.[49] For from the perspective of the new ascetics of southern Gaul, Paulinus was a success. The Gallic side of Paulinus's life had been regularly complemented by the very kind of Roman accolades that persistently fascinated and attracted the Gallo-Roman elite. As a younger man, Paulinus had seen his Bordeaux background enriched by an Italian governorship; now the septuagenarian Paulinus, many years after Severus's *vita Martini* had enshrined him as the ascetic friend of Tours's holy Martin, was a leading bishop of Italy. Moreover, the monastery at Nola was a clearinghouse on the road to the North Africa of Augustine, whose name remained powerful in Gaul even if his predestinarian theories were beginning to divide the monks and clergy of southern Gaul.[50]

It may, however, have been the deeper rhythms of Paulinus's story, with their subtle modulations between the private and the public, the intimate and the spectacular, that attracted Eucherius and Honoratus. Paulinus's claim on the contemporary imagination, and thus the late Roman mind and the public authority it conceded to designated individuals, arose from the same complex attitudes toward secular renunciation that animated the monks of Lérins. Several of them, beginning with Honoratus about 427, were soon to be propelled along the trajectory from the monastery to the episcopal cathedra; and more were to follow.[51] For such men, whose move away from the "din of the world" was temporary at best, the dramatic tale of Paulinus's own secular renunciation possessed immeasurable apologetic value. Thus when Eucherius, the "founder" of Lerinian discourse,[52] penned his *De contemptu mundi*, ostensibly to exhort the ascetic conversion of a high-ranking kinsman named Valerianus,[53] his treatise gave privileged place to "Paulinus, bishop of Nola, a special and blessed example from our Gaul." Rich and eloquent, as Eucherius dutifully reminded Valerianus (and his wider Gallic

48. R. Mathisen, "Epistolography, Literary Circles and Family Ties in Late Roman Gaul," *TAPA* 111 (1981): 95–109, esp. 104–8 on the circumscribed orbit of Lérins.

49. On Honoratus's quarrels see Mathisen, *Ecclesiastical Factionalism*, 77.

50. See, for example, Mathisen, *Ecclesiastical Factionalism*, 122–25.

51. On Eucherius's sons Salonius, bishop of Genava (Geneva) at least by 439, and Veranus, bishop perhaps of Vintium (Vence), for example, see: Stroheker, *Der senatorische Adel*, 213, no. 341, and 226, no. 406; Pricoco, *L'isola dei santi*, 46–48; *PLRE* 2, "Salonius 2" and "Veranius"; and *Patrology* 4: 527–28, all with further bibliography. Salonius's episcopate certainly overlapped that of his father, for they both attended the council of Orange in 441. It is possible, however, that Veranus became bishop only after Eucherius's death. For more examples see Mathisen, *Ecclesiastical Factionalism*, 85–92.

52. M. Vessey, "Eucherian (E)utopics: Place, Text, and Community in the Discourse of Lérins," paper delivered at the Annual Meeting of the North American Patristic Society, May 1993.

53. Both Valerianus's kinship with Eucherius and his high birth are signaled by the opening section of *De contemptu mundi* (*PL* 50. 711–712D): "Bene alligantur vinculo sanguinis, qui vinculo consociantur

readership), Paulinus brought himself to our *propositum* and subsequently scattered his speech and his deeds throughout the whole world.[54] Eucherius's text, it has been pointed out, now implicitly offered the same ecumenical ascetic glory to all Gallo-Roman readers, not just Valerianus, who might seek to occupy the "space of Christian fame" that the *De contemptu mundi* had fashioned for the "local hero" Paulinus.[55] Also implicitly, of course, Eucherius shouldered his way into that same space, for he spoke here as one already deeply committed.

Eucherius's *De contemptu mundi* is eloquent witness to the continuing attraction and utility of Paulinus's name in Gaul. It is also but one of a series of Gallic representations of Paulinus that, like Paulinus's portrait in Severus's baptistry at Primuliacum, established him as an iconic *exemplum* in his former homeland. Among Gallo-Roman writers this process of canonization now twists and turns through Julianus Pomerius, who in the later fifth century praised both Paulinus's renunciation of private wealth and his episcopal administration of ecclesiastical resources,[56] to Gennadius of Marseilles, who knew Eucherius's *De contemptu mundi* as well as various works of Paulinus,[57] and on to Gregory of Tours, who in the later sixth century was familiar with Paulinus's *natalicia* and had read a "long account" of his death (*transitus*), surely that composed by the Nolan presbyter Uranius.[58] As he composed his entry on Paulinus for his *De gloria confessorum*, Gregory further acknowledged that he had read no life of Paulinus but had listened to an account (*relatio*) of trustworthy men. It may be, however, that a *vita Paulini*, one written in verse, loomed somewhere behind that *relatio* and, perhaps, more generally behind the reputation of Paulinus in fifth- and sixth-century Gaul.

---

amoris. . . . Quamvis autem in maximos saeculi apices patre soceroque elatus illustribus ex utroque titulis ambiaris." Valerianus's father and father-in-law are unidentified. Stroheker, *Der senatorische Adel*, 225, no. 400, tentatively identified Eucherius's Valerianus with Priscus Valerianus, praetorian prefect under Avitus in 455–56. *PLRE* 2, "Valerianus 8," makes the identification without reservation but also without adequate explanation. The attempt of J.-P. Weiss, "La personnalité de Valerien de Cimiez," *Annales de la faculté des lettres et sciences humaines de Nice* 11 (1970): 160–62, to identify Eucherius's relative with Valerianus, bishop of Cemenelum (Cimiez) in the mid-fifth century is not fully convincing though accepted by R. Mathisen in "Petronius, Hilarius and Valerianus: Prosopographical Notes on the Conversion of the Roman Aristocracy," *Historia* 30 (1981): 106–12.

54. *PL* 50.718D–719A.

55. Vessey, "Eucherian (E)utopics."

56. *De vita comtemplativa* 2.9.1 (*PL* 59.453B–C).

57. *De vir. ill.* 64 (Eucherius) and 49 (Paulinus).

58. *Carm.* 15, 16, 18, and 23 inform Gregory's account of Felix at *De gloria martyrum* 103, but it is possible Gregory had to hand a synopsis rather than the poems themselves. For Gregory's *vita* of Paulinus see *De gloria confessorum* 108, in which he notes his possession of an account (*magna lectio*) of Paulinus's death (11). The identification with Uranius is also noted by Van Dam, *Gregory of Tours: Glory of the Confessors*, 110. Another candidate for this list of citations is Sidonius, *ep.* 4.3.7. Eutropius's *De contemnenda haereditate* (with *Paulinus noster* as an example) is early, ca. 400 (*PL* 30.48C).

DE OBITU

Paulinus died at Nola "about the fifth hour of the night" ten days before the Calends of July during the consulship of Bassus and Antiochus (22 June 431).[59] He was nearly eighty and severely ill. Several days before his passing, he was heard to call loudly for his "brothers" Martin of Tours and Januarius, Neapolitan martyr. Assured of their presence, he was at last "summoned from this body into the heavenly dwelling"[60] and joined the community of the saints. Not a year had passed on earth before Paulinus had returned to summon heavenward in turn the soul of John, bishop of neighboring Naples and recent impresario of the cult of Januarius. On the Thursday before Easter in 432, John reported that Paulinus had appeared to him "dressed in angelic dignity and completely distinguished in starry whiteness and resplendent with ambrosian odor." In his hand Paulinus had held a glistening honeycomb; he embraced John, placing some of the sweet, fragrant honey in his mouth. Two days later, on Saturday, John "breathed out his spirit" and heeded Paulinus's paradisiacal summons. The next day, Easter Sunday, 3 April 432, following a night vigil in the church, John was given a "glorious and praiseworthy burial."[61]

Just as Paulinus had assured others that death had no power over the tomb of Felix, the text that offered this story of Paulinus's epiphany at Naples offered similar assurance.[62] The church, it was duly noted, may have been weeping, but Paradise rejoiced to receive one so holy.[63] Indeed, the story of Paulinus's mystical visit to John of Naples subtly reinforced a claim that Paulinus himself had once made for Felix. As Felix's death had not deprived Nola of a beloved priest but secured her a heavenly patron, so on 22 June 431 Nola had not lost her bishop but acquired another friend in the halls of Christ.[64] Such a monumental passing as that signaled by Paulinus's death, ascension, and assumption of "angelic dignity" necessarily was registered on earth in more than just the tears of the church. Thus those gathered at Paulinus's bedside felt the earth shake at the very moment of his passing.[65]

To some in attendance, however, that tremor may also have portended the subtle displacement of Saint Felix that Paulinus's heavenly ascension ultimately brought about. Paulinus's visage, so familiar after thirty-six years at Nola, was more vivid than that of the ancient confessor Felix, which Paulinus himself had verbally sketched with such devoted attention; and the proof of Paulinus's *auctoritas* and prestige, as well as his *caritas,* was, of course, strikingly fresh and vital. He

59. *De obitu* 4, 12. A full translation is offered in appendix D.
60. *De obitu* 3, 8.
61. *De obitu* 11.
62. Cp. Sul. Sev. *ep.* 2, Martin's appearance to Severus.
63. *De obitu* 5.
64. Cp. Paul. *carm.* 18.102–12 on Felix.
65. *De obitu* 4.

who had enjoyed such intimate friendship with the saints while on earth, had exerted such tireless energy to succor and protect the poor, and had been so capable of working his influence at Ravenna as well as Rome would surely not be idle in the celestial halls of power. Ironically, it was a guarantee that reverberated back to Paulinus himself, for during his long residence at Nola as impresario of Felix, he had cast and refined the very religious, intellectual, and social structures that now gave meaning to his own death and allowed him to continue his patronal role from above. But, like the cults of Martin, Felix, and many other *sancti*,[66] the future of the cult of Paulinus at Nola hinged on the cooperation of Paulinus's episcopal successors, while his reputation in the wider Christian world depended equally on the literary endeavors of those he left behind.

It may have been with some such understanding that Uranius, a presbyter at Nola,[67] took on the daunting task of writing down the account of Paulinus's death cited above, for his report is equally a *laudatio funebris*, relating and illustrating the virtues Uranius deemed characteristic of Paulinus's entire Christian life.[68] But the sweep of Uranius's text from narrative to eulogy may also have been inspired by the opportunity for promotion offered by the circumstances that spurred him to undertake its composition, for Uranius's *De obitu Sancti Paulini* was designated grist for another's literary mill. Uranius's preface credits the origin of his short work to a request for information about Paulinus's passing that came to Nola from a certain *dominus illustris* named Pacatus. Pacatus was gathering material in order to compose a *vita Paulini* in verse.[69] The name and the aim tantalize. Although Pacatus's identity and provenance remain uncertain, there is good reason to suspect that he spent time in Aquitaine. Although Pacatus was surely not the Aquitanian orator Latinius Pacatus Drepanius—panegyrist of Theodosius in 389, *proconsul Africae* in 390, and *comes rei privatae* in the East in 393—[70]he may have been a descendant.[71] It is also tempting to identify Uranius's Pacatus with the Claudius Iulius Pacatus who served as *consularis Campaniae* and was honored as a *patronus* by the *ordo Beneventanus* "ob aequitatem iudicis et patrocinia iam privati."[72] A former governor of Campania might be particularly interested in the remarkable story of another

66. See, for example, R. Van Dam, *Saints and Their Miracles in Late Antique Gaul* (Princeton, 1993), esp. 11–49.

67. Uranius is otherwise unknown but perhaps to be identified with the delinquent letter carrier whom Paulinus was expecting to arrive from Bordeaux in the summer of 401 (*ep.* 19.1). An Aquitanian background for Uranius would fit the possible Gallo-Roman profile of Pacatus.

68. Especially *De obitu* 5–10.

69. Uranius, *De obitu* 1, 12: "Nunc autem veniamus ad ea, quae tibi, qui vitam eius versibus illustrare disponis, dicendi materiam subministrent" (1).

70. *PLRE* 1:272, "Drepanius."

71. So Stroheker, *Der senatorische Adel*, 197. He should be added to *PLRE* 2. See Mathisen, "*PLRE* II: Suggested *Addenda* and *Corrigenda*," *Historia* 31 (1982): 380.

72. *PLRE* 1:656, "Pacatus 3."

who had once held the post and exercised authority in Campania for so long in a rather different key. Indeed, as Uranius's Pacatus had only requested an account of Paulinus's death, he may have had the prior contact with Paulinus expected of a *consularis Campaniae*. But if Pacatus's possible connections to both Gaul and Campania remain speculative, his high rank and literary aspirations are self-evident.

The motives spurring Pacatus's desire to compose a verse *vita Paulini*, like the text itself, if it was ever completed, are lost. He may well have anticipated the fame and glory that Uranius assured him would be his—[73]after all, no lesser men than Jerome and Sulpicius Severus had gained renown (as well as rebuke) in such pursuit—but no evidence suggests he found it. Again it is tempting to speculate that Pacatus's poem made some contribution, perhaps still discernible in the idiosyncratic entry of Gregory of Tours's *De gloria confessorum*, to the Gallo-Roman versions of Paulinus's *vita*.[74] Still, while Pacatus's objectives and his work remain mysterious, Uranius's *De obitu*, which Gregory apparently did possess, reveals many of its author's aims, some expected but others perhaps more suggestive of the evolving local context of Paulinus's final years.

It is not surprising, for example, to find Paulinus eulogized for the virtues that dominate his own writings and self-representations.[75] Uranius's Paulinus emerges rich in humility and love. *Pius, misercors, humilis,* and *benignus,* Paulinus cared greatly for all men but especially for the poor, the weak, and the wretched (9). Even on his deathbed he was occupied with the financial details of charity (3). Uranius also deftly underscored Paulinus's place in the Christian moral tradition by comparison with an extensive set of patriarchs and apostles (8). The spiritual economics that Paulinus had advocated since his conversion are fully reprised here as well. Gold and silver, Paulinus understood, had value only as the material for performing those redemptive acts of liberality that benefited the rich far more than they helped the poor.[76] Thus when Paulinus was first converted to Christ, Uranius recalled, "he opened his storerooms to the poor, his warehouses to those who came," and as bishop he redeemed captives, freed debtors from their creditors, and clothed and fed the poor (6).

Uranius also testifies to the position of authority and leadership Paulinus had long held at Nola and in the region. Not only Christians, but Jews and pagans as well, Uranius proclaimed to Pacatus, lamented the death of their *dominus* Paulinus. They "bewailed the *patronus, defensor,* and *tutor* snatched from them" (9). And although the angels rejoiced, the people's tears were well justified, for Paulinus had exercised compassionately and fairly his episcopal duties: "He did not wish to present himself as a bishop who was feared by anyone. But he showed himself the

73. *De obitu* 12.
74. So much in Gregory's text occurs nowhere else.
75. A correlation well documented by Pastorino, "Il *De obitu sancti Paulini*," 115–41.
76. *De obitu* 8–9.

kind of priest who would be loved by all. . . . He maintained rigor in examination of justice, yet offered compassion in the framing of the sentence" (7). Thus news of his illness brought neighboring bishops to his bedside, their visit temporarily restoring his health (2). And when he died he was surrounded by those friends who felt the earth tremble as, "taken up by angelic hands, he breathed out the spirit he owed to God" (4). He who had received the saints Januarius and Martin on the eve of his death now offered his prayers for men in heaven (6).

In this manner Uranius's text reinforced familiar images of Paulinus. Similarly Uranius recalled Pacatus and other readers to Paulinus's extensive connections to the wider Christian world. "Truly what place is there in the world," he asked, "so remote, so hidden, which the passing of Lord Paulinus did not disturb?" (5). Not only all the provinces but even the barbarian nations were witnesses to his reputation (9). But in muted contrast to these assertions of worldwide renown, the *De obitu* has a decidedly local flavor. The introduction by name of such regional bishops as Symmachus, perhaps of Capua, and Acindynus is understandable for narrative purposes,[77] but the prominence given by Uranius to Saint Januarius and John, bishop of Naples, is more surprising. Indeed, Uranius's *De obitu* is the oldest surviving literary mention of Januarius, whose name never appears in Paulinus's extant writings. Moreover, John had but recently discovered the relics of Januarius and transferred them to the catacomb of Capodimonte, now S. Gennaro, where he himself was later interred.[78] Uranius's text, therefore, appears to have a secondary motive.

Uranius's dying Paulinus remarkably calls not on Saint Felix but on the saints Januarius and Martin. It is a choice that startles the modern reader conditioned by Paulinus's *natalicia*. Whatever Uranius's text may say about the political relationship between the church of Nola and that of Naples, the prominence its author gave to Saint Januarius and Bishop John must express a desire to bolster the status of this new Neapolitan cult by tying both the saint and his *inventor* to Paulinus.[79] If so, then Uranius presumably anticipated a Neapolitan audience for his text.[80] But promoting the stock of John and Januarius need not have entailed excising, as Uranius does, that of Felix.

It is impossible now to understand satisfactorily the abrupt reversal of expectations embodied in Paulinus's deathbed negligence of his heavenly *comes*, Felix. Only the view back through the glow of Paulinus's own subsequent success as a

77. On Symmachus see F. Lanzoni, *Le diocesi d'Italia* (Faenza, 1927), 1:102; *PL* 53.859–60.

78. See notices and bibliography at Saxer, "Januarius and Companions"; Zincone, "John I of Naples"; L. Pani Ermini, "Naples, Archaeology" in *Encyclopedia of the Early Church* (Oxford, 1992), 1:430, 1:438, 2:581.

79. Alternatively, Uranius may have been seeking to subordinate Januarius and John, but this could surely have been done more effectively either through silence or by introducing Felix.

80. Perhaps strengthening the possible Campanian ties of Pacatus if the Neapolitan leaning was induced by his interests.

saint at Nola suggests how Uranius's text may foreshadow Felix's fortunes in the aftermath of Paulinus's death. Fittingly enough, Paulinus's body was immediately laid to rest beside the tomb of Felix (figure 1c).[81] As the fifth century rolled into the sixth, to the tombs of Felix and Paulinus were added the tombs of Nola's successive bishops: Paulinus II (442), Felix (484), Theodosius (490), and Priscus (523).[82] About 500 a single altar and a surrounding mosaic-encrusted aedicula were erected over and around the tombs.[83] Then, at some point in the Middle Ages, Felix's remains may have been translated to an altar behind the original one.[84] In any case, when a Lombard prince of Beneventum was gathering relics in the late eighth or early ninth century, it was Paulinus whom he translated back to his capital.[85] Long before then, however, Paulinus's passing had given Nola a new and formidable heavenly patron, one whose renown soon rivaled the veneration he himself had bestowed on Felix.

News of Paulinus's failing health had brought a number of Campanian clergy to his bedside in the days before his death. His own cry, Uranius assures us, had summoned Martin and Januarius. When at last he was "taken up by angelic hands," he was surrounded by intimate friends, and his funerary rites were celebrated by pagans as well as Jews. Whatever the future might hold, the final images of Paulinus that Uranius offered to Pacatus, placing the dying bishop in the company of other bishops, saints, monks, and rustics, weave together the distinctive strands of the complex public life Paulinus had fashioned and refashioned since arriving at Nola in 395.

---

81. Uranius, *De obitu* 2.

82. Lehmann, "Lo sviluppo," 83; *CIL* 10.1340, 1344, 1345, and 1348.

83. Lehmann, "Lo sviluppo," 83–84; Lehmann, "Eine spätantike Inschriftensammlung," 246–55; Korol, "Alcune novità" 929–33.

84. Korol, "Alcune novità," 934.

85. Korol, "Alcune novità," 932. From the eleventh to the early twentieth century, Paulinus's body rested in the church of S. Adalberto (now S. Bartolomeo) in Rome on Tiber Island. In 1908 Pius X sanctioned its return to Nola, and it arrived there on 15 May 1909 to be placed in the new cathedral inaugurated only a week earlier. See Testini, "Note," 359 n. 69; and P. Palazzini, "La santità canonizzata e il culto di S. Paolino di Nola," *Atti del Convegno*, 22–23.

CHAPTER 10

⤙•⤚

Epilogue

In the late summer or autumn of 394 Paulinus of Bordeaux advertised his renunciation of the world and his rejection of his senatorial career. His intention henceforth was to live for Christ. His property would now be converted to heavenly treasure through the medium of alms and relief to the poor and needy. His poetry had already begun to forsake the fictions of the Muses in order to take up the eternal harmonies of Christ and the saints. He was in the process of reassessing and laying aside some old relationships and seeking new epistolary friendships with men he deemed to be learned in scripture and experienced in the ascetic life. Following his unanticipated presbyterial ordination at Barcelona on Christmas Day of 394, he prepared for his relocation to the outskirts of Nola in Campania. Passing through Rome and arriving there in mid- or late 395, Paulinus set about constructing a new life in a key both familiar and strange.

Paulinus's conversion captured the imagination of the age, and various observers quickly enlisted his example in defense of the emerging ideals and values of an ascetic movement that arose in tandem with the startling growth of Christianity after Constantine. His former high social rank ensured public scrutiny of his new way of life, and his undiminished literary aspirations contributed greatly to the emerging standards of monastic thought and practice. The influence of his endeavors to establish Felix and other saints as crucial intercessors in the unpredictable relationships that entwined God, man, and nature reached well beyond the Nolan countryside. In the presence of Paulinus, Nola became both an Italian way station for provincial clergy and a convenient focus of piety for the Christian aristocrats of the city of Rome, so many of whom owned ancestral estates in Campania. Inevitably, Paulinus's social relations required his participation in the debates and disputes then shaping some of western Christianity's characteristic doctrines. Thus Paulinus is unquestionably central among those advancing the Christianization of the late Roman world, even if influence in such matters hardly admits measure.

During the thirty-six years that Paulinus lived at Nola, the western half of the empire experienced political and military crises that proved irreversible. During the same period, Paulinus transformed himself from a Roman senator into a monk, cleric, and manager of a basilica complex and the cult apparatus focused on the tomb of a third-century confessor. Paulinus's turn away from traditional forms of social and political behavior, however, was complemented by his engagement in the new and evolving forms of aristocratic action that would provide one basis for order and continuity in the decades and centuries ahead. As urban topography shifted its weight subtly toward tombs, monasteries, and churches, so too were ecclesiastical offices beginning to offer the urban and even senatorial elite new opportunities for the exercise of leadership and patronage.

The boundaries between church and court were eroding even more quickly. The theological controversies of the last two decades of Paulinus's life and the papal schism of 419 reveal just how little proximity to the courts of secular authority Paulinus had sacrificed by his renunciation. It is a telling feature of the age that between Paulinus's consular *trabae* and the imperial letter summoning him to negotiate the settlement of a contested papal election lay the monastic *cilicium* and the episcopal *cathedra*. The world clung tenaciously to those accustomed to wielding power and privilege, even as the powerful collaborated in reconfiguring influence and prestige.

The biographer of Paulinus is tempted constantly to yield to hindsight, to impose a readymade pattern on his biography, and to smooth out the vital inconsistencies. Contemplated for any length of time, the dense mass of Paulinus's letters and poems becomes like a rough-cut precious stone. Turned before the eye these works reveal surfaces cast at different angles and reflecting multi-hued light. They flash images of a pious ascetic, a humble suppliant of men and God, an intimate companion of a caring saint, a highly self-conscious litterateur, a determined impresario and broker of holy power, a commanding episcopal presence, and any number of other facets. I have tried to resist leveling and reconciling all these presentations of Paulinus's persona, hoping to let the contrasts stand. For I believe that a life lived in collusion as well as collision with the spirits of its age must have presented many seemingly paradoxical faces to the world. Yet I suspect that I, like all who try to make a story of a life, have also heavily stamped Paulinus's biography with my own assumptions and attitudes. Others, no doubt, will see those more easily than I. In the end, this study can be only one more claim on Paulinus and his complex late-Roman world. I trust it displays some measure of accuracy and prudence and encourages further assessment.

APPENDIX A: THE CORPUS

Paulinus' *epistulae* and *carmina* are cited from the edition of G. de Hartel, *CSEL* 29 and 30 (1894), unless otherwise noted. Hartel's text is also now available, with some revisions as well as Italian translations and commentary, in the Strenae Nolanae series. The letters are translated by G. Santaniello, *Paolino di Nola: Le lettere* (Naples: Libreria Editrice Rendenzione, 1992), 2 vols. (= Strenae Nolanae vols. 4 and 5). The poems are translated by A. Ruggiero, *Paolino di Nola: I carmi* (Naples: Libreria Editrice Rendenzione, 1996), 2 vols. (= Strenae Nolanae vols. 6 and 7). English translations, with introduction and commentary, were prepared by P. G. Walsh for the series *Ancient Christian Writers* (New York: Newman Press), 35 (1966), 36 (1967), and 40 (1975).

Fifty-one letters and a single sermon can be assigned to Paulinus. Hartel's edition numbers Paulinus's letters from one through fifty-one, but *ep.* 34 is actually a sermon that was probably appended to *ep.* 33, while *epp.* 25 and 25* are two separate letters. Thus the number of letters remains at fifty-one, although *ep.* 48 is a fragment.

Hartel included thirty-three poems in his edition of Paulinus's *carmina* (and relegated three others to an appendix). Of these thirty-three, however, five have not been included in the present study for the reasons that follow:

Carm. 4: convincingly assigned to Paulinus of Pella by P. Courcelle, "Un nouveau poème de Paulin de Pella," *Vigiliae Christianae* 1 (1947) 101–13.

Carm. 5: almost certainly by Ausonius. See Fabre, *Essai*, 108; Green, *Ausonius*, 250.

Carm. 30: Recent study denies Paulinus's authorship of these two verse inscriptions, which eventually adorned a peristyle built about 500 to mark the vicinity of the tomb of Felix. See T. Lehmann, "Eine spätantike Inschriftensammlung und der Besuch des Papstes Damasus an der Pilgerstätte des Hl. Felix in Cimitile / Nola," *ZPE* 91 (1992): 248–55.

Carm. 32: Authorship of the so-called *poema ultimum* must be considered uncertain, but attempts to locate the poem include C. Morelli, "L'autore del cosidetto *poema ultimum* attribuito a Paolino di Nola," *Didaskalion* 1 (1912): 481–98, arguing that the piece must have been composed after 395; A. Chastagnol, "Le sénateur Volusien et la conversion d'une famille de l'aristocratie romaine au Bas-Empire," *REA* 58 (1956): 241–53, suggesting the addressee of the poem may be Volusianus; and F. G. Sirna, "Sul cosidetto 'poema ultimum' ps-Paoliniano," *Aevum* 35 (1961): 87–106, attributing the poem to Paulinus's correspondent Jovius (*ep.* 16).

Carm. 33: Authorship of the *obitus Baebiani* is also uncertain. Fabre, *Essai*, 130–34, seriously doubts its authenticity; R. P. H. Green, *The Poetry of Paulinus of Nola* (Brussels, 1971), 131, concedes at best an early date of composition by Paulinus. More recently, however, G. Guttilla, "Il *De cura pro mortuis gerenda* di Agostino e l'*obitus Baebiani* di Paolino di Nola," *Annali del Liceo Classico "G. Garibaldi" di Palermo* 25–27 (1988–90): 193–207, has argued for composition by Paulinus after ca. 421.

To Hartel's remaining twenty-eight *carmina*, however, may be added *CIL* 10.1370 (= *ILCV* 3482), the epitaph of Cynegius, most likely by Paulinus. See Green, *Poetry* 132; Walsh, *Poems*, 345; Ruggiero, *I carmi*, following p. 413. following p. 413. And we may now provisionally accept a recently uncovered poem published by T. Lehmann in the article "Zu Alarichs Beutezug in Campanien: Ein neu entdecktes Gedicht des Paulinus Nolanus," *Römische Quartalschrift* 93 (1998) 181–99. The six line epigram preserved in an eleventh century manuscript, and apparently once part of a late antique sylloge of *tituli* inscribed in the basilica complex, records the thanks given to Felix by Paulinus and the saint's *plebs* for the former's safe return *(pro reditu)* to the shrine. Lehmann's thorough argument, to which I hope to return elsewhere, situates this poem in the context of the Visigothic attack on Nola in late 410. The consequent figure of thirty *carmina*, however, is misleading, since *epp.* 8 (to Licentius) and 32 (to Severus) include poems.

APPENDIX B: EARLY CHRONOLOGY
AND *CURSUS HONORUM*

The majority of Paulinus's surviving letters and poems were written between 395 and 408. Thus the first fourteen years of Paulinus's residency at Nola are the best-documented years of his life. By comparison, reconstruction of the four decades that preceded Paulinus's move to Nola depends largely on several reminiscences presented in later works and a handful of contemporary letters and poems, most of which date from Paulinus's years in Spain (ca. 389–95). Many of the modern disagreements over Paulinus's pre-Nolan life have arisen primarily from variant interpretations of the lengthy autobiographical excursus that Paulinus included in *carmen* 21, the *natalicium* of January 407. This vignette in fact constitutes our richest source for reconstructing the shape and chronology of Paulinus's early public and private life, but objectives other than disinterested autobiography determined Paulinus's selection and presentation of information in this poem. Paulinus's words must be weighed carefully (see chapter 1). Still, if the sources for Paulinus's early life and his political career are recalcitrant and at times ambiguous, they are neither silent nor intractable.

Here I note and discuss the evidence that undergirds the chronological framework of the early chapters and justifies the political career assigned to Paulinus in chapter 2. The first section below lists some of the critical passages; the second offers the reasoning behind several chronological markers deemed sufficiently secure to serve as the basis for further construction. Section 3 develops the implications of these markers for Paulinus's social and public life before 395; and the fourth section considers in some detail the autobiographical section of *carmen* 21.

I. Select sources in chronological order

    A. Aus. *ep.* 18.3–4 to Paulinus (EW *ep.* 24);[1] composed 383–88.

> quamquam et fastorum titulo prior et tua Romae
> praecessit nostrum sella curulis ebur

---

1. Ausonius's works are cited from Green, *The Works of Ausonius*, with a cross-reference to the Loeb volumes of H. G. Evelyn White (Cambridge, 1919–21).

B. Aus. *ep.* 21.56, 60−61 to Paulinus (EW *ep.* 29); composed 392−93.

> ergo meum patriaeque decus columenque senati
> . . . .
> hic trabeam, Pauline, tuam Latiamque curulem[2]
> constituis patriosque istic sepelibis honores?

C. Paul. *carm.* 10.249−55 to Ausonius; composed 393−94.

> vel quia Pictonicis tibi fertile rus viret arvis,
> Raraunum Ausonia heu devenisse curules
> conquerar et trabeam veteri sordescere fano,
> quae tamen augusta Latiaris in urbe Quirini
> caesareas inter parili titulo palmatas
> fulget inadtrito longum venerabilis auro,
> florentem retinens meriti vivacis honorem?

D. Aus. *ep.* 24.56−57 to Paulinus (EW *ep.* 27); composed 394.

> Paulinum Ausoniumque, viros quos sacra Quirini
> purpura et auratus trabeae velavit amictus

E. Ambrose, *ep.* 6.27 to Sabinus (*CSEL* 82); composed 395.

> Paulinum splendore generis in partibus Aquitaniae nulli secundum. . . .
> Haec ubi audierint proceres viri, quae loquentur? Ex illa familia, illa pro-
> sapia, illa indole, tanta praeditum eloquentia migrasse a senatu, intercep-
> tam familiae nobilis successionem: ferri hoc non posse.

F. Sul. Sev. *V. Mart.* 25.4; composed 397.

> praestantissimumque nobis praesentium temporum inlustris viri Paulini . . .
> exemplum ingerebat.

G. Jer. *ep.* 118.5 to Iulianus; composed 406.

> Nec est, quod te excuses nobilitate et divitarum pondere. respice sanctum
> virum Pammachium et ferventissimae fidei Paulinum presbyterum

H. Paul. *carm.* 21.395−98 (*nat.* 13); composed 407.

> ergo ubi bis terno dicionis fasce levatus
> deposui nulla maculatam caede securim
> te revocante soli quondam genitalis ad oram
> sollicitae matri sum redditus.

---

2. Cp. Aus. *Praef.* 1.37, where Ausonius describes his own consulship as *Latiamque curulem*.

I. Uranius, *De obitu S. Paulini* 9; composed 432.

> Taceamus generis nobilitatem, paternis maternisque natalibus in senatorum purpuras admirabiliter rutilantem

II. Chronological markers

A. Paulinus was born at Bordeaux no later than 355.

In a letter to Augustine written at Nola in the fall of 395 (*ep.* 4.3), Paulinus equates his age then to the age of the man healed by Peter and John at the Beautiful Gate of the Temple.[3] According to Acts 4.22, this man was "more than forty years old (annorum enim erat amplius quadraginta homo, in quo factum erat signum istud sanitatis"). If Paulinus was speaking literally in 395, then he should not have been born after 355. Of course, Paulinus's remark in *ep.* 4.3 provides only a *terminus ante quem* and does not preclude a date of a few years earlier. In fact, as the next section argues, an earlier date is more likely.

B. Ausonius's pedagogical relations with Paulinus argue for a birthdate of about 352 or 353.

Paulinus studied literature at Bordeaux with Ausonius before the latter's departure to the court of Valentinian at Trier in 366 or 367.[4] Because the later relations of *amicitia* and literary sympathy between teacher and student run so deep, the duration of their early contact should be assumed to be long. If Paulinus had not been born until 355, then he would have been only eleven—the age at which a boy might normally begin literary studies with a *grammaticus*—when Ausonius left for Trier. Recognition of this discrepancy led A. D. Booth, who believed that Paulinus also studied rhetoric under Ausonius, to push back Paulinus's birthdate to 348.[5] Booth's solution, however, is too extreme. Such an early birthdate unnecessarily abuses the most likely chronology for Paulinus's *cursus honorum* (see below), and the evidence does not require Paulinus to have studied rhetoric as well as literature (*grammatice*) with Ausonius.[6] A birthdate of 352 or 353 allows sufficient time for Paulinus, clearly a precocious student, to pursue literary studies with Ausonius before the latter's departure from Bordeaux.

---

3. *Ep.* 4.3: "quippe aetas mihi secundum carnem iam ea est, qua fuit ille ab apostolis in porta speciosa verbi potestate sanatus." Trout, "The Dates."

4. On the date of Ausonius's departure for Trier see Étienne, *Bordeaux antique,* 342; Booth, "The Academic Career of Ausonius," 332; and Matthews, *Western Aristocracies,* 51.

5. A. D. Booth, "Sur la date de naissance de Saint Paulin de Nole," *Écho du monde classique* 26 (1982): 57–64.

6. For example, Aus. *ep.* 22.33–35 Green (EW *ep.* 25); and Paul. *carm.* 11.38–39 with discussion in chapter 4.

C. Paulinus held a curule office at Rome before January 379.

Writing to Paulinus in the 380s, Ausonius remarks that Paulinus's name comes before his in the *fasti* and that Paulinus's *sella curulis* preceded his at Rome (I.A above). Paulinus's office in question, therefore, must be placed before Ausonius's consulship of 379, to which these insignia should refer.

D. Paulinus was not at Nola for the feast of Felix (14 January) between 382 (or a few years earlier) and 396.

Paulinus relocated permanently to Nola in the summer of 395.[7] In the poem that Paulinus composed for the festival of Felix in January 396 (*carm.* 13; *nat.* 2), he claims that three *lustra* (at least fifteen years and perhaps as many as nineteen) had passed since "in person" (*coram*) he had dedicated his vows and his heart to Felix.[8] By this reckoning, Paulinus had not been present at the festival of Felix since at least January 382; this calculation of his absence from Nola fully accords with other indicators.

E. In the early 380s, but no later than the fall of 384, Paulinus was present in Milan.

In a letter written to Paulinus during the late summer or fall of 395, Alypius of Thagaste recalls that when he was in Milan, where he was baptized, he had heard the name of Paulinus.[9] The young *advocatus* Alypius had come to Milan with the aspiring rhetor Augustine in the fall of 384. Alypius's words eleven years later suggest that Paulinus was no longer at Milan when he and Augustine arrived but that his presence in the city was recent enough to have been recalled. On this and perhaps other earlier visits to Milan, Paulinus must have cultivated the relationship with Ambrose that later permitted him to claim that "he had always been nurtured in the faith" by the bishop of Milan (*ep.* 3.4).

F. Paulinus relocated to Nola from Spain in the summer of 395.

See D. Trout, "The Dates."

7. Trout, "The Dates."
8. *Carm.* 13.7–9:

tria tempore longo
lustra cucurrerunt, ex quo sollemnibus istis
coram vota tibi, coram mea corda dicavi.

9. Paul. *ep.* 3.4: "quod enim indicasti iam de humilitatis nostrae nomine apud Mediolanium te didicisse, cum illic initiareris." On the date see Trout, "The Dates."

G. Summary: The best evidence—offered by others as well as Paulinus—
argues for the reasonable surety of the following dates in the life of Paulinus:

ca. 352 or 353	date of birth
before 379	tenure of a curule office at Rome
ca. 383 or 384	visit to or stay in Milan
between ca. 382 and 395	no attendance at the Nolan festival of Felix
summer 395	relocation to Nola

III. Rank, *cursus honorum*, and chronological considerations

A. *puer clarissimus*

On the basis of the evidence at section I.E, I.G, and I.I above, we can reason-
ably assume that Paulinus was a *puer clarissimus;* that is, that he was the son of a
vir clarissmus (a member of the senatorial order in the broadest sense) and enti-
tled to the clarissimate by birth.[10] On this point Uranius (I.I) is explicit but late,
while Ambrose (I.E) and Jerome (I.G) are difficult to interpret in any other way.
Paulinus's tenure of the suffect consulship (see below) may be evidence not
merely of senatorial birth, but also of a father who was a member of the Sen-
ate at Rome.

Both Ambrose and Uranius indicate that Paulinus's family was *nobilis*, while
Jerome's use of Paulinus himself as an *exemplum* to convince Julianus that his *no-
bilitas* should not be an impediment to conversion depends for its force on the
assumption that Paulinus and Pammachius were *nobiles* at the time of conver-
sion. Although *nobilis* was used somewhat loosely by contemporaries, and does
not appear to be a term applied only to the holders of the higher senatorial
posts (and their sons),[11] it does normally indicate or intend to suggest a senato-
rial affiliation.[12] Symmachus, for example, accorded nobility to a nonsenator
adlected to the Roman Senate *inter consulares*, that is, at the level of a suffect
consul (a case that parallels Jerome's assertion for Paulinus, himself a *con-
sularis*).[13] Ambrose and Uranius, however, speak specifically to Paulinus's sena-
torial lineage.

---

10. On the order of *clarissimi* see Jones, *The Later Roman Empire*, 528–29; Arnheim, *The Senatorial
Aristocracy*, 9–10; Chastagnol, "Le Sénat dans l'oeuvre de Symmaque," 73–75; and P. Heather, "Sena-
tors and Senates," in *The Cambridge Ancient History*, vol. 13, ed. A. Cameron and P. Garnsey (Cambridge,
1998), 188–97.

11. As argued by T. D. Barnes, "Who Were the Nobility of the Roman Empire?" *Phoenix* 28 (1974):
444–49, limiting the term to holders of the ordinary consulate, the urban prefecture, or a praetorian
prefecture. On the complete unreliability of the term *nobilis* as a guide to senatorial affiliation in sixth-
century Gallic writers see Gilliard, "Senatorial Bishops," 163–66.

12. Arnheim, *The Senatorial Aristocracy*, 8.

13. Sym. *Rel.* 5 with Chastagnol, "Le Sénat dans l'oeuvre de Symmaque," 77–78.

B. *Consul suffectus*

Paulinus's curule office referred to by Ausonius (I.A) must be the suffect consulship. In two other references to Paulinus's Roman magistracy, Ausonius adds to the *sella curulis* the more specific distinction of the *trabea* (I.B and I.D). Paulinus himself (I.C) uses the *trabea* metonymically to indicate Ausonius's ordinary consulship; and in Ammianus,[14] Symmachus,[15] Claudian,[16] and four other references by Ausonius,[17] the *trabea* denotes the consulship exclusively.[18] As the ordinary consuls of these years are all known, however, Paulinus's consulship must have been suffect.[19]

The exact nature of the suffect consulship in the later fourth century remains obscure. Arguments for the social origins of post-Constantinian suffects[20] are vitiated by the inadequate statistical base; only three securely identified post-Constantinian suffects are indicated, for example, in the study of W. Kuhoff.[21] Nevertheless, one of these—Ragonius Vincentius Celsus—certainly held both the quaestorship and the praetorship before his consulship (*CIL* 6.1760); and all three (Ceionius Italicus, Insteius Pompeianus, and Celsus) belonged to established senatorial families.[22] Thus Paulinus's tenure of the office may be seen as further evidence of his family's senatorial rank.

The few fortuitously preserved references provide only scant information on the suffect's duties and responsibilties. The fifth-century calendar of Polemius Silvius (*CIL* I 2.1) places their nomination by the Senate on 9 January, also noting that the ordinary consuls laid down their fasces on 21 April. As often noted,

---

14. Amm. 14.11.27; 16.10.12; 21.10.8; 23.1.1; 25.10.11; 25.10.16; 26.5.6; 29.2.15; 30.3.1.

15. *Ep.* 9.112.1; *Or.* 2.1. *Or.* 1.23, contrasting *togae* with *paludamenta* and the *trabea* with *arma*, is less specific.

16. For the twenty-three references see P. G. Christiansen, *Concordantia in Claudianum* (Hildesheim, 1988), s.v. "trabea."

17. Aus. *Grat. Act.* 11, 18; *Protr.* 92.

18. The *trabea* clearly supplied contemporaries with a colorful and descriptive metonym for the consulship. See, for example, Amm. 23.1; Claud. *Eutr.* 2.10, praef.; *ILS* 1269 with Anicius Petronius Probus's remark on his consulship of 406; and Sid. *ep.* 8.6.5. For illustrations from the codex-calendar of 354 see Salzman, *On Roman Time*, figures 13 and 14.

19. For evidence that suffects were entitled to the *trabea* see Sym. *ep.* 6.40, where a suffect consul appears *palmata amictus*. The toga or tunica *palmata* is often introduced in conjunction with or as another name for the *trabea*. See, for example, Aus. *Grat. Act.* 11; Sid. *ep.* 8.6.5–6. Fabre's support of Reinelt's argument against Paulinus's tenure of a suffect consulship (Fabre, *Paulin de Nole*, 23–24) is founded on confusion about the nature of the office in the later fourth century.

20. A. Chastagnol, "Observations sur le consulat suffect et la préfecture du Bas-Empire," *Revue historique* 219 (1958): 231–37, depreciating its value, and M. T. W. Arnheim, "The Suffect Consulship in the Later Roman Empire," *Byzantine Studies* 1 (1974): 147–68, rehabilitaing the office as the "preserve of young men of senatorial origin" (168).

21. W. Kuhoff, *Studien zur zivilen senatorischen Laufbahn im 4. Jahrhundert n. Chr.* (Frankfurt, 1983), 37–38.

22. See Arnheim, "The Suffect Consulship," nos. 5, 8, and 9.

the evidence of Silvius and Symmachus, *ep.* 6.40—placing a suffect at the 21 April celebration of the *Parilia / Natalis urbis*—suggests that the suffects formally took office on 21 April. It need not follow that the ordinary consuls retired from office on that date, for the duties of the suffects were largely ceremonial and limited to Rome in the normal absence of the ordinary consuls from that city.[23] Even if the games alluded to by a Constantinian law were in abeyance by the later fourth century,[24] the office probably still required substantial financial outlay (pehaps in conjunction with the celebration of the *natalis urbis*) and may have been perceived as a *munus*.

Tenure of the suffect consulship implies membership in the Senate at Rome. If not through a previous (unattested) quaestorship or praetorship (see III.D), then through adlection before or as a result of his nomination to the suffect consulship Paulinus must have been enrolled in the Roman Senate.[25]

C. *Consularis Campaniae*

Paulinus's governorship of Campania is not in doubt, and it may be epigraphically attested.[26] In the autobiographical excursus of *carm.* 21, Paulinus rounds off a description of early building projects that he accomplished near the tomb of Felix (*carm.* 21.379–86, with a digression inserted from 386–94) as follows: "Consequently relieved of the sixfold fasces of authority, I laid down the ax stained by no slaughter (*ergo ubi bis terno dicionis fasce levatus / deposui nulla maculatam caede securim*), and with you [Felix] summoning me back to the region of my former native soil, I was restored to an anxious mother" (*carm.* 21.395–98 = I.H). The conjunction of "public works" at Nola and Paulinus's description of his office indicate clearly that he held the Campanian governorship with consular rank: the *ordo Beneventanus*, for example, honored the ex-governor Claudius Iulius Pacatus *post fasces depositos* (*ILS* 6505), and six fasces appear standard for *consular* governors in the fourth century.[27] (See below on two irregular *pro*consular Campanian governors.) If Paulinus in these lines were referring to

23. See R. Bagnall et al., *Consuls*, 20–21.

24. Kuhoff, *Studien*, 29.

25. See further Chastagnol, "Les modes de recrutement du Sénat," 187–211.

26. *CIL* 10.6088 from Formiae (Pontio Paulino cons . . .) could well be a dedication to Paulinus. See *PLRE* 1.681, "Paulinus 20." The other possible candidate, Pontius Proserius Paulinus (*consularis Campaniae* in 409), is styled Proserius Paulinus on all four inscriptions that record his name. See *PLRE* 2.848, "Paulinus 15," with the restoration of *CIL* 10.1128 and G. Cecconi, *Governo imperiale e élites dirigenti nell'Italia tardoantica* (Como, 1994), 70.

27. *ILS* 5535, 5536, 5555, et al., on the *sexfacilis consularis* of Numidia. The proconsul of Africa, who was distinguished by twelve fasces in the third century (Cyprian, *ep.* 15.2), apparently maintained this privilege in the fourth; see Sym. *ep.* 1.1.5 on his African proconsulship: "bis seno celsus, Symmache, fasce cluis." See also Chastagnol, "L'administration du diocèse italien," 362–65; and Cecconi, *Governo imperiale*, 68–70, on Paulinus's consular rank.

his suffect consulship, then twelvefold fasces would have been the required designation.[28]

D. *Quaestura* and *praetura* (?)

Whereas the Campanian governorship was almost certainly the final office of Paulinus's *cursus*, other earlier offices, particularly a quaestorship or praetorship at Rome, cannot be ruled out. There is no explicit evidence that Paulinus held either post, but they were regular avenues by which young *clarissimi* of established families entered the Senate at Rome.[29] Furthermore, among cases where fuller *cursus* documentation has survived, men who became suffect consuls often had held the *quaestura* or the *praetura*: thus eight of the sixteen suffects identified for the years 284–395 by one study held both offices (though most are early in this period);[30] and among the known suffects can be found no definite new senator.[31] It is therefore possible that Paulinus had held one or both offices. Ausonius's desire to reference the one magistracy the two men had held in common, the consulship (I.A, I.B, and I.D), sufficiently explains his silence about the *quaestura* or the *praetura*. Moreover, as *munera*, these posts were often bypassed even in honorific or dedicatory inscriptions.

Alternatively, Paulinus may have been adlected into the Roman Senate at the praetorian level before his nomination to the suffect consulship. *Adlecti inter praetorios*, however, while signaled by the law codes, are difficult to locate in the epigraphic evidence.[32]

E. The date of Paulinus's suffect consulship

As noted above (II.C), January 379 is the *terminus ante quem* for the curule office now securely identified as the suffect consulship. But Paulinus also most likely attained this office during the period of Ausonius's ascendancy, which began with the death of Valentinian and the accession of Gratian as senior Augustus in the West in late 375. Ausonius's delight in Paulinus's tenure of this office and Paulinus's ready acknowledgment of Ausonius's patronage are sufficient evi-

28. See, for example, *CIL* 6.32000 on the suffect consulship of Insteius Pompeianus: "bis senis fascibus auctus." Cp. Ovid, *Pont.* 4.9.4 ("bis senos fasces"); Martial, 7.63.9 ("bis senis fascibus"); 8.66.3 ("bis senos fasces"); Stat. *Sil.* 1.2.174–75 ("bissenos fasces"). Martial 11.98.15 refers to the six fasces of the praetorship with "senive fasces"; Symmachus refers to his son's praetorship as "fasces praetura tuae" (*ep.* 7.1.1; cp. *epp.* 5.9.1, 8.14.1, 8.71.1, 9.24.1, *Rel.* 45).

29. Jones, *The Later Roman Empire*, 530; Chastagnol, "Les modes de recrutement du Sénat," 191–94; Matthews, *Western Aristocracies*, 13–14; and Kuhoff, *Studien*, 26–27, 249, with just emphasis on the statistical inadequacy of the sources for drawing firm conclusions.

30. Arnheim, "The Suffect Consulship," 150.

31. Kuhoff, *Studien*, 41.

32. Against Chastagnol's optimistic advocacy of adlection *inter praetorias*, "Les modes du recrutement du Sénat," 194–201, see the reservations of Arnheim, "The Suffect Consulship," 147–50, and Kuhoff, *Studien*, 39–42.

dence of Ausonius's role at Trier. Therefore, Paulinus's consulship is best dated between 376 and 378, when (on the reckoning employed here) Paulinus would have been between twenty-three and twenty-six years of age.

F. The date of Paulinus's Campanian governorship

Paulinus's governorship should have followed his suffect consulship: for young *clarissimi*, the urban magistracies—the quaestorship, praetorship, and presumably the suffect consulship—were stepping-stones to the Italian governorships and beyond. The governorship, thus, could be placed any time between his consulship and late 381, the latest date at which we can reasonably place Paulinus at Campanian Nola (II.D, with the assumption that if present as *consularis Campaniae* Paulinus would have attended the January festival of Felix).

This magistracy, however, is best dated between mid-380 and late 381, following the *pro*consular governorships of Anicius Paulinus and Anicius Auchenius Bassus.[33] The governorship of Anicius Paulinus should be dated between November 378, when the governors of Campania were still *consulares* (*CTh* 9.40.12), and April 380, by which time Anicius Paulinus had been promoted to the urban prefecture at Rome.[34] Bassus's governorship, in turn, must be dated between January 379 (for his proconsulship followed the elevation of Theodosius [*CIL* 10.6656]) and November 382, for by then he, too, had become *praefectus urbi*.[35] Because of the uniqueness of their proconsular rank, Bassus probably directly succeeded Anicius Paulinus in the Campanian governorship, and therefore his tenure of that office is best placed before April 380, by which time Anicius Paulinus was already urban prefect. Thus the governorships of these two men should be placed in the 379 and early 380. If our Paulinus's governorship is placed before that of Anicius Paulinus, the chronology seems unduly compressed: Paulinus's suffect consulship and his governorship must be squeezed into the years 376–78. Moreover, the evidence of Paulinus's *carmen* 21 (I.H, and below) implies that Paulinus's activities as governor were conducted near the end of his Italian sojourn, which extended into the early 380s (II.D and II.E).[36] Thus 380 and 381 are the most likely years for Paulinus's Campanian governorship.

G. Summary

This analysis permits the following additions to and refinements of the chronological scheme presented at the end of the previous section:

---

33. So, too, Cecconi, *Governo imperiale*, 68–70, 216. On the elevation of the post to proconsular rank as a sign of imperial favor, see also Novak, "Anicianae domus culmen," 487.

34. On Anicius Paulinus see *PLRE* 1.678, "Paulinus 12"; and Chastagnol, *Les fastes*, 207.

35. On Bassus see *PLRE* 1.152, "Bassus 11"; Chastagnol, *Les fastes*, 211–16.

36. The exact period of the governorship of the Younger Nicomachus Flavianus, also *consularis Campaniae* during this period, cannot be determined beyond its *terminus ante quem*, February 383. See *PLRE* 1.345, "Flavianus 14."

ca. 352 or 353	date of birth
between 376 and 378	tenure of the suffect consulship at Rome
ca. 380 and 381	consular governorship of Campania
ca. 383 or 384	visit to or stay in Milan
between ca. 382 and 395	no attendance at the Nolan festival of Felix
summer 395	relocation to Nola

IV. The excursus of *carmen* 21.365–427 (*nat.* 13)

Carmen 21, thirteenth in the series of preserved *natalicia*, was written for the festival of Felix in January 407. Present at Nola for the celebration that year were a number of important visitors from Rome, family and friends of Melania the Elder: Melania's daughter-in-law, Albina; her niece and granddaughter, Avita and Melania the Younger; their husbands, the senators Turcius Apronianus and Valerius Pinianus; and the children of Avita and Apronianus, Asterius and Eunomia. For this audience, and for the less exalted crowd assembled for the day's diversions, Paulinus composed 858 lines in three different meters that variously praised Felix for his role in the destruction of the invading army of Radagaisus, surveyed the ascetic virtues of his esteemed guests, essayed the spiritual value of "poverty," described a recent examination of Felix's tomb, and thanked the neighboring Abellans for restoring an aqueduct that supplied Nola.

At the center of this poem, however, stands the most thorough formal autobiographical statement to be found in the extant works of Paulinus. This excursus provides unique evidence for the biography of Paulinus, but the passage must be approached with caution, because it is selective in its self-representation. Although its ostensible purpose was to document the persistent presence of Felix's guiding hand in the life of Paulinus (361–65), this retrospective public revelation of Felix's continual care for Paulinus—from his boyhood to the present time—also reinforced Paulinus's claim to be the special client of this otherworldly patron, the claim that undergirded Paulinus's social and religious authority in Campania. Paulinus's message in this poem was also intended for the ears of the wealthy Christian elite in his audience. The excursus is not, therefore, a straightforward autobiographical account, nor was it meant to provide posterity with a full or unambiguous record of the *cursus honorum* that Paulinus had abandoned more than twenty years earlier. Moreover, Paulinus could have expected the senators and aristocratic friends of his audience to appreciate the poem's allusiveness in ways that we, perhaps, cannot.[37]

A. Text

The lines of the excursus most relevant to the concerns of this appendix follow here. Spaces mark proposed divisions between discrete topics.

> tu mihi caelestum, si possem adtingere, rerum   365
> prima salutiferis iecisti semina causis.

37. See also chapter 1.

nam puer occiduis Gallorum advectus ab oris,   367
ut primum tetigi trepido tua limina gressu,
admiranda videns operum documenta sacrorum
pro foribus fervere tuis, ubi corpore humato
clauderis et meritis late diffunderis altis,
toto corde fidem divini nominis hausi
inque tuo gaudens adamavi lumine Christum.

te duce fascigerum gessi primaevus honorem   374
teque meam moderante manum, servante salutem,
purus ab humani sanguis discrimine mansi.

tunc etiam primae . . . libamina barbae[38]   377
ante tuum solium quasi te carpente totondi;

iam tunc praemisso per honorem pignore sedis   379
Campanis metanda locis habitacula fixi,
te fundante tui ventura cubilia servi,
cum tacita inspirans curam mihi mente iuberes
muniri sternique viam ad tua tecta ferentem
adtiguumque tuis longo consurgere tractu
culminibus tegimen, sub quo prior usus egentum
incoluit. . . .   386

[digression on Paulinus's building activities after
his arrival at Nola in 395]

ergo ubi bis terno dicionis fasce levatus   395
deposui nulla maculatam caede securim,
te revocante soli quondam genitalis ad oram
sollicitae matri sum redditus. inde propinquos
trans iuga Pyrenes adii peregrinus Hiberos.   399

B. Translation

(365–66) You [Felix] scattered the first seeds of heavenly things for me (if I might attain them) to be the causes of my salvation.

(367–73) For as a boy (*puer*) carried from the western regions of the provinces of the Gauls, as I first touched your threshold with fearful step, seeing the

---

38. Something is clearly missing from the text here, but as Fabre notes, *Paulin de Nole*, 15, Hartel's proposed *puerus* is hardly appropriate. Zechmeister's *iuvenis* at least better fits the context.

wonderful proofs of your holy works aglow before your doors, where with
body buried you are enclosed but are poured out widely through your lofty
merits, I drank in the faith of the divine name with my whole heart and re-
joicing in your light I loved Christ.

(374–76) With you as my guide, in my early years (*primaevus*) I conducted the
office that bears the fasces and with you governing my hand and preserving
my safety, I remained pure from the hazard of human blood.

(377–78) Then also I shaved the offering of my first beard before your tomb,
as if you were plucking it out.

(379–86) Already then, with a pledge promised to honor your abode, I de-
cided my dwelling place must be changed to the Campanian region; for you
established the future resting place of your servant when—breathing a com-
mission into my silent heart—you ordered a road leading to your dwelling
to be built and paved and a covering of great extent to rise up near to your
gables under which the poor then used to shelter.

(387–94) Digression

(395–99) Consequently relieved of the sixfold fasces of authority, I laid
down the ax stained by no slaughter; for with you summoning me back to
the region of my former native soil, I was restored to an anxious mother.
Then as a foreigner I traveled across the ridges of the Pyrenees to the neigh-
boring Spaniards.

C. Discussion

This part of *carmen* 21 selectively retails Paulinus's life from the occasion of a
first visit to Nola as a *puer* until his return to Aquitaine following his tenure of
the Campanian governorship.[39] Unfortunately Paulinus's treatment of events
suggests only a relative chronology; episodes appear to unfold in temporal
order, but Paulinus neither offers absolute dates nor provides the kind of infor-
mation that would allow us to reconstruct them. Much is ambiguous, yet most
previous readers have made two assumptions that have led to unnecessary diffi-
culties. First, it has become customary to identify both the "office that bears the
fasces" (*fascigerum honorem*) of l. 374 and the "sixfold fasces of authority" (*bis terno
dicionis fasce*) of l. 395 as references to the consular governorship of Campania.[40]

---

39. The remainder of the "autobiographical" section of this poem commemorates events in Pauli-
nus's life after his journey to Spain: his marriage, the death of a brother, his secular renunciation, and
the relocation to Nola. Thus Paulinus informs or reminds his audience of those events through which
Felix led him back to Nola.

40. So Fabre, *Paulin de Nole,* 17; Booth, "Sur la date de naissance," 56–58; Stroheker, *Der senatorische
Adel,* 210; *PLRE* 1.682, "Paulinus 21"; and Arnheim, *Senatorial Aristocracy,* 184.

Second, it is often held that the *depositio barbae* ceremony of ll. 377–78 corresponds to another moment in one of the earlier *natalicia*—the second *natalicium* (*carm.* 13.7–9) of 396. There Paulinus had recalled that three *lustra* had passed since he had last dedicated in person his heart and vows to Felix (see II.D).[41]

The result of the equation of the *fascigerus honor* with the *bis ternus dicionis fascis* has been the creation of a "unitarian" reading of lines 374–98. This reading relegates to the months of Paulinus's governorship all of the activities framed by the two references to the fasces—including the *depositio barbae* ceremony.[42] Furthermore, the conflation of *carm* 13.7–9 and *carm.* 21.377–78 forces a date ca. 381–82 for the *depositio barbae* ceremony, for according to Paulinus the act of self-dedication remembered and recorded in the *natalicium* of 396 had occurred three *lustra* before.

The "unitarian" reading of ll. 374–98, however, compressing all the events recalled here into Paulinus's months as *consularis Campaniae*, is untenable. It requires us to believe that Paulinus—intent on demonstrating to his audience the "gifts" he had received from Felix "with equal love" through the "various stages of his life"—presented merely the evidence of a single relatively brief period within the span of some thirty years that must separate his boyhood visit to Nola and his marriage in Spain. Moreover, anchoring the *depositio barbae* ceremony to Paulinus's days as governor generates a string of problems. Fabre, for example, doubted that this ritual would have been postponed much beyond the age of twenty-five, and he thus favored a date of 355 for Paulinus's birth.[43] As noted above (II.B), however, a birthdate of 355 yields its own problems by further limiting the time available for Paulinus to benefit from the tutelage of Ausonius.

To be sure, the scant evidence from the earlier empire suggests the mid-twenties were the latest age at which a young man should have performed the *depositio barbae*.[44] But a different reading of *carm.* 21 avoids using as chronological evidence a ceremony about which virtually nothing is known for late antiquity, and it eliminates the other difficulties attendant on the unitarian interpretation of this passage. First, Paulinus's *fascigerus honor* of l. 374 and his *bis ternus dicionis fascis* of l. 395 need not, and should not, reference the same office. Indeed as the first introduces and the second concludes the section on Paulinus's political life, these phrases are best seen as carefully chosen markers that

41. So Fabre, *Paulin de Nole*, 15–16; Booth, "Sur la date de naissance," 56–57.

42. For example, *PLRE* 1.682, "Paulinus 21"; Lienhard, *Paulinus of Nola*, 25–26; Booth, "Sur la date de naissance," 58, accepting the compression but apparently prefering a date ca. 375 for Paulinus's governorship.

43. Fabre, *Paulin de Nole*, 16.

44. Several sources of the earlier empire refer to the *depositio barbae* or *barbatoria* (Pet. *Sat.* 73, 29; Juv. 3.186, 8.166), but there was apparently no standard age for its performance: Octavian was twenty-four (Dio. 48.34); Caligula was nineteen (Suet. 10); and Nero was twenty-three (Suet. 12).

frame the presentation of a *cursus honorum* comprising at least two offices distinguished by the right to the fasces. The second reference clearly denotes Paulinus's Campanian governorship; the first, with the hapax legomenon *fascigerum*, should then gloss his suffect consulship. Nor is Paulinus's accompanying boast (ll. 374–76) that in the first office he remained "pure from the *discrimen* (crisis, danger) of human blood" an impediment to the separation of these two offices. The apparently similar claim advanced in relation to the Campanian governorship—"deposui nulla maculatam caede securim" (l. 396)—clearly echoes assertions made for or by other provincial governors and imperial officials[45] and alludes to Paulinus's judiciary powers of torture and capital punishment. The context of the potential blood-spilling in relation to the *fascigerus honor* of the suffect consulship is less clear, but it need not be connected to otherwise unattested powers of jurisdiction. Tenure of office in the capital (or any city) always had strong potential for associations with violence. Moreover, *discrimen* is a vague marker. Ammianus, for example, referring to the riots that disrupted Rome in 366–67, even noted that the papal contenders Damasus and Ursinus "went so far as conflicts (*discrimina*) resulting in bloodshed and death."[46] Paulinus elsewhere uses the term to describe the dangerous and false enticements that Rome presented to a young man.[47] Thus, rather than understand ll. 395–96 as a reprise of ll. 374–76 and connecting both to the Campanian governorship, we should read these as parallel, but carefully varied, glosses on the potential associations with violence and bloodshed that faced every holder of a curule office.

Second, the equation of the *depositio barbae* ceremony mentioned in *carm.* 21 with Paulinus's reference in the *natalicium* of 396 (*carm.* 13.7–9) to his last dedication of his *vota* and *corda* "in person" (*coram*) to Felix three *lustra* before is completely unfounded. The *natalicium* of 396, Paulinus's first since his relocation to Nola the previous summer or fall, emphasized his personal attendance at the festival after a long absence. The remembrance of the *natalicium* of 396, then, need only recall the occasion when Paulinus last "celebrated Felix's birthday within his threshold."[48] The *depositio* ceremony is irrelevant. Indeed, henceforth Paulinus customarily speaks of the composition and delivery of his *natalicia*

45. For instance, Aus. *Mos.* 405–6 ("innocuas secures"); Amb. *ep.* 25.3 ("quod incruentam de administratione provinciali securim revexerint"); Sym. *Or.* 3.2 ("incruentas secures"); and Rut. Nam. 1.159–60 ("nulla meum strinxerunt crimina ferrum").

46. Amm. 27.3.12: "ad usque mortis vulnerumque discrimina." Ammianius uses the term to mean simply "danger" (14.2.11; 30.1.9) or "distinction" between groups (28.1.45), although he also employs the term in the context of near-death under torture ("ad usque discrimen vitae vexatus" [14.9.7]; "non nullis usque discrimina vitae vexatis" [30.8.3]).

47. *Ep.* 8.3 (l.9) to Licentius: "tanta inter fragilis discrimina vitae." At *ep.* 32.15 and *carm.* 21.360, *discrimen* has its fundamental meaning of separation or division.

48. *Carm.* 13.6–7: "tandem exoratum est inter tua limina nobis / natalem celebrare tuum."

themselves as the annual renewal and fulfillment of his vow to Felix.[49] Paulinus could have performed this *depositio barbae* any time between ca. 376 and 381, when he was in his mid- or late twenties.

D. Summary

In sum, it is best to view the autobiographical excursus of *carm.* 21.374–96 as an impressionistic presentation of events and activities associated with the span of Paulinus's first period of Italian residency between ca. 376 and 383 and as selective reflections on a political career spanning several years. The passage provides a chronological arrangement of topics, but one that can hardly be pressed for precision. If the unitarian interpretation of the passage is jettisoned, the apparent discrepancies between this excursus and other evidence disappear, and the primary chronological markers of Paulinus's early life acquire further support. The evidence argues for the following final scheme:

ca. 352 or 353	date of birth
between ca. 359 and 367	educated by Ausonius
	boyhood visit to the shrine of Felix
between 376 and 378	suffect consulship at Rome
	depositio barbae
ca. 380 and 381	consular governorship of Campania
ca. 383 or 384	visit to or stay in Milan
	return to Aquitaine
between ca. 382 and 395	no attendance at the Nolan festival of Felix
summer 395	relocation to Nola

---

49. For example, *carm.* 18.1–3 (400); *carm.* 20.13–16 (406).

APPENDIX C:
SELECT CHRONOLOGY

352–82

ca. 352 or 353	Paulinus's birth
between 359 and ca. 366	Paulinus educated by Ausonius
	Paulinus's boyhood visit to the Nolan shrine of Felix
364	accession of Valentinian I and Valens
366 or 367	Ausonius summoned to Trier to educate Gratian
369	Ausonius and Symmachus meet at Trier
375	death of Valentinian I and accession of Gratian as senior emperor in the west
376–78	Paulinus's suffect consulship at Rome
August 378	death of Valens at Adrianople
January 379	accession of Theodosius I
379	ordinary consulship of Ausonius
380–81	Paulinus's consular governorship of Campania

382–89

382 and 383	Gratian's repudiation of the pontifical robe and removal of Altar of Victory from the Senate House
summer 382	Jerome's return to Rome
383	Augustine's arrival in Rome
spring 383	usurpation of Magnus Maximus in Britain
August 383	murder of Gratian at Lyon
383 or 384	Paulinus's visit to or stay in Milan
	Paulinus's return to Aquitaine

384	anti-Pricillianist synod at Bordeaux
late 384	Symmachus's third *relatio* to Valentinian II on restoration of the Altar of Victory
386 (?)	execution of Priscillian at Trier
28 August 388	death of Magnus Maximus
between 383 and 389	Paulinus's *carmina* 1–3
	Paulinus's marriage to Therasia
	meetings with Martin of Tours
	introduction to Victricius of Rouen
	Paulinus's baptism
	violent death of a brother (?)

389–95

ca. 389	Paulinus and Therasia's relocation to Spain
between 390 and 394	death of child Celsus at eight days
15 May 392	death of Valentinian II
22 August 392	elevation of Eugenius
summer 393 (?)	Paulinus's *carmen* 10 to Ausonius
fall 393–summer 393 (?)	Paulinus's *carmen* 11 to Ausonius
between 389 and 394	Paulinus's *carmina* 6-9
spring 394	Paulinus's first letter to Jerome
summer–fall 394	Jerome *ep.* 53
	Paulinus's renunciation made public
394	eruption of Origenist controversy in Palestine
September 394	Arbogast and Eugenius defeated at the Frigidus River
late 394 (or early 395)	Paulinus composes panegyric on Theodosius
25 December 394	Paulinus ordained as presbyter

395–432

25 December 394– 25 March 395 (Easter)	Paulinus's first *natalicium* (*carm.* 12)
	Paulinus's second letter to Jerome (carried by Vigilantius)
	Paulinus's *ep.* 1 to Severus
17 January 395	death of Theodosius I
spring–summer 395	Paulinus's relocation to Nola with stop in Rome
	Paulinus receives letter from Alypius, Augustine's anti-Manichean works, and Jerome's *ep.* 58
late 395	Paulinus sends *ep.* 3 to Alypius and *ep.* 4 to Augustine
winter 395–96	Paulinus's *ep.* 13 to Pammachius
396	Paulinus's second *natalicium* (*carm.* 13)

	episcopal ordination of Augustine
	Paulinus's *epp.* 7 and 8 to Romanianus and Licentius and *ep.* 5 to Severus
	Severus composes the *Vita Martini*
	Jerome's *ep.* 61 to Vigilantius
397	Rufinus's return to Italy
397 or 398	Paulinus's *ep.* 18 to Victricius of Rouen
between 397 and 401	Augustine's *Confessions*
January 398 and 399	Paulinus's *vita Felicis* (*carm.* 15–16)
399	Jerome's *ep.* 85 to Paulinus
November 399	death of Siricius and election of Anastasius at Rome
400	Nicetas of Remesiana and Melania the Elder visit Nola
	Paulinus's *propemptikon* (*carm.* 17) for Nicetas
between 400 and 402 (?)	Paulinus's *ep.* 16 and *carm.* 22 to Jovius
401	Alaric's first "invasion" of Italy, reflected in the *natalicium* of 402 (*carm.* 26)
401–3	Paulinus's major construction work at the shrine of Felix
ca. 402	the scandal of Boniface and Spes at Hippo
winter 402–3	Nicetas of Remesiana's second visit to Nola
ca. 405	Pelagius's letter to Paulinus (Aug. *de gratia Christi* 38)
406	the inspection of Felix's tomb
	a water dispute with Nola
	Jerome's *Contra Vigilantium*
August 406	Radagaisus's defeat at Faesulae, celebrated in the *natalicium* of 407 (*carm.* 21)
winter 406–7	Melania the Younger and family at Nola
between 406 and 408	Paulinus's *epp.* 46 and 47 to Rufinus
before 408	Paulinus's *epithalamium* (*carm.* 25) for Julian (later of Eclanum) and Titia
between 408 and 413	death of Therasia
	Paulinus's episcopal ordination
after 408	Paulinus's *ep.* 49 to Macarius on the adventures of Valgius / Victor
late 410	Gothic depredations at Nola
411	Council at Carthage censures Caelestius
415	Synod at Diospolis exonerates Pelagius
	relics of Stephen discovered
416	Councils at Carthage and Milevis condemn Pelagius and Caelestius
417	Pope Zosimus exonerates Caelestius and Pelagius
	ep. 186 of Augustine and Alypius to Paulinus

418	Pelagius is condemned by imperial rescript, a council at Carthage, and by Zosimus
26 December 418	death of Pope Zosimus
29 December 418	Boniface and Eulalius elected to papacy by rival groups
20 March 419	imperial court invites Paulinus to preside over synod to meet in June at Spoleto
3 April 419	imperial rescript resolves the dispute by recognizing Boniface
ca. 420	burial of Cynegius *ad sanctum* at Nola
	Paulinus sends *ep.* 51 to Eucherius (later of Lyon) at Lérins
ca. 422	Augustine's *De cura pro mortuis gerenda*
424	relics of Stephen arrive at Hippo
ca. 426	Augustine writes the final book of the *City of God*
ca. 430	Eucherius's *De contemptu mundi*
22 June 431	Paulinus's death at Nola
432	Uranius composes his *De obitu Paulini*

APPENDIX D: URANIUS'S
DE OBITU SANCTI PAULINI

Translation is based on the Latin text at *PL* 53.859–66. There is an Italian translation by M. Ruggiero, *Cipriano, Paolino di Nola, Uranio: Poesia e teologia della morte* (Rome, 1984).

THE LETTER OF THE PRIEST URANIUS
TO PACATUS ON THE DEATH OF SAINT PAULINUS

(1) Uranius[1] the presbyter to Pacatus,[2] illustrious lord [*dominus illustris*] and deservedly venerable in Christ. In reply to the letter of Your Nobility, I am moved to recount faithfully to you the death of Saint Paulinus. Indeed I will do what you order, but I fear that I may not do what I desire to do as effectively as you wish. Nevertheless, because you deigned to order, I will do so faithfully and without falsehood. And indeed I know it is better to keep silent than to tell lies to the sin of the soul. For the scripture says: "The mouth which lies kills the soul" [Wisdom 1.11]. And therefore I deeply beseech your Veneration that you deign to forgive my lack of skill. Yet if the meanness of my speech should begin to displease you, you will more properly charge not me but yourself, who demanded the water of the purest spring from a muddy brook. But let these things be said quickly. Now, moreover, let us come to those things which may furnish you the material for speaking, you who intend to illustrate his life in verse.

(2) The holy [*sanctus*] bishop Paulinus was born at Bordeaux, a city of the Gallic regions, but died gloriously and was buried in Campania at [the church of] the blessed confessor Felix. We know his life from the excellence of his death, and we take account of his death from the manner of his life. At last, when three days be-

---

1. On the identity of Uranius see chapter 9.
2. On the identification of Pacatus see chapter 9.

fore he was summoned from this world to that heavenly dwelling, when already all were despairing for his health and two bishops had come eager to see him— that is, holy Symmachus[3] and the blessed Acindynus—[4]he was so refreshed and renewed by their arrival that, all carnal infirmity forgotten, he showed himself to them to be completely spiritual and angelic. And as if about to set out to the Lord, he ordered the sacred mysteries to be celebrated before his little bed, certainly so that, when the Eucharist [*sacrificium*] had been offered together with the other bishops, he might commend his soul [*anima*] to the Lord and so that at the same time he might recall to the former peace those whom he had ordered through ecclesiastical discipline to be banished from the communion of the sacred mystery.

(3) And when the holy bishop had celebrated all these things in joyful and perfect order, suddenly he began to ask in a loud voice where his brothers were. Then one of those standing about who supposed that he was seeking his brothers, that is the bishops who were then present, said to him: "Behold, here are your brothers." And he replied: "But I am now calling my brothers Januarius and Martin who just now spoke with me and said they would come to me immediately." Of these, Januarius, bishop and martyr at the same time, distinguishes the church of Naples;[5] Martin, however, an apostolic man in everything, whose *Life* is read by all, was a bishop of the Gallic regions. After summoning these men he extended his hands and repeatedly sang this Psalm to the Lord, saying: "I have lifted my eyes to the hills, whence help will come to me. My help is from the Lord who made heaven and earth" [Ps 121.1–2].

Then, his prayer finished, he was reminded by the holy priest Postumianus that forty gold coins [*solidi*] were owed for the clothing that had been distributed to the poor. When holy Paulinus had heard this, smiling slightly, he said: "Rest easy, son. Trust me that there will be someone to pay the debt of the poor." And lo, before long a certain priest arrived coming from the region of Lucania, [and] sent by the holy bishop Exuperantius[6] or by his brother Ursatius, a most distinguished man [*clarissimus vir*], who had sent to him fifty gold coins through this man as a gift. When holy Paulinus had accepted these coins, he blessed the Lord and said: "Thank you Lord, you who have not abandoned one hoping in you." Moreover, from these fifty gold coins he gave two from his own hand to the priest who had brought them. But he ordered the rest to be given back to the merchants who had given the clothing to the poor.

---

3. Bishop, it seems, of Capua. See Lanzoni, *Le diocesi*, 859–60.

4. His see is unknown.

5. Uranius offers the earliest literary evidence for Januarius's cult at Naples. See notices and bibliography at Saxer, "Januarius and Companions," and L. Pani Ermini, "Naples, Archaeology," *Encyclopedia of the Early Church* (Oxford, 1992), 1:430, 2:581.

6. His see is unknown, but Paestum has been suggested. See Lanzoni, *Le diocesi*, 1:322.

(4) Meanwhile, however, since already night had followed day, he yielded somewhat to rest until the middle of the night. Then, awakened by the pain growing excessively in his side and worn out by the many unnecessary cauterizations of the physicians, he spent until about the fifth hour of the night exhausted and short of breath. Then, with dawn approaching, the holy man initiated his usual routine. And so, as he was accustomed, with all roused, he celebrated matins in the customary order. Moreover, when it became daylight he preached the peace inherited from the Lord's example [cf. John 14.27] to the priests and deacons and all the clerics. Then, as if roused from a dream, he recognized the time of evening devotion, extended his hands, and, although in a slow voice, [said]: "I have prepared a lamp for my Christ [Ps 132.17]; I have sung to my Lord." Then, after a considerable silence, about the fourth hour of night, with all who were present watching anxiously, suddenly his room was shaken by an earthquake so strong that those who were standing by his bed were terrified and disturbed, and all gave themselves to prayer. Those who were standing before the doors, however, knew nothing of this, for that earthquake had not been public but private in the room. He was taken up by angelic hands and breathed out the spirit he owed to God.

(5) We saw, dearest son, we saw, and amid our tears and sobbing we rejoice to have seen. We saw how a just man is raised up and no one understands. And just men are lifted up and no one reflects. Nor should it seem incredible to any Christian if in the passing of holy Paulinus one corner of the earth was specifically shaken by a tremor. Almost the whole world mourned his death. And truly what place is there in the world so remote, so hidden, that the passing of lord Paulinus did not disturb it? The entire Church wept because it lost such a bishop, but Paradise rejoices because it received one so holy. The people weep, but the angels rejoice. The provinces of men groan, but the sanctuaries [*loca*] of the saints rejoice, places to which he desired to fly away daily, when he said: "How lovely are your tabernacles, God, Lord of Virtues. My soul longs and faints for your halls" [Ps 84.2–3].

(6) O holy man and worthy of praise from every mouth, who so lived that he lived not only for himself but for all. And then because he lived for many in this world, he now lives for himself in Christ. And yet not for himself alone but for us as well, because he prays daily for us. He was a lamp burning in the house of the Lord, not placed under a bushel but placed on a lampstand, so that he even renders many lamps bright from his own brilliant light [cf. Matt 5.14–16]. For he was pleasant and gentle, even when he lived in the haughtiness of the world. When moreover he was converted to Christ, he opened his storerooms to the poor [and] his warehouses to those who came. For it was unimportant to him to nourish those close at hand if he did not also summon from all sides those whom he might feed and clothe. How many captives he redeemed! How many people entangled in debt did he free from their creditors by repaying the loan! Certainly with a single pious transaction he both wiped out the groans of the debtors and renewed the joys of the creditors.

(7) When, moreover, he had been promoted to the highest grade of the clergy, he did not wish to present himself as a bishop who was feared by anyone. But he showed himself [to be] the kind of bishop who was loved by all. Never was he so angered that he was not mindful of compassion in his anger, for never was that man able to be angered who despised insults and avoided hatreds. Never did he sit in judgment without compassion, because he knew that compassion was better than sacrifice. Every judgment of Christians must be clothed in compassion, as the venerable scripture says: "I will sing to you, Lord, of compassion and judgment" [Ps 101.1]. Justice also he tempered with kinder vows, knowing that the Holy Spirit as much favored fairness and justice as he kindly bestowed the favor of piety on his own [people]. And therefore he maintained rigor in his examination of justice, yet offered compassion in the framing of the sentence.

(8) O admirable man, to be judged by the praise of all virtues. For indeed he followed the examples of all the patriarchs. He was as faithful as Abraham, as trustful as Isaac, as kind as Jacob, as generous as Melchisedech, as foreseeing as Joseph, as grasping as Benjamin—for he seized from the rich and gave to the poor. And yet he is recognized to have benefited the rich more than the poor because he benefited the poor in this world but provided for the rich in the one to come. Therefore (as I began to say) he was as mild as Moses, as priestly as Aaron, as innocent as Samuel, as compassionate as David, as wise as Solomon, as apostolic as Peter, as lovable as John, as cautious as Thomas, as learned as Paul, as discerning as Stephen, [and] as fervent as Apollo. Concerning his responsibility and care for the churches, he imitated all the apostles and bishops in faith and love. He had all these qualities in himself; he guarded them faithfully during the length of his life. And therefore when (as I said above) he was summoned from this body into the heavenly dwelling, the earth grieved, but heaven rejoiced. The flesh wept, but the spirit exalted itself.

(9) For not only Christians, but even Jews and pagans came together for the last rites of Lord Paulinus, amid great weeping and tearing of clothing. With a single voice together with us, all bewailed the patron, defender, and guardian snatched from them. And truly he was such that he was loved by all. For everyone his life was an example of the acquisition of salvation and a source of refreshing consolation. Nor is my opinion that of a single person. All the provinces are witnesses; every land which the Roman world encompasses is a witness; even the barbarian nations are witnesses, to whom the reputation of lord Paulinus has penetrated. Nor undeservedly was he loved by all, he who was present for all. What suppliant did he not raise up with his right hand? What petitioner did he not comfort with his tender words? For he was pious, compassionate, humble, and kind. Spurning no one, despising no one, he gave to all, he bestowed on all. He encouraged the anxious, he tamed the fierce; the former he built up with words, the latter by his example. Some he supported with letters, others with his wealth. He admired no resources, no riches, except those which Christ had promised to his saints. He defined gold and silver and the rest in such a way that his liberality claimed them

for giving away, not his cupidity for hoarding them. And (to speak briefly) he had all good things in himself because he loved Christ; for he had faith, gentleness, concern for those closest to him, perpetual concern for the wretched, [and] compassion for the weak, looking to nothing else except peace and love. He alone was a beggar so that he might overflow for all. Finally, what place is there in the world, what solitude, which seas, that have not felt the gifts [*beneficia*] of holy Paulinus? All wished to know him, all desired to see him. Who did not come joyously to him? Who left him and was not about to miss him? For those who were not able to see him in the body at least desired to touch his letters. For he was pleasant and charming in his letters, sweet and very pleasant in his verse. What more? Credulity of faith would hardly admit those things which are said of him, did not his own deeds cast out the lie. Let us keep silent about the nobility of his birth—a nobility glowing admirably from paternal and maternal descent in the senatorial purple—and in addition the opulence of his riches, which he distributed to the poor on behalf of God. Now let us come to those matters which we began to say about his death.

(10) When holy Paulinus had given back the spirit owed to God, his countenance and his whole body were touched with such a snowy radiance that all among their sobbing and tears blessed God our Lord, God who leads forth his saints in magnificence to show his servants that this is the glory for all his saints. And so let his soul be praised in God and let his works be revealed among all who fear God, since he aspired to the commandments of his God, and he looked upon the needy and the poor so that his seed might be powerful in the earth and his justice remain for ever and ever.

(11) However, Your Veneration ought to know even this which pertains to the excellence of holy Paulinus, the fact that even holy John, the bishop of Naples, was acknowledged to have been summoned and called from this life to Christ by Lord Paulinus.[7] For three days before holy John migrated from this world to the Lord, he reported that he had seen Saint Paulinus dressed in angelic dignity, completely distinguished in starry whiteness, and resplendent with ambrosian odor and even holding in his hand a honeycomb shining brightly with honey. Paulinus was saying to him: "Brother John, what are you doing here? Loosen the chains of your weariness and now come to us. This food that I hold in my hand is abundant among us." And when he had said these words, he embraced him and put into his mouth part of that honeycomb, whose sweetness and odor Saint John said he so longed for that, if he had had the power in that very dream, he would not have failed to follow him. And yet he did not conceal it for long, for, aroused from sleep on the same day, that is the fifth day [Thursday], he paid all the clergy and the

7. On John I, bishop of Naples, 414–2 April 432, see Zincone, *Encyclopedia of the Early Church*, 1:438, with bibliography. John transferred the remains of Saint Januarius from near Puteoli to the catacomb of Capodimonte in Naples. Also see chapter 9.

paupers according to his custom, and in full health he celebrated the Lord's sup-
per. On the sixth day [Friday] he freed himself for prayer, but on the sabbath [Sat-
urday], at the second hour of the day, he joyously went forth to the church, and
having ascended the tribunal he greeted the people as was customary. Greeted in
turn by the people, he prayed, and when the prayer was finished, he breathed out
his spirit [2 April 432]. That night there was a vigil in the church, but on the next
day, that is, Easter, with lamps lighted, with a huge procession of neophytes and a
crowd of people following to the tomb, he received a glorious and praiseworthy
burial.

(12) These matters I have so commemorated for Your Nobility, so that you
might see even here the excellence of Saint Paulinus. You have the material for
speaking, but only if faith and belief are not lacking. And therefore I ask Your No-
bility that, as you deigned to promise, you consider it worthy to hasten the task of
your brilliant work. And you will pursue the rewards of fame and glory, if you il-
lustrate in verse the life of the holy man for the benefit of those to come. Would
that you may make me worthy of the reading of this work before I set out, because
if it pleases Christ I am ready to sail at once. Saint Paulinus the bishop died ten
days before the Calends of July [in the year] when Bassus and Antiochus, most dis-
tinguished men [*viri clarissimi*], were consuls [22 June 431].

SELECT BIBLIOGRAPHY

I have limited this bibliography to the secondary literature cited in the notes. More comprehensive bibliographical surveys can be found in the following: J.T. Lienhard, *Paulinus of Nola and Early Western Monasticism* (Köln, 1977), 192–204; C. Magazzù, "Dieci anni di studi su Paolino di Nola (1977–1987)," *Bolletino di studi Latini* 18 (1988) 84–103; and C. Iannicelli, "Rassegna di studi Paoliniani (1980–1997)," *Impegno e dialogo* 11 (1994–96): 279–321.

Alföldi, A. *A Festival of Isis in Rome under the Christian Emperors of the Fourth Century.* Budapest, 1937.
———. *A Conflict of Ideas in the Late Roman Empire: The Clash between the Senate and Valentinian I.* Oxford, 1952.
Argenio, R. "Il miracolo dei buoi nel xx [*sic*] natalizio di S. Paolino di Nola." *Rivista di studi classici* 17 (1969): 330–38.
Arnheim, M. T. W. *The Senatorial Aristocracy in the Later Roman Empire.* Oxford, 1972.
———. "The Suffect Consulship in the Later Roman Empire." *Byzantine Studies* 1 (1974): 147–68.
Babut, E.-C. "Paulin de Nole et Priscillien." *Revue d'histoire et de littérature religieuses* 1 (1910): 97–130, 252–75.
Bagnall, R. S., A. Cameron, S. R. Schwartz, and K. A. Worp. *Consuls of the Later Roman Empire.* Atlanta, 1987.
Balmelle, C. *Recueil général des mosaïques de la Gaule. Gallia* supp. 10.4.1 (1980): 58–83.
———. *Recueil général des mosaïques de la Gaule. Gallia* supp. 10.4.2 (1987): 151–94.
———. "L'habitat urbain dans le sud-ouest de la Gaule romaine." *Villes et agglomérations urbaines antiques du sud-ouest de la Gaule: Histoire et archéologie. Sixième supplément à Aquitania,* 335–64. Paris and Bordeaux, 1992.
Balmelle, C., M. Gauthier, and R. Monturet. "Mosaïques de la villa du Palat à Saint-Émilion (Gironde)." *Gallia* 38 (1980): 59–96.
Bammel, C. Hammond. "Rufinus' Translation of Origen's Commentary on Romans and the Pelagian Controversy." *Storia ed esegesi in Rufino di Concordia,* 131–42. Udine, 1992.
Bardy, G. In *Histoire de l'église; De la mort de Théodose à l'élection de Grégoire le Grand.* Ed. P. de Labriolle, G. Bardy, G. de Plinval, and L. Brehier. Paris, 1937.

Barnes, T. D. "Who Were the Nobility of the Roman Empire?" *Phoenix* 28 (1974): 444–49.

———. "The Historical Setting of Prudentius' *Contra Symmachum.*" *American Journal of Philology* 97 (1976): 373–86.

———. "Religion and Society in the Age of Theodosius." In *Grace, Politics, and Desire: Essays on Augustine.* Ed. H. A. Meynell, 157–75. Calgary, 1990.

———. "Augustine, Symmachus, and Ambrose." In *Augustine: From Rhetor to Theologian.* Ed. J. McWilliam, 7–13. Waterloo, Ontario, 1992.

Barnes, T. D., and R. W. Westfall. "The Conversion of the Roman Aristocracy in Prudentius' *Contra Symmachum.*" *Phoenix* 45 (1991): 50–61.

Barraud, D., and M.-A. Gaidon. "Bordeaux." *Villes et agglomérations urbaines antiques du sud-ouest de la Gaule: Histoire et archéologie. Sixième supplément à Aquitania,* 43–48. Paris and Bordeaux, 1992.

Barrow, R. H. *Prefect and Emperor: The Relationes of Symmachus A.D. 384.* Oxford, 1973.

Basson, A. "A Transformation of Genres in Late Latin Literature: Classical Literary Tradition and Ascetic Ideals in Paulinus of Nola." In *Shifting Frontiers in Late Antiquity.* Ed. R. Mathisen and H. Sivan, 267–72. Aldershot, 1996.

Baudrillart, A. *Saint Paulin: Évêque de Nole (353–431).* Paris, 1905.

Bloch, H. "A New Document of the Last Pagan Revival in the West, 393–394 A.D." *Harvard Theological Review* 38 (1945): 197–244.

Boissier, G. *La fin du paganisme: Étude sur les dernières luttes religieuses en occident au quatrième siècle.* 2 vols. 3d ed. Paris, 1898.

Booth, A. D. "Notes on Ausonius' *Professores.*" *Phoenix* 32 (1978): 235–49.

———. "The Date of Jerome's Birth." *Phoenix* 33 (1979): 346–53.

———. "The Academic Career of Ausonius." *Phoenix* 36 (1982): 329–43.

———. "Sur la date de naissance de Saint Paulin de Nole." *Écho du monde classique* 26 (1982): 57–64.

Bordeaux: 2000 ans d'histoire. Bordeaux, 1973.

Bowersock, G. W. "Symmachus and Ausonius." *Colloque genevois sur Symmaque à l'occasion du mille-six-centième anniversaire du conflit de l'autel de la Victoire,* 1–15. Paris, 1986.

Bradbury, S. *Severus of Minorca: Letter on the Conversion of the Jews.* Oxford, 1996.

Brown, P. "Aspects of the Christianization of the Roman Aristocracy." *Religion and Society in the Age of Augustine,* 161–82. New York, 1972.

———. *Augustine of Hippo: A Biography.* Berkeley, 1967.

———. "Pelagius and His Supporters: Aims and Environment." *Religion and Society in the Age of Augustine,* 183–207. New York, 1972.

———. "The Patrons of Pelagius: The Roman Aristocracy between East and West." *Religion and Society in the Age of Augustine,* 208–26. New York, 1972.

———. *The Cult of the Saints: Its Rise and Function in Latin Christianity.* Chicago, 1981.

———. "The Saint as Exemplar in Late Antiquity," *Representations* 2 (1983): 1–25.

———. *The Body and Society: Men, Women, and Sexual Renunciation in Early Christianity.* New York, 1988.

———. *Authority and the Sacred: Aspects of the Christianisation of the Roman World.* Cambridge, 1995.

Brückner, A. *Julian von Eclanum: Sein Leben und seine Lehre. Texte und Untersuchungen zur Geschichte der altchristlichen Literatur* 15.3a (Leipzig 1897): 1–180.

Burn, A. E. *Niceta of Remesiana: His Life and Works.* Cambridge, 1905.

Burrus, V. *The Making of a Heretic: Gender, Authority, and the Priscillianist Controversy.* Berkeley, 1995.

Buse, A. *Paulin, Bischof von Nola, und seine Zeit (350–450).* 2 vols. Regensburg, 1856. French translation by L. Dancoisne, *S. Paulin, évêque de Nole, et son siècle (350–450).* Paris, 1858.

Callu, J.-P. "Les préfectures de Nicomaque Flavien." *Mélanges d'histoire ancienne offerts à William Seston*, 73–80. Paris, 1974.

Cameron, Alan. "The Roman Friends of Ammianus." *Journal of Roman Studies* 54 (1964): 15–28.

—————. "Gratian's Repudiation of the Pontifical Robe." *Journal of Roman Studies* 58 (1968): 96–102.

—————. "Theodosius the Great and the Regency of Stilico." *Harvard Studies in Classical Philology* 73 (1969): 247–67.

—————. "Paganism and Literature in the Fourth Century." *Christianisme et formes littéraires de l'antiquité tardive: Entretiens sur l'antiquité classique XXIII*, 1–30. Geneva, 1977.

—————. "Polyonomy in the Late Roman Aristocracy: The Case of Petronius Probus." *Journal of Roman Studies* 75 (1985): 164–182.

—————. "The Date and Owners of the Esquiline Treasure." *American Journal of Archaeology* 89 (1985): 135–45.

—————. "Pagan Ivories." *Colloque genevois sur Symmaque à l'occasion du mille-six-centième anniversaire du conflit de l'autel de la Victoire*, 41–64. Paris, 1986.

—————. "Filocalus and Melania." *Classical Philology* 87 (1992): 140–44.

Cameron, Averil. *Christianity and the Rhetoric of Empire: The Development of Christian Discourse.* Berkeley, 1991.

—————. "Eusebius' *Vita Constantini* and the Construction of Constantine." In *Portraits: Biographical Representation in the Greek and Latin Literature of the Roman Empire.* Ed. M. Edwards and S. Swain, 145–74. Oxford, 1997.

Carrese, L. "I carmi profani di Paolino di Nola." *Annali della facoltà di lettere e folosofia dell' Università di Napoli* 28, n.s, 16 (1985–86): 5–14.

Casati, G. "S. Agostino e S. Paolino di Nola." *Augustinianum* 8 (1968): 40–57.

Caspar, E. *Geschichte des Papsttums von den Anfängen bis zur Höhe der Weltherrschaft.* 2 vols. Tübingen, 1930.

Cattaneo, E. "Il *Christus patiens* nel giusto perseguitato: reminiscenze melitoniane in S. Paolino di Nola." *Koinonia* 9 (1985): 141–52.

Cavadini, J. "Simplifying Augustine." Paper delivered at meeting of the North American Patristic Society, Loyola University of Chicago, 31 May 1996.

Cavallera, F. *Saint Jérôme, sa vie et son oeuvre.* 2 vols. Louvain, 1922.

Cébeillac, M. "Quelques inscriptions inédites d'Ostie." *Mélanges de l'école française de Rome* 83 (1971): 39–88.

Cecconi, G. *Governo imperiale e élites dirigenti nell'Italia tardoantica: Problemi di storia politico-amministrativa (270–476 d.C.).* Como, 1994.

Chadwick, H. *Priscillian of Avila: The Occult and the Charismatic in the Early Church.* Oxford, 1976.

—————. "Oracles of the End in the Conflict of Paganism and Christianity in the Fourth Century." *Mémorial A.-J. Festugière*, 125–29. Geneva, 1984.

Chadwick, N. *Poetry and Letters in Early Christian Gaul.* London, 1955.

Charlet, J.-L. "Prudence, lecteur de Paulin de Nole: A propos du 23e quatrain du *Dittochaeon*." *Revue des études augustiniennes* 21 (1975): 55–62.

Chastagnol, A. "Le sénateur Volusien et la conversion d'une famille de l'aristocratie romaine au Bas-Empire." *Revue des études anciennes* 58 (1956): 241–53.

—————. "Observations sur le consulat suffect et la préfecture du Bas-Empire." *Revue historique* 219 (1958): 221–53.

—————. *La préfecture urbaine à Rome sous le Bas-Empire.* Paris, 1960.

—————. *Les fastes de la préfecture de Rome au Bas-Empire.* Paris, 1962.

—————. "L'administration du diocèse italien au Bas-Empire." *Historia* 12 (1963): 348–79.

———. "La restauration du temple d'Isis au *Portus Romae* sous le règne de Gratien." *Hommage à Marcel Renard.* Vol. 2. *Collection Latomus* 102 (1969): 135–44.

———. "Le diocèse civil d'Aquitaine au Bas-Empire." *Bulletin de la société nationale des antiquaires de France.* (1970): 272–92.

———. "Les modes de recrutement du Sénat au IVe siècle après J.-C." *Recherches sur les structures sociales dans l'antiquité classique,* 187–211. Paris, 1970.

———. "L'évolution de l'ordre sénatorial aux IIIe et IVe siècles de notre ère." *Revue historique* 244 (1970): 308–10.

———. "La carrière sénatoriale du Bas-Empire (depuis Dioclétien)." *Tituli* 4 (1982): 167–94.

———. "Le Sénat dans l'oeuvre de Symmaque." *Colloque genevois sur Symmaque à l'occasion du mille-six-centième anniversaire du conflit de l'autel de la Victoire,* 73–96. Paris, 1986.

———. *Le Sénat romain à l'époque impériale.* Paris, 1992.

Chierici, G. "Lo stato degli studi intorno alle basiliche paoliniane di Cimitile." *Atti del IV congresso nazionale di studi romani,* 236–43. Rome, 1938.

———. "Di alcuni risultati sui recenti lavori intorno alla basilica di san Lorenzo a Milano e alle basiliche paoliniane di Cimitile." *Revista di archeologia cristiana* 16 (1939): 51–72.

———. "Sant'Ambrogio e la costruzione paoliniane di Cimitile." *Ambrosiana. Scritti di storia, archeologia ed arte pubblicati nel XVI centenario della nascita di Sant'Ambrogio, CCCXL–MCMXL,* 315–31. Milan, 1942.

———. "Metodo e risultati degli ultimi studi intorno alle basiliche paleocristiane di Cimitile." *Atti della pontificia accademia di archeologia (Serie 3). Rendiconti* 29 (1956–57): 139–49.

———. "Cimitile." *Palladio* n.s. 7 (1957): 69–73.

———. "Cimitile, I. La Necropoli." *Revista di archeologia cristiana* 33 (1957): 99–125.

———. "Cimitile." *Archivio storico di Terra di Lavoro* 2 (1959): 159–69.

———. "Cimitile: La seconda fase dei lavori intorno alle basiliche." *Atti del 3 congresso internazionale di studi sull'alto medioevo,* 125–37. Spoleto, 1959.

Clark, E. A. "Ascetic Renunciation and Feminine Advancement: A Paradox of Late Ancient Christianity." *Anglican Theological Review* 63 (1981): 240–57.

———. *The Life of Melania the Younger.* New York, 1984.

———. "Authority and Humility: A Conflict of Values in Fourth-Century Female Monasticism." *Byzantinische Forschungen* 9 (1985): 17–33.

———. *The Origenist Controversy: The Cultural Construction of an Early Christian Debate.* Princeton, 1992.

———. "Reading Asceticism: Exegetical Strategies in the Early Christian Rhetoric of Renunciation." *Biblical Interpretation* 5 (1997): 82–105.

Clark, E. A., and D. Hatch, *The Golden Bough, The Oaken Cross: The Virgilian Cento of Faltonia Betitia Proba.* Ann Arbor, 1981.

Clemente, G. "Le carriere dei governatori della diocesi italiciana dal III al V secolo." *Latomus* 28 (1969): 619–44.

Comaroff, J., and J. Comaroff. *Modernity and Its Malcontents: Ritual and Power in Postcolonial Africa.* Chicago, 1993.

Consolino, F. *Ascesi e mondanità nella Gallia tardoantica.* Naples, 1979.

———. "Modelli di santità femminile nelle più antiche Passioni romane." *Augustinianum* 24 (1984): 83–113.

———. "Il monachesimo femminile nella tarda antichità." *Codex Aquilarensis* 2 (1988): 33–45.

———. "Sante o patrone? Le aristocratiche tardoantiche e il potere della carità." *Studi storici* 30 (1989): 969–91.

Conybeare, C. "The Expresssion of Christianity: Themes from the Letters of Paulinus of Nola." Ph.D. diss. University of Toronto, 1998.

Cooper, K. "Insinuations of Womanly Influence: An Aspect of the Christianization of the Roman Aristocracy." *Journal of Roman Studies* 82 (1992): 150–164.

————. *The Virgin and the Bride: Idealized Womanhood in Late Antiquity.* Cambridge, Mass., 1996.

Corsaro, F. "L'autore del *De mortibus boum:* Paolino da Nola e la politica religiosa di Teodosio." *Orpheus* 22 (1975): 3–26.

Costanza, S. "Dottrina e poesia nel carme XXXI di Paolino da Nola." *Giornale italiano di filologia* 24 (1972): 346–53.

————. "I generi letterari nell'opera poetica di Paolino di Nola." *Augustinianum* 14 (1974): 637–50.

————. "Aspetti autobiografici nell'opera poetica di Paolino di Nola." *Giornale italiano di filologia* 27 (1975): 265–77.

————. "I rapporti tra Ambrogio e Paolino di Nola." *Ambrosius Episcopus: Atti del congresso internazionale di studi ambrosiani nel XVI centenario della elevazione di sant'Ambrogio alla cattedra episcopale,* 220–32. Milan, 1976.

————. "Rapporti letterari tra Paolino e Prudenzio." *Atti del Convegno: XXXI Cinquantenario della morte di S. Paolino di Nola (431–1981),* 25–65. Roma, 1982.

————. " *Pax romana–pax christiana* in Paolino di Nola." *Studi tardoantichi* 1 (1986): 55–71.

Coster, C. H. "Christianity and the Invasions: Paulinus of Nola." *Late Roman Studies.* Cambridge, Mass., 1968.

Countryman, L. W. *The Rich Christian in the Church of the Early Empire: Contradictions and Accommodations.* New York, 1980.

Courcelle, P. "Paulin de Nole et Saint Jérôme." *Revue des études latines* 25 (1947): 250–80.

————. "Un nouveau poème de Paulin de Pella." *Vigiliae Christianae* 1 (1947): 101–13.

————. "Fragments historiques de Paulin de Nole conservés par Grégoire de Tours." *Mélanges d'histoire du moyen age dédiés à la mémoire de Louis Halphen,* 145–53. Paris, 1951.

————. "Les lacunes de la correspondance entre saint Augustin et Paulin de Nole." *Revues des études anciennes* 53 (1951): 253–300.

————. "Nouveaux aspects de la culture lérinienne." *Revue des études latines* 46 (1968): 379–409.

————. *Recherches sur les* Confessions *de Saint Augustine.* 2d ed. Paris, 1968.

————. *Late Latin Writers and their Greek Sources.* Trans. H. E. Wedeck. Cambridge, Mass., 1969.

————. "Jugements de Rufin et de Saint Augustin sur les empereurs du IVe siècle et la défaite suprême du paganisme." *Revue des études anciennes* 71 (1969): 100–130.

Cracco Ruggini, L. "Il paganesimo romano tra religione e politica (384–394 d.C.): Per una reinterpretazione del Carmen contra paganos." *Mem. dell' Accademia Nazionale dei Lincei.* Classe di scienze morali, storiche e filologiche. Ser. 8, vol. 23. Rome, 1979.

Cristo, S. "Some Notes on the Bonifacian-Eulalian Schism." *Aevum* 51 (1977): 163–67.

Croke, B. "Arbogast and the Death of Valentinian II." *Historia* 25 (1976): 235–44.

Crouzel, Henri. "Chronologie proposée du prêtre commingeois Vigilance de Calagurris (Saint-Martory)." *Bulletin de littérature ecclésiatique* 73 (1972): 265–66.

————. "Saint Jérôme et ses amis toulousains." *Bulletin de littérature ecclésiastique* 73 (1972): 125–46.

————. "L'epitalamio di San Paolino: Il suo contenuto dottrinale." *Atti del Convegno: XXXI Cinquantenario della morte di S. Paolino di Nola (431–1981),* 143–48. Roma, 1982.

————. "Un 'piccolo cliente' di San Paolino di Nola: Vigilanzio di Calagurris." *Paolino di Nola: momenti della sua vita e delle sue opere,* 199–219. Nola, 1983.

D'Arms, J. H. *Romans on the Bay of Naples: A Social and Cultural Study of the Villas and Their Owners from 150 B.C. to A.D. 400.* Cambridge, Mass., 1970.

Debord, P. and M. Gauthier. *Bordeaux Saint-Christoly: Sauvetage archéologique et histoire urbaine.* Bordeaux, 1982.

de Bruyn, T. *Pelagius's Commentary on St. Paul's Epistle to the Romans.* Oxford, 1993.

Delehaye, H. "Les premiers 'libelli miraculorum.'" *Analecta Bollandiana* 29 (1910): 427–34.

———. "Saint Martin et Sulpice Sévère." *Analecta Bollandiana* 38 (1920): 5–136.

———. "Les recueils antiques de miracles des saints." *Analecta Bollandiana* 43 (1925): 5–85.

de Ligt, L. *Fairs and Markets in the Roman Empire: Economic and Social Aspects of Periodic Trade in a Pre-industrial Society.* Amsterdam, 1993.

Desmulliez, J. "Paulin de Nole: Études chronologiques (393–397)." *Recherches augustiniennes* 20 (1985): 35–64.

De Vooght, D. "Les miracles dans la vie de Saint Augustin." *Recherches de théologie ancienne et médiévale* 11 (1939): 5–16.

———. "La théologie du miracle selon Saint Augustine." *Recherches de théologie ancienne et médiévale* 11 (1939): 197–222.

di Ferrante, E. "Il restauro delle basiliche di Cimitile." *Akten des XII. internationalen Kongresses für christliche Archäologie,* 746–55. Rome, 1995.

Dionisotti, A. C. "From Ausonius' Schooldays? A Schoolbook and Its Relatives." *Journal of Roman Studies* 72 (1982): 83–125.

D'Isanto, G. *Capua romana: Ricerche di prosopografia e storia sociale.* Rome, 1993.

Doignon, J. "'Nos bons hommes de foi': Cyprien, Lactance, Victorin, Optat, Hilaire (Augustin, *De doctrina christiana,* IV, 40, 61)." *Latomus* 22 (1963): 795–805.

———. "Un récit de miracle dans les 'Carmina' de Paulin de Nole: Poétique virgilienne et leçon apologétique." *Revue d'histoire de la spiritualité* 48 (1972): 129–44.

———. "Oracles, prophéties, 'on-dit' sur la chute de Rome (395–410): Les réactions de Jérôme et d'Augustin." *Revue des études augustiniennes* 36 (1990): 120–46.

Dolbeau, F. "Damase, le carmen contra paganos, et Hériger de Lobbes." *Revue des études augustiniennes* 27 (1981): 38–43.

Drinkwater, J. F. *The Gallic Empire: Separatism and Continuity in the North-Western Provinces of the Roman Empire.* Stuttgart, 1987.

———. "The Bacaudae of Fifth-Century Gaul." In *Fifth-Century Gaul: A Crisis of Identity?* Ed. J. F. Drinkwater and H. Elton, 208–17. Cambridge, 1992.

Duchesne, L. *Fastes épiscopaux de l'ancienne Gaule.* 2d edition. 3 vols. Paris, 1910.

Duncan-Jones, R. *The Economy of the Roman Empire: Quantitative Studies.* Cambridge, 1974.

Duval, Y. *Loca sanctorum Africae: Le culte des martyrs en Afrique du IVe au VIIe siècle.* Rome, 1982.

———. "Flora était-elle africaine? (Augustin, *De Cura gerenda pro mortuis,* 1, 1)." *Revue des études augustiniennes* 34 (1988): 70–77.

———. *Auprès des saints: Corps et âme. L'inhumation "ad sanctos" dans la chrétienté d'Orient et d'Occident du IIIe au VIIe siècle.* Paris, 1988.

Duval, Y.-M. "L'éloge de Théodose dans la *Cité de Dieu* (V, 26, 1): Sa place, son sens et ses sources." *Recherches augustiniennes* 4 (1966): 135–79.

———. "Recherches sur la langue et la littérature latines: Bellérophon et les ascètes chrétiens: 'Melancholia' ou '*otium*'?" *Caesarodunum* 3 (1968): 183–90.

———. "Julien d'Éclane et Rufin d'Aquilée: Du Concile de Rimini à la répression pélagienne. L'intervention impériale en matière religieuse." *Revue des études augustiniennes* 24 (1978): 243–71.

———. "Pélage est-il le censeur inconnu de l'*Adversus Iovinianum* à Rome en 393? Ou: du 'portrait-robot' de l'hérétique chez S. Jérôme." *Revue d'histoire ecclésiastique* 75 (1980): 525–57.

———. "Les premiers rapports de Paulin de Nole avec Jérôme: Moine et philosophe? Poète ou exégète?" *Studi tardoantichi* 7 (1989): 177–216.

Edwards, M., and S. Swain. *Portraits: Biographical Representation in the Greek and Latin Literature of the Roman Empire.* Oxford, 1997.

Eiswirth, R. *Hieronymus' Stellung zur Literatur und Kunst.* Wiesbaden, 1955.

Eno, R. *Saint Augustine and the Saints.* Villanova, 1989.

Erdt, W. *Christentum und heidnisch-antike Bildung bei Paulin von Nola.* Meisenheim, 1976.

Errington, R. M. "The Praetorian Prefectures of Virius Nicomachus Flavianus." *Historia* 61 (1992): 439–61.

Étienne, R. *Bordeaux antique.* Bordeaux, 1962.

———. "Ausone et l'Espagne." *Mélanges d'archéologie, d'épigraphie et d'histoire offerts à Jérôme Carcopino,* 319–32. Vendôme, 1966.

Evans, R. *Pelagius: Inquiries and Reappraisals.* New York, 1968.

Evenpoel, W. "The Vita Felicis of Paulinus Nolanus." *Aevum inter Utrumque: Mélanges offerts à Gabriel Sanders,* 143–52. Steenbrugis, 1991.

———. "La phrase et le vers dans les Carmina de Paulin de Nole." *Eulogia: Mélanges offerts à Antoon A. R. Bastiaensen,* 95–108. Steenbrugis, 1991.

———. "Saint Paulin de Nole, *carm* 18, 211–468: Hagiographie et humour." *La narativa cristiana antica: Codici narrativi, strutture formali, schemi retorici,* 507–20. Rome, 1995.

Exner, M. "Il convegno paoliniano XVI centenario del ritiro di Paolino a Nola." *Kunst Chronik* 49 (1996): 145–53.

Fabre, P. *Essai sur la chronologie de l'oeuvre de Saint Paulin de Nole.* Publications de la faculté des lettres de l'Université de Strasbourg, 109. Paris, 1948.

———. *Saint Paulin de Nole et l'amitié chrétienne.* Bibliothèque des écoles françaises d'Athènes et de Rome, 167. Paris, 1949.

Favez, C. "Note sur la composition du *carmen* 31 de Paulin de Nole." *Revue des études latines* 13 (1935): 266–68.

Fedalto, G. "Rufino di Concordia: Elementi di una biografia." *Storia ed esegesi in Rufino di Concordia,* 19–44. Udine, 1992.

Ferrua, A. *Epigrammata damasiana.* Rome, 1942.

———. "Graffiti di pellegrini alla tomba di San Felice." *Palladio* n.s. 13 (1963): 17–19.

———. "Cimitile ed altre iscrizioni dell'Italia inferiore, I." *Epigraphica* 33 (1971): 99–104.

———. "Cancelli di Cimitile con scritte bibliche." *Römische Quartelschrift* 68 (1973): 50–68.

———. "Le iscrizioni paleocristiane di Cimitile." *Revista di archeologia cristiana* 53 (1977): 105–36.

Flury, P. "Das sechste Gedicht des Paulinus von Nola." *Vigiliae Christianae* 27 (1973): 129–45.

Foerster, F. and R. Pascual. *El naufragio de Valgius: Estracto comentado de la Epistola n. 49 de San Paulino de Nola.* Barcelona, 1985.

Fontaine, J. *Suplice Sévère: Vie de saint Martin. Sources chrétiennes* 133. Paris, 1967.

———. "Valeurs antiques et valeurs chrétiennes dans la spiritualité des grands propriétaires terriens à la fin du IVe siècle occidental." In *Epektasis: Mélanges patristiques offerts au Cardinal Jean Daniélou.* Ed. J. Fontaine and C. Kannengiesser, 571–95. Paris, 1972.

———. "Les symbolismes de la cithare dans la poésie de Paulin de Nole." *Romanitas et christianitas: Studia J. H. Waszink,* 123–43. Amsterdam and London, 1973.

———. "Société et culture chrétiennes sur l'aire circumpyrénéenne au siècle de Théodose." *Bulletin de littérature ecclésiastique* 75 (1974): 241–282.

———. "L'affaire Priscillien, ou l'ère des nouveaux Catilina: Observations sur le 'Sallustianisme' de Sulpice Sévère." In *Classica et Iberica: A Festschrift in Honor of Reverend Joseph M. F. Marique, S.J.* Ed. P. T. Brannan, 355–92. Worcester, Mass., 1975.

———. "La conversion du christianisme à la culture antique: la lecture chrétienne de l'univers bucolique de Virgile." *Études sur la poésie latine tardive d'Ausone à Prudence,* 214–39. Paris, 1980.

———. *Naissance de la poésie dans l'Occident chrétien.* Paris, 1981.

Fouet, G. *La villa gallo-romaine de Montmaurin. Gallia* supp. 20. 1969.

———. "Le sanctuaire des eaux de 'la Hillère' à Montmaurin (Haute-Garonne)." *Gallia* 30 (1972): 83–124.

————. "Exemples d'exploitation des eaux par de grands propriétaires terriens dans le sud-ouest au IVe siècle." *Caesarodunum* 10 (1975): 128–34.

Frayn, J. M. *Markets and Fairs in Roman Italy.* New York, 1993.

Frend, W. H. C. "Paulinus of Nola and the Last Century of the Western Empire." *Journal of Roman Studies* 59 (1969): 1–11.

————. "The Two Worlds of Paulinus of Nola." In *Latin Literature of the Fourth Century.* Ed. J. W. Binns, 100–33. London, 1974.

Gabba, E. "Mercati e fiore nell'Italia romana." *Studi classici e orientali* 24 (1975): 141–63.

Gadeyne, J. "Alcuni considerazione sulla descrizione Paolina del mosaico absidiale di Fondi." *Boreas* 13 (1990): 71–74.

Gamble, H. *Books and Readers in the Early Church: A History of Early Christian Texts.* New Haven, 1995.

Gaudemet, J. "La condemnation des pratiques païennes en 391." In *Epektasis: Mélanges patristiques offerts au Cardinal Jean Daniélou.* Ed. J. Fontaine and C. Kannengiesser, 597–602. Paris, 1972.

Geiger, J. *Cornelius Nepos and Ancient Political Biography.* Stuttgart, 1985.

Gelsomino, R. "L'epitalamio di Paolino di Nola per Giuliano e Titia (Carme 25)." *Atti del Convegno: XXXI Cinquantenario della morte di S. Paolino di Nola (431–1981),* 213–30. Rome, 1982.

Gentili, B. and G. Cerri. *History and Biography in Ancient Thought.* Amsterdam, 1988.

Gersch, S. *Middle Platonism and Neoplatonism: The Latin Tradition.* Notre Dame, 1986.

Ghizzoni, F. *Sulpicio Severo.* Rome, 1983.

Gilliard, F. "Senatorial Bishops in the Fourth Century." *Harvard Theological Review* 77 (1984): 153–75.

Goldschmidt, R. C. *Paulinus' Churches at Nola: Texts, Translations and Commentary.* Amsterdam, 1940.

Gorce, D. *Vie de Sainte Mélanie.* Sources chrétiennes 90. Paris, 1962.

Gordini, G. D. "Origine e sviluppo del monachesimo a Roma." *Gregorianum* 37 (1956): 220–60.

Grabar, A. *Martyrium: Recherches sur le culte des reliques et l'art chrétien antique.* 2 vols. Paris, 1946; reprint, London, 1972.

Green, R. P. H. *The Poetry of Paulinus of Nola: A Study of his Latinity.* Brussels, 1971.

————. "Paulinus of Nola and the Diction of Christian Latin Poetry." *Latomus* 32 (1973): 79–85.

————. "The Correspondence of Ausonius." *L'antiquité classique* 49 (1980): 191–211.

————. "Still Waters Run Deep: A New Study of the *Professores* of Bordeaux." *Classical Quarterly* 35 (1985): 491–506.

————. *The Works of Ausonius.* Oxford, 1991.

————. "The Christianity of Ausonius." *Studia Patristica* 28 (1993): 39–48.

Griffe, E. *La Gaule chrétienne à l'époque romaine.* 2d ed. 3 vols. Paris, 1964–1966.

Grünewald, T. "Der letzte Kampf des Heidentums in Rom? Zur postumen Rehabilitation des Virius Nicomachus Flavianus." *Historia* 41 (1992): 462–87.

Guttilla, G. "Una nuova lettura del *carme* 31 di S. Paolino di Nola." *Koinonia* 11 (1987): 69–97.

————. "Il *De cura pro mortuis gerenda* di Agostino e l'*obitus Baebiani* di Paolino di Nola." *Annali del Liceo Classico G. Garibaldi di Palermo* 25–27 (1988–90): 193–207.

————. "S. Paolino e i barbari nei *Natalicia.*" *Koinonia* 13 (1989): 5–29.

————. "I tituli in onore del *presbyter Clarus* e la datazione del carme 31 di Paolino di Nola." *Bollettino di studi latini* 19 (1989): 58–69.

————. "Il *Panegyricus Theodosii* di S. Paolino di Nola." *Koinonia* 14 (1990): 139–54.

———. "Preghiere e invocazioni nei *carmi* di S. Paolino di Nola." *Annali del liceo classico G. Garbaldi di Palermo* 28–30 (1991–93): 93–188.

———. "Paolino di Nola e Girolamo." *Orpheus* 13 (1992): 278–94.

———. "Tre naufragi di contenuto cristiano del IV secolo d.C. (Ambrogio, *de exc. fratr.* 1,43–48; Paolino, *carm.* 24,1–308 ed *epist.* 49)." In *Anchora vitae: Atti del II Convegno Paoliniano nel XVI Centenario del Ritiro di Paolino a Nola (Nola / Cimitile 18–20 maggio 1995).* Ed. G. Luongo. Naples, 1998.

Guy, J.-C. "La place du 'mépris du monde' dans le monachisme ancien." *Le mépris du monde: La notion de mépris du monde dans la tradition spirituelle occidentale,* 5–17. Paris, 1965.

Guyon, J. "Saint-Bertrand-de-Comminges." *Villes et agglomérations urbaines antiques du sud-ouest de la Gaule: Histoire et archéologie. Sixième supplément à Aquitania,* 140–45. Paris and Bordeaux, 1992.

Hammond, C. P. "The Last Ten Years of Rufinus' Life and the Date of his Move South from Aquileia." *Journal of Theological Studies* 28 (1977): 372–429.

Harries, J. "Prudentius and Theodosius." *Latomus* 43 (1984): 69–73.

———. "'Treasure in Heaven': Property and Inheritance among Senators of Late Rome." In *Marriage and Property.* Ed. E. Craik, 54–70. Aberdeen, 1984.

———. "The Roman Imperial Quaestor from Constantine to Theodosius II." *Journal of Roman Studies* 78 (1988): 148–172.

———. *Sidonius Apollinaris and the Fall of Rome.* Oxford, 1994.

Heather, P. *Goths and Romans, 332–489.* Oxford, 1991.

———. "Senators and Senates." In *The Cambridge Ancient History,* vol. 13, ed. A. Cameron and P. Garnsey, 184–210. Cambridge, 1998.

Heffernan, T. *Sacred Biography: Saints and Their Biographers in the Middle Ages.* New York, 1988.

Heim, F. *La théologie de la victoire de Constantin à Théodose.* Paris, 1992.

Heinzelmann, M. "Gallische Prosopographie: 260–527." *Francia* 10 (1982): 531–718.

Herrmann, L. "Claudius Antonius et la crise réligieuse de 394 ap. J.-C." *Mélanges Henri Grégoire.* Vol. 2, 329–42. Brussels, 1950.

Herval, R. *Origines chrétiennes: De la IIe Lyonnaise gallo-romaine à la Normandie ducale (IVe–XIe siècles).* Rouen, 1966.

Herzog, R. "Probleme der heidnisch-christlichen Gattungskontinuität am Beispiel des Paulinus von Nola." *Christianisme et formes littéraires de l'antiquité tardive: Entretiens sur l'antiquité classique XXIII,* 373–423. Geneva, 1977.

———. *Restauration et renouveau: La littérature latine de 284 à 374 après J.-C.* Vol. 5 of *Nouvelle histoire de la littérature latine.* Ed. R. Herzog and P. Schmidt. Paris, 1993.

Heylin, C. *Bob Dylan: Behind the Shades.* New York, 1991.

Honoré, T. "Some Writings of the Pagan Champion Nicomachus Flavianus." *Xenia* 23 (1989): 9–17.

Hopkins, M. K. "Social Mobility in the Later Roman Empire: The Evidence of Ausonius." *Classical Quarterly* n.s. 11 (1961): 239–49.

Hubaux, J. "La crise de la trois-cent-soixante-cinquième année." *L'antiquité classique* 17 (1948): 343–54.

Hunter, D. "Resistance to the Virginal Ideal in Late-Fourth-Century Rome: The Case of Jovinian." *Theological Studies* 48 (1987): 45–67.

———. "Helvidius, Jovinian, and the Virginity of Mary in Late Fourth-Century Rome." *Journal of Early Christian Studies* 1 (1993): 47–71.

Iannicelli, C. "Note al lessico Paoliniano: Indagine su alcuni apellativi riferiti a S. Felice." *Impegno e dialogo* 8 (1990–91): 183–204.

Inglebert, H. *Les romains chrétiens face à l'histoire de Rome: Histoire, christianisme et romanités en Occident dans l'antiquité tardive (IIIe–Ve siècles).* Paris, 1996.

Irvine, M. *The Making of Textual Culture: "Grammatica" and Literary Theory, 350–1100.* Cambridge, 1994.

Jäger, F. *Das antike Propemptikon und das 17 Gedicht des Paulinus von Nola.* Rosenheim, 1913.

Jameson, M. H. "Sacrifice and Animal Husbandry in Classical Greece." In *Pastoral Economies in Classical Antiquity.* Ed. C. R. Whittaker, 87–119. Cambridge, 1988.

Jay, P. "What's the Use: Critical Theory and the Study of Autobiography." *Biography* 10 (1987): 39–54.

Jenal, G. *Italia ascetica atque monastica: Das Asketen-und Monchtum in Italien von dem Anfangen bis zur Zeit der Langobarden.* 2 vols. Stuttgart, 1995.

Joannou, P.-P. *La législation imperiale et la christianisation de l'empire romain (311–476).* Rome, 1972.

Jones, A. H. M. *The Later Roman Empire, 284–602: A Social, Economic and Administrative Survey.* 2 vols. Norman, 1964.

Junod-Ammerbauer, H. "Le poète chrétien selon Paulin de Nole: L'adaptation des thèmes classiques dans les *Natalicia.*" *Revue des études augustiniennes* 21 (1975): 13–55.

———. "Les constructions de Nole et l'esthétique de Saint Paulin." *Revue des études augustiniennes* 24 (1978): 22–57.

Kaspin, D. "Chewa Visions and Revisions of Power: Transformations of the Nyau Dance in Central Malawi." In *Modernity and Its Malcontents.* Ed. J. Comaroff and J. Comaroff, 34–57. Chicago, 1993.

Kaster, R. A. "Notes on 'Primary' and 'Secondary' Schools in Late Antiquity." *Transactions of the American Philological Association* 113 (1983): 323–346.

———. *Guardians of Language: The Grammarian and Society in Late Antiquity.* Berkeley, 1988.

Kee, H. C. "Rich and Poor in the New Testament and Early Christianity." In *Through the Eye of a Needle.* Ed. E. A. Hanawalt and C. Lindberg. Kirksville, 1994.

Kelly, J. N. D. *Jerome: His Life, Writings, and Controversies.* London, 1975.

Kessler, H. "Pictorial Narrative and Church Mission in Sixth-Century Gaul." In *Pictorial Narrative in Antiquity and the Middle Ages.* Ed. H. Kessler and M. Simpson, 75–91. Hanover, 1985.

Kirsch, W. "Paulinus von Nola und Nicetas von Remesiana: Zur Literaturauffassung zweier Christen des 4. Jahrhunderts." *From Late Antiquity to Early Byzantium: Proceedings of the Byzantinological Symposium in the 16th International Eirene Conference,* 189–93. Prague, 1985.

Kohlwes, K. *Christliche Dichtung und stilistiche Form bei Paulinus von Nola.* Bonn, 1979.

Konstan, D. "Problems in the History of Christian Friendship." *Journal of Early Christian Studies* 4 (1996): 87–113.

———. *Friendship in the Classical World.* Cambridge, 1997.

Korol, D. "Zu den gemalten Architekturdarstellungen des NT-Zyklus' und zur Mosaikausstattung der 'Aula' über den Gräbern von Felix und Paulinus in Cimitile / Nola." *Jahrbuch für Antike und Christentum* 30 (1987): 156–71.

———. "Alcune novità riguardo alla storia delle tombe venerate e del complesso centrale nel luogo di pellegrinaggio di Cimitile / Nola." *Akten des XII. Internationalen Kongresses für christliche Archäologie,* 928–40. Rome and Münster, 1995.

Krautheimer, R. *Three Christian Capitals: Topography and Politics.* Berkeley, 1983.

———. *Early Christian and Byzantine Architecture.* 4th ed. London, 1986.

Kuhoff, W. *Studien zur zivilen senatorischen Laufbahn im 4. Jahrhundert n. Chr.* Frankfurt, 1983.

Labriolle, P. de. *La correspondance d'Ausone et de Paulin de Nola: Un épisode de la fin du paganisme.* Paris, 1910.

Labrousse, M. *Toulouse antique.* Paris, 1968.

Lagrange, F. *Histoire de Saint Paulin de Nole.* Paris, 1877; 2d ed. 1882.

Lambot, C. "Les sermons de Saint Augustine pour les fêtes de martyrs." *Analecta Bollandiana* 67 (1949): 249–66.

Lana, I. "La storiografia latina pagana del IV sec. d.C." *Koinonia* 3 (1979): 7–28.

Lane Fox, R. "The *Life of Daniel.*" In *Portraits: Biographical Representation in the Greek and Latin Literature of the Roman Empire.* Ed. M. Edwards and S. Swain, 175–225. Oxford, 1997.

Langlois, P. "Les poèmes chrétiens et la christianisme d'Ausone." *Revue de philologie* 43 (1969): 39–58.

Lanzoni, F. *Le Diocesi d'Italia.* Faenza, 1927.

Leanza, S. "Aspetti esegetici dell'opera di Paolino di Nola." *Atti del Convegno: XXXI Cinquantenario della morte di S. Paolino di Nola (431–1981),* 67–91. Rome, 1982.

————. "Una pagina di Melitone di Sardi in Paolino di Nola." *Orpheus* 5 (1984): 444–51.

————. "Una precisazione a proposito di due recenti articoli su Melitone di Sardi e Paolino di Nola." *Koinonia* 10 (1986): 89–90.

Lehmann, T. "Lo sviluppo del complesso archeologico a Cimitile / Nola." *Boreas* 13 (1990): 75–93.

————. "Eine spätantike Inschriftensammlung und der Besuch des Papstes Damasus an der Pilgerstätte des Hl. Felix in Cimitile / Nola." *Zeitschrift für Papyrologie und Epigraphik* 91 (1992): 243–81.

————. "Der Besuch des Papstes Damasus an der Pilgerstätte des Hl. Felix in Cimitile / Nola." *Akten des XII. Internationalen Kongresses für christliche Archäologie,* 969–81. Rome, 1995.

————. "Zur Genese der Trikonchosbasiliken." *Innovation in der Spätantike: Kolloquium Basel 6. und 7. Mai 1994,* 317–57. Wiesbaden, 1996.

————. "Paolino di Nola: poeta architetto e committente delle costruzioni." In *Anchora vitae: Atti del II Convegno Paoliniano nel XVI Centenario del Ritiro di Paolino a Nola (Nola / Cimitile 18–20 maggio 1995).* Ed. G. Luongo, 95–104. Naples, 1998.

————. "Zu Alarichs Beutezug in Campanien: Ein neu entdecktes Gedicht des Paulinus Nolanus," *Römische Quartalschrift* 93 (1998): 181–99.

————. *Paulinus Nolanus und die Basilica Nova in Cimitile / Nola.* Forthcoming.

Lepelley, C. *Les cités de l'Afrique romaine au Bas-Empire.* 2 vols. Paris, 1981.

Lienhard, J. T. "Paulinus of Nola in the Literary Tradition." In *Paradosis: Studies in Memory of Edwin A. Quain,* 35–45. New York, 1976.

————. *Paulinus of Nola and Early Western Monasticism.* Köln, 1977.

————. "Paulinus of Nola and Monasticism." *Studia Patristica* 16 (1985): 29–31.

————. "Friendship in Paulinus of Nola and Augustine." *Collectanea Augustiniana: Mélanges T. J. van Bavel,* 279–96. Leuven, 1990.

Lietzmann, H. "Zur Entstehungsgeschichte der Briefsammlung Augustins." *Sitzungsberichte der preussischen Akademie der Wissenschaften, philo.-histor. Klasse* (1930): 356–88.

Lippold, A. *Theodosius der Grosse und seine Zeit.* 2d ed. Munich, 1980.

Lizzi, R. "Una società esortata all'ascetismo: misure legislative e motivazioni economiche nel IV–V secolo d.C." *Studi storici* 30 (1989): 129–53.

————. "Ascetismo e monachesimo nell'Italia tardoantica." *Codex Aquilarensis* 5 (1991): 53–76.

Lorenz, R. "Die Anfänge des abendländischen Mönchtums im 4. Jahrhundert." *Zeitschrift für Kirchengeschichte* 77 (1966): 1–61.

Loyen, A. "Bourg-sur-Gironde et les villas d'Ausone," *Revue des études anciennes* 62 (1960): 113–26.

Luongo, G. *Lo specchio dell' agiografo: S. Felice nei carmi XV e XVI di Paolino di Nola.* Naples, 1992.

Luongo, G., ed. *Anchora vitae: Atti del II Convegno Paoliniano nel XVI Centenario del Ritiro di Paolino a Nola (Nola / Cimitile 18–20 maggio 1995).* Naples, 1998.

MacCormack, S. *Art and Ceremony in Late Antiquity.* Berkeley, 1981.

MacMullen, R. *Paganism in the Roman Empire.* New Haven, 1981.

————. *Corruption and the Decline of Rome.* New Haven, 1988.

————. "The Preacher's Audience (A.D. 350–400)." *The Journal of Theological Studies* 40 (1989): 503–511.

―――. "Some Pictures in Ammianus Marcellinus." In *Changes in the Roman Empire,* 78–106. Princeton, 1990.

Maillé, M. *Recherches sur les origines chrétiennes de Bordeaux.* Paris, 1959.

Marandino, R. "I dolci colloqui di Paolino nell'epistolario." *Impegno e dialogo* 9 (1991–92): 141–48.

Marcone, A. *Commento storico al libro VI dell'epistolario di Q. Aurelio Simmaco.* Pisa, 1983.

Markus, R. "Gregory the Great and a Papal Missionary Strategy." *From Augustine to Gregory the Great: History and Christianity in Late Antiquity,* ch. 9. London, 1983.

―――. "The Legacy of Pelagius: Orthodoxy, Heresy and Conciliation." In *The Making of Orthodoxy: Essays in Honour of Henry Chadwick.* Ed. R. Williams, 214–34. Cambridge, 1989.

―――. *The End of Ancient Christianity.* Cambridge, 1990.

―――. "How on Earth Could Places Become Holy? Origins of the Christian Idea of Holy Places." *Journal of Early Christian Studies* 2 (1994): 257–71.

Martinetto, G. "Les premières réactions antiaugustiniennes de Pélage." *Revue de études augustiniennes* 17 (1971): 83–117.

Massie, M. "Vigilance de Calagurris face à la polémique hiéronymienne." *Bulletin de littérature ecclésiastique* 81 (1980): 81–108.

Mathisen, R. "Epistolography, Literary Circles and Family Ties in Late Roman Gaul." *Transactions of the American Philological Association* 111 (1981): 95–109.

―――. "Petronius, Hilarius and Valerianus: Prosopographical Notes on the Conversion of the Roman Aristocracy." *Historia* 30 (1981): 106–12.

―――. "*PLRE* II: Suggested *Addenda* and *Corrigenda.*" *Historia* 31 (1982): 364–86.

―――. *Ecclesiastical Factionalism and Religious Controversy in Fifth-Century Gaul.* Washington, D.C., 1989.

―――. *Roman Aristocrats in Barbarian Gaul.* Austin, 1993.

Mathisen, R., and H. Sivan, eds. *Shifting Frontiers in Late Antiquity.* Aldershot, 1996.

Matthews, J. "The Historical Setting of the 'Carmen contra Paganos' (Cod. Par. Lat. 8084)." *Historia* 20 (1970): 464–79.

―――. "The Letters of Symmachus." In *Latin Literature of the Fourth Century.* Ed. J. W. Binns, 58–99. London, 1974.

―――. *Western Aristocracies and Imperial Court:* A.D. 364–425. Oxford, 1975.

―――. "Symmachus and His Enemies." *Colloque genevois sur Symmaque à l'occasion du mille-six-centième anniversaire du conflit de l'autel de la Victoire,* 163–75. Paris, 1986.

―――. *The Roman Empire of Ammianus.* Baltimore, 1989.

―――. "Nicomachus Flavianus' Quaestorship: The Historical Evidence." *Xenia* 23 (1989): 18–25.

―――. "The Poetess Proba and Fourth-Century Rome: Questions of Interpretation." *Institutions, société et vie politque dans l'empire romain au IVe siècle ap. J.-C.,* 277–304. Rome, 1992.

McCarty, T. "The Content of Cornelius Nepos' *De Viris Illustribus.*" *Classical World* 63 (1973–74): 386–91.

McLynn, N. *Ambrose of Milan: Church and Court in a Christian Capital.* Berkeley, 1994.

―――. "Paulinus the Impenitent: A Study of the *Eucharisticos.*" *Journal of Early Christian Studies* 3 (1995): 461–86.

Meiggs, R. *Ostia.* 2d ed. Oxford, 1973.

Meigne, M. "Concile ou collection d'Elvire?" *Revue d'histoire ecclésiastique* 70 (1975): 361–87.

Mercogliano, A. *Le basiliche paleocristiane di Cimitile.* Rome, 1988.

Merdinger, J. *Rome and the African Church in the Time of Augustine.* New Haven, 1997.

Miller, P. Cox. "'Differential Networks': Relics and Other Fragments in Late Antiquity." *Journal of Early Christian Studies* 6 (1998): 113–38.

Misch, G. *A History of Autobiography in Antiquity.* Trans. E. Dickes. London, 1950.

Mitchell, W. *Peasants on the Edge: Crop, Cult, and Crisis in the Andes.* Austin, 1991.

Moine, N. "Melaniana." *Recherches augustiniennes* 15 (1980): 3–79.

Momigliano, A. "Christianity and the Decline of the Roman Empire." In *The Conflict Between Paganism and Christianity in the Fourth Century*. Ed. A. Momigliano, 1–16. Oxford, 1963.

———. *The Development of Greek Biography*. Cambridge, Mass., 1971.

Mommsen, T. "Carmen codicis Parisini 8084." *Hermes* 4 (1870): 350–64.

Monturet, R. and H. Rivière. *Les thermes sud de la villa gallo-romaine de Séviac. Aquitania* supp. 2. Bordeaux, 1986.

Morelli, C. "L'autore del cosidetto *poema ultimum* attribuito a Paolino di Nola." *Didaskalion* 1 (1912): 481–98.

Moricca, U. "Il *votum* di Sulpicio Severo e di S. Paolino da Nola." *Didaskalion* n.s. 3 (1925): 89–96.

———. "La morte violenta di un fratello di Paolino di Nola." *Didaskalion* n.s. 4 (1926): 85–90.

Mratschek, S. "Einblicke in einen Postsack: Zur Struktur und Edition der 'Natalicia' des Paulinus von Nola." *Zeitschrift für Papyrologie und Epigraphik* 114 (1996) : 165–72.

Murphy, F. X. *Rufinus of Aquileia (345–411): His Life and Works*. Washington, D.C., 1945.

———. "Melania the Elder: A Biographical Note." *Traditio* 5 (1947): 59–77.

———. "Rufinus of Aquileia and Paulinus of Nola." *Revue des études augustiniennes* 2 (1956): 79–91.

Näf, B. *Senatorisches Standesbewusstsein in spätrömischer Zeit*. Freiburg, 1995.

———. "Paulinus von Nola und Rom." *Studia Patristica* 33 (1997): 448–53.

Nautin, P. "Études de chronologie hiéronymienne (393–397): I. Le livre de Jérôme contre Jean de Jérusalem." *Revue des études augustiniennes* 18 (1972): 209–18.

———. "Études de chronologie hiéronymienne (393–397): II. La controverse origénienne de 393 à 396." *Revue des études augustiniennes* 19 (1973): 69–86.

———. "Études de chronologie hiéronymienne (393–397): III. Les premières relations entre Jérôme et Paulin de Nole." *Revue des études augustiniennes* 19 (1973): 213–39.

———. "Études de chronologie hiéronymienne (393–397): IV. Autres lettres de la période 393–396." *Revue des études augustiniennes* 20 (1974): 251–84.

Nazzaro, A. V. "La parafrasi salmica di Paolino di Nola." *Atti del Convegno: XXXI Cinquantenario della morte di S. Paolino di Nola (431–1981)*, 93–115. Rome, 1982.

———. "Orazio e Paolino." *Impegno e dialogo* 10 (1992–94): 239–52.

Nicols, J. "Pliny and the Patronage of Communities." *Hermes* 108 (1980): 365–85.

Nissen, H. *Italische Landeskunde*. 2 vols. Berlin, 1902.

Novak, D. "Anicianae domus culmen, nobilitatis culmen." *Klio* 62 (1980): 473–93.

Nugent, S. G. "Ausonius' 'Late-Antique' Poetics and 'Post-Modern' Literary Theory." *Ramus* 19 (1990): 26–50.

Nuvolone-Nobile, F. "Problèmes d'une nouvelle édition du *De Induratione Cordis Pharaonis* attribué à Pélage." *Revue des études augustiniennes* 26 (1980): 105–17.

O'Donnell, J. J. "The Career of Virius Nicomachus Flavianus." *Phoenix* 32 (1978): 129–43.

———, ed. *Augustine: Confessions*. 3 vols. Oxford, 1992.

O'Meara, J. J. "Augustine's *Confessions:* Elements of Fiction." In *Augustine: From Rhetor to Theologian*. Ed. J. McWilliam, 77–95. Waterloo, Ontario, 1992.

Oost, S. I. *Galla Placidia Augusta: A Biographical Essay*. Chicago, 1968.

Palanque, J.-R. "Sur l'usurpation de Maxime." *Revue des études anciennes* 31 (1929): 33–36.

———. In *Histoire de l'église: De la paix constantinienne à la mort de Théodose*. Ed. J.-R. Palanque, G. Bardy, and P. de Labriolle. Paris, 1950.

———. "L'empereur Maxime." *Les empereurs romains d'Espagne*, 255–67. Paris, 1965.

Palazzini, P. "La santitá canonizzata e il culto di S. Paolino di Nola." *Atti del Convegno: XXXI Cinquantenario della morte di S. Paolino di Nola (431–1981)*, 11–23. Rome, 1982.

Palmer, A. M. *Prudentius on the Martyrs.* Oxford, 1989.

Paschoud, F. *Cinq études sur Zosime.* Paris, 1975.

————. *Zosime: Histoire nouvelle.* 3 vols. Paris, 1979–1989.

Pastorino, A. "Il *De obitu sancti Paulini* di Uranio." *Augustinianum* 24 (1984): 115–41.

Patlagean, E. *Pauvreté économique et pauvreté sociale à Byzance, 4e–7e siècles.* Paris, 1977.

Patrucco, M. and S. Roda. "Le lettere di Simmaco ad Ambrogio: Vent'anni di rapporti amichevoli." *Ambrosius Episcopus: Atti del Congresso internazionale di studi ambrosiani nel XVI centenario della elevazione di Sant'Ambrogio alla cattedra episcopale.* Vol. 2, 284–97. Milan, 1976.

Pavolini, C. *Ostia.* Roma-Bari, 1983.

Penco, G. "La vita monastica in Italia all'epoca di S. Martino di Tours." *Studia Anselmiana* 46 (1961): 67–83.

Perler, O. *Les voyages de Saint Augustine.* Paris, 1969.

Perrin, M.-Y. "*Ad implendum caritatis ministerium:* La place des courriers dans la correspondance de Paulin de Nole." *Mélanges d'archéologie et d'histoire de l'école française de Rome, Antiquité* 104 (1992): 1025–68.

Petersen, J. M. "The Garden of Felix: The Literary Connection between Gregory the Great and Paulinus of Nola." *Studia Monastica* 26 (1984): 215–30.

————. *The Dialogues of Gregory the Great in Their Late Antique Cultural Background.* Toronto, 1984.

Pflaum, H. G. "Q. Planius Sardus L. Varius Ambibulus, légat de la *legio IIIa Augusta,* à la lumière de découvertes récentes." *Bulletin archéologique du comité des travaux historiques et scientifiques* 1963–64: 141–151.

Pietri, C. *Roma christiana: Recherches sur l'Église de Rome, son organisation, sa politique, son idéologie de Miltiade à Sixte III (311–440).* Paris, 1976.

Pietri, L. "La succession des premiers évêques tourangeaux: Essai sur la chronologie de Grégoire de Tours." *Mélanges de l'école française de Rome, moyen age–temps modernes* 94 (1982): 586–605.

————. *La Ville de Tours du IVe au VIe siècle: Naissance d'une cité chrétienne.* Rome, 1983.

Piscitelli Carpino, T. *Paolino di Nola: Epistole ad Agostino.* Naples and Rome, 1989.

————. "La figura di Maria nell'opera di Paolino di Nola." *Impegno e dialogo* 9 (1991–92): 197–218.

Pizzolato, L. *L'idea di amicizia nel mondo antico e cristiano.* Turin, 1993.

Plinval, G. de. *Pélage: Ses écrits, sa vie, et sa réforme.* Lausanne, 1943.

————. *Essai sur le style et la langue de Pélage.* Fribourg, 1947.

Prete, S. *Paolino di Nola e l'umanisimo cristiano: Saggio sopra il suo epistolario.* Bologna, 1964.

————. "Vittricio di Rouen." *Bibliotheca Sanctorum* 1969: 12.1310–15.

————. "Paolino di Nola: la parafrasi biblica della *Laus Iohannis* (carm. 6)." *Augustinianum* 14 (1974): 625–35; reprint, *Motivi ascetici e letterari,* 19–34.

————. "I temi della proprietà e della famiglia negli scritti di Paolino di Nola." *Augustinianum* 17 (1977): 257–82; reprint, *Motivi ascetici e letterari,* 53–86.

————. "Il Carme 20 di Paolino di Nola: Alcuni aspetti letterari e culturali." *Augustinianum* 21 (1981): 169–177; reprint, *Motivi ascetici e letterari,* 87–99.

————. "Paolino agiografo: Gli atti di S. Felice di Nola (*carm.* 15–16)." *Atti del Convegno: XXXI Cinquantenario della morte di S. Paolino di Nola (431–1981),* 149–59. Rome, 1982; reprint, *Motivi ascetici e letterari,* 101–16.

————. *Motivi ascetici e letterari in Paolino di Nola.* Naples and Rome, 1987.

Pricoco, S. *Per una nuova edizione del "De contemptu mundi" di Eucherio di Lione.* Turin, 1967.

————. *L'isola dei santi: Il cenobio di Lerino e le origini del monachesimo gallico.* Rome, 1978.

————. "Aspetti culturali del primo monachesimo d'Occidente." *Società romana e impero tardantico,* vol. 4: *Tradizione dei classici: Trasformazioni della cultura.* Bari, 1986.

————. *Il rifuto del mondo: De contemptu mundi.* Florence, 1990.

Quacquarelli, A. "Una *consolatio* cristiana (Paul. Nol., *Carm.* 31)." *Atti del Convegno: XXXI Cinquantenario della morte di S. Paolino di Nola (431–1981),* 121–42. Rome, 1982.

Ramsey, B. "Almsgiving in the Latin Church: The Late Fourth and Early Fifth Centuries." *Theological Studies* 43 (1982): 226–59.

Rebenich, S. *Hieronymus und sein Kreis.* Stuttgart, 1992.

Rees, B. R. *Pelagius: A Reluctant Heretic.* Bury St. Edmunds, 1988.

Refoulé, F. "Julien d'Éclane, théologien et philosophe." *Recherches de sciences religieuses* 52 (1964): 42–84, 233–47.

Reinelt, P. *Studien über die Briefe des hl. Paulinus von Nola.* Breslau, 1903.

Richardson, L. "Nola." *Princeton Encyclopedia of Classical Sites.* Princeton, 1976.

Roberts, M. "Paulinus Poem 11, Virgil's First *Eclogue,* and the Limits of *Amicitia.*" *Transactions of the American Philological Association* 115 (1985): 271–82.

————. "The Use of Myth in Latin Epithalamia from Statius to Venantius Fortunatus." *Transactions of the American Philological Association* 119 (1989): 321–48.

————. "Barbarians in Gaul: The Response of the Poets." In *Fifth-Century Gaul: A Crisis of Identity?* Ed. J. F. Drinkwater and H. Elton, 97–106. Cambridge, 1992.

————. *Poetry and the Cult of the Martyrs.* Michigan, 1993.

Roda, S. "Una nuova lettera di Simmaco ad Ausonio? (a proposito di Symm., *Ep.* IX, 88)." *Revue des études anciennes* 83 (1981): 273–80.

Rougé, J. "*Periculum maris* et transports d'état: la lettre 49 de Paulin de Nole." *Studi tardoantichi* 2 (1986): 119–136.

Rousseau, P. *Ascetics, Authority, and the Church in the Age of Jerome and Cassian.* Oxford, 1978.

Rousselle, A. "Deux exemples d'évangélisation en Gaule à la fin du IVe siècle: Paulin de Nole et Sulpice Sévère." *Béziers et le Biterrois, Fédération historique du Languedoc méditerranéen et du Roussillon, XLIIIe Congrès,* 91–98. Montpellier, 1971.

————. "Aspects sociaux du recrutement ecclésiastique au IVe siècle." *Mélanges de l'école française de Rome: Antiquité* 89 (1977): 331–70.

————. "From Sanctuary to Miracle-Worker: Healing in Fourth Century Gaul." Trans. E. Forster. In *Ritual, Religion, and the Sacred.* Ed. R. Forster and O. Ranum, 95–127. Baltimore, 1982.

————. *Croire et guérir: La foi en Gaule dans l'antiquité tardive.* Paris, 1990.

Ruggiero, A. "Carme 21: Nola crocevia dello spirito." *Atti del Convegno: XXXI Cinquantenario della morte di S. Paolino di Nola (431–1981),* 183–212. Rome, 1982.

————. "La 'Vita Felicis' di Paolino di Nola come fonte per la conoscenza della religiosità popolare in Campania nei secoli IV e V." *Paolino di Nola: Momenti della sua vita e delle sue opere,* 163–97. Nola, 1983.

————. *Paolino di Nola: I carmi. Testo latino con introduzione, traduzione italiana, note e indici.* 2 vols. Naples, 1996.

Ruggiero, M. *Cipriano, Paolino di Nola, Uranio: Poesia e teologia della morte.* Rome, 1984.

Salvatore, A. "Due *omelie su Sansone* di Cesario di Arles e l'*epistola* 23 di Paolino da Nola." *Vetera Christianorum* 7 (1970): 83–113.

————. "Immagini bibliche e strutture discorsive: la lettera 11 di Paolino." *Atti del Convegno: XXXI Cinquantenario della morte di S. Paolino di Nola (431–1981),* 253–80. Rome, 1982.

Salzman, M. "Aristocratic Women: Conductors of Christianity in the Fourth Century." *Helios* 10 (1989): 207–220.

————. *On Roman Time: The Codex-Calendar of 354 and the Rhythms of Urban Life in Late Antiquity.* Berkeley, 1990.

————. "How the West Was Won: The Christianization of the Roman Aristocracy in the West in the Years after Constantine." *Collection Latomus 217; Studies in Latin Literature and Roman History VI,* 451–79. Brussels, 1992.

———. "The Evidence for the Conversion of the Roman Empire to Christianity in Book 16 of the *Theodosian Code.*" *Historia* 42 (1993): 362–78.

Santaniello, G. "La prigionia di Paolino: Tradizione e storia." *Paolino di Nola: Momenti della sua vita e delle sue opere,* 221–49. Nola, 1983.

———. *Paolino di Nola: Le lettere. Testo latino con introduzione, traduzione italiana, note e indici.* 2 vols. Naples, 1992.

———. "Momenti del percorso teologico di Paolino nel dialogo epistolare con Agostino." *Impegno e dialogo* 11 (1997): 259–77.

———. "Un'amicizia sofferta in silenzio: Rufino di Concordia e Paolino di Nola." *Teologia e vita* 5 (1997): 71–128.

Saxer, V. *Morts martyrs reliques en Afrique chrétienne aux premiers siècles.* Paris, 1980.

Schmid, W. "Tityrus Christianus: Probleme religiöser Hirtendichtung an der Wende vom vierten zum fünften Jahrhundert." *Rheinisches Museum für Philologie* 96 (1953): 101–65.

Seeck, O. *Geschichte des Untergangs der antiken Welt.* Vol. 5. 2d ed. Stuttgart, 1920.

Seeck, O., and G. Veith. "Die Schlacht am Frigidus." *Klio* 13 (1913): 451–67.

Seston, W. "Jovius et Herculius, ou l'"épiphanie' des Tétrarques." *Historia* 1 (1950): 257–66.

Sgobbo, I. "L'acquedotto romano della Campania: 'Fontis Augustei Aquaeductus.'" *Notizie degli scavi* 16 (1938): 75–97.

Shanzer, D. "The Anonymous *Carmen contra paganos* and the Date and Identity of the Centonist Proba." *Revue des études augustiniennes* 32 (1986): 232–48.

———. "The Date and Composition of Prudentius's *Contra Orationem Symmachi Libri.*" *Rivista di filologia e d'istruzione classica* 117 (1989): 442–62.

———. "'*Arcanum Varronis iter*': Licentius's Verse Epistle to Augustine." *Revue des études augustiniennes* 37 (1991): 110–43.

———. "The Date and Identity of the Centonist Proba." *Recherches augustiniennes* 27 (1994): 75–96.

Shaw, B. "The Family in Late Antiquity: The Experience of Augustine." *Past and Present* 115 (1987): 3–51.

Shelton, K. "The Esquiline Treasure: The Nature of the Evidence." *American Journal of Archaeology* 89 (1985): 147–55.

Sheridan, J. J. "The Altar of Victory: Paganism's Last Battle." *L'antiquité classique* 35 (1966): 186–206.

Simon, M. "Bellérophon chrétien." *Mélanges d'archéologie, d'épigraphie et d'histoire offerts à Jérôme Carcopino,* 889–904. Paris, 1966.

Sirna, F. G. "Sul cosiddetto 'poema ultimum' ps-Paoliniano." *Aevum* 35 (1961): 87–107.

Sivan, H. "Town, Country, and Province in Late Roman Gaul: The Example of CIL XIII 128." *Zeitschrift für Papyrologie und Epigraphik* 79 (1989): 103–13.

———. "Town and Country in Late Antique Gaul: the Example of Bordeaux." In *Fifth-Century Gaul: A Crisis of Identity?* Ed. J. F. Drinkwater and H. Elton. 132–43. Cambridge, 1992.

———. *Ausonius of Bordeaux: Genesis of a Gallic Aristocracy.* London, 1993.

———. "Anician Women, the Cento of Proba, and Aristocratic Conversion in the Fourth Century." *Vigiliae Christianae* 47 (1993): 140–57.

———. "The Last Gallic Prose Panegyric: Paulinus of Nola on Theodosius I." *Collection Latomus* 227; *Studies in Latin Literature and Roman History* 7 (1994): 577–94.

———. "Nicetas' (of Remesiana) Mission and Stilicho's Illyrican Ambition: Notes on Paulinus of Nola *Carmen* XVII (*Propemticon*)." *Revue des études augustiniennes* 41 (1995): 79–90.

Skeb, M. *Christo vivere: Studien zum literarischen Christusbild des Paulinus von Nola.* Bonn, 1977.

Smith, R. R. R. "Late Roman Philosopher Portraits from Aphrodisias." *Journal of Roman Studies* 80 (1990): 127–55.

Smith, T. *De Gratia: Faustus of Riez's Treatise on Grace and Its Place in the History of Theology.* Notre Dame, 1990.

Sorrentino, D. "L'amore di unitá: Amicizia spirituale ed ecclesiologia in Paolino di Nola." *Impegno e dialogo* 9 (1991–92): 149–69.

Springer, C. *The Gospel as Epic in Late Antiquity.* Leiden, 1988.

———. "Jerome and the *Cento* of Proba." *Studia Patristica* 28 (1993): 96–105.

Stancliffe, C. *St. Martin and His Hagiographer: History and Miracle in Sulpicius Severus.* Oxford, 1983.

Starobinski, J. "Le style de l'autobiographie." *Poétique* 3 (1970): 257–65.

Stein, E. *Geschichte des Spätrömischen Reiches.* Wien, 1928; translated as *Histoire du Bas-Empire* by J.-R. Palanque. Paris, 1959.

Stowers, S. "Greeks Who Sacrifice and Those Who Do Not: Toward an Anthropology of Greek Religion." In *The Social World of the First Christians: Essays in Honor of Wayne A. Meeks.* Ed. L. M. White and O. L. Yarbrough, 293–333. Minneapolis, 1995.

Straub, J. "Eugenius." *Reallexikon für Antike und Christentum* 6 (1966): 860–77.

Stroheker, K. *Der senatorische Adel im spätantiken Gallien.* Darmstadt, 1948.

Swain, S. "Biography and the Biographic in the Literature of the Roman Empire." In *Portraits: Biographical Representation in the Greek and Latin Literature of the Roman Empire.* Ed. M Edwards and S. Swain. Oxford, 1997.

Testini, P. "Cimitile: L'antichità cristiana." *L'art dans l'Italie meridionale: Aggiornamento dell'opera di Émile Bertaux sotto la direzione di Adriano Prandi*, 163–76. Rome, 1978.

———. "Note per servire allo studio del complesso paleocristiano di S. Felice a Cimitile (Nola)." *Mélanges de l'école française de Rome, Antiquité* 97 (1985): 329–71.

———. "Paolino e le costruzioni di Cimitile (Nola): Basiliche o tombe privilegiate?" In *L'inhumation privilégiée du IVe au VIIIe siècle en Occident. Actes du colloque tenu à Creteil les 16–18 mars 1984.* Ed. Y. Duval and J.-C. Picard, 213–19. Paris, 1986.

Thélamon, F. "L'empereur idéal d'après l'*Histoire ecclésiastique* de Rufin d'Aquilée." *Studia Patristica* 10 (1970): 310–14.

———. *Païens et chrétiens au IVe siècle: L'apport de l'"Histoire ecclésiastique" de Rufin d'Aquilée.* Paris, 1981.

Thompson, E. A. "Christianity and the Northern Barbarians." In *The Conflict between Paganism and Christianity in the Fourth Century.* Ed. A. Momigliano, 56–78. Oxford, 1963.

Thonnard, F.-J. "L'aristotélisme de Julien d'Éclane et Saint Augustin." *Revue des études augustiniennes* 11 (1965): 296–304.

Tibiletti, C. "Motivazioni dell'ascetismo in alcuni autori cristiani." *Atti della accademia delle scienze di Torino* 106 (1972): 489–537.

Traube, L. "Zu alten Philologie I.3: Zu Cornelius Nepos." *Kleine Schriften. Vorlesungen und Abhandlungen.* Vol. 3, 20–30. Munich, 1920.

Trompf, G. W. "Rufinus and the Logic of Retribution in Post-Eusebian Church Histories." *Journal of Ecclesiastical History* 43 (1992): 351–71.

Trout, D. "Augustine at Cassiciacum: *Otium Honestum* and the Social Dimensions of Conversion." *Vigiliae Christianae* 42 (1988): 132–46.

———. "The Dates of the Ordination of Paulinus of Bordeaux and of His Departure for Nola." *Revue des études augustiniennes* 37 (1991): 237–60.

———. "*Amicitia, Auctoritas,* and Self-Fashioning Texts." *Studia Patristica* 28 (1993): 123–29.

———. "Re-textualizing Lucretia: Cultural Subversion in the *City of God.*" *Journal of Early Christian Studies* 2 (1994): 53–70.

———. "Christianizing the Nolan Countryside: Animal Sacrifice at the Tomb of Saint Felix." *Journal of Early Christian Studies* 3 (1995): 281–98.

———. "Town, Countryside, and Christianization at Paulinus' Nola." In *Shifting Frontiers in Late Antiquity.* Ed. R. Mathisen and H. Sivan, 175–86. Aldershot, 1996.

———. "History, Biography, and the Exemplary Life of Paulinus of Nola." *Studia Patristica* 32 (1997): 462–67.

Van Bavel, T. J. "The Cult of the Martyrs in St. Augustine: Theology versus Popular Religion." In *Martyrium in Multidisciplinary Perspective: Memorial Louis Reekmans*. Ed. M Lamberigts and P. Van Deun, 351–61. Leuven, 1995.

Van Dam, R. *Leadership and Community in Late Antique Gaul*. Berkeley, 1985.

———. *Gregory of Tours: Glory of the Confessors*. Liverpool, 1988.

———. *Gregory of Tours: Glory of the Martyrs*. Liverpool, 1988.

———. *Saints and Their Miracles in Late Antique Gaul*. Princeton, 1993.

Vera, D. "La carriera di Virius Nicomachus Flavianus e la prefettura dell'Illirico orientale nel IV secolo d.C." *Athenaeum* 61 (1983): 24–64.

———. "Simmaco e le sue proprietà: Struttura e funzionamento di un patrimonio aristocratico del quarto secolo d.C." *Colloque genevois sur Symmaque à l'occasion du mille-six-centième anniversaire du conflit de l'autel de la Victoire*, 231–76. Paris, 1986.

Vessey, M. "Conference and Confession: Literary Pragmatics in Augustine's *Apologia contra Hieronymum*." *Journal of Early Christian Studies* 1 (1993): 175–213.

———. "Eucherian (E)utopics: Place, Text, and Community in the Discourse of Lérins." Paper delivered at the Annual Meeting of the North American Patristic Society. May 1993.

———. "The Forging of Orthodoxy in Latin Christian Literature: A Case Study." *Journal of Early Christian Studies* 4 (1996): 495–513.

Volbach, W. *Elfenbeinarbeiten der Spätantike und des frühen Mittelalters*. Mainz, 1976.

Walsh, P. G. *Livy: His Historical Aims and Methods*. Cambridge, 1961.

———. "Paulinus of Nola and the Conflict of Ideologies in the Fourth Century." *Kyriakon: Festschrift Johannes Quasten*, 565–71. Münster, 1970.

———. "Paulinus of Nola and Virgil." *Studia Patristica* 15 (1984): 117–21.

Ward-Perkins, B. *From Classical Antiquity to the Middle Ages: Urban Public Building in Northern and Central Italy, A.D. 300–850*. Oxford, 1984.

Weintraub, K. "Autobiography and Historical Consciousness." *Critical Inquiry* 1 (1975): 821–48.

Weiss, J.-P. "La personnalité de Valerien de Cimiez." *Annales de la faculté des lettres et sciences humaines de Nice* 11 (1970): 141–62.

Westra, H. "Augustine and Poetic Exegesis." In *Grace, Politics and Desire: Essays on Augustine*. Ed. H. A. Meynell, 87–100. Calgary, 1990.

White, C. *Christian Friendship in the Fourth Century*. Cambridge, 1992.

Winkler, J. *Auctor & Actor: A Narratological Reading of Apuleius's* The Golden Ass. Berkeley, 1985.

Wiseman, T. P. "Viae Anniae." *Papers of the British School at Rome* 32 (1964): 21–37.

Witke, C. *Numen Litterarum: The Old and the New in Latin Poetry from Constantine to Gregory the Great*. Leiden, 1971.

Wolf, E. *Peasants*. Englewood Cliffs, N.J., 1966.

Wright, J. "Saint Paulinus of Nola." In *Classica et Iberica: A Festschrift in Honor of the Reverend Joseph M.-F. Marique, S.J.* Ed. P. T. Brannan, 417–23. Worcester, Mass., 1975.

Yarbrough, A. "Christianization in the Fourth Century: The Example of Roman Women." *Church History* 45 (1976): 149–65.

GENERAL INDEX

Abella, 192–94

Achilleus, bishop of Spoleto, 255–56

Acindynus, Italian bishop, 266, 294

Aemilia Hilaria, 122

Aemilius of Beneventum, 225, 232

Alaric, 117–20, 227, 229, 253, 272

Albina, daughter-in-law of Melania the Elder, 119, 142, 207, 208, 226, 231

Alethius of Cahors, correspondent of Paulinus, 201

Alingo (Langon), 27, 148–49, 200

Altar of Victory, 40, 45, 50, 54, 107

Alypius of Thagaste, 49, 67, 116, 187, 202–5, 210, 276; signatory of Aug. *ep.* 186, 229, 233, 247

Amandus, correspondent of Paulinus, 138–42

Amandus of Bordeaux, 15–16, 64–66, 84, 86, 90, 95, 130, 148–49, 195, 200–1

Ambrose of Milan, 54, 60, 63, 95, 100, 124, 127, 163; and Eugenius, 107n13, 108–13; and Magnus Maximus, 54; and Paulinus, 49–50, 52, 116, 206; on Paulinus's background and wealth, 26; on Paulinus's conversion, 3–4, 19, 94, 274; and Petronius Probus, 39

amicitia (friendship), 35–45, 56–59, 68, 88, 89, 169, 170, 191, 198–200, 209–18, 259, 275

Ammianus Marcellinus, 36n81, 37, 187, 286

Anastasius, bishop of Rome, 115, 189, 199, 206, 224

Anicius Paulinus, 35, 281

Anicius Auchenius Bassus, 35, 281

Aper and Amanda, correspondents of Paulinus, 142–45, 154, 156, 157–58, 168, 200

Aphrodisias, 9

Aquitaine: prosperity, 24–25; *villae*, 27–28, 55–59

Arbogast, 64, 105–10

Arcadius, 117

Asterius, son of Avita and Turcius Apronianus, 282

Athanasius, 122–123; *Vita Antonii*, 9, 123, 135

Athaulf, 252–53

Augustine: at Cassiciacum, 134, 137; correspondence with Paulinus, 101, 116, 203–5, 211, 229–30, 235, 237–38, 244–51; and cult of the saints, 236–38, 244–51; *ep.* 186 (to Paulinus), 229–30; in Milan, 5, 49, 53, 67, 78, 83–84, 94, 122, 124, 276; on Paulinus's conversion, 4–6; and Pelagian controversy, 227–32; in Rome, 36n81, 37, 53, 123; at Thagaste, 28, 29, 67

Augustine, select works: *Confessions*, 5n13, 16–17, 21, 72, 122, 204, 210, 231; *De civitate Dei*, 7, 8, 111n36, 112n41, 120, 245, 248n299, 250–51; *De cura pro mortuis gerenda*, 15, 42, 120, 203, 230, 238, 245–47, 250, 272; *De gratia Christi*, 231, 232; *De Trinitate*, 247–48; *De vera religione*, 237–38, 248

Aurelius of Carthage, 116, 202–3, 205

Ausonius, 27n25, 49–51, 103; death, 89; and Paulinus in 380s, 55–59, 63; and Paulinus in 390s, 68–84, 86–89, 103, 140–41, 212; political career, 32–33, 187; promotion of family and friends, 33–36; and Symmachus, 33, 35–38; teacher at Bordeaux, 28–29; teacher of Paulinus, 29–30, 275; teacher at Trier, 28

Auxentius, bishop of Milan, 124

INDEX LOCORUM

Text:	Baskerville
Display:	10/12 Baskerville
Composition:	Impressions Book and Journal Services, Inc.
Printing and binding:	Edwards Brothers, Inc.
Maps:	Bill Nelson Cartography